The SAGE
Handbook of

Social Work
Research

This is an ambitious book. It aims at nothing less than a comprehensive account of the state of the art of social work research internationally and an intellectually original statement that will help to define and shape social work research. Those with a serious interest in social work research will agree that this is a major undertaking and one that should put social work research 'on the map'.

Ian Sinclair, University of York

This terrific Handbook provides an essential map for navigating the complex currents of social work research today. It resists polemical and simplistic binaries to chart a course that emphasizes diversity, pluralism and sensitivity to political contexts in many featured exemplars. As key chapters note, inherent tensions at the heart of social work itself are mirrored in current debates about the purposes and methods of social work research. Rather than patch over differences, the volume invites us to understand historical roots of unresolvable tensions, and live with them. The international scope of the volume is unique – scholars from more than a dozen different countries were involved – and its broad scope counters the tendency toward parochialism of much North American literature. The Handbook should be essential reading for students and academics.

Catherine Riessman, Boston University

The SAGE
Handbook of

Social Work
Research

Edited by
Ian Shaw,
Katharine Briar-Lawson,
Joan Orme and Roy Ruckdeschel

Los Angeles | London | New Delhi
Singapore | Washington DC

First published 2010

SAGE Publications Ltd
1 Oliver's Yard
55 City Road
London EC1Y 1SP

SAGE Publications Inc.
2455 Teller Road
Thousand Oaks, California 91320

SAGE Publications India Pvt Ltd
B 1/I 1 Mohan Cooperative Industrial Area
Mathura Road
New Delhi 110 044

SAGE Publications Asia-Pacific Pte Ltd
33 Pekin Street #02-01
Far East Square
Singapore 048763

Library of Congress Control Number: tbc British Library Cataloguing in Publication data

A catalogue record for this book is available from the British Library

ISBN 978-1-4129-3498-5
ISBN 978-1-4129-3499-2 (pbk)

Typeset by Glyph International, Bangalore, India
Printed in Great Britain by the MPG Books Group, Bodmin, Cornwall
Printed on paper from sustainable resources

Contents

Notes on Editors

Katharine Briar-Lawson is Dean and Professor of the School of Social Welfare at the University at Albany, State University of New York. She is co-editor of two forthcoming books on *Practice Research* and also on *Globalization, Human Service Professions and Social Justice*. She has helped lead several national grants including the National Child Welfare Workforce Institute. She is the immediate past president of the National Association of Deans and Directors of Schools of Social Work. Her research interests focus on family centered practice and family support, school based services, as well as poverty and unemployment. In addition, she is concerned with the professionalization of child welfare in the U.S.

Joan Orme is currently emeritus Professor of Social Work in the Glasgow School of Social Work having been a social work academic for over thirty years. Her interests have been in the quality of practice for those who are recipients of services. To this end she has researched workload management, social work practice and social work education. Professor Orme has written major texts for social workers on workload management, social work practice and gender and is currently co-authoring a text on social work research for qualifying practitioners. All of her writing has been informed by her study of the contribution of feminist theory to social work and to this end she has also explored feminist approaches in research. Her other major research involvement has been to work with the UK research council (the Economic and Social Research Council, ESRC) in a number of funded projects to develop the quality and quantity of social work research.

Roy Ruckdeschel is Professor of Social Work at the School of Social Work of the College of Education and Public Service of Saint Louis University. His early social work career was in community organizing. In addition to an MSW, his PhD is in sociology. He has tried throughout his career to bridge that academic discipline with the profession of social work. He has been strongly influenced by the Chicago tradition and symbolic interactionism. His current interests in social constructionism and postmodernism are in large part an outgrowth of those influences. Professor Ruckdeschel is co-editor of the *Qualitative Social Work* journal (Sage Publications), and on the editorial board of the newly minted *International Review of Qualitative Research* (Left Coast Press) edited by Norman Denzin. He has published numerous articles on research in social work and was an early advocate of the application of qualitative methods in social work. His substantive interests lie in evaluative research and case study method. His most recent interest is in the application of emergent computer and media technologies in social work education and research.

Ian Shaw is Professor of Social Work, University of York, England. His primary academic interests lie in the extensive borderlines between social work practice and research. This includes research involving older people, children and young people, offenders, mental health sufferers, hospital and primary care patients, and people with learning disabilities. Professor Shaw has written extensively on qualitative methods, evaluation and practice/research relationships in social work and related fields, aspects of evidence and knowledge for practice, and the character and history of social work research. He has also written or edited about a dozen books and eighty peer reviewed papers. He co-edits the *Qualitative Social Work* journal (Sage Publications), and was lead editor with colleagues in the USA for the *Sage Handbook of Evaluation*. He is presently preparing a new edition of his *Evaluating in Practice* (Ashgate), as well as co-authoring books on evidence and knowledge for social work (Polity Press), and *Social Work and ICT* (Sage Publications). He is following up a completed national evaluation of the Integrated Children's System – part of the UK government's e-Government programme – and a study of practitioner research networks in Scotland.

Notes on Contributors

CHAPTER 1

Nigel Parton is Foundation NSPCC Professor of Applied Childhood Studies at the University of Huddersfield, England. A qualified and registered social worker, he has written and researched on social work, child welfare and child protection for over thirty years. Previously he was Professor in Child Care Studies at the University of Keele and Professor in Child Care and Director of the Centre of Applied Childhood Studies as well as being head of social work research for fifteen years at the University of Huddersfield. He is the author of numerous books including *The Politics of Child Abuse* (Macmillan, 1985, with Patrick O'Byrne) and *Constructive Social Work: Towards a New Practice* (Palgrave/Macmillan, 2000). His most recent books are *Safeguarding Childhood: Early Intervention and Surveillance in a Late Modern Society* (Palgrave/Macmillan, 2006, with Bob Lonne, Jane Thomson and Maria Harries), *Reforming Child Protection* (Routledge, 2008), and (with Nick Frost) *Understanding Children's Social Care: Politics, Policy and Practice* (Sage, 2009).

Stuart A. Kirk is Distinguished Professor and Marjorie Crump Chair in the Department of Social Welfare, School of Public Affairs at the University of California, Los Angeles. He has served as Chair of the Department and as Director of the doctoral program at UCLA. Formerly, he was Dean of the School of Social Welfare at SUNY at Albany and was on the faculty at Columbia University. Among his academic interests are the interplay of science, social values and professional politics in the creation of psychiatric diagnoses and in the development and uses of knowledge in social work. He has published widely in social welfare, psychology, psychiatry and other journals. His books include *The Selling of DSM* (Aldine, 1992), *Making Us Crazy* (Free Press, 1997), *Science and Social Work* (Columbia University Press, 2002) and an edited book, *Mental Disorder in the Social Environment* (Columbia University Press, 2005).

CHAPTER 2

Annette Boaz is a social scientist with an interest in the relationship between research evidence policy and practice. Annette Boaz has recently taken up a new post as lecturer in translational research at King's College London. Prior to this she was a senior research fellow in the UK Economic and Social Research Council funded Centre for Evidence and Policy, also based at King's. At the Centre she was involved in a programme of training, development and methodological work relating to evidence based policy and practice. Annette has conducted research for the UK Social Care Institute for Excellence (SCIE) on the types and quality of social care research. She is also a member of the SCIE Quality Assurance Advisory Board. Annette is a member of the editorial board of the journal *Evidence and Policy*.

James Blewett is a registered social worker who is currently national chair of Making Research Count, a research dissemination network in the UK which in London is based at the Social Care Workforce Research Unit, Kings College London. This has involved him working closely with practitioners and managers around the dissemination and utilization of research. Prior to this James spent many years working in different social work settings in children's services. James has taught extensively on social work qualifying and post qualifying programmes at a number of universities. James co-authored the literature review that informed the English consultation about the roles and tasks of social work and recently led a national evaluation of the codes of practice for social workers on behalf of the four care councils in the UK. James' other research interests have been around child welfare policy, family support and the impact of poverty on parenting.

CHAPTER 4

Daniel Gredig, PhD, Social Worker, is Professor and Head of the 'Institute Integration and Participation' in the School of Social Work at the University of Applied Sciences Northwestern Switzerland (FHNW). He was trained in social work at the University of Fribourg (Switzerland) and at the Freie Universität Berlin (Germany). He received his PhD from the University of Zurich. In 2000 he joined the University of Applied Sciences Northwestern Switzerland and held appointments at the School of Social Work and the University of Zurich. His fields of special interest include history and theory of Social Work, research-based intervention development and innovation, social work and health, HIV prevention and social services for people living with HIV/Aids. His publications in the last years have focused on HIV protection behavior, HIV prevention, support needs of people living with HIV/Aids and evidence-based intervention development in social work.

Jeanne C. Marsh, MSW, PhD, is Dean and George Herbert Jones Distinguished Service Professor in the School of Social Service Administration at the University of Chicago. Her fields of special interest include services for women and families, service integration in service delivery, social program and policy evaluation, and knowledge utilization in practice and program decision making. Professor Marsh joined the University of Chicago faculty in 1978 and held appointments in both the School of Social Service Administration and the Committee of Public Policy Studies. She served as Dean of SSSA from 1988 to 1998 and from 2006 to present. She also has served as Visiting Professor in the London School of Economics and at Clare Hall, Cambridge University. Professor Marsh publishes broadly on issues of substance abuse, social service provision for women and children, evidence-based practice and the evaluation of social work interventions. She is recipient of the NASW Award for Excellence in Social Work Research, has served as Editor-in-Chief of *Social Work*, the journal of the National Association of Social Workers, and served on the Board of the Society for Social Work and Research.

CHAPTER 5

Gerhard Riemann is a sociologist and presently professor of social work at the Georg-Simon-Ohm University of Applied Sciences in Nuremberg, Germany, after having worked at the social work departments of the Universities of Bamberg and Kassel for two and a half decades. He has taken part in the development of biographical research on the basis of narrative interviews and has a long-standing interest in the uses of interpretative approaches and qualitative methods for fostering skills of case analysis among students of social work and social workers. He has been quite involved in working with students of social work in the context of research work-shops and seminars on practice analysis and has written extensively about these styles of research discourse and practice reflection. Gerhard Riemann published research monographs on mental patients' biographies (based on autobiographical narrative interviews with patients) and recurring problems of professional work in the practice of social workers in family coun-selling. He presently participates in an EU sponsored research project on European identity work which is carried out by groups of social scientists in different countries.

Susan White is Professor of Social Work at Lancaster University in the UK. Her primary research interest is in ethnographic and discourse analytic studies of clinical and professional decision making and, particularly, professional talk. She has recently completed an Economic and Social Research Council funded ethnographic study of electronic information sharing in multidisciplinary child welfare practice and is Principal Investigator on a further ESRC Public Services Programme study of 'error and blame' in child welfare practice. This latest study focuses on the relationship between the performance management of public services responsi-ble for safeguarding children and the impact of anticipated blame within the decision-making practices of those providing, supervising and managing these services.

CHAPTER 6

Bob Pease is Chair of Social Work at Deakin University in Australia. His main research inter-ests are in the fields of critical masculinity studies and critical social work practice. In the former area, his specific research focus is on men's violence against women, cross-cultural and global perspectives on men and masculinities and post-Vietnam military masculinities. In the latter area, he is interested in the application of critical theories to progressive social work practice and profeminist approaches to working with men in the human services. His most recent books are *International Encyclopedia of Men and Masculinities* (co-edited, Routledge, 2007); *Critical Social Work Practice* (co-edited, Allen and Unwin, 2003) and *Men and Gender Relations* (Tertiary Press, 2002). He is currently co-editing a book titled *Migrant Men: Critical Studies of Masculinities and the Migration Experience* and writing a book titled *Undoing Privilege: Facing the Predicament of Unearned Advantages*.

CHAPTER 7

Joan Levy Zlotnik, PhD, ACSW is the Executive Director of the Institute for the Advancement of Social Work Research (IASWR). Leading the organization since 2000, she works in the national policy arena with colleagues from other disciplines to promote social work research and behavioral and social science research opportunities. Within the profession she works with schools of social work and other national organizations to build and enhance research infra-structure and foster applicants' success at garnering federal research grants. She previously worked at the Council on Social Work Education and National Association of Social Workers and has directed federal grants as well as projects supported by the Annie E. Casey Foundation, John A. Hartford Foundation, Gill Foundation, Kellogg Foundation, Casey Family Programs and the Ford Foundation. Her areas of interest include building a competent health and human services workforce, promoting community–university partnerships, evidence-based practice, and dissemination and implementation research.

CHAPTER 8

Haluk Soydan is Research Professor and Director of the Hamovitch Center for Science in Human Services, USC School of Social Work, Los Angeles. He has a PhD in sociology from Uppsala University in Sweden. Before joining the USC School of Social work he served for the last ten years as Research Director at the National Board of Health and Welfare, Stockholm. His scientific publications include more than two dozens of books, authored or co-authored by him, and a large number of journal articles. He is a co-founder of the international Campbell Collaboration which he served as co-chair for six years. His meta-analysis article together with colleagues on what works among ethnic juvenile delinquents was awarded the Pro Humanitate Award for 'Intellectual Integrity and Moral Courage'. He is a three times award receiver of the Swedish Association of Textbook Writers. In 2004 he was honoured by the Swedish Government for 'Zealous and Devoted Service to the Nation'. In 2008 he was given the Recognition of Outstanding Contribution to the Campbell Collaboration Award.

CHAPTER 9

Richard Hugman is Professor of Social Work at the University of New South Wales, Sydney, Australia. He has practised, taught and researched in various aspects of social work, in the UK and in Australia. Recent publications have mostly been in the area of professional and applied ethics. For six years he was a member of the Australian Association of Social Workers national ethics committee and also currently serves on the International Federation of Social Workers panel on ethics. Since 2004 Richard has been working with UNICEF Vietnam to advise the government of Vietnam about the development of professional social work in a way that is appropriate for that country.

CHAPTER 10

Steve Trevillion is Professor of Social Work and Dean of the School of Social Sciences, Media and Cultural Studies at the University of East London. He started his social work career in Plymouth and worked as a neighbourhood social worker in London before he began to focus on teaching and research. He has held personal chairs at Brunel University, London South Bank University and the University of Leicester. From 2002 to 2005 he was Head of Social Work Education at the General Social Care Council. During this time he took the lead role in developing the Post-Qualifying Framework of Education and Training for Social Workers. His major research interests lie in partnership working and social work theory. He is the author of *Networking and Community Partnership* (1999) and his most recent work is a reappraisal of concepts of prevention.

CHAPTER 11

Mikko Mäntysaari is Professor of social work at the University of Jyväskylä, Finland. His academic career started at 1982 after three years of experience as a child welfare social worker. He has been working in the University of Tampere (1982–1995), National Research and Development Centre for Social Welfare and Health (Stakes) (1995–2001), and from the year 2001 in University of Jyväskylä. His research interests have been in social philosophy, social welfare administration and evaluation studies.

Richard Weatherley is Professor emeritus at the University of Washington, School of Social Work. He has an MA in social work from the University of Chicago, School of Social Service Administration; and a PhD in political science from the Massachusetts Institute of Technology. His research focuses on the adoption and implementation of social policies, and especially the role of human service organizations and front-line workers. The substantive areas of his research include special education reform, mental health policy, adolescent pregnancy programs, child abuse prevention, income maintenance and social security. Work experiences in Africa, Asia, Australia and Europe, as well as the US, have contributed to his appreciation for a comparative perspective. He is currently a visiting Professor at the University of Malaya, Department of Social Administration and Social Justice.

CHAPTER 12

Adrienne Chambon is Professor at the University of Toronto's graduate Faculty of Social Work, where she is also director of the PhD Program. Her research interests have been in critical theory, specifically in narrative and discourse approaches to social work practice and policy. She co-edited Essays on *Postmodernism and Social Work* with Allan Irving, and *Reading Foucault for Social Work* with A. Irving and L. Epstein. More recently, she has received several grants from the Social Sciences and Humanities Research Council of Canada as P.I. to inquire into the links between social work knowledge and art forms, in particular, socially engaged arts. She has extended her previous research on immigration and refugees to delve into a transnational perspective on the circulation of people and ideas. One of her grants on 'solidarity across the disciplines', a cultural-studies approach to social work, focuses on a historical re-reading of agency and community archives and practices, drawing on visual along with textual materials.

CHAPTER 14

Jackie Powell is Professor of Social Work Studies and a co-director of the ESRC funded National Centre for Research Methods located within the School of Social Sciences at the University of Southampton, UK. She is a professionally qualified social worker and has practised in a number of mental health settings. Prior to taking up an academic appointment more than a decade ago, she was a 'contract researcher' in various organizational settings. Her particular interests include interagency working at the health and social care interface and the impact of changing policy and organizational structure on patterns of service provision and professional practice. She also has a long-standing commitment to promoting older people's involvement in the research process and facilitating the greater utilization of research by practitioners. She is active in the implementation of a range of capacity-building activities to promote social work research within both academic and practice settings.

Blanca M. Ramos is Associate Professor at the School of Social Welfare, State University of New York at Albany. She holds a Master's in Social Work and a Doctorate in Social Welfare. She has conducted research on health, mental health, and domestic violence with multicultural populations in the U.S. and in Latin America. She has served in local, regional, national, and international boards and commissions and has extensive experience as a practitioner and community advocate. She has served as the first Vice President of the U.S. National Association of Social Workers (NASW) and on the National Board of the Institute for the Advancement of Social Work Research and the NASW National Ethics Committee. She has developed collaborative partnerships with higher education institutions, non-governmental organizations, community advocates and social work professionals to further social work research in Mexico and Peru.

CHAPTER 16

Jennie Popay is Professor of Sociology and Public Health, Institute for Health Research, University of Lancaster, United Kingdom. She spent five years working in East Africa and New Zealand before returning to the UK in the 1970s. She has worked as a sociologist in social policy and public health in academia, the voluntary sector and the NHS. Her research interests include social inequalities in health, the sociology of knowledge with a particular focus on lay knowledge, the evaluation of complex social interventions, community engagement/empowerment and methods for the synthesis of diverse evidence. She is currently working with the WHO Commission on the Social Determinants of Health co-ordinating a global knowledge network on social exclusion and has undertaken an extensive review of evidence on community engagement for the National Institute for Public Health and Clinical Excellence. She has held public appointments as a commissioner with the Commission for Health Improvement, Vice Chair of the Commission for Patient and Public Involvement in Health, Chair of the Salford Early Years Partnership and a Non-Executive Board Member of the Mancunian NHS Community Health Trust.

Geraldine Macdonald is Professor of Social Work and Director of the Institute for Child Care Research at Queen's University Belfast. After working first as a qualified social worker she began her academic career at Royal Holloway, University of London. She moved to the Chair at the University in Bristol in 1997 where she stayed until April 2004 when she was appointed Director of Information and Knowledge Management at the newly established Commission for Social Care Inspection. Her research interests are effectiveness research, professional decision-making and child protection. She has published and presented nationally and internationally on each of these areas. She was a founding member of the Campbell Collaboration and is Coordinating Editor of the Cochrane/Campbell Developmental, Psychosocial and Learning Problems Systematic Reviews Group. Geraldine Macdonald has been a Board Member of the Social Care Institute for Excellence; is a Trustee of Coram (England's oldest Children's Charity) and Chair of Coram's Children's Services Committee.

CHAPTER 17

Jane F. Gilgun, PhD, LICSW, is Professor, School of Social Work, University of Minnesota, Twin Cities, USA. She does research on the development of violent behaviors, the meanings of violence to perpetrators, and how children overcome adversities, with a particular interest in prevention and intervention. She also collaborates with social service agencies to develop theories of change (what works with whom under what conditions) and clinical assessment instruments. She has published and presented nationally and internationally on qualitative research methods and methodologies and on her violence research and writes for the general public through the internet (Kindle, triond, helium, and lulu). She has taught qualitative research and evaluation methods on the master's and PhD level for more than 20 years. She has bachelor's and master's degrees in English literature (poetry), a master's in social work from the University of Chicago, a licentiate in family studies and sexuality from the Catholic University of Louvain, and a PhD in child and family studies from Syracuse University.

CHAPTER 18

Carmen Lavoie is a PhD candidate in Social Work at McGill University in Montréal. Carmen's dissertation examines the construction of race and ethnicity in neighbourhood community organizing practice. Before her PhD, Carmen worked for five years as a community organizer in several low-income neighbourhoods. During this time, she was the coordinator of a participatory study examining the experience of residents in one neighbourhood. Her areas of interest include anti-oppressive social work, community organizing, racism, migrant issues, poverty, social work education, participatory approaches to research and models of community–university collaboration.

Judy MacDonald is an Associate Professor at the School of Social Work, Dalhousie University, where she is currently the Undergraduate Coordinator. She has been a practicing social worker for over twenty years, working in medical social work and feminist based practice. (dis)Ability rights and inclusion have been Judy's primary focus in both teaching and research. She identifies as a woman with a (dis)Ability using this location to inform her research, practices and teachings. Examples of her research experience consist of: (dis)Ability inclusion, survey of Schools of Social Work in Canada; community response to woman abuse; women in the helping professions as sufferers of chronic pain – (re)storying (dis)Ability; healthy balance: caregivers portraits; and (dis)Ability accessibility in on-line teaching.

Elizabeth (Bessa) Whitmore, Professor Emerita at Carleton University School of Social Work, Ottawa, Canada, has been teaching community-based approaches to research and evaluation for many years. She has conducted a number of participatory research and evaluation projects, and is currently evaluating a banking accessibility project for people living with 'severe mental illness'. Book chapters include 'Six street youth who could ...' in the *Handbook of Action Research* (2001), 'Some contradictions in conducting a short term participatory evaluation' in *Knowledge Shared: Participatory Evaluation in Development Cooperation* (1998), and 'To tell the truth: Working with oppressed groups in participatory approaches to inquiry' in *Participation in Human Inquiry* (1994). She co-authored, with B. Cousins, the lead chapter 'Framing participatory evaluation,' in her edited volume *Understanding and Practicing Participatory Evaluation* (1998). Among her local activities, she co-chairs the Community-based Research Network of Ottawa.

CHAPTER 19

Jennifer C. Greene is a Professor of Educational Psychology at the University of Illinois, Urbana-Champaign. She has been an evaluation scholar–practitioner for over 30 years. Her work focuses on the intersection of social science methodology and social policy and aspires to be both methodologically innovative and socially responsible. Her work in mixed methods well engages this commitment. Greene's conceptual methodological work has concentrated on advancing the qualitative and mixed methods approaches to social inquiry, as well as participatory–democratic commitments in evaluation practice. Greene has held leadership positions in the American Evaluation Association and the American Educational Research Association. She has also provided considerable editorial service to both communities, including a six-year position as co-editor-in-chief of *New Directions for Evaluation*. Her own publication record is extensive and includes a co-editorship of the recent *Sage Handbook of Program Evaluation* and authorship of *Mixed Methods in Social Inquiry*.

Peter Sommerfeld is Professor of Social Work at the University of Applied Sciences Northwestern Switzerland, School of Social Work, and head of the institute for 'Social Work Research and Cooperative Knowledge Creation'. His research interests are grouped around the development of Social Work as a profession and the theory–practice link. Knowledge production and knowledge transfer in Social Work therefore are of special interest to him. Recent research has been completed in the fields of probation services, psychiatry and occupational social work. Following the idea of 'cooperative knowledge creation' these recent research projects also are conceived as huge development projects on the level of concept and methods in these practice fields. He mostly published in German on a broad variety of themes such as social work research, professionalism, adventure pedagogy, social work and psychiatry, social work and urban development. In English he published on Evidence-based Social Work. He is co-president of the Swiss Society for Social Work.

Wendy Haight is Professor of Social Work at the University of Illinois, Urbana-Champaign. She received her BA from Reed College and her PhD from the University of Chicago where she studied cultural developmental Psychology. Her current research focuses on vulnerable families involved with public child welfare systems in the U.S. and Japan. Using a mixed method approach, she examines socialization beliefs and practices and children's development in cultural context. Several representative publications are: Haight, W. (2002). *The Socialization of African-American Children at Church: A Sociocultural Perspective*. New York : Cambridge University Press; Haight, W., Ostler, T., Black, J. and Kingery, L. (2009). *Children of methamphetamine-involved families: The case of rural Illinois*. New York: Oxford University Press; and Bamba, S. & Haight, W. (2007) Helping maltreated children to find their Ibasho: Japanese perspectives on supporting the well-being of children in state care, *Children and Youth Services Review*, 29(4): 405–427.

CHAPTER 20

Robyn Munford is Professor of Social Work, School of Health and Social Services Massey University, Palmerston North, New Zealand. She has qualifications in social work and sociology and lectures in social and community work, research methods and disability studies. Robyn has extensive experience in disability and family research and has worked for the past decade on a family wellbeing research program that utilizes participatory and action research methodologies. She is currently engaged in an action research project exploring social and community practice in community-based settings and is co-director of a five-year research programme investigating resilience pathways for young people who are service users of community-based and statutory agencies. This is a multi-disciplinary study involving researchers and practitioners from a range of disciplines and practice settings. Robyn has published widely on social and community work theory and practice including strengths-based practice; disability studies; community development and bicultural practice; research methods; young people; and family research.

Jackie Sanders is a Senior Researcher in the Social Work and Social Policy Programme, School of Health and Social Services at Massey University, Palmerston North, New Zealand. Her research examines changing patterns of family life and the different ways in which parents and children/young people respond to these changes. She has a particular interest in well-being and resilience for young people and manages a large five-year research programme examining pathways to resilience for vulnerable young people. Her research interests also include different aspects of social work practice and she works with a number of social care organizations in the non-profit sector in New Zealand. Jackie has twenty years experience in health and social service planning and management.

CHAPTER 21

Linda Briskman is the Dr Haruhisa Handa Chair of Human Rights Education at Curtin University in Perth, Australia. She previously held social work academic appointments at other Australian universities and her practice background is in the area of child and family welfare, particularly with Indigenous Australians. Her main areas of research are asylum seeker rights and Indigenous rights within the Australian context and she publishes widely on these issues. She is a convenor of the People's Inquiry into Detention under the auspices of the Australian Council of Heads of Schools of Social Work, which challenged Australian government policies on immigration detention. Recent books include *Social Work with Indigenous Communities, 2007; and Human Rights Overboard: Seeking asylum in Australia*, 2008 (co-authored with Susie Latham and Chris Goddard).

CHAPTER 22

Karen M. Staller is Associate Professor of Social Work at the University of Michigan School of Social Work. She holds degrees from Columbia University (PhD) and Cornell Law School (JD). She has published articles and book chapters on runaway and homeless youth, child abuse and neglect, qualitative methods, and the intersection of law and social work. Her book *Runaways: How the Sixties Counterculture Shaped Today's Practices and Policy* (2006) published by Columbia University Press reflects her long-standing practice and scholarly interests in runaway and homeless youth as well as qualitative and historical methods. Her forthcoming book, co-edited with Kathleen C. Faller, is an in-depth historical, community-based, case study on the prosecution of child sexual abuse cases in a small, rural U.S. community. Her teaching interests include the history and philosophy of social policy, social welfare policy, children, youth and family policy, law and social work and qualitative research methods.

Tracie Mafile'o researches culture and social work, in particular, Pacific Islands and Tongan social work – including Mafile'o, T. (2008) 'Tongan social work practice,' in M. Grey,

J. Coates, and M. Yellowbird (Eds) *Indigenous Social Work around the World: Towards Culturally Relevant Education and Practice*. Williston, VT: Ashgate Publishing, Mafile'o, T. (2005) 'Community Development: A Tongan Perspective,' in M. Nash, R. Munford and K. O'Donoghue (Eds) *Social Work Theory in Action*. London: Jessica Kingsley Publishers, and Mafile'o, T. (2004) 'Exploring Tongan Social Work: Fakafekau'aki and Fakatokilalo.' *Qualitative Social Work: Research and Practice*, 3(3), pp. 239–257. Dr Mafile'o is currently based in Papua New Guinea, Pacific Adventist University as Director of Counselling and Senior Lecturer, while on extended leave from Massey University, New Zealand, Social Policy and Social Work Programme, School of Health and Social Services. Of Tongan and New Zealand Pakeha descent, Dr Mafile'o is involved in a number of groups promoting the wellbeing of Pacific peoples in New Zealand and beyond.

CHAPTER 23

June Thoburn is Professor Emeritus in the School of Social Work at the University of East Anglia, Norwich, England. She recently completed a Leverhulme Emeritus Fellowship to undertake an international comparison of children in out-of-home care in 25 jurisdictions. A qualified child and family social worker, she has been teaching on and researching across the field of child welfare since 1978. She is involved in the training of the judiciary and is frequently asked to provide expert evidence in complex foster care and adoption cases. She has just completed a seven-year term as a founding member of the General Social Care Council and was awarded the CBE in 2000 'for services to social work'. Her research (covering family support, child protection, adoption, foster care and services to minority ethnic families), employs quantitative and qualitative methodologies. She has a long-standing interest in the re-analysis of routinely collected administrative data.

Mary C. Ruffolo, PhD, LMSW is an associate Professor at the University of Michigan School of Social Work, Ann Arbor, Michigan, USA. Her research studies focus on adapting efficacious interventions, evaluating effectiveness, and addressing ways to disseminate efficacious interventions with at-risk populations (e.g., families of children with serious mental illness, adults with severe mental illness). She is committed to research that addresses the needs of vulnerable populations served by the public systems. Her research activities address (a) testing the effectiveness of interventions and services for at-risk populations and (b) disseminating empirically supported interventions. Current funded intervention and dissemination studies include: evaluating the Support, Education and Empowerment intervention for parents of youth living with a serious emotional disturbance in public mental health settings; adapting and evaluating cognitive-behavioral interventions in school-based health clinics for youth living with depression or anger management problems; and a Statewide Multiple Family Group Psychoeducation dissemination evaluation project.

Paula Allen-Meares is Dean Emeritus, Norma Radin Collegiate Professor of Social Work, and Professor of Education at the University of Michigan. In January, 2009 she assumed Chancellorship of the University of Illinois Chicago. Research interests include functions of social workers employed in educational settings; psychopathology in children, adolescents, and families; adolescent sexuality and parenthood; and social work practice. She has published extensively on these topics, as well as issues in higher education, and contributed to numerous editorial boards. She is principal investigator of the Skillman Foundation funded Good Neighborhoods Technical Assistance Center, and previously served as PI on numerous federal and foundation grants. Allen-Meares has served on national professional and scientific committees promoting social work advancement, such as the Society for Social Work Research, the Council on Social Work Education, the National Association of Social Workers, and others. Presently, she is a trustee and fellow of the New York Academy of Medicine and a member of the Institute of Medicine of the National Academies.

CHAPTER 24

Paul Bywaters is Emeritus Professor of Social Work at Coventry University and Honorary Professor at the University of Warwick in the UK. His research has explored different aspects of social work's contribution to people's health, and particularly social work's role in combating health inequalities. He was co-founder and first Convenor of the Social Work and Health Inequalities Network (www.warwick.ac.uk/go/swhin).

Michael Ungar, PhD, is a University Research Professor and Professor in the School of Social Work at Dalhousie University, Halifax, Canada. His research is focused on understanding resilience among children, youth and families across cultures and contexts. Currently he leads several studies (www.resilienceproject.org), including an eleven-country program of research on positive development among youth-at-risk and an Atlantic Canada study of how clusters of mandated services and community supports relate to resilience. Dr. Ungar has authored more than 60 peer-reviewed articles and book chapters, as well as six books for parents, educators and helping professionals.

CHAPTER 25

Sally French started her working life as a care assistant working with disabled children. She then became a physiotherapist and later a physiotherapy lecturer. Over the years she specialized in teaching and researching the social sciences applied to health and illness. Her major interest during the last 20 years has been Disability Studies where she has written and researched extensively. She has also co-authored two books on research which are aimed at health and social care workers.

John Swain is Professor of Disability and Inclusion at Northumbria University. He has taught and researched in the area of Disability Studies for over thirty years at both Northumbria University and the Open University. He has published widely in this field, particularly co-authoring and co-editing texts with Sally French, and he is executive editor for the *Disability and Society* journal. His current research interests include the experiences of disabled people as health and social care service users and the development of participatory research approaches to working with disabled people.

CHAPTER 26

Peter Huxley is Professor of Social Work and Social Care and Director of the Centre for Social Work and Social Care at Swansea University in Wales. He was previously (1999–2006) at King's College in London where he held a Chair in Social Work at the Institute of Psychiatry, and was also Director of the Department of Health funded Social Care Workforce Research Unit. Between 1995 and 1998 he was the first social worker to be head of a UK School of Psychiatry (at Manchester University, where he trained as a social worker). He has research collaborations with colleagues in Norway, Italy, the Netherlands, Germany, and Australia, and between 1989 and 2004 he worked on a continuous series of mental health service evaluations with Dr. Richard Warner at the Mental Health Centre of Boulder County, Colorado. He has published internationally on social work and social aspects of psychiatry and community mental health services.

Michael Sheppard has been Professor of Social Work at the University of Plymouth since 1997. Before becoming an academic he worked as a social worker. He has had particular interest in the areas of child care, mental health and social work theory and much of his writing falls into these areas. In addition to research he has been involved in editorial and advisory work, as well as teaching and management at university.

Martin Webber is Programme Leader of the MSc in Mental Health Social Work with Children and Adults at the Institute of Psychiatry, King's College London. He teaches research methods and supervises practitioners' research projects on the programme. He is also the Teaching and Learning Co-ordinator for the Institute of Psychiatry. His PhD research was on the role of social capital on the process of recovery from depression research. Broadly, his research interests lie in the impact of social phenomena on mental health and the role of social workers and other professionals in their amelioration. Martin is a qualified social worker with experience of working with people with mental health problems and those who have a learning disability.

CHAPTER 27

Philip McCallion, PhD, ACSW is Professor in the School of Social Welfare at the University at Albany, and is Director of the Center for Excellence in Aging Services. A Faculty Scholar and National Mentor in the John A. Hartford Geriatric Social Work Faculty Scholar Program, Dr. McCallion's research falls into three areas: 1. Making communities more aging prepared and measuring the effectiveness of related interventions including evidence based health promotion programs. 2. Examining the experiences of multi-cultural and multi-generational families and of aging families supporting persons with developmental disabilities. 3. Evaluation of interventions for persons with dementia. Dr. McCallion's research has been supported by the John A. Hartford Foundation, National Institute for Drug Abuse, Agency for Health Quality Research, Administration on Aging, Joseph P. Kennedy, Jr., Foundation, Alzheimer's Association, New York State Health Foundation, and New York State's Department of Health, Developmental Disabilities Planning Council, Office of Children and Family Services and Office for the Aging.

CHAPTER 28

Fergus McNeill is Professor of Criminology and Social Work and Deputy Head (Research) in the Glasgow School of Social Work (a joint venture of the Universities of Glasgow and Strathclyde) and a Network Leader in the Scottish Centre for Crime and Justice Research (at the University of Glasgow). Prior to becoming an academic in 1998, Fergus worked for a number of years in residential drug rehabilitation and as a criminal justice social worker. His research interests and publications have addressed several of the interfaces between social work and criminal justice, including sentencing, community penalties and youth justice. Latterly his work has focussed on the policy and practice implications of research evidence about the process of desistance from offending. His first book, *Reducing Reoffending: Social Work and Community Justice in Scotland* (co-authored with Bill Whyte), was published by Willan in April 2007.

Denis Bracken has been teaching criminal justice social work at the University of Manitoba for 29 years. He holds postgraduate degrees from the University of Toronto and the LSE. Recent research has been in the area of desistance from crime by inner city aboriginal gang members, and social work training and community justice. He is the co-author of two reports for the Manitoba Government on working with domestic violence offenders. He is on the Editorial Advisory Board of the *British Journal of Community Justice* and the Specialist Assessment Panel of the *Probation Journal*. Professor Bracken has been an academic visitor at De Montfort University, Trinity College Dublin and the Glasgow School of Social Work. At the University of Manitoba he was director of the Inner City Social Work Program and later Associate Dean responsible for Distance Education and undergraduate programs. Presently he is the Rector of St. Paul's College at the University of Manitoba.

Alan Clarke, BA (Hons), BPhil, PhD is Professor of Criminology in the Department of Law and Criminology, Aberystwyth University. His main research interests are in the field of crime and criminal justice. He has been involved in a variety of research studies including an evaluation of a mentoring intervention project for young people at risk of offending, a study of the nature and effectiveness of drugs throughcare for prisoners, a qualitative survey of attitudes towards relationship rape, a study of the implementation of a Youth Inclusion Programme in a rural area and an investigation into local responses to school exclusion. He is the author of *Evaluation Research: An Introduction to Principles, Methods and Practice*, published by Sage (1999) and a co-editor of *The Economic Dimension of Crime*, published by Macmillan (2000). He has also published numerous papers in a number of key academic journals.

Handbook Advisory Board

Kazimiera Wódz, MA in Psychology, PhD in Humanities, Professor of Sociology, Head of Social Work Unit, Institute of Sociology, University of Silesia, Katowice, Poland.

Walter Lorenz is Professor for the sociology of cultural and communicative processes at the Free University of Bolzano/Bozen, Italy, and Principal of the same university. He co-edits the online journal *Social Work and Society*.

Jeanne Daly, Adj. Professor, mother and child health research, La Trobe University, Australia.

Mapping Social Work Research: Pasts, Presents and Futures

Ian Shaw, Katharine Briar-Lawson,
Joan Orme and Roy Ruckdeschel

INTRODUCTION

The *Sage Handbook of Social Work Research* aims to provide a comprehensive account of the state of the art of social work research internationally, and in doing so to craft an intellectually original statement that will have a defining and shaping role for social work research, and thus provide an agenda-setting framework for the medium-term future. The *Handbook* reflects the concept and readership level of the publisher's handbook series, as it offers a defining statement on the theory and practice of social work research for the first decades of the twenty-first century. It is written for academics, advanced postgraduate students, social work researchers, experienced practitioner and user researchers, and commissioners and end users of social work research.

The *Handbook* aims to map social work research. To our knowledge this has not been done previously. From their first beginning, maps have been made for some particular purpose or set of purposes. In so mapping our intention is not simply to portray, nor just to describe the 'topography', but to actively form and shape the landscape. Rather like the work of the cartographer, mapping a field of research entails a diversity of modes of representation. The success with which the intent of the mapping is accomplished rests in the extent to which the user – in cartographic terms the percipient – understands, and is able to assess and engage with its purpose/s.

Maps carry their own symbology – projection, scale, compass bearings and so on. Our intention in this essay is to suggest the symbology through which the *Handbook*-as-map may be read. The elements in the map space shift – we variously differentiate texture, shade and orientation throughout the *Handbook*. The central significance given to the idea of context in the second part of the *Handbook* illustrates this extensively.

We accept that there is no final consensus on the purposes of social work research. Still more, we realize that there is no consensus on which methods of research 'fit' particular purposes or contexts. But we believe there is sufficient consensus, from different standpoints, that social work research and practice are always enhanced when purpose, method, context and domain[1] are brought together in the practice of research.

In speaking of social work and of research, we find it helpful to distinguish:

- social work research as empirically apparent;
- social work research as theoretical discourse; and
- social work research as social and moral practice/s.

Reflecting and developing these distinctions, the four key questions the *Handbook* addresses are:

1. What is the role and purpose of social work research?
2. What contexts shape the practice and purpose of social work research?
3. How can we maximize the quality of the practice and method of social work research?
4. How can the aims of social work in its varied domains be met through social work research?

These questions move in and out of focus throughout the *Handbook*, although each in turn provides the primary focus for the four *Handbook* sections – the purposes, contexts, practice and domains of social work research. The writers, board members and editors of the *Handbook of Social Work Research* aspire to a diverse, coherent, critical and comprehensive benchmark statement about the nature and role of social work research and evaluation in contemporary twenty-first century societies around the globe.

The *Handbook* is necessarily diverse and pluralist, as social work research has many representations, multiple stakeholders and audiences, and diverse ideologies. It is also necessarily dynamic. It traces recent and on occasion more distant historical shifts, and projects future pathways. The *Handbook* does not say everything there is to say about social work research, for even a relatively comprehensive project must leave out some perspectives, some ways of knowing, and some spheres of action and interest. As with any decent map, we were faced with judgments about what to include, what to leave

out and where to place items of interest, for we cannot emulate Lewis Carroll's fictional map that had the scale of one mile to a mile.[2] To change the metaphor from map to building, we say more about foundations, superstructure, roofing and borders with neighbours, and less on internal room layouts, furnishings and *decor*.

Yet the *Handbook* strives for coherence – a unity enhanced through the organizing framework. In addition, although the *Handbook* specifies important differences among alternative approaches, it also endeavours to specify major commonalities. The emphases in the *Handbook* at different moments are international, national, or local in scope. They find their primary impetus from practitioners, service users, policy makers or the university community. They may be established or innovative in demeanour. But they share the commonalities of commitment to shared social work values and of seeking to foster the highest standards, quality and value of social work research. Moreover, in each of the four major sections of the *Handbook*, an anchoring chapter offers a critical synthesis of the ideas and discourse presented in that section. Through these framing guidelines, the *Handbook* seeks to make a major contribution to coherence in the field.

We aspire to counter ethnocentrism of various kinds. The field of social work research has sometimes been limited by boundaries of disciplinary domiciles, professional interest and paradigmatic location. National boundaries also have sometimes served to introduce an unnecessary parochialism into the development of the field. The *Handbook* contributors stand against naïve pragmatism on such matters and have been asked to avoid a tendency toward the lowest common denominator. We have sought to resist ethnocentric tendencies through the cultivation of a critical (rather than polemical) and open stance. We asked contributors to include critical, reflexive assessments of positions with which they themselves are associated. Writers were also asked to consider the overall gains and deficits in the field in which they are writing and, where appropriate, to set out their aspirations as to what developments would make for substantial gains in the medium term future.

The *Handbook* aims for an integration of theory, research and practice within each chapter (although the relative mix of theory, research and practice varies from chapter to chapter). Further, social work research is part of different changing social and political contexts. The *Handbook* contributors acknowledge these contexts. They look backward as well as forward as they overview the field. They also explore linkages with other disciplines and fields of practice. In several of the chapters one of the writers is writing from 'outside' social work.

SOCIAL WORK RESEARCH?

Social work research is identifiable through a set of features, none of which exclusively or exhaustively characterizes it, but which can be seen to typify its scope and character. These general features include:

- The use of a broad range of research methods and an acceptance of different linkages between research method and research questions in the contexts, practices and domains of social work research.
- Underpinned by the quest for both usefulness *and* theoretical contributions so that research is not categorized as only 'pure' or 'applied'.
- A pervasive concern with social inclusion, justice and change.
- Work with stakeholders in different aspects of the research process and managing the complex power relationships involved.

The following definition is helpful as a starting point:

Research is understood as original investigation undertaken in order to gain knowledge and understanding. Social work is an applied policy and practice-oriented discipline, which is strongly theoretically informed and can generate further developments in

theory, policy and practice. Research in social work covers:

a. theory, methodology, ethics and values, and pedagogy as they apply to social work and social care and to substantive issues in these areas of study;
b. relevant links with other disciplines – most importantly anthropology, criminology, demography, development studies, economics, education, gerontology, health studies, history, law, penology, philosophy, politics, psychology, social policy and sociology;
c. relevant links with other stakeholders, professionals, service users and carers;
d. policy-making processes, practice, governance, and management, service design, delivery and use, and inter-professional relationships; and
e. comparative research and research into international institutions, policy and practice. (JUC SWEC, 2006: 3)

Definitions almost without fail give hostages to fortune. They tend to fall into the standard trap of confusing the descriptive and the normative, and too often take the form of staking territorial claims. The JUC SWEC definition is less vulnerable to the second problem but there are apparent tendencies to normative statements – for example in the claim that it is 'strongly theoretically informed' and in the aspirational 'can generate further developments in theory, policy and practice'. It also has a slightly detached feel. It is quite different from other definitions on offer. Take, by way of contrast, the following statement from within a statement on doctoral training requirements:

The focus of social work research is often on those with asymmetrical, stressful or divergent relationships with their fellow citizens, the formal agencies of the local or national state and the formal and informal institutions, processes and structures of the communities and societies in which they live. This requires social work researchers to be aware of and responsive to differences that arise through the lived experience of gender, race, ethnicity, physical and mental capacity and disability, sexuality, age, culture, beliefs and values.[3]

How far do such statements carry global meaning and agreement? The IFSW/IASSW series of statements (2007) that stem from the core statement setting out an 'International Definition of the Social Work Profession' does not include a specific definition of social work research. However, they include within the definition a paragraph headed 'Theory' which starts with the statement that:

> Social work bases its methodology on a systematic body of evidence-based knowledge derived from research and policy evaluation, including local and indigenous knowledge specific to its context. (IFSW/IASSW, 2007: 6)

The 'Global Standards' include as one of five points under the methods of social work practice the statement that these methods include:

> Knowledge of social work research and skills in the use of research methods, including ethical use of relevant research paradigms, and critical appreciation of the use of research and the different sources of knowledge about social work practice. (IFSW/IASSW, 2007: 21)

Two points may be offered by way of reflection. First, the statements are fairly cross-cultural. For example, knowledge is said rather uncontroversially to 'include' local and indigenous knowledge, rather than to consist entirely in such knowledge. The appeal to 'systematic' and 'evidence-based' alike suggests a foundational role for mainstream science models. This suggests that the main international groupings of social workers and social work academics accept that the social work profession and its associated research-related roles and activities carry a large degree of common ground across cultures and nations.

Much the same can perhaps be said of statements emerging from individual countries where social work is relatively well established.[4] Superficially, this may not seem to be the case, as in the following statement about social work from the Finnish National University Network for Social Work (SOSNET):

> In Finland, social work has been developed as an independent field of study with its own problem-setting, epistemological and ontological assumptions, research targets and ways of knowledge formation. (http://www.sosnet.fi/?deptid=22096)

But this claim to independence may be speaking more to an intra- than inter-national audience.

Second, the IFSW/IASSW statements seem to have an aspirational dimension. They illustrate the problem we referred to above of including rhetorical, normative statements in definitions. The SOSNET statement seems to engage in similar rhetoric when it asserts that 'Social workers are involved in producing information with scientific methods and they apply this information in their work'. This is not necessarily a weakness. It would be naïve to expect or even wish for rhetoric-free statements, but we should recognize and respect different categories of claims.

We are not wholly convinced of the wisdom of demanding a single global definition of social work research. This is not in the interests of fuzzy thinking, but more from a fear that such statements are likely to prove bland and unduly rounded. Local and national statements (e.g. Karvinen et al., 1999) are more likely to engage the mind and promote conversation. International statements also risk obscuring the local and the national, often in the name of a variety of pluralism that 'confuses issues of interests with conflicts of power' and 'can balance only those interests that are represented – typically those of the powerful' (House, 1991: 240).[5]

For some, a priority is to link any defining features of social work research to social work practice. 'Practice research', for example, is often associated with strongly voiced discussions about ways of evidencing and knowing. This is as it should be, but it ought not to make us exclusive in our view of the scope of the project. Practice research may be accepted as comprising any disciplined empirical inquiry (research, evaluation, analysis), conducted by researchers, practitioners, service users/carers, which is intended, wholly or to a significant degree, to shed light on or explain social work intervention/ practice with the purpose of achieving the goals of social work within or across national cultures.

However, practice or intervention research in the USA is the design and testing of interventions rather than this more general and inclusive definition. In this context, practice research encompasses multiple levels of interventions from the individual, to families and groups, to organizations, communities and policy involving specific programmes. Intervention or practice research is a Design and Development (D&D) study process that uses both quantitative and qualitative research. It may require in-depth interviews with practitioners and literature reviews in the 'engineering' phase in which a practice design occurs of the intervention to be tested. Fashioned as an iterative, sequential approach to developing, designing, testing, refining and retesting of an intervention, intervention research builds on knowledge utilization, outcome evaluation and proceduralization along with field testing. Such D&D is also critical to the adaptation of interventions to diverse populations. Interventions may be retested and reformulated for new populations as well as new target problems.

An alternative way of capturing the nature and field of social work research is to see it as possessing two general identifiers – for example, as addressing characteristic *substantive* fields, and doing so with one or more characteristic *problem foci* (Shaw and Norton, 2007). From this perspective any given research project or program can be identified against two definers. Some early work has been done along these lines, distinguishing the *substantive* fields into eight actual or potential service user or carer groupings, three citizen, user and community populations, and four professional and policy communities. The *problem foci* are also distinguished into fifteen categories. Cross referring the two sets of defining categories yields a mathematical possibility of 225 different kinds of research, although the maximum meaningful number is much less than this although as yet cannot be affirmed with any confidence.[6] The following examples illustrate the category levels:

Substantive fields

- Adult offenders/victims (service user/carer category)
- People as members of communities (citizen populations)

- Social work practitioners/managers (professional/ policy communities)

Problem foci

- Understand/explain issues related to equality, diversity, poverty and social exclusion
- Understand/develop/assess/evaluate social work practices, methods or interventions
- Understand/promote learning and teaching about social work or related professions

This framework is at an early stage of development. There are no inter-rater measures between different stakeholder groups. Furthermore, for it to be used across countries then inter-cultural ratings will be an essential prior requirement. But it may hold promise of a more evidenced approach to important discussions regarding cultural competence in research, and for understanding the extent of common ground between different national and indigenous social work research visions and practices.

Valuable as these approaches may be, the writers of a *Handbook* that purports to identify social work research as a field with discipline-like qualities cannot avoid questions of where social work research sits in relation to other fields or disciplines.[7] For example, should we conclude from the foregoing that social work research is and ought to be different from research in social science disciplines, and even from other areas of 'applied' research, such as education or health?

An illustration may clarify. It has sometimes been suggested that social work research has a distinctively radical critique of positivism. The references to positivism in social work are almost always negative, as when the broadside is fired that 'positivists not only see their work as uncontaminated: they see themselves as pure and safe in their objectivity, an elite who have managed to transcend the constraints of subjectivity' (Everitt et al., 1992: 6).[8]

We have two problems with this and similar arguments. First, the key terms – positivist, objectivity and subjectivity – tend to be treated as self-explanatory, and in need of no unpacking. Arguments become a form of sloganizing – 'a swearword by which no-one is swearing' (Williams, 1983) – and leave proponents vulnerable to being regarded as partial, and as a consequence run the risk of being ignored. Second, it undermines a culture of reciprocal exchange and argument that should mark social work activity at all levels. Lying behind claims to social work's special character is, we suspect, an old heresy that for many years was prevalent – the belief that social work has a basic value position that has greater merit/greater human authenticity/is more whole-person oriented, etc. than other professions and disciplines. Even when the term 'paradigm' is not used, these sorts of arguments have the marks of a naïve paradigm position. Hammersley is right to warn that paradigm talk on this level 'obscures both potential and actual diversity in orientation, and can lead us into making simplistic methodological decisions' (Hammersley, 1995: 3). To pick up his second point, this problem is apparent when one hears the occasional argument that quantitative analysis is inherently 'positivist', whereas qualitative methodology is somehow more reflective of social work values.

Social work and social work research will be the poorer if we over-emphasize their distinctives. It will make us disinclined to listen to the voices of colleagues in other disciplines and professions. If we espouse professionally joined-up services, why not disciplinarily joined-up research? On most occasions the right question to ask is not what makes social work research distinctive, but what might make it distinctively good?

There are advantages stemming from the conventional view that social work is a multidisciplinary field that draws reflectively on a wide range of disciplines, rather in the way that the JUC SWEC definition of social work research suggests. The advantages arise from the differences between one field or discipline and another. For example, disciplines vary in how far their identities are respectively empirical, hermeneutic or critical. From this distinction we can draw on a plausible interdisciplinary rationale to conceptualize social work research as being committed to evidence, learning/reflection and emancipation without having to set these commitments in a hierarchy. Of course, this only takes us so far. Evidence does not make us free in the absence of other conditions; neither does reflection guarantee we will reach the truth. Perhaps a theory of communicative action and of discourse ethics, following Habermas, will do – not as solutions to concrete issues 'so much as a set of recommended practices within which such solutions may be pursued' (Outhwaite, 2000: 657). One such recommendation for standards of discourse, advocated by Martyn Hammersley, is summarized in the 'Places in Time' chapter that explores an overview of contextual issues in social work research. Deliberative processes of this kind are, of course, close to democratic theory. They also have been applied to and developed in the field of evaluation (e.g. House and Howe, 1999).

Social work research in time and place

Social work research adjoins – and is challenged by – other contemporary fields and disciplines. It also has a history – indeed, histories – and a place that suggest the nature of social work research is not always similar from time to time or from place to place. Feminist histories of social work research go to figures such as Jane Addams,[9] when the politics of gender were brought to the fore especially through 'settlement sociology' (Lengermann and Niebrugge, 2007). Mainstream academic histories may cite Charles Loch in the UK or Edith Abbott in the USA. Histories of social work research also vary by country. Nordic histories trace the origins of later distinctives in earlier moments and people. The recent development of social work in countries of the Asia Pacific Rim will develop their own narratives. One stream within the UK has been the policy research tradition that goes back to the Fabian impact on policy from the late years of the nineteenth century, with Beatrice and Sydney Webb, and the relationship of social work to the emerging discipline of social policy. Other histories set social work in a related or more widely encompassing social category – human services in the USA, social care in the UK, social pedagogy in the Baltic States and elsewhere in Europe.

But despite this multiplicity of histories, we think it is possible to argue for a common approach to 'doing history' in social work research. The point is made elsewhere in this *Handbook* that to insist on the importance of history is not simply a point about methodology, but has regard to a way of thinking – of 'focusing "upstream" on the historical roots of contemporary relationships' (Mallinson et al., 2003: 773). Walter Lorenz has pressed this point effectively (Lorenz, 2007). He complains that it is as if we are 'too embarrassed to look seriously at our history, afraid of the disorder we might find, too eager to distance ourselves from the pre-professional beginnings' and are, in consequence, homeless and 'disembedded' (Lorenz, 2007: 598, 599). He concludes that 'All social work practices are deeply embedded in historical and cultural habits from which we cannot detach ourselves at will', and aptly infers from this that we should be practising history 'in the dual sense of positioning ourselves in a historical context and of giving our interventions a historical dimension' (Lorenz, 2007: 601).

But in speaking about the history of social work research, we are on uncertain ground. While there are some valuable parts of a jigsaw in place (e.g. Diner, 1977; Lubove, 1965; Kirk and Reid, 2002: Ch 2; Timms, 1968), these tend to take social work in general as their reference point. We are not sure when 'social work research' achieved common currency in social work, though it was probably associated with the slippage of 'case work' from a term for the whole to a term for a part ('casework') of 'social' work.

Standard accounts of the history of social work research lack depth. Some of the central questions are scarcely asked:

- To expand the argument made by Lorenz, what role does research play in the collective memories of social work?
- How does social work research relate historically to the emergence of research in other social science disciplines?
- What are the main themes in a critical narrative of social work research's past and its relation to other disciplines?
- Were certain knowledge conditions necessary for the emergence and development of social work research?

On the fourth question, it is likely that the growing hold of modern rational philosophy was a major contributing knowledge condition for social work research, with its basic 'proposition that humans interact and that their interactions have, over many centuries, become more and more complex, more and more rational, and, with it, more and more able to use rationalism to resolve their differences' (Wickham and Freemantle, 2008: 924).[10] There are various forms of social work research that are clear heirs to rational philosophy, and it is plausible to interpret the emergence of the early university-linked social work programmes in Chicago, Boston, Minnesota, New York and the London School of Economics as seeking, and to a fair extent gaining, credibility through their commitment to a strong intellectual and rational stance.

Yet almost from day one, social work research sat uncomfortably between the social sciences and the world of practice and policy. For example, the early USA social work pioneer at Chicago, Edith Abbott, complained that 'some of our social science friends are afraid that we cannot be scientific because we really care about what we are doing ...' (Diner, 1977: 11). In addition to the doubts of their 'social science friends' Abbott and her colleague Sophonisba Breckinridge famously referred to 'our eastern colleagues' (the social work programmes at Boston and New York) who 'told us we could not have casework and fieldwork in a university' (Diner, 1977: 7; c.f. Lubove, 1965: 265).[11]

Being simultaneously 'scientific' and 'really' caring may have gone hand in hand for Abbott, but the two have more often been uneasy bedfellows. We have aspired to a position that has affinity with that held by Abbott, in ways that we sketched in the early part of this introductory essay. But we do not wish to dissolve contrasting commitments – for example, to rigour or to emancipatory research. Indeed, different manifestations of research as heirs of rational philosophy are not sufficient as an explanation of the knowledge conditions for social work research. Wickham and Freemantle (2008) detect in earlier sociology, through at least to Weber, a domain of the social that owes much to voluntarist philosophy going back to Thomas Hobbes – where the stress lies on the will rather than the mind. It may not be unduly simple to suggest that several of the major debates among social work researchers have their ground in whether their advocates are primarily influenced by rationality or voluntarism. But even if this general interpretation stands up following further work, such historical work will doubtless prove 'a process so full of surprises that no theory or set of protocols can ever anticipate it' (Baehr, 2008: 947).

DIVERSE, COHERENT, CRITICAL, COMPREHENSIVE – IDENTIFYING TENSIONS

We have tried throughout the process of crafting this *Handbook* to sustain a sense of a recognizable field, but of unresolved and probably best-left-unresolved tensions. This is reflected among the contributors, the advisory board and within the editorial team. In an early exchange of thinking we set out our aspirations for the *Handbook* as a diverse, coherent, critical and comprehensive project. We expressed these aspirations in a form that

has proved enduring over the three years it has been in development. We said that the *Handbook of Social Work Research* would offer in one volume a coherent benchmark statement about the nature and role of social work research and evaluation in contemporary twenty-first century societies in many countries around the globe. There are deliberate oppositional elements in this way of conveying the project – diverse *but* coherent; comprehensive *but* critical; coherent *but* dynamic.

To flesh out these necessary tensions within the *Handbook*, we pursue just one of them. The melding of criticality and comprehensiveness was perhaps the most demanding fusion asked of contributors. Our stance on criticality has aimed to sustain how a position can be advocated but not in partisan way. Thus, even *within* given stances – critical practice, evidence-based practice, etc. – there are diverse debates. We will be satisfied if the *Handbook* proves comprehensive in that sense among others. We invited contributors to give recognition to seriously held justice-informed positions that have been present in social work research, but which may be ones that the writers did not hold.

Taking a UK example,[12] the Fabian tradition of research linked to the welfare state formed the core of the emerging discipline of social policy in the UK. The influential research of people such as Richard Titmuss, E.H. Halsey, Peter Townsend and others – embodied in the Fabian Society – was characterized by a realist trust of empirical evidence and scepticism of theoretical stances. The Fabian Society is a democratically constituted membership organization. It is affiliated to the British Labour Party but is organizationally independent. George Bernard Shaw, H.G. Wells, Beatrice and Sidney Webb, Oscar Wilde and all Labour prime ministers have been members of the society. It is an intellectual socialist movement, whose purpose is to advance the principles of social democracy via gradualist and reformist, rather than revolutionary means. It represents a justice-informed position for social research and one that is alive and well in the social work research community. The dominance of left-leaning political positions among social work academics has been a continuing strand here.

Holders of the Fabian position have been forcefully criticized by Marxists as 'drawing room socialists'.[13] Yet there is diversity even here. There are those Marxist academics who decline to adopt an activist position as part of their research or take a direct and explicit involvement in transformative action through their research. Popkewitz illustrates this position. We do not do justice to his position by a single quote, but he argues that 'social scientists are partisans in the forming of social agendas through the practices of science' (Popkewitz, 1990: 50).

This does not exhaust justice-based stances. There are older traditions. Robert Dingwall discusses the moral discourse of interactionism and draws on Adam Smith for how the moral and the empirical plug together. He concludes 'If we have a mission for our discipline, it may be to show the timeless virtues of compromise and civility, of patient change and human decency, of a community bound by obligations rather than rights' (Dingwall, 1997: 204). This example is taken from sociology and may have as few direct parallels in social work as it does in sociology. But the diversity of positions – UK Fabianism, differences on partisanship within Marxism, and the more conservative position of Dingwall – illustrate how general commitments can be part of a research community without requiring the same stance on the part of everyone.

We wanted writers to acknowledge these tensions and positions. We did not expect writers to consent to them in a pluralist fashion, but we *did* want them, where appropriate, to accept that they are positions that can meaningfully be held and contested. We had this in mind when we asked contributors to include critical, reflexive assessments of positions with which they themselves are associated. Needless to say, we did not expect all the contributors to sign up to every detail of our position, and we were content that differences between contributors should

remain within the *Handbook*. By way of illustration, we engaged in a lengthy and eventually unresolved discussion with the authors of one chapter regarding ways in which a critical stance on the social model of disability and related questions might be expressed within the *Handbook's* commitment to melding criticality and comprehensiveness. It remains reasonable to us to acknowledge the force of the comments on the chapter from one Board member who reflected from within a critical commitment that:

> The medical model once represented an enormous advance over the moralising approach which connected disability to metaphysical forces and causes. The medical model contributed towards the regaining of dignity by disabled people by making their condition treatable. This must be seen as an attempt of inclusion, belonging to the general project of modernity – with all its ambiguity! It is the crisis of modernity … which facilitated the demise of the individual model and the rise of a constructivist view of a whole range of social realities, including disability (but also gender and ethnicity for instance).

This takes us back to our assumptions about the advisability of a form of scholarly discourse that includes such exchanges. We are not sure that there is unanimity regarding such terms of discourse. Researchers who hold a strong standpoint position, for example on issues of race or gender, or who believe that the more important differences underlying debates within the social work community are epistemologically paradigmatic in nature, would probably have difficulty in conceding this position. Researchers who hold a diametrically different position, and believe that research pragmatics permit unanimity on all key issues, would also, we think, find it difficult to align with our position that closure on debates and differences is premature – indeed, perhaps inappropriate. Hence, while assuming that a real, mutually understood conversation regarding big questions is possible, we stand against such closure.

We may perhaps describe this as a 'coalition'[14] though this unhelpfully suggests something temporary and entered into for some immediate purpose. The kind of community we have in mind calls for a term that suggests that this is something about the essence of how things ought to be (and therefore not temporary) but also avoids assuming a united alliance. Another way of expressing this mode of containing matters is to see it as a position on the *levels* at which debates can be taken forward – at a 'middle-range' of generality, whereby differences of approach can be acknowledged, without requiring an abandonment of the quest for collective positions.

MAPPING THE *HANDBOOK*: PURPOSES, CONTEXTS, PRACTICES AND DOMAINS

The purposes of social work research

The chapters in this section are organized around distinct but not exclusive traditions and ways of doing, thinking and knowing within social work research. Each represents a particular role or purpose for social work research in society. For each tradition, contributors were asked to consider issues of philosophy and paradigm, theory, practice and critique. We expressed these issues in the form of questions. What is the philosophical framework justifying this tradition? What major research approaches characterize this intellectual tradition? What does research practice within this intellectual tradition look like? Whose interests does it serve? What major questions does it answer? What are important critiques of this understanding of the purpose of research? What are its particular benefits and limitations? What are important future areas for development?

Social work research will be distinctive insofar as, *inter alia*, it achieves a thoroughgoing consistency with broader social work purposes. It will do so when it severally aims to:

- generate or enhance theory and knowledge about social work and social care;

- provide impartial evidence about and for decision-making;
- instrumentally improve practice and organizational learning;
- highlight the quality of lived experience and advance practical wisdom; and
- promote justice, social change and social inclusion.

The chapters in the opening section directly reflect these benchmarks. We have not asked writers to present these in a pragmatic 'pick-and-mix' manner. Indeed, as we elucidate below, thinking of social work research as a purposeful enterprise is one area of the *Handbook* where the intended tensions of the project come to the surface. Are differences in research purpose paradigmatic in nature? How do we respond to diversity if we espouse a form of pluralism? Is social work research a discipline?

Part of our response to these enduring questions is to enter a plea that social work research should be conceptualized in such a way that 'pure' and 'applied' research are not in conflict, and applied research is not seen in deficit terms as a methodologically lesser form of research. But this does not tell us whether some ways of expressing research purpose in social work ought to be given greater weight than others. We suggest that there are, in fact, three possible positions on this question, rather than just two.

Some research purposes carry greater weight than others. This may be argued from a belief that scientific knowledge always takes precedence over, for example, knowledge based on experience (hence rigour, accuracy and other 'inner-science' criteria, on this view, will always be more important than 'outer-science' criteria). The same general stance may also be argued from, for example, a strong 'standpoint' position that the knowledge of the oppressed will always carry greater validity than that of the oppressor – though of course the direction indicators are in quite the reverse, giving precedence to 'outer-science' purposes over 'inner-science' ones.

The weightiest research purpose in social work will always be contingent on local context and the perspectives of the stakeholders, and cannot be 'assigned' in advance. This position is sometimes loosely referred to as a 'postmodern' position – 'loosely' because typically under-developed and perhaps assumed to be beyond countermanding.

A third position – and one with which we find ourselves in broad sympathy – is that:

'Inner' and 'outer' science criteria of quality are both indispensable, and they should be brought to bear on any given research project or output. However, they should not be applied through a framework of 'criteriology' (Stake, 2004), but at a level of generality that does not require us to 'weight' dimensions against one another. On this premise, 'outer-science' norms or purposes (e.g. being useful or emancipatory) are neither more nor less intrinsically important than 'inner science' epistemic norms.[15]

Stuart Kirk and Nigel Parton set the scene for this in their opening chapter where they reflect upon the nature and purposes of contemporary social work as a context for thinking about the role of research. Their primary aim is to provide some thoughts on what they see as the nature and purposes of social work and how these have developed both historically and comparatively. The central argument of the chapter is that debates about the nature and purposes of social work research cannot be separated from debates about the nature and purposes of social work. Their secondary aim is to outline how research can be seen to have contributed to the enterprise and might do so in the future.

Annette Boaz and James Blewett draw on their different perspectives in elaborating how providing objective, impartial evidence for decision making, and providing public accountability, form a core organizing purpose for social work research. Boaz and Blewett note how the relationship between *knowledge* and differing research traditions influences social work decision making. Social work traditions which might be characterized as the therapeutic, the social order

and the emancipatory, each have their own perspective on evidence. In the authors' view, the challenge of enhancing the decision-making process by practitioners will require systematic efforts at improving the quality and synthesis of evidence. In one of several chapters contributed by the editors, Joan Orme and Katharine Briar-Lawson explore ways in which generating or enhancing theory and knowledge about social problems and social policy and how best to enhance policy development acts as a driver for much social work research. In an exploration of the history of the relationship between research, policy and practice they argue for an iterative dialogue between the three which reflects the complexity of researching the personal and political dimensions of social work practice.

Daniel Gredig and Jeanne Marsh interweave their European and North American outlooks in unfolding the improvement of social work intervention and practice as a recurrent purpose of social work research. Offering four conceptualizations of research for practice, and their critique, they explore the relationship between research and practice and the contribution of empirical research to the development of practice. Underpinning the discussion are distinctions between 'intervention' and 'professional practice' and an exploration of the extent to which research approaches reflect a commitment to professional values and ethics.

Taken together these three chapters broadly, though not unconditionally, represent different manifestations of commitment to rigour and rationality: The following two chapters reflect more the influence of voluntarist philosophy. Sue White and Gerhard Riemann start from the general stance that a defining purpose of social work research is highlighting and advancing the quality of lived experience, practical wisdom, and personal and organizational learning. They develop this through depicting what they regard as the intrinsic affinity between the activities involved in the reconstructive analysis and assessment of single and collective cases in social work and related processes in research. Bob Pease's chapter concludes this framework-setting opening section of the *Handbook*. Recent years have witnessed a proliferation of books and articles advocating broadly justice-based and critical standpoints for social work research. Pease does not simply *reprise* these arguments. Rather, he places the debates and issues in ways that both challenge social work readers and researchers of whatever hue, and creatively takes the research agenda forward for critical researchers and others influenced by developments in this field. He outlines some of the implications of theories of knowledge and structural and discursive locations on the ethics and politics of how we do research.

Contexts

The *Handbook* aspires to reflect the diversity within social work research while having, as we have mentioned earlier, a coherence and comprehensiveness. This diversity is mirrored in the social, relational, political, intellectual and ethical dimensions of social work research as a practice engaged with people. These rich and challenging contexts are explored in this section of the Handbook. By devoting a quarter of the *Handbook* to research contexts, we are signalling our seemingly paradoxical belief that the more one endeavours to understand social work research in ways that speak to the international social work community, the greater becomes the significance of contextual issues.

We remarked at the beginning of this essay that the *Handbook* is diverse and pluralist, as social work research has many representations, multiple stakeholders and audiences, and diverse ideologies. Pluralism is, to borrow Popper's term, a 'bucket' word, too often left as if it spoke for itself.[16] For us, we can comfortably adopt for social work research a statement on pluralism from a discussion of evaluation, as having:

... many countenances, multiple vested audiences, and diverse ideologies. Part of this pluralism is

indeed ideological ... Part of this pluralism is temporal, as evaluation is intrinsically linked to changing societal and international ideals and aspirations. And part of this pluralism is spatial, as evaluation is inherently embedded in its contexts, which themselves vary in multiple ways (Mark et al., 2006: 10).

We have sought to engage with this pluralism in different ways, perhaps most obviously by representing different social work research traditions, purposes, domains and practices. We have also aimed to respect and highlight different differences and commonalities. Finally, we have aspired, as explained elsewhere, aspired to counter ethnocentrism of various kinds, most persistently through the collaborative forms of authorship to which we refer later in this essay.[17] In casting pluralism in these terms, we distance ourselves from the soft relativism that would allow all ideologies an equal chance of expression. Relativism can helpfully be adopted as a way of thinking when one is trying to understand another culture (c.f. Hacking, 1999). But this willing suspension of belief as an attitude of mind should not be confused with relativism – that combination of 'intuitionism and alchemy' (Geertz, 1973: 30).

The section opens with an overview by Ian Shaw and Joan Zlotnik of the government context for research. The structural context of government and its reciprocal relationship with social work research is the focus of this chapter. The writers distinguish between research as a means of governing, and research as the evaluation of government, and concentrate primarily on the former – the uses that governments make of evaluation and research as a means of governing. They include a review of general government approaches to research funding.

Other structural contexts, for example, regarding wider political contexts, and social science disciplines, are dealt with in the chapters by Soydan, Mäntysaari and Weatherley. Haluk Soydan analyzes the nature and role of politics and values, both as critical contextual features of social work research practice and as intertwined with knowledge claims associated with research. Cross-national ideological differences and the consequences for social work research are also considered. The chapter concludes that values and politics impact on social work research practice, but this does not necessarily lead to biased research results in social work. Application of what are described as extra-scientific and intra-scientific norms and criteria can help to recognize, control for and eliminate biases in social work research. This chapter may be read in conjunction with Mikko Mäntysaari and Richard Weatherley's analysis of the role of theory and theoretical knowledge in social work research. They trace the historical evolution of theory in social work in light of debates about the nature of theory, and examine current trends in theorizing. Social work writing on research has on occasion been unduly parochial, as if social work is a hermetically sealed field of action and study, with its own values, methodology, preoccupations and historical lineage. Mäntysaari and Weatherley serve to disabuse us of that fallacy. Like a number of chapters, they offer a perspective born of European/North American collaboration.

Political and intellectual contexts both pose questions of ethics. Richard Hugman majors on this in his chapter on ethics as context for social work research. He locates ethics within social relationships, especially those constituted by power, and examines processes and procedures in research to explore this. Acknowledging the challenges presented by developments in applied ethics the chapter emphasizes ethics as process rather than event and highlights connections between ethics of social work research and the wider professional field of social work.

One of the most self-evident contexts for social work research is social work practice and institutions and settings in which it takes place. Yet scarcely anything has been written that foregrounds this. Steven Trevillion expresses the point succinctly in his contribution to the *Handbook*. He remarks that 'The relationship between research and the practice contexts in which it takes place is one of the most important and yet poorly understood issues facing social work researchers. In particular, we seem to know very little about the ways in which practice influences research'. His starting point is the idea that it is possible (even necessary) to conceive of research about practice as an outcome of what goes on in the practice domain. In response to the ways that social work practice needs to be understood at different levels, he suggests a three-level model of practice with each level linked to particular examples of emergent research. His argument integrates the practice context with research in ways that open up the scope for more coherent research – and practice.

Almost all of this section envisages contexts as either contemporaneous with, or precursors to, the research act. Roy Ruckdeschel and Adrienne Chambon's chapter on the uses of social work research is located in this part of the *Handbook* because research takes a major part of its character from context as futures. Ruckdeschel and Chambon identify three aspects of research utilization, these being knowledge development, 'use' in the sense of how knowledge is incorporated into social work practice and knowledge dissemination. Utilization is illustrated through exemplars involving social work professionals and service users with a particular emphasis on community-based activist research. The challenges presented by the internet and the evolving forms of media for the dissemination of social work knowledge on a global level are explored.

The final chapter offers a big-picture appraisal of how social work researchers have shaped – and ought to shape – their work in the light of these contexts. Ian Shaw adopts a moderately strong position on context. He acknowledges the influence of wider social theorizing for thinking and living in time and place, before reflecting on context as the focus and concern of the research act – both methodological and substantive. The ensuing part of the chapter considers social work practice as context for research, before turning to the varied elements of the social work and wider academic communities. The closing part of the chapter considers those contexts extrinsic to the immediate research act – the state, city, rurality and the community – and includes aspects of race and politics.

The practice of social work research

The distinctive character of this *Handbook* – mapping social work research as a discipline-like field of study – has meant that tracts of literature normally central to the landscape of social work research texts appear here in more general, discursive forms or in some cases not at all. This applies most obviously to methods for the collection and analysis of data. This is not because we are indifferent to either the importance or indeed attraction of 'methods-talk', and we have made our own efforts to contribute to that literature elsewhere. It is rather because we have chosen to explore questions of methodology and methods *within the identity of the discipline-like field of social work research*. Hence we say much more about methodology than methods, and what we and contributors do say is in almost all cases embedded within the larger fields of purposes, contexts and research domains.

A central assumption we bring to this section is that social work research methodology generally does not draw on methods original to social work, but on the range of social science fieldwork choices in, for example, sociology, policy analysis, education, health and psychology. It is the core purposes (Section I) and contexts (Section II) of social work that give its research methodology a distinctive 'shape' and which give a distinguishing mix to the palette of methods. Positions regarding methodology are also entailed in the final section of the *Handbook*. For example, the writers of the chapters for that section were invited to reflect on how particular domains of social work research gave identity and character to the methodology of the research enterprise. Social work research is therefore likely to draw more

extensively on some fieldwork methods than on others, or at least draw on them in characteristic ways. Writers for this part of the *Handbook* were asked to exemplify this illustratively, rather than comprehensively. However, they were encouraged to develop consideration of how the contexts and purposes of social work have contributed to a distinctive 'set' of methodological interests, and to suggest possible future developments. For this reason, the chapters in this section partly mirror in an overt way those in the opening section.

Thus, methodology is not described out of context or in the usual form of a research methods text. Instead, methods are discussed in relation to the purpose, context and value considerations raised in the preceding sections. In doing so, we do not wish to plead for a one-to-one matching of method and purpose. For example, we emphatically do not want to present restrictive visions of qualitative methods as suited only for the purpose of highlighting and advancing the quality of lived experience, or of randomized control trials as fit simply for the purpose of providing objective, impartial evidence for decision making. Indeed, a major editorial agreement for this proposal was to avoid presenting methods under the conventional rubrics of qualitative and quantitative. This is not because we think the distinction no longer matters, nor even because we think that we no longer have any lessons to learn from paradigm thinking. We see a degree of continuing sharp debate over such matters as healthy and recognize the value of not prematurely resolving basic differences in positions (c.f. Arnd-Caddigan and Pozzuto, 2006).

The *Handbook* does, as we indeed hoped, include a range of positions on these issues, and would not take the position, popular in the social work community at the time of writing, that mixed methods are by definition stronger than quantitative or qualitative methods to the exclusion of the other. This decision is linked to our aspiration that the *Handbook* will help shape and (re)define social work research. We intend that it should be methodologically comprehensive. We have endeavoured to ensure the *Handbook* addresses newer developments and neglected methodologies, and that it does not give undue space and weight to familiar territory such as evidence-based practice, interview methods, randomized control trials and research assumptions stemming from western experience of social work research.

The third *Handbook* section opens with a wide-angle reflection on the practice of social work research. Jackie Powell and Blanca Ramos – drawing on experience in England, South and North America – focus primarily on what we know of the experience of doing social work research. They consider the experience of a range of stakeholders including career researchers, practitioners, social work faculty and social work users. They reflect on how the researcher manages the tensions arising from different and often competing interests within the research process in the pursuit of generating knowledge that is both rigorous and relevant, and conducted in ways that seek to make the research process both transparent and inclusive. An appreciation of the competing values, ideologies and commitments of the various interests involved in research serves to underline the multiple obligations of the researcher and the complex issue of accountability.

This research practice-led chapter is following by an attempt by Ian Shaw to place social work research in the context of the extensive literature regarding the logic of social research, and judgments regarding its quality. The purposes of this chapter are twofold. First, to explore the nature of and requirements for good-enough reasons for thought and action in social work research. Second, to deliberate whether there are general criteria that provide a framework for reaching considered judgments regarding the quality of social work research. In doing so, he sets out to stand against naïve pragmatism and avoid any tendency toward a lowest common denominator. His hope in doing so is to resist ethnocentric tendencies through

the cultivation of a critical (rather than polemical) and open stance, and to include reflexive assessments of positions with which he has associated himself.

The section then opens up with a short series of direct parallels between this section – the nearest we get to a conventional discussion of methodology – and the opening section on the purposes of research. Geraldine Macdonald and Jenny Popay's chapter on methods for providing evidence of effectiveness and improving social work intervention echoes the chapters by Boaz and Blewett, and Gredig and Marsh. Jane Gilgun's chapter on methods for enhancing theory and knowledge about problems and policies calls back to Katharine Briar-Lawson and Joan Orme's discussion in Chapter 3 of generating or enhancing theory and knowledge about social problems and social policy and enhancing policy development. The chapter by Carmen Lavoie, Judy MacDonald and Elizabeth Whitmore develops the methodological implications of the chapters by White and Riemann, and Pease. How well the *Handbook* works depends in part on this connectivity – a central driver of the project – that methodology is most helpfully considered as related to judgments regarding purpose.

We have set out our stall to discuss methods in relation to the purpose, context and value considerations raised in the preceding sections. In doing so, we stressed that we do not wish to plead for a one-to-one matching of method and purpose. Having taken this approach, a natural question arises regarding the approach social work researchers ought to adopt towards the proliferating literature on mixed-methods research. Peter Sommerfeld joins forces with Jennifer Greene – a leading writer and thinker on mixed methods research within the international evaluation community – and Wendy Haight, to develop a position on methodological decision making that avoids the distracting naïve pragmatism and provides an intelligence-led stance that will add to the coherence of the arguments in this section. The chapter on mixing methods in this section takes a position with which we would generally concur.

The opening chapter by Powell and Ramos and the closing chapter by Katharine Briar-Lawson, Robyn Munford and Jackie Sanders together provide the book-ends for this section, looking around and forward, respectively. The final chapter addresses challenges and directions in the practice of social work research. The authors lay out challenges in advancing research that is relevant, inclusive and practice based. Intervention or practice research strategies are discussed along with systematic research reviews. In addition, exemplars include approaches to participatory research and developmental research.

Domains of social work research

This section includes chapters reviewing some of the major practice and service domains in which social work research has been carried out. The *Handbook* authors recognize the creative potential of diverse locations for social work research. However, a central agenda has been to counteract any limiting tendencies to professional insularity within the fields of both practice and research. The nature and boundaries of social work services is perhaps the area where there is the greatest degree of diversity between and even within countries. The risk of ethnocentrism is pervasive in a project of this kind, but nowhere more so than in this section. Hence, the editors emphasized consideration of the analytic problems of generalizing from research in one social work domain to that in another, as well as the prospect of cross-domain research, cross-national transfer of learning and social work research that is both domain-specific and in a global context. Hence, the emphasis on integrative developments is not at the expense of necessary distinctions about the development of social work research in different domains.

The chapter themes are presented in a relatively context-free frame of reference to avoid the hazards touched on above. Each of the chapters in this section addresses problems and services. 'Health and Well-being', for example, includes both health *problems* and health *services*. Put slightly differently, each chapter has something to say that links back to the varied purposes of social work research covered in the opening section.

Contributors to the section were asked to include a concise historical outline of the development of research and evaluation in their field, as well as a substantial section exploring likely future developments including key research and other agendas, with exemplars. Contributors were also asked to bear in mind the structure of the volume as a whole. For example, they may have addressed, as appropriate, the roles and *purposes*, social and disciplinary *contexts*, and research *practice* issues that have most influenced social work research *in their field*. This is intended to add to the coherence of the volume as a whole, and contribute to the adequate coverage of different traditions. Writers were asked to consider a number of permeating dimensions, including social exclusion, diversity, poverty, race, gender and indigenization, while recognizing that these are not unproblematic terms.

Linda Briskman opens this last section of the *Handbook* with a forceful discussion of nation as domain for research. There are superficial overlaps with the early chapter in Section Two, but in that case government, politics and so on were under consideration as *contexts* for research. In this final section they are present as the organizing key category for the focus of the research itself. The 'Nation' chapter challenges the 'orthodoxy' of all aspects of social work research: ethics, epistemology and methodology. Drawing on examples of research in the areas of people movements, asylum seekers and refugees; indigenous peoples; and development, world poverty and aid the chapter argues that it is necessary to go beyond traditional research paradigms to develop research to challenge 'evidence' presented to support policies antithetical to human rights.

The collaboration between Karen Staller and Tracie Mafile'o has enabled the project to include a chapter where the domain of community has been explored from the very different national contexts of the USA and Tonga and New Zealand. They consider the different ways in which community is conceptualized in social work practice and research. This leads them to an overview of the historical unfolding of community-based research, including discussions of the settlement house movement, and developments in ethnographic practices, participatory action methods, feminist and standpoint theories, and indigenous/non-Western research, each as part of the evolving landscape of research methods as they relate to community domain. They helpfully turn in closing to consider future directions.

The subsequent chapters treat domains in somewhat more discrete terms – children, young people and families, health and well-being, disability, mental health and ageing. Mary Ruffolo, June Thoburn and Paula Allen Meares bring together themes and issues from the very substantial array of social work research in the domain of children and families. They address studies that advance service access and effective interventions across diverse systems and settings. Cross-national and cross-jurisdiction research initiatives are cited, which promote knowledge brokering for effective practices. Major longitudinal surveys and systematic reviews are also discussed. Research gaps in rigour are also addressed.

Paul Bywaters has collaborated with Mike Ungar – a UK/Canada nexus – to address the equally extensive domain of health and well-being. Although they omit issues regarding disability and mental health – both of which fall in subsequent chapters – in other respects they set their terms broadly. Reflecting the *Handbook*'s notion of domain, they not only discuss research about health *care* or social work activity in health *settings* (such as primary care teams or hospitals) but also care provided in communities by informal providers. They are particularly illuminating in

their identification of a number of areas where it can be argued that social work is breaking new conceptual and methodological ground in health research. Among these are service user involvement, resilience (positive growth under stress) and the indigenization of health knowledge.

The chapters on disability and on mental health are contributed by Sally French and John Swain (disability) and Peter Huxley, Michael Sheppard and Martin Webber. French and Swain capture the positions with which they have been associated in their previous collaborative work. They present their perspective on the centrality of consumer-driven research. They discuss their views of participatory research and the necessity of involving participants with disabilities in all phases of the research. They advocate for emancipatory research as a preferred form of participatory practices. While Huxley, Sheppard and Webber are all working in different locations within the UK, their links with researchers in several countries give a breadth to their discussion of the domain of mental health. The authors describe the important contributions of mental health social work research (MHSW) and discuss its interface with other social work research domains. They also explore contributions to transferable service development and organization, to clinical and practice research, to diversity and equity-related issues, and consider future prospects for MHSW research. Ageing is addressed by Phil McCallion who illustrates the range of social work research approaches in this area. The growing potential for secondary data analysis, the value of longitudinal studies and the need for different frameworks and research approaches to support translational research work are highlighted as are the benefits of multidisciplinary research teams.

The chapter on criminal justice has been accomplished by collaboration that perhaps more than any other in the *Handbook* delivers new collaboration. Fergus McNeill (Scotland), Denis Bracken (Canada) and Alan Clarke (Wales) also cross the disciplines of social work (McNeill and Bracken) and social policy (Clarke). They present compelling arguments for desistance research and address the need for effective interventions and studies on effectiveness. They examine traditional programme evaluation studies against the backdrop of desistance research and argue for approaches that can be tailored to the individual needs and attributes of offenders.

The *Handbook* closes with reflections from three of the editors on the connections and disconnections between research domains in social work. These highlight a dynamically changing picture of social work research, but one that is in the main positive. Writers covering diverse fields identify challenges in methodological developments that have to address multi-disciplinary approaches and be meaningful to multi-professional working. The need for more culturally inclusive research is cited along with more cross-national studies. Other challenges include the demands of policy makers and funders, and the readiness of the workforce to embrace research agendas. However overall there is a sense of robustness in both the nature of the research being undertaken, and social work's ability to respond to the challenges.

DEVELOPING AND WRITING THE TEXT

The reading and navigating of the *Handbook* may be facilitated if we say a little about how we organized the project. The overall direction of the project lay with the editors. Editorial collaboration has been marked by a strong collegiality with extended periods of face-to-face work and audio conferencing. In addition we worked in close collaboration with an international Advisory Board appointed by the publishers. The role of the Board included giving guidance and advice on the purpose, structure and content of the project; advising on contributors; and acting as editorial readers of chapter drafts. This last proved the most significant.[18]

The *Handbook* contributors are in most cases in university posts. While they have been asked to cultivate responsiveness to the research perspectives of policy makers, service user researchers and practitioners (and no doubt in several cases do not see themselves as occupying a solely academic role), the project has been academic-led. The contributions have been subject to demanding standards of peer review. We divided responsibility for each chapter such that each of us acted as lead editor for a quarter of the chapters, and each chapter had a linked Board member who was asked to review the drafts in the role of an intelligent general reader rather than as a specialist in the area covered by the chapter.

Although a minority of chapters are single authored, the great majority are co-authored. The nature of this collaborative writing is unusual. Of the twenty-nine chapters at least fourteen involve newly minted collaborations, and in most of those cases the writers were personally unknown to each other prior to this venture. In each case this has required exchange and negotiation by writers. Given that in most cases they are also domiciled in different countries, the demands of writing have been stringent. Numerous times we have been told by writers that the task of writing has proved very demanding. This is as we hoped. We were determined to avoid established senior academic writing partners producing the latest version of a familiar overview of their field. There are over sixty different people involved in this project, from twelve different countries. The Project Board included senior advisors from fourteen countries.

The form of collaboration was left to writers. If there is a lead writer the pattern of collaboration ranges from a second or third writer acting as resource consultant to the lead writer to full sharing in the development and writing of the chapter. These collaborations were partly a way of operationalizing our vision for the project and partly a reflection of the fact that the breadth and scope of almost all chapters made it overly demanding for one writer to cover the ground.

Consistent with our views regarding the relationship between social work and other fields and disciplines, there is a significant interdisciplinary dimension within the *Handbook*. There are perhaps half a dozen writers who would not regard themselves as social work researchers, plus two or three of the Board. We have asked all contributors to draw on key ideas from other intellectual traditions, in relation, for example, to knowledge, theory, practice, welfare, well-being, technology, health, care, social justice, language, culture, communication, time, place and community.

We asked lead writers to prepare a chapter abstract within two months of agreeing to take on the work. The lead editor, usually in consultation with the co-editors, provided detailed feedback on the abstract. Part of our reason for this was to ensure that the principles of coherence and comprehensiveness were met. On receipt of the first chapter draft, the linked Board member was asked to provide a full review and to suggest how the revision should proceed. The lead editor also reviewed the draft, and provided a consolidated feedback to the writers. We conducted this process without anonymizing either the chapter authors or the Board members. Contributors and writers were sent copies of the full file of writers and advisors.

One of the tensions in the project is that between the general and the specific. One of the main ways we endeavoured to manage this was through asking contributors, wherever it was possible, to include a number of exemplars in their chapter. These take a range of forms – a synopsis of linked research in the area of the chapter with the aim of lending greater specificity and grounding to the discussion; or the development of a model position on something; or a brief narrative of a key research experience. We invited contributors to exercise creativity in developing apt exemplars for their chapter, and welcome the diversity in how this dimension of the *Handbook* has been accomplished.

Each section of the *Handbook* includes a chapter that provides an overview of the themes in that section, and a future look. We regard these chapters as crucial to the overall success of the project. We do not regard the synthesis chapter simply as a commentary on the other section chapters but as a chapter in its own right.

FUTURE CHALLENGES

Niels Bohr, the Danish physicist, was among those who remarked to the effect that 'Prediction is very difficult, especially about the future'. Bearing in mind that caution, the relative space we have devoted to different issues, here and through the *Handbook*, is the best indicator of the questions we believe to be important now, and which we anticipate will remain so for the foreseeable future. Newer issues and the differentiation and expansion of existing ones, can be provisionally identified. The challenge of faith issues may prove a major challenge to social work research. We touch elsewhere on the significance of developments in ICT and the Internet (e.g. in Parton and Kirk's reflections on the growth of surveillance in the opening chapter, in Ruckdeschel and Chambon's chapter on the uses of research, and in passing elsewhere in the chapters on community and on the intellectual contexts of social work research), though this is part of the research map that continues to extend by the day. The relationship of the state and social work research is not easy to anticipate. The discussion above of pluralism and diversity reflects the present predominance of social work research as a western phenomenon. The consequences of the world recession in the latter years of the first decade of this century may well see countries such as China and India emerge as leading economic powers that hence become significant in how the state/citizen relationship plays out in social work research.

As these social forces and forms take shape, who are likely to prove the 'best' – and 'worst' – scholarly allies for the social work research community? We have produced a handbook that despite its originality has been written largely in the familiar scientific voice. This may not be true of future statements. There is an emergent interest in 'voice' issues in writing, and this is having a growing visibility in social work research, where social work may justly claim to be among the field innovators (c.f. Witkin, 2000, 2001, Witkin et al., 2007). Whether social work research hangs together as a field or discipline will be shaped by much that is entailed in these developments, as will the wider question of the future identity of social work as an occupation and profession. Yet it remains our modestly upbeat conviction that:

> Science can be socially framed, possess political meaning, and also occasionally be sufficiently true or less false, in such a way that we cherish its findings. The challenge comes in trying to understand how knowledge worth preserving occurs in time, possesses deep social relations, and can also be progressive ... and seen to be worthy of preservation. (Jacob, 1992: 501)

NOTES

1   The term 'domain' is used primarily in this *Handbook* to refer to the broad practice contexts and also forms of service delivery within which social work research often takes place. See Section IV of the *Handbook*. The term is used in the 'Global Standards' statement by IFSW/IASSW (2007), but does not appear to be defined.

2   We find it hard to resist offering Carroll's text from his *Sylvie and Bruno Concluded*.

'That's another thing we've learned from your Nation', said Mein Herr, 'map-making. But we've carried it much further than you. What do you consider the largest map that would be really useful?' *'About six inches to the mile'.*

'Only six inches!' exclaimed Mein Herr. 'We very soon got to six yards to the mile. Then we tried a hundred yards to the mile. And then came the grandest idea of all! We actually made a map of the country, on the scale of a mile to the mile!' *'Have you used it much?' I enquired.* 'It has never been spread out, yet,' said Mein Herr: 'the farmers objected: they

said it would cover the whole country, and shut out the sunlight! So we now use the country itself, as its own map, and I assure you it does nearly as well'.

3   http://www.esrcsocietytoday.ac.uk/ ESRCInfoCentre/Images/Postgraduate_Training_ Guidelines_2005_tcm6-9062.pdf.

4   We are indebted to Synnöve Karvinen and Mikko Mäntysaari for pointing us to Finnish thinking and statements.

5   For an earlier, thoughtful discussion of social work research in an African state, see Brand (1986).

6   The framework was developed as a means of understanding social work research in universities. It has been applied without any apparent problems in a review and study of practitioner research in Scotland (Mitchell et al., 2008).

7   Mäntysaari and Weatherley discuss social work as a discipline or field (Chapter 11).

8   For an interesting example of a social work researcher wrestling with what she describes as the embedded culture of positivism in the face of her own varied practices see Fook (2001: 123–7).

9   We have been struck by the number of times Addams' role has been discussed by different contributors.

10   This quotation is from a recent exchange regarding the knowledge conditions for the emergence of sociology that bears reading in this connection (c.f. Baehr, 2008; Wickham, 2008).

11   We develop this point further in Chapter 15 in discussing the logic of social work research.

12   Chapter 7 has an example of politics and research from the Soviet era.

13   The phrase was Leon Trotsky's in his essay on 'The Fabian theory of socialism'. He concludes, 'Poor, wretched, feeble-minded Fabianism – how disgusting its mental contortions are!' Accessed at http:// marxists.anu.edu.au/archive/trotsky/works/britain/ ch04.htm.

14   Or possibly a collaborative or a co-operative.

15   This argument is developed in Shaw and Norton (2007).

16   On this occasion the Wikipedia entry is helpful.

17   In its strict philosophical meaning pluralism refers to a system of thought that recognizes more than one ultimate principle, over against philosophical monism. Pluralism in its primary uses seems to refer to the distribution of power in western society. See Cronbach et al. (1980) and House (1991) for illuminating engagements with political pluralism in its relation to research and evaluation.

18   We take this opportunity to record our appreciation of the indispensable advice provided for the project by the Board members.

Purposes of Social Work Research

The Nature and Purposes of Social Work

Nigel Parton and Stuart Kirk

INTRODUCTION

Our aim in this chapter is to reflect upon the nature and purposes of contemporary social work as a context for thinking about the role of research. During social work's history not only has there been considerable debate about its primary purposes and the way it should be organized, but also about the philosophical premises on which it should be based. Many of the arguments about the nature and purposes of social work are reflected in debates about the nature and purposes of social work research. Clearly the two are intimately related and, in many respects, research is now centrally implicated in debates about the practice and future directions of social work in ways which have not been evident previously.

It is not the aim of this chapter to provide an overview and critical analysis of the different approaches and methodologies which might come under the umbrella of social work research. This will be a central focus for several of the other chapters in this *Handbook*. Our primary aim is to provide some thoughts on what we see as the nature and purposes of social work and how these have developed both historically and comparatively. A secondary

aim is to outline how research can be seen to have contributed to the enterprise and might do so in the future.

Our discussion is organized into five substantive sections. First, we outline a wide variety of different approaches to and contexts for social work and outline some of the key themes which have characterized its development since the late nineteenth century. We emphasize the importance of locating social work in its changing social and political contexts. Second, we discuss how certain approaches to 'science' were taken up during the twentieth century, particularly in the USA, as a way of trying to establish social work's professional status and knowledge base. The late twentieth century witnessed an increasing emphasis on the importance of 'evidence-based practice'. Third, we critically analyse the growing importance of population-based research which aims to identify people 'at risk'. We argue, fourthly, that such approaches are in great danger of both de-emphasizing an understanding of clients in their particular social contexts and of the crucial 'relational' elements to the work, while contributing to the growth of surveillance networks. Fifth, we draw attention to other approaches to research which explicitly try to give voice to clients and thereby attempt to democratize both research and social work itself. The central argument of the chapter is that debates about the nature and purposes of social work research cannot be separated from debates about the nature and purposes of social work, and that these are very much tied up with epistemological and value issues, themes which we underline in the conclusion.

THE HISTORICAL ROOTS AND DIFFERENT CONTEXTS OF SOCIAL WORK

Unlike a number of traditional professions such as medicine, law, teaching, pharmacy and engineering that can be traced to classical Greece and Rome and throughout the medieval period in Europe, the emergence of social work did not take place until the second half of the nineteenth century. Moreover, there are still areas of the world that do not have social workers and, of those that do, many have seen its (re)introduction during the second half of the twentieth century.

It is important to recognize that both the nature and purposes of social work are constructed within diverse social and political environments (Payne, 2006) and take rather different forms in different societies. In England, which was one of the first countries to have identifiable social work activity, and which we will discuss in more detail later, and in the USA, it originally manifested itself as voluntary and predominantly middle class female work and its focus was the undesirable individual and the social consequences of industrialization and urbanization. By the second half of the twentieth century, however, it had been transformed into a predominantly professional activity, organized in large, bureaucratic, local government public sector agencies. By contrast, in continental Europe, Australia and the 'developing' world it continued to be carried

out primarily in smaller voluntary agencies with professional staff working with volunteers, while in the USA there also developed a distinctive private and commercial sector alongside the voluntary and public sectors. Most western countries have seen a growth in the commercial sectors and a growing reliance on private sector business practices. Social workers in all advanced industrialized states are located in a range of statutory public bodies, voluntary agencies, community associations and commercial enterprises, working alongside or under the supervision of a number of other professionals, and accountable to regulatory frameworks of law and guidance. The range of activities is considerable and the focus of the work includes individuals, families, groups and communities.

This diversity is particularly evident in Europe, where a range of terms are used and which cover a variety of different practices. For example, in nearly all European countries the terms 'social work' and 'social pedagogy' are both used, but the differences between them are not used in a consistent way. This means that in some countries, including Germany, the use of the two titles does not necessarily correspond to differences in forms of practice and areas of responsibility. In other countries, differences in titles do correspond more clearly to differences in practice, but not necessarily on the social work/social pedagogy axis (for example, 'socionom' in Sweden or 'socialradgiver' in Denmark). Care workers in the residential child care field might, therefore, be regarded as belonging to the broad field of social work in one place, and to a different professional group in another.

As Walter Lorenz (2008) has argued, the different titles in use within the broad domain of what is increasingly being referred to as the 'social professions' (which include: social work, social assistant, social pedagogue, social educator, youth worker, community worker, social adviser, care worker) are expressions of both different histories of practice and different academic, analytic and conceptual fields. There are now a number of studies which attempt to describe these different forms of practice and which attempt to analyse the different prevailing perspectives and themes in European social work (Erath et al., 2005; Hamburger et al., 2004–2007; Lyons and Lawrence, 2006; Lorenz, 2006).

A common thread is that social work emerges at times of rapid social change, at the time of war, or when communities break up under pressure from increased market forces and where industrialization and urbanization are rapid. This latter was particularly evident in England and the USA in the second half of the nineteenth century where traditional communities based on kinship and geographical proximity were no longer able either to meet the needs of their members or provide appropriate social order. It was also evident in the late twentieth century when the more regulated and compulsory communities forged by the coercive collective inclusionary policies of state communist societies began to collapse under the demands of liberalization and privatization in the post-Soviet era. Social work has also grown in 'developing' societies where rapid urbanization, industrialization and changes in the labour market have taken place and traditional community networks related to kinship, a rural way of life and religion have proved inadequate for the tasks expected of them.

Social work has often been used following periods of major social unrest or war to support the establishment of nationhood and mould citizens (Satka, 1995). Invariably, social work has been heavily implicated in the processes of both colonization and imperialism (Midgley, 1981; Gray et al., 2008). It is one of the measures which emerges as societies experience rapid social change and seek both to shore up social order and also compensate their most vulnerable members in the face of the socially undesirable consequences of capitalist contractual relations, where the primary way of meeting needs is via earning money in the commercial labour market (Jordan, 1997).

In the process, there is something of a tension at the heart of social work. While it emerges primarily in contexts where market-orientated economic individualism becomes the dominant form of social relations, its values are informed by those of a caring, inclusive, reciprocal community that wants to take collective responsibility for its members. This is reflected in many of the central tensions that have been evident throughout the development of social work and continue to the present day. In many respects not only do these tensions and how they are addressed help us to characterize social work, they are also key to differentiating social work from other practices. They take us to the heart of what is distinctive about the 'nature' and 'purposes' of social work.

As one of us has argued previously (Parton, 2000), social work develops as a hybrid in the 'social' intermediary zone or space between the private sphere of the household and the public sphere of the state and wider society. It evolves through new relations between the law, social security, medicine and the school but cannot be reduced to these other practices. Social work is seen as a positive solution to a major problem for the liberal state (Hirst, 1981). Namely, how can the state establish the health and development of individuals who are weak and dependent, particularly children, while promoting the family as the 'natural' sphere for caring for its members, but in a way which does not require intervention in all families? Social work develops at a midway point between individual initiative and an all-encompassing state. It provides a compromise between the liberal vision of unhindered private philanthropy and the socialist vision of the all-pervasive state that would take responsibility for everyone's needs and hence, potentially, undermine individual initiative and family responsibility.

Originally, in nineteenth-century England, these activities were carried out through voluntary philanthropic efforts, and were primarily carried out by educated middle-class women. In many fields the work was providing help via personal relationships and offering good advice, what Bill Jordan (1984) has called 'perfect friendship'; Elizabeth Fry with prisoners, Josephine Butler with prostitutes, Octavia Hill with slum tenants and Mary Carpenter with delinquents, are good examples. Victorian charity played an important role in the social policy of the era. Industrialization was accompanied by a political commitment to individual rights and liberties, and to increasing economic freedoms. As a consequence the rapidly growing urban proletariat were required to throw themselves into the free market, unprotected by the state. The new Poor Law of 1834 in England was primarily a system for excluding the able-bodied from relief and defining eligibility for assistance in terms requiring personal degradation and loss of citizenship. At the same time there was a fear that the growth in the *dangerous classes* would threaten social cohesion, security and public morals. Maintaining social order was a growing challenge (Stedman Jones, 1971). The task of classifying the poor and giving 'scientific assistance' according to moral status complemented the narrow exclusiveness of the poor law and provided a network of inclusion and distribution through voluntary agencies, which subtly reinforced the moral regime of the middle classes.

Social work thus occupied the space between the respectable and the dangerous classes (Pearson, 1975; Jones, 1983) and between those with access to political influence and voice and those who were excluded. It provided an essentially mediating role between those who were excluded and the mainstream of society, a role which it has fulfilled in different ways in the different cultures and societies throughout its history. Part of what social workers have traditionally sought to do has been to strengthen the bonds of inclusive membership by nurturing reciprocity, sharing and small-scale redistribution between individuals, in households, groups and communities. At the same time, social work has also been concerned with the compulsory enforcement of social obligations,

rules, laws and regulations. It is in this sense that social work has always involved both *care* and *control* (Garland, 1985). For, while social work has always been concerned to liberate and empower those with whom it works, it is also concerned with working on behalf of the state and the wider society to maintain social order. We can therefore see that one of social work's enduring characteristics is its contested and ambiguous nature (Martinez-Brawley and Zorita, 1998). Most crucially, this ambiguity arises from its commitment to individuals and families and their needs on the one hand and its allegiances to and increased legitimation by the state in the guise of the court and its 'statutory' responsibilities on the other. This ambiguity captures the central, but sometimes submerged, nature of modern social work.

In the twentieth century the more explicit moral analysis of relationships and behaviour was replaced by a psycho-social approach where the inner world of the individual was given as much focus as the relationships between people. 'Casework' became the dominant form of social work in England and the USA. Its 'theory' was informed by an optimistic view of human nature, which thought the best of people, and saw social problems as examples of individual dysfunction, divorced from issues of class, conflict, oppression, exploitation or discrimination (Mills, 1943; Pearson, 1973). Social work aimed to present a client in objective terms, but also had a built-in belief in the fundamental good in humanity. While social work had regarded itself as a carrier of the human tradition of compassion, it increasingly drew on the social sciences for its 'knowledge base'. As Philp (1979) has argued, social work was concerned with 'common human needs', with 'people not cases' and with a 'truly human response to suffering'. It tried to produce a picture of the individual which was both *subjective* and *social* and where the use of the professional *relationship* provided the key mechanism to help individuals be integrated back into the mainstream of society. But in conveying this perspective to the public, social work itself needed to address its social status in society. On what grounds did social work speak and with what authority? The answer to this question offered by the leaders of social work was that it constituted a profession and like other professions drew its legitimacy from knowledge, skill and the ideal of service.

SCIENCE AS A BASIS FOR PROFESSIONAL HELPING

The dilemma for those engaged in responding to human needs in the late nineteenth and early twentieth century was to distinguish their work from the domains of the church and clergy, on the one hand, and from political and social advocates, on the other hand. The clergy ministered to the individual needs of the poor, disabled, dispossessed and anguished, while political activists rallied for collective social justice and reform. As an aspiring profession concerned with care and control, social work needed a modern grounding, distinct from religion and political advocacy. For this purpose they adopted, however tentatively, the rubric of science. First, as Leiby (1978) indicates, social work attempted to find its distinctive social niche and propel itself into the status of an independent profession with scientific philanthropy and scientific charity.

Professional status and grounding in science were modern and synergistic, and also the pathway that medicine had taken. But the road to professional status was not smooth for social work. Abraham Flexner, who had just spearheaded an effort that transformed medical education in the USA into a scientifically based profession, declared in 1915 that social work 'is hardly eligible' for the status as a profession (Flexner, 1915: 588). Flexner faults social work for its mediating role, for being unspecific in its ends, and for failing to have an organized educational agenda. Although one might quibble with his criteria for professional status, for those wanting to declare that

social work was a profession, particularly in the USA and, to a lesser extent in the UK, the white-coated physician became and remained the subliminal image of a professional who has rigorous training, systematic procedures for diagnosis, deliberately developed practice skills, a black bag of technical interventions, independence and autonomy, while serving the best interests of clients. In fact, for nearly a century the language of social work practice, particularly in the USA, has borrowed the language of medicine: cases, diagnosis, treatment, symptoms, pathology, recovery and rehabilitation. This image emphasizes care, not control, and presents the professional relationship as a medium of detached, disinterested competence.

If science was to be the foundation, or at least a guide for social work practice, how was that to be accomplished? Following medicine, in the USA, professional social work training was transferred into major research universities, where the education could be grounded in the latest knowledge and theories of human behaviour and where, ostensibly, professors would oversee both classroom and field/clinical learning, as they did in medicine. For a variety of reasons, transferring social work education into universities failed to transform the profession as much as it had done for medicine. Social work faculty were drawn largely from practice not research settings; there were few doctoral programs in social work and almost no research infrastructure; most graduate programs in the USA did not even have a majority of their faculty with PhDs; and field education took place not in university hospitals and clinics, but in social agencies where supervisors rarely had any involvement in scientific research. Consequently, most social work practitioners have been educated without a research or scientific orientation and have pursued careers in settings in which they were unlikely to develop one. Relatively little has changed in recent decades in this regard, except that the social work professoriate in North America, the UK and across Europe has grown more research capable.

Responding to the need to be more embedded in science, social work has taken two distinct approaches (Kirk and Reid, 2002). The first involves using *science as a model of practice*. Since the Charity Organization Society (COS), social work has borrowed scientific techniques such as careful observation, gathering objective data about a case, and intervening in systematic ways. Mary Richmond's *Social Diagnosis* (1917), for example, concentrated on individual clients and treated each case as a focus of inquiry. Assessment involved gathering all the relevant facts to be used to form hypotheses about the causes of the client's problems; this diagnosis would then guide intervention. Such careful case analysis and deliberate methods of inquiry also served as a basis for hypothesis generation in early psychoanalysis, which presented itself in the early twentieth century as a scientific method of inquiry and treatment that had many adherents, particularly in American social work.

This modelling of practice as a form of scientific inquiry was elaborated in the later twentieth century in the USA among proponents of using single subject designs (SSD) in clinical practice (Blythe et al., 1994; Tripodi, 1994). In this elaboration, each client was treated as a quasi-experiment, where objective measures are taken of the client's problem behaviours before, during and after providing service. Although this practice-as-science approach has its critics (Wakefield and Kirk, 1996), the general aspiration to represent professional helping as a problem-solving process (fact gathering, rational and systematic inquiry, followed by action) is certainly well founded. Indeed, these methods certainly appeared to be more secular and rational and less sentimental and dogmatic. But in using scientific techniques as practice techniques, the role of the professional relationship can be overshadowed.

The second approach in social work to using science was as *a source of knowledge*, rather than as practice techniques. With this approach practice methods draw on scientific knowledge about how to intervene most effectively. The knowledge which sustains scientifically based professionals is based on the accumulation of diverse studies over time. The challenge in using science as a source of knowledge hinges on a myriad of connected problems, involving developing a scientific infrastructure to produce knowledge, synthesizing findings from diverse studies and making them available for use by practitioners in appropriate ways. These efforts have been variously described as integrating research with practice, bridging the gap, linking researchers with practitioners, and other such rubrics of improving the use of science in and for practice. To build these links, advocates have championed programme evaluation (Suchman, 1967), research utilization and dissemination (Grasso and Epstein, 1992), design and development models (Thomas and Rothman, 1994), agency–researcher partnerships (Hess and Mullen, 1995) and single subject designs for use by practitioners (Bloom et al., 1999). One of the latest strategies of making social work practice more scientific, once again following the lead of medicine, is promoting practice guidelines (Rosen and Proctor, 2003; Howard and Jenson, 1999) and evidence-based practice (Rubin, 2007; Walker et al., 2007). The heart of these efforts is to critically evaluate existing intervention outcome research, synthesize the evidence from them, derive action or behavioural guidelines from these studies, and insist that educators and practitioners base their helping efforts on these guidelines and practices. These efforts are unmistakeably the twenty-first century descendants of Abraham Flexner's work.

Medicine continues to provide the image of a science-based profession, not only in its singular authority in the realm of health matters, but also in the character of its research methods, such as use of scientific laboratories for biomedical discoveries and the rigours of randomized clinical trials as the gold standard for the evaluation of the effectiveness of interventions. Although in recent years the medical scientific establishment itself has suffered a series of scandals involving conflict of interests arising from the corrosive influence of the wealthy pharmaceutical companies, which have suppressed and distorted research findings, compromised university researchers and government scientists and influenced medical practice and health policy in ways that have harmed patients and the public (Angell, 2004; Bekelman et al., 2003; Kassirer, 2008; Greene, J.A., 2007). Nevertheless, medicine still provides an allure to social work which retains aspirations of using science to make social work practice a technical, rational, uniform and accountable activity.

Among the scientific templates that medicine provides have been the search for the causes of diseases, the development of diagnostic tests, and the evolution of effective prevention and treatment protocols. An important part of medical inquiry has been the identification of risk factors to health in the general population as a method of uncovering probable causes, identifying those who may be vulnerable, and for guiding preventive efforts. Risk connotes the probability of an unwanted outcome (i.e. the onset of disease, relapse, disability or death) and a risk factor refers to a particular agent or exposure that increases the probability of that outcome. The architecture of this medical schema, particularly the search for risk factors, has been adopted for studying many non-medical human problems. There are potential problems – you might say risks – of social work adopting this schema, involving such ingredients as assuming that the causes of human problems are internal to the individual (e.g. as yet undiscovered genetic defects, chemical imbalances, cognitive or affective dysfunctions) and that the solutions are some form of individual treatment rather than institutional or structural reform. Despite the attractions of importing medicine's research strategies, they may not, especially in the USA, be fully suited for social work's purposes. In this regard, the search for and uses of risk factors should alert social work to ways in which the purpose of controlling can undercut caring.

THE RISKS OF RISK FACTORS

While social work has looked to science to professionalize, it has also been driven by the bureaucratic demands of organizations and governments that fund and regulate it. Governments have an interest in monitoring the health and welfare of their citizens and in providing needed services. State monitoring routinely tracks such social problems as alcoholism, drug abuse, child neglect, mental disorder, crime, obesity, unemployment, and so on. There are many uncertainties and controversies about the nature, immediate causes or explanations of these problems. These uncertainties frequently misguide risk research in the following ways. First, in order to study any problem it must be well defined. Typically, arbitrary and expansive definitions of the problem are used with high sensitivity (includes many false positives), but low specificity (few false negatives). Second, researchers study large samples of the population to identify who appears to fit within the expansive definitions of a 'case'. Third, a vast quantity of demographic and behavioural information is gathered from each respondent in the sample. Fourth, data dredging compares those identified as 'cases' with the non-cases to uncover any distinguishing variables between the two groups, a procedure likely to uncover 'statistically significant' but meaningless associations (Ioannidis, 2005). Fifth, those variables found to be associated with 'caseness' are used to identify people in the population who may be 'at risk'. Finally, those considered potentially at risk are the subject of increased state surveillance, intervention and control, even though many, if not most of them, are not and will never become 'cases' of the problem. Examples from medicine of these processes of expanding definitions and the number of people at risk are detailed in Jeremy Greene's (2007) analysis of the history and treatment of hypertension, diabetes, and cholesterol, in which the expansion of the definition of disease allowed even those without symptoms to be defined as 'cases' and be subject to treatments which were at times actually harmful.

Such expansion of the number of people who may be at risk is facilitated by the confused and misleading terminology of risk factors found in both the scientific and popular literature (Kraemer et al., 1997). It is not uncommon for any correlate of the unwanted outcome to be presented as a causal risk factor, when it may have no bearing on causing the problem. In fact, it may be spuriously associated with the problem or even a consequence of the problem. These misinterpretations and misuses of population data become more common with the growth of government and industry funded population-based studies, surveys, epidemiological studies, and studies based on service utilization and administrative records. Although such studies are necessary ingredients of state and professional accountability and control, there are occasions when such population-based information may undercut or impede the social work profession's mission for caring for individuals and jeopardize their privacy and well-being. Thus, there are potential misuses of research in which the functions of caring for individuals get overshadowed in the pursuit of the control of populations, as may happen if medical records containing personal medical information are used by insurance companies to deny coverage.

Let us offer two examples drawn from problems of children which will illustrate how research using expansive definitions of problems and the notion of risk factors may potentially undercut the objective of caring.

Exemplar 1: Children's psychiatric disorders

After decades of biological, psychological and social research, no definitive cause or biological marker has been identified for virtually any mental disorder of adults or children (APA, 2000). Even the definition of mental illness has been disputed for many decades and is still unresolved (Rounsaville et al., 2002). In this vacuum, psychiatry has opted to use ambiguous lists of behaviours as 'symptoms' or indicators of undefined, presumed, underlying illnesses. This approach to medicalizing many behaviours received official approval from the American Psychiatric Association in the publication of the third edition of the *Diagnostic and Statistical Manual of Mental Disorders* (DSM-III) in 1980 (APA, 1980), a development that is discussed in many publications (for example Conrad, 2007; Horwitz, 2002; Kirk and Kutchins, 1992; Wilson, 1993). The diagnostic indicators, which represent many normal behaviours, serve as the definition of illnesses, but are used in various ways, sometimes as symptoms of the disorder, as the actual target of treatment, and as risk factors for the disorder, among others. Such ambiguities allow for many misuses.

One of the results of this descriptive approach to mental disorders has been that the boundaries of mental disorders are easily and arbitrarily expanded, undercutting the accuracy of psychiatric diagnosis, which had never been particularly impressive. Diagnostic accuracy requires both validity and reliability. *Validity* refers to whether the distinctions among disorders and between disorders and non-disorders make conceptual sense and can be used appropriately by clinicians. *Reliability* refers to the extent to which actual clinicians can agree on the diagnoses of a series of cases. How accurate is the use of the most prevalent DSM diagnoses for children?

The standard way of measuring accuracy is in terms of the amount and type of error that can be expected, referred to as the sensitivity and specificity of the diagnosis. *Sensitivity* is the term used to indicate the extent to which a measure captures all true cases (true positives), even though in doing so it may also capture many false positives (people who truly don't have the disorder but are identified as having it). *Specificity* is the term used to indicate the extent to which a measure captures only true cases, even though it may classify many people as not having the disorder when they truly do have it (false negatives). Together sensitivity and specificity indicated the amount of error that can be expected in the diagnostic classification of children. Using the sensitivity and specificity estimates from the Spitzer et al. (1990) study, we calculated the expected rates of diagnostic error in the use of the diagnoses Attention Deficit Hyperactivity Disorder, Conduct Disorder and Oppositional Defiant Disorder (for details, see Kirk, 2004). If we assume that the true prevalence rate of the disorder in a population of a 1000 children is 5%, a common figure in many studies (Roberts et al., 1998), the number of children from a population of 1000 who would be *incorrectly* diagnosed using the DSM indicators would be 375 for ADHD, 110 for Conduct Disorder and 210 for Oppositional Defiant Disorder. Within each of these three diagnoses, the majority of errors were in the direction of false positives: many children who did not have that disorder would be receiving a mental disorder diagnosis. These are the known and expected error rate built into the formal diagnostic criteria for these disorders. But this does not exhaust the extent of diagnostic errors that undoubtedly occur regularly.

There are also reliability errors in which clinicians assessing the same children fail to agree on the proper diagnosis. There have been many different kinds of studies of the reliability of diagnoses of children and most have concluded that diagnostic reliability has ranged from less than good to dismal, with great variability across studies (Kirk, 2004). Thus, in addition to the high level of false positives from the expansive diagnostic criteria for children's disorders, there are other unintentional and

intentional (Kirk and Kutchins, 1988) errors made by clinicians. Because of the high rate of diagnostic error inherent in identifying children who have mental disorders, studies that search for risk factors associated with these false positive and false negative 'cases' will themselves flounder and be misleading.

More importantly, there are other negative consequences for the individual children as well. Many children may be inappropriately labelled as mentally ill, some may receive the wrong diagnosis and be inappropriately treated, epidemiological estimates of disorder may be distorted, and children's medical records may contain errors that could harm them in later life by stigmatizing them as mentally impaired as children. In short, a seriously flawed, medicalized approach to children's problems, with expansive and arbitrary definitions of mental illness, compounded by measurement errors that produce many false positives, few or no causal explanations, and no guiding validated theory.

Exemplar 2: Child welfare and early intervention

Similar problems can be found in other areas of child welfare, where individuals or families are determined to be 'at risk' based on correlates found in large samples, which, however valid, will not apply to all individuals, particularly in the case of behaviours that have low base rates (prevalence). If, for example, there is a correlation between ethnicity and adolescent violent behaviour, using ethnicity as a predictor of violence will produce a sizable population of false positives (that is youth of that ethnicity who truly are not violent) and will fail to identify those who will be violent, but are of other ethnicities (false negatives). The identification of false positives has enormous implications for civil liberties, whether in relation to crime and

anti-social behaviour or other problems that would introduce mandatory
intervention:

> Any notion that better screening can enable
> policy makers to identify young children destined
> to join the 5 per cent of offenders responsible for
> 50–60 per cent of crime is fanciful. Even if there
> were no ethical objections to putting 'potential
> delinquent' labels round the necks of young chil-
> dren, there would continue to be statistical barriers.
> Research into the continuity of anti-social behaviour
> shows substantial flows out of – as well as into –
> the pool of children who develop chronic conduct
> problems. This demonstrates the dangers of assum-
> ing that anti-social five-year-olds are the criminals or
> drug abusers of tomorrow. (Sutton et al., 2004: 5)

In relation to trying to prevent poor outcomes for children and young people more
generally, Feinstein and Sabates conclude
that:

> Children move in and out of risk in terms of their
> own development and their levels of contextual
> risk. Therefore, it is important that the policy
> mechanisms allocating interventions and support
> to children and families are flexible and able to
> track and monitor levels of risk, not always inter-
> vening at the first sign of risk but equally able to
> provide early interventions that may reduce the
> need for more substantive and costly later inter-
> ventions. *This requires a considerable degree of
> local practitioner skill.* (Feinstein and Sabates,
> 2006: 35, emphasis added)

So, while research is helpful in identifying
who *might* be 'at risk', these probabilities are
very inexact, requiring a 'considerable degree
of practitioner skill' in knowing when and
how to intervene effectively with clients in
such a way that the work is of benefit to
them. The point is that by the final quarter of
the twentieth century we began to see significant changes in the way social work was
thought about and practised. There was a de-
emphasis on the importance of the worker/
client relationship as the medium for helping
and an abandonment of attempts to explain
and understand clients' problems. Developing
in its place is an emphasis on describing
people with unwanted behaviour, attempts to
predict who is at risk, and, with the advent of
computer information systems, the growth of
surveillance as a central purpose.

THE DE-EMPHASIS OF THE RELATIONSHIP, THE ABANDONMENT OF EXPLANATION, AND THE GROWTH OF SURVEILLANCE

Since the mid 1970s across western Europe
and North America, there have been growing
and often very public criticisms of social
work and increased attempts to improve its
accountability and closely monitor its spheres
of discretionary decision making. Nowhere
have these changes been more evident than in
child welfare, particularly following a series
of high profile public inquiries into child
abuse and the subsequent failures of child
protection systems to protect children and
provide appropriate and sensitive help
(Parton, 1985; Waldfogel, 1998).

An analysis of press reporting of social
work in national daily and Sunday newspapers in England between 1 July 1997 and 30
June 1998 is particularly instructive (Franklin
and Parton, 2001). There were nearly two
thousand articles measuring 97,932 column
centimetres (ccm), of which 6995 ccm were
devoted exclusively to discussions of social
work and social services. The 15 most
common messages, accounting for 80% of the
total, were negative with regard to social work
and included: 'incompetent', 'negligent',
'failed', 'ineffective', 'misguided', 'bungling'.
Over 75% of the stories were related to children where the dominant concerns were about
child abuse, paedophiles, adoption and fostering. Media stories about the nature, purposes
and efficacy of social work were, almost without exception, negative and critical.

In part as a defensive response to such
criticism, social work practice has increasingly adopted a procedural mentality, which
emphasizes the need to follow administrative
protocols, to ensure that practice is made
accountable. While the technical requirements in the job have increased, space
for professional judgement has decreased
(Howe, 1992: 492).

David Howe (1996) has argued that social
work has undergone a number of major

changes in its character from the late 1970s onwards; performance has become the dominant criterion for knowledge evaluation, both in relation to clients and of social workers themselves. No longer is the focus on trying to understand or explain behaviour, for social workers are less concerned with *why* clients behave as they do than with *what* they do. *Depth* explanations drawing on psychological and sociological theories are being superseded by *surface* descriptions. Coherent causal accounts which attempt to provide a picture of the subject in their social context have become of declining importance, for the key purpose of the social worker is increasingly to classify clients for the purpose of judging the nature and level of risk and for allocating resources. The emphasis on the professional worker/client relationship – previously the central feature of social work practice – is being stripped of its social, cultural and professional significance. Knowledge for practice is relevant only in so far as it aids the gathering, assessing, monitoring and exchange of information and is closely related to the central role now given to managers in most agencies.

By the early/mid 1990s in North America, Australia, the UK and other countries in Europe, it was clear that social work practice was becoming much more routinized and formalized. Increasingly, the changing social, political and economic climate in which social work operated and the introduction of a variety of new technologies meant that the nature of the work itself began to change. As Carol Smith (2001a, 2004a) has argued, the situation is full of paradox, for while most agree that certainty in many areas of social work is not possible, the political and organizational climate increasingly demands it. The result is that many of the changes introduced act to sidestep the paradox and substitute *confidence in systems* for *trust in individual professionals*.

Such developments have become even more evident with the growing influence of information and communication technologies (ICTs) and the requirement that practitioners input, manage and monitor a whole variety of information via the new electronic systems. Not only does this mean that practitioners are spending more time in front of the computer on bureaucratic tasks (Samuel, 2005), but that a greater proportion of time is now accounted for by assessment activities and less on ongoing contact, counselling and support (Statham et al., 2006).

With the introduction of ICT there is an expectation that as information becomes more accessible, the agencies, professionals and their decisions should become more transparent and accountable. In the process, there is less discretion for the individual professional for identifying what information is relevant as the required information is predetermined by the structure of the database and the algorithm. The identities of clients as people with needs and problems in contexts are superseded by accounts constructed by the fields that constitute the database. In striving for clear and objective representations and decision making, the client's views and social context are reduced to what can be captured by lists and factors associated with 'need' and 'risk'. Categorical thinking, based on the binary either/or logic, dominates. Individuals are placed into master categories that obscure any ambiguities. Rather than presenting a picture of the client as subject in social context, as previously, social work increasingly acts to reassemble clients' identities according to the requirements of the database. In the process, the embodied subject is in danger of disappearing and we are left with a variety of surface information which provides little basis for in-depth explanation or understanding. As one of us has argued elsewhere (Parton, 2008), the key focus of social work is in danger of shifting from the 'social' to the 'informational'.

Not only does the growing use of computerized information systems mean that the traditional boundaries between the 'public' and 'private' – the key space in which social work has traditionally operated – become blurred, but social work becomes increasingly involved in ever wide-ranging, complex and unstable systems of surveillance, particularly where such systems are used to enhance strategies for early intervention (Parton, 2006). Policy and practice are increasingly premised on the need to identify 'at risk' individuals or groups in the population and engage in early intervention before the onset of problems or to prevent problems getting worse. The sharing of information between different professionals and health, welfare and criminal justice agencies takes on a strategic role in trying to enhance and implement such practices. For example, in England since the mid 1990s there has been an emphasis on trying to improve policies in relation to 'early childhood' prevention based upon, the 'risk and protection-focussed prevention paradigm' (France and Utting, 2005). The approach has been influenced by research on what affects children's development. The belief is that not only will this ensure that children develop appropriately, but that they achieve both at school and in later life, avoid mental health problems and do not engage in criminal or anti-social behaviour.

PRACTITIONER AND SERVICE USER VOICES AND THE IMPORTANCE OF THE RELATIONAL

While it is clear that the nature and purposes of social work have undergone significant reconfiguration over the last thirty years, there is also a growing recognition that this has been at a cost, and research has played its part in opening up these debates. For example, both Scotland and England have engaged in major reviews which have direct implications for the nature, purposes and future directions of social work and how research might be drawn upon to aid both understanding and future planning (Asquith et al., 2005; DfES and DH, 2006).

In particular, in late 2006 the General Social Care Council (GSCC) took the lead in a project which aimed to describe the roles and tasks of social work (GSCC, 2008). The project was commissioned by the Department of Health and the Department for Education and Skills and was to apply to England, though it would take into account developments in Scotland and related work in Wales and Northern Ireland. It was the first high-level official analysis of social work in England since the Barclay Report in 1982 (Barclay, 1982) and took place in the context of the major changes instituted by the New Labour government in the provisions and organization of social care services for both children and adults since it came to power in 1997 (GSCC, 2008).

Two literature reviews were commissioned by the project: one which derived from the mainstream professional and policy literature (Blewett et al., 2007) and the other based upon service users' perspectives (Beresford, 2007b). Research on the views and experiences of 'service users' is particularly instructive; for while social workers now seem to undertake less direct support and face-to-face work, this is precisely what service users valued most. They valued the wide range of approaches used by social workers and the breadth of tasks undertaken. These included:

- offering information, advice and advocacy;
- helping people negotiate with other state agencies, particularly over benefits and financial support, housing and other services;
- providing counselling and other psycho-therapeutic support;
- providing practical guidance and help;
- referring service users to other relevant agencies and service providers; and
- accessing financial support to service users.

Service users placed a particular value on social work's 'social' approach, the relationship and the positive personal qualities they associate with social workers. The latter included warmth, respect, being non-judgemental, listening, treating people with equality, being trustworthy, openness and honesty, reliability and communicating well (Beresford, 2007b: 5–6). This all seems quite different from the somewhat distant, procedure-bound role which we discussed earlier and which is primarily concerned with gathering, sharing and monitoring information and identifying 'risk factors'. Service users welcomed a 'hands-on' approach which takes account of both personal and social issues and their complex interrelationships. It is this which is seen to define the core of social work and which makes it distinctive from other professions.

Service users see social work as an essentially human rather than a technological or scientific activity. In their view it is primarily about talking to or communicating with each other and is more likely to be successful when carried out in partnership with the service user and with the maximum participation of all parties. The central message that comes across time and time again from client studies is that it is not the particular model or technique used by the social worker which is significant but the quality of the experience. The key themes which service users identify for success can be summarized as 'accept me, understand me and talk with me' (Howe, 1993; Seligman, 1995). This is not simply saying that good social work is only about establishing relationships, but studies which attempt to identify what service users find helpful repeatedly identify this as a necessary component. In this respect the 'principles of social work' espoused by Biestek (1961), which include good individualized listening, availability, being non-judgemental and non-directive, and working on the basis of trust and confidentiality, still seem to have relevance today, and closely echoes Bill Jordan's characterization of nineteenth-century social work as 'perfect friendship'.

The two 'literature informed discussion' papers prepared for the GSCC also demonstrate that the type and range of research both about and for social work is much more diverse and heterogeneous than studies which inform the evidence-based practice movement in which experimental approaches are awarded paramount importance. There are growing debates about the most appropriate forms and methodologies to develop knowledge for practice and increasing sympathy for ensuring there are pluralistic sources of knowledge and therefore different types of research. There is a growing argument that not only are the views and experiences of service users important, but that they should be the starting point for any research.

> A starting point for research suitable for social work then, is that it should be concerned ultimately with a concern to alleviate suffering and to put power in the hands of those often excluded from influence in social processes. The underlying principle in participative research rests on the emphasis on research participants and researchers attempting to collaborate as equals, through sharing power in decision-making and by drawing on each others' knowledge and insights. (Humphries, 2003: 84)

Whether research is qualitative, quantitative or mixed-method in approach, the key issues relate to epistemological concerns and the priority to give voice to those who would otherwise be silent.

CONCLUSIONS

What becomes evident is that debates about the most appropriate form(s) that social work research should adopt very much reflect debates about the nature and purposes of social work itself. These tensions have been at the heart of social work since its emergence. While approaches to social work are now much more explicitly based on the assumption that practice should be informed by research evidence than previously, there is considerable debate about the most appropriate form this evidence should take. While social work is much less 'moralistic' than it may have been in the nineteenth century, it is also recognized that social work is centrally concerned with making moral and professional judgements and that the work is contested and complex. The relational aspects of the work have remained central.

As we argued, social work has always involved both *care* and *control*. For, while it attempts to liberate and empower those with whom it works, it also works on behalf of the state and the wider society in order to maintain social order.

Walter Lorenz (2004), drawing on the work of Habermas (1987), argues that this tension closely reflects the profession's ambivalent position between 'the lifeworld' (the realm of society in which people take care of their own affairs, individually and collectively) and 'the system' (where organized control and rationalist governing mechanisms operate). The concept of 'the lifeworld' tries to capture those elements of day-to-day existence where people experience themselves as communicating actors capable of expressing intentions and giving meaning to their world. In contrast, 'the system' refers to those aspects of the world which aim to ensure the material reproduction of society and is based on notions of instrumental rationality. Habermas argues that these two domains have become increasingly uncoupled from each other and that we have witnessed an increasing 'colonization' of 'the lifeworld' by 'the system'. While far more sophisticated, the domains of the 'the lifeworld' and 'the system' can be seen to capture many of the characteristics which we discussed in relation to *care* and *control* earlier. According to Lorenz, social work, from the time of its emergence, has occupied an intermediary position between 'the lifeworld' and 'the system' sharing in the differentiation and specialization of both but also developing its mediating functions.

Similar ambiguities and tensions can be found in social work research. For example, when studies emphasize the service user's voice, empowerment and partnership, we sense the promise of these reference points resonating from their 'lifeworld' qualities and roots. But it is always important to see how such ideas are applied and played out in practice. Upon closer inspection of their use in particular contexts ideas which may appear emancipatory may be used instrumentally with regard to social control. Conversely, adhering to the principles and criteria of objectivity and rationality, which are key elements enabling 'the system' to legitimize power relations, can at times act as a key element by which social work research aims to bolster and enhance the profession and 'service users', and so resist colonization by 'the system' which seeks to use the profession primarily for the purposes of social control and regulation. As Lorenz argues:

> ... the wider significance of discourses on research methodology cannot be elaborated adequately without reference to the intersection of these two sets of dynamics. They play a role on the one hand in the epistemological ambiguity between what has been described classically as the alternatives of social work as art and as science, and on the other hand in the ambivalence between striving for the status of a full, autonomous profession and retaining the empowering elements of 'voluntarism' and the solidarity with service users which they convey. (Lorenz, 2004: 148)

What is of particular interest is that at a time when there is considerable debate about the nature and purposes of social work, and evidence of the growing fragmentation and differentiation of social work, there is also considerable debate about the nature and purposes of social work research. In many respects the current discussions about social work research can be seen as key elements in debates about the nature and future identity of social work itself. The two are intimately connected. Because social work is such a rich tapestry of practices it is important that these debates remain open and active. Because social work is always likely to have a close, if highly ambivalent, relationship with 'the system' and notions of social control and instrumental rationality, it is vital that it maintains its close relationships with 'the lifeworld' of those with whom it works. A key element of social work's energy and vitality comes from continually engaging in critical debate about its epistemologies and methodologies in both research and practice and how both contribute to its nature and purposes.

Providing Objective, Impartial Evidence for Decision Making and Public Accountability

Annette Boaz and James Blewett

INTRODUCTION

Social workers take a variety of professional and administrative decisions within a policy and organisational context. Although in reality any absolute divide will be artificial and arbitrary, in the context of this volume the focus of this chapter is decisions taken by individual social workers in respect of individuals and/or families. The identity of *social work* is a very complex phenomenon, which it has been suggested, occupies somewhere between 'art and science'. Within this complexity the understanding of roles and tasks in social work will vary greatly. This chapter reviews the nature of the *knowledge* which underpins the process of decision making at the individual level. It highlights the varying compatibility between research traditions and social work decision making, whilst acknowledging that other forms of knowledge such as the views of services users also impact on the decision-making process. It also provides brief examples of current strategic initiatives in the US and UK which are intended to optimise practitioner access to knowledge with a view to facilitating its application to practice. The chapter concludes with an exploration of the concept of the public accountability of social work practitioners at the level of state, community and individual.

What does it mean to promote objective impartial evidence for decision making? We distinguish between concerns about the nature and quality of the evidence and its application in social work practice. This chapter draws together two very different sets of experience (one academic, the other rooted in social work practice) to consider the impact on theory and practice of a more evidence-based approach to practice. In doing so it spans (sometimes uncomfortably) two worlds: one concerned with finding a role for the best available evidence and the other more focused on the business of social work. It is with these different worlds in mind that we have spent some time thinking about evidence from a practice perspective, rather than (as is more often the case) from an evidence perspective. However, we begin with the philosophical traditions that have led to a renewed interest in the use of evidence in social work practice.

THE PHILOSOPHY AND PARADIGM

The arguments in favour of greater use of more objective evidence to inform decision making in social work practice range from the ethical and ideological to the highly practical. In particular, experimental methods have been promoted in order to generate more objective evaluations of interventions. Prominent exponents of evidence-based policy and practice (Chalmers, 2005) have argued that social workers and other social care professionals are responsible for intervening in peoples' lives at critical points and that these interventions should always be based on a *robust* knowledge base. They argue that it is unethical to proceed with untested interventions. In fact one of the most worrying consequences of experiments for practitioners is that they have concluded that some established interventions were not just ineffectual, but harmful to service users. For example, Oakley (2000) gives the example of Blenkner's study of older people receiving a bundle of social, medical and psychiatric services. The study found that on a range of outcome measures the older people in the control group (i.e. those not receiving the intervention) faired better (Blenkner et al., 1974). The capacity of services to do more harm than good is a compelling argument for collecting rigorous evidence of effectiveness. However, service users need to retain a voice in the research process, in order that the acceptability as well as the effectiveness of services is tested.

In practical terms, experiments and systematic reviews also offer some tantalizing outcomes in terms of, for example, effect sizes for interventions. Dubois et al. (2002) pooled together a range of very different outcome measures (such as school achievement, attendance and employment) in order to calculate an effect size for youth mentoring interventions. The prospect of knowing that, for example, ten per cent of young people participating in a mentoring scheme might achieve better educational outcomes is attractive to practitioners trying to choose between different interventions designed to help young people. Combined with cost benefit data this information can also support decisions in terms of making the best use of limited resources.

Ideologically, experimental methods have been aligned with positivism on one side of the great (if artificial) divide between quantitative and qualitative approaches to research. The former is considered to be mimicking natural science in the pursuit of real, measurable truths while the latter is characterized as a softer, more context-sensitive approach to understanding. Much intellectual energy has been expelled in heated debate about the relative contribution of these different approaches (Chalmers, 2005; Hammersley, 2005). This debate has taken place in its current form for over a decade and as a result can feel both 'tired' and remote from the realities of everyday practice. Nevertheless it is important to recognize that this debate is not simply an expression of academic rivalries or an abstract and somewhat pedantic discussion of research methodologies and philosophy. Tunstill (2003) and Trinder and Reynolds (2000) argue that this debate is a response to, and has been shaped by developments in social policy. That is, they argue that particularly in the UK there has been a move away from Cochrane's (1979) original strong practitioner focus on the use of randomized control trials to improve outcomes for patients to the use of 'evidence' in a much more overtly organizational and managerial role. They argue that this growth of managerialism has implications for how research is funded and carried out, particularly in relation to the definition and measurement of *outcomes* and how the findings of research are then disseminated into practice. There are, as we will go on to illustrate, expressions of this shift in terms of how practitioners utilize research in their decision making.

However, the debate about methods (randomized controlled trials versus more conventional methods of social work research) has shifted attention away from perhaps a more challenging question of how evidence can be used to support policy making and the implementing of policy into practice. While it is widely accepted that policy is rarely 'made' to pre-agreed recipes and practice is complex and often messy (Shaw and Shaw, 1997) a gulf remains between most conceptual writing about policy and practice and the day-to-day realities of making and taking decisions. Indeed:

> ... the literatures of decision making, policy formulation, planning and public administration formalize the [rational, linear] approach ... leaving public administrators who handle complex decisions in the position of practicing what few preach (Lindblom, 1959: 80).

In the US, in particular, there has been recognition that there remains a gulf between an abstract adherence to the *idea* of evidence-based practice in the context of both social work education and in agencies and the reality of how far this translates into day-to-day practice within either professional training or practice. There is an increasing recognition that the barriers to working in a more evidence-based, research-minded way are complex and multi-facetted (Barratt, 2003; Gibbs and Gambrill, 2002) with the barriers ranging from the conceptual in terms of what is counted as evidence, the cultural in terms of the extent to which this knowledge is both accepted and promoted in the field and the practical in terms of how practitioners are able to access this knowledge base.

A second strand therefore of research within evidence-based policy has been less concerned with research methods and more focused on improving connections between good quality research and practice. This research suggests that increasing the uptake of social work research is about much more than arming social workers with the critical appraisal skills required to read academic papers. In the US, Rubin (2007) among others distinguishes between what he describes as 'bottom up' and 'top down' approaches to promoting research mindedness amongst practitioners. The 'bottom up' is an approach in which the focus is on training and equipping practitioners with the skills to locate and utilize applied social research in their practice. It entails therefore being able to critically appraise research-based knowledge and adapt it to their specific context (Sackett et al., 2000). In contrast the 'top down' approach entails the development of practice guidelines and other toolkits developed by managers and policy makers that social work practitioners then implement. These tools are based on a robust research knowledge base. In the UK context Walter et al. (2004) identify similar typologies but propose three models for understanding the contribution of research might make to social care practice. These are:

- The research-based practitioner model
- The embedded research model
- The organizational excellence model

First they identified the research-based practitioner model, which to some degree is similar to Rubin's 'bottom up approach'. They argue that it is where practitioners take sole responsibility for and ownership of their professional development. In this model, practitioners seek continually to update their knowledge base. The practitioners themselves therefore make choices as to what areas of research are pertinent to their practice and they play a large role in determining the weight of competing areas of research-based and other 'evidence'. The strength of such an approach is that it *can* promote the professional authority and self esteem of the social worker. It fits with a perception of the expert practitioner and is particularly relevant to the independent social worker model. The disadvantages of such an approach is that the possibilities for testing the knowledge base of the practitioner can be limited and there can be a danger that employers will absolve themselves of responsibility for the professional development of their workforce and recognizing the importance of promoting a learning culture in their agencies as a prerequisite for high quality practice.

Exemplar 1: A pilot study of working with practitioners in New York: an example of the research-based practitioner

The nature of this model is such that it has not been as widely researched as the other two approaches. It involves an individualistic approach by social work practitioners to the task of increasing their levels of research mindedness. Mullen et al. (2007) provide a very interesting example of a small-scale project with which they have been involved in New York. Although the project involves elements of the top down and organizational excellence models, it is largely based on the bottom up or research-based practitioner model. The research team selected three contrasting welfare agencies in New York. They then worked closely with managers to identify some of the main challenges and practice issues that faced them in their work. The team then delivered training to practitioners in the following areas (based on Gibbs, 2003):

- motivation for evidence-based practice;
- how to convert information need into a search question;
- evidence search tools;
- evidence appraisal skills;
- information integration skills; and
- self-evaluation.

The project is still in its early stages, but the authors report very positive initial findings. The teaching of research evaluation skills was evaluated by participants as being successful. One of the main early benefits identified is that while the project has not necessarily led to practitioners proactively using research in their decision making, it did lead to higher levels of analysis and more awareness of the relevance of research. Nevertheless the practical challenges to using research on a systematic basis in the workplace remain very real.

Second, the embedded research model, which reflects Rubin's 'top down approach' represents the opposite end of the continuum, where practitioners take no *individual* responsibility for the integration of research into practice. Rather, managers and policy makers ensure that research is embedded in practice through policy and procedures. The strength of such an approach is that it can ensure that service design and within that decision making is based upon an evidence base that is tested and potentially robust. This can enhance the credibility of an intervention and also promote partnership working with the users of services in that practitioners can justify and explain their work in relation to 'objective evidence'. The weakness of this approach is in the nature of the 'evidence' in terms of its validity and durability and can imply a simplistic, linear and, to a degree, de-politicized relationship between research, policy and practice. Furthermore, there is danger that the role of practitioner could be reduced to that of technician, minimizing the scope for continuing professional development.

Exemplar 2: Early intervention service in child welfare in the US: an example of embedded research

Over the last 20 years, there has been an emerging body of research-based evidence in the US that has demonstrated the effectiveness of early intervention services for families whose children are vulnerable. The most well known of these is *Head Start* but there are a wide range of others such as *Homebuilders* and the *Nurturing Parent Programme*. The research base has helped define and shape these services as well as convincing funders of their worth. However this example also shows the shortcomings of such an approach.

Policy makers have often been selective as to the messages they have taken and the implementation of programmes has been patchy and geographically uneven, with some minority ethnic groups not receiving an equitable service. The evidence base has promoted 'joined up' homogenous services but these have rarely been achieved in practice. Although by and large positively evaluated the piecemeal nature of the development of these policies has posed methodological difficulties for researchers attempting to measure outcomes that are in themselves complex in their nature and relationships (Hanson et al., 2006).

The third model identified by Walter et al. (2004) is the organizational excellence model. This model is in some respects a combination of both the bottom up and top down approaches. This also puts agencies 'at the centre', but the crucial role they can play is in developing a research-minded culture through training, supervision and clear leadership. Research is seen as contributing to service development, but it is recognized that findings need to be adapted to the local context. Knowledge brokering organizations, such as in the UK, Making Research Count (See Exemplar 3) and Research in Practice, are seen as having an important part to play in supporting the management of agencies in developing this culture, and in assisting practitioners in applying research to their work with clients. They have the potential of combining the strengths of both the other approaches and minimizing their weaknesses. However, the challenges of successfully promoting a research-based learning culture should not be underestimated in complex and often pressured practice environments (Humphries et al., 2003).

Exemplar 3: Making research count in London – an example of the organizational excellence model

Making Research Count is a university based research dissemination network that works with health and social care agencies in England. Its aim is to promote evidence or more accurately knowledge informed practice at both the service design and delivery levels of social care services. The network is guided by a belief in the legitimacy of a pluralistic knowledge base and that dissemination can be most effectively promoted at the local level within agencies themselves. Each of the universities that make up the MRC network acts as a 'hub', working with a group of local agencies to deliver research-based services and models of working, which vary across the country. The London hub is based in the Social Care Workforce Research Unit, Kings College, London. As examples of MRC's work last year in London:

- 72 seminars were delivered in-house in the agencies on a broad range of policy and practice-based topics.
- Six regional conferences and 13 seminars drew an audience of 1900 practitioners and managers.
- An email enquiry service was provided whereby practitioners could make requests for references about specific areas of their work.
- A reflective practitioner group composed of managers in London met every month around a specific area of practice.
- Researchers have provided consultation to specialist working groups in agencies such as those in protection of vulnerable adults (Blewett, 2007).

THEORY

This chapter is focused on a particular perspective on the role of the contribution of social work research. While part of a longer tradition (Fischer, 1984), there has been a recent resurgence of interest in objective, impartial evidence for decision making. In particular, the international interest in evidence-based medicine and the focus on improving accountability make a consideration of these issues timely. The terms 'objective' and 'impartial' reflect an interest in rigorous evidence that 'speaks truth' to power.

This has very much focused at the level of individual practitioners and managers faced with dilemmas in treatment and intervention. In particular evidence-based medicine has advocated systematic reviews of evidence (Haynes, 2005; Egger et al., 2001) and randomized controlled trials to improve the quality of evidence available to practitioners. This chapter argues that while much can be learnt from the experience of this approach, and indeed the wider moves towards evidence-based practice in public policy, in relation to social work, a narrow conception of evidence should be avoided. This is both in terms of the methodologies employed to generate that evidence and the need for empirical evidence to be used alongside other areas of expertise including that of practitioners and the users of services or as Preston-Shoot (2007) describes 'experts by experience'.

One of the dangers in the debate in relation to the promotion of a more evidence-based approach to decision making amongst social work practitioners is that there can be a confusion between *technical* and *conceptual* challenges faced by both the research and practice communities. This is to a degree understandable in that the two are closely entwined with one another. However, if we are to understand ways in which professional decision making can be made more rigorous and therefore accountable then we need to understand the nature and complexities of the relationship between the two. There can be a danger with both the 'top down' and 'bottom up' approaches that they are interpreted crudely and are based on a mechanistic understanding of the relation between research and practice. This can then in turn lead to practical but ultimately simplistic solutions such as attempting to resolve complex practice issues by either only making more training available or promoting ever more prescriptive practice guidelines and toolkits within which research findings are embedded. Instead there needs to be, as Proctor and Rosen (2008) argue, a debate which combines both knowledge production and implementation, while recognizing the

political and organizational context in which practitioners are operating.

The debate is further complicated in that there are differences in approaches to objective, impartial evidence across the world. For example, in the UK social work research has traditionally been characterized as favouring qualitative methodologies over quantitative, with the concept of what counts as evidence often being hotly contested (Davies et al., 2000). By contrast in the US there has been more of a quantitative tradition in social work research (Shaw, 2006). The increased interest in the nature and utilization of research reflects a shift in social work and other fields of practice away from a faith in professional decision making based on experience, or decision making guided by political ideology. We will explore the professional context of this debate further but the argument that what matters should be what is effective in terms of improvements for service users has struck many commentators as extremely persuasive (Smith, 1996). However, putting this theory into action has been challenging for all concerned, not least because the pressures of politics and practice have not gone away. While the evidence might suggest a particular course of action, politicians continue to want change today, resources are limited, and organizations are caught up in a constant process of change and reorganization. In practice, a Swedish study suggested that fewer than 10% of practitioners read research-oriented books or journal articles more than once or twice a year (Bergmark and Lundstrom, 2002).

One response which has been at the heart of the evidence-based practice 'movement' over the past 15 years has been to promote the use of research evidence derived from social experiments rather than encourage more use of research per se. Randomized controlled trials, used widely in medical research and, in the US, to assess social interventions, have been promoted as a method for really understanding whether or not social interventions actually work (Macdonald, 1997b). Similarly, systematic reviews have been conducted as a means of pulling together a wide body of knowledge related to a given intervention. This focus on interventions (and systematic reviews of intervention studies) has been attractive to many commentators, particularly as it helps to focus service providing organizations on desired outcomes of specific services.

Early attempts to generate a rigorous evidence base for social interventions occurred in the United States in education policy (Oakley, 2000), where schools were considered to be natural laboratories for experimental interventions. Elsewhere, the shift has been more a case of debate and pronouncement than the widespread use of experimental methods. For example, the 1999 UK White Paper on Modernising Government encouraged a greater use of evidence in policy making:

> This Government expects more of policy makers. More new ideas, more willingness to question inherited ways of doing things, better use of evidence and research in policy making and better focus on policies that will deliver long term goals (Cm 4310, para 6, 1999).

This more general encouragement to greater use of evidence has been interpreted in different ways by those wishing to promote the use of all different types of research relevant to policy making (Pawson, 2006) and others who saw an opportunity for greater experimentation (Macdonald and Sheldon, 1998). However, perhaps the greatest note of caution has come from those arguing that promoting a greater use of evidence in practice is altogether more complex than improving the availability of appropriate evidence to practitioners (Rubin, 2007; Mullen et al., 2007).

CHANGING CONTEXTS OF SOCIAL WORK PRACTICE

This section argues that an understanding of the role of social work research should be grounded in social work traditions rather than social work research traditions. The activity of social workers lies very often at the interface between the individual citizen and the state, and the profession has been difficult to assign a single role or set of roles and tasks; indeed its nature is complex and fluctuating (Asquith et al., 2005). Butler and Drakeford (2005) argue that this represents both its strength and weakness in that social work can on the one hand be perceived as adaptable, durable and capable of acting as a key mechanism for meeting the aspirations of macro social policy. On the other hand it can appear rootless, vague and at worst built on superficial foundations. This dichotomy has been reflected in the debate about the nature of the 'expertise' of social work practitioners and the way that this expertise is executed in the course of their work. In particular the knowledge base that underpins this expertise and the extent to which this informed by, and *the way* that is informed by, applied social work and other social research has been at the heart of the discussion about the nature and role of social work.

One of the striking features of the social work profession has not only been its growth internationally but also the globalization of the debate about the nature of its theory and practice to the point where there is now an internationally recognized definition of the profession (IFSW, 2000). Nevertheless theorists and commentators, including the users of services and practitioners but primarily academics and policy makers have explored and at times polemicized about the role and identity of social work as a profession (Lavalette and Ferguson, 2007). Social work, intervening as it so often does at the interface between the private lives of individuals and the state, is therefore inherently political. Questions about the extent and nature of the involvement of the state in individual's lives are central to the shaping the roles and tasks of social work. It is therefore unsurprising that over the last 50 years (and to some degree before) different traditions have emerged within social work. These traditions reflect the different positions not only towards state involvement but also within social work on the status of different spheres of knowledge and the dynamic between knowledge, values and skills.

In the context of the complexity and fluidity of both, the role and identity of the social work identifying typologies within the profession can always be problematic and potentially simplistic or reductionist. Nevertheless Dominelli (2002) and Payne (2006) have developed a helpful framework that identifies three broad traditions within social work: the therapeutic; the social order or maintenance; and the emancipatory or transformational tradition (see Table 2.1). The relative influence of each varies over time and internationally. The therapeutic tradition, with its roots in psychodynamic theory, casts social workers in the role of helping the individual manage and cope with adversity. The emphasis is on addressing individual psychological functioning, and the social worker's role is to maximize the individual's capacity to live with difficulties in their past and present. The role of research in such a tradition is to provide frameworks for the social worker to understand these processes and models for intervention at the individual level.

The second trend Dominelli and Payne identified was that of the social order or maintenance tradition. Within this model the social worker occupies a different role of 'expert' in relation to the user of services. The expert social worker is there as a source of information and knowledge and provides solutions to problems the individual faces. Within this tradition the social worker is not so much concerned with personal empowerment but solving difficulties on *behalf* of the service user and where appropriate on behalf of society such as in cases, for example, of adult and child protection. It therefore purports to represent a more pragmatic perspective on social work practice. This tradition has become most commonly associated with state social work, particularly in Western Europe, North America and Australasia, and establishing public accountability for assessments and interventions carried out on behalf of the state have been crucial. The development of an evidence base for applied social research with the emphasis on 'what works' has been an important feature of social work and other professions in the public services (Davies et al., 2000).

The third position identified within the social work literature is the emancipatory or transformational tradition (Payne, 2006; Dalrymple and Burke, 2006). This tradition sees social work as an inherently more politically orientated profession than the other two traditions. The starting point is that those who use social work services do so largely because of difficulties that are defined or significantly influenced by the unequal and discriminatory nature of societies in which we live. Social work is therefore centrally concerned with issues of social justice

Table 2.1 Social work and evidence

Three traditions in social work	Three perspectives on evidence
Therapeutic Facilitation of the individual to find ways of dealing with difficulties facing them in their lives	Evidence should be used to generate frameworks or models that help social workers understand processes and interventions
Social order or maintenance The 'expert' practitioner facilitating change through the provision of services and information. This includes taking coercive action on behalf of the state where necessary	Evidence should show which interventions work and which do not. This perspective is most closely aligned with objective, impartial evidence
Emancipatory or transformative Based on principles of social justice the activity of the practitioners is based on the concepts of empowerment and promoting the self efficacy of the individual	Evidence should be produced by practitioners or service users (or at least with practitioner or social worker involvement) and should be part of practice development and improvement

and this position asserts that individual problems can only be understood and addressed within their wider social context, even if social workers are not necessarily in a position to influence or change that context. The proponents of this tradition, which is strongly reflected in the international definition, argue that social workers cannot afford to be neutral on issues of inequality and discrimination. On the contrary Banks (2006), for example, links emanicipatory social work to reflective practice and argues that a central feature of the reflective practitioner is their preparedness to take 'moral blame', a theme echoed by Clarke (2006) who argues that social work has, as distinct to other professions a 'moral character' in both theory and practice.

Humphries et al. (2003) argue that applied research within this more radical tradition is key to social work maintaining both its clarity and integrity in the decision-making process. She argues that public accountability is wider than practitioners' responsibilities toward those prescribed by any given state. While a feature of many social workers' practice environments is the statutory framework within which they practice (Thompson, 2000) social workers have a wider professional responsibility that transcends day-to-day policies and procedures, which interestingly is reinforced by many national codes of professional conduct and registration processes. The nature of the research that is utilized is also an important dimension of this tradition. Qualitative as well as quantitative methodologies are identified as being useful in the decision-making process but in particular participatory models are promoted. These, it is argued, both articulate the perspectives of those who use social work services and challenge the position of those users as the passive objects of research (Beresford et al., 2007).

These different perspectives involve different actors (academics, practitioners, service users) and come in and out of favour at different points in time. As we discuss here, evidence-based social work had seen a renewed interest in evidence that demonstrates the effectiveness of social care interventions. Like many typologies these three traditions are rarely to be found in pure or separate forms with most practitioners working in a combination of the three. Payne (2006) characterizes them as three poles between which practitioners move, depending upon their circumstances. 'Expertise' and its role within a broader social work identity need to therefore be understood within any given practitioner's geographical and political context. However, the status of knowledge and its relationship to practice also has to be understood within the broader context as to how practitioners make decisions.

There is a danger when discussing decision-making processes that the relationship between research and practice is perceived as linear, with at its extreme the practitioner seen simply as the conduit of research (Lawrence, 2006). Jordan and Jordan (2000: 209) comment:

> Evidence based care would be a very good way to tie the profession ... into a conception of their tasks that effectively de skilled and shackled them, while seeming to raise their status to that of scientific researchers.

However many writers have recognized that in the course of their work the reality for social work practitioners is that they draw upon a number of different areas of knowledge (Gilgun, 2005; Drury-Hudson, 1999). Certainly social workers may well utilize research-based knowledge but they do so alongside their practice experience and knowledge, local and national procedures (usually based upon legal frameworks) and their personal experience. The relationship towards and between each of these 'spheres' of knowledge varies greatly and all are mediated by the influence of professional and personal values.

The pluralistic nature of the knowledge base that underpins practice is widely recognized by policy makers. In the UK, the Social Care Institute of Excellence validated such a view in a published knowledge review (Pawson et al., 2003). Moreover the General

Social Care Council in the same national context recognized that the post qualifying social work education programmes needed to be developed on the basis of the integration of research, theory, practice and values (GSCC, 2005). What is striking when looking at the international definition of social work and many of the curricula of social work programmes is the influence and near hegemony of at least the language of emancipatory and transformational approaches to research.

Statham et al. (2005), in the context of the debate regarding the role of social work in Scotland, argue that this is to some degree the consequence of the nature of the social work task. Social work practice is by its very nature complex and requires a model of knowledge utilization that is more sophisticated than the linear relationship that some models (particularly of dissemination) suggest. Munro (2002) has taken this forward and explored the decision-making process in social work from the perspective of generic decision-making theory. In particular she looks at the inter-relationship between intuitive and analytical reasoning and the use of emotional intelligence. Munro argues that many social workers rely upon intuitive reasoning. This reflects the low status that knowledge has in many practice environments and that the emphasis in many settings is on social workers' activism and pragmatism rather than their view of either themselves or by others as being an expert profession. Munro does however recognize the utility and validity of intuitive reasoning and that its speed and basis in empathy and rapport building fits closely and comfortably with the social work role. Munro does, however, argue that social work practice and the perception and reputation of the profession can be enhanced by greater use of analytic reasoning in social work decision making. It is not a case of counter posing analytical reasoning to intuitive processes but rather that the former can be an important check and balance on the latter. The systematic utilization of research is an important dimension of moves towards a more analytical

model of reasoning in the decision-making process that is at the core of social work practice.

Although not accidental, it is perhaps unfortunate that attempts to increase the rigour of both the knowledge base itself and the process of its application to decision making have been in the context of an increased emphasis on audit and performance management. Tillbury (2005), writing from an Australian perspective, comments that performance management can militate against the execution of professional judgment and discretion. Tillbury (2005) and Allnock et al. (2005) make the point that performance indicators can be important tools for increasing public accountability and raising awareness and increasing understanding about the impact of social policy and social work practice. As such they play a valuable role in providing 'objective evidence' for informing the development of policy. The gathering of such evidence takes place within a political and organizational context and this will inevitable impact on what is measured, how it is measured and any findings that are applied. Bullock for example comments in relation to the impact of research on recent UK child care policy:

> Those [studies] that produced recommendations that were costly and difficult to implement, such as the overview for children cared for away from home, had little impact whereas the adoption studies had a delayed but major effect owing to a change of Government and the Prime Minister giving it his personal attention. (Bullock, 2006: 19)

In terms of both evaluation and performance management, care needs to be taken that any criteria for assessing services and practice need to be based upon appropriate indicators in terms of what they are seeking to measure, and that there is recognition for example that there is often a complex relationship between costs and outcomes. If they are used as a crude managerialist tool then they will not only provide misleading data but the prescriptive way that they are used will also have consequences for professionals and their practice. If an 'audit culture' develops (Munro, 2004) then the corrosion of practitioners' capacity to exercise their professional expertise and judgment will impact on the *way* that those practitioners utilize knowledge, and an unintended consequence could be a diminution of expertise rather than its enhancement in the decision-making process.

The interest in performance management has partly been driven by a desire to increase the efficacy and accountability of agencies providing care services. However, the management of risk and more specifically its aversion has become a widely recognised and well documented concern in the public sector (Beck, 1992) and the evidence base has been identified as one of the mechanisms of monitoring and managing risk. There is an emerging body of literature that has focused on agencies that need to be perceived as high reliability organizations (Roberts and Bea, 2001). In these organizations, (typically airlines, fire services and the nuclear power industry), failure to manage risk can be catastrophic. In social work, systemic failure can be very serious and traumatic, particularly in cases that involve maltreatment. Research-based evidence can help equip social workers with the knowledge necessary to identify and intervene in situations in which risk is a strong feature. Similarly, it can be used to build dynamic, responsive organizational structures that seek to learn from systems failures. Parton (2005) and Hendrick (2003) both warn against welfare systems being shaped by these most serious cases in that living with a level of risk is not only necessary but desirable. For example the early removal of children from the care of parents with difficulties such as addiction problems may minimize risk in one sense but that course of action will carry a number of other risks such as disrupted attachments and a burgeoning population in state care. Research-based evidence can give practitioners the confidence in both their own but also their managers' and the wider public's eyes to live with and manage levels of risk in the community.

CRITIQUES

Debates about the provision of more objective, impartial evidence for decision making have elevated research as a source of knowledge for social work practitioners. Promoting objective, rigorous social work research has gained support amongst researchers and research users and the notion of systematic reviews producing syntheses to support practice has proved particularly attractive.

More recently the debate has shifted to consider the challenging issue of how to better support the use of evidence in decision making. It quickly became apparent that this was about more than promoting critical appraisal skills for social work practitioners, but required a whole set of individual, organizational and wider structural barriers to be addressed. The three models proposed by Walter et al. (2004) go some way to addressing these barriers.

Evidence is often inconclusive. However, when it is clear, there is still a lot to be learnt about how to promote changes in practice. In medicine, professional guidelines have been used to channel new research to practitioners; in social work in the UK this development has been mirrored by the development of evidence-based resources by organizations such as the Social Care Institute for Excellence (SCIE). The effectiveness of strategies to promote the use of good quality research in practice (and ultimately outcomes for service users) has been given very little attention (Nutley et al., 2007).

And what of the far more frequent occurrence – when the evidence is inconclusive and does not lend itself to neat 'guidelines' for practitioners? It has been suggested that it might be helpful in cases such as these (and perhaps for all evidence) to think in terms of contributing new complex, inconclusive information to the 'mindlines' of practitioners (Gabbay and le May, 2004) – the complex web of understanding that is shaped by not only evidence (of all sorts) but also professional practice, context, etc. This would involve a more fluid approach, involving for example professional networks, continuing professional development and staff exchanges.

It is now more widely accepted that evidence will never be capable of replacing professional judgement, particularly for professionals tasked with complex decision making in the inherently risky situations encountered by social workers every day. However, there is scope for social work organizations to encourage an enhanced use of evidence to support professional judgement and improve services. At the same time it is clear that there is a role for individuals in making the best use of the evidence available to them.

There is still a challenge in providing more objective, impartial evidence through improvements in the quality and synthesis of evidence. In particular, the role of systematic reviews as rigorous syntheses to inform practice has been promoted and supported through the Campbell Collaboration social welfare group. Ventures such as the Campbell Collaboration reflect the international demand for objective, rigorous evidence to support policy and practice. The next step will be to ensure that this evidence makes a meaningful contribution to social work practice.

Theory and Knowledge about Social Problems to Enhance Policy Development

Joan Orme and Katharine Briar-Lawson

INTRODUCTION

This chapter will consider the role of social work research in generating theory and knowledge about social problems to enhance social policy. In doing so it will consider the relationship between social work research and the wider social sciences and explore the role of both in informing policy.

In the first instance the position of social work in the wider social sciences is explored by reflecting on perceptions of social work as a research discipline. Contextualizing social work research in this way involves discussion of the distinction between basic and applied research and the implications for the relationship between research and policy development.

The chapter goes on to explore specific inter-relationships between social work research, theory, knowledge and policy. This has been organized around three overarching themes: researching interventions, the personal/political divide and the process of democratizing knowledge production. These headlines represent some of the distinctive aspects of social work research that arise out of its position between policy and practice.

They are large fields in their own right, but they are discussed here as illustrative of debates within social sciences and social work research about knowledge and theory for policy.

The conclusion provides an overview of imperatives for, and the complexities of, enhancing policy development through social work research.

CONTEXT: RESEARCH, PRACTICE, POLICY AND THEORY

A distinctive feature of social work research is that its focus is, or at least should be, on both policy and practice; the structural and the individual. This dual focus, and the use of theory generated by other social sciences, has led to social work inhabiting a rather contentious place. The closest relationships between social work and other social science disciplines in terms of theoretical relevance have been with psychology, sociology and social policy but in that these are underpinned by philosophy, political and economic theory the connections are more diverse. However, because it draws significantly on other subjects social work is sometimes said to have no distinctive theoretical base of its own. In the UK social work has at times been dismissed by other social scientists as merely the 'appliance' of social science (Orme, 2000a,b).

However, social work is both a field of study and a field of practice, and this has often led to new questions emerging regarding social work's relation to psychology, sociology and related social science disciplines. Disciplinary boundaries are being renegotiated. The power and authority of the field are thus undergoing change. There are opportunities and challenges faced by social work shared by both the UK and US. When seen as an arm of the social sciences doing technical or applied research, the profession or discipline of social work has had a subservient status. On the other hand, the social responsibility of the field to ameliorate social problems is an attribute that creates disciplinary credibility as the field of practice attempts to generate knowledge involving problem solving. Thus, instead of always being perceived as a field that is subservient, its relational and integrative characteristics place social work in a special role as it promotes interdisciplinary integration and knowledge generation regarding social problem solving. This role means social work is an 'interstitial' profession working at the interface of public and private issues (Butler and Pugh, 2004: 67). This has implications not only for knowledge generation but also for research for and on policy and practice. The relational attribute helps social work transcend the theory/practice debates as it contributes both applied and explanatory knowledge of social problems. Also because it is the very site of the inter-relationship between research, policy and practice social work has the potential to contribute to theory and knowledge that enhances both.

Applied research

The theory/practice tension within the social sciences is important in that it has implications

for which knowledge and theory are recognized as valid. The tradition of distinguishing between different types of research, defined predominantly by purpose, is underpinned by distinctions made between research deemed to be basic and that which could be applied. Janowitz (1972) redefines this as the difference between enlightenment and engineering models. The latter provides applications of theoretical knowledge, while the former supplies resources, such as theoretical concepts which lead to understanding of the situation and the role of practitioners in it. In enlightenment models research impact is pervasive rather than direct (Hammersley, 1995: 119).

Such distinctions have been influential in perceptions of the relationship between research, policy and practice. Basic, enlightenment or theoretical research is often given the status of 'proper' research, with applied research being seen to be inferior, because of its lack of distance and/or objectivity from the subject of the research. The epithet of social work as the 'appliance' of social science therefore diminishes its importance in contributing to knowledge generation. The suggestion is that social work research draws on other theoretical traditions to describe or explain social work, rather than contributing to or generating new knowledge about the social problems with which it deals, or any theoretical understanding of these. This therefore denies the contribution it can make to enhancing policy. Such knowledge hierarchies exist in the US where what is known as 'explanatory' (similar to enlightenment) research is often seen as more scholarly than applied or 'engineering' research.

Policy research

The theory/applied distinction has been challenged by expanded of notions of policy research or policy-oriented research (Becker and Bryman, 2004). This involves research designed to inform and understand one or more aspects of the public and social policy process. This understanding assumes a direct relationship between research and policy; an instrumental use of research by policy involving the direct application of research results. Nutley et al. (2007) argue that there now exist many typologies of the relationship between research and policy which highlight the different and subtle ways in which research can inform, influence and enhance policy.

This expansion of the understanding of the relationship between research and policy is helpful to social work research in that social work research is not necessarily or perhaps more accurately not primarily about researching for policy or researching policy directly. Social work research is more often focused on the effects of policy, or on the interventions into the social contexts and problems that are, or should be, the subject of policy.

This, however, raises further tensions. For example, Hammersley (1995) questions the relationship of research and policy that assumes that all policy interventions will have a positive impact, what Finch (1986) calls the 'amelioration' tradition. He argues that this implies that social improvement is a given outcome of research and can be achieved primarily through the application of theory and research results (Hammersley, 1995: 137). Such a position seems to be supported by Becker and Bryman (2004) in their assertion that social policy research is both descriptive and prescriptive (Becker and Bryman, 2004: 5). However, Hammersley argues that there is no certainty about the appropriate person(s) to make decisions or prescriptions about 'improvement' and/or what is 'right' or 'good' in intervening in social problems. He further questions this as a function of academic research (see Hammersley, 2003 for discussion of these, what he calls, 'dilemmas').

However, a different approach is that of Kurt Lewin's (1946) action science ideas which led the way for some researchers to subscribe to the notion that the best way to understand a problem is to try to solve it. Thus explanatory or enlightened knowledge can be informed if not enhanced by applied (or engineering) knowledge.

Hence in the US there is a more positive orientation to research that has the potential to inform public policy. Such a goal is consistent with the practice research orientation in the profession, and empirically-based practices and programs have the potential to become the basis for public policy.

However, there are legitimate concerns about the appropriate relationship between research and policy. Having too close an association with the status quo risks research being seen to legitimate and support policy implementation (Finch, 1986). It might also lead to certain social problems being at best ignored, or at worst denied. It is because of this that the relationship between research and practice is crucial in surfacing social problems. The knowledge held by social work practitioners and those experiencing social problems can contribute to the generation of theories for policy development and practice intervention.

The relationship between theory, research and policy

The relationship between research and policy is often assumed to refer to (research) evidence *for* policy or evidence-based policy. This is often associated with a commitment to empirical, deductive, positivist research. While knowledge generated from such research is necessary and relevant there is also a place for theory in the development of policy. However the status of theory in influencing policy is tenuous. It has been suggested that the decline in the influence of social science generally is related to its inability to engage in and influence important agendas. The usefulness of knowledge in the social sciences and its capacity to enhance policy is related to its capacity to contribute to significant debates (Delanty, 1997).

In social work, it has been argued that those undertaking research and generating knowledge have also failed to influence the profession of social work and those formulating policy for the profession. In the opinion of these critics it should be possible to have practice (dictated by policy) circumscribed by research. In an overview of social work research utilized in the UK, Macdonald and colleagues (1992) subscribe fully to an engineering model. They suggest that, given the right methodological approaches, there is sufficient evidence to be prescriptive about practice and that it would be:

> ... entirely reasonable that the proposers of a new training course, or a member of staff being supervised, be asked to explain why a particular approach has been chosen and whether there is any evidence to back it—just as, on a different scale, any practising architect or engineer proposing to build a high-rise residential block or a two-lane motorway would be expected to say why previous experience does not apply. (Macdonald et al., 1992: 638)

However, the criticism is that theory generated is rarely based on rigorous high-quality research (Macdonald, 1999; Khinduka, 2007); the knowledge base is seen to advance slowly involving sporadic additions to knowledge (Reid, 2002a). An alternative critique is that practice and policy do not always articulate theory (Lovelock et al., 2004).

These different perspectives reflect inherent tensions in the rigor–relevance relationship (Schön, 1983). For example, relevant translations of research into compelling stories may constitute rigor among some stakeholders, including policy makers. The faculty researcher who can present stories for policy makers at a legislative hearing along with the more rigorous findings from research may address some of these tensions. However, if rigor is measured by scholarly peers and scientific criteria these may not suffice. This illustrates the complex intersections that have to be addressed by research-generated theory and knowledge in order to have an impact, to bring about change and, in doing so enhance policy development.

A wider role for practice-focused intervention and different kinds of knowledge generation could be supported by Rist (2000) who would challenge Macdonald et al.'s (1992) assertion above. He questions the assumption that policy making requires applied research as conceptualized in the engineering model. He argues that early analyses in social welfare simplistically fixated on technical adequacy without commensurate concern for utilization. In the engineering model of research, he suggests, it is presumed that sufficient data can be brought to bear to determine the direction and intention of the intended policy. If policy making is seen not as a single event but as a process then research has to perform an 'enlightenment' function which will: 'create a contextual understanding about an issue, build linkages and strive to educate about developments and research findings' (Rist, 2000: 1003).

Shaw and Norton (2007) however suggest that the distinction between applied and basic is unhelpful in social work research on two levels. The first is, as has been said, that the distinction has not served social work well in terms of the status of the knowledge generated. Second, it does not encapsulate the complexity of the iterative process of identifying and intervening in social problems, in ways that inform and are informed by policy.

Shaw and Norton (2007) draw on educational research (Furlong and Oancea, 2005) which identifies distinctions between 'research inspired by consideration of use' and 'research seeking fundamental knowledge'. They suggest that this helps to conceptualize social work research in ways that do not construct basic and applied as being in conflict, but can be seen as compatible and possibly synergistic dimensions (Shaw and Norton, 2007: 10). This is helpful in that research to generate knowledge about social problems and policy requires fundamental knowledge. It also requires reflection on the ways in which that knowledge is utilized, by both policy makers and practitioners.

The implications of this for social work are that social work research in a variety of traditions could contribute knowledge to inform and enhance policy. It challenges the assumption that there are 'right' methodological approaches that will produce evidence about social problems to inform policy. An examination of social work research reveals that there are traditions of social work research contributing to knowledge, theory and policy development in different ways.

TRADITIONS IN SOCIAL RESEARCH

Debates about the status, rigor and approach of social work research highlight that there is a corpus of social work research. However, this corpus consists of different traditions. This should not be considered as negative. In many ways the traditions in social work research can be seen to have their roots in the general trends of social research. A broad-brush backdrop of developments in social research is therefore provided here, focusing on the specific links between research and policy before discussion of how specific aspects of social work research have built on these developments.

Trends in social research

Significantly, the origins of social work practice could be said to be associated with early traditions in social research. The quantitative traditions of data collection that commenced with the Royal Commission on the Poor Law (1832) were reflected in early social work traditions represented by the Charity Organisation Society and its confidence in 'the science of life' (Shaw, 2008b).

Scientific traditions were continued in the form of surveys of social conditions undertaken by, among others, Chadwick, Rowntree and Booth (see Bulmer (1982) for discussion of these traditions and their implications).

Such approaches were predominantly structural and descriptive, and were underpinned by an assumption that describing and documenting social conditions caused them to be known. That such descriptive studies had an impact on policy decisions is illustrated by the work of Chadwick whose report on *The Sanitary Condition of the Labouring Population* (1842) brought about massive improvement in public health in Britain. In the US, surveys that exposed social ills were the predominant form of research in the early years of social work and are evident in the work of Jane Addams (1910). Like those in the UK, these focused on economic conditions and the social consequences for individuals, families and communities.

This use of research to look at the causes of social and health problems was followed through in the work of the Fabian Society in the UK at the end of the nineteenth century. Research moved from the descriptive and began to question the causes of the phenomena described in ways that both problematized and required a response. Such research used the findings to underpin arguments for social policy through a commitment to social reform.

During the nineteenth and twentieth centuries a number of competing traditions related to research for policy became evident. Collection of data through mass observation and the organization of, for example, census data and household surveys continued to produce statistics which were predominantly (or allegedly) 'neutral'. However during the 1970s methods of enquiry were developed to help understand and interpret the conditions that were revealed (Townsend, 1979). Differences among such research were not necessarily about method, but about a commitment to a particular value base, and to constructing explanations or theories about the existence of social conditions and the potential responses to them.

A third tradition and one which had implications for the place of social work research in social work more generally was the distinction between research addressing macro and micro issues. In an important critical review of welfare research undertaken toward the end of the twentieth century, Williams et al. (1999) identify two distinct patterns of research:

- research in structuralist mode which addresses structural and policy matters; and
- individual welfare research that focuses on individualised and privatised issues (Williams et al., 1999: 157).

While this is a rather dichotomized perception of welfare research, it does help to illuminate a potential place for social work and social work research in welfare research more generally. Williams et al. (1999) identify what they describe as attempts to mediate the relationship between agency and structure: to acknowledge that welfare research has to capture both individual biographies, identities and values but understand these in prevailing structures informed by policy and discourse (for example the discourse of social care). Making direct reference to social work research they suggest that debates that appear to be about the salience of different research questions reflect more fundamental debates about the contested nature of legitimate knowledge about the social world (Williams et al., 1999: 159).

The framework produced by Williams and colleagues to try and reconcile the disparity between research traditions incorporates consideration of four interconnected analytical levels: the welfare subject; the social topography of enablement and constraint; institutional and discursive context of policy formation and implementation and the contextual dynamics of social and economic change. Such a framework acknowledges a characteristic that could be said to be distinctive of social work research and its position between practice and policy: research not only has to address the individual as a welfare subject, but also as an individual in their own right, experiencing and contributing to social problems (such as abuse, family dysfunction)

and evaluate the implications and effect of interventions in these situations.

Acknowledging mediating concepts is important not only in breaking down the dichotomy between agency and structure, but also in trying to identify how social work research can influence policy and practice. The focus on the individual resonates with social work's commitment to see 'the person in their environment' and suggests this could be an important strand of social work research. This might involve researching the nature of social work interventions and developing theory and knowledge about these. However social work research is much broader than this, and is required to be so if it is to enhance social policy more generally.

ASPECTS OF SOCIAL WORK RESEARCH

To explore the relationship over time between social work research this section focuses on three aspects of social work research:

- researching interventions;
- the personal/policy interface; and
- democratizing the process of knowledge production.

RESEARCHING INTERVENTIONS

There is a limited tradition of social work research that provides either complex statistical analysis or empirically-based analysis of those who are in receipt of social work services, their social conditions and the effectiveness of interventions.

Effectiveness

For example in the US studies of the effectiveness of the dominant intervention of the time, individual casework (Fischer, 1973) were designed to bring about effective change. While in the UK, Robinson (1970) explored how scientific evaluation may be applied to social work to test whether social work intervention did bring about change for the better.

More influential in the UK were government-funded studies of social conditions that caused individuals to be in touch with services. Those undertaken by Davies (1969) and others were part of government funded research program of effectiveness studies into probation. This research was impressive for its volume and methodological seriousness and diversity (Shaw, 2008b). That of Folkard (1974), for example, involved a form of randomized control trial in the allocation of intensive services to offenders on probation supervision orders. In terms of policy influence the aim was to provide arguments for greater resources to support community supervision.

Another form of research which investigated the relationship between social conditions and micro interventions focused on structural issues that cause individuals and families to require services and advocated changing the nature of intervention in communities (Hadley and McGrath, 1984). Although the research had informed a government think tank considering the role and tasks of the social services in the UK (Barclay, 1982), neither the research recommendations nor the policy report were ever put into effect.

This can be compared with the work of Reid in the US, whose evaluation of practice interventions and testing out new models informed not only the micro practices of social workers (Reid and Shyne, 1969; Reid and Epstein, 1972) but also the organization of social work services into intake teams.

More recent examples of empirical work to test out, or introduce methods of intervention, have been advocated by those committed to producing a certain kind of 'evidence' for practice interventions and policy decisions about service provision. In an example, again from the probation service, McDonald (1994) empirically tested the use of behavior modification techniques with offenders, and argued that this should be the prime mode of working with offenders. Such research ultimately led to a raft of policy changes that introduced programmatic work with offenders and changes in the organization of services for offenders (Furniss, 1998).

The need to be seen as addressing major social issues such as poverty, crime, substance abuse as well as having to respond to demographic changes has created continuing pressure from legislature and policy makers in the US for the advancement of knowledge about what social work interventions are effective. In such a climate the paucity of research studies published or submitted for presentation at social work conferences reveals the problematic nature of generating more intervention research (Fortune et al., in press). To be influential in policy agendas researchers are compelled to undertake more practice or intervention research.

In addition to ideological resistance to such intervention research the labor-intensive nature of the work, from intervention design to testing and retesting, may impede such research in the academy. While governmental funding and research council sources affirm the importance of intervention research by issuing special proposal requests, with the social work community as one of the target disciplines, such grants are very competitive and out of reach for many academics. Conferences (Fortune et al., in press), workshops (Fraser, 2005) and national strategies (Bywaters, 2008) also reflect efforts to advance more intervention research. Social work has been slow to develop sustainable solutions to systematically address this deficit.

Despite this intervention knowledge gap, there is a compelling need for social work to demonstrate effectiveness and thus to build the knowledge base about practice interventions with tested interventions. The need for such knowledge generation about practice effectiveness is heightened by growing emphasis on the promotion of evidence-based practice (EBP). The demand, if not requirement, for EBP to guide funding decisions by some policy makers may usher in a different approach to research which may in turn influence the nature and content of social work fostered intervention research. The implications of such agendas are that social work's role in enhancing policy development may be overshadowed by systematic studies and applied research knowledge from psychology, economics and sociology.

These developments would curtail the influence of social work knowledge and theory and this could have implications for future developments in research. For example, while intervention studies are important, Proctor argues that there are other questions germane to the study of practice. This includes questions about the practices of social workers, the taxonomies of practice by site, what practices should be used and how these can be improved (Proctor, in press). Kirk and Reid (2002) also remind us in the US that very little is known about practice epistemologies including bias, error, notions of truth and objectivity. If the opportunity to pursue such research agendas is lost, then knowledge about and policies pertaining to social problems and those who experience them will be severely limited.

It has been argued, on the basis of the US experience, that intervention research is necessary. This can not only involve evaluation of individual programs but can also involve overviews of extant research. An example of research synthesis in the UK involved social work researchers reviewing the evidence and informing policy changes in child care (DHSS, 1985; DoH, 1995). However, specific intervention research was also undertaken. Innovations in assessment were developed, evaluated and tested (Ward, 2000), and frameworks and tools for practice developed (e.g. in England the DoH *Framework for Assessment of Children in Need and their Families*). The purpose of this research was to inform policy under an agenda of *Quality Protects* and according to Sinclair (2000) is significant because the targets and performance

measures arrived at were informed by social work research.

Evidence

As indicated above, a significant influence on social work research has been the pressure from the EBP movement. As EBP is dealt with in some depths at different points in the *Handbook* the intention here is not to discuss it in detail, but to look briefly at the implications of evidence in social work research for the development and enhancement of policy.

Knowledge or evidence to enhance policy development can be derived from both explanatory and applied research. For example, epidemiological and etiological knowledge is critical to understanding problem prevalence and incidence and the cause and effect relationships that need to be altered. Social policy studies involving the testing of an intervention or a cluster of interventions can also be seen as applied research. For example, Campbell (1969) wrote about 'reforms as experiments' wherein social policy initiatives can often be subjected to the same experimental and quasi-experimental conditions as other interventions. Thus on the surface what may appear to have a very different purpose, such as applied research, may actually have as a prerequisite the building of explanatory knowledge. In other words, sound intervention research in social policy requires solid explanatory studies.

In fact, analysis of social work research might suggest that the dichotomies of enlightened versus engineering research or explanatory versus applied research may actually prove to be false. Applied research such as intervention or practice research embraces both. For example, in order to undertake practice or intervention research, knowledge is required about the social problem, its etiology and epidemiology. Knowledge of culture and context is vital and this may be informed by explanatory knowledge. In prevention science, for example, explanatory research may be a prerequisite for interventions as chains of risk and protective factors are studied and mapped and then informs the selection of the interventions to be tested (Fraser, 2005).

While identifying many caveats to the use of quantitative research, Sinclair (2000) argues that it can have a vital role by demonstrating, for example, frequency of occurrence of phenomena or circumstances. This can ensure they become a priority for policy and/or further research. However quantitative research, he argues, tends to concentrate the mind on the final outcome as evidence and not on the processes by which the outcomes are reached. Also, what Sinclair calls the 'slipperiness' of the activities to be measured in social work means that outcome measurements have limited value. Ideally quantitative approaches should be part of wider data collection. Hence in evaluation of policy Pawson and Tilley (1997) argue that attention should be given to the contexts and mechanisms in which the policy is implemented, and not just to the numeric outcomes.

Having highlighted some of the limitations to using measurement in social work research to support policy change, Sinclair sees a clear role for quantitative research as part of preparatory descriptive research. This can prepare the way for other evaluation studies and sometimes helps sharpen the hypothesis. Also, in a positive sense, he suggests social work research presents challenges to quantitative approaches. These challenges enable social work to contribute to the wider social sciences by stimulating development of other approaches. These include analytic description and approaches to evaluation that value the complimentary contribution of different methodologies (Sinclair, 2000). Such approaches reflect opportunities to develop methodologies in researching practice that surface other knowledges.

THE PERSONAL/POLICY INTERFACE

Critiques of the distinction between the enlightenment and the engineering model are predicated on the assumption that the most effective basis for improvement in policy is through generated knowledge. Discussions have focused on whether scientific (rational, theoretical) knowledge is achievable through social research and if so how (Hammersley, 1995: 122). However, researching practice brings another dimension to research informing policy and, as Williams et al. (1996) identify, the need to generate knowledge from the individual welfare subject is as important for policy development as the large scale datasets about the social conditions which contribute to social problems.

Social work frequently draws on Schön's conceptualizations of professional practice (Schön, 1983, 1987) to argue against the use of technical–rational approaches to knowing. His concepts of knowing-in-action and reflection-in-action put greater emphasis on building up professional skill and knowledge (or more accurately wisdom) from the experiences of practice rather than either theoretical or technical, rational knowledge gleaned through research. His influence is seen in reflective approaches to social work (Fook, 2000a) and social work research (Fook, 1996) which change the research emphasis from the production of knowledge for practice, to the recognition of different kinds of knowledge. They also change the focus from research for, or on, policies and their impact on individuals to ways of knowing about the situations *of* individuals (and families and groups), often referred to in social work as 'the person in their situation' configuration.

However, the complexity of drawing on professionals' (practitioners and/or researchers) capacity to know individual experiences and theorize from them is challenged by Bourdieu's theory of practice (Bourdieu, 1990). While Bourdieu's work is much wider than social research and draws on many other philosophers (see May, 1996 for a critical synthesis), his interpretation of agency-structure is particularly relevant to discussions of how knowledge generated in social work practice can inform policy. It is also pertinent because Bourdieu's theories of individual experience arise out his own empirical work. This demonstrates the potential for transcending the theory/practice/evidence divide.

When Bourdieu refers to 'practice' he redefines it as the experience of individuals rather than professional interventions in that experience. His empirical work leads him to suggest that the principles on which individuals structure their world (the person in their situation) cannot necessarily be known, either by empirical research or by reflection in action. What he calls 'the objects of knowledge' are constructed over time in and by their *habitus* (Bourdieu, 1990: 52). Attempts to know and understand at any one time impose understandings on individuals and their situations, which totalizes the *habitus* in ways that are contrary to the ways in which it evolves: 'Science has a time that is not of that practice' and because it ignores time and detemporalizes, scientists arrive 'after the battle is over' (Bourdieu, 1990: 81).

Bourdieu therefore refers to the totalization by science, or the inquiry relationship, which produces a neutralization by setting up a situation of theoretical questioning. For him any methodological approach can take away the structuring of the situations by the individual through the very process of enquiry (or research). Enquiry also resorts to 'instruments of eternization', that is by trying to use knowledge about situations it enshrines momentary experiences and understandings in time. Hence Bourdieu questions the very process of attempting to generate knowledge.

This is not to say there are not patterns. For Bourdieu the practical world has structures – organizing principles which do not necessarily fall into the grand categories of sociology. While experiences are 'regulated' they do not necessarily follow formal or informal rules but are the response to the influence of early personal history. Bourdieu refers to the notion of *habitus* which incorporates a person's experience and her/his learning. Although people might experience the same conditions, barriers, etc.

their personal style or unique integration, based on earliest experiences, is influenced because individuals defend themselves against change (Bourdieu, 1990: 60–1).

At first sight, this appears to be a rather nihilistic position to academic enquiry – or even reflective practice; it suggests the very process of attempting to discern truth is counter to the process of practice: 'Simply because he is questioned – or questions himself – about reason he cannot communicate the essential point: the very nature of practice is that it excludes questions' (Bourdieu, 1990: 91).

However, there is point in trying to understand, as opposed to know. Bourdieu suggests that researchers can develop different means of receiving communications about practices while recognizing that these means will construct the communications in particular ways. In a set of arguments that have implications for methodological approaches he urges researchers to recall that their constructions are the product of responses to individual *habitus* and do not necessarily create structured rules in generative principles. This gives particular purpose to social work research that focuses on practice interventions, which involve practitioners entering and becoming part of individual *habitus*.

Bourdieu opposes the objectivism/subjectivism dichotomy and challenges both the 'lofty distance' of objective hermeneutics and 'participant' anthropology (Bourdieu, 1990). This lends weight to the attempts within social work to use discourse and narrative to discern how individuals within situations construct such situations. However, knowledge generated in such a way is not always acceptable to government departments. Focusing on individuals' experiences in this way precipitates a different emphasis on what is, or can be known, about social problems and how that knowledge is, or can be, constructed and utilized. Exploring how knowledge of social problems can be generated from the process of social work interventions could bring a different dimension to policy development.

Such an approach has relevance for social work research because it constitutes a challenge to the acceptance that there is either a single event of 'knowing' as represented in the 'findings' of a research project or that there is an iterative process of knowing which is the result of reflecting on interventions. There is a need to identify research traditions that facilitate understanding of the ways that individuals respond to their *habitus*, the deeply personal, private and individualized circumstances in which social workers intervene. These understandings have been applied to processes of desistance in criminal justice (see Chapter 28) and are crucial when trying to enhance knowledge about situations which involve, for example, abuse or the way that the world is experienced by people with mental health problems.

There are other approaches in the social sciences that have contributed to understandings of how to generate knowledge from and about individual experiences in order to understand social problems. Work on personal construct theory (Kelly, 1955) is used as a practice intervention, but can also be used as a research tool to discern the way individuals choose to construct their own world. Houston (2001), discussing social work practice, argues that social and psychological sciences have had to face the challenge of how to promote a theory of human agency whilst at the same time taking into account the impact of social structure. In his suggestion that practitioners draw on theories of 'critical realism' he echoes Delanty (1997), who argues that the role of social science is to provide explanatory knowledge, but also to dig deeper into social structures of social reality identifying generative mechanisms for causal laws. Underpinning all this is the recognition that knowledge is not context free: social action and structures are mutually implicated. This is as true for the social work researcher as it is for the social work practitioner.

One consequence of critical realism in social work research is that it emphasizes

that knowledge gained from research into individual experience, be that ageing, poverty, violence (as survivor or perpetrator) is crucial in informing policies that address social conditions. It also recognizes that policies in some ways construct that experience and that this also needs to be a focus for research. Finally research itself can be part of that construction – of both individual experiences and policy impact. Therefore, whatever methods are used, to be effective social work research has to 'mine' the data or description, by critically reflecting on the meaning of the data for and from different contexts. This reiterates calls for a reflexive, dialogic approach (Powell, 2002) or an interactive approach (Orme, 2004).

DEMOCRATIZATION OF KNOWLEDGE PRODUCTION

The focus on knowledge acquired from exploring individual contexts could be seen to be part of a tradition in social work research that has surfaced the voice of those who are recipients of services. However, this focus on individual experience has also been associated with aspects of post modern thinking. As such it is seen to represent a form of relativism that challenges approaches that have emphasized group experience and standpoint knowledge. In that this has been said to weaken the political influence of research it is useful to explore the development of research approaches that have sought to involve stakeholders.

Early trends to critique policy led to radical movements within policy and practice. In social work this is reflected in the development of 'radical' stances represented first by Marxist analysis (Bailey and Brake, 1975) and then feminist critiques (Wilson, 1980). These positions involved not only an analysis of the status quo, but interpretations from specific political perspectives of the causes and implications of the 'evidence'. Theoretical critiques were paralleled in practice by methods in the

US and the UK which challenged discrimination and worked with marginalized groups. Practice moved from individualized clinical work to include community-based projects, in some ways building on the beginnings of social work in the settlement movement. These developments reflected a positive inter-relationship between policy and practice but did not necessarily draw on a research base.

Approaches to research that developed from feminism and social movements such as disability rights have been influential in welfare research generally (Williams et al., 1999) and in social work research in particular (Orme, 2004). Early examples of research representing the views of clients, or service users, and others (see Mayer and Timms, 1970; Sainsbury et al., 1982; Croft and Beresford, 1984) embrace both enlightenment and engineering approaches. They change the process and purpose of knowledge production by imbuing research with a purpose, not just of eliciting knowledge, but of giving voice to those who are the object of research. This includes privileging the knowledge that is surfaced from practitioners, service users and carers.

In doing this they maintain that it is not just research that informs policies that will bring about 'good': the research process itself is to be a force for change. This occurs either by liberating individuals and groups, or bringing to the fore knowledge about social circumstances that require policy interventions. For some the claims for a 'tradition' of social work research, its distinctiveness, would centre on epistemological and methodological developments associated with the work of Foucault. Social work has been at the forefront of identifying subjugated knowledges (Foucault, 1980) and has developed methodological approaches and methods that help surface and value these knowledges. Such approaches also adopted Foucault's (1980) analysis of power to challenge the status quo of policy and practice. The contention of these approaches is that they give more in-depth understanding of social problems and social issues than

more positivist social science approaches. The feminist mantra, based on Marxist philosophy, that 'the personal is the political' resonates with social work's involvement with individuals whose circumstances are created by, or are the object of, policy contexts and political decisions. Accessing that personal experience generates and enhances knowledge about them.

The democratizing process also challenges power dynamics within the research process. For example, in arguing for a feminist *praxis* in research Stanley (1990) concentrates her critique on the academic mode of production. She argues that the construction of separations between knowers and what is known/who is known leads to 'alienated knowledge'. This knowledge bears no relation to the conditions of its production or the social relations that give rise to these (Stanley, 1990: 11). Outside of the academic mode feminism insisted on useful knowledge, theory and research as practice, or as a form of *praxis* which involves the need to 'understand the world and then change it' (Stanley, 1990: 13). This political position is not allied with any one feminist position but is one which rejects the theory/research divide. This has been attractive to social work research both because social work is predominantly the domain of women (as both workers and service users) and because social work attempts to bridge the theory/practice/research divide not only in its work with social work practitioners as researchers, but also in its quest to ensure research and its outcomes are meaningful to those who are in receipt of services (Orme, 1997).

In many domains of social work practice and research the participation of service users has been developed over time and has led to methodological approaches that attempt to give voice to 'hard to reach groups' such as those in the mental health system (Tew, 2008), and to guidelines for research processes that ensure full participation (Fisher, 2002b). The involvement of service users has also figured prominently in reviews of social work itself, and related research. For example the twenty-first century review of social work in Scotland (Scottish Executive, 2006), which had a strong service user involvement, drew on commissioned research for all aspects of social work organization and practice. Such developments have influenced and been influenced by policy thinking that has reconstructed those who are in receipt of government services (e.g. health, education or social work) as consumers or stakeholders (Field, 1996). In social work this is reflected in the consumer movement in mental health in the US and in the UK in the discourse of care management and related policies such as 'direct payments' to service users to purchase their own services rather than relying on state provided services.

The commitment to change and political action reflected in research underpinning these policies is described by Hammersley (1995) as involving an 'instrumentalist' view of the relationship between 'theory' (as constituted by research) and 'practice' (Hammersley, 1995: 63). For Hammersley, research undertaken by anyone other than academics does not constitute 'proper' research because, he argues, the research process must be given some autonomy from practical concerns (Hammersley, 2003).

The dislocation of research from practice is unhelpful and unproductive for social work research and its role in enhancing policy. For social work research to generate knowledge about social problems to inform social policy requires engagement with practice in both the organization and utilization of research (Mullen, 2002; Walter et al., 2004). Otherwise research remains irrelevant to, and under-utilized by, practitioners and policy makers. Therefore, no matter how much knowledge is generated, there will be little or no engagement with policy.

A further conundrum for social work research is the tension between democratizing or emancipatory approaches to research based on standpoint politics or group identity and postmodern tendencies to celebrate diversity and, as was illustrated in the discussion in the previous section, work at the level of individual knowledge and experience.

SYNTHESIZING KNOWLEDGE

In order to influence policy, it is unhelpful for social work researchers to become embroiled in internecine conflict. What is important is to recognize that knowledge generated at all levels *may be* seen as valid knowledge, contributing to the development and enhancement of policy.

An example of a global social problem where policy has been influenced by knowledge generated from a variety of sources, building on different methodological approaches is the response to domestic violence.

In the 1970s and 1980s, feminists in the UK and the US identified and shared experiences of, among other things, domestic violence. Personal experiences were then documented in research emanating from practice with women survivors that identified their experiences (Edwards, 1987) and documented social work's response to it (Maynard, 1985).

This was paralleled by the work of the Dobashes commenced in the 1970s in the US (Dobash and Dobash, 1979) and continued in the UK (Dobash et al., 1985). They developed research methodologies to capture the extent of the violence, and the way that it was experienced by women. In doing so they challenged some of the myths and stereotypes about women's role in attracting or inciting violence and documented women's treatment by a variety of public sector agencies.

The growing amount of research evidence led to this very personal issue being identified as a public/policy issue and led to investigation of 'measuring' the scale of the problem through data collection to calculate the incidence and complexity using large scale data sets. Policy initiatives included definitions and guidelines on staying safe, public campaigns to draw attention to the issues and ultimately legislation to make domestic violence a criminal offence (see Mullender, 1996 for a comprehensive account of the inter-relation of practice, research and policy in this area).

At the same time practice interventions such as the Domestic Abuse Project in Minneapolis, Minnesota and the Duluth projects in Minnesota using specific practice methodologies (Pence and Paymar, 1986; Pence, 1987) were developed, tested, evaluated and disseminated. They provided the foundation for interventions with women and children survivors and male perpetrators.

Having said that, research and theory developments in this area are not without disagreements (Orme, 2004), but these reflect the complexity of the social issue and the different theoretical traditions that can be drawn on. In the context of these theoretical discussions the need for different knowledges and different theoretical analyses are crucial to ensure a continual dialogue with and enhancement of policy in this area.

THE RELATIONSHIP BETWEEN SOCIAL WORK RESEARCH AND POLICY

The complexity of the role of social work research in generating knowledge about social policy and social problems is highlighted by Powell (2002), who suggests that underpinning the analyses of social work research is the widely held view that the primary purpose of social work research is to 'promote the development and improvement of social work practice' (Powell, 2002: 21) rather than inform policy. But to do this risks marginalization of social work as an academic discipline (Orme, 2000b) and leaves social work as a profession open to changes implemented on the basis of policy research into which social work has had no input.

On the one hand it is acknowledged that policy makers often require evidence of outcomes and effectiveness: seeking both the 'truth' of situations and evidence of effective interventions that will bring about change. On the other, attention to practice at the micro level of interpersonal relationships informed and constituted by policy is at the heart of social work research. To be effective in informing, challenging and changing policy social work research has to develop ways of understanding the intimate and personal relations that are the subject of micro practice in the context of wider social, economic and political contexts and changes. In doing this social work research becomes both an intellectual project and a political practice (Butler and Pugh, 2004). However, it should approach both with caution. While it is important for practice research to inform policy it is necessary to avoid the possibility of a 'cosy confidence' of interest between policy makers, social work practitioners and researchers (Butler and Pugh, 2004: 55).

To date such a comfort zone has not been reached. Political changes that have underpinned developments in social policy and social work can threaten the link between social work research and policy enhancement. Politicians can misunderstand, misuse and misappropriate research findings in order to support their own political view point, or support policy principles. An 'academic' approach might involve social research, and social work research within it, as objective critical commentary on policy development and not be implicated in it. However, it is arguable that profession (or practice)-based social research such as social work should do more than commentate when the interests of the profession are implicated in the continuation of certain policies. The research needs of policy can sometimes be seen to be focused on the outcomes of interventions in a negative way in that they are framed around a series of questions/invocations.

What works? Where policy makers genuinely seek answers to questions about social problems and the nature of interventions that might be effective.

Does it work? Where policy makers 'cherry pick' research evidence to fit the political context, or require researchers to undertake quick and limited evaluations of particular approaches.

Make it work! Where policies are decided on little or no research evidence, but managers and practitioners are required to implement policy and collect 'evidence' of the effectiveness of the interventions (Orme, 2006).

Mullen's (2002) analysis of stages of the relationship between research and practice in the US is not dramatically different from that in the UK, but the consequences for the role of research in policy and practice in the US seems to have been more positive. One way to achieve this influence is to ensure the rigor of the research undertaken, and the methodologies used. Trinder (1996) has suggested that in the UK there is an eclectic, pragmatic approach to research. This may be no bad thing: to be truly effective social work needs to be involved in a raft of research programs that not only evaluate the outcomes of practice interventions or policy initiatives, but also generate research that surfaces knowledge about social conditions and social problems – knowledge that practitioners are accumulating on a daily basis. This might constitute the rapprochement referred to by MacDonald (1999) and Qureshi (2004).

CONCLUSION

This chapter has acknowledged that in discussions about knowledge to enhance policy, social work research has at times been marginalized because of its close relationship with practice. However, the chapter has sought to challenge this view and argued that the position that social work research occupies between practice and policy enables it to make a distinctive contribution to developing knowledge about social problems, and thus enhancing policy. The three strands of social work research discussed above have illustrated the inter-connections between researching practice and policy enhancement. They have also demonstrated opportunities for methodological developments that arise out of the need to acquire knowledge at both the individual and structural level.

This examination of the contribution that social work can and does make to understanding social problems and policy development leads to two major conclusions. First, collaboration, reciprocity and dialogue between researchers, policy makers, practitioners and service users is necessary to examine the implications of existing theory and knowledge about social problems and to develop ways of undertaking research that will continue to contribute new knowledge to enhance policy. Second, social work needs to build a robust defense of the variety of methodological approaches and to construct powerful arguments for research agendas over and above those set by policy makers. Only when this is achieved will policy be truly enhanced by knowledge about understandings of the social situations experienced by those who are recipient of services.

Improving Intervention and Practice

Daniel Gredig and Jeanne C. Marsh

INTRODUCTION

From its earliest origins, the field of social work has developed through the conduct and use of empirical research. Early pioneers of social work insisted that the practice should be grounded on systematic, scientific analysis. Those then in charge of training people for these new professions and the first scientists working on the question of social welfare agreed that social work is situated in an area where science and practice converge and interact (Abbott, 1930; Feld, 1925; Salomon, 2003 [1933]; Karpf, 1931). Research in social work almost invariably claims to be of use for the professional context or to have at least some implications for the conduct of practice and professional intervention (Lüders and Rauschenbach, 2001: 572). This has prompted some to refer to social work as a 'science of action' (Sommerfeld, 1998; Staub-Bernasconi, 2007b) or a 'professionalized reflection science' (Dewe and Otto, 2002: 186).

Despite the widespread agreement that social work develops through the conduct of empirical research, the conceptualization of the relationship between science and intervention and practice is evolving. A number of specific models and approaches have been developed to describe the integration of research-generated knowledge and intervention and practice in social work. Reid (1994) reviews the development of empirical practice approaches in the United States of America. Some of the more salient approaches include the work of Rothman and Thomas (1994b) on social work intervention research, Reid and Epstein's (1972) work on task-centered practice, Jayartne and Levy's (1979) approach to empirical clinical practice, Gambrill and Thyer's writings on evidence-based practice (Thyer, 2003; Gambrill, 1999).

This chapter will describe and discuss four conceptualizations of the relation between research and intervention and social work practice. The focus is on conceptualizations that capture the diversity between the models and approaches: conceptualizations with marked contrasts, for example, in the way they perceive the interface of research and intervention and practice and the necessary knowledge they consider. Further conceptualizations that represent different generations of thinking are included, two of which are still in discussion and refinement today. Finally, approaches that have currency in

Europe and the United States of America and are referred to with different intensity in the respective scientific communities are considered. Viewing them equally is intended to overcome barriers to communication among the various scientific communities in the world today.

First we will examine conceptions of the relation between scientific, research-generated knowledge and intervention and practice enshrined in the terms 'knowledge transfer' and 'action research'. Then we will talk about a model widely discussed in English-speaking countries, that of 'evidence-based practice', proceeding from there to outline a model seeking to reconcile the claims of science and practice under the heading of 'reflective professionalism' (*Reflexive Professionalität*), which currently is more intensively discussed in some European scientific communities. By comparing and contrasting these approaches, we seek to point the way to advancing the use of empirical research to improve social work intervention and practice.

DIMENSIONS OF THE DISCUSSION

In examining the different approaches, we will first describe the emergence and underlying philosophy of each approach and then provide a critique and an exemplar. This will involve consideration of four basic questions:

(1) To what extent is the concept concerned with improving intervention and practice?
(2) What type of knowledge (e.g. evidence of problems and life situations, social service organizations, social work interventions, and effectiveness) is foregrounded?
(3) To what extent are professional values and ethics considered as part of the model?
(4) Who ultimately makes the decisions (practitioner as professional, practitioner as tool of the state, practitioner in collaboration with service user, or service user independently)?

The chapter closes with a summary of the discussion of the four models in terms of

these four questions and an outline of a number of ideas for advancing the relationship between research and practice and for evolution and innovation in the practice of social work.

For the purposes of this chapter, research is viewed as a knowledge-generating process that uses the principles of science to claim the knowledge is valid, i.e., robust, sound and trustworthy (Creswell, 1994; Richards, 2005). The validity claim can be upheld to the extent that:

(a) the process is governed by theory;
(b) the procedure is explicitly and plausibly justified in all its stages;
(c) the capture, description, and reconstruction of the issue under consideration is subjected to methodological control; and
(d) the conclusions drawn contain no contradictions.

The question of which methods are accepted as reliable is subject to ongoing critical discussion in the scientific community and is, thus, in a constant state of flux, change, and development. (Lüders and Rauschenbach, 2001; Friedrichs, 1990; Diekmann, 1995).

Given the extensive nature of social work practice, empirical research on the subject is focused on the development of knowledge in at least three areas:

(1) The dimension of *the life-world or environment of service users*. '*Service users*' encompasses not only individuals but also families, other primary groups, peer groups, or even whole communities. This embraces research of the life situations of the addressees of social work, plus the description of social problems, investigations of the dynamics and causes of those problems, assessment of everyday coping strategies employed by those affected by such problems, and on the need and demand for services supplied by social workers.
(2) The dimension of *social work practice and professional action*. This dimension covers investigations of services offered, procedures, and interventions, including the course they take, their repercussions, effectiveness, and efficiency. It also includes studies on the professionals

themselves, ranging from a reconstruction of the logic(s) on which their activities are based and the institutional impact on the way in which they pursue those activities, to the self-image of the profession, the cooperation with other professions, honorary commitment, or the development of the labor market.

(3) The dimension of *social work organizations*. Studies in this field focus on the institutional and organizational framework in which social work is performed. This includes investigating the institutions providing social work, the historical dimension of the origins of such institutions and the changes they undergo, as well as the internal structures of organizations and the decision-making paths and dynamics that characterize them. This dimension also encompasses studies of the local and supra-regional structures identifiable in social work offerings, their development, and their tendencies to interlink or screen themselves off from one another (Lüders and Rauschenbach, 2001).

Research-generated knowledge on these different dimensions produces:

(a) descriptions of facts and existing states/conditions;
(b) explanations, i.e., statements on regularities in the origination of phenomena and the changes they undergo; and
(c) evaluations of the development, repercussions, effectiveness, and efficiency of services, interventions, and procedures.

It is important to note that scientific research is only one source of knowledge on these dimensions. In a practice profession like social work, knowledge derives from numerous other sources: service user reports, practitioner observation, theoretical perspectives deriving from educational preparation and experience of professionals, and the policies and procedures of organizational settings. For the purposes of this chapter, we are discussing only research-generated knowledge.

Furthermore, 'practice' is viewed as action taken by professionals while working with service users, i.e., individuals, families, groups, or communities, while 'intervention' is viewed as a circumscribed course of action

that can be named, evaluated, and learned so that professionals can have recourse to them for the purpose of solving problems.

KNOWLEDGE TRANSFER AND TRANSFORMATION

A common conceptualization of the relationship between research and practice is the model of 'knowledge transfer'. The notion of knowledge transfer was operative in the initial establishment of social work training courses. It was still influential in the 1970s, notably in Europe, when such study programs were established at universities, and when universities of applied sciences began to spring up. Today, it still figures in discussions on the benefit and utility of research for social work in certain contexts. Thus, the term continues to reflect diverse understandings.

For this chapter 'knowledge transfer' relates to academization as a step in the process of professionalization of social work. Central to this notion of knowledge transfer is the stance that everyday knowledge ('common sense') and understandings acquired and passed on in concrete professional activity is no longer adequate for dealing and coping with problematic and complex situations encountered in practice. Critics of a conventional practice relying on common sense and personal experience contend that, to be effective, social work needs to take its bearings from scientific findings on the societal and economic causes of social problems. Scientific or research-generated knowledge is proclaimed to be more rational than other kinds of knowledge and hence capable of increasing the effectiveness and rationalism of professional practice (Dewe et al., 1993).

This model of 'knowledge transfer' builds upon the assumption of a simple, unidirectional relationship between research and practice: research supplies factual and explanatory scientific knowledge that satisfies its own validity standards and serves to guide practitioners in their activities. The assumption is that there is a direct connection between the results of research and theory-formation in the social sciences on the one hand, and practical implementation in decision-making and professional action on the other (Lüders, 1987: 639). Accordingly, transcending the boundary between science and practice should take the form of a knowledge transfer. Scientific knowledge should be purveyed via the medium of language, from the sphere of scientific research to the sphere of practice, and guide the activities of social workers. The practitioner 'in action' *applies* the explanatory knowledge thus placed at his/her disposal, 'deriving his/her activities rationally' from 'abstract theoretical knowledge'[1] provided by science and research (Otto, 1971: 89). Put trenchantly: research is the sender, while practitioners are the receivers of research-generated knowledge.

In the German context, for example, where the model was prevalent in the 1970s, knowledge transferred in this way stems primarily from research on the conditions leading to the evolution of social problems (i.e. research on the life-world of the service users) and on analysis of, and reflection on, the societal function of social work (Otto and Schneider, 1973; Hollstein, 1973). A tendency associated (though not invariably) with this view is to regard social workers as 'experts'. As experts, social workers undertake the technical or instrumental application of their scientific knowledge, thus following a pattern of action aimed at relieving their service users of practical decisions connected with their lives and solving problems on their behalf. In so doing, social workers behave in a manner that is tantamount to the incapacitation of their service users (Dewe et al., 1993: 13).

Exemplar 1

The lifecycle of an intervention named 'coolness-training' exemplifies the 'knowledge transfer' model.

Empirical studies identified a set of determinants of adolescent aggressive behavior and violence committed which included diverse causal factors. One research strand identified personal characteristics and deficient interactive competences in young men committing violence including repeatedly deficient empathy; low frustration tolerance; low tolerance for ambiguity and ambivalences; little capacity for role distance, and strong neutralizing techniques. On the basis of this research-generated knowledge-for-understanding some authors conclude that anti-aggressive trainings should aim at a modification of these personal characteristics: enhancement of empathy for the victim and reduction of neutralizing techniques (Weidner and Malzahn, 2004). A set of practice principles, called 'coolness-training' (Weidner et al., 2003) was devised to produce enhanced capacities of empathy and strengthening moral norms and is recommended to practitioners as the appropriate response to adolescents displaying aggressive behavior.

Critics of the knowledge transfer model contend that it overlooks the fact that scientific knowledge, whether factual or explanatory, is designed in the first place to provide answers to questions posed by the researcher. As such, it contributes nothing to the concrete knowledge-for-action required by practitioners in successfully coping with problems. Accordingly, the benefit of factual and explanatory knowledge derived from scientific research cannot be implemented in the form of practical action: 'In principle, explanatory knowledge defies application' (Pieper, 1988: 180) and must not be 'equated with knowledge-for-action' (Dewe, 2005: 369). The model of a uni-linear transfer of knowledge from the knowledge-generation context to the application context proves to be a technocratic misconception and involves problems that its advocates have tended to attribute either to resistance or to obstacles militating against its reception. This conviction comes in a variety of different guises. Abstract, scientific knowledge claiming to function as a template for action can be accused of irrelevance, dismissed as unrealistic, and discredited as a typical product of the ivory tower. On the other hand, a form of practice that displays reluctance to 'implement' the latest and best evidence available can be accused of ignorance, pilloried as incompetent, and criticized as irresponsible.

Adherents of the knowledge transfer model normally attempt to overcome resistance and transfer obstacles by means of communicative strategies (Beck and Bonss, 1989). But as Gira et al. (2004) indicate with reference to the health professions, these attempts to integrate scientific knowledge into the interpretation repertory of professionals by 'persuasive' means (Dewe, 2005: 369) have had little success.

Elaborations of this model ultimately led to differently accentuated notions of a *transformation* of knowledge, which recognize the structural difference between scientific knowledge-for-understanding and practical knowledge-for-action. Accordingly, the provision of scientific knowledge-for-understanding should be made compatible with the practitioner's fund of knowledge. One example of this is the 'dissemination and utilization approach', according to which new insights should be passed on to practitioners making connections with everyday knowledge, thus making it possible to incorporate these insights into the body of knowledge on which practitioners base their courses of actions. The point is 'not to find a new model of professional development, but simply to reinforce and professionalize the one that is already there'. Huberman (1985: 261) Other elaborations acknowledge that practitioners are highly selective in their use of scientific knowledge, drawing upon it not so much for guidance purposes but rather to legitimize practice institutionally imposed on practitioners.

A more radical approach to the use of scientific knowledge in contexts of action is one that abandons the idea that science has a

guiding influence on practice. It is assumed practitioners will avail themselves of scientific knowledge and incorporate it into their practical activity themselves, *adapting* it for their purposes in the process (Dewe et al., 1992).

Fueled by criticism of the idea of social workers as 'experts' and increasing interest in a professionalism oriented to the lifeworld and the encouragement of service user autonomy approaches placing professional actors in the foreground and eschewing any further reference to the transfer program became prevalent (Böhm et al., 1989; Lüders, 1991).

ACTION RESEARCH

Another approach referred to as *action research* emerged from theses critiques. Some proponents of action research explicitly rejected the idea of a knowledge transfer. They also rejected critical rationalism (Popper, 1966) and its contention that science could, and should, be neutral. Particularly, they rejected the notion of technology implicit in that epistemological position which posits that technological propositions inform about the means to reach a certain goal while abstaining from reflection on the legitimacy of that goal and the means implemented (Albert, 1967). Further, action research was to transcend 'the separation between thought and action that underlies the pure and applied distinction that has traditionally characterized management and social research' (Coghlan and Brannick, 2005: 8). Put trenchantly, action research calls upon researchers not only to investigate social reality but also to change it (Greenwood and Levin, 1998). 'Those who do the research also do the action' (Dick, 2007).

Representatives of action research identify with a tradition dating back to Kurt Lewin (1953). Action research has, however, taken on a number of different materializations, and the ground it covers is extensive

(Greenwood and Levin, 1998; Palshaugen, 2007). In social work action research should initiate a process of politicization in which service users achieve self-determination and experience liberation, the nature of social problems is addressed head-on, and socio-political reform leads to a new form of social work practice (Fuchs, 1970–1971). In this light, action research is understood as 'a complex strategy for orchestrating processes of democratizing social reform' (Greenwood, 2007: 146).

It is not possible to discuss all facets and ramifications of action research but our interest here is in how action research relates to the integration of research and social work practice.

Action research is conceived as an approach designed to address the complexity of practice, as well as to engineer a close relationship between scientific reflection and practical action. Also, the knowledge generation process is designed to embed investigation of practice in an analysis geared toward social theory and social criticism which focuses on new creative perspectives for social work practice (Von Wensierski, 1997). Research was intended to be critical and activating, aimed directly at ongoing practice development and at reform and innovation of specific fields of activity in social work and its organizations.

At a methodical level, action research is based on three principles (Moser, 1977a,b, 1995). First, research should approach the life-world of the social work service users with the goal of achieving *comprehensive and holistic understanding*. Second, the discourse between researchers and the people who are the focus of the research should be *symmetrical* and avoid degrading persons to the status of research 'objects'. Persons and groups on which research focuses are not merely sources of information for the researchers, but individuals joining the researchers in their quest for enlightenment (Moser, 1977b) and should participate in research communication on an equal footing. Action research takes the form of self-enlightenment on the part of social

work practitioners leading to a new form of professional practice in the real-life context. Accordingly – and thirdly – existing practice was thought to be changed *directly* by this kind of research (Moser, 1995).

Action research takes the form of an iterative process of information collection and discourse between the actors involved. Information is retrieved by recourse to as many methods of social research as possible, making statements both about the facts relating to a specific field and about action rules and events in the sector of professional practice under observation. Methods used range from questionnaires and non-standardized interviews, to role games and crisis experiments in order to generate data not only describing facts but also revealing implicit action rules and the fragility – and hence changeability – of facts and processes (cf. Moser, 1977b; Greenwood, 2002). However, the information thus retrieved makes no claim to be the valid outcome of the research process but is viewed as an interpretation of real-life contexts forming a basis for subsequent egalitarian, or 'non-hierarchical' discourse (Habermas, 1981) between the actors engaged in the research process. The validity of the information and interpretations must be established in discourse by critical argumentation. Discussions on the validity of interpretations lead to the development of practical options and new and improved courses of action (Moser, 1977b). In this way, discourse produces orientations that can provide guidance in the field and the basis for improvements in practice.

Exemplar 2

In an early action research project in Switzerland in the late 1960s and early 1970s institutions of residential care were criticized for their educational conceptions and practices. Motivated by social workers a group of researchers approached staff working in different Swiss residential care institutions to determine the social workers' views of the problems in residential care, an analysis of prevailing practice and the subsequent initiation of process of problem solving and change. Initially data was collected on problems and their causes identified by the social workers. In the second step the information was analysed and the third step involved organized data feedback. The information presented by the research team was discussed with the social workers to validate the problems identified and to initiate a discourse on the problems to facilitate reflection and change. The reactions ranging from 'I'd never have thought that' or 'We need to talk about that', all the way up to 'We've got to do something about it' and 'We need to ask ourselves whether perhaps' this or that procedure might be more appropriate, opened the way for development of a different, improved practice (Schellhammer et al., 1978).

For its proponents, action research leads directly to changes and to greater justice in practice. Therefore there is no problem of the interface of research and practice outlined in the first part of this chapter. Action research sees research and action as forming a part of *one and the same* trajectory. Or, as Moser (1977b: 51) states, 'Action research projects are about planning for action in the social field'. Action research entertains the conviction that practitioners investigating their own practice in conjunction with social scientists will arrive, in the course of discourse with researchers, at a formulation of critical theorems on their practice and then engage in a process of enlightenment and reflection leading to an awareness of alternatives for action and finally to changes and improvements to practice. The starting point for this discourse is action research-generated knowledge about events taking place in practice, and results in – and this is crucial – the reconstruction of the (implicit and explicit) rules underlying action in the field.

Criticism of this reconciliation of research and practice contends that such research is so closely bound up with planning for action that it is deprived of the objectivity thought fundamental to the traditionally defined research enterprise. The independence from action that constitutes research in the first place is no longer assured. Research is subjected to the imperatives of a system of practical action, which means that it is expected to fulfill the utility criterion of practice rather than the truth criterion of science. In short, action research at least tends to mutate into a program for making research and practice indistinguishable (Moser, 1995; Sommerfeld and Koditek, 1994). One might even go further and object that action research has, for all intents and purposes, done away with research. Essential knowledge results not from scientific research but from discourse. In addition, in the conception of action research, a systematic engagement with the problem of scientific standards and quality criteria is absent (Von Wensierski and Jakob, 1997). Also, the conduct of this kind of research has shown that the corresponding projects have failed to live up to the claims of equality in the communication between researchers and practitioners (Moser, 1995). Finally, the proponents of action research acknowledge that one question remains unanswered: if and how results of action research processes can be generalized (cf. McLaughlin et al., 2007) and how the reformed practice can be communicated to and implemented in other organizations.

In parts of the scientific community, in the German speaking community, for example, problems besetting action research were identified and led to a withdrawal from the program asserting the unity of research and the improvement of practice.

This brings us to conceptions of the relation of scientific knowledge and practice in social work currently being debated. First, we turn to evidence-based practice: a widely considered and much-discussed approach to social work that has made the relationship between science and practice the focus of its concerns.

EVIDENCE-BASED PRACTICE

The discourse on evidence-based practice (EBP) in social work emphasizes the reliance on research, scientifically generated knowledge, or evidence as a means to develop and improve practice that has characterized the social work profession since its inception in the United States (Reid, 1994). Evidence-based practice represents one approach to the identification and utilization of scientific knowledge in practice that can take different forms and is itself evolving (Briggs and Rzepnicki, 2004). In this chapter, evidence-based practice is defined as a process of using research findings to assist in clinical decision-making. It promotes the collection, interpretation, and utilization of scientifically generated knowledge relevant to practice. As discussed in Berlin and Marsh (1993) and Briggs and Rzepnicki (2004), evidence-based practice also recognizes that knowledge relevant to practice derives from multiple sources, including extant social science theories, service user reports, and clinician observations, in addition to scientific research. Further, evidence-based practice is concerned with the specific nature of clinical decision making whereby various types of knowledge contribute to particular decisions. Thus, EBP is an approach to practice that views scientifically generated knowledge as one source of information for decision making, while recognizing that knowledge alone is never sufficient to make a clinical decision (Berlin and Marsh, 1993; McCracken and Marsh, 2008).

Evidence-based practice is grounded in basic assumptions about the nature of social work practice. Social work practice is viewed as a problem-solving process where the practitioner and service user work together to address three questions:

(1) What are the nature and circumstances of problems?
(2) What is the appropriate course of action to resolve the problem?
(3) What, if any, change has occurred that is relevant to adjusting or shifting the course of action and understanding the outcome?

Thus, social work practice focuses on a problem or problems defined or co-constructed through collaboration between social worker and service user. The ultimate purpose of this collaboration is to enable the service user to achieve his or her goals. Further, social worker and service user engage in a process of ongoing monitoring and evaluation to determine whether, indeed, service user goals are met. In the profession of social work in the United States, practitioners are ethically obligated to provide service users with the best available services according to the best evidence available (Berlin and Marsh, 1993).

Consistent with this perspective of social work practice, three fundamental elements illustrated in Figure 4.1 define the process of using research findings to aid clinical decision-making: best available evidence, the practitioner's knowledge and judgment, and service user values and expectations. As Gibbs (2003) notes, these elements are grounded in the Code of Ethics of the U.S. NASW (1999) in the sections focusing on concern for service user preferences, professional expertise, and use of research evidence.

Much of the discussion of evidence-based practice has focused on the first element, best available evidence, or specifically, what scientifically generated research is available, how it is collected, and how its quality is identified (Gibbs, 2003). Further, significant attention has been focused on research evidence about specific interventions and about a set of procedures that have been tested to evaluate the practice question, 'What is the appropriate course of action to resolve the problem?' or 'What works?' Nonetheless, in EBP, evidence refers to information deriving from a number of sources: service user reports and practitioner observations, as well as scientifically generated knowledge or research that is relevant both to the question of 'What is the nature of the problem?', as well as the question, 'What is the appropriate solution?', or what we describe in this paper as knowledge-for-understanding versus knowledge-for-action.

Figure 4.1 Three elements of evidence-based practice[2]

Gibbs, in particular, provides explicit practical guidelines to the conduct of evidence-based practice that emphasize a focus on available scientifically generated evidence: how to identify it, how to collect it, and how to assess its quality. He provides the following conceptual definition for EBP:

> Placing the service user's benefit first, evidence-based practitioners adopt a process of lifelong learning that involves posing specific questions of direct practical importance to service users, searching objectively and efficiently for the current best evidence relative to each question, and taking appropriate action guided by evidence. (Gibbs, 2003: 6)

The first phrase in the definition focuses on welfare of service user signalling that improving practice and advancing service user welfare are the ultimate aims of social work and of an EBP approach to social work. However, the phrase 'searching objectively and efficiently for the current best evidence' is a central component of the definition and places in the foreground the EBP process of collecting evidence and assessing its quality. The guidelines that Gibbs provides for finding and assessing the best available evidence

focus entirely on electronic searches of databases and rely on prevailing quality standards in social sciences. For example, the highest points for effectiveness studies go to research where subjects are randomly assigned to experimental or control groups (the 'gold standard' of research designs), where subjects do not know whether they are in the treatment or control group and where the psychometric properties of outcome measures have been assessed. To make this search and assessment process as clear and as systematic as possible, Gibbs has developed a set of rating forms and checklists. These forms are designed to enable the practitioners to evaluate and use both quantitative and qualitative studies. They include a worksheet to appraise treatment effectiveness studies that give the highest ratings to randomized controlled trials (RCTs). Although some advocates of EBP use these ratings to advocate for the use of RCTs, Gibbs advocates their use to promote the consistent evaluation of evidence quality. The expectation is that by following procedures, social work practitioners will be able to identify a set of research findings, 'the current best evidence', that will help them make decisions about which course of action to take or which intervention to deploy.

The second consideration in understanding the process of evidence-based practice is related to the knowledge, experience, and judgmental strategies the practitioner brings to the practice situation. This is the reserve of practitioner expertise that all professionally prepared social workers bring to practice from academic learning and professional experience. In *Informing Practice Decisions*, Berlin and Marsh (1993) focus significant attention on the particular knowledge types and judgment processes that social workers use to make practice decisions. In particular, they describe the types of judgments practitioners make and the structures and processes they use to make them. They recognize that in the problem-solving process of practice, practitioners make numerous judgments, both large and small. The research literature on perception, problem-solving, and judgment shows that these judgments are influenced by universal structures and mechanisms of human information-processing: the explicit fund of theoretical and substantive knowledge the professionals bring to practice, the implicit practice wisdom developed through experience, and the practitioner's individual inference strategies (Hogarth, 1985; Kahneman et al., 1982; Nesbitt and Ross, 1980). Social science research on decision-making indicates that most decisions are based on a limited number of cues and a small number of thinking strategies (Kahneman et al., 1982). Even though a social worker may gather a great deal of information about the service user's problems, strengths, and situation, she or he will necessarily be selective in what is ultimately considered. A rational thinking process is inevitably dominated by prior knowledge and information-processing shortcuts. Understanding her/his own processes of judgment and decision-making permits the social worker to use available scientific and other evidence more critically and

reflectively. Indeed, instead of following an unconsidered first inclination to fit incoming information into routine patterns of thought and action, the practitioner can expand professional discretion by reflecting on how she or he is thinking and consider additional information or additional ways of understanding the problem. Although these ideas related to practitioner reflection and critical thinking are not well-developed in the EBP literature, it is increasingly recognized that practitioner expertise is essential to implementing EBP in real-world clinical practice. McCracken and Marsh (2008) define practitioner expertise as a set of cognitive tools that aid in the interpretation and application of evidence and in the overall conduct of social work practice. These tools for thinking develop over a period of extended practice such that the individual with experience in a given area is likely to respond to a situation very differently from a novice.

Placing the concerns, values, expectations, and goals of the service user first is the third major component of EBP. Discussions of evidence-based practice in the U.S. typically reference the NASW Code of Ethics. While this third component of EBP has been a consistent element of the approach, it is an element that has not been as well developed or acknowledged as other elements.

Exemplar 3

McCracken and Marsh (2008) provide an example of the use of the EBP process to aid clinical decision-making in the provision of services in a private, non-profit, community-based agency serving children and parents involved in the state Department of Children and Family Services. The social worker, Ms. W. (pseudonym), was collaborating with foster parents who were in the process of adopting a five-year-old Mexican-American girl, Maria (pseudonym). With the family, the social worker moved through the five decision-making steps in evidence-based practice: (1) convert the need for information into an answerable question; (2) track down with maximum efficiency the best evidence with which to answer that question; (3) critically appraise that evidence for its validity and usefulness; (4) integrate the critical appraisal with practitioners' clinical expertise and with the client values, preferences, and clinical circumstances and apply the results to practice; and (5) evaluate the outcome. Ms. W. developed a working alliance with the family and considered the range of information she needed to tailor services to this family – including clinical information about Maria, her foster parents, and their interaction; parent preferences for treatment; and the Department of Children and Family Services' expectations for treatment. Based on the information gathered during assessment, Ms. W. and the family determined the clinical goals were (a) monitoring and strengthening the attachment between Maria and the foster parents and helping Maria process the abuse trauma she had experienced, (b) teaching parenting skills and providing information to parents, and (c) modifying/ regulating Maria's anxious and inappropriate sexual behavior at home and school. Ms. W. then used the electronic search strategies and supports learned in graduate school and described by Gibbs (2003) in order to identify relevant interventions and appraise their quality. Ultimately, Ms. W. found promising research supporting two different interventions addressing the treatment of children who had been abused or who had been targeted for increasing the bonding/attachment between child and parent: one a cognitive behavioral treatment and the other a child–parent psychotherapy intervention. Throughout this process, Ms. W. made numerous decisions and exercised significant clinical judgment. For example, initially Ms. W. had to draw on her expertise to determine whether evidence existed to guide decision-making in this

case and then to formulate a question to search and provide the relevant information for this particular family. In the electronic search, she had to use expertise to develop potentially useful search terms and reject those that did not fit the family's situation. Ultimately, she used her expertise to involve the family in selecting one of the two interventions identified, in balancing potential benefit versus harm, in taking into account family values and preferences, and in assessing the feasibility of implementing the intervention in the particular practice setting. As Guyatt and Rennie (2002) note, while the principle of service user involvement in EBP is clear, engaging the service users in decision making, in communicating their preferences, and in ensuring they receive adequate information to make informed decisions requires considerable expertise on the part of the practitioner. Throughout this process, Ms. W's substantive knowledge of human judgment and information processing enabled her to assess and use the available scientific evidence more critically and reflectively than would have been possible in a less formalized and deliberate decision-making process. In the end, the use of an explicit decision-making process enabled Ms. W. to bring the best available knowledge to bear to address the question of greatest relevance and to tailor services for this particular family.

Critics of EBP typically restrict their focus to the first element of this decision-making process, the search for current best evidence. They object to definitions of 'best available evidence' that describe hierarchies or levels of evidence and place results of RCTs as the 'gold standard' of evidence (Otto and Ziegler, 2008). They further object to the use of checklists (Howard and Jenson, 1999) and forms in the search for relevant evidence, positing these forms give more weight to RCTs and ultimately narrow and restrict practitioner discretion. Finally, critics challenge the ecological validity of RCTs and are concerned that findings from group studies may not generalize to single-service users (Schnurr, 2005; Otto and Ziegler, 2008).

Critics of EBP typically ignore, negate or misrepresent the role of practitioner thinking processes and expertise in clinical settings. Rather than contributing to routinized, automatic decision-making that can characterize conventional approaches to practice, evidence-based practice requires reflection and critical thinking. Although the exigencies of everyday helping requires some reliance on short-cuts or 'tried-and true' methods, evidenced-based practice pushes the practitioner to improve the quality of decisions made by systematically reviewing information from rigorous data gathering efforts instead of relying on customary practice or agency policy (McCracken and Marsh, 2008: 301).

In sum, critiques of EBP tend to ignore two of the three fundamental elements of the approach and focus narrowly on *best available evidence* and on the use of checklists and measures in the practice decision-making process. Bloom provides an efficient analysis of the fundamental debate between those who support and critique EBP when he states:

> Extreme empiricists box themselves into a position that reduces complex social environments to a set of relatively understandable but context-stripping measurable events. Practitioners at the other extreme resist the valuable, albeit partial, knowledge that is communicated through such measurable events and mistake the immediacy of the individual experience for the efficacious 'knowledge' of what to do about problems. (Bloom, 1995: 3)

Evidence-based practice is located at the intersection of the best available evidence, practitioner expertise, and the service user's values and expectations. Evidence consists of scientifically generated research that provides both knowledge-for-understanding and knowledge-for-action as we have been discussing it in this paper. Proponents of EBP have developed explicit protocols for identifying, collecting, and assessing the quality of

this research. Service user values and expectations represent a second fundamental consideration along with practitioner expertise. Ultimately, then, decisions are made when the service user and practitioner consider together the evidence available.

REFLECTIVE PROFESSIONALISM

We now turn to the utilization of scientifically generated knowledge for practical purposes contained in the model of 'reflective professionalism'. In so doing, we enter into a discourse that enshrines the issue of utilization of science in practice in consideration of the nature of a profession providing social services. Theories of professions seek to explicate professions, professionalism, and professional action. Accordingly, these models are not designed in the first instance to make detailed statements about the connections between research findings and interventions. But the relation of research-generated knowledge and professional action form a part of this discourse, although the nature of the connection between research-generated knowledge and professional action depends on the model of professionalism advocated (see Chapter 1). In contemporary models of professions, the relationship between scientific knowledge and practice is central to the debate on professionalism by placing the 'use of knowledge' at the heart of the definition (Dewe and Otto, 2002). This model is therefore relevant to understanding the relationship between research and practice.

Fundamental to a reflective professionalism approach to social work practice is the understanding that social work is a supportive process for individuals coping with crises occurring in the practical conduct of their lives. The aim of professional action is to indicate to the service users new and more extensive options for conduct leading to broader participation and prospects, in short, to establish or re-establish autonomy in leading their own lives (Dewe and Otto, 2002;

Schnurr, 2005). Services of this kind are invariably provided in direct relation to or interaction with the service user. This service user or case orientation is constitutive for social work. Cases are diverse, heterogeneous, and discrete. Accordingly, in their communication with service users, social workers attempt to identify the problem and an appropriate solution from the perspective of the service user. Central significance is accorded to a process of mutual communication on the problem itself and the options for change that are available. This is indispensable because the intended effect of the action undertaken by social workers cannot be achieved except through cooperation between social workers and service users (Schnurr, 2005). The key purpose is to *interpret* the problem and discern potential solutions to it on the basis of such interpretations and to develop in communication with the service user's 'genuine, i.e., situationally and emotionally sustainable justifications for the practical coping strategies envisaged' (Dewe and Otto, 2002), which are to be compatible with the service user's life perspectives.

Overall, in the reflective professionalism approach, professional action is conceptualized as an assisted interpretation of a problem and a subsequent supportive process, compared to the EBP approach which is more closely conceptualized as a problem-solving process. However, the service user orientation of reflective professionalism is consistent with the focus on service user values, expectations, and goals identified in the EBP approach outlined above.

Thus, it is crucially important in this approach that the social work professional sees the service user's problem in context, understands what is specific and special about it, and delivers an interpretative reconstruction of the problem on behalf of the service user. Reflective professionalism asserts this can only be done *rationally* if the professional dealing with case can draw upon a fund of *scientific knowledge-for-understanding*. Scientific knowledge refers to the evidence that has been generated through controlled research designs and has proven to

be sound in rigorous tests (Oevermann, 1996: 124). By relying on scientific knowledge-for-understanding, the findings of empirical research, i.e., the evidence on the regularities in the origins and development of a given problem, descriptive and explanatory information *about the problem* comes into operation. Reflective professionalism involves incorporating research results into the process of reconstructing a problem with all the case-related features that make it special, and producing an understanding of that problem that takes full account of its setting. From this perspective, the use of research results and their influence on practice play a very different role from the one accorded to them in conceptions such as the knowledge transfer model that assume that knowledge generated by research will actually tell practitioners how to take effective action. Research findings can only have a genuine impact when they have been made relevant for the problem in hand in the course of problem definition or case reconstruction. Thus, in reflective professionalism, the function performed by research findings is not so much to guide professional courses of action but to underpin the professional's understanding of the specificities of a case in light of generalizing scientific knowledge about social problems. To this extent, generalizing scientific knowledge is refracted in the *hermeneutic approach* to the case itself. Generalizing abstract, explanatory knowledge is compounded with the understanding of the case.

Those advocating the idea of reflective professionalism accordingly contend that by virtue of its specific structure, social work practice will invariably need to satisfy two requirements *at the same time*. It will need to be justified in terms of the trustworthiness of the scientifically generated knowledge-for-understanding, as well as appropriate in terms of the compatibility with the specifics of the service user's situation, perspective, and goals. Accordingly, in radicalized professionalization theory on which reflective professionalism draws, professional action is also referred to as the 'locus of reconciliation between theory and practice' under the conditions imposed on practice to produce scientifically justifiable problem solutions (Oevermann, 1996: 80). This operation is undertaken in the framework of a working alliance between the professional and the service user, an alliance that essentially takes the form of a relationship in which diffuse and role-type relationship components exist side by side (Oevermann 1996: 109).

Exemplar 4

One of the few examples of this approach is in a description of professional action in the context of family counselling.

Placed in the context of contemporary society that is marked by increasing social change and individualization leading to a devaluation of traditional patterns of problem solving, family counselling is offered to family systems confronted with social problems. Its aim is providing families support in decision making and adequate practical problem solving.

The task of a social worker is to contribute to provide the family system with possible interpretations of the problem they face and to stimulate the self-interpretation of the family and identification of possible and alternatives of problem solving and everyday practice adequate to the situation and the needs and compatible with the visions of the given family. Therefore, first, the social worker offers interpretations of the problem. S/he reconstructs the problem together with the family while referring to the information given by the service users and to research-generated knowledge-for-understanding about societal and structural context conditions of families in place today, the societal trends affecting families, the problems resulting off these conditions and ways of overcoming demanding situations (relating also to partner, gender and generation problems) in different societal

milieus. S/he uses her/his knowledge-for-understanding in order to come up with a interpretation of the single case and so produces case-related new knowledge. Second, on the basis of an interpretation of the case and the identification of the problem, the social worker develops options for actions. Then it is up to the family to weigh the options and to make the decisions about the action taken. The end of this process is the commitment on the next steps to be realized in order to change the problematic situation and the implementation of the correspondent courses of action (Dewe et al., 1993: 100–10).

In contrast to the evidence-based practice approach which focuses on professional decision making and the essential knowledge-for-action, the discourse on reflective professionalism basically focuses on the *reconstruction* of service users' problems and the essential knowledge-for-understanding. Although it is taken for granted that professionals are taking supportive action, professional decision making and the role of knowledge-for-action is not well developed in the literature: in some papers, knowledge-for-action is left out completely.

Where knowledge-for-action is considered, even empirical findings on the effectiveness of interventions are not understood to be a *direct* source of *guidance* for professional action. Of course they help in reflecting on the options for action available in preparing and substantiating decisions (Dewe et al., 1993), but this generalization of scientifically generated knowledge-for-action brought to bear on interventions is also refracted to the extent that the goals of an intervention are subjected to the criterion of situational and case-related appropriateness. The goals must be legitimate and appropriate in terms of the specifics of the case and the service user's context.

Thus, in the model of reflective professionalism, different types of knowledge become related. It makes apparent that empirical research findings alone are not sufficient as a basis for successful professional action. It is crucial that in this model professional action is considered to be guided on a form of knowledge that *differs systematically* from both knowledge-for-understanding and knowledge-for-action. This form of knowledge is *professional knowledge*. Professional knowledge is a sector of knowledge in its own right that is located between scientifically generated knowledge-for-understanding and practical knowledge-for-action. It materializes from the encounter between those two forms of knowledge and the way they are collated (Dewe et al., 1992). What it has in common with practical knowledge-for-action is the permanent pressure to make decisions. What is has in common with scientifically generated knowledge-for-understanding is the imperative of justification (Dewe and Otto, 2002). In the last resort, it is acquired in the course of the vocational routine acquired by a professional social worker (Schön, 1987).

In this model, research findings flow into the *professional knowledge* guiding the actions of practitioners and are collated with practical knowledge-for-action (knowledge of methods and procedures) and other types of knowledge (like knowledge on organizational contexts, legal regulations, and ethical considerations or goals of social work). Thus, scientifically generated knowledge becomes part of professional knowledge, which is *hybrid* because it is the outcome of an encounter (collation) between knowledge from different reservoirs, of which research is only one instance (Gredig and Sommerfeld, 2008). The hybrid knowledge produced by such a collation displays a quality of its own that cannot be reduced to one of the other forms of knowledge that originally went into it (Dewe, 2005: 371). In categorical terms, this professional knowledge belongs not to the province of 'knowing *that*' but to the province of skill, of 'knowing *how*'.

Forms of knowledge characterized in the model of reflective professionalism are no longer restricted to scientifically generated knowledge but also encompass practical knowledge-for-action and – at a crucial juncture – the professional knowledge that guides professional action. Indispensable as scientifically generated knowledge is, it cannot provide a sufficient grounding for action in itself. However, in the model of reflective professionalism the focus is on empirically based explanatory knowledge (Oevermann, 1996: 124), the empirical, factual, and explanatory knowledge that professionals draw upon when providing an interpretation of the problematic situations their service users find themselves in. By contrast, little reference is made about interventionist knowledge and the explicit scientific knowledge about options for action and solution strategies or their effects. The concrete options for action are revealed *in the process* of professional action. Knowledge-for-action is mentioned as something that needs to be incorporated into professional knowledge. But where it is referred to at all, this knowledge takes the form of practical methodical knowledge, i.e., knowledge of how to proceed when dealing with a case. It does not take the form of empirical knowledge of what results can be achieved in a given case with a given procedure and what unintended effects may materialize in the process (scientifically generated knowledge-for-action).

It is significant that from a reflective professionalism perspective, this understanding of the matter makes reference to 'professional action' or 'professional practice', whereas the term 'intervention' is conspicuous by its absence. This reflects the persuasion that, at its core, professional social work is a dialogic form of practice in which professionals and service users cooperate to generate solution options that they then intend to put into practice. Here there is no place for *interventions*, meaning circumscribed courses of action that can be named, evaluated, and learned so that professionals can have recourse to them for the purpose of solving problems. The same is true of empirical research findings on the effects of clearly identifiable approaches and forms of intervention (interventionist knowledge).

Critics of reflexive professionalism could view this neglect of interventions as not only due to the fact that these models are theoretical approximations of the ideal type of professional action that admittedly abstain from presenting methodical procedures. The fact of the matter is that this openness or indeterminacy of case-related action squares with the essential features of reflective professionalism outlined above. The postulate of the specific, case-oriented design of supportive strategies proposed by social workers centers on the conviction that social workers are always *developing* (not applying) specific, case-oriented, and hence *new* courses of action, constantly renewing their approaches, and in fact continuously reinventing the action they engage in. Concrete problem-solving action results from connections posited and conclusions reached in the course of assisted reconstruction of a given problem by professionals engaging in dialogue with the service users. The requisite strategies for action materialize of their own accord, as it were, once the case has been understood. This implies that professional action is always creative.

Similarly, critics of reflective professionalism could posit that no attention is given to the question of what 'coming up with options for action' actually implies, to the judgment and decision-making processes that underlie the devising of courses of action. Also, 'reflection' is given no methodical consideration – unlike the discussion in English-speaking countries, where critical reflection is also thematized in methodical terms (Fook and Gardner, 2007). This is in marked contrast to the analysis of the processes involved in case reconstruction, which are subjected to close scrutiny under the heading of 'reconstructive social work' (Jakob and Von Wensierski, 1997). In reflective professionalism, the proposal is that phenomenological, hermeneutic, and qualitative *research* methods should be drawn upon for case reconstruction and professional understanding and also turned to account for practical action; qualitative research methods aimed at the

comprehension of characteristics and properties displayed by persons and institutions can also serve the purposes of practical anamnesis, diagnosis, and intervention planning in social relations (Miehte, 2007; Jakob and Von Wensierski, 1997). The exponents of this approach thus act on the assumption that a 'structural homology' exists between research geared to understanding and social work practice geared to understanding. However, this equation is hardly convincing as there are significant differences between research and practice in terms of their preconditions (pressure to act and pressure to decide) (Lüders, 1998; Miethe, 2007).

This neglect of the decision-making process leading to a selected course of action is one limitation of the reflective professionalism approach. Although there are no known published critiques of reflective professionalism in the English-language literature, there are some additional limitations that should be noted here related to the creativity of professionals and their ability to constantly re-devise their practice in line with the specific demands of the cases involved. The expected creativity hardly corresponds with the empirical description of reality in social work. A look at the relevant research suggests rather that, in everyday professional contexts, routine replaces the constant reinvention of action. Practitioners will tend to apply the repertory of courses of action at their disposal to all cases they are confronted with, even when new problems crop up. In addition, institutional regulations, liaison with colleagues, and organizational cultures and policies also have a major influence on practitioners' action (Thole and Küster-Schapfl, 1997; Ackermann and Seek, 1999; Gildemeister, 1989). These are the experiences criticized by representatives of EBP, e.g. when they critique authority-based practice or the tendency in social work to pass certain procedures off as appropriate although there is no way of substantiating whether these procedures can claim to bring about the desired effect.

The statements made by advocates of reflective professionalism indicate that service user autonomy is not only the aim of solution-oriented cooperation between professionals and service users but insist that the process itself must not be 'incapacitating', and that personal autonomy should be assumed, preserved, and restored in that process, even if the facts appear to militate against it (Dewe et al., 1993: 37). The crucial significance accruing to communication and negotiation in this notion of professionalism is that professionals and service users should come to an agreement on potential options for action in light of the interpretation of the case proposed.

The overlap with EBP as presented in this chapter is the recognition that research is only one instance of the types of knowledge that professionals use. Similarly, the construct of 'professional knowledge' as developed in this approach points to the importance of understanding the decision-making processes of professionals and the role that evidence plays in these processes. Thus, in reflective professionalism, research serves not as a 'guide for action' as in other models, but as an 'underpinning' that is 'compounded' with the understanding of the case.

THE WAY FORWARD: USING RESEARCH TO IMPROVE PRACTICE

In this chapter we have discussed four different conceptualizations of the interface of research on the one hand and intervention and social work practice on the other. We highlighted the background and to some extent the roots of the outlined models, considering their strengths and declaring the critiques they meet. We discussed the type of research-generated knowledge that in the different models is considered to contribute to the improvement of professional courses of action. We considered the place that is given to professional values and ethics and, finally, who is making the decisions about the action to be taken. Table 4.1 provides a summary of the results of these deliberations.

Each model assumes an interface of research and intervention and practice. This reflects the large consensus existing in social work that social work practice and intervention has its foundation in research-generated knowledge. However, none of the models outlined here conceptualizes the interface in a way that would not be subject to critiques. Nevertheless, the two models still in refinement, EBP and reflective professionalism, certainly merit further attention in striving for an accurate and sound conceptualization of the interface of research and social work practice. They hold promise for advancing the integration of research and practice and as a justification for interventions.

These two perspectives emphasize different features of professional practice in social work and display the biases and weakness outlined above. The discussion on reflective professionalism emphasizes the use of scientifically generated knowledge-for-understanding, knowledge-for-action, and professional knowledge. In so doing, it operates with an extensive notion of empirical knowledge encompassing knowledge gained by the methods of both quantitative and qualitative social research. With regard to the diversity of problems that can confront service users, it effectively pinpoints the necessity for collaborating with the service user in defining the individual problem and arriving at an agreement with the service user on what an appropriate approach to, and solution of, the problem constellation might look like from the viewpoint of those affected before proceeding to a concrete course of action. Evidence-based practice has emphasized the development of scientifically generated knowledge-for-action, the use of circumscribed and well defined procedures that have been investigated for their effects, both desirable and undesirable. The relative emphasis of these two perspectives provides direction for ongoing work on the relation between research and practice and

Table 4.1   Summary of four conceptions of the relationship between science and practice

	Knowledge transfer	Action research	Evidence- based practice	Reflective professionalism
(1) To what extent is conception concerned with improving practice?	Research results can be 'transferred' directly and automatically to guide practice.	Research and practice are indistinguishable and aimed at social change.	Evidence used to guide practice decisions and improve practice.	Evidence used to interpret service user problems and develop solutions.
(2) What type of knowledge is foregrounded?	Knowledge on conditions leading to social problems and on societal function of social work.	Knowledge-for-action: Research relevant to planning for action.	Knowledge-for-action: Scientifically generated knowledge on interventions and their outcomes, one-source information for decision-making.	Knowledge-for-understanding: Research about nature of problem, as well as strategies for action.
(3) To what extent are professional values and ethics part of the model?	Minimal attention to values and ethics.	Values and ethics set prior to research and action: self-determination and liberation.	Service user values and professional ethics explicitly considered.	Attention to service user perspective, including service user values, and professional ethics.
(4) Who ultimately makes the decisions?	Social workers alone operating as experts.	Researchers and practitioners make decisions through mutual discourse.	Service users and practitioners collaborate to make decisions.	Service users and practitioners collaborate to make decisions.

the contribution of empirical research to the development of practice.

It would be useful to continue to develop practice approaches and intervention strategies focused on the types of problems and groups typically served by social workers. Against the background outlined here, it would also be valuable to inquire how courses of action are developed that are investigated empirically for their effects and offered to practitioners for use. In other words, we need to elucidate how courses of action are justified in terms of their basic approach. How must the evolution of interventions be devised and designed so that the interventions themselves are based on evidence in the sense of knowledge about the causes of problems and crises? Which actors need to be involved in the development of interventions? What stages need to be reviewed

in the process of work on this development? Prospects for work in this direction can be found in the deliberations on cooperative, research-based *intervention development* in the intermediary space between research and practice (Gredig, 2005; Gredig and Sommerfeld, 2008).

Further investigation also needs to be done on the way in which evidence-based interventions previously tested for their effects could be disseminated so that professionals can appropriate such approaches and include them in their repertoire of courses of action. With reference to the training and ongoing education of professionals, we also need to ask how practitioners can be enabled to draw upon such validated forms of intervention in the framework of their professional discretion. How can social workers be trained to develop the ability to adapt circumscribed procedures they have appropriated to the specifics of a given case and its context? Answers to most of these questions have not yet materialized, but are the subject to debate in other parts of this *Handbook*. Thus, we see that this chapter on improvement of intervention and practice via research is anything but closed. In fact, the interconnections between research, intervention, and practice are themselves a field that requires further scientific research and development.

ACKNOWLEDGMENTS

The authors wish to thank Ms. Tanya Hines of the University of Chicago School of Social Service Administration for able editorial assistance and the Förderverein Fachhochschule Nordwestschweiz (Friends of the University of Applied Sciences Northwestern Switzerland) for financial support which rendered possible our transatlantic discussion and co-authorship.

NOTES

1 Quote translated by the authors.
2 From: Haynes, R. B., Sackett, D. L., Gran, J. M., Cook, D. J. and Guyatt, G. J. (1996) Transferring evidence from research to practice: 1. The role of clinical care research evidence in clinical decisions. *ACP journal Club*, 125, A14–A16. Adapted with permission as cited in L. E. Gibbs, *Evidence-based Practice for the Helping Professions.*

Researching Our Own Domains: Research as Practice in 'Learning Organizations'[1]

Susan White and Gerhard Riemann

INTRODUCTION

In this chapter, we are charged with the task of helping to articulate 'the purposes of social work research'. As discussed elsewhere in this volume, there are many and various ways in which research into modes of service delivery, intervention and outcome can contribute to sound, evidence-informed practice. However, our own take on 'the purposes of social work research' somewhat reframes the research/practice relationship. We argue that there is an intrinsic affinity between the activities involved in the reconstructive analysis and assessment of single and collective cases in social work and related processes in research. In many important ways, professional practice is research. For example, we suggest that disciplined and rigorous assessment should be treated as small-scale, but powerfully consequential qualitative and sometimes quantitative enquiry. Conducted well, for example, it will involve a period of immersion in an unfamiliar cultural context, the negotiation and comprehension of different ways of being and doing, the formation of

a range of candidate interpretations, hopefully a rigorous approach to confronting them with new data, of testing their fallibility or of specifying and refining them, and crucially some attention to wider applicability and generalizability. These bear striking similarity to criteria for assessing the quality of, particularly qualitative, research (e.g. Glaser and Strauss, 1967).

This does not mean that we ignore the differences between different 'finite provinces of meaning' (Alfred Schutz) and the 'systems of relevance' of social scientists (in a more narrow sense) and professional practitioners, who have to act and to decide under heavy time pressure. The types of relationship between social work practice and research have been discussed in a number of publications (cf. among others Goldstein, 1991; Fuller and Petch, 1995; Shaw and Gould, 2001a; Anderson-Nathe and Abrams, 2005; Atkinson, 2005).

Moreover, just as the quality of research output depends on the capacity of the researchers to choose wisely and reflect upon their methods and analyses, so does ethical practice depend on practitioners developing their capacity to interrogate how they use and *make* knowledge in their practice (Taylor and White, 2000). There are arguably tendencies in the prescriptive curriculum design of much social work education and the economization and bureaucratization of the social work role, which militate against practitioners acquiring the skills for careful social scientific analysis. We argue here that there is a pressing need to develop forms of organizational learning and social work education, which inoculate practitioners against becoming passive vessels into which 'increasingly obsolete ... propositional knowledge' (Eraut, 1994: 113) may be poured. We contend that there is considerable innovative potential for both social work and social work research if practitioners themselves become researchers as well as research users. We will present a number of examples to illustrate how this could be done. These are offered not as the philosopher's stone, but as suggestions to encourage readers to reflect upon their own educational and practice domains.

RESEARCH AS PRACTICE

There is a robust tradition in the social scientific study of professional practice of the synthesis of the roles of practitioner and researcher and of the mutual stimulation of practice and research. For example, the seminal research of Anselm Strauss on the social organization of medical work and of living with chronic illness involved close collaboration with social scientists, who had also been trained and worked as nurses, and could continuously use their practical experiences as resources for analysis (cf. Fagerhaugh and Strauss, 1977; Strauss et al., 1985; Corbin and Strauss, 1988). An early example of this tradition (Strauss and Glaser, 1970) demonstrates quite clearly how student nurses, who participated in the unfolding drama around a dying patient during their work placements, were not just providers of data but became

involved in reflecting on and analysing their experiences when Strauss interviewed them and commented on what they told him.

In recent years, there has been a growing recognition, first that professionals and future professionals have widely contributed to the development of new approaches in the social sciences like biographical research (cf. Dausien et al., 2008) and second, that certain approaches associated with interpretative social research like narrative analysis, biographical research, interactional analysis and ethnographic studies of milieus and social worlds can become very important building blocks for professional sensemaking in human service contexts, since they provide skills for a more careful, self-reflective and rigorous analysis of single and collective cases (Sheppard, 1995; White, 1997). This topic has been widely discussed in different countries, for example, Germany – especially with regard to social work (Jakob and Von Wensierski, 1997) and teacher training. Schütze, whose work has been especially influential in the analysis of professional work and its paradoxes (Schütze, 2000), emphasizes the affinity between case analysis in social work and social scientific case analyses, which can be traced back to Mary Richmond's (1922) 'quasi-ethnographic conception of "social case work" and case analysis' (Schütze, 1994: 196–204).[2]

The dynamic of certain strands of social work research owes a lot to the fact that it has become a legitimate domain for (future) practitioners. Schools of Social Work and other professional schools have been fertile grounds for the emergence of new forms of research communication – like research workshops (cf. Reim and Riemann, 1997; Riemann, 2005b) – settings in which students are drawn into an ongoing discussion and joint work on primary data (transcriptions, fieldnotes etc.), which have been collected in the projects of the participants.[3] There have been quite a few attempts in different departments of social work, for example, in Germany, to devise settings in which students are encouraged to make use of interpretive social research to reflect on their own practical experiences (Giebeler et al., 2007; Miethe, 2007; Völter, 2008) and to do empirical studies on research problems which have emerged in situations of their professional practice. It is part of our contention here that such pedagogic approaches produce practitioners better equipped to make sense of the complex social worlds in which they must work.

Lamentably, at the same time, it has become clear that there are certain obstacles to these endeavours, such as the widespread introduction of more bureaucratized ways of 'student processing' in seemingly more 'efficient' social work courses.[4] The latter trend is arguably writ large in the UK, where at least to date, the General Social Care Council has resisted lobbying by social work academics to have a research pathway on its post-qualifying programmes, seeing this as somehow antithetical to the needs of employers. Moreover, there is a backcloth in both our countries of service reform which pushes social workers increasingly towards precipitous bureaucratic categorizations – a tendency exacerbated by the implementation of various electronic recording systems. These embed decisions in software, taking them out of the dialogical space and rendering them immune from reflexive analysis.

So, we must exercise caution in conflating the skills of practitioner and researcher, because the ability to analyse one's own sense-making requires particular conditions to flourish and, as Shaw and Faulkner (2006) note, there is not a consensus from practitioners on these matters:

> There has been serious discussion in the social work literature as to whether the skills required of an evaluator are similar to or different from those required of a practitioner. Hazel, in a passing aside that nobody else in her working agency had 'the capacity or the ability to undertake practitioner research,' would presumably have felt that the two kinds of work required rather different qualities and skills, whereas Catherine, in her observation that 'the research in many ways mirrored my professional training course,' seemed to find important resonance and echoes of inquiry skills in her learning of social work skills. (Shaw and Faulkner, 2006: 52)

Thus, in due course we will reflect on the types of education which may help to foster a social scientific approach to professional work, which we argue is so valuable, but first, we examine the nature more generally of the organizational environments which may foster the kinds of approaches we are describing.

Organizational learning and the learning organization

The term 'organizational learning' was first coined by Argyris and Schon (1978), when seeking to articulate how practitioners may be enabled to interrogate the impact upon their everyday activity of practice cultures and organizational structures.[5] A pivotal concept here, 'tacit knowledge', is derived from the work of Michael Polanyi (*inter alia*, 1958, 1967). The 'tacit' aspects of knowledge cannot be apprehended through instruction, or by consuming bites of propositional knowledge, but can only be transmitted through personal experience. Tacit knowledge is embedded in and reproduced by activities within a culture and is difficult to share with people outside that culture. It has been described as 'know-how' (as opposed to 'know-what' (facts), 'know-why' (science) and 'know-who' (networking). Riding a bicycle is an oft-cited example. Polanyi, however, prefers the example of facial recognition: 'We are somehow able to make sense of the human face and its moods without being able to tell, except quite vaguely, by what signs we know it' (Polanyi, 1967: 7).

This allusion to the *embodiment* of knowing, is an aspect of Polanyi's work that is less frequently discussed, but is pivotal to our position in this paper. Polanyi's project is to dispose of the mind/body dualism bequeathed to us by Descartes. We cannot step outside our bodies into some objective, rational domain, rather we assemble, *ex post facto*, a 'rationale' for decisions we take in part, and often substantially, on other (*emotional and cultural*) grounds.

> Within the framework of a commitment, to say that a sentence is true is to authorize its assertion. Truth becomes the rightness of an action; and verification of a statement is transposed into giving reasons for deciding to accept it, though these reasons will never be wholly specifiable [they are tacit]. We must commit each moment of our lives irrevocably on grounds which, if time could be suspended, would invariably prove inadequate; but our total responsibility for disposing ourselves makes these objectively inadequate grounds compelling (Polanyi, 1958: 320).

In other words, our imperative to 'perform ourselves' means that we assemble *from culturally available materials* a 'reason' for our actions. It was Polanyi's reflections on his practice as a physical chemist that caused him to question the notion of a disembodied objectivity and his arguments now have considerable empirical support from cognitive neuroscience and experimental psychology. The perspectives, closely allied to each other, carry a number of appellations, for example, the 'sentimental rules hypothesis' (Nichols, 2004) 'social intuitionism' (Haidt, 2001), or 'constructivist sentimentalism' (Printz, 2007). In the words of neuroscientist Antonio Damasio:

> At their best, feelings point us in the proper direction, take us to the appropriate place in a decision-making space, where we may put the instruments of logic to good use. (Damasio, 1994: xiv–xv)

The social intuitionist approach articulated by psychologist Jonathon Haidt (e.g. 2001) is particularly apposite for social work. Haidt shows that *reasoning* follows moral judgement not the other way round.

Moreover, and crucially Haidt's hypothesis is not some crude evolutionary position which banally posits that our emotions are functional, naturally selected products of our biology (see also Printz, 2007), nor is it a leap back into unreconstructed cognitivism which posits that all that is meaningful is formed *de novo* inside the individual's head. Rather, morals are often the product of 'moralising' – *cultural (group or organizational) storytelling*.

So, let us sum up what we are arguing here. There is now clear evidence that a good deal of decision-making relies on our capacities as human beings to make sense of the world using our emotions, but this does not mean we wash around the world a swirl of individual biological primary drives. Rather, our emotions and the social world, the cultures in which we live and work are connected:

> Because people are highly attuned to the emergence of group norms, the model proposes that the mere fact that friends, allies and acquaintances have made a moral judgement exerts a direct influence on others, even if no reasoned persuasion is used (Haidt, 2001: 819).

A shared taken-for-granted store of simplified easy-read text book knowledge exacerbates this problem (Fleck, 1979; White, forthcoming 2009). These tendencies are amplified still further when practitioners are under pressure to categorize and make decisions quickly, as Eraut notes:

> The process of becoming a professional involves learning to handle cases quickly and efficiently, and this may be accomplished by reducing the range of possible ways of thinking about them to manageable proportions. This leads to intuitive reliance on certain communal practitioners' concepts …, while apparently more valid theoretical ideas get consigned to 'storage' and never get retrieved. (Eraut, 1994: 43)

In other words, cultural norms and cant phrases are all the more sweet and heady when supped in the company of friends. This means the normative responses of social workers and managers as they go about their work are the proper business of *social* science and it makes a lot of sense that practitioners and managers turn into social scientists of their own domains.[6]

It is here that the work of Argyris and Schon becomes important. Their approach draws on understandings derived from systems theory, which stresses the interconnected and self-sustaining nature of social life. For example, Argyris and Schon distinguish between single-loop and double-loop learning, these are related to Bateson's (e.g. 1972) systemic concepts of first and second order learning. In single-loop learning, actions are modified when achieved outcomes differ from those expected and valued within an organization or culture. In double-loop learning, the actors question the very values and assumptions which led to the action being desirable in the first place. Thus, second-order or double-loop learning has transformative potential. When achieved it helps us to 'see what we don't see' (Varela, 1992: 19) about our organizational and occupational modi operandi. But, there are huge barriers to double loop learning.

There have been some attempts to theorize what characteristics an organization should have and what activities it should promote to create the conditions for double loop learning – that is, for the interrogation of its own cultures, values and dominant knowledges. One product of this theorizing is the notion of the 'learning organization' (Senge, 1990), defined thus:

> At the heart of a learning organization is a shift of mind – from seeing ourselves as separate from the world to connected to the world, from seeing problems as caused by someone, or something 'out there' to seeing how our actions create the problems we experience. A learning organization is a place where people are continually discovering how they create their reality. And how they can change it. (Senge, 1990: 12–13)

INTERROGATING THE TACIT DIMENSION

In the concept of a learning orgnization, we can see familiar themes starting to emerge – for example Polanyi's notion of sense-making as embodied and connected, not objective and detached. Senge makes a number of very practical suggestions for the kinds of activities that should be encouraged in a learning organization, which share the goal of seeing what we know in a new light, or at least seeing what is it that we think we know, so that we can decide whether it is still what we want. Whilst there has been a degree of interest in the concept of the learning organization,

as Nick Gould (2004) notes, social work has been ambivalent and somewhat suspicious of some of the vocabulary associated with Senge's work. Senge is writing from a North American business perspective which can sit uncomfortably alongside social work's discourses. However, as Gould notes, the learning organization is brought to life by the people who work in it and it must be acknowledged that Senge has some important practical messages for those of us who want to keep professional language lively. Indeed, the rejection of Senge's work on the grounds that it comes from the wrong stable may be one example of the censorious impact of dominant ideas on debate in social work. For example, when we compare the forms of reflexive inquiry commended by Senge with those recently adopted by the Social Care Institute for Excellence in England (http://www.scie.org.uk/publications/learningorgs/know/know12.asp), the former are far more refreshing, offering real possibilities for making the familiar strange.

There are, however, some important and cogent criticisms of Senge on the grounds that his somewhat utopian enthusiasm for innovation and learning does not take account of the sometimes malign, or selfish 'get on' motives of those at the top, or even in the middle, of organizational hierarchies who may harness Senge's powerful language from strategic positions to dress up top down change. As Fielding notes:

> [T]he self-induced invisibility of power may well turn out to be the ghost of Banquo at the table of the learning organization. (Fielding, 2001: 22)

For this reason, we advocate below that it is vital that both practitioners and managers have a repertoire of methods by which they can shake up and re-examine organizational and cultural life. Cultural games must be able to be named by all, not just by the movers and shakers in the managerial hierarchy and their votaries.

If we take this as read, then what Senge gives us are some really useful and impassioned ideas about how to engage empirically with what we take for granted and how to spot a stale discourse. For example, he makes use of Argyris' notion of 'defensive routines', which sustain established patterns and are usually so taken-for-granted they are difficult to spot. He notes:

> To retain their power, defensive routines *must remain undiscussable.* Teams stay stuck in their defensive routines only when they pretend that they don't have any defensive routines, that everything is all right, and that they can say 'anything'. But how to make them discussable is a challenge. (Senge, 1990: 255, original emphasis)

Senge may be referring to American corporations here, but social work too has its defensive routines and, if our agencies are to become learning organizations, we are going to have to develop ways to make them visible. Research can help us to do this.

It is necessary, but necessary to note:

> [T]here is a need for professionals to retain critical control over the more intuitive parts of their expertise by regular reflection, self-evaluation and a disposition to learn from colleagues. This implies from time to time treating apparently routine cases as problematic and making time to deliberate and consult. It is partly a matter of lifelong learning and partly a wise understanding of one's own fallibility. (Eraut, 1994: 155)

Yet, as Senge notes, this is easier said than done, as cultures continually sustain and reproduce their own normative domains. For example, social work cultures create rhetorical trump cards (White and Wastell, forthcoming, White, forthcoming) in the form of potent moral tales, or 'defensive routines' which are difficult to 'see' except when they are breached.

Let us give an example from child care social work in the UK. In this context, there is a powerful professional discourse of 'child-centredness', a common-place opprobrious statement in such contexts is the accusation that a practitioner is being 'too parent-centred', or 'losing the child'. This accusation is difficult to challenge without appearing to devalue the 'child-centred' doctrine. The invocation of children at risk is used routinely to account for decisions taken on other

grounds. Let us look at an example of this 'trump card' phenomenon. The following account was given by a team manager in children's services in the UK. The data are taken from an ongoing study[7] (by White and colleagues, 2006) of professional reasoning in children's services:

> Adolescents are difficult because they do not always get the service they deserve...if they are breathing, fed, clothed, got money in their pockets and a B[ed] and B[reakfast], I will say, 'that's it, see you in another life'... Really these cases need more care... The life skills they would have got from their parents. But I can't do that. *I've got a baby in a crack house. I've got to deal with that.* (emphasis added)

The Assessment Team Manager contrasts the limited service that is provided for adolescents, here invoked as one that does at least ensure that their basic needs are met, with the riskier situation represented by the graphic description 'baby in a crack house'. The moral dilemma facing the manager is evident, as clearly both types of cases would benefit from a service. The florid categorization of a 'baby in a crack house' is a rhetorically potent visual allusion, removing at a stroke any ambiguity about social work priorities. We have said that double-loop learning requires the actors to question the values and assumptions which sustain routine action, yet these values and assumptions are continually reproduced in the talk of the organization and the organization is obviously an accomplice.

There is no doubt that the tacit dimension of practice is often very difficult to extract and articulate. However, precisely because it is social, it cannot be located entirely inside the social worker's head. It must in some way, at some times be visible, available and reportable – how else do we account for the induction of novices into established ways of working? Therefore, if we are to develop the capacity of social workers to evaluate whether they want to make changes to tacit aspects of their practice, we need techniques to help them make what is familiar strange. However, we also need spaces and places where this work can take place. We will show below how simple techniques like taping a team meeting might help practitioners to begin to interrogate some of their assumptions, but this will not take place if organizational life precludes it. Obviously, spaces like professional supervision provide opportunities to bring 'the learning organization' to life, but if the familiar has not in some way been made strange, these arenas can reinforce, rather than shake-up dominant organizational stories (cf. Jones, 2004).

RESEARCH AND THE DEFAMILIARIZATION OF PRACTICE

It is in making the familiar strange that practitioners may usefully become researchers of their own affairs. This research may be quantitative or qualitative in form. The eclectic field of evaluation incorporates both approaches and when undertaken in a proper spirit of enquiry, rather than simply to prove that what we are doing was right all along, it can have huge transformative potential, as this practitioner researcher/evaluator describes:

> I think it made a huge, huge difference of how I sit with families and I learnt through doing the research that people love to pass their views. So that's made really a big difference. It has also made a very big difference doing the research to my understanding of when one can appropriately ask children to speak of you in the presence of their parents or even when not in the presence of their parent. (Shaw and Faulkner, 2006: 59)

There is an extent to which we are arguing that when undertaken by practitioners or students themselves all research is (self) evaluative, in that even descriptive research like ethnography, which focuses on what *is*, rather than what *ought* to be the case will inevitably spark debate and new possibilities. Let us briefly illustrate our argument with various studies from a number of traditions. This is clearly not an exhaustive list!

Using number to unsettle practice

Quantitative work may look for pattern and difference in numerical data. In our performance management culture, management information is routinely collected. Yet aside from this audit orientation, such data can be used to open up areas for debate.

For example during 2007, Kellie Thompson, a PhD student at Lancaster University, completed as yet unpublished research in two co-located children's services 'Referral and Assessment' teams in a UK local authority. The teams had identical roles and remits (to screen and assess referrals to the service and refer on to other teams as necessary) and also identical management structures and information systems. Yet, in Team A, of 2393 contacts to the service, only 789 became referrals, whilst in Team B of 2014 contacts, 1502 became referrals. Despite serving very similar populations the teams seemingly undertake very different decision-making in relation to the number of cases receiving a response. This kind of simple counting can be very valuable in opening up practice to debate, and by analysing that debate in turn, we can render visible important aspects of team culture. It is noteworthy that, to date, the teams have found this rather threatening seeing the process to be part of performance management culture. This is not surprising since target setting and the tyranny of performance indicators driven by central government are an increasingly pervasive feature of local authority organizations in the UK. This illustrates how very challenging are these times for developing dialogical spaces in social work organizations.

When such dialogue can be achieved, qualitative inquiry can add considerably to the understandings derived from quantitative work. For example, Bilson and Barker (1994, 1995, 1998) studied the levels of contact between 1068 looked after children and their parents in five UK local authorities. They found wide variations between teams, which they argue could not be explained by the factors usually linked to differing levels of contact (these include the age of the child, reason for becoming looked after, time in care, etc.). For example, in one local authority half the teams had levels of contact between 32% and 38% of children seeing their parents at least once a month, whilst the other teams had levels of between 69% and 71%. It seems that team culture was a very important variable. Teams with low levels of parental contact accounted for this by referring to the need to help children come to terms with parents' poor commitment. In contrast, teams with high levels of contact stressed the value of making a great deal of effort at the beginning of a placement to gain parental co-operation and build up a positive pattern of contact. Whilst, clearly the exemplars we have given are both *investigator* stories, where the research sheds light 'on' practice, there is no reason, in this 'information age', why social work teams cannot undertake this kind of comparative analysis themselves. Research then can provide new vocabularies to describe the social world and hence potentially open up democratic, discursive spaces and new possibilities (cf. Romm, 1998). But if social workers and managers are themselves to undertake this kind of reflexive enquiry, they will need time and space to do it and it will need to be valued by the organization and seen as real work.

Qualitative inquiry: describing the social workings of social work

As a social work student, I was confused by professional ways of talking, writing, analysing and describing people's lives... Even after graduating and working as a front line social worker, I remained unable to muster the authority of my education and the power of my organizational mandate to make 'true' pronouncements, to produce unequivocal case 'facts' and to work with certainly and confidence in my authority and power. I remained confused by the worlds of my clients... Perhaps it was my own sense of being confused, and thereby of being fallible, that continued to make me angry when I heard the pretentious authority and certainty that accompanied the

pronouncements of experts and officials. (De Montigny, 1995: 5)

Perhaps this quotation from the introduction to an ethnographic study of social work cuts to the quick of what we are trying to argue. In order to practise with care and humility it is important to attend to how work gets done in everyday situations (for a further exemplar of ethnographic work on everyday practice, see Pithouse, 1999).

Students of social work have found it worthwhile to utilize different approaches of interpretive research to gain a deeper understanding of processes of professional work and their subject matter: biographical research based on narrative interviews (Riemann, 2003; Schütze, 2007a, b) has served as a resource for discovering and analysing processes and problems of life histories of clients and patients. Students found it useful to study the narratives of social workers and other professionals to learn about their 'arcs of work' (Strauss et al., 1985) and the recurring problems of their work. Ethnographic studies based on participant observation have shed light on the everyday life and the practices of survival of marginalized groups and milieus. And conversational analysis, an analytical method derived from ethnomethodology, sensitized them to the ways in which professionals and clients understand – and sometimes misunderstand – each other.

We consider here a brief exemplar of how qualitative enquiry can assist practitioners and students to think about how they do what they do.

In the analysis below, Lloyd (1992) uses conversation analysis to study in detail the way talk is assembled in sequence over 'turns'. Here, it is applied to the linguistic practices of therapists and social workers in the USA during forensic interviews with children in cases of suspected sexual abuse. His data illustrate how denials from children that abuse had taken place were 'dispreferred' by the adult interviewers, who would respond to such denials with subtle censure or with further questions. Lloyd summarizes his findings as follows:

> The adults elicit children's confirmations by producing candidate response initiations [suggesting the answer], ratifying confirming turns, censuring children's non-confirming responses, producing subsequent versions of initiations [suggesting the answer again] and treating children's weak agreements as strong agreements. (Lloyd, 1992: 109)

The techniques in vogue at the time for eliciting children's accounts involved the use of puppets and play acting. The following is an example of an adult censuring a child for producing a non-confirming response:

(Adult treats Nicole as animating the Houndy puppet)

ADULT: Do you remember that part?

CHILD: No I don't

ADULT: Oh Houndy. You were doing so good. I think you're losing your memory. How about …

(Lloyd, 1992: 115)

Lloyd does not pass judgement on whether abuse had actually taken place. He does not have the data to support such an assertion. Does this make his analysis irrelevant to practitioners? No, it does not. Lloyd's data illustrate perfectly the local reproduction of certain ideas that were dominant at the time, which were treated by practitioners working with sexual abuse as the only right and proper way to think. It makes this process transparent – it makes the familiar strange.

Exemplar: Ethnographies of professional practice

We will focus now on a more extended example of another approach to the 'defamiliarization' (White, 2001) of practice, which can be regarded as a project to encourage students of social work to become 'ethnographers of their own affairs' (Riemann, 2006). Our discussion begins with a brief extract from a reflective account of a final year Masters student in social work at the University of Lancaster.

The student has given her permission for us to use this extract. The student is placed in a youth offending service which undertakes preventive work. She is describing her efforts to persuade an Initial Assessment team to respond to a situation about which she was concerned and the evaluation of these efforts by her Practice Assessors:

> My interaction with the Initial Assessment team had been observed as competent, compelling and thoughtful. It did not induce the same impression on me, at the time or afterwards. Further down the line, I have questioned what competence is. Is it getting the support the family have asked for? Is it using 'culturally' specific language to persuade? Is it recognizing my own and the agency limitations? Eadie and Lymbery (2002) state that in preparing students to function as *competent* social workers, educators need to communicate social work values and that education must not simply prepare students to conform. In reality the above situation included the need to conform to the linguistic 'repertoire' required by Initial Assessment and to get, in Bourdieu's terms, a feeling for what was required to trigger 'eligibility'. Whether this is conforming; being culturally competent … or creative is subject to debate …

Clearly, the student brings vast personal resources to the party. This cannot be underestimated. Yet we can see clear evidence of ability to interrogate her own practice. Not just to get by, but to articulate the tensions. Let us show one of the ways in which we may nurture this kind of understanding and humility.

In the following example we will present excerpts from the fieldnotes of a German female social work student, Daniela Scherbel, who had been supervised by one of us (G.R.) during her specialization in working with people with mental health and/or substance misuse problems during her undergraduate training.[8]

While the student was on a short work placement in a psychiatric hospital for a couple of weeks, in order to become familiar with the practice of psychiatric social workers, she wrote a field protocol. During her placement she spent most of her time on one ward (S2) in the company of one social worker (Nina), but had the chance to spend time on another ward (the 'general psychiatric ward') and the social worker there, Antonia. The following excerpt is taken from her observations on this other ward:

> After the lunch break (at a quarter past one) the admission interviews start on the general psychiatric ward. Antonia proceeds on the basis of a similar form as I had seen used by Nina on ward S2. I already notice during her talk with the first patient that the patient is annoyed by some questions. The woman who is about fifty years old and has been diagnosed as 'paranoid schizophrenic' hesitates again and again in answering some questions and looks at her with a sharp eye which Antonia apparently does not notice. She is much too busy taking notes. The following scene which I reconstruct from my memory serves as an illustration:
>
> 'What is the occupation in which you are working?'
>
> *'After getting married I have been working as a housewife. Shortly afterwards I got the children.'*
>
> 'That means no work. You have got your insurance through your husband, right?'
>
> *'Yes.'*
>
> 'How do you earn your living?'
>
> *'My husband goes to work. He has a very good job.'*
>
> 'That means you live on your husband's money.'
>
> Doesn't Antonia notice how offensive her summaries are? It is so obvious that she works against the patient's pride that I would like to say something. In order to show that Antonia really means no harm. I do feel how the patient forces herself to stay calm.
>
> Afterwards we have a short conversation with the 'anorectic' girl. (...) The last patient for this day is supposed to be the young woman with a 'burnout' who shares a room with the first patient. When Antonia opens the door to her room, the client whom she is looking for is not there. The older woman (mentioned above) says that her room-mate has gone out for a walk. Shortly before she leaves the room she stops and approaches Antonia. The following conversation develops between the two of them (I reconstruct it from my memory):
>
> 'What are you actually doing here?'
>
> Antonia seems to be confused for a moment. *'I am the social worker here.'*
>
> 'And it's your job to ask all people the questions which you asked me?'
>
> Antonia nods shortly. *'Sometimes.'*
>
> I watch the patient stretch herself as if she wanted to grow a few inches for what she planned to do. 'If that's the case I don't understand why they employ such unfriendly persons like you.'
>
> She sails past us, her head erect, neither looking at me nor Antonia. I am bewildered and look at Antonia. What's that? She remains cool and unmoved. She explains that you have to take such things when doing this kind of job. The patients would attack you personally because they are ashamed of their current state. This has to leave you cold.
>
> *That's probably the case. But I think it would have served Antonia right to get rid of her arrogance for a short while and to ponder over what the woman just said. The woman is right after all. I also believe that taking the patients' – and not just the doctors' and other social workers' – criticism seriously does contribute to assuring the quality of the work.*

The student presented these fieldnotes in a practice analysis seminar (cf. Riemann, 2005a: 95–7; 2006) in which the participants took turns to share and discuss observations which they had written down during their work placements. These meetings were supposed to help them get some analytical distance from their notes, so they could write a final report in which they were to present parts of their experiences, to analyse certain situations and processes,[9] and to reflect on what they had encountered and had gone through. When talking about such fieldnotes the instructor and the students focused on (a) features of the text with regard to its textual validity, (b) the realities of the setting, situation, actions and structural conditions which the student writer had got to know as a trainee and (c) what the text revealed about the student writer – her presuppositions, typifications, sensibilities, 'hang-ups' and possible 'blind spots'. (The participants made sure that the style of the discussion was respectful and non-confrontational and never resembled any sort of confessional ritual.)

When we look at features of this particular text, for example, it can be noticed that the writer used elements of a quasi-transcription for recollecting and highlighting sequences of dialogues which had impressed her in the past situations (without pretending that this was a transcription) and that she commented on the social worker's behaviour. Her first commentary ('Doesn't Antonia notice …') refers to her inner state while participating in the encounter, the second commentary, which she italicizes ('*That's probably the case* …'), acquires the quality of a more generalizing proposition formulated in retrospect ('*I also believe that* …'): She uses this particular instance to explicate how things should get done according to professional standards and to invoke the basic ethical postulate that it is necessary to take into account patients' perspectives, not just the perspectives of those who are in a position of authority.[10]

The text reveals the student's sensibility for something important which happens when the social worker interviews the patient and comments and codes her answers. She notices that the patient experiences some pressure to save her face and to offer accounts (in the sense of Scott and Lyman, 1968) when the social worker's moves appear face-threatening. It could be criticized that the social worker does not sufficiently work on assuring a basis of trust. One does not need to share the student's indignation to arrive at the conclusion that when the social worker normalizes or trivializes the patient's confrontation by subsuming it under a pattern which appears familiar to her – the *pattern of patients' shame* – she fades her own contribution to *shaming the patient* out of her awareness. She has developed a firm theory which serves to immunize herself against criticism by patients. This was one of the things which were spelled out and abstracted in the seminar. The participants also used this example to talk about types and functions of typifications and theories which professionals have developed about their work and their clients.

But there was another important issue which came up in the seminar discussion: in asking her questions and summarizing and coding the patient's answers the social worker had used a standardized form (like other social workers do) which had been created for these occasions. The instructor suggested that the student try to get hold of one of these forms in order to get a deeper understanding of the situation. The student followed this lead. The following is a small excerpt of her final report:

> Later on I looked at the admission form once again. As a matter of fact it also contains these categories which Antonia had created. It means it is not an open form which does justice to the client's individuality, but Antonia had to choose among the available options by ticking them off. With regard to the sequence which I described above the following alternatives are relevant:
>
> Occupation
>
> Steady employment, since ……………………………
> Unemployed, since …………………………………
> last employment: ……………………………………
>
> Subsistence
>
> Secure
>
> Endangered
>
> Kind of income: ……………………………………
>
> When looking at his part of the form it appears quite obvious that it induces professionals to lose their sensibility – especially if they have to work under time pressure. The form does not allow for the possibility to fill in 'housewife and mother' as an 'occupation', therefore the client is put into the box 'unemployed'. Her subsistence is secure nevertheless because of her husband. That means that she lives on her husband's money as a matter of fact. The work which the patient has performed as a housewife and mother is not sufficiently appreciated by the form (and the professional who asks her these questions).

Maybe some readers might regard this part of her final report as somewhat too conciliatory and forgiving because of a shift of responsibility (e.g. 'it induces professionals to lose their sensibility'). But it is important that she now focuses on an issue which she had not paid much attention to in her original fieldnotes: the tendency towards a standardized interaction because of the requirement to fill out a given standard form and the possible consequences of routine procedures which have emerged in this context. And by generalizing this topic she hits upon something which is highly relevant in current developments in social work and offers it as a topic for a self-reflective professional discourse.

This example was used to give a sense of what is involved in this kind of ethnographic work; how observing, writing, and discourse are integrated; and how gradually new insights emerge. It is not unimportant that the work is carried out by future practitioners who are still 'on the margin' in the settings of their work placements[11] and are not yet 'blinded by routine' even though this is a matter of degree and differs from case to case.

Some of this might sound familiar to readers: for example, writing about one's practice placements in personal terms might resemble the wide-spread practice of keeping 'learning journals' (Moon, 2006), which have proved useful in professional education in order to encourage reflective practice. But usually such journals are not shared with fellow students in the context of a practice analysis seminar but are merely kept for oneself, one's practice teacher or mentor. And while such ethnographic fieldnotes are also supposed to be written down spontaneously and in a personal manner, students are reminded of certain features that they should keep in mind[12]. They are advised (Riemann, 2005a: 94–5):

- to overcome the tendency to take things for granted;
- to write their notes for readers whom they should assume are not familiar with this respective field of practice or the history of their work placement, want to learn more about them and are sympathetic;
- to avoid 'polishing' observations in order to save face etc.;
- to write in the first person and to clearly differentiate between the 'first persons' at different

times: as actor in the depicted situation and during the later 'inscription' and reflection of their experiences;
- to avoid giving in to the tendency to 'self-absorption' that might be appropriate in writing a private diary;
- to systematically focus on sequences for the sake of discovering the order, but also the disorder of social processes (e.g. the unfolding of everyday conversations, the course of professional types of action, the development of narrative and argumentation in certain types of action, long-run collective processes, the history of a relationship or a project);
- to take into account and to differentiate the perspectives of different actors without privileging certain powerful and established perspectives as natural, authoritative and normal which would mean validating the established 'hierarchy of credibility' (Becker, 1967);
- to differentiate the language of the field from their own observational language;
- to present social processes, interactions, situations, organizational contexts, milieus, inner states and reflections in such a way that it is possible for outside readers to analyse the text by themselves; and
- to change the names of persons, organizations and places (before presenting the fieldnotes to others) in order to ensure confidentiality.

This list emerged when comparing and reflecting about a large number of fieldnotes of students of social work. It should be kept in mind that this project of turning students into self-reflective ethnographers of their own affairs should not be mixed up with current tendencies in some varieties of 'auto-ethnography' – exactly because of the quality of confessional writing and self-absorption in 'auto-ethnography' which often resembles a kind of 'writing cure' (if we are allowed to play with the term 'talking cure' which is important in the history of psychoanalysis)[13]. So, what kinds of educational approaches are appropriate to developing reflexive skills which go beyond self-indulgent confessional disclosures of the type anthropologist Clifford Geertz dubs 'the diary disease' (1987: 90) (see also, Taylor, 2006)?

Educating for research-minded, humane practice

One of the authors (S.W., with Carolyn Taylor) has written elsewhere on the kinds of educational approaches (and we include here post-qualifying education and staff development) which may nurture the sort of culturally reflexive practice we have described here (e.g. Taylor and White, 2006; Balen and White, 2007) and much of the discussion below rehearses these arguments.

We have argued that the parallels between research, particularly of the qualitative variety, and social work assessment can fruitfully be explored to encourage better understandings of the ways in which social workers generate knowledge about cases, thus helping to promote a more rigorous and questioning approach to practice. We have said that we must give students and practitioners techniques for examining what they cannot see for, as Varela notes:

> ... most of our mental and active life is of the immediate coping variety, which is transparent, stable, and grounded in our personal histories. Because it is so immediate, not only do we not see it, we do not see that we do not see it, and this is why so few people have paid any intention to it ... Yet the question remains: how can this distinction between coping behaviours and abstract judgement, between situatedness and morality, be applied to the study of ethics and the notion of ethical experience? (Varela, 1992: 19)

For this reason, it is also important for students to learn to interrogate their own case stories as texts. This is not in place of the dissemination of formal knowledge, but the balance between didactic 'textbook' approaches and the kinds of activities we have suggested needs to shift and research methods are thus absolutely core to the curriculum. Students do need to learn things, but they then need to interrogate how they use them. This shifts focus from knowledge using per se (the conventional basis for educational programmes) to an acknowledgement of the *knowledge-making* processes inherent in practice. By examining their case talk, reports and files for taken-for-granted assumptions, in the manner we have illustrated, students may be encouraged to explore how formal knowledge gets used in practice, how it interacts with moral reasoning, and what is the relationship between certainty and uncertainty. They could subsequently extend this by making recordings of interviews and case discussions and use them for reasoned debate as a further means to interrogate their practice (for examples of and exercises in the practical application of discourse analytic techniques, see Taylor and White, 2000).

But, we also need to attend to the quantitative skills of students and practitioners. Vast amounts of data are being collected in the interests of performance management and audit. If we are to nurture a democratic version of the learning organization these data need to be accessible to practitioners *and comprehensible to them*. Because numbers and counting have become new sources of potential blame in a target-driven culture, and because practitioners cannot easily interpret numerical data, vast reservoirs of information on pattern and difference remain inaccessible. Again, this can be remedied by putting research skills at the centre of professional education.

We argue that these reflexive skills are particularly important in occupations like social work which rely to a large extent on moral judgement and exoteric (commonsense and taken-for-granted) knowledge where there is a real danger that the apparent certainties produced by the uncritical use of this popular knowledge prematurely forecloses alternative readings of cases. We therefore need to place much greater emphasis on the critical evaluation of how research and theory get invoked in practice to *make* knowledge about service users and their difficulties.

A final note: this is a chapter in a handbook of social work research. Since we focused so much on practice and the uses of our stance for understanding and coping with practical professional problems, some readers might ask, 'What do you regard as the implications of your stance for *research*? And for social science more widely?'

When we chose the title of our chapter – 'researching our own domains' – we wanted to convey that it is vitally important for the collective project of social work that practitioners and future practitioners acquire and use research skills that help them 'to make their own practice strange'. This does not just include focusing on their own work routines and strategies, it also means to preserve an attitude of respect for the 'otherness' of clients or users (who must not be totally reduced to their membership in a given system of classification) and for the complexity of their biographies which can be understood nevertheless. We could not go into details with regard to the scope of such skills and approaches and we could not sufficiently take into account different ways of approaching and understanding 'lived experience', but at least we tried to share with readers some ideas of how to go about this task.

We have argued that professional practitioners and practice could definitely profit from acquiring and using research skills in order to understand the complexity of individual and collective cases. Social workers could become better and more circumspect professionals by turning into researchers. Of course there are many open questions: how is it possible to develop and preserve practice cultures which are open with regard to researching their own domains? Our own experience is mostly based on working with students of social work – students whom we hope will acquire and maintain elements of a 'research habitus'.

But we are also convinced that the acquisition of such skills leads to interesting methodological and practical innovations and substantive discoveries when students and practitioners engage in research themselves. Just think of the features of social workers' ethnographies and their implications for fostering a self-critical discourse among professionals on what can go wrong in professional practice and 'what could be done about it'.

(This is necessarily different from ethnographies of sociologists or anthropologists who have arrived 'from the outside'.) Just think of settings of critical reflection of practice and 'de-familiarization' of taken for granted assumptions (Taylor and White, 2000). The range of potential methods to be deployed is extensive (for an inclusive review of methods for 'evaluating in practice' see Shaw, 2009).

The widespread acquisition of such skills would have wider consequences as well – consequences for the place of social work in the division of labour of the professions and in the ensemble of the social sciences (cf. Dausien et al., 2008).

NOTES

1   We would like to thank Tomofumi Oka and Ian Shaw for their very helpful comments on an earlier draft of this chapter.
2   This remark about one of the pioneers of professional social work might appear surprising. Of course Mary Richmond did not use the concept of 'ethnography', but a close scrutiny of her case illustrations (in Richmond, 1922) reveals her appreciation of features in case reports which are characteristic of careful ethnographic texts since they pay attention to key markers and 'contextualization cues' (Gumperz) in unfolding situations, take into account different perspectives and are sensitive to biographical developments. Schütze (1994) demonstrates this by focusing on her detailed description of the case of Mrs. Winifred Jones (Richmond, 1922: 68–80). Mary Richmond (1922: 227–8) had in mind that social workers could make important contributions to the social sciences: 'There can be no question that family case workers are in an exceptional position to make valuable observations upon family life at first hand where they are protected, as they should be, from too large a case-load, and where they have had the kind of theoretical training in social science and practical training in social work which supplies them with the necessary background. "The interplay," says Professor Park, "of the attractions, tensions, and accommodations of personalities in the intimate bonds of family life have up to the present found no concrete description or adequate analysis in sociological inquiry."' It is interesting that she quotes Robert Park at this point in order to argue that social workers might fill a gap which sociology had left open – Jennifer Platt notes that the term 'case study',

which became so important in early sociological monographs at the University of Chicago, 'probably had a lot to do with the social worker's "case history" or "case work".' (Platt, 1996: 46).

3   Many studies which have come out of these research workshops are biographical analyses based on autobiographical narrative interviews (cf. Prins, 2008). See Schütze (2007a,b) for the methodological underpinning of these studies.

4   The authors observe these tendencies (which are detrimental for processes of personal and collective professionalization) not only in their own countries, the UK and Germany, but in other European countries as well (cf. the overall introduction of Bachelor programmes of social work in the European Union in the context of the so called 'Bologna process'). Tomofumi Oka informed us about very similar developments in Japan which contribute to a widening of the gap between the worlds of academia and professional practice.

5   Organizational learning is a systemic concept referring to the way an organization learns and adapts. That is, how an organization may be enabled to sense fluctuations in the signals it receives from its internal and external environment and produce productive adaptations to these. For this to happen we argue, the familiar must be made strange.

6   Of course we do not claim that this is a new position in the history of the profession of social work (cf. the quote of Mary Richmond in earlier footnote). But it needs to be spelled out how this can be accomplished. Our chapter is an exercise in this regard.

7   The study referred to here is: White, S., Wastell, D., Pithouse, A., Hall, C., Peckover, S and Broadhurst, K. (2006–2008), ESRC, Public Services Programme, *Error Blame and Responsibility: The Problematics of Governance in an Invisible Trade*. Outputs are beginning to be prepared but none are currently published.

8   The work which we refer to was carried out at the Department of Social Work of the University of Bamberg in which one of us (G.R.) had been teaching since 1997. (This specific work is not being carried on due to the dissolution of this department.) We wish to thank Daniela Scherbel for allowing us to use her fieldnotes. We will present a somewhat

longer excerpt in order to provide readers with enough material, so they can develop their own interpretations and have a basis for assessing the following commentary.

9   This included raising 'generative questions' in the sense of Strauss (1987: 40–54) and discovering and discussing general features of professional work beyond the particularities of the scenes which students had observed.

10   Participants in the seminar discussion also referred to another element in the text: when the patient is quoted with the question, 'What are you actually doing here?' one gets the impression that the social worker had not introduced herself in her first meeting with the patient. But maybe this had not been noticed by the patient or it might have been left out in the fieldnotes which just focused on a small part of the 'admission interview'. The student writer only referred to the circumstances, equipment ('form') and development of the 'admission interview' in vague terms and she left out how the participants had opened the encounter and brought about its closure.

11   Sometimes it is not easy for them to reconcile their sympathy and loyalty with staff members in the settings of their work placements with the requirement 'to make their practice strange' – or the practice of people whom they followed around. They might experience some uneasiness and suspect that they should become disloyal to people whom they trust and sometimes even admire. And after having become familiar with the language of the settings, e.g. the terminology of psychiatry, which helps practitioners to make sense of persons whom they encounter, it might be unsettling to be expected to put such terms in quotation marks again. There have been moral and intellectual 'investments'.

12   The 'art' of writing ethnographic fieldnotes has long been regarded as something to be primarily passed on by word of mouth. This has changed in the last two decades (cf. Van Maanen, 1988; Sanjek, 1990; Emerson et al., 1995; Wolfinger, 2002; Tjora, 2006).

13   Cf. Anderson (2006) as a succinct critique and Ellis et al. (2008) as a collection of self-presentations, self-reflections and mission statements of protagonists of the movement.

6

Challenging the Dominant Paradigm: Social Work Research, Social Justice and Social Change

Bob Pease

INTRODUCTION

In recent years we have witnessed a revival of critical and anti-oppressive approaches to social work theory and practice in the United Kingdom (Dominelli, 2003; Webb, 2006), North America (Mullaly, 2006; Wood and Tully, 2006; Baines, 2007) and Australia (Fook, 2002a; Allan et al., 2003; Healy, 2005; McDonald, 2006). Critical social work is informed by a wide range of theoretical frameworks, including Marxism, critical theory, feminism, critical-race theory, radical humanism, liberation theology, postmodernism, postcolonialism, Green political theory and anti-globalization theory. Modernist perspectives give more emphasis to material conditions, social structure, structural location, top-down power and dominant ideology. Postmodernists give more attention to culture, agency, subject positions, localized power and discourses.

The various approaches, however, all share a commitment to social justice, human rights

and social transformation. The critical tradition in social work thus emphasizes: the role of economic and political systems in shaping experiences and social relationships; the impact of structural oppression such as class, race, gender, age, disability and sexuality on people's lives; a commitment to working alongside oppressed populations to challenge the processes and structures that perpetuate oppression; the importance of challenging the power imbalance between practitioners and service users by forming egalitarian relationships and validating people's lived experiences of oppression.

While critical theories have gained prominence in social work practice, social work research texts have on the whole failed to make links with critical social theory and anti-oppressive practice. Generic social work research texts tend to be located within a positivist paradigm (Monette, 2002; Grinnell and Unrau, 2005). Some writers have even argued that the positivist approach to social work research is the only way to construct a knowledge base for social work (Marlow and Boone, 2005).

While most generic social work research texts do distinguish between quantitative and qualitative approaches (Thyer, 2001b; Neuman, 2003; Engel and Schutt, 2005; Grinnell and Unrau, 2005), the logic of most of these books remain within a positivist notion of scientific inquiry. They also tend to differentiate these approaches more in terms of methods rather than paradigmatic underpinnings about the nature of knowledge and the social world. As such, they ignore the influences of critical social theories noted above and their implications for social work research. Anti-oppressive research methodologies are thus rarely mentioned in most generic social work research texts (Brown and Strega, 2005),[1] while fewer authors still advocate a critical-theory informed position in relation to social work research.[2]

Most of the challenge to the dominant positivist paradigm in social work research has come from constructivist and qualitative approaches, within which critical-theory informed research is some times articulated (Denzin and Lincoln, 2005). We have in recent years witnessed an increase in qualitative social work texts (Shaw and Gould, 2001d) and we now have an international refereed journal (*Qualitative Social Work*) devoted to qualitative research in social work. Critical-theory research paradigms and methodologies are more prominent, however, in the disciplinary fields of gender studies, education, disability studies, postcolonial studies and even management studies than they are in social work.

In arguing for a critical-theory informed social work research in the tradition of critical social work, I acknowledge that there are other approaches to social justice-based research. In the United Kingdom, there is a long history of Fabian social policy research informed by the Titmuss tradition. While this research has made a significant contribution to our understanding of social divisions and class-based inequalities, it is argued here that such research has an element of structural determinism. This approach to social policy research in the United Kingdom has tended to neglect the role of human agency in response to widening inequalities (Welshman, 2004). Martin (2004) maintains that this social policy research tradition over-emphasizes the impact of structural constraints on human behaviour. Thus, there seems to be little place in this tradition for those who are excluded to be active participants in challenging the material conditions of their lives through social movements and activist-based research.

The same neglect of agency can be seen in some elements of the Marxist analysis. Shaw (1999) has noted the tension between Marxists who focus on structural conditions and those critical theorists who rely more upon subjective meanings that people attach to these conditions. Scientific Marxists maintain that the laws of economic development are analogous to the laws of the natural sciences. They thus attempt to develop a Marxist science in contrast to what they see as the bourgeois science of positivism (Burawoy, 1990). This stands in contrast to critical-theory informed Marxists who use qualitative and ethnographic methods to research people's experiences (Atkinson et al., 2008). We need approaches to research, that bridge the tension between structure and agency. Williams (1999) has emphasized the capacity of service users to move welfare research in new directions, while retaining an analysis of structural inequalities.[3]

A number of critics within social work have raised concerns about the capacity of social work research to contribute to the social justice and human rights imperatives of the profession (Brown and Strega, 2005; Strier, 2007). Social work has also been challenged by scholars outside of the profession to explore ways to integrate critical theory and qualitative research to promote social justice and social change (Denzin, 2002). This call is reminiscent of a challenge issued almost thirty years ago by Galper (1980) who outlined the roles that research and writing could play in building a radical social work practice. It would appear, however, that the dominant trend in social work research is more towards empirical evidenced-based and scientific forms of research.

INTERROGATING THE EVIDENCE-BASED RESEARCH AND PRACTICE TRADITION IN SOCIAL WORK[4]

While critical social work educators and writers have articulated the socially constructed nature of knowledge and moved away from positivism, many forms of social work research and practice have moved in the opposite direction to embrace scientific and evidence-based approaches (Trinder, 2000a). In this chapter I argue that the research paradigm underpinning evidence-based social work practice does not adequately address the social justice and human rights imperatives of social work practice. If social work research is to contribute to social justice and social change, we must first challenge the dominant view of evidence.

Munro (1998: 23) says that evidence-based practice 'encourages social workers to use empirically-tested methods of helping to formulate their reasoning and to evaluate their own work rigorously'. In this view, social work interventions should be based on the best evidence available (McDonald, 2006). At first glance, it is hard to argue against the idea that social work should be based on evidence. However, what constitutes evidence and who chooses it? The dominant view of evidence-based practice originating in North America emphasizes the importance of 'empirically supported' interventions that are able to be validated by research evidence through randomized controlled trials (RCTs). Randomized controlled trials have become accepted in medicine as providing the best evidence for medical interventions. They are at the top of the hierarchy of levels of evidence, with RCTs cohort and case studies at the top of the pyramid with ideas and opinions at the bottom (Webb, 2001).

This form of evidence-based practice in the social work is analogous to drug trials and is thus predicated on a pharmaceutical model (Western and Bradley, 2005). While it can be argued that patho-physiology and pharmacology can establish relationships between cause and effect in bodies and forms of treatment (Meagher, 2002), how transferable are the principles of evidence-based medicine to the human services and social work? (Marston and Watts, 2003).

Evidence-based practice in social work promotes individualism because the interventions are all focused on work with individuals (Witkin, 1996). Collective work and collective solutions are thus neglected. How might community development approaches that emphasize empowerment and participation be evaluated in relation to evidence where outcomes are hard to define? Furthermore, some critics of evidence-based practice have expressed concern about the lack of attention to consumer perspectives (Trinder, 2000b). Although there have recently been some moves to incorporate consumer views within the Cochrane collaboration, their perspectives are not allowed to inform what is regarded as a scientific process (Trinder, 2000b).

Any consideration given to the role of social and political forces on people's problems is likely to be denigrated as being unscientific in evidence-based research. McDonald (2006) asks how working with indigenous people, one could consider the impact of alienation or dispossession on people's lives within an evidence-based practice model. How might the experiences of people with disabilities and others have their experiences validated by the epistemological standards of evidence-based research? As I have written elsewhere, listening to people's stories is an important source of knowledge because the subjugated knowledge of service users can challenge the dominant understandings of social problems (Pease, 2002).

Evidence-based research must also be seen in the historical context of attempts by social work theorists to formulate a scientific foundation for social work practice in the context of the on-going debate about whether social work is a science or an art (McDonald, 2006). Thus, any discussion of evidence-based practice and research must take place within an epistemological debate about the foundations of appropriate knowledge for social work (Gray and McDonald, 2006).

Evidence-based practice is located primarily within a functionalist research paradigm and it is based on positivist assumptions about the nature of social reality. In the positivist view, facts are independent of theory and are able to constitute knowledge on their own. The key question here is whether we can separate evidence from beliefs. Is it possible to have objective knowledge in the social sciences? As Gonzales et al. (2002) note, while the notion of scientific evidence implies objectivity, it is also premised on epistemological assumptions and subjective understandings of what constitutes reality and what should be studied. I challenge the view that evidence is value neutral and argue that RCTs are located within a theoretical framework and value system that is unacknowledged and which influences the reality it seeks to understand (Witkin, 1996). The view of the individual in evidence-based practice is of a rational and autonomous being and consequently social work practice is defined as a rational project with behavioural objectives and measurable outcomes. However, I argue that all knowledge is located within an historical, cultural and political context, and is shaped by the experiences and values of those who create it (McNeill, 2006b). There is thus no such thing as 'the' evidence. It is not a matter of the use of evidence. Rather, the issue of concern here is about who controls the definition of what constitutes evidence (Denzin and Giardina, 2008).

Evidence-based research does not usually recognize the competing epistemological assumptions about knowledge and the contested nature of social reality (MacDonald, 2003). Because positivists have such a narrow view of science, they are unable to engage with knowledge derived from constructivism, critical theory or postmodernism. They do not seem able to grasp the reality that single system designs and RCTs are also partial ways of understanding the world (Gray and McDonald, 2006).

In arguing against the dominant view of evidence, I am not suggesting the whole notion of evidence should be rejected. Clearly, survey data, longitudinal studies and official statistics can be important sources of information about oppression and discrimination (Oakley, 2000). As someone who is committed to social justice, I am interested in empirical data about the experiences of oppression and marginalization and how they are connected to institutionalized processes of discrimination. What I am challenging here is the hegemonic status given to experimental ways of knowing above other approaches to knowledge development.

Oakley believes that quantitative and experimental ways of knowing can be reshaped to promote emancipatory purposes. Humphries (2008) also argues that concerns about experimental methods are more to do with the ways in which they are used than the methods themselves. Such methods can be used effectively to measure inequality and disadvantage. The problem is that when they are used to inform policy and practice, they tend to concentrate on individual and behavioural risk factors. Furthermore, Oakley (2000) maintains that RCTs produce the best knowledge for emancipatory practice. I maintain that evidence is a social construct (Gibbs, 2001a) and that not all forms of knowledge can be measured by quantitative methods. We need to be aware of other paradigms and different ways of knowing to understand why and how any research has political and ethical dimensions (D'Cruz and Jones, 2004).

SOCIAL CONSTRUCTIONISM, QUALITATIVE RESEARCH AND CRITICAL REFLECTION

Qualitative approaches to social work research have challenged narrow forms of evidence-based research which rely solely on scientific evidence and RCTs. We see an attempt to embrace a wider notion of knowledge that includes qualitative research and professional expertise (Eisler, 2002). Some advocates of evidence-based practice have argued for the inclusion of qualitative research as sources of evidence. Larner (2004) says that it is not a choice between science and non-science but rather between a narrow positivist construction of science which only recognizes RCTs and a wider notion of evidence that includes qualitative research. Certainly, some researchers use the language of 'evidence-based practice' as inclusive of qualitative methods (Meagher, 2002).

From an interpretative perspective, social work practice and research are moral rather than technical activities. Gray and McDonald (2006: 15) emphasize the importance of ethical reasoning in social work and argue that social work is primarily 'a practical-moral activity'. Most social workers emphasize the importance of values in interpreting the world. Many practitioners are concerned that scientific knowledge will take attention away from the caring and emotional dimensions of social work where the importance of humanistic responses, feelings and interpersonal relationships are valued. Taylor and White (2000) locate evidence-based practice in the context of technical rationality as the dominant form of professional knowledge. Schön (1983) argued over twenty years ago that technical knowledge was unable to address the complexity of professional work and unable to access the tacit knowledge

internalized often unconsciously that informed practice.

In empirically supported versions of evidence-based practice, social workers use knowledge developed by experts by applying it to practice, rather than being the makers of knowledge (Healy, 2005). An alternative tradition in social work for the development of practice knowledge is critical reflection and reflective practice. In this view, importance is placed on recognizing 'practitioners' lived experience or practice as a basis for making and using 'knowledge' (Healy, 2005). Fook (2004), for example, makes the case for narrative and reflective methods to analyse practitioners' accounts of their practice as a contribution to knowledge development.

Avis (2006) argues that it is important to construct an epistemology for critical reflection that can provide an alternative to RCTs. In this view, critical reflection is seen as a form of 'expert practice' that is able to interpret the diversity of evidence before making a decision about how to intervene. Thus, it is said, we need to develop an 'an epistemology of practice' that recognizes and validates ways of knowing that are embedded in professional practice (Clegg, 1999). I have suggested elsewhere that this reflexivity should be extended to encompass the privileged positioning of the professional worker (Pease, 2006a).

Plath (2006) argues that it is possible to blend critical reflective approaches with evidence-based practice, arguing that practitioners utilize both sources of knowledge in their practice. However, where other forms of evidence and knowledge are recognized, RCTs are still regarded by most adherents of evidence-base practice as 'the gold standard'. I am not convinced that evidence-based research and practice can incorporate other forms of knowledge and values alongside scientific knowledge without being devalued when references to practitioner-based knowledge and service users' views are regarded as 'grey literature' (Feltman, 2005).

CAN WE MOVE BEYOND THE PARADIGM WARS?

The debate over what constitutes appropriate evidence and knowledge in social work is located in the wider divisions between positivists/objectivists and interpretivists/subjectivists about the nature of social reality. From an interpretivist perspective, positivism does not have a valid claim to objective knowledge. Social constructivists and postmodernists have emphasized the importance of seeing science and knowledge as being socially constructed (Lopez and Potter, 2001). This debate between universalism and relativism has plagued the social sciences for many years.

Shaw (1999) raises the question of whether researchers need to choose between paradigms in conducting research and whether there is a determining relationship between paradigm and methodology. Thirty years ago Burrell and Morgan (1979) maintained that paradigms were incommensurable. Those who hold to purist positivist and constructivist perspectives will certainly maintain that there is no possibility for accommodation between the epistemological paradigms.

Shaw and Gould (2001b) argue against a strong defence of paradigms because they believe such positions do not do justice to opposing paradigms and do not encourage reflexivity about one's own positioning. To me it is not a question of either taking a closed system approach to paradigms or a multi-paradigm position as Shaw and Gould pose the issue. Martin and Nakayama (1999) have identified four quite different approaches to the use of multiple paradigms in research. A liberal pluralist position values the contribution of each paradigm to our understanding of a phenomena without attempting to connect them. A paradigm-borrowing approach encourages the taking of particular methods from one paradigm and adapting them to the edicts of another paradigm. A multi-paradigm collaboration endeavours to develop multiple perspectives.

Alternatively, one can opt for a dialectical perspective that transcends the limitations of single paradigms.

We need to untangle a number of different issues here. First, there is the issue of epistemology. My view is that realist and constructivist paradigms are not necessarily incompatible. Humphries (2008) notes that many realists do acknowledge that some aspects of reality are socially constructed and that many constructionists recognize a reality that is external to subjective experience. Kazi (2000) also differentiates social constructionism from constructivism, pointing out that the former accepts the existence of an external reality. It is thus possible to hold an ontological realism and at the same time accept a form of epistemological constructivism (Maxwell, 2008).

In critical social work research, we need to transcend the limitations of these objective–subjective and universalist–relativist dichotomies. Alston and Bowles (2003) argue that critical research needs to be situated between purist objectivist and subjectivist approaches. While people are shaped by external social forces, they can become aware of the sources of their oppression and attempt to resist the dominant ideologies that define their reality.

From a critical social work perspective, if there is no objective reality, how can we develop the foundations for emancipatory projects (Oakley, 2000)? Parker (2001) argues that an uncritical pluralism undermines progressive social movements. It has the danger of leading to what some writers refer to as the 'abyss of relativism' (Peile and McCouat, 1997; Sheppard, 1998b; Taylor and White, 2000). The relativist position considers all views as being equally valid and does not allow us to develop standards to determine what is just or unjust.

Second, there is the connection between epistemological paradigm and method. Shaw (2003a) supports a cross-paradigm, multi-methods approach to research and argues that paradigms should not necessarily determine methods. D'Cruz and Jones (2004) argue, however, that the theoretical, political and ethical positionings arising from particular paradigms will shape the methodological choices the researcher makes. In their view, one thus needs to be aware of how one's own epistemological assumptions and political values shape the process of knowledge construction. For example, when positivists use constructivist and qualitative methodologies, they sometimes subordinate these approaches to a positivist logic. This is not to suggest that the epistemological stances of researchers alone will determine methods. Methodologies will also be influenced by the political realities and social pressures of sponsoring organizations and funding bodies (D'Cruz and Jones, 2004).

Third there is the relationship between purpose and method. Shaw and Norton (2007) argue that methods should be related to the research question and the purpose of the research. In this chapter, I am interested in how the purposed-method connection works in relation to the promotion of social justice and equality. There are many research methods that can be used towards this end. What is required is an ability for practitioners to understand the various ways in which power operates through whatever methodologies we use (Humphries, 2008).

Shaw (2007) argues against what he sees as a polarized attachment to particular methods and methodologies in social justice-based research. He questions whether naturalistic paradigms are more ethical than realist perspectives (Shaw, 2003b). Shaw and Gould (2001a) have also questioned whether qualitative methodologies are more congruent with the promotion of social justice than quantitative approaches. If we are focusing on epistemology, I agree with Shaw (1999) that no one paradigm is more suited to social justice-based research than any other. However, I would argue that some political perspectives are inconsistent with social justice research.

We thus come to the fourth issue, which is the politics of paradigms. The challenges I pose to positivism here are not based on epistemological differences. As a critical social work researcher, I acknowledge the existence of an external reality. My concerns are more about the ways in which positivism has been used to maintain repressive regimes of power (Strega, 2005). We should be careful to untangle a critique of positivism on political grounds from a critique of all realist post-positivist perspectives.

Realist and constructivist epistemologies can both be used for conservative and progressive political purposes. Thus, the epistemological dimensions of paradigms can support a variety of different political positions (Firestone, 1990). However, I argue here that the transformative agenda of critical theory, in either its realist or constructivist guise, is incommensurable with those paradigm positions which argue for detached and disinterested research. I thus argue against Padgett (1998) who believes that methodological rigour is compromised by advocacy-based research and Hammersley (1997) who argues that the political goal of emancipation undermines the legitimacy of research as the objective production of knowledge. I rather believe that social work researchers should take sides and embrace the values of promoting social justice and human rights.

Given that critical research is concerned with transforming the world, rather than studying it, we need to articulate the links between critical epistemological stances and emancipatory methodologies (Alston and Bowles, 2003). As someone who is committed to emancipatory research, my own work has been informed by four philosophical approaches: postmodern critical theory (Pease and Fook, 1997; Allan et al., 2003), standpoint epistemology (Pease, 2000; 2002), critical realism (Pease, 2007) and indigenous epistemologies (Atkinson and Pease, 2001). I am not proposing a synthesis between these different epistemological perspectives or suggesting that there is one best way to provide an alternative knowledge base for critical social work research. Thus, I am not arguing here that these epistemological perspectives are necessarily the correct stances for undertaking social justice-based research.

Rather, like Lather (1992), I believe that we should encourage a critical pluralism to allow a variety of approaches to be developed that challenge the dominant way of knowing.

TOWARDS POSTMODERN CRITICAL THEORIES

One of the biggest challenges to critical social work is that the vision of emancipatory politics in critical theory has been rethought by many theorists in light of postmodernism. Some writers talk about the need to envisage a progressive politics that is appropriate to postmodern conditions (Leonard, 1997), while other critical theorists are concerned that postmodern perspectives obscure the material reality of oppression (Mullaly, 1997). Others are concerned that the commitment to social justice and human rights may be undermined by the postmodern rejection of the meta-narrative (Ife, 1997).

However, there are many forms of postmodernism reflecting the extent to which they break with notions of modernity and the extent to which they retreat from an emancipatory politics. These distinctions have been variously articulated as 'weak' and 'strong' postmodernism (Benhabib, 1992) and 'progressive versus reactionary appropriations' (Giroux, 1990). I have sided with those expressions of postmodern thinking that do not totally abandon the values of modernity and the Enlightenment project of human emancipation. I have argued that a 'weak' form of postmodernism informed by critical theory can contribute effectively to the construction of an emancipatory politics concerned with political action and social justice (Pease, 2000).[5]

One of the most useful methodological tools in this epistemological approach is discourse analysis which examines the assumptions, language and myths that underpin particular positions in order to show that discursive practices are ordered according to underlying codes and rules which govern what is thought or said at any time (Tilley, 1990). Often the prevailing view is only able to prevail because people are unaware that it is only one of the several possible alternative views. Dominant discourses involve processes of domination whereby the oppressed often collude with the oppressor taking for granted their discourse and their definitions of the situation (Gitlin, 1989). The recognition of discourse as a dimension of the real does not lead to abandoning attempts of understanding an extra-discursive reality and the impact of powerful social and institutional forces shaping people's lives. I have used discourse analysis to analyse the ways in which members of oppressed and dominant groups are positioned to adopt particular subject positions (Pease, 2000).[6]

DEVELOPING STANDPOINT EPISTEMOLOGIES

Standpoint theory and critical realism are two other approaches to epistemology that recognize the social constructed nature of knowledge while at the same time asserting that some forms of knowledge are more valid than others in challenging oppression and social injustice (Sprague, 2005). A standpoint involves a level of awareness about an individual's social location, from which certain features of reality come into prominence and from which others are obscured. A researcher's standpoint 'emerges from one's social position with respect to gender, culture, colour, ethnicity, class and sexual orientation and the way in which these factors interact and affect one's everyday world' (Swigonski, 1993: 179). Researchers are required to reflect upon the implications of their social position for both their motives for undertaking the research and the consequences for the conduct of their research.

There are a variety of standpoint theories that range from essentialist expressions and materialist analyses to postmodern variations. While earlier versions of feminist standpoint theory did have an essentializing tendency, more recent interpretations have located women's experience in concrete, historical contexts. Furthermore, postmodern developments have led to the rejection of a single female perspective and to the acknowledgement of a plurality of female standpoints (Grant, 1993: 91). Thus, there is considerable convergence between recent versions of standpoint theory and postmodernism in that both emphasize multiple interpretations and multiple subjectivities.

Standpoint epistemologies that privilege the views of marginalized groups have been criticized by some writers who illustrate the ways that oppressed people may internalize the dominant viewpoints (Gopalkrishna, 2002). In some versions of standpoint theory and empowerment approaches to research, the subjective views of the participants in the research are given unquestioned validity and truth status (Sprague, 2005). I do not support those standpoint positions that maintain that social position solely shapes one's level of understanding (Shaw and Gould, 2001). Rather, I argue that discursive frameworks are as important as structural locations in developing a stance on research. Participants may articulate views shaped by hegemonic discourses rather than social justice informed perspectives. Also, Golpalkrishna (2002) maintains that marginalized people's views are only superior in a context where dominant groups do not interrogate their own dominant position. As I discuss elsewhere in this chapter, I have used standpoint theory to inform the construction of a profeminist standpoint to research men's lives.

FOSTERING CRITICAL REALISM AS AN ALTERNATIVE TO POSITIVISM

Critical realism also provides an alternative to the dualism of the objectivist–subjectivist dichotomy by combining elements of positivism and constructivism (Sheppard, 1998b; Lopez and Potter, 2001; Wright, 2004).

Critical realism acknowledges that knowledge is socially and culturally situated but at the same time asserts that social structure exists. Wright (2004) sums up critical realism as comprising three basic premises: that a reality exists outside of human perception, that our ability to comprehend that reality requires subjective understanding and that reality cannot be understood without critical and reflexive thinking that goes beyond the positivist notion of scientific detachment. So while there is an independent reality, research cannot accurately observe it (Parker, 2001).

Critical realism enables us to retain the possibility of human knowledge of the world while at the same time acknowledging the provisional nature of that knowledge (Cooling, 2005). Because human beings produce knowledge, they can be wrong. Unexamined assumptions and ideology can distort knowledge. Thus, we should be cautious and critically interrogate claims about objective evidence. Critical realism offers a reconciliatory position between positivism and social constructionism (Houston, 1995; Willson, 2006). McNeill (2006b) formulates this as a 'humble realism' in that although multiple realities are acknowledged as people endeavour to make sense of the social world, an external world does still exist even if we can only understand it in partial ways.

Parker (2001) articulates the notion of 'critical pluralism', as distinct from an 'uncritical pluralism' which acknowledges the need for tolerance with respect to knowledge but at the same time takes a position from which to challenge dominant and oppressive forms of knowledge. In a critical realist approach, knowledge should serve the purpose of emancipatory practice (Clegg, 2005; Wilson, 2006). In this sense, 'evidence' outside of its narrow positivist connotations can be used for social critique and emancipatory projects (Hollway, 2001; Marston and Watts, 2003; Clegg, 2005). As Peile and McCouat (1997) acknowledge, critical theorists do not see their analyses just sitting alongside political conservative positions.

From a critical realist position, some theoretical explanations of the world are more accurate than others and thus there are rational grounds for preferring one theory over others (Cooling, 2005). Thus, critical pluralism does not celebrate all forms of difference and diversity, and it actively challenges anti-democratic and oppressive discourses (Connelly, 2001). I have used critical realism to develop the epistemological foundations of an alternative knowledge base for critical social work practice (Pease, 2007).

EMBRACING INDIGENOUS EPISTEMOLOGIES

Traditional research epistemologies constructed within the West have come under criticism by indigenous and postcolonial scholars. Rigney (1999) says that research epistemologies should be critiqued in the context of colonialism and racism. Mutua and Swadener (2004) argue that research itself can be considered to be a colonizing construct. Clearly, as a result of different histories, experiences, values and cultures, indigenous people are likely to interpret reality and the world differently (Rigney, 1999). Thus, they should explore the implications of anti-colonial epistemologies and methodologies to validate their local knowledge and experiences.

A number of writers have identified the importance of indigenous knowledge as a resource for developing strategies of social change (Rigney, 1999; Bishop, 2005; Yang, 2000; Kincheloe and McLaren, 2005). Tuhiwai Smith (1999) provides an extensive critique of Western paradigms of research and knowledge from the position of a Maori woman. She challenges traditional Western ways of knowing and calls for a 'decolonisation of methodologies' by developing new non-Western epistemologies and methods of inquiry. Such work provides substantial challenges to non-indigenous researchers.

In response to such critiques, Connell (2006) has talked about 'Northern theory' as a way of explicitly naming the way in which most social theory is produced in the global North. She says that the 'northernness' of social theory is reflected in the claim to universal relevance, a tendency to 'read from the centre' and an exclusion of texts from the non-Metropolitan world.

In supervising doctoral research on the relationship between indigenous and non-indigenous activists promoting justice and self-determination in Australia, I have been grappling with some of the dilemmas and tensions facing non-indigenous researchers who are committed to conducting culturally sensitive and anti-racist research. My Anglo-Celtic views have also been challenged by supervising a Sudanese PhD student who is conducting research on young African refugee men from within an Afrocentric epistemology (Brown, 2007).

SITUATING OURSELVES

A number of writers emphasize the importance of providing a sense of where are located when we undertake research (Cox and Hardwick, 2007). If all research reflects the standpoint of the researcher, researchers should be clear about their own beliefs regarding the nature of the phenomena under investigation and their relationship to it. Our research questions will be directly connected to our assumptions about life and what is important to us.

As I argue that knowledge is socially and historically situated, I should make clear my own geo-political and social position. I am an able-bodied white male heterosexual Professor of Social Work at a university in a regional city in Australia. Because of my positioning, I cannot do justice to feminist, indigenous, disability-based and consumer-led research. Such methodologies must be articulated by those positioned within these locations. We must all recognize the politics of our own societal–political location (Herising, 2005) and, if appropriate, interrogate and decentre the privileged spaces that construct our identities and subjectivities (Pease, 2004, 2006b; Flood and Pease, 2005).

I thus occupy multiple positions of privilege. I also come from a working-class background and as I approach 60 years of age, I find myself subjected to various embodied limitations and occasional health scares. The future of my health and able-bodiedness feels increasingly uncertain. As an espoused pro-feminist man, I have endeavoured to 'walk the talk' in relation to gender relations. Thus, I have at times eschewed full-time work to care for my now two adult children when they were young and now as an older parent of an eight year old daughter, I continually endeavour to achieve some form of work-life balance as I confront the work-load demands of university life with the demands of parenting a primary school age child and the challenge by my partner for complete equality in our relationship.

Our location in relation to gender, class and culture will influence our interests in either maintaining or challenging the current social order. By making oneself visible in the text and describing what stakes we have in the research, others, as well as ourselves, may be more able to identify the blind spots that hinder our investigations (Sprague, 2005).

CHALLENGING THE DOMINANT PARADIGM

Many writers argue that the knowledge that gets legitimated is biased towards the interests of privileged and dominant groups (Sprague, 2005). Kincheloe and McLaren (2005: 306) identify critical approaches to research as those that seek to interrogate the 'social structures, discourses, ideologies and epistemologies that prop up both the status quo and a variety of forms of privilege'. Alvesson and Geetz (2000) also argue that dominant discourses and social practices

should be the focus of critical research. Ladson-Billings and Donnor (2005) maintain that interrogating the dominant social order is important to enable us to understand the ways dominant discourses distort the experiences of marginalized groups and so unwittingly reproduce the power relations which sustain their oppression. Brown and Strega (2005) suggest that to challenge the relations of dominance and subordination, research must also challenge the dominant place of traditional research paradigms.

In response to this challenge, Oyen (2002) poses some questions about why different discourses in research become dominant.

- Why was a certain discourse opened up in the first place?
- Who introduced it and what kind of impact does it have on the questions researchers pose?
- What kind of interests lay behind it?
- Why did a certain set of arguments become so powerful that they dominate our way of thinking and the choice of analytical approaches?
- Why are certain concepts and strategies pushed upfront and others made invisible?
- Who adopts a certain discourse and why?
- What is the impact of certain discourses on policy making?
- How much power is invested in keeping the discourse alive?
- Who are the benefactors of a certain discourse?
- Who is excluded through such a discourse?

Weber (2006) challenges us to critically examine the ways that our own understanding is infused with dominant discourses, and thus shapes what we regard as data and whose voices we privilege.

EMPOWERING THE OPPRESSED

Critical research, like critical social work, is concerned with empowering the oppressed and promoting social justice (Strega, 2005). McLaughlin (2007: 127) says that 'anti-oppressive research ... seeks to build partnerships with service users and oppressed communities to promote empowerment'. Some critical researchers argue that the focus of critical and anti-oppressive research should be on those who are most socially excluded and oppressed to ensure that they do not unwittingly reproduce oppression (Strier, 2007). Thus, research questions should be analysed to determine whether they empower or oppress marginalized groups. The association of critical research with empowerment is clear in other approaches. Ristock and Pennell (1996) articulate empowerment as a framework for community research and Fetterman et al. (1996) formulate what they call 'empowerment evaluation' as a conceptual framework for self assessment and accountability.

As I have written elsewhere, however (Pease, 2002), some practices of empowerment may have unintended disempowering effects. We can sometimes contribute to dominance in spite of our liberatory intentions. Foucault (1980) alerts us to the potentially oppressive role of professional and scientific discourse in the power to define the social world. The professional knowledge claims of social work can become a means of ideological domination. This can also happen when the intentions of the researchers are emancipatory. Foucault's analysis of how marginalized knowledges are affected by dominant cultural practices suggests a redefining of empowerment as the insurrection of subjugated knowledge (Pease, 2002).

INTERROGATING PRIVILEGE

The emphasis on empowerment can underemphasize the role that privileged groups play in reproducing oppression. Generally, researchers study down rather than up, focusing on those with less power as opposed to those in privileged positions (Sprague, 2006). Why do we focus on why women are disadvantaged as opposed to why men are overly advantaged? Thus, we also need to interrogate privileged social locations and find ways of undoing privilege (Flood and Pease, 2005, 2006a). Carniol (2005) says that a critical consciousness of oppression *and* privilege is

central to understand the ways in which our world views are shaped by our social positioning. This means that to be truly reflexive, we must consider 'our own complicity in systems of domination and subordination' (Strega, 2005: 229). Those of us who benefit from unearned privileges should interrogate the ways that our research practice may unwittingly reproduce the exploitative relationships that we are challenging (Carey, 2004). This can be another form of decolonizing research (Mutua and Swadener, 2004). We can cross boundaries, engage in dialogues across differences and attempt to understand our position from the perspective of those who are marginalized.

METHODOLOGIES FOR CRITICAL SOCIAL WORK RESEARCH

Critical research utilizes a variety of research methodologies including feminist methodologies, critical ethnography, action research, participatory research, collaborative inquiry, experiential research, auto-ethnographic approaches, memory work, consciousness raising and sociological intervention, to name just a few. Potts and Brown (2005) note that there are no distinctive anti-oppressive methods of inquiry. In their view, it is the epistemological stance that differentiates anti-oppressive research from traditional forms of inquiry. In addition to the above, I have also used more traditional life history and narrative methods (Pease and Crossley, 2005; Pease, 2006b; Rees and Pease, 2007). I have been particularly interested, however, in the use of participatory research methods.[7]

Participatory research encourages the development of practice that is informed by consumer knowledge where consumers are full participants in the creation of knowledge. Participatory approaches to research are concerned with the involvement of consumers in formulating the research questions and in determining whether their interests are served by the research (Scheyett, 2006).

Such participatory research is seen as essential if social work is to promote equality and social justice (Meagher, 2002).

I am not suggesting here that participatory methodologies are the only way to pursue social change agendas. Popkewitz (1990) has pointed out how political commitments can also be expressed in how we develop the agenda of our research projects beyond researchers' direct association with social movements.

Doing participatory research with critical social workers

My first use of participatory research methodologies was in the late 1980s, when I undertook a collaborative inquiry with social work practitioners who were attempting to formulate radical approaches to their practice (Pease, 1990). My specific interest was in how radical social workers related critical theories to practice. This interest stemmed from my own political commitments and my experiences of teaching critical social work. Practitioners with radical political commitments rarely wrote about their attempts to develop a radical practice and I thought that this was a significant gap in the literature.

From the beginning of the research process, I believed that there was an important relationship between the purpose of the research and the method of study. I was aware of studies which had liberating objectives but which used questionable research studies to pursue them. My concern about research methodology was that it should constitute an emancipatory political practice. I wanted to contribute to an educational process for the practitioners and I wanted to assist the practitioners who participated in the study to grapple more effectively with the tensions and conflicts in their work.

To stimulate a dialogue with practitioners, I wrote a discussion paper outlining my engagement with the radical debates in social work and my journey towards participatory research methodologies. Through a snowball sampling process, I generated a list of 30 potential research participants. I contacted each of these people by phone, asked them if they would like to receive a copy of the discussion paper and come to a meeting to discuss it. Of the 30 people who received the discussion paper, 21 people came to the initial meetings to discuss it and of those 14 people became involved in the on-going group process.

Throughout the meetings, we explored a number of themes related to radical theory and practice in social work: structural limitations on the possibilities for radical practice; social activism outside the state and working in and against the state; working with conflicting interests of multiple stakeholders; the construction of clients' interests; the role of unionism in supporting progressive social work, among many others. I recorded these discussions, transcribed the tapes and fed back to the participants summaries of the issues we explored.

Doing participatory research with profeminist men

I further used participatory research methodologies in my research with profeminist men. Truman and Humpheries (1994) identify research on men and masculinities as an exemplar of research into privilege. While it is generally accepted that men cannot do feminist research, they are encouraged to evolve approaches based on feminist standpoint epistemology to research men's lives. Wadsworth and Hargreaves (1993) suggest that the methodological approaches of feminism will be relevant to men who are seeking to transform subordinating practices, whilst Maguire (1987) also encourages men to use participatory research to uncover their own modes of domination of women.

I invited self-defining profeminist men to participate in a collaborative inquiry group to examine how men who were supportive of feminism were responding to the feminist challenge through an exploration of their experiences and dilemmas of trying to live out their profeminist commitment. The aim was to explore the extent to which it was possible for men to reposition themselves in patriarchal discourses and to reformulate their interests in challenging gender domination. To link the process of personal transformation to the collective politics of change in gender relations, I explored these experiences and dilemmas through three participatory methodologies: anti-sexist consciousness-raising, memory-work and dialogues with allies and opponents of profeminism.

Consciousness-raising enabled the men to explore issues in relation to their own lives and to link these issues to the wider social and political context. Through our discussions, we strengthened a profeminist discursive framework as an alternative subject position. Memory-work provided an opportunity to reframe some of the content of our memories to facilitate a process of challenging dominant social relations. By asking men to reflect on their understandings of the ways in which they accommodated to or resisted the dominant constructions of masculinity, we were able to understand the ways in which new subject positions could be created. Dialogue with allies and opponents of profeminism contributed to the development of new spaces for the collective positioning of profeminist men's work in the ongoing public debates about masculinity politics.

Attempts to formulate progressive standpoints among dominant groups are not without controversy. According to Morgan (1992: 29), when dominant groups research their own position in society, 'these considerations may be more in terms of justifications than in terms of critical analysis [and] their investigations may always be suspect'. He goes on to raise questions about the extent to which it is possible for men to develop those forms of self knowledge which could lead to the erosion of male power and privileges. However, I make a case that men can change their subjectivities and practices to constitute a profeminist men's standpoint (Pease, 2000).

CONCLUSION

I do not propose that the epistemologies and methodologies I have utilized represent a definitive plurality of research strategies for addressing social injustice. Rather the conceptual frameworks and methodologies I have outlined are simply those understandings and practices that I have found useful in my specific geo-political and structural location to enable me to connect my research to social justice and social change. In this chapter I have identified some of the key tensions and dilemmas associated with these approaches and some of the criticisms that have been leveled against them.

We know that research can promote social change and social justice. However, we also know how it can be used to reproduce relations of domination and injustice (Potts and Brown, 2005). Given the human rights imperatives of our profession, social workers must think seriously about the epistemological and political assumptions embedded in their research practices. There is no theory-free or value-free knowledge. We thus need to be clear about our own beliefs regarding the phenomena we are investigating and our relationship to it. I have endeavoured to outline some of the implications of our theories of knowledge and our structural and discursive locations on the ethics and politics of how we do research. I hope that this chapter assists readers to think about how their own structural location and subjective positioning influences how *they* do research and how that research might contribute to challenging rather than reproducing social injustice.

NOTES

1   Three recent generic texts do attempt to articulate critical alternative approaches to social work research. D'Cruz and Jones (2004) outline feminist and indigenous perspectives. Alston discusses emancipatory, feminist and postmodern approaches; and McLauglin (2007) has a chapter on anti-oppressive research. However, the implications

of these alternative approaches for research practice are not elaborated. The only exception to this general trend is Morris's (2006) recent book which identifies four alternative paradigms, one of which is critical theory.

2   Notable exceptions are Ristock and Pennell (1996); Brown and Strega (2005) and Humphries (2008).

3   The theoretical approaches to social justice-based research discussed here are only some of the many perspectives. Shaw and Gould (2001c) also discuss the reformist approach of House (1993) and Dingwall's (1997) reference to the work of Adam Smith as social justice-based approaches.

4   An earlier longer version of this critique of evidence-based practice was published in Pease (2007).

5   My weak form of postmodernism, which I call postmodern critical theory, is in tension with Fook's (2002a) notion of critical postmodernism in which the critical theory is encompassed by the epistemological premises of postmodernism.

6   See Phillips and Jorgensen (2002) for an outline of the implications of discourse analysis for critical research.

7   Heron and Reason (1997) argue that participatory research constitutes a separate paradigm, what they call a participatory/cooperative paradigm. They posit an epistemology of experiential, propositional and practical knowing. In this chapter I am outlining participatory methodologies that can be informed by other paradigms.

Contexts for Social Work Research

Research and Government

Ian Shaw and Joan Zlotnik

INTRODUCTION

The structural context of government and its reciprocal relationship with social work research is the focus of this chapter. An important distinction needs making at the outset, between research as a means of governing and research as the evaluation of government. Our concern is primarily with the former – the uses that governments make of evaluation and research as means of governing. In illustrating these themes we review the government context for social work research, including research infrastructure enhancements, research agenda development and research training. We aim to embed reflections on implications for the future throughout the text including the development of more linkages between the social work research community and government agencies at all levels and across nations.[1] We acknowledge that our focus is largely on research – government relations in democratic states where social work is established as an occupation and profession, and where it is to a considerable degree recognized as a distinct field of study.

We open the chapter with a glance at the way wider social theories have shaped our assumptions regarding the interface of government and social research, and move to consider how far these preoccupations and concerns have parallels in contemporary arguments regarding the social (and social work) research agenda in government. We then offer a relatively detailed case study of how specific government-sponsored structures have emerged in the USA. Funding mechanisms lie at the centre of government, and we proceed to explore these through examples of government efforts to shape fundable research. We reflect on contemporary research priorities within government, and illustrate ways in which such priorities are by their nature shifting and ambiguous. We close with a consideration of how the social work research community can practice advocacy within this context. This returns us full circle to the nature of government – and to closing thoughts of national strategy development.

GOVERNMENT AND RESEARCH IN SOCIAL THEORY

The broad question of the governmental context for research includes several areas for deliberation. What assumptions are entailed regarding 'government' in social work and social science research? What do governments typically want from social work research? How do governments traditionally manage social work services by research and evaluation? How is research used to inform resource allocations? How does government manage social work research and evaluation? What are some of the pitfalls facing governments' management of social work research and evaluation? What is the impact of interest in 'evidence-based policy' on the use of evaluation processes by and for governments (cf. Davies et al., 2006)?

The relation of social research to government and the state has been a recurring strand through much of the development of social theory. Early social science theory in the work of Auguste Comte, and his heirs and successors, was a direct response to the upheavals of the French revolution. Comte viewed sociology, through positivism, as the basis for a new secular social consensus. 'He created sociology and positivism to give the world ... stability, order and harmony' (Pickering, 2000: 43). One line of continuing Comtean influence was to the Fabian socialists, Beatrice and Sydney Webb. Edith Abbott visited London (the London School of Economics) in 1906, and on her return reproduced Beatrice Webb's course in 'Methods of Social Investigation' in Chicago at the School of Civics and Philanthropy. Comte's influence on the model of the relationship between government and research can also be traced, if more tenuously, to mainstream post Second World War social policy research in the UK, where the Fabian[2] model of the researcher–policymaker relationship has been dominant (Finch, 1986). Sydney and Beatrice Webb articulated and consolidated a model which became tied in to British Labour Party policy. It influenced Labour especially when in opposition and to some extent when in power. Figures such as Richard Titmuss, A. H. ('Chelly') Halsey and David Donnison were part of a small elite of high status academics with congenial political positions, wishing to act as professional advisor and expert to those in power. They represented a social engineering model aimed at social justice through the Fabian belief in the 'inevitability of gradualness' and research

which was both partisan and rigorous. This tradition inherited the assumption of factually unproblematic data which would speak for themselves.

Theories of government and its relation to social work research have been perhaps at their most explicit and transparent in some forms of critical and neo-Marxist research, and often associated with skepticism for most forms of government under western capitalism (e.g. Garrett, 2003a,b, 2006). More frequently, theories of government within social work research have been common sense, unstated or treated as unproblematic. Probably without having read Max Weber, social work researchers sometimes share his seventy-year-old concern about the growth of a pragmatic approach to public life, and the conviction that means–end rational calculations will neither offer dignity to persons nor prevent the rule of force. Rationalist ideas of efficiency, for many though not all, do not sit comfortably with ideas of democratic participation. Cronbach and his colleagues went as far as to say that, 'Rationalism is dangerously close to totalitarianism' (Cronbach et al., 1980: 95). Weber detected and feared the rise of specialists without spirit, and advocated strong parliaments, not dominated by the state's civil servants or authoritarian rulers, and hence wanted strong democracies. He argued for the restriction of the role of science. In his classic *The Methodology of the Social Sciences* Weber argued that 'Science cannot – and *must* not – inform us how we *should* live' (Kahlberg, 2000: 189). This risk occurs, he believed, when science is seen as offering objectively valid knowledge through a caste of experts.

Government and the social research agenda

How far do these preoccupations and concerns have parallels in contemporary arguments regarding the social (and social work) research agenda in government?

Chelimsky (2006) argues – to state her argument in slightly less USA-contextualized terms – that a democratic government needs research and evaluation for four purposes:

1. support parliamentary and government oversight;
2. build a stronger knowledge base for policy making;
3. help agencies develop improved capabilities for policy and program planning, implementation and analysis of results, as well as for greater openness and a more learning oriented direction in their practice; and
4. strengthen public information about government activities through dissemination of research and evaluation findings.

She suggests three conceptual frameworks for evaluators in their relations with government (Chelimsky, 1997), viz. evaluation for accountability, evaluation for development, and evaluation for knowledge. She reviews the kinds of studies government actually wanted in her experience in the GAO in parallel terms as accountability studies, development studies and knowledge studies (Chelimsky, 2006).

Within the general purpose of promoting accountability, social work program and policy initiatives are designed, implemented, and then assessed to see if they yield expected outcomes or effects. These three stages together constitute a strategy for promoting or preventing social change. On the assumption that government has made strategic decisions and that some kinds of intervention are thought necessary, the question follows: What kind of policy instruments can be used to substantiate, implement and effect change? Vedung differentiates between regulations, economic means, and information as generic clusters of public policy instruments (Vedung, 1998). Policy instruments are named as Sticks, Carrots, and Sermons, referring to regulations, economic means, and information, respectively (Davies et al., 2006). From a western government perspective, this means collecting data to inform the public, decision makers, taxpayers, service users, and other

stakeholders about the worth of government policies, programs, interventions, and any other measures taken to impact the state of affairs in society.

In the following paragraphs we move still further from social theory and models of government–social-research relations, with an account of how specific government-sponsored structures have emerged in the USA. It serves to illustrate the diversity of arrangements from one nation to another and the work necessary to articulate general principles and discrete forms of governance.

THE USA AND FEDERAL STRUCTURES FOR SOCIAL WORK RESEARCH

With impetus from the report of the Task Force on Social Work Research (1991), the social work profession has undertaken strategic efforts to expand the contributions of social work research and the connections between social work research and governmental agencies, especially at the federal level. The Institute for the Advancement of Social Work Research (IASWR) mission is particularly to represent social work within the national scientific community and to link with government agencies. The social work research enterprise in the USA vis-à-vis the government is perhaps at its strongest point in the history of the profession and almost certainly at the strongest point in the two decades prior to writing.

NASW has on occasion maintained a less optimistic stance.

NASW's position is that the federal, state, and local governments must play a role in developing policies and programs to expand opportunities, address social and economic justice, improve the quality of life for all people, and enhance Communities and been ready to criticize those policies they viewed as 'antithetical to social work values'

(NASW – http://www.socialworkers.org/resources/ abstracts/abstracts/role.asp)

Building capacity might be viewed as an interplay between advocates outside of the government, and the government's legislative and executive branches. Identified needs, be they substantive, for example autism spectrum disorders, or perspectives, for example behavioral and social science research, might receive little government attention and funding without external advocates working with Congress. The legislative branch then uses its mechanisms (laws, letter writing to high level officials, appropriations, hearings) to guide the actions of the executive branch.

For social work research, there are not consistent research investments and levels of available government funding across fields of practice or government agencies. The Children's Bureau, for example, has recently enhanced its focus on research and evaluation (Brodowski et al., 2007). While some social work researchers may be the beneficiary of the Quality Improvement Center grants and the recent funding of regional Implementation Centers, the majority of the agency's funding is targeted to services, with limited investments in research. This is juxtaposed to the National Institutes of Health (NIH), whose sole mission is the support of research to improve the health of the nation.

The growth in social work research enterprise can be partly explained in relation to the catalytic role played by key federal agencies in the USA, especially the National Institute of Mental Health (NIMH), just one of 28 institutes of the NIH.

National Institute of Mental Health

Since the inception of NIMH, in 1948, there was support for the social work profession including support for social work research. This has included:

- a committee which recommended that research competence be expected of all doctoral students;
- An NIMH supported publication (Maas, 1966) of systematic reports of research in family services,

public welfare, child welfare, neighborhood centers and social planning; and
- research relevant projects at both the National Association of Social Workers (NASW) and the Council on Social Work Education (CSWE). Conferences, monographs and other projects (e.g. Fanshel, 1980) emerged from these developments. A report on *Research Utilization* in *Social Work Education* (Briar et al., 1981) emerged from a CSWE project supporting the development of empirically based models of social work practice and research among social work educators.

In 1988, concerned that the social work profession needed a greater focus on knowledge development and that there was a 'disconnect' between the practice efforts of the profession and its involvement in science, especially related to mental health, NIMH funded the creation of the Task Force on Social Work Research (TFSWR). It undertook a three-year information gathering effort to address support for social work research across multiple federal agencies and to assess the capacities, within social work and through interdisciplinary collaborations, to launch a more robust research enterprise. The resulting report declared that there is both 'a crisis in the current development of research resources in social work' and that 'the contributions of practice-relevant research to the knowledge base of social work practice lags far behind the dynamic growth of the profession and professional education' (Task Force on Social Work Research, 1991: viii). The report stimulated responses from within the social work profession and from federal agencies. Not only did NIMH expand its investments in social work, but other institutes gave increased attention to social work research, eventually culminating in the implementation of recommendations from the 2003 NIH Plan (see Box 7.1).

Building social work research capacity

NIMH created Social Work Research Development Center grant funding for mental

---

Box 7.1   Example of an NIMH Funded Advanced Research Center at a School of Social Work

Washington University Center for Mental Health Services Research supported under the NIMH's Advanced Centers for Interventions and Services Research (ACISR) announcement. The Center undertakes research that examines the quality of care for persons with mental disorders who are served in non-mental health settings, e.g. child welfare and nursing homes, recognizing that service delivery is challenged by 'competing demands, co-occurring psychosocial problems, and resource constraints'.

(CMHSR, 2008)
http://gwbweb.wustl.edu/cmhsr/cmhsr_overview.html

---

health research infrastructure in schools of social work and provided some initial support to the emergence of two organizational entities, the IASWR and the Society for Social Work and Research (SSWR).

NIMH also funded initiatives such as mentoring, researcher training, and guidance to deans and directors, to enhance research infrastructure. The institutes also supported, *inter alia*, summer workshops to help infuse mental health research findings into the curricula. These broad activities demonstrate both a commitment to research as well as research/practice linkages.

Corresponding developments can be linked to other national institutes, such as the National Institute on Drug Abuse (NIDA). It has funded research infrastructure developments, doctoral initiatives, travel awards, and mentoring.[3]

National Institutes of Health

To broaden social work research opportunities across NIH, a premier funder and catalyst for bio-medical, behavioral, and social science research in the USA, Congress requested a plan and agenda for social work research. The 2003 *NIH Plan for Social Work Research* specifically articulated the value of social work research to NIH's overall mission, stating 'Social work research as it relates to health of individuals sheds light on the behavioral and social determinants of wellness and disease and helps to develop effective interventions for improving health outcomes' (NIH, 2003: 5). This pronouncement helped to broaden the visibility and relevance of social work research at NIH beyond its links with its more traditional homes at the National Institute on Mental Health (NIMH), National Institute on Drug Abuse (NIDA), and the National Institute on Alcohol Abuse and Alcoholism (NIAAA). Social work research was seen as fitting within the NIH Office of Behavioral and Social Sciences Research (OBSSR) mission 'to stimulate behavioral and social science research throughout NIH and to integrate these areas of research more fully into others of the NIH health research enterprise, thereby improving our understanding, treatment, and prevention of disease' (OBSSR, 2008).

This analysis illuminates the most extensive and developed framework for a national infrastructure of financial and policy mechanisms for government–research relations. Yet even in such cases the relationship is far from straightforward. Exemplar 1 offers an intentionally impressionistic and critical comment on the relationship between social work research and government in another country where social work research has a relatively long history.[4]

Exemplar 1: Research and government in England and the UK

For many observers, the perception is that 'social work' as an occupational category has been weakened from the mid 1990s to the time of writing. This is in part due to a splitting of responsibility for children and adult services at central government level, and a consequent unhelpfully wide diversity of local arrangements. Second, the emergence of the category of *'social care'* has been helpful in some regards, but it remains unclear in the public eye, and is interpreted in diverse ways by government. Important government developments increasingly proceed through consultation and policy development phases without consulting the social work academic community. The 'majority holding' in central government departments (e.g. Department of Health and Department for Children Schools and Families) of large practice/professional fields (health and education) and the lead influence in government of disciplines whose members are typically unfamiliar with social work research (e.g. economists within the Cabinet Office) alike lead to imbalanced expectations and input to policy advice.

This is complicated by the way *social work employers* at national levels have generally displayed a parlous lack of commitment to understanding, supporting and participating in the development of helpful and rigorous policy-relevant research. In addition, national 'post-qualifying' frameworks for social work employees stop well short of recognizing that strong policy-relevant research will not develop without opportunities for a small proportion of practitioners to move into those fields.

Social work academics also need continued development in awareness of the processes of government and policy. We are conscious of how the academic community is sometimes perceived by the policy world. For example, Duncan and Harrop (2006) insist that policy users of research are essentially pragmatic, and want research that is 'clear, useful, timely and usable' (2006: 160).

'Policy makers and practitioners are usually untrained in research methods and so

often cannot assess the quality of the evidence from a methodological perspective. Indeed, they are not particularly interested in doing so' (2006: 162).

Furthermore, 'those responsible for policy and practice will never depend on research evidence alone. Research always competes with "common-sense" views of the world' (2006: 163). Yet they conclude both sides need to understand the different perspectives of researchers and practitioners. 'Unless we understand the different natures of these two worlds, we risk forever misunderstanding each other and failing to draw on joint strengths' (2006: 161).

More established social science communities tend to operate from limited and traditional conceptualizations of research use and dissemination (e.g. Shaw et al., 2006). Relatively passive notions of research dissemination will prove inadequate. And more active notions of *research utilization* are required. However, reference to the idea of *research 'user'* within much of UK government remains largely limited to the funding commissioner and the agencies/organizations that commission or deliver services. Active notions of research utilization are rarely budgeted into commissioned research – a necessity if academics are not to be sucked into a treadmill of research-and-report.

There remains an inappropriate set of prejudgments within government regarding the *kinds of research* that are likely to prove 'useful' – one weighted unduly towards measurement-oriented outcome research. While this will remain a central part of policy-relevant research, the understandings of the micro-worlds of practice and services that are yielded by a diversity of qualitative as well as quantitative methods too often remain under-used.

There is need on all 'sides' for fresh thinking on the optimum points at which the policy and research communities should engage in order to be constructive. The perceived issue of the 'gagging' of unwelcome findings would benefit from an honest and open airing, along with its counterpoint – the risk that 'government-friendly' researchers may be co-opted into the policy community.

Chelimsky's 'final thought' on the political climate for evaluation strongly resonates with this.

> Evaluation is a fragile reed to send up against all those giant oaks ... and evaluators need to be ingenious, lucky and much better protected than they currently are if they are to survive in any government. Alas, we make a lot of enemies, although we try hard not to ... (Chelimsky, 2006: 53)

Public mistrust of government is not new. Indeed, it was precisely this mistrust that brought to the UK the Magna Carta, and to France the 1689 Bill of Rights. 'Public distrust is ... a positive not a negative element in a democratic society. In that larger sense, the search for political balance and open government makes evaluators of us all' (Chelimsky, 2006: 54).

The relationship between social work research and government in large areas of the world will be shaped differently from that in western democracies – for an earlier, thoughtful discussion of social work research and government in an African state, see Brand (1986). This issue was acknowledged a generation or more ago in discussions of political science and sociology in the USSR. Ermarth (1965) reviews the enthusiasm in the 1960s for increasing the influence of social science on Soviet policy. He cited a long article in Pravda demanding the pragmatic application of sociological research to aid the Party in fulfilling its mission. In carrying out 'concrete sociology' the standard caveats were that a Leninist spirit must be invoked in this research, that empiricism must be avoided – as a relic of bourgeois western positivist ideology – and that the 'essence' of a problem had to be discovered in each case. But 'philosophy' was to be left to philosophers and the Marxist social scientist was to devote much attention to the collection of facts, the digesting of facts, and the experimentation with facts.

Within this analytical and factual approach, favored methodologies were survey-oriented, and the possibility of a cautious critique of government was left to the facts to speak for themselves. It is possible that similar safeguards may continue in contemporary social inquiry in one-party states.

Changing political contexts make the positions discussed and recommended in this part of the chapter provisional. Cronbach and colleagues remarked with the irony of hindsight that 'Our theses will have to be revised to fit the United States of the year 2000' (Cronbach et al., 1980: 14). Hammersley is sympathetic to the argument that suggests high expectations regarding influencing policy are misguided, and that research is not a primary source of consideration in the policy process. He occasionally leaves the impression that this is only as it should be (Hammersley, 1994, 1995).

GOVERNMENT AND RESEARCH FUNDING ALLOCATIONS

There are increased expectations in universities in many countries that faculty should access external funding to support their research. Faculty across multiple departments, including social work, are encouraged to pursue research grant funding from a range of funding sources each with its own particular relationship to government. Within this span of funders there will be national hierarchies with certain funders generally regarded as the 'Gold Standard' for research funding, whether they are bodies such as Suomen Akatemia (the Academy of Finland), the NIH or National Science Foundation in the USA, or the Economic and Social Research Council in the UK.

Covering the period of 1993 to the time of writing, more than 600 NIH grants have been identified as being funded. They span diverse areas including HIV/AIDS, criminal justice, homelessness, cancer survivorship, poverty, violence, maltreatment, substance use and abuse, serious mental illness, family-focused service delivery, and lesbian, gay, bisexual, and transgender issues. In 2008, there were approximately 125 active grants to social work researchers funded by NIH (IASWR, 2008).

However, estimating government investment in social work research is at best something of a hit and miss process. In one of the most serious efforts to do so, Marsh and Fisher (2005) compared the government research investment in social care with investment in primary care. The results do not suggest that the UK government gives priority to research investment.

> For example, as a proportion of total annual spend, investment in research and development (R&D) runs at about 0.3% in social care compared with 5.4% in health. The overall annual spend per workforce member stands at about £25 in social care compared with £3,400 in health. Using the more specific comparison with primary care, the annual R&D spend per social worker is about £60, compared with £1,466 per general practitioner (GP); annual university research income from the Higher Education Funding Council … Quality-related Research (QR) is £8,650 per social work researcher and £26,343 per primary care researcher. (Marsh and Fisher, 2005: ix)

Orme and Powell develop the implications of this and related analyses for capacity and capability building in social work research (Orme and Powell, 2008).

Government efforts to enhance research are sometimes in tension with parts of the social work research community. For example, qualitative social work research is in various parts of the world a poor relation to quantitative research. Qualitative social work research is at its strongest in the Nordic countries, the UK, in vigorous corners of work in Europe (e.g. Spain, Switzerland and Germany) and in Canada, Australia and New Zealand. In Eastern and parts of Southern Europe, in South America, and in large areas of the Asia-Pacific region it is parlous or at best a noisy infant. Within the USA there is generally a prioritizing of scientific practice,

and measurement oriented approaches (Shaw, 2006), but there is a strong emerging minority community of qualitative scholars associated, in the USA, with the Qualitative Interest Group in the Society for Social Work and Research (SSWR), and internationally through the journal *Qualitative Social Work*.

One of the more encouraging signs in the decade prior to this *Handbook* has been the interest of some western governments in developing standards and guidance for qualitative research bids in welfare and human services fields. In the UK the Economic and Social Research Council has long recognized the role of qualitative methods as central to all good social science. In 2005 the council for the first time recognized social work as a distinct field of study/discipline. This meant that alongside the generic standards for research methods training there was also a set of parameters for social work research.[5]

The UK Cabinet Office published the results of a report group on quality standards for qualitative methods (Spencer et al., 2003). In the USA the National Institutes for Health published the results of a working group on qualitative research in health that aimed in large part to advise on how qualitative applications should be prepared in a way that are more or less compatible with the NIH application format (OBSSR, 2001).

Before referring to these reports we want to identify why such initiatives are sometimes not received as an unmixed blessing for qualitative social work researchers. First, commissioning staff of funding agencies may themselves lack adequate expertise in qualitative social science. This can lead to a mistrust of qualitative designs and charges of 'anecdotalism' or a suspicion of 'bias' based on a general notion that a lack of 'objectivity' will be associated with insufficient rigor, even in cases where funders are not familiar what is entailed in a specific proposed design.

Second, organizational and policy end users sometimes believe that qualitative research has no clear commitment to being 'useful'. This may be related to a belief that the essential question in applied research is 'Does it work?' Research that is assumed to be good at throwing light on process is thus less respected.

This relates to a third area of concern – the hierarchy of evidence problem, marked by a perception that there is a more or less absolute hierarchy of kinds of evidence with systematic reviews/meta-analyses at the top, closely followed by randomized control trials, with qualitative research very near the foot of the table.

The problems are not solely with funders and end users. There are serious weaknesses in qualitative skills in the social work community, even in countries where qualitative methods are often the methodology of choice (Shaw, 2003b; Kvale, 2004). The NIH report from the USA highlights several weaknesses of qualitative research applications. They are of interest for how they illustrate likely government ways of valuing certain stances within methodology.

- Failing to 'strike a balance among well-defined areas of inquiry, achievable aims, and openness to unanticipated findings' (OBSSR, 2001: 2).
- Failing to tie methods, procedures, and analysis to the aims. Not explaining why a particular data collection method is the most appropriate one to answer the specific questions.
- Having an unduly broad range of cited literature insufficiently organized in relation to the aims. Also lack of consistency in how concepts are described and used throughout the proposal.
- Insufficient attention to showing how the applicant's past qualitative work has led to useful findings.
- Insufficient description of what the methods will entail.
- When proposing combined methods one method is well described but the other is only superficially addressed. Also the contribution each method is to make to the study problem is not well described.

Jane Gilgun wrote a critique of the NIH report (Gilgun, 2002) and the chair of the working party, Suzanne Heurtin-Roberts

(2002) gave a brief rejoinder. The report and the exchange that followed show that there is a serious interest in finding a place for qualitative research, but also that the issue is not a straightforward dimension of relations between social work research and government. The NIH report provides a welcome effort to build bridges, but much work needs to continue in regard to research review strategies and expanding qualitative research's contribution. Addressing health disparities and issues of treatment adherence are areas where qualitative studies have a central role (see Chapter 24). The overall advice of the report writers about completing applications is sensible and well worth taking on board even in countries outside the USA. They offer some sound counsel, for example on sampling and ethics. But the assumptions about quality criteria may be too narrow.

Responsible conduct of research and research ethics

If the NIH report indicates how methodological stances are influenced by government interests, developments over the decade previous to this *Handbook* also illustrate a corresponding influence and interest around research governance and ethics. Governments in the majority of countries where social research is an established part of the policy process are taking and increased interventionist interest in safety, governance, and research ethics. A spate of concerns has run through social and medical research in the West over consent for storage of body organs, developments in genetics, and linked innovations in technology; and new problems in privacy issues have destabilized confidence in the ethical regulation of medical research. Concerns range from the use of chemicals in international sport to university science that could be exploited by terrorist networks. Mark Walport (Director of Wellcome Trust, a major UK medical research charity) reflected the growing recognition within the research community that these developments have led, perhaps ineluctably, to a growth of regulation when he remarked that 'Scientists have responsibilities. If the scientific community is resistant to self regulation it can't complain if governments with legitimate concerns decide to intervene' (*Times Higher Education Supplement*, 14/11/03). Within the health research fields this has led to a growth of national and state level governance frameworks.

In the USA this increased focus is partly due to the lasting impact of past research abuses such as the Tuskegee Syphillis Study. Concern about potential harm and risks has created a focus on issues of research ethics, responsible conduct of research and research integrity. The government response to this within the Department of HHS is carried by the Office of Research Integrity which 'promotes integrity in biomedical and behavioral research funded by the U.S. government, monitors institutional investigations of research misconduct, and facilitates the responsible conduct of research (RCR) through educational, preventive, and regulatory activities' (HHS, 2008).[6]

CONTEMPORARY GOVERNMENT RESEARCH PRIORITIES

The development of government research priorities and the interplay in this process between the social work community, government and other key stakeholders has been understood in different ways. For example, from the perspective of the IASWR in the USA, four distinct but overlapping approaches to research can be priorities in the medium term.

1 Evidence-based practice

Government attention to focusing on investing in programs and policies that will improve outcomes for those in need of health and social services in the most efficient and cost-effective ways appears to be increasing. Thus there is increasing attention to evidence-based practice (EBP). EBP is regarded by its many adherents as a three-legged stool – combining the best available research with practitioner knowledge, values and ethics and client/consumer/community culture, characteristics, values and preferences in order to make decisions about what services should be provided (IASWR, 2007). We could of course draw on statements to the following effect from several countries, when observing from the USA the National Association of Social Workers statement on EBP, which says circumspectly:

> Some states, government agencies, and players have endorsed certain specific evidence-based treatments such as cognitive behavioral therapy for anxiety disorders and community assertive treatment for individuals with severe mental illness and thus expect that practitioners are prepared to provide these services.[7]

This attention to EBP gives greater attention to both findings from research and the need to adopt and adapt research findings to ensure there is a focus on what works for whom and under what conditions. In the USA, as federal and state policies require attention to EBP, there have been developments such as the California Evidence-Based Clearinghouse for Child Welfare (http://www.cachildwelfareclearinghouse.org/), funded by the California Office of Child Abuse Prevention, and the Center for Mental Health Quality and Accountability of the National Association of State Mental Health Program Directors Research Institute (NRI-INC).

2 Translational research

With the concern that there is a gap between the outcomes of research and getting that research into practice (IOM, 2001), many federal agencies are increasingly focusing on translational research. The concept of 'translational research' is gaining a foothold within universities in the West (cf. Chapter 2). The goal of translational science is 'to speed the use of findings from our best science into usual care settings' (Brekke et al., 2007: 123) and these authors suggest that social work is ideally positioned to significantly influence the translational research agenda. Closely aligned with translational research that moves the study from academic into real world settings, there is growing attention to knowledge transfer and dissemination and implementation research. A wide range of US government agencies are investing in research that is intended to create ways to 'identify, develop, and refine effective and efficient methods, structures, and strategies that test models to disseminate and implement research-tested [health behavior change] interventions and evidence-based prevention, early detection, diagnostic, treatment, and quality of life improvement services into public health and clinical practice settings' (NIH, 2007).[8]

3 Interdisciplinary research

There is an increased view within western governments that one discipline or one researcher, working in isolation, limits the level of scientific discovery that can be achieved. Funders of research in western governments are increasingly advocating the importance of interdisciplinary research. This presents both a challenge and opportunity for social work.

4 Community-based participatory research

Community-based participatory research (CBPR) strategies are gaining increased visibility across several government agencies, including several institutes and centers. CBPR as a research design is also used in

studies on environmental, housing and community development issues in a number of countries. According to NIH (2008)[9] Community Participation in Research (R01), CBPR is defined as:

... scientific inquiry conducted in communities and in partnership with researchers. The process of scientific inquiry is such that community members, persons affected by the health condition, disability or issue under study, or other key stakeholders in the community's health have the opportunity to be full participants in each phase of the work (from conception – design – conduct – analysis – interpretation – conclusions – communication of results).

CBPR approaches are seen by some government agencies as an effective means to better address health disparities and to capitalize on the strengths and uniqueness that each of the partners brings the research endeavor.

Elucidating government priorities entails more than grasping and tracking favored approaches of the kind we have sketched above. Indeed, policy priorities are typically fluid, generalized, and dependent on a wide range of drivers of which an evidence base is only one and often not the most influential. Hence, even research and evaluation that starts with a confident understanding of relevant policy priorities can easily become sunk in a morass of ambiguity and subject to the push and pull of important figures in the political and policy community. This is illustrated in Exemplar 2.

Exemplar 2: Policy aspirations and government research

England and Wales saw the introduction in the first decade of this century of the Integrated Children's System (ICS) – designed in a systematic manner, to enable practitioners and managers to collect and use information systematically, efficiently and effectively.[10] There are analogous systems in some American states, Sweden, and Australia. The ICS is a 'bucket' of

---

Box 7.2   Policy aims of the UK Integrated Children's System

Needs-led, child-focused services	'It benefits children and families by enabling them to understand what information agencies are seeking and why, and helps them to judge whether they are getting the services they require'
Standardizing good practice	The ICS 'will assist us with developing a common language to describe children's needs within and across agencies'. It provides 'common terms … which can be used by all those who work with children in need and their families'
National database	The ICS will enable 'aggregated data for local service planning and for national statistical returns'
Joined up working at central and local government	The ICS involves looking at 'how we can work across government to ensure coherence' (Policy Officer). Also 'it is critical that this is seen as a multi-agency system'
Accountability/transparency/ outcomes	To deliver 'effective services' and 'to improve outcomes for children and families'
Government-driven policy	'It is important to point out that the development of the Integrated Children's System is a government led initiative … It is unusual … to do that on a national basis and have it driven by government'

---

diverse aspirations that move in and out of focus. It exemplifies how numerous policy 'goods' tend to get linked to major policy initiatives. In this case the ICS has been claimed (by officials and protagonists) to be all of the following (Box 7.2):[11]

The difficulty facing relationships between the policy and research communities is that no one policy is likely to achieve all this. Presumably, on quiet days, the policy community is well aware of this. Policy language is, of course, rhetorical, although this does not imply that it is thereby 'false'. In addition, central policy positions on this case did not seem to be 'fixed'. Priorities at the operational level moved in and out of focus, and mid-level government ministers changed. The policy community is not homogenous and may be marked by major changes (e.g. three different central government departments were responsible for this policy initiative during a three-year evaluation), and shifts whereby ministers quickly move on, officials become marginalized. These processes may not be well understood by the academic community, and when they *are* then there is a risk that they become co-opted into the policy community.

ADVOCACY AND GOVERNMENT FUNDED RESEARCH

Professional associations and scientific societies play important roles in expanding the government's research capacity. They provide input to research priority setting by working through *coalitions* of varying levels of formalization, *briefing* activity, *lobbying*, and so on. In the USA, coalitions exist such as Friends of NIDA, Friends of NIAAA, and the Coalition for Health through Behavioral and Social Sciences Research or the Foundation for Mental Health. These networks sponsor briefings on Capitol Hill, drawing attention to the important research contributions emerging from the studies within their spheres of interest. These external groups also meet with members of Congress to provide input on issues and problems that need further attention as well as levels of funding that should be established for various institutes and agencies.

However, there are underlying agenda within such developments that have been the focus of necessarily sharp debate. One of the significant developments in analysis of the relationship between government policy and social work research has been the development of a critique of undue reliance on accountability models of the purpose of research. Cronbach, because he believed that evaluation is to be 'judged by its contribution to public thinking and to the quality of service provided subsequent to the evaluation' (Cronbach et al., 1980: 64), regarded accountability as a limited view of program evaluation. 'Evaluation is not best used, we think, to bring pressure on public servants' (1980: 17). 'All too often, assignment of blame to individuals becomes the prime use of the accounts, while system improvement is forgotten' (1980: 135). The evaluation then falls heavily on the wrong person. 'Accountability is most demanded of those public servants condemned to farm rocky ground, under capricious weather conditions' (1980: 137). His conclusion was that a demand for accountability is a sign of pathology in the social system.

> Such a demand, each time it has occurred during the past century, has been a sign of discontent: those in charge of services are believed to be inefficient, insufficiently honest, or not self-critical. (1980: 139)

The work of Carol Weiss, and others who addressed similar problems, changed the face of evaluation in the 1970s.[12] She addressed various issues. For example, she delineated the political context in which evaluation is located. Although she has been primarily concerned with evaluation and policy research at the federal level, her empirical work with policy and program staff resonates more widely with social research. She also exposed the limitations of conventional instrumental views of the political use of information, through her conceptualization of use as enlightenment (cf. Chapter 12). To similar effect, Finch criticized knowledge-driven and problem-solving models of research use for their basis in a rationalistic model.

> The rationalist model of policy making sees it as a series of discrete events, where each issue to be decided is clearly defined, and decisions are taken by a specific set of actors who choose between well-defined alternatives, after weighing the evidence about the likely outcome of each. (Finch, 1986: 149–50)

There may also be concern about the greater role given to large national surveys and reviews of administrative data rather than field-focused intervention research. The enlightenment model 'offers far more space to qualitative research, through its emphasis on understanding and conceptualization, rather than upon providing objective facts' (Finch, 1986: 154). Finch's tentative alignment with a reformist position would probably not persuade Hammersley. 'It is becoming increasingly difficult to defend this enlightenment optimism' (Hammersley, 1994: 146).

Finally, Weiss imbued models of use with a realistic view of the public interest. 'More than anything she has struggled towards a realistic theory of use. These shifts started a debate in evaluation that goes on to the present day about the role in evaluation of idealism and pragmatism' (Shadish et al., 1990: 207–8).

Cronbach and colleagues argued how evaluation enters a context of governance that is typically one of *accommodation* rather than *command*. They complained that evaluation theory had been developed 'almost wholly around the image of command', with an associated view of managers and policy officials having a firm grip on the decision-making controls. On the contrary, they believed that 'most action is determined by a pluralistic community, not by a lone decision maker' (Cronbach et al., 1980: 84).

In a modified version of Cronbach's argument, we suggest that the audience for social work research consists of public servants and the public. Public servants include elected members, policy officials, responsible program officials, and operating personnel, such as teachers, social workers, nursing staff, and housing managers. The relevant public for a program includes the immediate constituencies of the program clientele, and those Cronbach describes as illuminators (e.g. reporters, academics, some novelists and dramatists, media commentators). We might also include the major lobbying groups which in some cases may be close to public servant roles (arm's length political 'think tanks', or non-governmental organizations, for example), and in other cases more associated with illuminators (as in the example of lobbying groups for the homeless). It is important to recognize that the policy-shaping community will expand and contract according to both the issue and the phase of any program.

Chelimsky makes some valuable points arising from her long experience in perhaps the most influential evaluation post, as Assistant Comptroller General for Program Evaluation and Methodology in the United States General Accounting Office (GAO). For instance, she suggests that evaluation use can operate by means of a *deterrence* function. 'In other words, the mere presence of the function, and the likelihood of a persuasive evaluation, can prevent or stop a host of undesirable government practices' (Chelimsky, 1997: 105). Chelimsky adds, 'More importantly … it is often the case that both accountability and knowledge evaluations are undertaken *without any hope of use*'. Expected non-use is characteristic of some of the best evaluations, including 'those that question widespread popular beliefs in a time of ideology, or threaten powerful, entrenched interests at any time' (1997: 105). Thus, 'there are some very good reasons why evaluations may be expert, and also unused' (1997: 105). Chelimsky's comments are both sane and plausible.

> To justify all evaluations by any single kind of use is a constraining rather than an enabling idea because it pushes evaluators towards excessive preoccupation with the acceptability of their findings to users, and risks turning evaluations into banal reiterations of the status quo. (Chelimsky, 1997: 106)

We are familiar with the arguments for ways in which the political process may act in negative ways. They include:

- pressures to limit the scope of an evaluation;
- demand that evaluators meet unrealistic time frames;

- indirect pressure to distort the study results through requests that alternative interpretations of the data are considered;
- the selective dissemination of evaluation results; and
- the suppression or critical delay of publication of the report.

Yet Hedrick, who notes all these negative influences and others beside, suggests ways in which politics can provide paradoxical support for evaluation. His basic case is that evaluation often functions as a solution to political disagreement. While this may itself be a negative consequence, it can have positive effects. For example, political disagreements can serve as stimuli for the initiation of evaluative studies.

While it would be reassuring to believe that evaluation studies are done primarily to find out whether a particular programme is working, or what a specific policy change has wrought, it is likely that many studies are initiated to confirm existing beliefs or a policy position (Hedrick, 1988: 9). In addition, the political use of research and evaluation as a delaying tactic can have the positive result that 'the scope of questions to be addressed can be expanded and researchers can adopt a long-term perspective of adding to the knowledge base about a social program or problem' (1988: 9). In other words, political fire-fighting to limit the direct instrumental utilization of evaluation may unwittingly feed longer term enlightenment uses of evaluation.

A look to the future

Advocacy work is sometimes developed slightly detached from government. A long term social work research strategy in the UK (Bywaters, 2008) was developed around a series of relatively long term objectives, linked to a series of operationalized aims derived from each general aim:

1. Increase the spend on social work and social care R&D to 2.5% of the total social services budget

by 2014 in line with the Science and Investment Innovation Framework.[13]

2. Secure the position of UK higher education institutions as world leaders in social work research and the contribution of social work research to methodological development in the social sciences.

3. Increase the proportion of social work educators in higher education institutions with postgraduate research qualifications to a minimum of 80% by 2020.

4. Establish a minimum of 300 social work practice posts across the four countries of the UK with some responsibility for undertaking research included in contractual duties by 2012.

5. Secure for social work full institutional recognition as a research discipline from national funding and quality assurance bodies and individual universities.

6. The establishment of robust, appropriate and accountable systems of social work/social care research governance that are agreed and accepted by all stakeholders.

7. Ensure that social work research has a high positive public profile reflected in exposure through a variety of media.

8. Ensure that all social work research builds in effective approaches to knowledge transfer (Joint University Council Social Work Education Committee, 2006).

Each of the underlying dimensions of resources, capacity, governance, and public profile were subsequently linked to ongoing implementation groups.

Research investments make a difference in the daily lives of our society. Medical and genetic breakthroughs help to eliminate disease and increase longevity, with more people living with chronic conditions. Poverty continues to be a root problem for health disparities and neglect across the lifespan, despite more than 30 years of targeted efforts to prevent abuse and address its consequences. Emerging policy categories like 'well-being' are susceptible to careful exploitation by social work researchers (Bywaters, 2007). This may provide the circumstances that will set the stage for greater support for social work research across government entities at local and national levels. The attention to EBP, translational and interdisciplinary

research as well as forms of participatory research, may all prove congruent with values implicit in social work research.

Yet if the profession is to truly become a strong player in the government research world it must clearly articulate its research perspective from both a systems and methodological perspective. Research goals need to be constantly set in active conversation with the priorities of the funding agencies. Sustaining research strengths may require enhancing university/agency/community research partnerships, sharing lessons learned and strategies to sustain capacity beyond single projects and one-time funding opportunities. Social work leaders and researchers need to shape the research agenda and help foster more funding through vigorous outreach to the legislative branch.

NOTES

1 Broader political contexts for social work research are considered by Haluk Soydan in Chapter 8.

2 For the Fabian Society see http://fabians.org.uk/about-the-fabian-society.

3 Similar analyses can also be offered of the role of the National Institute on Alcohol Abuse and Alcoholism, the National Cancer Institute, and the National Institute on Ageing.

4 We suggest that the basic elements of this analysis, taken out of their immediate context, will transfer at least to the larger states in the EU.

5 See http://www.esrcsocietytoday.ac.uk/ESRCInfoCentre/opportunities/postgraduate/ and 'Postgraduate Training Guidelines'.

6 For an interesting discussion of governance issues from the European Union see http://ec.europa.eu/governance/index_en.htm.

7 The full NASW pages on evidence based practice can be located at http://www.socialworkers.org/research/naswResearch/0108EvidenceBased/default.asp.

8 Accessed at http://grants.nih.gov/grants/guide/pa-files/PAR-07-086.html.

9 Accessed at http://grants.nih.gov/grants/guide/pa-files/PA-08-074.html.

10 See 'About the Integrated Children's System' at http://www.everychildmatters.gov.uk/socialcare/integratedchildrenssystem/about/. Accessed 18 August 2008. Key findings from the evaluation can be found at Shaw et al. (2009).

11   All quotations are taken from official government sites or from presentations by policy officers and are in the public domain. However, because we do not wish to focus on the views of individuals we have not made specific identifications.

12   For an interesting conversation with Carol Weiss on policy making and research see http://

www.idrc.ca/en/ev-43607-201-1-DO_TOPIC.html. Accessed 28 August, 2008.

13   This framework was a ten-year investment framework for science and innovation issed by HM Treasury, the UK finance ministry. It can be accessed at http://62.164.176.164/3015.htm.

Politics and Values in Social Work Research

Haluk Soydan

INTRODUCTION

This chapter discusses one of the most debated issues in the philosophy and sociology of science, that is, the nature and role of politics and values in science. The nature and role of politics and values in social work research is part of the more general issue as treated in terms of social sciences. However, social work research practice takes an outstanding locus in this discourse. This is determined by the fact that the main subject matter of social work research is social work practice, which is about social action and interventions for the purpose of changing the life situations of disadvantaged human beings and communities. And, as it will be argued in this chapter, social change and social interventions are intimately related to values and politics. Thus, values and politics are critical contextual features of social work research and are intertwined with knowledge claims associated with social research.

The chapter sets out a brief presentation of core concepts such as values, politics, value systems, morality, and ethics. In addition, social work practice and social work research practice are defined and briefly related to the question of how they interact with politics and values. A presentation of science as a social institution serves as a general frame to understand science, and illustrates how social work research practice is embedded in the world of values and politics. Three classical questions of how values and politics are associated with knowledge production are raised and approached by using Jurgen Habermas' concept of 'knowledge interest'. Thereafter, social work research practice is discussed in light of historically central scientists whose work impacted social work research practice: Comte de Saint-Simon, Karl Marx, and Ronald Campbell. The controversy of 'objectivity' in social science is referred to by relating to the work of Max Weber and Gunnar Myrdal. The concluding section is on multiculturalism in social work, one of the well known controversies of social work research in which values and politics plays an outstanding role.

This chapter relates to a number of others in the *Handbook* especially 9 on ethics, 7 on research and government and 13 on the intellectual contexts. Also others would take a different stance in terms of methodological rigor.

VALUES AND POLITICS

Values and politics are two concepts that are intertwined with a web of other concepts such as values systems, norms, ethics, authority, change, and action, some of which we need to examine briefly. In diverse contexts the relative importance of any of these and other related concepts might be perceived and emphasized differently. Individuals dealing with these concepts might have different tastes or take a different stand so as to emphasize the primacy and importance of any of these concepts differently. It seems to me that two concepts, 'value' and 'morality' open up a sensible approach to understand values and politics in social work research.

Values

The concept of value refers to beliefs that human beings as individuals or human societies as collective systems internally and cohesively maintain, cherish and expect others to accept. One of the classical debates in philosophy and later in sociology is about whether values are embedded in human nature (values that are God given), or if human beings simply create values through social interaction. Modern understanding of this question is based on more empirically supported scientific models although other co-existing types of knowledge systems such as religion maintain traditional stands. In social and behavioral sciences it is asserted that human beings in social interaction generate values and integrate them in structured systems. Values are either personal, that is, maintained by individuals and not necessarily shared by others, or are cultural, that is, they are shared by a group of people who define themselves as an in-group and are perceived as a distinct group by other groups. Values then are embedded as a system or web by cultural, societal, religious, ideological and other contexts in human societies. Driven and empowered by values individuals, groups

and large constituencies of human beings make choices and decisions, thus generating politics.

Related to the concept of value is the concept of morality. Morality refers to human actions based on dichotomized or paired values such as 'good and bad', 'right and wrong', and 'disgusting and admirable'. Our personal morals such as our consideration of what is 'good and bad' operate as compasses of our actions, intentions, decisions, non-decisions as we seek to discriminate between good and bad in all these and other contexts.

One may say, personal values and personal morals reflect *choices*, albeit not always explicitly: whether it is about buying a new car ('I should choose a smaller car to try to limit my contribution to air pollution'), casting a vote for a political party ('I should vote for AKP in Turkey because they want to expand the human rights of ethnic minorities'), implementing a social work intervention model ('I should not prescribe psychotherapy to my client Malinda because she couldn't afford it as a single mother with four children and a low income'), or preparing a research proposal ('I should propose a multi-site randomized controlled study of Multi-systemic Theory because it seems to be promising but needs further independent investigation'). Choices are related to politics, the other main concept this chapter elaborates on when it comes to social work research.

Value systems are often attributed to specific social aggregates (e.g. social classes, 'diversity'-labeled groups such as ethnic minority groups, older age groups, gays, and lesbians), and societies and cultures in general. One specific instance of value systems involves professionals and organizations; social work professionals and social scientists, including social work researchers, they all operate within given and relatively well defined organizational value systems. For instance, in an interesting survey of Norwegian and American corporations, Wenstrop and Myrmel (2006) identified three basic types of values that constitute an organizational values system: core values (the character and attitude of the organization), created values (especially created and tailored for stakeholders), protected values (codified in code of ethics, and they refer to health, safety, and environment). For example, in the context of social work research, organizations' core values would refer to commitment to scientific rigor, accountability to knowledge users, ability to deliver in a timely manner, scientific trustworthiness, respect for peers, and for tax-payers' funds; created values would involve dissemination of social work interventions that work, have a high degree of client acceptance, and be ethically sensitive, and less costly to social work agencies; protected values would involve rejection of interventions that harm (see Chapter 9), promotion of translational research to secure social worker and client participation in contextualizing generalized knowledge, and designing, for example, motivational interview methods to protect the safety of social workers in high risk environments.

The complex relationship between ethics and values and their significance for social work research is explored in the following chapter. Suffice to say here that national and international social work organizations have developed a complex set of ethical standards of conduct for the profession and disseminated codes of ethics to guide and protect the interests of individuals and groups exposed to social research, to ensure that research results are generated accurately and truthfully by using consistent and rigorous scientific methods, to urge scientists to awareness of appropriate use and misuse of research results, and to conduct pertinent research to serve human needs in a world of troubles and economic constraints, among others.

Politics

Politics is a human process through which people make decisions. Some decisions might be the sole business of individuals without explicitly involving other human beings. An example of such decisions would be when a client makes an ultimate decision to quit alcohol use or abuse. A long disputed type of decision is an individual's free will to commit suicide. Although for professional social workers the answer might be clear and self-evident that no individual should be left to his or her free will in such a decision-making situation, the complexity of the phenomenon is reflected in the philosophical position that rational human beings (agents) master their own actions and decisions. From a social worker's perspective, a value conflict might emerge because of the respect for the client's free will and agency, and the social work profession's dedication to help. Clearly, any action taken by social workers in such an instance is based on values held by the workers themselves and the profession.

However, one might have strong arguments for the case that no decision is made in a social vacuum and that all decisions are socially circumstantial. Therefore, the concept of politics refers to decision making as an inter-human process or interactive behavior that takes place in groups, organizations, and institutions. Politics necessarily involves power, authority, and legitimacy. These are all complex concepts and have been an object of study of the social sciences for centuries (e.g. see Giddens, 1979); it is not the purpose of this chapter to explore these concepts in depth. However, briefly, power is the capacity of an individual or an aggregate to control the environment in order to reach certain intended outcomes. In order to function smoothly power must be associated with authority, that is, a source that provides justification to the exercise of power. When power is justified it means that it has legitimacy, generally recognized by other agents and institutions. For example, in a case of child maltreatment a social worker might need to remove the child from the family and for this purpose s/he would need the power to do so; authority and legitimacy of such a coercive exercise of power would emanate from the child protection legislation and the worker's professional standing including the institutional framework of the social work agency. Ultimately, such an action is based on the value of human rights and right to protection of the children as reflected in the legislation of a country.

By its very nature politics may involve many dimensions, multiple stakeholders and take place in the context of diverse structural value systems; thus, its outcome(s) may not be given a priori and may temporarily or permanently change in a necessarily dynamic social environment.

In social work, most decision making is related to decisions for and/or with clients for the betterment of the client, and the purpose of developing and implementing, and sometimes enforcing (social) policies. This specific aspect of decision making in social work is intertwined with and has implications for aspects of social work research practice, a topic to be elaborated on in the next section of this chapter.

In general, a policy is a well thought-out program to guide action steps and generate intended outcome(s). Social work practice might be impacted by policies implemented by governments, organizations, and institutions. For example, social work practice might be impacted by social policies of government to eradicate poverty or unemployment, knowing that more financially secure neighborhoods or low unemployment rates make a good framing to control crime, truancy, unwanted teen pregnancies, and so forth. These types of policies are referred to as public policy. An interesting example that illustrates great variances pertains to income support policies also known as social assistance/social security. A cross-national study of six countries and 13 cities in those countries reveal that institutional frameworks for social assistance varies a great deal.[1] Variations include factors such as legal basis, universal vs. discretionary measures, enforcement of entitlements, target populations, and individuals' age limits, waiting time between request and first payment, etc. Social workers' decisions and actions in terms of supporting clients with social assistance/social security are thus contingent on and impacted by the national policy frames. Social work practice might also be impacted by the internal policies of a social work agency: for example, lack of planned and funded organizational support for implementation of evidence-based practice may lead social workers to use opinion-based practices.

It is worth noting, as well experienced social workers know, not all public policy is implemented successfully, fully or at all, due to processes intrinsic to the nature of organizations. As Lipsky (1980) so aptly analyzed, on the organizational level, including social work and social welfare agencies, large gaps might exist between intentions of written policy documents, other agency policies, and what is being implemented by social workers during policy implementation! In other words, we would expect a continuous exchange and tension between macro and micro levels of policy making and values maintained at all levels of a social system.

In sum, values and politics are intertwined, embrace all social institutions and human life and are intertwined with activities and outcomes of human processes. Social work research practice is not an exception.

SOCIAL WORK RESEARCH

To understand what social work research is, one needs to explore the nature of social work as a professional practice (see Chapter 1 for a discussion of the purposes of social work). The International Federation of Social Workers, the worldwide organization that gathers social workers around the globe, defines social work as:

> The social work profession promotes social change, problem solving in human relationships and the empowerment and liberation of people to enhance well-being. Utilizing theories of human behavior and social systems, social work intervenes at the points where people interact with their environments. Principles of human rights and social justice are fundamental to social work. (IFSW, 2000: 1)

In a nutshell, this definition captures three dimensions of social work practice indicating how and why values and politics, and social work research are intimately locked to each other.

First of all, the social work profession's foremost aim is to infuse social change in order to liberate people from hardship and enhance well-being. As we have already seen social change is closely related to values and to social workers' individual or collective understanding of what is good (e.g. well-being) and what is bad (e.g. poverty), and to politics, that is, the web of multiple structures involving power, authority, and legitimacy.

Second, the principles of human rights and social justice are fundamental to the social work profession. Typically, for both human rights and social justice, whenever they were historically achieved in societies, it was as a result of long and hard political struggles. The history of human societies is a history of struggles to secure human rights and to design and enforce policies for social justice. Values and politics are essential to this aim of the social work profession.

Third, the social work profession is dependent on high quality knowledge and skills to understand problems to be solved and the solutions that are viable, do not harm, and work. In fact, social work practice has been moving from being an authority-based to an evidence-based profession (Gambrill, 1999, 2001).

The scope of social work research is very broad and multi-disciplinary. The mission of social work research is to deliver practice pertinent knowledge on multiple phenomena, problem-generating processes, problem identification and diagnosis as well as intervention models that work, and most importantly, do not harm the client.

Modern social work research includes descriptive studies of social environments of individual clients and families; descriptive studies of psychological states of individual clients and their families; descriptive studies of social units such as neighborhoods, large urban environments; descriptive studies of patterns of deviant behavior; organizational studies; epidemiological surveys; process studies of interventions; and effectiveness studies of interventions.

Interestingly, several decades ago Sidney Zimbalist (1977) summarized the scope of social work research as an inquiry into the causes of poverty, measurement of the distribution of poverty, surveys of social movements, quantification and indexing of social work, evaluation research into the effectiveness of the social services, and studies of multi-problem families.

In sum, the very nature of social work involves both values and politics, and social sciences. The most tangible dimension of social work as a scientific discipline (and its associated professional social work practice) is that it is a social institution. Like other scientific disciplines social work research has the attributes of an institutionalized scientific discipline; these attributes include specific research institutions, research chairs, doctoral programs, own journals, scientific conduct codes, etc.

Science as social institution

John Ziman, a New Zealander and British theoretical physicist, defined the ultimate purpose of science as the solving of problems. In his remarkable book *Real Science: What it is, and what it means*, he places science in the complexity of value systems and politics by making clear its social character. Science, he writes:

> ... involves large numbers of specific people regularly performing specific actions which are consciously coordinated into larger schemes. Although research scientists often have a great deal of freedom in what they do and how they do it, their individual thoughts and actions only have scientific meaning in these larger schemes. Like many facts of life, this is so obvious that it was for long overlooked! (Ziman, 2000: 4)

Paraphrasing Ziman, we could say that social work as a scientific discipline is somewhat similar to other institutions such as organized religion, law, and the humanities in producing knowledge. Typically, knowledge is the principle purpose and outcome of social work as a scientific discipline. This certainly defines the locus of social work research in society as well as impacting on the type of knowledge it produces.

The notion that social work research can be defined as a problem solving social institution is embedded in the funding of research in terms of projects. The researchers are expected to present detailed proposals for funding of particular projects. Project writing has almost become a specialty occupation, especially in countries such as USA and Europe where large, centralized public funding institutions are major funding engines with complex and sophisticated mechanisms of soliciting research (based on policy principles drawn by federal decision-making institutions), review systems, post-award follow-up mechanisms, and network building programs to promote research administration in the short term but also research advancement in much longer terms.

Typically, research proposals are expected to indicate questions that might be solved by what might be discovered. Thus, the presumed purpose of research is to solve problems that can be formulated in advance. Social work research as a social institution is independent; at least in the sense that it manages its own internal affairs. The fundamental principle of operation is transparency, meaning that all patronage, public and private, is channeled through communal scrutiny. Benefactions (public and private funds) are handed over to academic committees and councils of scientific notables. Academics themselves are the peer judges of scientific activities: they develop research programs; they assess research proposals; they award research grants.

Does this means that the scientific community is totally disconnected from the society in the sense that it is apolitical? Or, for social work research, are social work researchers totally disconnected from social service agencies, clients and all other individuals or social entities that social work research is meant to serve?

Ziman (2000: 54) argues that 'science' is not disconnected from 'society', and attributes the main bridge between science and society to the system of teaching and training. Teaching activities connect scholars and professional practice intimately. For instance, the faculty of social work as well as other disciplines with a professional practice such as law, engineering, and medicine must have experience as practitioners, and very often focus their research on practical problems of the professional practice. Furthermore, as noted below, Mode 2 research entities such as centers of excellence and specialized research centers increasingly broker knowledge exchange between researchers and end-users.

Furthermore, the principle of academic freedom is especially invoked when science impinges on practice. Especially in terms of the social work profession, science and social work practice have multiple two-way connections.

'State patronage inevitably brings politics into science – and science into politics' writes Ziman, (2000: 74). Furthermore: 'By accepting state patronage on a large scale, scientists have become very vulnerable to the demands of their paymasters. Science policy unveils apparent discrepancies between what science might possibly produce, and what society actually gets … In other words, considerable pressure is put on scientists to work on problems favored by the government, rather than problems of their own choosing' (Ziman, 2000: 76). And, social work research practice is no exception in this context!

Today social work researchers around the world rely heavily on research funds made available by major national research foundations and government agencies. As an example, let's take the National Institutes of Health (NIH) in the United States (http://www.nih.gov/). By all means NIH is the world's largest research funder in health, mental health and related human services. In 2009 its total research budget was over USD 32 billion, it had 18,000 employees, and more than 325,000 researchers at over 3000 universities and laboratories were on NIH grant payrolls. Typically, NIH operates with mechanisms that steer the direction of the research it funds. Most dominant mechanisms are funding opportunity announcements (FOAs), program announcements (PAs) and request for applications (RFAs). Directions and research areas defined by these mechanisms reflect the values and policies of the involved decision-makers including the US Congress, the US Department of Health and Human Services, and various bodies within NIH. One of its larger institutes, the National Institute of Mental Health (NIMH) is a major funder of social work research (http://www.nimh.nih.gov/). In 2008 NIMH was focusing on 13 research topic areas (such as anxiety disorders, depression and post-traumatic stress disorder) thus prioritizing considerable amounts of tax money to these 13 topic areas and consequently excluding other topic areas. Furthermore, NIMH prioritizes randomized controlled studies, thus steering the methodology to be used by the researchers as well. The methodological priority is based on an understanding that randomized controlled studies are better fit to measure effects of mental health and social work interventions – traditionally a very different stand than what many European countries' research policies dictate. Social work researchers who conduct research on social work in mental health are thus heavily dependent on what is being decided and offered by these government bodies.

A second example comes from another part of the world; Sweden's Council for Working Life and Social Research (FAS) is the main funder of social work research (http://www.fas.se/). Compared to its American counterpart, FAS is a relatively small foundation with an annual budget of approximately SEK 95 million (an equivalent of USD 13 million at 2009 exchange rates). Typically, this foundation's main research topic areas focus on macro systems and structures such as 'work and health', 'labor market', 'public health', etc. thus strongly reflecting the emphasis by the society on social policy. In a database scan conducted by the author in July 2007 the Council listed 100 ongoing research projects classified under its social work program. The research projects listed in the FAS website were consistent with the policies of the foundation!

These two examples illustrate how values and policies held by government bodies constitute critical contextual features of the practice of social work and determine the direction of knowledge made generated for the profession.

THE CLASSICAL ISSUE OF VALUES AND POLITICS IN SCIENTIFIC PRODUCTION OF KNOWLEDGE

Three questions will be discussed in the following:

1) Do a social work researcher's values and political preferences influence his/her research activities?
2) Does the social work profession's universal values, political preferences and circumstantial/contextual political preferences impact its research activities?
3) If social values and political preferences influence the social worker's research, does this necessarily lead to biased research results?

One basic assumption about the mission of social sciences is that social sciences are committed to explore 'truth' by producing 'objective' and unbiased research results. However, this specific stand is contested as we shall see later in this chapter when reviewing standpoints taken for example by the Marxist tradition. It is useful to classify values, political preferences, and personal tastes in terms of extra-scientific and intra-scientific factors. Extra-scientific values refer to value systems such as political, religious, cultural, ethnic, and so forth. Intra-scientific values refer to science's internal assumptions about scientific methods. In one sense, it is not completely adequate to call these assumptions values because scientific methods are about rules and criteria that are assumed to lead us to less biased possible research results. Scientific methods are based on assumptions developed during the history of modern social sciences. These assumptions are paradigmatic, they come as a package and persist over a very long time until a new paradigm comes and replaces the current one, and involve basic assumptions about human nature, the nature of the society, the relationship between society and human beings, and the ability of scientific methodology to generate knowledge (Kuhn, 1962).

In general, academic science has become an integral part of techno-science; industrial as well as the human services. Most researchers in techno-science are trained in academia. Many techno-science centers are prominent research institutions where scientific problems to be solved are generated in close collaboration with end-users of knowledge, work is trans-disciplinary, the research results are transferred to the end-users during the process of knowledge production, and accountability to stakeholders is an important quality (Gibbons et al., 1994). This specific mode of knowledge production came to be called Mode 2 production of knowledge (Gibbons et al., 1994). In fact, social work research is taking the first steps of more explicitly creating its own mode of production, translational research, pertinent to the conditions of social work practice (Brekke et al., 2007; National Institute of Mental Health, 1999; New Freedom Commission on Mental Health, 2003).

The most basic intra-scientific value cherished by the scientific community is the commitment to 'truthful', unbiased and 'interesting' (useful, meaningful, pertinent) knowledge. In particular, the knowledge interest involves the relationship between (social) sciences and politics. The perspective of the knowledge interest of science relates to the rationality of human beings in terms of what the meaning and use of

knowledge is. In social work research this would generate questions such as: what is the relationship between explaining and understanding social phenomena, and impacting and changing the course and nature of social phenomena? How can the search for truth (scientific evidence) and achievement of political intentions such as attaining betterment of human beings be integrated?

The German social scientist and philosopher Jurgen Habermas (1984, 1987) has developed a typology of knowledge interest that provides a useful framework to understand the location of different types of social work research. Habermas differentiates between three generic types of knowledge interest: technical, practical, and emancipatory.

Technical knowledge interest refers to our purpose of explaining, controlling, and manipulating our physical environment. Knowledge is generated by empirical research using analytic, hypothetical–deductive theories and experiments. Habermas' intention is to classify the knowledge interest of natural sciences such as biology and physics in this domain. However, in my view social work research at times relates to this knowledge interest for the purpose of explaining how destructive processes and social structures can be blocked, changed, or controlled; what interventions work to control destructive and negative behaviors, attitudes, and social circumstances. Research on social work has a bounty of examples. For example, research on Life Skills Training programs demonstrate that this program is successful in training adolescents to resist peer pressure to smoke, drink alcohol and use drugs. These programs support students to develop self-esteem and self-confidence so that they can cope with anxiety and reduce health risk behaviors (Botvin et al., 2006; Griffin et al., 2006).

Practical knowledge interest in Habermas' typology refers to social actors (agents such as social workers or clients) strivings to *understand* communicative social action and behavior patterns. Social norms are studied empirically and analytically but they are grounded in the inter-subjective symbolic worlds of human beings. Habermas classifies historical–hermeneutic sciences such as sociology, ethnography, and history in this category. Social work research should be located in this domain as well. In particular, social work research is well situated in this domain because social work practice is embedded in organizations and uses organizational mechanisms to impact the betterment of societies and people.

Emancipatory knowledge interest refers to an individual's biography, roles, and expectations and uses self-reflection, self-knowledge, and critique as vehicles of emancipation from institutional and psychological constraints. Typical disciplines with emancipatory knowledge interest are ideology critique, psychoanalysis, feminist theory, and action research. As many people understand the knowledge interest of social work research it has a clear locus in this category as well as exemplified by the chapter on disability research in this handbook. A few outstanding examples of social work research with emancipatory knowledge interest include Paulo Freire's (1970) pedagogy for and by oppressed populations, Karl Marx's (Marx and Engels, 1969) political action for abolition of private property and the oppression of the working class in the capitalist society, and Kurt Lewin's (1946) and John Dewey's (1929) action research methodology.

I shall come back to give a response to the questions that are raised in this section; I kindly ask the patience of the reader for the delay. For now, in the next few sections, some historically important inputs that directly involve social work research will be viewed.

MODERN SCIENCE IN THE SERVICE OF HUMANITY[2]

While curiosity about human beings and societies might be as old as human history itself, the genesis of modern empirical social science is relatively recent. As commonly known, the emergence of social analysis is attributed to the Enlightenment and to the French Enlightenment philosophers. While this account might have some credit, our current understanding of modern empirical social science was more sharply formulated in Scotland by contemporary thinkers than by philosophers from the French Enlightenment. Most prominently, Adam Smith, but also, Adam Ferguson and John Millard, formulated the foundations of modern social sciences. These economists/philosophers, known as The Scottish School, were active during the second half of the eighteenth century, and put forward a four-stage theory of society.

The Scottish School laid the foundation of modern empirical social science, but they did not develop a theory about predictions based on scientific analysis of society. We had to wait for years, for the linkage between modern social scientific analysis and its planned use of research results for social change and the betterment of human conditions. There was, it is true, ideas and utopia about human progress. Yet, the Western history of social science for the service of human beings had to wait a few more decades to come to surface (Soydan, 1999).

The period at the end of the eighteenth and beginning of the nineteenth centuries, was a time of great upheaval in Europe. The French Revolution affected the entire European stage. Awareness of better human conditions assumed a prominent place in many political agendas.

Marquis Marie Jean de Condorcet, a French thinker and agitator, whose small pamphlet (written in 1793, and published posthumously in 1795) is a historical milestone in this context. It reads:

> The idea of human perfectibility is similar to the thought of the desire for change, the law of progression, but is more demanding and, to a certain extent, has more consequences. The desire for change is aimed at man's external conditions. People constantly attempt to alter the conditions of their lives so that they can function a little more simply, a little more efficiently, produce considerably

better results for slightly greater effort etc … The thought of perfectibility is also aimed at the inner consequences of external work; people will be ethically and existentially better, so to speak, and more perfect from this work. (Soydan, 1999: 20)

The Scottish School's contributions and Condorcet's input fused and emerged in the earlier years of the new century, as the catalyzing element of social science and planned social change. Today, the utilization, implementation, and translation of research results into practice contexts would be the terminology (we would prefer to use) to indicate the marriage between the social sciences and social change. Several others took over from this point. However, again another Frenchman was first on the stage, and leaving an impressive legacy with longstanding implications for social work practice. This man was Claude Henri de Rouvroy, Comte de Saint-Simon, simply known as Saint-Simon.

Saint-Simon – the earliest and most accomplished model of transporting research to practice

Saint-Simon's fundamental concepts were: society is sick; social science can cure the sick society, the organized authority, and the total organization of people's lives. The metaphor of the time was 'sick' in contrast to characterizing the state of the society as dysfunctional and attacked (what we today define as), social problems. The state of 'sickness' was attributed to the structure of the society (as opposed to other attitudes that social problems were generated by the individual him/herself). Saint-Simon perceived his historical role, or his calling, as a role of a social scientist that could and should 'cure' the sick society.

The major vehicle for curing society was modern social science which was just about to be shaped, and was later to take off. It is worth pondering the fact that only a few decades ago (Saint-Simon's work was accomplished basically during the first two decades of the 1800s), the use of social science to cure societal problems was an unknown theme. With Saint-Simon, social science made its definitive entry into the service of the society. Using Jurgen Habermas' terminology, it might be suggested that the social science of Saint-Simon had developed one distinct knowledge interest: the practical!

Given the sense of calling, and the spirit of the era, maybe it is not surprising that Saint-Simon vividly advocated an order which would be challenged by later generations of social scientists. Saint-Simon believed that social scientists should be given the power to transform society because they were the bearers of knowledge and thus best suited to plan, organize, and change.

However, the prototype model of (a) a social scientific knowledge-base, (b) a program for change, and (c) professionals whose job it is to implement intervention, survived. It ultimately increased in its sophistication, and continues to advance. Over the decades, especially after World War II, many models have been developed and launched to block or eradicate negative mechanisms and induce positive change in society. Two such examples in the tradition include the concepts of social engineering, which is especially favored in Europe, and the experimental society (see below) favored particularly in the United States (Soydan, 1999). More recent efforts to develop implementation and translational research, as well as the use of higher quality scientific evidence (EBP) could also be seen in this perspective. Social work and social policy are two areas of research and practice among several human services related disciplines and professions where practical knowledge interest is outstanding.

Marxism – a promise of emancipatory knowledge

Marxism, as a study of class struggles and the capitalist economic system, is a political ideology, and a revolutionary political action strategy emerged from the mid-1800s in response to a number of phenomena that included: the positivist social sciences and bourgeois class dominance in Europe and societal cleavages based on disfranchise, underprivilege and extreme poverty. Karl Marx and Friedrich Engels (1969) were its pioneering thinkers and agents who clearly advocated an emancipatory knowledge interest when it came to the social theory and empirical studies conducted especially by Karl Marx. Historical materialism was developed as a methodology to study history, society, and economic systems. The ultimate purpose of historical materialism was to produce emancipatory knowledge to liberate oppressed and underprivileged classes. Furthermore, at least in theory, Marxism was related to concepts such as social justice, equality, freedom, liberation from alienation, and oppression. Some of these cardinal values and concepts in the core of Marxism were also to be found among core values of the social work profession. Originally, for obvious reasons, social work as a profession and its emerging research discipline were not on the agenda of Marxism, other than its strong interest in social reformation (in more modern terms, social policy). However, much later, values, concepts, and politics that were cherished by Marxism and explicitly advocated for, by at least some groups in the social work profession, gained prominence.

For example, Jane Addams, one of the pioneering classics of social work, introduced and used radical methods for working with impoverished groups (most of them new immigrants) in neighborhoods of Chicago. Addams was not a Marxist, rather a sociologist and social worker associated with the Chicago School of Sociology (Soydan, 1999), but advocated a clearly emancipatory approach.

Another example of community social work, also originating from Chicago, is provided by Saul Alinsky's work (Alinsky, 1969; 1971). Alinsky has focused on models organizing the underprivileged and poverty stricken populations in neighborhoods and work places. The Industrial Areas Foundation that

he developed was committed to organizing radical leftists around the country on the principle of self-help and for the purpose of changing working and living conditions. Association of his approach with values such as social justice and the liberation of working men and women are very similar to those values found in the Marxist tradition.

A final example I would like to draw attention to is the work of Paulo Freire, because his approach impacted social work substantially although they were originated as pedagogical models. Paulo Freire, a Brazilian, started his professional trajectory as the Director of the Department of Education and Culture of the Social Services in the city of Refice, in Brazil. Typically, the name of the department indicated the locus of education and culture in the social services system of this specific country at that specific time. His major theoretical work published as *Pedagogy of the Oppressed* (Freire, 1970), was explicitly influenced by Marxist teaching, as well by related literature on the post World War II anti-colonial movements and politics. His discussion focused on the liberation of the oppressed; rejection of dominance by the powerful; and on the under-privileged. Eradication of unilateral and unbalanced dominance of the student by the teacher was a dear topic for Freire's writings. His legacy has an impressive presence in many countries around the world, and his work is referred to in international social work conferences, albeit not as much among American scholars and practitioners as among social workers in developing countries and to some extent among European social workers.

The emancipatory approach and the values associated with it have been a major driving factor of community and neighborhood based social work projects in European countries during the 1970s and early 1980s. Such projects were supported with government funding in especially social-democratic regimes such as Sweden. Interestingly, many non-governmental organizations that work currently with victims of human trafficking in the United States base their activities on values very similar to those advocated by Addams and Freire. Such NGOs focus their effort to free victims of human sex trafficking from individuals and mechanisms hurting them, and provide services to enable re-entry to a social situation free of oppression. Indeed, the definition of social work adopted in July 2000 by the International Federation of Social Workers expresses and supports similar values: 'In solidarity with those who are dis-advantaged, the profession strives to alleviate poverty and to liberate vulnerable and oppressed people in order to promote social inclusion' (http://www.ifsw.org/en/p38000208.html).

In recent decades much of social work research has been projected on the issues of groups and communities organized around identity. Examples of such groups are people of color, immigrant women, lesbian women, gay men, disabled people, and elderly. In fighting racism, at times, black women have, for example, based their methods for knowledge generation and social change on 'race' rather than gender as a priority (Collins, 1991). Another illustrative example may be found in the research area of strengths and resilience building among social work clients. Social work research shows that most children and adolescents exposed to violent and disorganized family and neighborhood environments do well when supported by mechanisms that reinforce self-esteem, self-confidence and values of salutary lifestyle (Peele and Brodsky, 1991).

THE EXPERIMENTING SOCIETY – SOCIAL EXPERIMENTS IN SOCIAL WELFARE AND SOCIAL WORK

Interestingly, Habermas limits the concept of 'technical knowledge interest' to the explanation, control and manipulation of the physical environment. However, it could be argued that there is also an explicit human interest in explaining, controlling and manipulating the social environment (including the psychological environment). This rationale is based on the perception that certain social and psychological mechanisms generate outcomes that are perceived as negative and destructive factors impacting society and human beings. True, what is negative to whom is a complex question, and such definitions evidently vary in time and space. Having recognized this complexity, it is sensible to suggest that there is broad consensus among considerably large groups of populations across time and space, in the perception of a large number of problems as being negative and destructive. The social work profession and social policy have a long list of such problems, a few of which include: poverty, child molestation, violence, suicide, commercial sexual exploitation of children, genocide, ethnic cleansing.

In my view, intervention research is the most sophisticated expression of social sciences' interest in 'technical knowledge' as a Habermasian perspective. In fact, it can be argued that intervention research is right in the core of social work practice (Soydan, 2008b).

Intervention research (Soydan, 2008b) in the human services field was shaped during the post World War II era. Presidents Kennedy and Johnson, and later to some extent president Nixon launched nationwide programs to improve the conditions of the most needy and underserved cross-sections of the American population. These social reforms aimed to induce change constitute an important backdrop to what later came to be defined as intervention research. Sponsors of social programs wanted to understand whether the programs they funded had any positive and intended outcomes.

The American psychologist and methodologist, Donald T. Campbell, has coined the concept of 'the experimenting society' meaning that the eradication of societal problems should be based on the scientific principle of experimentation and evaluation of intervention outcomes.

The expansion of welfare state reforms has involved many areas of human and social services. Experimental studies or field trials were launched to study the effects of welfare reforms, and have continued to be conducted ever since. Research on social work practice has highly benefited from and should continue to capitalize on experiences of neighboring fields areas such as education (Boruch et al., 2002), public assistance programs (Greenberg and Shroder, 1997), poverty reduction programs (Blank, 2002; McKernan and Ratcliffe, 2006), crime prevention programs (Lipsey and Wilson, 1993), housing programs (Friedman and Weinberg, 1985), wage subsidy programs (Burtless, 1985), and mental health programs (Solomon and Marshall, 2002; Solomon and Draine, 2004). All these and other social welfare reform areas, directly or indirectly related to social work practice, involve multi-disciplinary researchers from economics, psychology, psychiatry, criminology, and sociology as well as social work. The Campbell Library's systematic research reviews in the field of social welfare include many examples of fine experimental studies in social work practice (retrieved May 25, 2009 from: http://www.campbellcollaboration.org).

Outside the United States, the idea of intervention studies took somehow a different trajectory, in the beginning by confining itself to program evaluation, and later by developing better understanding for experimental studies and the idea of evidence-based practice (Davies et al., 2006). Awareness of effectiveness of social interventions was early in Sweden as illustrated by the evaluations conducted by government commissions. An early example was the study of the effectiveness of post-institutional care for juvenile delinquents who had been in the care of specially tailored institutions following the Parliament's 1937 reform (Davies et al., 2006). In other Scandinavian countries this process was slower (Schwandt, 1998). In other parts of the world, especially in developing countries, adaptation of Western models of evaluation and cultural competency issues came to the foreground (Thompson-Robinson et al., 2004).

Nevertheless, there has been a major shift in many countries. In an internal report Boruch et al. (2004) reported the existence of randomized and possibly randomized trials pertaining to human services in a number of countries, including Australia (82), Canada (94), Denmark (4), Finland (8), Germany (19), Mexico (41), Netherlands (57), New Zealand (9), Spain (16), Sweden (23), and Turkey (3).

Similarly, the Institute for Evidence-Based Social Work Practice (IMS) in Sweden carried out an inventory of Swedish effect studies in 2008 to assess the body of experimental studies in human services and social work in particular. The inventory covered the period 1996–2007 (IMS, 2008). The studies identified in the inventory refer to a wide range of social welfare interventions. The tendency from 1996 to 2007 shows a large increase of effect studies and today RCT studies are dominating. While only one experimental study was published in 1996, the number of ongoing or published experimental studies was 45 in 2007.

This development means that in many countries among social work researchers, research founders as well end-users such as social workers, social work agency managers and social policy-makers, there is a growing awareness of the value of experimental studies in understanding the effects of social work interventions.

A SOLUTION? THE VOCATION LECTURES BY MAX WEBER

In previous sections, I have referred to imposing traditions: the first one going back to the ideas of social progress, The French revolution, and the genesis of modern social sciences, the second emanating from a reaction to the first tradition and positioning itself on values such as liberation and social justice (among others) while developing radical politics. The third one is much more recent with the advances in effectiveness studies of social work interventions, evidence-based practice (EBP), implementation research, and translational research. All three traditions have substantially impacted, and continue to impact, the direction of the social sciences including social work research as reflection of choices, politics and values. Social work was not an exception in this historical process; rather, for reasons already given, social work has been intimately intertwined with values and politics. More precisely, values and politics set out by all traditions constituted a critical contextual framework for social work research practice and have always been associated with knowledge claims of social work research.

Earlier I raised three questions of pertinence: do social work researchers' values and political preferences influence their research activities; do the social work profession's universal values and political preferences and circumstantial/contextual political preferences impact on its research activities; and if social values and political preferences do influence research, does this necessarily lead to biased research results?

So far, the historical trajectory of the social sciences that has been elaborated on might suggest that answers to the first two questions are affirmative! More precisely, the traditions that we have referred to make explicit the presence of values and politics in social sciences including social work research.

But, what about the third and crucial question: If social values and political preferences influence research, does this necessarily lead to biased research results?

Max Weber, one of the most influential scientists of the modern social sciences, has delivered two long lectures. In these lectures ('Science as a vocation' (Weber, 2004) and 'Politics as a vocation' (Weber, 2004) at the University of Munich) Weber elaborates on: what is the relationship between science and politics and what is the meaning and value of science? Especially, the former question relates to the issue of whether science can be

the basis of human action, and ultimately of politics. Could science be the mechanism by which human actions and politics could be motivated and underwritten?

In the lectures, Weber assertively concluded that politics and science were two separate vocations, almost callings, with their own characteristics. Generation of scientific knowledge was the professional ('vocational') activity and duty of the scientist, while politics was reserved for citizens and their politicians. The duty of the scientist was to produce pertinent policy knowledge, demonstrate scientifically (based on scientific evidence), the estimated consequences of different types of actions or policies in order to reach specific aims, or achieve specific values. The homo politicus, that is, citizens and politicians would take over from there and make decisions. Thus, for Weber, the ultimate purpose of science was to serve politics, but politics was not the activity of scientists. A scientist could be engaged in politics, not as a scientist but only as an ordinary citizen.

Weber's stand was therefore completely different than what Saint-Simon and later Positivists, and Marx and Marxists argued for, as discussed above. For Weber, applying the results of scientific research in the making of policy decision was not the task of the scientist but it was rather the task of the willing, acting person. Again and again, Weber emphasized:

> An empirical science cannot tell anyone what s/he *should* do – but rather what s/he *can* do – and under certain circumstances – what he wishes to do. (Weber, 1949: 54)

In sum, a Weberian response to the question: 'if social values and political preferences influence research, does this necessarily lead to biased research results' should be yes. It certainly will influence research, and research results influenced by values and political preferences will lead to bias. The salvation would be the strict separation of these two activities.

The Weberian position may be seen as idealistic especially in the light of how research results are used to impact the life of people. States, in general, and welfare states in particular, are keen to use research results to change behavior, structures, and processes in societies. Governments operate to pursue policy goals and to promote or prevent social change. For example, the government might wish to change sexual behavior patterns in the population in order to prevent the proliferation of HIV. In this and many other instances, governments commission research, and use research results in policy making. As we have seen, the Weberian position to separate research and politics is one of the several positions one may choose in pursuit of knowledge.

Scientific controversies; the case of multiculturalism in social work

With the growth of scientific knowledge, proliferation of all sorts of social work methods, and the advancement of professional and organizational tools, one growing problem social work practitioners encounter is to understand the scientific credibility of knowledge and technologies. Professionals and the public are compelled to leave it to experts and scientists to understand the rigor and credibility of scientific social work research results. The scientific community, however, is often stricken by scientific controversies.

But scientific controversies are often generated by positions based on different and opposing values or commitment to different and opposing policies. For example, the question of 'Are practitioner intuition and empirical evidence equally valid source of professional knowledge?' has been around for almost a century (Flexner, 2001 [1915]; Allen-Meares, 1994; DeRoos, 1994). Scientific controversies are fueled by lack of or limited scientific evidence: an illustrative example of this is the controversy on the effectiveness of Multi-systemic Therapy (Littell et al., 2005; Littell, 2006; Henggeler et al., 2006).

In my view, scientific controversies illustrate the intimate relationship between (social) sciences and values and politics. The case of multiculturalism in social work is probably one of the most debated, persistent and at times messy scientific controversies. It is therefore warranted to look at values and politics in social work research practice in the context of the controversy on multiculturalism. The issue at stake here is whether the clients from ethnic and cultural minority groups should and could be treated with social work methods and intervention programs as the mainstream, majority population of a given society and setting. Or, seen from the opposite perspective, whether clients of ethnic and cultural minority groups should be treated with ethnically and culturally tailored intervention methods.

This example raises many complex issues. Other differences – including gender – would challenge a 'one size fits all' approach to methods. This is of course at the heart of the politics of the debate about the relationship between research (science) and practice.

Historically, social workers have always worked with ethnic and cultural minorities, especially in Western immigration countries around the world. Minority groups are often under-privileged, underserved, and marginalized because they were ethnically and culturally different from, and not welcomed by, the majority population. It is then assumed by the proponents of ethnically tailored social work intervention methods that ethnically and culturally diverse groups, especially if they also are exposed to hardships of exclusion, have different needs and therefore respond differently to social work services and interventions. This assumption is based on the perception that ethnically diverse groups have ethnically determined values and needs and that these values and needs are fundamentally different than the values and needs of the majority population. Others assume that this is not the case. Opposing values among social work researchers and professionals generate a scientific and political controversy!

Especially in Europe (Williams et al., 1998) and the Unites States (Wilson et al., 2003) the debate on tailored vs. mainstream intervention methods for clients of ethnically and culturally diverse groups has been much debated. There is also a relatively rich flora of handbooks that advocate specific models of tailored service delivery: for example, Cultural Awareness (Green, 1995), the Process Stage Approach in Minority Treatment (Lum, 1996), and Ethnic-Sensitive Social Work Practice (Devore and Schlesinger, 1996). These approaches are generic models of social work practice for ethnic and cultural minority groups, and can be used in multiple intervention areas (e.g. family counseling, behavior contracting, interpersonal skills training, group counseling, and substance abuse treatment). None of these approaches are based on high quality outcomes studies to determine whether they work, and if they work whether they work better than mainstream, universal models of intervention. Rather, these approaches are products of commonsense and assumption of what would work with ethnic minority clients.

Nevertheless, the controversy is there! A detailed account of some of the controversies in this field is aptly laid out in a collection of papers in *Controversial issues in multiculturalism*, edited by de Anda (1997). In this book the controversial questions raised include: whether programs and social delivery services should be culture-specific in their design; whether the therapeutic process is more effective if the client and the social worker are of the same ethnic or cultural group; and, whether ethnic agencies can more effectively serve ethnic clients than mainstream social work agencies.

The question of whether the introduction of multicultural social work practice has resulted in more effective and appropriate services for ethnic minority clients is intensively debated. However, when it comes to available and pertinent scientific evidence, the results may often be surprising. For instance, in the area of foster care for children

(who are assessed by social workers as maltreated or whose parents are not fit to care for them) shows that differences between ethnic groups in terms of outcomes of mainstream programs, if they occur at all, do not necessarily favor majority group clients. Barth and Blackwell (1998) showed that White and Hispanic children in foster care have higher rates of death than their age group in the general population. However, the death rates of African American foster care children are no worse than those for the African American children in the general population. Also, the risk of incarceration following foster care was greater for African American youth than for Hispanic or White youth, even when researchers controlled for gender, age at first placement, and characteristics of placement history (Jonson-Reid and Barth, 2000).

Yet, the controversies in this field go on as exemplified by John Longres' argument:

> Dr. Brown argues that multiculturalism has brought about more effective and appropriate services. I argue that it has not ... In the first place, Dr. Brown is largely talking about appropriateness, not effectiveness. She offers anecdotal evidence to demonstrate that her students, her colleagues, and apparently their clients seem to be satisfied with the counseling they are receiving. This anecdotal evidence hardly stands up to rigorous evaluation and so has to be taken for what it is, the opinion of an educator. Even if her evidence were more rigorously represented, Dr. Brown supplies no evidence of effectiveness: the clients and their helping professionals may feel good, but do the clients behave differently, and have their lives been changed for the better? The evidence suggests that as a collective, people of color are treading water; their lives have not been improved by the growth of a new multicultural sensitivity, however more appropriate it may appear to be. (de Anda, 1997: 18–19)

When Longres suggests that Brown 'offers anecdotal evidence' he is referring to what Brown writes earlier in the debate: 'Common voices of ethnic minority clients who have worked within the context of multicultural practice are:' (de Anda, 1997: 15) and then she quotes three clients, one of whom says: 'I feel like I have been born again!' (1997: 15). Another clients says: 'I feel comfortable and affirmed working in a helping environment that not only sees me, my race, and my ethnic heritage, but understands and appreciates my realities in terms of who I am and how I approach and perceive life' (1997: 15). Brown concludes: 'Clearly in these statements, multicultural work is perceived to be effective and appropriate in that there is a sense of comfort, affirmation, spirituality, and connectedness expressed' (1997: 15).

In the core of this controversy there are differential assumptions as to what constitutes evidence in terms of measuring and understanding the effectiveness of 'multicultural work'. Brown uses three client voices as evidence to suggest that 'multicultural work' is effective, while Longres demands 'rigorous evaluation' (yet what constitutes a 'rigorous evaluation' is not defined by Longres). Differential valuing of what constitutes scientific evidence in the context of what interventions work in social work practice remains an issue of values and related politics, fueling scientific and political controversies.

Scientists make up the major driving force of scientific controversies. When they do so, they do exactly the opposite of the model suggested by Max Weber. When scientists get involved in scientific controversies, they do so not only as scientific experts, but also often or exclusively as political human beings defending or opposing one side over the other. Their activities are based on values, ethics, or politics that they are committed to and advocate.

As described in the beginning of this chapter, because values and politics are intertwined critical contextual features of social work practice, they also become critical features of social work research. Thus, scientific controversies in social work research are an extra burden to the profession of social work. As Hammersley (2003) points out, research often generates complex and fallible results that need to be associated with multiple qualifications. Complex findings can be a problem for end-users such as social workers and social work agency decision-makers since they don't have the time, willingness

and at times training to read and integrate lengthy research accounts. Practitioners often expect research results to be simple, to the point, and self-explanatory bullet points. Complex scientific controversies can thus be very confusing and burdensome.

CONCLUDING REMARKS

In this chapter, social work research practice is treated as a legitimate part of the social sciences in general. Politics, values, and social work research practice simultaneously operate in one and the same social context: values and politics are critical contextual features of social work research as well as being intertwined with knowledge claims associated with social research. I raised the following questions:

1) Do the social work researcher's values and political preferences influence his/her research activities?
2) Does the social work profession's universal values and political preferences and circumstantial/contextual political preferences impact their research activities?
3) If social values and political preferences influence their research, does this necessarily lead to biased research results?

I concluded that values and politics impact social work research practice, but this does not need to lead to biased research results in social work. Recognizing, controlling, and eliminating biases in social work research results are associated with conscientious application of extra-scientific and intra-scientific norms and criteria. Naturally, this position has been challenged and will be challenged. For instance, the evidence-based social work practice movement argues that the least biased evidence may be generated by randomized controlled studies of the effects of social work interventions – a position that is being challenged by questioning the ability of randomized controlled studies.

Furthermore, some social work researchers and social work practitioners may argue that certain values and associated policies should be imperative in social work practice fields such as child welfare, human trafficking, social work with ethnic minority groups.

NOTES

1 Social assistance dynamics in Europe 2002.
2 This and the next section on Saint-Simon are based on my previous work (Soydan, 1993, 1999).

Social Work Research and Ethics

Richard Hugman

INTRODUCTION

Issues of ethics have become a major concern in social research in recent years. Questions about the ethical dimension of research projects now often assume a significance as great as that of defining research aims or methodology. This chapter examines the way in which ethics has grown in importance as a dimension of research, specifically focusing on social work research. The chapter considers ethics as an aspect of research practice, locating it within social relationships, especially as these can be understood as constitutive of power dynamics such as the capacity of some people to affect the lives of many others for better or for worse. So the chapter first examines reasons why we ought to be concerned about ethics in social (work) research. Second, it considers ways in which institutional processes have come to dominate thinking about research ethics and briefly explores the positive as well as the negative implications of this phenomenon. Then the complexities of seeking 'informed consent' are examined as a core issue in research ethics, using an example from practice to illustrate some of the current debates. In the next part of the chapter consideration is given to the challenges presented by recent developments in applied ethics and this is illustrated by a further detailed example. The chapter concludes by re-emphasizing the way in which the ethics of social work research connects research to the wider professional field of social work.

WHY SO MUCH CONCERN ABOUT ETHICS?

All research is about the creation of knowledge, no matter which paradigm informs the aims and methodology. Whether research is qualitative or quantitative, whether it seeks to answer research questions or to test hypotheses, however it builds theory, research is undertaken in order to find new ways to understand the world. Moreover, in applied fields such as social work, research is not done simply for the sake of developing social theory in itself but for the ways in which this might inform changes in practices, institutions, policies and laws, however directly or indirectly. Normally the justification for making such changes would be that they constitute 'improvements' in some way. That is, a primary reason for undertaking research in a field such as social work is the belief that, by asking the right sorts of questions about the rights sorts of evidence, social work and human services can be made better as a consequence of findings that are produced. Therefore, the choice of topics for inquiry and the selection and implementation of appropriate methods for investigation are points at which options of the future shape of social work theory and practice are determined. In this sense research is one of the sites of power to influence the creation and sustaining of practices and institutions and, from that of, social work as a profession.

As Soydan has already argued in Chapter 8, for these reasons research must be recognized as inherently political. It is part of the means by which different groups and individuals within society evaluate and assert their preferences for action. Moreover, as Soydan also recognizes, such preferences are not only formed through the consideration of research findings but these themselves are understood in terms of the values that people hold about the sort of society in which they wish to live. In this way, research is both constituted by and reflects the political and moral values of those who undertake research as well as those who commission, use or form the subjects of that research. Soydan concludes that although 'value-freedom' is not possible (or desirable) this does not invalidate the research effort, because good research practice enables us to move beyond the problem of 'bias' in both the technical and the moral senses. In short, politics and ethics are necessarily two sides of the same coin; to expect one, or either, to be absent from research is the same as expecting any other aspect of society to be exempt from such considerations.

There are several core ethical issues for research that are derived from the liberal individualism of western society. These are: honesty and integrity; utility and futility; the right to know versus the right to withhold information; competing and conflicting interests; the relationship between ends and means in research as a social activity. These issues are central to understanding the specific debates about ethics in research that have developed in recent decades. (Later in the chapter some more recent developments in applied ethics will also be considered as a means of thinking about future possibilities.)

Before we examine these issues, however, it is important to note that there are different underlying approaches competing for our attention in any debate about ethics. The two predominant liberal approaches are:

- the ethics of inherent duty – this is usually termed 'deontology', which holds that something is right because it accords with the duties that follow from the moral nature of humanity (the 'good' here is that of human moral autonomy);
- the ethics of consequences – this is usually termed 'teleology', which holds that something is right because it leads to good outcomes (where the 'good' is the sum of human well-being, whether this is defined according to some objective standard or in terms of each person's preferences).

At times research ethics may also draw on:

- the ethics of character – this is usually termed 'virtue ethics', in which what is right is encountered in the qualities of the person acting (where the 'good' is understood as the flourishing of the human person).

As we will see below, aspects of these different approaches are often combined in the practical ethics of professions, including social work.

Honesty and integrity. Quite simply, these notions together refer to the 'truthfulness' of research, both as process and as product, and of researchers. They focus on the question of whether something is actually the case, as it is stated in the descriptions of a project, the data that are presented, the interpretations placed on data and the conclusions drawn from them. It matters that we can trust the information that is provided in any report of research, such as the descriptions from interviews or observations, or the figures in a table or graph. As with truth-telling in other areas of social life, we tend to proceed on the basis that this does not need constantly to be negotiated (to use a contemporary phrase, it is the 'default position'). In this respect everyday life is an ethical domain and research is an ordinary social activity. Thus, in so far as we may be angered, shocked, dismayed, or perhaps just irritated when we discover that another person has lied to us in other situations, so we will tend to react similarly in a research setting. However, research also carries with it specific obligations concerning truth-telling and trustworthiness that derive from the power of research to impact on people's lives, directly and indirectly. These can only be addressed by making ethics specific to the research context and not simply by relying on 'ordinary' ethics to do the job.

One example of this can be seen in expectations that methods used and the resulting data will be presented in ways that are capable of being checked. In other words, the standards of evidence are necessarily much more stringent in research than in an everyday conversation. In the research setting it is vital to ask if numbers add up, or if inferences are supported by examples of the ideas presented by interviewees. We are required to show explicitly how we reached our conclusions, for ethical as well as methodological reasons.

Another example is the assumption that, unless there is a very strong methodological argument to do otherwise, research involving human subjects should not involve deception (see Butler, 2002: 243). Where deception is used it should not cause distress to subjects and there should be immediate thorough debriefing so that the deception is removed at the earliest possible opportunity (Barnes, 1979: 98; Butler, 2002: 246). It now appears to be standard practice to place the burden of the argument on the researcher who wishes to use deception.

Utility and futility. Ethical questions about the way in which research is conducted also concern the potential for projects to produce findings that can be used (have *utility*) because they can be relied on as sound methodologically. There is a strong line of argument, drawing on a combination of ideas of duty and of consequences, that where a project is based on an unsound methodology then it should be considered *futile* in that it cannot achieve the purpose of research to

advance meaningful knowledge. Futility in this sense is 'bad' for a number of reasons:

1. it wastes the time of human research subjects (an argument from duty);
2. it leads to harmful outcomes in practices that are not soundly supported (a consequence);
3. it wastes resources that might be used more effectively in research that does have usable outcomes (another consequence); and
4. it lowers the credibility of all research (a combination of duty, consequence and virtue).

For Macdonald and Macdonald (1995: 49) only randomized controlled trials provide really robust conclusions about what works and what does not work. This leads them to an ethical defence of the use of this method as the missing ingredient of social work research. Their argument is illustrated with examples of poor practice in the use of statistical inference of selections between possible interpretations of otherwise sound data. They conclude that 'sloppy research' cannot by definition be 'ethical', even if it otherwise meets ethical criteria such as informed consent or confidentiality (1995: 61). Just so, but by implication Macdonald and Macdonald are leaving open the suggestion that other forms of research are ethically not acceptable because they lack the predictive rigour of randomized controlled trials. This seems to take the matter too far. While an ethical defence of the inclusion of randomized controlled trials for the purposes to which they best fit is entirely plausible, to take it to the level of generality across all methods is to make an unwarranted assumption that 'knowing what works' defines all that social work research is needed to achieve. The randomized controlled trial in bio-medical science works by taking the key variable (a treatment) as a closed box. When that variable is a measured dose of a drug, for example, the method is sound. However, in social work this is largely untenable because the comparable variable is an intervention and these are frequently social processes which exist only as they are produced. These are actions where *what* is done cannot be separated from *how* it is done. (Macdonald and Macdonald refer only to administrative decisions as their examples.) So we also need good quality descriptions of what is happening in social work practice, for example, which can only be produced by qualitative studies (Shaw and Gould, 2001d).

Without doing them too much of a disservice, Macdonald and Macdonald (1995) might also be read as containing an argument that 'good' research is that in which ethical and methodological criteria of the good can be brought together. If the assumption that there is only one goal for research is removed, we can see that the issues of utility and futility are actually addressed by ensuring that methods are applied appropriately to the questions asked and the purposes of inquiry. 'Poorly done' research of any kind is ethically unacceptable, on grounds of duty, consequence or virtue, and this ought to be our main concern.

The right to know versus the right to withhold information. Researchers may assume that their interest in a topic or the obvious benefits to be derived from new knowledge in themselves justify the collection and use of information about people (or derived from other living animals). Yet from both the ethics of duty and the ethics of consequences we can see that there are limitations on the extent to which any interest or 'need to know' creates a 'right to know'. This is not to say that the counter argument holds, that seeking information about people in order to create data is 'wrong'. What is being suggested is that the interests of social researchers have to be understood as positioned by their role as researchers; such interests may or may not be capable of being reconciled with the interests of others to provide information about themselves, or the communities or institutions of which they are part, for the purpose of it being turned into data.

From the ethics of duty, it can be argued that because each subject is a human being there are various duties owed to them by researchers. Information about a person and the social relations in which they are situated is a property of the person (both in the sense of being an attribute of their humanity and of being something over which they have ownership). So unless subjects have the capacity to make their own decisions about the conditions under which such properties of themselves may be used to serve purposes that have been established by others, then researchers will be failing to accord the respect to their capacity to be autonomous moral agents that is a primary ethical duty. In short, from this perspective, all people should always be regarded as ethical 'ends-in-themselves' and not be used as the means for others to achieve their own ends.

From the ethics of consequences, the rights of individuals to set limits on the use of information about themselves could be seen as restricted by the actual or intended benefit to be gained from the research for all members of society as a whole. On what basis, it could be asked, should someone claim the right not to be used as the basis for data when research will be to the benefit of the whole society. This is the classic utilitarian idea of what is 'right' being defined in terms of 'the greatest [good] for the greatest number' (Freeman, 2000: 51). At the same time, contemporary arguments for utilitarianism set some boundaries around this, balancing the pursuit of the 'greatest good' with that of the 'least harm', so that the cost to any individuals in having their interests subordinated to those of the society more generally should not be disproportionate (*loc. cit.*). The cost of any sort of compulsion, for example by requiring people to participate in research in order to get a service, is that of undermining basic assumptions about liberal western-style democracy and runs counter to the prevailing international standards (see below).

The way in which these two predominant ethical approaches are reconciled normally is reached through the practice of *informed consent*. That is, each person who participates in research as a subject is expected to agree knowingly to allow various properties of themselves to become constructed as data. Under many institutional processes (see below) this practice is often a major element in ensuring ethical standards in research. Informed consent is grounded in the ideas that agreement to participate as a subject is given explicitly, that agreement can be withdrawn at any time and that it is based on the subject being fully informed about the nature, purposes and procedures of the research. This connects with the principles of honesty and integrity (discussed above) as it assumes that there is a full disclosure of all the factors in which a research subject could reasonably be expected to have an interest when making a decision about participation.

Competing and conflicting interests. In all areas of life we face competing interests. For example, we may want to achieve several goals but only have the resources to pursue one. So we must choose between those goals that we value; where values appear equal but distinct, we may then make decisions based on the contribution they make to other values (such as taking into account the values of other people who are important to us). Such dilemmas may be difficult to resolve, but they do not of themselves present a problem for our ethics.

There are other situations, however, in which our values may conflict (rather than simply compete). In these situations we experience both compelling and repelling values about the same matter. In social work research there are two main ways in which we experience conflicting interests in this way. The first is in working with people with whom it is difficult to have empathy (men who have abused their partners or small children are one such example – see Orme, 2003b). To what extent is the importance of understanding people who act in unacceptable ways reconcilable with a commitment that the researcher might have to the rights and needs of those who have been harmed by them? Orme (2003b) argues convincingly that this is more complex than simply an 'either/ or' choice and concludes that in the case of men who perpetrate domestic violence it is possible to engage in such research without abandoning such commitments to the women

and children against whom such violence has been perpetrated.

The second dilemma is experienced when conflicting values relate not to emotions or commitments but to the requirements of two or more aspects of a role. For example, how can the roles of researcher and social worker be combined? As Shaw and Gould note (2001d: 161), there are difficulties when the researcher is also providing interventions, as service users may give consent in the belief that this will benefit them in getting help. But even where the social worker is in a distinct research role there may still be dilemmas such as how to respond to evidence of actual or potential harm to service users. Responses vary enormously, from those who argue that the prevention of any harm is paramount (a duty based argument) to those who claim that where a harm is remediable it may be better not to intervene in a single instance in order to have a stronger basis for using research to create more systemic change (a consequential argument). Indeed, both arguments can be made in compelling ways, but we should note that the question of whether harm can be judged to be 'remediable' is vital here.

The relationship between means and ends. The fifth aspect of ethics that is crucial for social work research is that of the appropriateness of the relationship between the methods and processes (means) and the goals (ends) of any project. In many ways this is a linking principle, which ties together the other issues that have already been discussed. For each issue it has been suggested that for the goals of research, that is the objectives of advancing knowledge, improving services, or whatever, to be morally credible then there is a corresponding moral requirement on researchers to act with honesty and integrity, to use methods that can produce plausible and useful outcomes and to involve research subjects only on the basis of informed consent.

The concern with these principles across all areas of research involving human subjects has been heavily influenced by biomedical ethics. The origins of this lie in the involvement of medical researchers in Nazi atrocities in the mid-twentieth century and the post-war response (Nuremberg Code, 1949). From this came the Declaration of Helsinki (WMA, 1964), in which researchers committed themselves to high standards of moral conduct, based on notions of human rights and the corresponding responsibilities of researchers to put such rights before their interests to extend knowledge. The most influential development of bio-medical research ethics that follows from the Helsinki Declaration is widely regarded as that of Beauchamp and Childress (2001), in their synthesis of duties, consequences and virtues into the principles of autonomy, beneficence, non-maleficence and justice. (I have discussed this approach in more detail elsewhere, see Hugman, 2005: 10.) In this form bio-medical ethics has had enormous impact in other disciplines, especially where these concern questions of health and human well-being (for example, in the context of social work research, see Butler, 2002). However, it can be argued that as a result social sciences have been caught up in an approach derived from research that has a different epistemological basis (Redwood and Todres, 2006; Hardwick and Hardwick, 2007: 304).

Yet, although there is some merit in this criticism, it can also be said that social research bears similarly important responsibilities to those of medicine. To start from Nuremberg and Helsinki, it is the case that social workers, along with nurses, teachers, clergy and other professionals, were also implicated in the atrocities of central Europe in the 1930s and 1940s. *All* research is located in power relations and so has capacities to be used in various ways. We may agree that there is a particular responsibility placed on researchers in a field such as medicine arising from the potential, however slight, for someone to be killed or physically harmed through being a research subject. But the difference between this and the harms, physical, social, psychological or moral, which can be perpetrated by other forms of research, is a matter of degree and not substance. Although we may wish to believe that

decent people do not need to be told how to act, there is ample historical evidence that some public yardstick is useful if any profession or discipline is not simply to be an unaccountable community of self-interest (cf. Barnes, 1979: 163).

The importance of all these issues for social work research is that social work as a profession tends to be concerned with people who are disadvantaged, marginalized, excluded or otherwise not in positions where they can routinely exercise a wide range of choices in dealing with powerful social institutions. Conversely, social workers, including social work researchers, tend to be in positions in which they can exercise power in many respects, as individuals and as members of organizations. Although social workers may at times be conscious of constraints on their power, through organizational policies and procedures for example, this imbalance in social power as the potential to make choices and exercise one's will in the world is always present in comparison to service users, who (necessarily) are the subjects of social work research. Broader social work values, as expressed in codes of ethics (see, for example: NASW, 1999; AASW, 2002; BASW, 2002), emphasize a core professional commitment to serving the community and practice that enables people to be empowered. For social work research to have integrity it ought to be undertaken in a way that is congruent with this goal (Butler, 2002). Ethics in research that enables social work to promote the human agency of service users therefore is called for by the moral claims the profession itself makes. So practices that embody respect for the moral autonomy of subjects in research, such as honesty, competence, informed consent and so on can inform 'good' research in social work.

ETHICS AS GOVERNANCE

The Helsinki Declaration (WMA, 1964: §13) enshrines the notion that all research involving human subjects should be accountable through a formal process of ethical review. It is quite specific, detailing that:

- such committees should have the right to be provided with relevant information, including the topic and its justification, the methodology (including access to subjects), sources of funding and any conflicts of interest;
- committees also should have right to monitor the process and progress of a project; and
- most of all, committees should be one key means by which researchers are held to account ethically.

Since the mid-1960s such committees have become routinized, especially but not solely in 'western' countries. Where such committees have become the norm it is now the case that it is not only medical and health research, but all research involving human subjects which is scrutinized in this way. To examine the role of committees as a vehicle for ethical oversight of research, we will look briefly at the formal requirements in three countries: the USA; the UK and Australia (HSS, 2004; DH, 2005; ESRC, 2005b; NHMRC/ARC/AVCC, 2007).

First, we can note that there is very widespread use of such committees. While in the early stages of responding to the Helsinki Declaration such measures were almost entirely directed towards bio-medical research, they rapidly developed to include concerns with the social sciences and other areas that impact directly on social work (cf. Barnes, 1979). It is now highly unlikely that any social work research would not be subject to some type of institutional process of accountability.

Second, the rules which inform these ethics review procedures are in each of these countries established by government or para-governmental organizations. Where researchers depend on government bodies as sources of funding or for access to participant groups, this gives enormous power to these organizations to enforce the rules. Quite simply, if a project is not given 'ethical clearance' then it will not be given funds or access.

Third, there is a high degree of conformity with the Helsinki Declaration. In each of these countries, the regulations not only require that committees are established, but they specify the composition of such bodies and the way in which they may proceed. Common features include:

- broadly similar accounts of what researchers are required to do to meet their ethical obligations, including respect for moral autonomy (through informed consent and confidentiality), minimization of risk, using sound research design and ensuring those undertaking research are competent to do so;
- both expert and lay membership in order to balance the necessary depth of knowledge about research procedures with an 'ordinary' perspective on what is acceptable in the wider community;
- continuing accountability, that is throughout a project and not only at the point of commencement, with expectations that changes will be reported and reconsidered;
- independent (third party) points of complaint, grievance or appeal by participants or anyone not immediately part of the project;
- an expectation that both individual researchers and their employing agencies are ethically accountable for a project; and
- measures to deal with specific issues, such as a perceived need to expedite ethical clearance and 'special' categories of methodological issues.

Having already dealt with some of these points above, we will focus here on two matters that have implications for social work research: the institutionalization of ethics, and the notion of 'special' categories of research for ethical consideration.

Challenges are frequently posed to the idea of ethics as an appropriate object for institutional or bureaucratic processes (Barnes, 1979; Redwood and Todres, 2006; Hardwick and Hardwick, 2007). Put simply, such arrangements are questioned on the grounds that ethics is a matter of personal judgement and responsibility. Our moral values, it is asserted, cannot be subject to such direction. It is not argued that researchers should not be accountable, but that this should be a matter between the researcher and the participants in a project. To do otherwise is not a matter of ethics but of law, policy, bureaucratic rules or even of gross interference and unwarranted control of some researchers by others ('ethics' as a vehicle for epistemological and political struggles).

The counter argument is that such a position makes assumptions about human agency that are untenable. Social research takes place within a network of relationships, in which funders and gatekeepers have an interest because they too, whether as individuals or as organizations, bear great responsibilities for the conduct and outcomes of research. Where a researcher is an entirely free agent, for example not employed by a service agency or a university and not in receipt of funds from any other source, then perhaps it might be tenable to claim that ethics is a matter solely between that person and research participants. However, it is highly unlikely that this will be the case in social work research. So at best this argument is a misunderstanding of what is being implied and at worst it seems disingenuous (perhaps almost a claim not to have to be accountable). If accountability to service users is at the heart of such criticisms that is another matter and one to which we will return below.

The other frequent problem for many researchers is the place of qualitative research in research ethics processes (Mason, 1996; Shaw and Gould, 2001d; Redwood and Todres, 2006)[1]. The most important difference between the two broad paradigms is the way in which for qualitative studies it is methodologically inappropriate for too much to be specified in advance while for quantitative studies as much as possible must be so specified. The former is seeking an open-ended inquiry, in which the emerging data can guide further data collection as well as analysis; the latter seeks the maximum possible control over variables so that the relationship between them can be stated clearly. It is because the specification of all possible eventualities is precluded in qualitative methodologies that formal institutional ethics review procedures

as often currently constructed may be experienced as overly constrictive, even where they do not simply rule out such methodologies on grounds of futility (see above). In contrast, the very prescriptive nature of quantitative techniques make them entirely congruent with the expectation that ethical aspects (such as mechanisms for informed consent or exactly what questions are to be asked) can be defined in advance of any contact with research subjects/participants.

The solution to the long-standing concerns of qualitative researchers that their work is often inappropriately judged (and found wanting) has been to recognize such distinctive aspects. In the major guidelines that establish institutional ethics processes *for universities* in the UK (ESRC, 2005b: §4.2.2.2) and Australia (NHMRC/ARC/AVCC, 2007: Ch.14) there are sections specific to qualitative research. These state particular requirements to take account of the ways qualitative research differs from other types of research. (The Australian document also contains a brief but very clear description of qualitative methodology that deals with possible inappropriate charges of futility.) Recent recommendations in the UK seek to extend this type of broader thinking to research that does not come under the auspices of universities (Pahl, 2007).

Exemplar 1: Practical ethics in mental health research

The implications of these arguments can be illustrated by considering some of the complexities in research in social care. The present author has undertaken a number of such studies and this chapter will draw on one of them, a participant observation study of a community-based mental health rehabilitation service located in the north of England (Hugman, 1992).[2]

The use of ethnographic methods in this context presented several challenges. Although initial ethical clearance was obtained through the agency that was responsible for the service, this was based on gaining informed consent from each member of staff and service user. The process was that presentations about the project were made separately to service users and staff in groups following which individual responses were invited through a third party in the agency. All members of staff gave consent, as did all but one of the service users. The quandary was that the one person who declined to give consent was resident in the service's core unit. There were two crucial elements to the dilemma created by this response. The first was that the person concerned was in an active phase of a severe mental health problem. There was a tangible risk that the presence of the researcher might prove too intrusive. As the person was using the service in order for mental health needs to be met and not to take part in a research project it was agreed by the agency, the service staff and the researcher that this person's needs were paramount. The second element was that it would not be possible to undertake the research without long periods of participant observation in the core unit. The dilemma was resolved through informal negotiations involving a friend of the service user and a member of staff as third party channels of communication, in which it was agreed that no observations would be recorded in any situation where this service user was present and that the researcher would withdraw from such situations. The project then began in this way and after two months the service user, whose mental health had improved, asked to be included and on occasions directly provided information to the researcher in one-to-one conversations.

From this example I want to draw out three main points about practical ethics in social work research. First, 'informed consent' should be seen as a process as much as it is an event. That is, simply having obtained an initial agreement is not a sufficient basis to conclude that all the responsibilities of the researcher have been discharged. Second, formal processes for gaining informed consent may not always be appropriate. In this instance briefing meetings followed by the provision of consent recorded by a third party was not the way in which consent was finally given by one participant, yet the principles both of autonomy and of not causing harm were maintained and could be accounted for.

Not only should it be the case that a participant can refuse consent or withdraw it at any point but we can also observe that in work that involves vulnerable people who experience disadvantage and marginalization in their lives there can be said to be a duty on the part of researchers actively to ensure that informed consent is ongoing. One way of doing this is by reminding participants in whatever ways appropriate that they are in the role of research subject and this was necessarily repeatedly in this study. However, it seems difficult to be sure that the dynamics of relationships between staff and service users, or between staff and their managers, do not create an implicit 'compulsion' to give consent. Similarly, the researcher's identity as a social worker (disclosed in response to questioning in both service user and staff group briefings) might also have encouraged people to greater disclosure (see Shaw and Gould, 2001d: 161). In response, reflexive checking that pays attention to such ethical questions is part of good qualitative methodology and in this sense ethics has to be a continual practice not simply a set of procedures.

How different can research ethics be?

While the above example is a single instance, it portrays issues that continue to be discussed widely among social researchers. For example, Redwood (writing as a health researcher) emphasizes the value of qualitative research in terms of the 'possibility of practitioner-led inquiry and the development of practitioners' sensitivities of [sic] the realities of patients' and clients' lives' (in Redwood and Todres, 2006: §§10–11). This is clearly relevant for social work research.[3] The solution she proposes is to go beyond notions of harm and consent to ideas of ethics as 'caring for'. We are shifted into the realm of relational ethics. Such an argument appears to point to the 'ethics of care' as an alternative model for research. But what would such a model look like? How different can research ethics be?

The 'ethics of care' is grounded in feminist theory (for example, see: Tronto, 1993; Sevenhuijsen, 1998). Its basic premises are that traditional liberal ethics, whether of duties, consequences or virtues, portrays each person as if they were an isolated individual. As a result rights and responsibilities come to be understood in the abstract, as disembodied principles. In contrast the 'ethics of care' asserts that what is 'good' is to be found in the way that relationships are nurtured and that others are cared for. The core principles of the ethics of care, which are attentiveness, responsiveness, responsibility and competence (Tronto, 1993: 127–36), must be encountered in concrete, lived human relationships. These are not matters that can be dealt with simply by following a procedure, such as getting research subjects to sign a form to record informed consent, but must be realized throughout the interactions between the researcher and each participant continually throughout a research project.

Although this approach to ethics has not been widely addressed in depth within social work (for notable exceptions see Orme, 2001: Parton, 2003; and Banks, 2006) it appears to have much to offer, especially in the detail of relationships between practitioners and service users (Hugman, 2005). However, while an ethics of care may be enormously enriching to social work practice, where relationships may develop over time, it may be less easy to see how it can be applied in all research situations. Qualitative research methodologies could be said to reproduce the characteristics of social work practice, especially in long-term studies where ongoing working relationships develop, but in quantitative approaches,

including surveys and secondary analysis, the relevance of an ethics of care may be less immediately obvious. The problem is that the ethics of care is derived from thinking about the morality of close relationships, whereas in the context of professional work, including research, at least a degree of social distance remains an inherent aspect of relationships (for a more extended discussion of this issue, see Hugman, 2005: 75–81). This sense of social distance is more pronounced in positivistic methods.

Yet, ironically, it is for exactly this reason that we might consider that in long-term participant observation, such as that discussed above, the researcher has obligations continually to remind participants of her or his identity as a researcher, for example on grounds of honesty and integrity so that they do not come to think of the researcher as a co-worker or just as a friend (Hugman, 1992). In other words, it re-introduces an element of social distance that is sufficient to 'care for' participants in the sense intended by Tronto (1993) or Sevenhuijsen (1998), precisely because of the way in which they ground abstract notions of honesty and integrity in the specific relationship of *this* research situation involving *these* people. At the same time, the practice of reminding participants about the research relationship pursues a good outcome, in that the participants are less likely to be surprised later in discovering that what was said has been recorded and used as data; it also fulfils the duty that the researcher has to the moral standing of participants. As both Tronto and Sevenhuijsen argue, an ethics of care also attends to questions of rights and justice, but does so in the social context of everyday life, not in the abstract.

So, we are moving towards the idea that if we consider the ethics of care not as an either/ or alternative to the more traditional, abstract liberal ethics but as an addition to our ethical vocabulary then it might indeed have something practical to offer social work research. If this is so, then in turn it leads us to a further question: how can different ethical approaches be reconciled when they appear to present competing arguments about what is right/good?

Banks summarizes this issue when she observes that the various approaches to ethics each have something to contribute overall 'but none seems complete on its own' (2006: 66). A solution to this challenge is offered by the idea of 'moral pluralism'. This is a notion that seeks to find an alternative to the either/or choice between assertions that there is one over-arching ethical approach that must be found and which would subordinate all other approaches (one best way of looking at all moral issues) or that there is no way to distinguish between approaches, and ethics is simply a matter of localized preference (anything goes). In moral pluralism it is recognized that in any situation there may be many competing values, each of which must be considered in deciding how to act. In this sense, moral pluralism is a method of practical ethics rather than a position, in which the various factors of any given situation are weighed in terms of duties (including rights and responsibilities), utilitarian objectives, ideals (which would include religious values), caring for relationships, personal obligations and commitments (which would include ideas of virtue) (Banks, 2006: 67). To this we might also add the ethical implications of emotions, such as empathy and compassion (Hugman, 2005: Ch. 4).

In the example above we considered a situation in which it appears that the requirements of several of these approaches were able to be satisfied at the same time. However, moral pluralism also addresses those situations in which we have to choose between values that cannot be satisfied simultaneously. In the research context this can be effectively illustrated by returning to the differences between qualitative and quantitative methodologies, by briefly examining the implications of the logic that each follows. We noted previously that a major difference between qualitative and quantitative methods is that in the former as little as possible and in the latter as much as possible ought to be

specified prior to obtaining data. So ethical dialogue based on moral pluralism ought to allow us, for example, to give greater weight to the ways in which a researcher might deal with ethical issues as they arise during the course of an open-ended study and greater weight to formal procedures specified in advance in projects where this is appropriate.

Does moral pluralism therefore lead to the conclusion that an ethics of care is necessary for qualitative research while abstract, impersonal ethics is appropriate for quantitative studies? In response to this question I want to look briefly at four reasons why such a conclusion is too simplistic and that moral pluralism needs to be more carefully understood if it is to benefit ethics in social work research.

First, other ethical matters also affect qualitative research. As Todres notes (in Redwood and Todres, 2006: §10) questions of duty and consequences still are important. When we consider the ethics of care we are adding an additional layer of complexity to an already complex situation rather than removing all the questions raised by more abstract approaches (cf. Mason, 1996: 31). Moral pluralism does not let qualitative methodologies off the ethical hook of needing to attend to notions of how we might understand what is good/right using ideas such as rights and responsibilities, justice and so on (compare with Tronto, 1993 or Sevenhuijsen, 1998). Moreover, some aspects of ethics in qualitative research can be specified prior to obtaining data, such as how research participants are to be recruited to a study; at this stage of a project an institutional ethics review can reasonably require researchers to be able to say how they will act. Indeed, the institutional processes require qualitative researchers to attend to the same broad underlying principles as other forms of research, even when there are special terms to ensure such research is appropriately evaluated (for example, in: ESRC, 2005b; NHMRC/ARC/AVCC, 2007).

Second, other ethical matters also affect quantitative research. In particular, the ethics of care is not confined to qualitative studies but can inform practice in positivistic research, especially in a field such as social work where topics frequently focus on matters of disadvantage, marginalization, exclusion and so on. It can be argued that there is as much a need to be attentive, responsive, responsible and competent in dealing with questionnaire material or the conduct of an experiment as there is in qualitative studies. Providing clear explanations and safeguarding people's identities are examples of this.

Third, as noted above, it is implausible to see any individual researcher as a free-floating agent. Even in the most unstructured and open-ended inquiry the researcher remains part of one or more professional communities (of social work, of researchers and so on) and such relationships are intermeshed rather than discrete. While the researcher is responsible for her or his own views and actions, we cannot practically restrict to which of our overlapping communities we will allow ourselves to be accountable. So, while I may wish to see the service users who participate with me in a project as the primary group to whom I owe such a responsibility, my employing agency (and all social work researchers have an employer of some sort) will have a reasonable expectation that I am also accountable to them. This problem is only partly removed when service users are my employer. But even then what I do as a researcher has implications for other researchers, for others in the wider society and for future service users who may be affected by the impact of my findings (for a more extended discussion of this latter notion see Hugman, 2005: Ch. 6).[4]

Fourth, although as a researcher I may develop close relationships with participants, even in action research or a co-participation model I am there as a researcher and so my interests may not be identical to others with whom I am interacting. While I can conclude that I should be attentive and responsible to the group, it does not seem reasonable that I should be required to give up my own rights,

interests and so on, any more than I should be required to do so if employed by a large bureaucracy. Moral pluralism provides a way of thinking about the task of balancing competing values in such a situation but by definition it does not give a single model from which to work; nor does it privilege individual researchers as the sole arbiters of their own ethical standards.

In summary, the addition of approaches such as the ethics of care to the vocabulary of social work research will enrich our moral conversation. However, it does not erase the importance of considering other approaches, nor does it remove the difficult task of making judgements about the balance of the (potentially) competing moral claims of different groups who are part of the research field. Having presented some of the issues in rethinking research ethics, the chapter will now look briefly at a further concrete example in which some of these ideas are illustrated.

Exemplar 2: Participatory research with refugee women

Research concerning refugees is vital as the number of refugees continues to rise rapidly. A group of researchers in this field[5] have recently argued that, although often well-intentioned, many refugee studies have caused harms that could have been anticipated but were not considered (Mackenzie et al., 2007). Particular problems are encountered by refugee women, whose position is especially vulnerable because the implications of being refugees are compounded by the social realities for them as women (Pittaway et al., 2007). The impacts of research vary from the use of women as sources of data, including photographic images, in ways that degrade women's sense of self-worth and/or raise expectations about benefits that might follow, through to exposing women to heightened risk of rape and other forms of violence by the way in which information is not well-handled. These studies voice similar criticisms of research ethics review processes to those already discussed, in particular limitations on the extent to which the ethical issues of qualitative methods are accurately grasped by those whose background is in other methodologies, but they also note the way in which some qualitative researchers act inappropriately in terms of principles such as respect, autonomy, honesty, integrity and justice (Mackenzie et al., 2007: 300).

In response, the development of an action research model in which refugee women are involved as co-researchers is advocated. The background to this research consciously involves an ethical dimension to the research design, which is in itself grounded in a collaborative process. Core principles, such as integrity, respect or justice, are not questioned: what is being sought is to apply these skilfully in the context of working with refugee women. In short, such research, it is argued, should go 'beyond harm minimization' to actively promoting benefits for participants and refugee communities more widely (Mackenzie et al., 2007: 301). In response, this research group suggests a form of collaborative research based on certain key elements:

- dialogue with local communities and involving refugees themselves as co-researchers as much as possible in all aspects of a research project;
- an ongoing (iterative) process of informed consent through negotiation involving all parties in the research (compare with the example from the mental health service discussed above);
- a relational understanding of autonomy, which seeks to affirm the agency and resilience of participants but at the same time respond appropriately to the way their capacities for this are affected by experiences of trauma (compare with the 'ethics of care' discussed previously);
- seeking to promote reciprocity by focusing on benefits to participants arising from their participation; and
- reinforcing the connections between sound methodology and advocacy resulting from research

outcomes (as opposed to seeing the goal of advocacy as introducing 'bias').

There are similarities here with arguments from the service user movements, particularly in the UK (Beresford, 2000). What is significant in this work is the way in which questions of politics and epistemology are integrated with research ethics. This is done in such a way that the argument can be used to inform future debates not only within social work, but more widely in other social science research and in institutional ethics processes. It builds on more established principles by grounding them in the concrete situations of refugee women rather than attempting to 'apply' them from an external standpoint. Of particular interest, I suggest, is the way in which the notion of 'relational autonomy' is congruent with an ethics of care, connecting that with principles of respect, justice and so on. Similar approaches have been developed in recent years to inform the governance of research with Aboriginal Australians and Maori in New Zealand/Aotearoa (for example, see: NHMRC, 2003; Massey University, 2006).[6]

ACCOUNTABILITY AND INTEGRITY IN SOCIAL WORK RESEARCH

In this discussion, one thing has been absent so far, namely, a consideration of the way in which the professional ethics of social work itself addresses research. In fact, there appears to be a wide consensus among professional associations regarding ethics in social work research. Taking the codes of ethics from Australia, the UK and the USA as examples, we can see that many of the ideas discussed in this chapter are present in the profession's ethical codes (NASW, 1999; AASW, 2002; BASW, 2002; also see Butler, 2002).

The areas of broad consensus include attention to the moral autonomy of participants (for example, through the use of informed consent and the right to withdraw consent, or through ensuring anonymity, privacy and confidentiality for participants), honesty and integrity (for example, by ensuring accuracy in reporting findings, or by submission of proposals to ethical review committees where required) and consideration of the impact of research on the relationships between service users and social workers (for example, taking steps to avoid conflicts of interest and to maintain appropriate relationships). In summary, we can observe that the ethical statements of the profession are congruent with the intent of the prevailing norms of social research.

So, although there are some textual differences these codes can be regarded broadly as similar. The British code (BASW, 2002) contains an exception to this, in that it includes statements about the utility and intent of social work research, specifying that social work research ought to:

- be based on the perspectives and lived experience of the research subject except where this is not appropriate;
- seek to ensure that [social work research] contributes to empowering service users, to promoting their welfare and to improving their access to economic and social resources; and
- seek to work together with disempowered groups, individuals and communities to devise, articulate and achieve research agendas which respect fundamental human rights and aim to towards social justice (BASW, 2002: §4.4.4(b)).

In other words, social work research ought always to support the wider goals of social work, to promote well-being, human rights and social justice (IFSW/IASSW, 2001).

The section on research in the UK code is based very closely on the work of Butler (2002). Butler reviews contemporary debates about ethics in social work as his starting point and concludes by making a very strong statement that any ethical statement is 'provisional' (2002: 243) in that it must be subject to constant testing, debate and reconsideration by all morally engaged members of the profession. He also takes as the only plausible basis for such a code the set of four core principles derived from the bio-medical field that are discussed elsewhere in this chapter

(see above). Such a code of ethics is, therefore, one that embraces a pluralist approach of specifying core values from diverse (and at times competing) approaches. All the codes discussed here share this position. At the same time, Butler acknowledges that ethics is not simply a matter of a framework or rules but also of using these as the *minimum* statement of values (cf. Mason, 1996: 31). Not only is it possible for national or regional emphases to be addressed, but, beyond this, it is still necessary for each social work researcher to engage actively as a 'moral practitioner' (cf. Husband, 1995). Taking each national code of ethics as a basic minimum in this way then opens up the potential to develop our thinking further about the complexity of ethical responsibilities, using an ethics of care and other ideas that help us to grasp the relational dimensions of research in practice.

CONCLUSION

This chapter began by recognizing the connection between ethics and politics (understood as power relations, at both the personal and structural levels). From this, the importance of ethics in research was explained in terms of responsibility and accountability for all aspects of how research is undertaken. The underlying argument has been informed by the view that while the principles derived from traditional, liberal ethics are necessary they are not sufficient to inform research in social work. What is also required is a more skilful, relational approach that is able to ground principles such as respect, integrity and justice in the concrete social relationships of actual research. With a pluralist framework, the ethics of care adds to rather than replacing other sets of ideas.

Arguments that privilege the voices of participants, especially when these are service users from disadvantaged, marginalized or excluded social groups, make a particular political claim about research relationships. It has been suggested here that shifting in this

direction is ethically desirable and, by implication, methodologically plausible. Research
in social work that does not potentially benefit service users in some way, however indirectly, does not accord with the profession's
ethics more generally. However, while in the
past some researchers may have paid insufficient attention to the ethical claims of participants, it should also be recognized that this
imbalance cannot be redressed by denying
the appropriate ethical claims of institutions,
the profession or the wider community of
researchers. What has been outlined here
enables these more complex implications to
be grasped. The idea of ethics as process still
leaves open the relevance of ethics as an
event (institutional approval) and the value of
ideas such as informed consent. Yet by
making ethics procedures within institutions
more subtle and responsive to the nuances of
research that is ethically concerned with
those who are affected by it will not only
benefit service users and social work, but also
social science more broadly as well as the
wider community.

ACKNOWLEDGEMENTS

I would like to thank Lesley Hughes and
Alexandra Hugman for their perceptive comments on an original draft of this chapter.
Mark Lymbery, Joan Orme, Eileen Pittaway
and Wheturangi Walsh-Tapiata provided
helpful information on crucial points.

NOTES

1   This point seems to be a major factor in the
recent debates in the UK about the impact of the
Department of Health ethics framework (DH, 2005)
on social work research (Hardwick and Hardwick,
2007). These debates have led to a review that, at
the time of writing, is approaching the point of resolution based largely on consideration of the various
issues discussed in this chapter (Pahl, 2007).

2   This example is offered not to suggest that it
provides the definitive model, but rather because it
reveals ways in which challenges are encountered in
practice. In addition, by using my own practice I am
intending to 'take responsibility', in keeping with the
ethical arguments that I make in this chapter. I am
adopting an approach of providing a 'natural history'
of these processes following the style developed,
inter alia, by Bell and Encel (1978).

3   This is not to suggest that positivistic research
has no place in social work. Clearly, hypothesis testing
and quantitative surveys are part of the range of useful
methodologies. The point is that post-positivistic techniques are also very important as part of this range of
methodologies, perhaps more so in a profession such
as social work than they might be in some other professions (cf. Hardwick and Hardwick, 2007).

4   In this context Todres' criticism of institutions
as 'officious gatekeepers' (in Redwood and Todres,
2006: §22) seems curiously at odds with the contextualization of ethics implied in a relational approach.

5   This group is based primarily between the
Centre for Refugee Research at the University of
New South Wales (Australia) and the Information
Centre on Asylum and Refugees at the City University
of London (UK). On the basis of ethical disclosure,
it should be noted that the present author has at
the time of writing (2007) been invited to act as a
co-researcher with associated projects, specifically to
act as an 'internal ethical auditor' to the developing
process, but has had no role in the work reported
here.

6   This point raises the question of approaches to
ethics in non-Western contexts. While ethics in
research globally tends to be dominated by the
Declaration of Helsinki (WMA, 1964), there are
important issues about how the principles discussed
in this chapter can be achieved in diverse cultural
settings (cf. Barnes, 1979). This requires further
detailed work, but the example chosen here has
been selected partly because it represents cross-
cultural research practice. Research that is accepted
as ethically sound cross-culturally is likely to be seen
as such also in culturally specific contexts.

From Social Work Practice to Social Work Research: An Emergent Approach to a Basic Problem

Steve Trevillion

INTRODUCTION

The relationship between research and the practice contexts in which it takes place is one of the most important and yet poorly understood issues facing social work researchers. In particular, we seem to know very little about the ways in which practice influences research. Why has so little progress been made? This is particularly puzzling because there are many different questions that could be asked. For example:

- How have the needs of particular service user or client groups helped to shape research questions, research ethics and research processes?
- How do organisational and research typologies relate to one another – are some methods more suited to exploring some practice organisations than others?
- How do the structural and historical characteristics and traditions of particular social welfare sectors influence research?
- How do research sponsors gather intelligence about practice in order to formulate their funding priorities?

Why is it that questions like these have not been asked? Is it because they do not translate well into an international context?

Different countries define service user or client groups in different ways. Different 'welfare regimes' have generated different kinds of service systems embedded in different ethical and legal codes, making it very difficult to create a single organizational typology. It is also very difficult to generalize about social welfare sectors; for example the 'voluntary sector', may be significant in some countries, but almost completely absent in others.[1] Finally, questions about the funding of research are not easy to pursue in an international context where funding regimes vary from country to country.

But, if the problem were solely one of comparison then one might expect to find a range of single country studies looking at the ways in which practice contexts influence research. Yet these too are largely conspicuous by their absence. Perhaps the problem is more fundamental and we simply do not know how to frame meaningful questions about the way that practice influences, shapes or drives research?

This chapter aims to supply the basic intellectual scaffolding that is currently missing and its starting point is the idea that it is possible (even necessary) to conceive of research about practice as an outcome of what goes on in the practice domain. The peculiarities of this argument are obvious. Instead of looking at practice through the prism of research (asking familiar questions about the application of research findings to practice issues and problems), the reader is asked to suspend disbelief and look at research through the prism of practice (cf. Chapter 1). This *emergent*[2] approach to research may be counterintuitive, but it enables practice–research relationships to be analysed in different contexts and at different levels of complexity – horizontally (across a range of international examples) and vertically (using examples from the history of social work).

The extent to which practitioners draw on research and the uses researchers make of evidence drawn from practice are important questions. However, this chapter is not a contribution to the debate about 'evidence-based practice'. The focus here is on practice as a shaper and driver of the research enterprise. This means that many examples of high-quality, evidence-based research are excluded because they cannot be classified as *emergent research*.

TOWARDS SOME FOUNDATIONAL QUESTIONS

There is now a large and growing literature on the subject of how social work research *should* be influenced by practice and/or the way in which research *should* contribute to practice (e.g. Parton, 2000; Sheppard et al., 2000). This forms part of a wider literature that concerns itself with what sets social work research apart from the research traditions of other disciplines – a set of issues that remains unresolved in spite of the intensity of the debate (Thyer, 2002).

In contrast, there have been relatively few attempts to straightforwardly describe the nature of the practice–research relationship. One of the most interesting contributions to this relatively small descriptive literature has been the suggestion that the relationship between research, practice and theory is an 'open triangle' where no element is privileged at the expense of another (Powell, 2002: 30). This model appears to offer a way out of the tensions between theory, research and practice that have bedevilled the social work discipline from its inception. It also feels right. Social workers instinctively identify themselves with the democratic and inclusive values that underpin it. However, it does not sit very comfortably with what is known about the politics of research. This suggests that the theory–practice–research relationship is often characterised by a high level of tension and conflict in contrast to the egalitarian assumptions lying behind the 'open triangle' hypothesis.

Lyons has noted that social work, like other research areas linked to professional activity, has an active practitioner community that helps to set the research agenda. She has also shown that tensions between 'the field' and 'the academy' appear to be rife in many countries, including Sweden, Australia and the UK (Lyons, 2000: 438). We also know that the pedagogic practices of social work continue to divide research, theory and practice from one another (Trevillion, 2007).

Overall, while social work may aspire to ideal knowledge production conditions the real world picture is both more complex and more conflict-ridden. Demonstrating that research theory and practice can all have an influence on one another does not take us very far if what we want to know is how and in what ways practice contexts help to shape the research enterprise. It does not help us to understand the emergent characteristics of social work research.

We know much more about how research influences practice than how practice influences research. Thanks to the evidence-based practice movement practice is now more likely to be influenced by research than it was in the past,[3] but we still know very little about how practice influences (shapes and develops) either specific research projects and programmes or wider research preoccupations and priorities.

In order to establish our bearings in this relatively unknown territory we need to find answers to five basic or *foundational* questions. They are, as follows:

1. Practice is to some extent shaped by changes in government policy and a considerable amount of research is paid for by national governments with the explicit purpose of helping to achieve policy-driven objectives. In this situation, can we distinguish between policy-driven and practice-driven research, and if so how?
2. Practice is increasingly interprofessional and multi-disciplinary. What does it mean to talk about a specifically social work practice domain in an increasingly interprofessional and multi-disciplinary context?
3. The practice context may look very different to practitioners, service users, carers and managers. Is there a way of describing the influence of practice on research that does justice to all these different perspectives?
4. In order to examine the influence of the practice context on research there is a need to model the relationship between the two. How do we go about building a model based on the idea that research is an emergent property of practice?
5. Practice means different things at different levels of social reality. How do we incorporate the concept of 'different levels of practice' in our emergent model?

The first three questions focus on problems of definition; questions four and five focus on the substantive issues. The argument is not that these are the only questions that can be asked, but that we need to find at least some answers to them before we can ask others in a meaningful way. The following sections look at each of these foundational questions in turn and try to supply some preliminary answers.

DEFINING THE PRACTICE DOMAIN: THE PROBLEM OF POLICY

A considerable amount of research could be described as 'policy-driven'. Projects of this kind tend to focus on what Hudson has described as 'the implementation gap' (Hudson, 2007: 34) or the gap between government intentions and service outcomes. In effect this type of research defines 'practice' as little more than an extension of the policy domain. Many of the links between policy formation, policy implementation and policy implementation research are well documented. In comparison, the influence of the practice domain on research can seem diffuse and difficult to pin down.

There is a sense in which all social domains are connected with one another (Layder, 1997) and so looking for any absolute boundary between policy and practice is probably foolish. However, it would be equally foolish to conclude that there is no difference between the policy and practice domains.

The practice domain can be provisionally defined as *the product of all the social interactions associated with the work of social workers, including the delivery of services to service users/clients and interactions with other professionals*. This domain is clearly influenced by other domains (not just the policy domain but also the legal and economic domains). However, it retains its own characteristics and internal dynamics. Focusing on the practice domain involves excluding research that is much more obviously policy-driven than practice-driven. This is a difficult step to take because policy implementation research includes some very significant and high-quality research. However, it does avoid a study of the practice/research interface turning into a study of the policy/research interface.

There are ambiguities and complexities. A good example of these is the shift towards the idea of 'evidence-based services' in the USA. Important initiatives have taken place in both Oregon and Hawaii. In both cases the State Government took a lead role and specific legal and policy instruments were put in place to make sure that service development was increasingly research-led and 'evidence-based'. However, the presence of clear political and policy imperatives in both Hawaii and Oregon does not mean that practice imperatives (whether articulated by practitioners, managers or service users) did not also play an important part in creating the initial demand for a new policy direction (for details see the websites of the State of Hawaii, Department of Health, 2008; and the State of Oregon, Department of Human Services, 2008).

Adopting an emergent perspective does not resolve all these ambiguities. However, it does enable a line to be drawn between research rooted in the practice domain and research that has its origins in the political sphere.

Defining the practice domain: the problem of interprofessionalism and multi-disciplinarity

Recognizing that the practice domain is connected to but nevertheless distinguishable from the policy domain only solves one problem. Even if practice is conceptualised as a relatively autonomous domain, why should it be seen as specific to social work? With the rise of interprofessionalism, multi-disciplinarity and inter-agency working is it not anachronistic to even talk about a distinctive social work practice domain?

The practice domain is defined by interactions of one kind or another but it does not (and never has) consisted solely of interactions between social workers and service users. For most social workers the practice domain is increasingly characterised by interactions with other professionals and other organisations as well as with service users, their families and communities. This phenomenon has been recognized by the World Health Organization and has changed the nature of the practice domain in the USA and many parts of Europe (Engel, 1992). If the space occupied by practice is increasingly characterised by complex inter-agency and cross-professional networks then it follows that knowledge about practice not only includes knowledge about these 'interdependencies' and 'complexities' (Trevillion, 2000) but is itself a form of shared knowledge

that no single profession can lay claim to (Thyer, 2002). This appears to call into question the very idea of social work practice as a discrete field of research and by implication, perhaps, 'social work research' itself.

Alternatively, it could be argued that the rise of interprofessionalism is not where the threat to the validity of the idea of social work practice lies. If social workers are able to operate confidently within a recognized sphere of competence then this will automatically validate the idea of a field of social work practice even in a highly interprofessional, multi-agency or multi-disciplinary environment.

This can be well illustrated by looking at what happens when these conditions are not present. In Italy it seems that the territory of what would in many other countries be defined as 'social work practice' is fought over by a range of competing disciplines:

> Several professions are currently contesting the ground of social services, among them social pedagogy, educators and care workers, sociologists and latterly also community nursing (Facchini et al., 2007: 1).

Situations of this kind pose as many problems for interprofessionalism as they do for social work; where professions are involved in zero sum games it is difficult for the practice domain to be conceptualised in either professional or interprofessional terms. It follows that attempts to create a stronger commitment to the idea of a 'social work practice' domain in Italy are likely to make it easier both to generate an interest in social work research and to establish a sense of interprofessionalism based on mutual respect.

The importance of this point is that it shows it is meaningful to continue to ask questions about *social work* practice in an increasingly interprofessional practice universe.

Defining the practice domain – the issue of multiple perspectives

Social work practice is rooted in respect for and engagement with a wide range of different views and perspectives and some of the most important strands of social work research engage directly with the way in which the social work practice space is characterized by (even to some extent defined by) multiple perspectives and contested viewpoints.

In the social work literature different versions of this issue have been articulated, but all of them have grappled with the socially situated nature of social work knowledge and the need to generate critically reflexive accounts of professional practice. This preoccupation with diversity (frequently linked to structured inequality) has been at its most obvious where research has been used to develop strategies to enable social workers to challenge discrimination and oppression (Thompson, 2003), but it goes wider than the specific literature on anti-discriminatory or anti-oppressive practice.

Social work research is a product of complexity because social work practice is complex. Social work research emerges out of a range of different experiences, 'discourses' (Best and Kellner, 1991) and 'standpoints' (Harding, 1986; Haney, 2002) because social work practice itself exists at the intersection between these. Not only have the experiences and viewpoints of service users, carers and communities played a significant part in shaping the social work research domain, but the practice domain itself also cannot, finally, be separated from the multiple subjectivities of its key actors.

RESEARCH AS AN EMERGENT PROPERTY OF PRACTICE

The 'emergent' thesis

How do we go about building a model based on the idea that research is an emergent property of practice and what might be the implications of this?

To argue that the practice domain can give rise to and subsequently shape research is to make a strong claim both about the nature of

social work research and about the nature of the practice domain. This claim goes well beyond suggesting that social work research uses material drawn from practice to develop theory or to test out hypotheses (evidence-based research) that can then be applied to practice (evidence-based practice). To suggest that practice can have a significant formative influence on research is to suggest that we think about research as a particular kind of practice outcome. This is a startling proposition. It runs counter to the rather romantic idea that research is the outcome of an independent community of scholars exploring issues in a process driven exclusively by intellectual curiosity. It also challenges the assumption that the world of research is essentially rational and linear and that the researcher is in control of the research agenda by suggesting that research is a product of the same messy world that social workers and service users inhabit.

This is not an argument about cause and effect. To argue that practice exercises a formative influence on research is not the same as claiming that practice determines or causes research. Moreover, to suggest that research is an emergent property of practice does not invalidate other ideas about research. What it does, however, is to link the research process to particular social contexts. This is not to deny that research is an attempt to understand practice, but rather a way of pointing out that the process of searching for knowledge is itself rooted in the conditions being examined.

From complexity to empowerment

Many years ago Norbert Elias pointed out that complexity in social affairs leads to disempowerment as individuals lose sight of the role played by others and themselves, and experience social life as a product of impersonal forces or rules enforced in some mysterious way from above (Elias, 1978: 71–103). This insight makes it possible to see social research as a way for individuals and groups to regain some sense of control over their lives. From this point of view, all forms of social research can be seen both as a product of complexity and as a partial solution to the problems associated with it.

Whatever the truth of the general argument that research is a response to the disempowering effects of complexity, in relation to social work, the argument that there is a link between research and empowerment is more specific. It is that social work practice has grown up in and continues to exist in conditions of marginalisation and disempowerment (which includes the position of social workers in their organisations and in society) and that research is, to some extent at least, a response to the way in which these conditions are experienced in the practice domain. In effect, it commits us to an image of social work research as dynamic and empowering and links these characteristics to its emergent properties.

The next section examines these characteristics in a historical context.

SOME HISTORICAL EXAMPLES

Modern social work can be seen as having grown out of the community-based initiatives of the settlement movement and the more individual and family-based work associated with the casework tradition. The history of the profession shows that from the beginning its identity was constructed around key questions, problems and issues which came out of the concrete social experiences of its practitioners and went on to form the basis of its research traditions.

Combating poverty

The settlement movement began in nineteenth-century England, spread through several parts of the British Empire and had a major influence on the development of social work in the USA. By the early years of the twentieth

century there were settlement houses in London, Glasgow, New York, Boston, Chicago and elsewhere and it was Samuel Barnett, the founder of the movement who laid the foundations of an organizational culture in which research on poverty and a commitment to combating social injustice could go hand in hand (Thane, 1982: 23).

If we think of settlements as operating in and helping to create specific kinds of practice domains, then it is clear that some of the most influential research on poverty emerged out of a practice domain characterised by beliefs in partnership, community living and, especially in the USA, the creation of strong neighbourhood-based organisations to fight for improvements in the lives of the poor. These researchers were therefore approaching their work through a particular kind of lived experience in which they had first-hand knowledge of the effects of marginalisation and poverty on individuals, families and communities, and a desire to do something about it.

The strong relationship between research, practice and personal experience characteristic of the settlement movement was particularly influential in Chicago. It is possible to see a strong link between the work of the Hull House Settlement and the founding vision of the first social work journal the *Social Service Review* which sought to promote the value of research for social work and to champion the idea that social workers should be equipped to undertake research (Shaw, 2008a: 3).

The emergence of the 'social dimension' in casework

The second example illustrates very clearly how the first generation of social workers were influenced not just by their encounters with service users but also by their relationship to wider organizational and professional systems.

In its early days the casework model was little more than an attempt to separate out the 'deserving' from the 'undeserving'. It certainly contained no analysis of the social forces operating which might make it difficult for people to improve their lives. However, in the early years of the twentieth century a strong vision of 'the social dimension' emerged as the core of casework practice in the USA. Recent research by Praglin (2007) has shown how this idea came about and the critical role played in this process by the structural position of the first social workers in their organizations.

Ida Cannon and Ethel Cohen, two pioneers of casework practice, were based in hospital settings and developed their ideas about casework partly in response to the difficult and sometimes overtly hostile environments in which they both worked. Their rigorous focus on the 'social dimensions' of illness was not only a direct response to the needs of those whom they tried to help, it also provided a meaningful narrative to underpin their resistance to the dominance of the medical profession in the hospitals where they worked. This early version of a social model of illness and disability also enabled the casework pioneers to challenge the dominant medical model of illness. The opening of the first social services clinic in Boston in 1905 provided an organizational, professional and conceptual base for the casework pioneers both to resist their medical colleagues and to articulate their ideas about social work and social work education.

This example, drawn from the early history of social work, shows that key aspects of its basic theoretical framework were laid down in the context of gender-based inequalities and the way they informed day-to-day casework practice. The doctors in Boston were male: the social workers were female – as were many of those the social workers were trying to help (Praglin, 2007). In this way a distinctive research vision emerged out of an ongoing struggle against gender-based inequalities. The subsequent history of social work has continued to show the influence of gender on both theory and practice (Lyons and Taylor, 2004).

THE DIFFERENT LEVELS OF ANALYSIS

The three-level model

Relationships between practice and research can only be discussed in a meaningful way if they are linked to a specific level of analysis. In this section the practice domain is divided into distinct levels and each of these is related to certain forms of social work research and bodies of social work theory. These levels are:

- The micro-level that links the day-to-day work of the individual practitioner with the field of practitioner research.
- The meso-level where the focus is on the influence of the team or organizational context on research.
- The macro-level associated with two major types of practice context:
  - The practitioner community context: this kind of context arises when individuals or teams of individual practitioners forge links across organizational boundaries and begin to identify with one another. The community level can also be thought of in more dynamic terms as a social movement linking together practice innovation and innovation-focused research.
  - The national context: this refers to the way in which practice is shaped by specific national socio-legal traditions and welfare cultures. This can only be dealt with by cross-national research.

PRACTITIONER RESEARCH – THE RELATIONSHIP BETWEEN RESEARCH AND PRACTICE AT THE MICRO-LEVEL

In some respects, the relationship between practice and social work research is clearer at the micro-level than at any other level. At its best, practitioner research at the micro-level brings to life the complex interplay between social context and the consciousness of the individual practitioner, including his or her professional capacities, values and attitudes (Dadds and Hart, 2001: 143–59). However, the very closeness of the practitioner researcher to the practice context of the research brings with it a range of complications. Three broad types of practitioner research are considered here: reflective practice, critical practice and action research. All raise specific issues and challenges.

The reflective practitioner

For some, the concept of 'reflection' effectively integrates research and practice processes with one another so that 'the epistemological process in the therapeutic encounter can be seen as akin to the research process' (Yelloly and Henkel, 1995: 6–7).

The implication is clear. No hard and fast distinction between research and practice exists (cf. Sue White and Gerhard Riemann's consideration of this issue in Chapter 5). In so far as a distinction between the two is made, research is envisaged as an extension of the process of reflective engagement with practice material. The difficulty posed by this for an emergent model of research is that it is not clear whether we should see the research process as a product of the dynamics of the practice context or as another one of those dynamics. To put this another way: is the research process associated with reflective practice so embedded in the practice process that it has not yet fully emerged from it?

The critical/sceptical practitioner

When practitioner research goes beyond reflection and begins to question some of the most basic features of the practice encounter it could be said to occupy a clearer space as a form of research. This shift from reflection to criticality is not necessarily linked to the adoption of a particular practitioner research methodology. In the introduction to her reflections on the Tarantula Project, designed to tackle domestic violence in Hamburg, Germany, Sabine Stövesand outlines the rationale for the project but then describes

how 'the impetus for this paper was given by my growing scepticism towards this approach' (Stövesand, 2007: 1). She argues strongly for a community work approach to domestic violence that would challenge what she describes as the 'security discourse' – a discourse that merges the functions of social workers with those of the police.

One of the interesting aspects of this paper is the way that the threat to the social nature of the practice field and the perceived need to protect it from the new 'security discourse' become key drivers of the research process. This is strongly reminiscent of the way that the early caseworkers sought to promote the value of the social dimension in the face of threats from the medical establishment and the medical discourse.

The differences between critical and reflective research are not always as clear as this and in many cases attempts have been made to link the two together in an integrated critical–reflective paradigm. In the present context probably the best way of thinking about these issues is in terms of a continuum from practitioner research that is almost entirely *embedded* in practice to evaluative/critical research that has clearly *emerged* from practice.

Action research – between the individual and the team

It has always been difficult to differentiate between practitioner research in general and action research in particular (Dadds and Hart, 2001: 6–7). Published action research crosses most of the geographical, cultural and organizational boundaries of social work. Drawing together the various strands of thinking about action research from its origins in the work of Kurt Lewin, Stringer and Dwyer have recently emphasised both its focus on social change and its 'collaborative' nature, arguing that it is these attributes that distinguish it from other examples of practitioner research (Stringer and Dwyer, 2005: 1–4).

Because it is both collaborative and change-oriented a good example of action research is the team approach to helping children who have witnessed domestic violence described by Childs (2001: 102–15). The project began with the day-to-day experiences of an individual practitioner, but was designed to find a solution to pressing problems shared by the team as a whole. In order to mobilize support for the project in the team the initial researcher/practitioner became a champion of the research in the team and developed team ownership of it. Although it could be said that this example of action research emerged at the individual, micro-level of practice, it also shows how a project can be taken forward into other levels of practice. This is what action researchers refer to as 'working developmentally' (Stringer and Dwyer, 2005: 11) and it means that action research straddles the divide between the micro- and meso-levels of analysis.

TEAM OR ORGANISATIONAL RESEARCH – THE MESO-LEVEL OF ANALYSIS

From an action research perspective the boundary between team, organizational and practitioner research is somewhat blurred. As the last example showed, action research tends to collectivise the concepts of both 'practice' and 'research' and can therefore be situated anywhere between the individual, team and organizational levels. So, it is only when we consider organizational research outside the framework of action research that some of the distinctive characteristics of this meso-level of analysis become clear.

The problems posed by domain boundaries are particularly difficult to resolve at the organisational level of practice. The issues associated with differentiating between policy-driven and practice-generated research, which have already been discussed, have to be dealt with once again at this level of analysis.

Many organizations will initiate research only in response to an external pressure. Very often this means that organizational research is described as a response to a new policy. This makes it seem as if organizational research is really little more than policy implementation research – a form of research that has already been excluded from this discussion because of its association with top-down government-driven political processes rather than bottom-up, practice-driven or practice-generated research. However, there is a major difference between a situation where an organization is simply one among many sites for a government-directed research programme and one where a research project is part of an organization's response to a change in the external environment (which can include policy changes).

Research linked to or emerging out of the organisational level of practice can be seen as a form of organizational learning. An organization that critically reflects on its performance is frequently classified as a 'learning organization' (Senge, 1990) and so all forms of practice research at the organizational level can be understood in terms of positive feedback loops in which needs and problems generate research and research generates improvement. Of course, in reality, the extent to which organizations learn from mistakes or make good use of research findings is very variable.

An interesting example of the complexities associated with both the organizational ownership of research and the relationship between organizational research and organizational learning comes from Germany. In recent years the Federal Government in Germany has developed a new programme, the Bund-Laender-Prohgramm Soziale Stadt (Social City Programme) focused on urban regeneration. What separates this from some other national programmes is that individual regions have to actively apply to be part of the programme and if they are accepted they have to bear part of the cost themselves, so it can be seen as an example of local/regional decision-making even though it is a national programme. In a recent article Evers et al. (2006) looked at the experiences of one region.

The Social City programme in Hessen aimed to promote community development as well as economic development (2006: 185). One anticipated outcome was the emergence of a new 'networked mode of governance' in these urban centres. However, the project had only limited success and the research demonstrated very clearly that in order to create genuine participatory decision-making there needed to be a much wider involvement of social workers in the programme. This was the message of the research, but there is no clear indication that this message was heeded.

Research can emerge at the organizational level of practice, but the conditions that allow it to do so appear to be relatively rare. Many organizations remain indifferent to research and disinclined to use research findings to shape their practices. For example, few organizations seem willing to encourage the development of a cadre of 'evidence-based practitioners' (Mullen et al., 2005) and in the absence of evidence-based or research-literate practitioners it is difficult to see how research findings can be effectively integrated into organizational learning.

A noticeable exception to this widespread organisational resistance to research was that associated with a UK initiative on the part of the County of Wiltshire to 'make research findings count in the development of services'. This was described as a 'journey' showing 'how children's services attempted to expose themselves to lessons from research' (Fanshawe, 2002: 23). The project had a national influence and informed a series of publications including *What Works for Troubled Children* (Buchanan and Ritchie, 2004) and *Seen and Heard 2* (Buchanan et al., 2002). Unusually, the findings focused on both the needs of the families and the development of 'new service initiatives' to help them.

The themes of empowerment and change may be less evident in research projects generated at the organizational level than in those generated at the practitioner level. However, these two examples show that dissatisfaction with the *status quo* and a clear desire for change also play a key role in the emergence of research projects at this meso-level of practice.

THE MACRO-LEVEL

Practitioner communities and research

The history of social work is in part a history of practitioner movements. These movements can also be thought of as dynamic *practitioner communities*. A practitioner community of this kind is an active network or 'action set' (Trevillion, 1999: 49–50) mobilized around a central body of practice or practice paradigm which is frequently conceptualized by those involved as fundamentally *new* and *different* to anything that has come before. These claims cannot, of course, be taken at face value but they are important ingredients of the underlying ideologies that help to mobilise specific practitioner communities. The research associated with practitioner movements or communities has a number of distinctive purposes. It is a way of disseminating new practices, legitimating them in relation to identifiable bodies of theory and continuing to develop them through research.

Some of the best known examples of practice-generated research projects can be situated at this community level. These kinds of research initiatives are typically characterized by a combination of strong individual practitioner commitment, support from organizations and teams and the presence of a national or even international community of interest to whom much of the research is addressed.

Two examples illustrate the way in which practice communities can effectively drive research agendas: the model of the family group conference that originated in New Zealand and the patch or neighbourhood social work model that originated in England. There are many other examples, including the research associated with a wide range of campaigning networks. However, these examples have been selected because they focus on the activities of social work practitioners.

Exemplar 1: Family group conferencing – an example from New Zealand

The family group conferencing method and the wider school of family decision-making have been described as emerging out of a search for 'culturally synchronous and ecologically valid methods of intervention that built on client strengths' (Whittaker, 1999: xiv).

Family group conferencing has been described as 'a new way of thinking and behaving' (Connolly and McKenzie, 1999: 20). This practice and its associated research originated in New Zealand. It was developed by practitioners working with Maori families who were disappointed with the range of options on offer. They felt that current family support practices did not focus enough on the day-to-day realities of dealing with child abuse. At the same time, they felt strongly that there had to be a way of helping Maori children to access the 'cultural strengths' of Maori families and communities (Connolly and McKenzie, 1999: 14).

In 1986 the Puao-te-Ata-tu or 'Daybreak Report' was published. This report argued strongly for a focus on the needs of Maori children and the importance of finding a way for these children to be cared for in their own communities. The publication of the Daybreak Report was a paradigm-changing event that led to an upsurge of practitioner experimentation. Social workers began to invite 'cultural consultants' from the Maori community to professional meetings and out of this unique chemistry the first versions of the family group conferencing model began to develop.

The rapid spread of family group conferencing seems in large part to have been due to the dissemination of 'practice wisdom' through practitioner networks (Connolly and McKenzie, 1999: 20). This process also seems to have enabled the original research paradigm to change and diversify.

Although it was originally conceived of as a distinct theoretical and research paradigm, like other areas of social work research linked to practitioner movements it grew organically and soon developed synergistic links with other theoretical and research paradigms. In turn, these synergies led to a number of new areas of practice/research. The idea of increasing the safety network surrounding children at risk of harm, which was originally part of the family group conferencing approach (Connolly and McKenzie, 1999) fused with aspects of family systems work, the family network assembly approach and networking theory (Trevillion 1992: 58–60) to became part of mainstream child protection practice (Gardner, 2005). As a result, network-based approaches to child protection can now be considered to be a distinct field of research. Another idea, which can also be traced back to family group conferencing, is that of 'participatory decision-making' (Connolly and McKenzie, 1999). Over time this has also fused with other traditions so that the idea of family-led solutions to social problems has joined with ideas about service user-led approaches (Beresford, 2000) to enter the mainstream of ideas about 'emancipatory practice' (Thompson, 2003: 40–2).

Exemplar 2: Patch social work – an example from England

A few years before the family group conferencing method began to develop in New Zealand, another practitioner community, enthused by the transformative potential of new 'neighbourhood' or 'patch' models of social work practice began to develop in the UK. Like family group conferencing, this movement was associated with an effort to think outside the narrow confines of professionally led care and to make use of the strengths of disadvantaged and marginalized social groups. Practitioners, researchers and managers were all involved in championing the new model and making the case for its adoption by local government as the preferred way of delivering services to individuals and families.

In 1979 a key conference took place at the Commonwork Conference Centre in Kent, which brought together the first patchwork enthusiasts and in 1980 a linked research seminar took place at the National Institute of Social Work in London. Out of these events came two key publications: *Going Local* (Hadley and McGrath, 1980) and *Perspectives on Patch* (Sinclair and Thomas, 1983). These became the key theoretical/research texts of the patch movement and provided the intellectual basis for the community social work approach (Barclay, 1982).

The patch model was summed up at the time as the 'decentralisation of services to small units and the fusion of statutory work with voluntary action' (Hadley and McGrath, 1980: 1). Like family group conferencing it was born out of a widespread sense of frustration and concern about the direction of social care and its inability to achieve the ambitions it had set itself. At the core of the movement was a critique of what was seen as the bureaucratic, overly professional, centralized and hierarchical systems of state social work in Britain in the 1970s.

The original body of research associated with 'patch social work' incorporated an attempt to evaluate the effectiveness of small community-based teams in comparison to traditional casework services. One of the features of patch research was that managers, practitioners and professional researchers were all involved with it (Hadley and McGrath, 1980).

Patch social work quickly became popular and for a short period of time looked set to become the dominant model of social work in the UK. Nevertheless, a few years later it fell victim to a decisive shift in UK policy-making that prioritized specialist services over community-based resources. In part, its rapid fall from grace was a consequence of its dependence on its practitioner community rather than support from government and the research-base of the movement disappeared with it. The international impact of patch was limited. Unlike family group conferencing it was too rooted in the unique practice context of the UK to develop a strong international network of champions. However, Cooper's idea of finding a way to create 'a lively partnership of the statutory, voluntary and informal sections of communities' (Cooper, 1980: 30) has continued to be a key driver for research in the UK and internationally. In this way the modest research tradition associated with patch played an important part in the development of a bigger story. Just as family group conferencing became linked to other ecological systems and network-based approaches, so too did patch social work research eventually join forces with a wide range of other research traditions in the fields of social inclusion, community development and community care.

THE NATIONAL CONTEXT AND CROSS-NATIONAL RESEARCH

The influence of national traditions and specific welfare cultures on practice only becomes truly apparent when these contexts are compared with one another. While the national context of practice can be assumed to exercise a pervasive influence on research, the way in which it does so is so firmly embedded in the taken for granted universe of researcher assumptions that it can be difficult to see how it actually operates to shape research. Cross-national research makes these influences explicit and, in many cases, turns what would normally lie in the background into the subject matter of the research project. Some of the best examples come from the field of comparative child protection research.

Positive Child Protection: A View from Abroad (Cooper et al.) was published in 1995. At the very beginning of this study, the authors make clear that what brought them to the subject was a sense of crisis within the English child protection system and an urgent need to find ways of resolving it: 'This book is concerned with the crisis in the child protection system of England and Wales and how it might be overcome' (Cooper et al., 1995: viii).

The authors realized that one of the things that was wrong was the way in which the problem of child protection was being conceptualised and so for them one of the main outcomes from comparing the English and French systems was the new light it cast on the English system. As they put it:

> In our experience an initial fascination with the discovery that thirty miles from Folkestone they do things very differently was quickly supplemented by an enduring process of critical reflection on how we ourselves do things (Cooper et al., 1995: vii).

The use of a vignette-based methodology allowed the researchers to focus on the views and experiences of practitioners in both France and England.

The second study is more recent but also had its origins in concerns about the operation of child protection systems. 'Co-operation in a child welfare case: a comparative cross-national vignette study' is a cross-national comparison of approaches to collaboration between different organizations and professions (Glad, 2006). It involved researchers from Denmark, Germany, Sweden, Texas and Britain, and like the earlier work it made use of a vignette methodology to illuminate national practices. The impetus for the research was a concern with the problems associated with communication between professionals in child protection cases and the project was coordinated from Sweden.

Although the research problem was one that all the participants recognized as relevant to their own countries, the drive for this piece of research seems to have been rooted in specific research findings from Sweden demonstrating that 'cooperation seems to be very difficult to establish and that the outcome is frequently doubtful' (Glad, 2006: 225).

These studies indicate that cross-national research tends to arise at moments of crisis and renewal in specific national traditions, but may gain added momentum when these perceptions of crisis have resonance across state boundaries.

DOMAIN-WIDE PROCESSES

A focus on specific levels of practice can be informative, but it may also make it difficult to identify issues that cut across different levels. Focusing on practice at the national or international level does not entirely solve this problem as the specific issues associated with particular working environments tend to disappear in the search for generalised mindsets or cultures of practice. This might not matter if the questions that drove research emerged only or mainly at one level of practice. However, it could be argued that many of the issues that have already been examined here exist at more than one level and that choosing to locate them in a specific type of practice context runs the risk of losing sight of other equally significant ways in which the practice domain, as a whole, shapes the research agenda.

Domain-wide processes operating at a number of different levels of practice can be identified by their close association with shifts in the way in which the aims, objectives and even values of practice are understood by individuals, teams, organizations and communities of practitioners. The impact of these domain-wide practice shifts on research can be very significant. They have the potential to change the way research topics and questions are formulated and to mobilize resources behind new research projects and programmes. By definition, there are relatively few examples of this kind of domain-wide change and even fewer where the changes can be seen to subsequently influence research at an international as well a national level.

Over the course of the last fifty years perhaps the single most important domain-wide change in practice has been the emergence of *community care* as a central organizing principle of social welfare. It is often argued that community care is not a universal phenomenon. The language associated with it is often too closely identified with particular welfare regimes or welfare cultures to have universal currency. However, many countries have experienced a move away from institutionalized responses to human need in favour of flexible, human alternatives and it is this rather than any specific model for delivering or funding social welfare services which has been the true paradigm shift.

The move from an institutional to a community-based approach to social welfare not only transformed the orientation of social work in many countries, it also created a complex web of new practice problems and dilemmas at the micro-, meso- and macro-levels which fundamentally re-shaped social work research in this period.

Ways of achieving community care ambitions with limited resources became an increasingly pressing issue for individual social workers, social work organizations and practitioner communities as the pace of decarceration and hopes for the wider social impact of the social work profession both increased in the 1970s, and it was during this period that an identifiable social work research tradition in the field of community care first began to emerge (Bayley, 1973).

The concept of 'social support' was an early focus of community care research. By the early 1980s research in the United States by Whittaker, Pancoast, Froland, Gottlieb, Garbarino, Auslander, Lewin and others had developed sophisticated models of social support which were able to draw on advances in network analysis and systems theory. This in turn fed into other work in the UK, where by the late 1980s Sharkey, Seed, Smale, Trevillion and others had all built on and developed these ideas. Interest in these approaches was further stimulated by vision of a flexible integrated form of localised community care first put forward by Cooper (1980) as part of his argument for patch social work.

Community care developments from the 1970s onwards also spawned another major school of practice/research. This was focused less on patterns of care and more on changing the way in which people related to one another. Drawing on the values of community care this was the 'normalization' or 'social role valorization' movement in practice and research. 'Social role valorization' has been defined by its founder Wolfensberger as 'the creation, support and defense of valued social roles for people who are at risk of social devaluation' (Wolfensberger, 2003: 81). He has gone on to say that it focuses both on 'the enhancement of people's social image or personal value in the eyes of others' and the 'enhancement of their competencies' (Wolfensberger, 2003: 82).

If research on social support could be seen as responding to the problems of potential isolation and marginalization following on from decarceration, then normalization and social role valorization could be seen as responding to the problems of stigma and segregation which have always been associated with residential care (Wagner, 1988: 1–6) but which also pose risks to community-based initiatives.

At the beginning of this chapter it was noted that social work research frequently emerges as part of a reaction against experiences of oppression and marginalization and sometimes forms part of a concerted effort to promote change. The history of research linked to the early history of community care shows that this basic model of how research emerges out of practice can also be applied to domain-wide change processes. All the social work research associated with community care in this period focused on the ways in which individuals and groups could connect with others, be treated with respect and access the means by which they could create new and better lives for themselves. Taken as a whole, this body of research tried to show that there was no need to choose between the dehumanizing disciplines of life in a 'total institution' or the loneliness and isolation of life on the margins of society that was very often the only alternative offered. It therefore contained a profound and radical vision of change.

Although community care can be seen as global phenomenon, it also has a very particular history in specific countries and this illustrates the general point that domain-wide developments can sometimes be more appropriately analysed at the level of the single nation state or the single welfare regime than at the international level where comparison is often so difficult. Whereas the early research on community care focused on issues that were readily understandable anywhere in the world, the next phase of research was much more obviously a product of particular sets of changes in specific societies and therefore much more limited in its international impact.

In 1983 Austin published one of the first accounts of case management, describing it as 'a mechanism for linking and coordinating a service delivery system' (1983: 16). Case management emerged as a practical tool for coordinating care around the needs of individuals in the radically pluralistic and market-dominated environment of social care in the USA. Some of the early case management research had strong links with the broader area of research on social support and maintained a focus on informal as well as formal care (for example, Steinberg and Carter, 1984: 24–6), but, over time, case/care management practice began to develop a very distinct preoccupation with the assessment of care needs, the commissioning of services, the 'packaging' of formal care services and workload management (Orme and Glastonbury, 1993). This preoccupation led to research that was also focused on these issues. The driver for

this research was domain-wide but the domain was now limited to Anglo-American market-based models of social care and had little resonance outside this sphere.

CONCLUSION: FROM PRACTICE-DRIVEN RESEARCH TO RESEARCH-DRIVEN PRACTICE

This chapter has tried to lay the foundations for an emergent theory of social work research by examining the ways in which the characteristics and dynamics of the social work practice domain have shaped the social work research enterprise from its earliest days. This has not been a mechanistic process. From the beginning, experiences of marginalisation and disempowerment coupled with a commitment to and hunger for change have been powerful shapers of social work research.

This chapter has shown how deeply enmeshed social work research has been with the development of the profession, but it has also shown that research comes out of and feeds back into day-to-day practice.

Social work practice can be conceptualized at a number of different levels and this poses a distinct challenge for any attempt to show how research emerges from practice. This problem has been addressed by introducing a three-level model of practice with each level linked to particular examples of emergent research.

The phenomenon of 'domain-wide' processes and their impact on research has been looked at by examining the ways in which social work research has responded to the paradigm shifts associated with the development of community care.

In the introduction to this chapter it was noted that very little progress had been made in understanding how practice influenced research. Adopting an emergent approach does not by itself answer all the questions we may have. However, it does make it possible to at least have a meaningful discussion about the ways in which social work research is shaped by social work practice.

NOTES

1 In response to these kinds of considerations this *Handbook* has developed a less contextually specific category of 'domain' to capture the substantive, practice and service-delivery agenda for social work research. See Section IV.

2 The term 'emergent' is generally associated with the idea of multiple causality. In this chapter the more specific reference point is the figurational sociology of Norbert Elias (Elias, 1978).

3 The work of the international Cochrane Collaboration in health care and its sister organization the Campbell Collaboration are the best-known examples of this (see http://www.campbellcollaboration.org). However, within many countries a wide range of services are now on offer to help practitioners use research evidence to improve their practice (see for example the Social Care Institute for Excellence in the UK).

11

Theory and Theorizing: Intellectual Contexts of Social Work Research

Mikko Mäntysaari and Richard Weatherley

INTRODUCTION

This chapter considers the role of theory and theoretical knowledge in social work research. It traces the historical evolution of theory in social work in light of debates about the nature of theory, and examines current trends in theorizing. Theory, as a concept, is best understood in the context of philosophical debates about knowledge, the nature of reality, and how we know and represent that reality. We begin with a discussion of 'theory' and consider the uses of theory in the social sciences and in social work. We examine the historical development of social work in the US and Europe, and recent international trends. We conclude with some thoughts about the current state of theorizing and possible future directions.

Why theorize? Is it not more important for the social work researcher to simply get to the facts? Yet we do theorize whether or not we are aware of it. We interpret facts in the light of theories, implicit or explicit, that give them meaning (Skidmore, 1975: 12). Theories enable us to move back and forth from statements in a theoretical vocabulary to statements about our observations (Johnsson and Svensson, 2005). Theories tell us what to look for and where. Once we have made our observations, they help us organize and make sense of what we have seen. They provide explanations about causation and the relationships among phenomena.

Theory is a central element of the research process. To some, the development of theory is *the* basic aim of science. Sellars (1963: 106) states that theories have a family resemblance that is easy to discern but difficult to describe. 'Theory' is like 'time' was for St. Augustine – we know what it means, but cannot easily define it (von Wright, 1982: 23).

THE ROLE OF THEORIES IN THE SOCIAL SCIENCES

What does it mean to theorize?

Research in social work is part of a larger family of sciences, namely the social sciences

(Johnsson and Svensson, 2005). The roots of modern social sciences lie in ancient Athens, where philosophers like Plato and Aristotle established the fundamental elements of a philosophy of science. Originally, 'to theorize' meant to contemplate, to think about the nature of things, but not in a passive sense. For the Greeks, 'theory' involved observation, as for example observing stars and planets, or watching a play or a festival. It also carried the connotation of participation. To think 'theoretically' is to observe and at the same time to take part in what is being observed. According to the German philosopher Gadamer 'theorizing' always involves taking part in something, being present in a situation (Gadamer, 2004: 167). To theorize meant to understand the plot of the play, to anticipate what is going to happen. Theorizing was always directed toward something outside ourselves, as for example, watching others closely and clearly (Gadamer, 2004: 171).

According to the traditional view of science, scientific activities aim at true descriptions of the world. This goal can be attained through empirical investigation and by constructing theories based upon these observations. Concepts, their relationship to each other, and hypotheses about the state of affairs provide us with theories, which other researchers can use in their investigations. This basic and common understanding of science considers theories as a central feature of research (Kerlinger 1973: 8). This view, while not totally incorrect, is today considered too limited.

Empirical testability of theories

The role of theories in human and social sciences has undergone deep structural changes for a quite some time, affecting social work research along with other disciplines. One of the most intriguing questions about the changing role of theory has to do with the empirical testability of theories. The common understanding used to be that theories can and should be empirically testable. The traditional

view of science also held that the selection of theoretical hypotheses could be done with the support of empirical evidence. The hypotheses should either be verified (by *induction*) or falsified (by *Popperian deduction*). Popper considered empirical testability as a criterion of the scientific nature of a system:

> I shall certainly admit a system as empirical or scientific only if it is capable of being *tested* by experience. These considerations suggest that not the *verifiability* but the *falsifiability* of a system is to be taken as a criterion of demarcation. (Popper, 1980: 40)

The empirical testability of theoretical claims has also been an issue in social work. Thyer, one of the central figures in promoting evidence-based practice, maintained that theories used in social work were shallow and did not enhance the value of the research. Thyer claimed that social work research was unnecessarily striving for theories and should instead concentrate on measuring service outcomes (Thyer, 2001a). Gomory took issue with Thyer from a Popperian perspective contending that since all perceptions are colored by theoretical elements, research cannot be undertaken without an element of theory (Gomory, 2001a). Social work researchers should accordingly strive for falsifiability of theoretical claims (Gomory, 2001a,b; see also Munro, 2002a).

The case against empirical testability

The view that theoretical terms and empirical observations can and should be separated became problematic with the recognition that this is an impossible condition to achieve (Kiikeri and Ylikoski, 2004: 29).

The Duhem-Quine thesis states that it is not possible to falsify single hypotheses because it is invariably conjunctions of hypotheses which are being tested. No single empirical test or observation can alone define the fate of a hypothesis (Quine, 2008 [1951]; Cross, 1982: 320). In the Duhem-Quine thesis, claims are testable, but only within an entire network of propositions (Morad, 2004: 664). In the encounter of hypothesis with observation, there is always a set of implicit helping hypotheses within the observation tools, test-situations and so on. If the empirical test does not support the prediction, we know that something is wrong, but we do not know which of the set of hypotheses is false (Kiikeri and Ylikoski, 2004: 33). Quine pushed this thesis to its limits suggesting that a very stubborn person can always change the set of hypotheses to match the evidence.

The theory-ladenness of observations thesis states that even the most basic observations presuppose some kind of conceptual framework. There is no such a thing as pure empirical observation; observation is always observation in the light of theories (Popper, 1980: 59). Previous experience, expectations and presuppositions influence observations. Theoretical frameworks also influence the definition of the research topic, and the selection of data. Thomas Kuhn (1994) used the term paradigm to signify that not just theories but rather the questions considered worth asking and the rules by which they can be answered are important (Somers, 1998: 728).

There are many methodological orientations in the social sciences (e.g. ethnography, discourse analysis, phenomenology, historiography) which do not consider testability of hypotheses as criteria for assessing the fruitfulness of a theory. The central value of theories, their predictive capability, is not now considered quite as important in social sciences. The empirical testability of predictions can as a rule be seen as suitable for quantitative, hypothetic-deductive oriented research. However, qualitative research is not usually concerned with prediction, testing theories or validating hypotheses, but instead, seeks to understand the meaning immanent in the researched phenomena. This does not mean that qualitatively oriented research should be considered theory-free. Theories may be employed in designing the research and in reporting the findings. Theories may help researchers select among possible research topics and methodologies. Most qualitative methods yield theoretical constructs, with some (Grounded Theory) aiming at generating theories (Glaser and Strauss, 1967).

Unified science – or not? A central question in the philosophy of social sciences is whether society can be studied in the same way as nature (Bhaskar, 2000). There are (at least) two answers. The naturalist tradition claims that there is no basic difference between ways of scientific knowing, and that there is an essential unity of method between the natural and the social sciences (Bhaskar, 2000: 2). The anti-naturalists hold that the subject matter of the social sciences is embedded with meaning, and the aim is to elucidate the meaning (Bhaskar, 2000: 1). The anti-naturalist tradition calls attention to the 'double hermeneutics' where the objects of our research, the social life-forms, are full of meaning and interpretations, and cannot be studied outside of culturally defined practices (Alasuutari, 2004). Naturalist and anti-naturalist traditions have different views of role of the theories.

The possibility of a general theory Is a general theory in social sciences possible? In physics, Einstein tried to create a general theory of 'everything'. According to Finnish sociologist Alasuutari, a great deal of social research and theorizing share a common viewpoint, even to the extent of converging toward a single theory (Alasuutari, 2004). A general social theory would involve two elements: habitual behavior as a building block of society; and language, conveying information, coordinating action and forming human reality (Alasuutari, 2004: 7). Both behavior and language are also central to social work. Social workers struggle with the problems of everyday life, and the primary tool they employ is language (Timms, 1968; Fargion, 2007).

THEORIES IN SOCIAL WORK AND SOCIAL SCIENCE

What kind of science is social work – or is it science at all? Fargion (1968: 58–75) gives three possible answers. First, social work can claim to be science on the ground that social workers' knowledge-base is scientific. Second, social workers' ways of working resembles scientific problem solving. Scientists and social workers alike seek evidence and use similar reasoning and data-gathering methods. Third, social work can claim to be an applied science. In applied science, it is not so much a strict doctrine or propositions of social science which are being applied, but rather a method of enquiry based on a few general concepts. But social work is not only applied science, it is also art (Timms, 1968; England, 1986).

Social work studies describe, analyze and understand social conditions, assess the efficacy of alternative interventions, and suggest new intervention models. Social work draws upon theories from many different disciplines, including philosophy, sociology, psychology and education. What sets social work apart from other fields is that a concern for intervention is always present (Johnsson and Svensson, 2005: 420).

DISCIPLINARY AND NON-DISCIPLINARY CONTEXTS

Disciplinary context

Is social work an independent discipline? Shaw et al. (2006), citing the *Shorter Oxford English Dictionary* definition, suggest that while social work may indeed be a discipline in the sense of 'a branch of instruction', as a '"department of knowledge" social work's disciplinary identity raises numerous awkward questions.' Sunesson, a central figure in Swedish social work research, maintains that social work is a *field* of research, not an independent discipline. He uses the analogy of map and landscape by way of illustration. A map can give us an overview of the landscape, and can also guide us through the very narrow streets of a medieval town. There are many possibilities for map drawing: historical,

political, topographical, as well as for showing the way from one place to another (Sunesson, 2006: 334). Each map offers a different view of the same landscape that is an approximate description of a particular reality. Social work research can provide descriptions based upon theories and methods of sociology, psychology or social policy. Each aims at a true description of the world, but each gives only a partial view.

Theorizing in social work draws upon various intellectual traditions. While sociology and psychology have provided the primary intellectual context for social work research, philosophy, social pedagogy, social policy, indigenous thinking and feminist scholarship continue to play an important role.

Philosophy Developments in the philosophy of science have always influenced social work research, and this influence can currently be seen in articles appearing in leading social work research journals.

Social pedagogy has an important position in Europe, especially in Germany, Austria, Switzerland and some countries in Eastern Europe.

Social policy once providing the context for social work teaching is still considered an independent discipline in some European countries (e.g. Finland). Elsewhere, social policy research is based in various social science disciplines.

Sociology has probably been the most important disciplinary context for social work research, especially in parts of Europe. The situation has been changing, though, as the central role of sociology among the social sciences is nowadays not as unchallenged as before. Giddens, Habermas, Bourdieu and Foucault, probably the four most important European social theorists of the past 30 years, have had a significant impact on social work research. Their collective work explores sources of power and domination in social relations; the nature of truth, objectivity and subjectivity; the need for researchers to engage in critical self-reflexivity; the possibility of progress; tensions between agency and structure; and tensions between the actual and the normative, what is and what should be. Their theories illuminate power relations that are embedded in social work practice through the control of dominant discourses on normality, ethnicity, gender and sexuality (Houston, 2004: 262; Lovelock and Powell, 2004; Parton, 2000: 460).

Structural theories The question of structure and action is central to social work theory, with one or the other tending to dominate the discourse at various times and in different places. Structural theories focus attention on social structure and its contribution to social problems, while individual (or action) theories are connected with psychotherapeutic methods (Johnsson and Svensson, 2005, 421).

In the 1960s, European university students protested and read works neglected by the previous generation. Marx, Mao Zedong and Lenin became influential, even in social work. One central text of Marxist social work was Paul Corrigan and Peter Leonard's *Social Work Practice under Capitalism: A Marxist Approach* (Corrigan and Leonard, 1978). Marxist theories have continued to influence social work research, albeit from the margins (Ferguson and Lavalette, 2007: 25).

Postmodern theories developed as a response to the recognized uncertainties in societies and day-to-day practices in social work. The perspective gained wide recognition with French philosopher Lyotard's (1924–1998) book *The Postmodern Condition* (Lyotard, 1984; Parton, 2002: 238). Some advocates of social work radicalism felt that Marxism undervalued the salience of gender and ethnicity (Fook, 2002a: 7–8).

Ferguson and Lavalette (2004: 298), however, contend that postmodern or post-structuralist theories lack the capacity to replace Marxism insofar as they substitute individualist, subjective notions of identity and difference for Marxist concepts of structural oppression. In so doing, they fail to offer a collective response to oppression, but instead mirror right wing ideologies that hold individuals responsible for their own poverty (Ferguson and Lavalette, 2004). Some researchers today combine Marxist analysis with postmodern or critical theories and feminist theories (e.g. Cox and Hardwick, 2002).

Psychology has been influential in social work since the early days of the profession. Sylvia Staub-Bernasconi (2007a: 4542–3) lists what she considers the most important theoretical perspectives focusing on individuals:

- *Psychodynamic concepts* became after the pioneer contributions of Richmond and Salomon the first strong explanatory theory for many practice concepts.
- *Psychoanalytic social work:* Florence Hollis adapted psychoanalytic theory for social work practice in developing the notions of sustaining relationship, techniques to reduce anxiety, low self-esteem and lack of confidence.
- *Behavioral theories* and methods derive from the work of experimental behavioral psychologists, which criticized the diffuse, un-testable conceptions of psychoanalytic theory.
- *Cognitive theories* work with the assumption that people construct their own versions of reality and problems through what they have learned.
- *Task-centered social work* sought to replace psychodynamic social work based on a 'time-consuming' supportive relationship by a rationally planned 'short-term therapy' with a clear time limit. Central is what the client presents or accepts as a problem and wants to change.
- *Strength development:* strength or resilience is seen as a product of facing adverse life events and traumatic situations which can be used as a resource for actual problem-solving.

The governmental context of social work research

Social work research today is to a large extent commissioned and/or paid for by governments (Powell, 2002; cf. Chapter 7). While academic freedom is a shared value in Western democracies, research that is 'too theoretical' is not generally found on the wish list of purchasers of applied science. Even when universities are guaranteed freedom in research and teaching, the research agenda is heavily influenced by governmental priorities. This agenda-setting influence is exemplified by the growth of government-funded research (Powell, 2002).

The governmental context can be crucial. In Sweden, for example, social work research has been driven by the welfare state and the profession on the grounds that sociology and psychology did not produce knowledge relevant to social work practice (Bäck-Wiklund, 1993; Dellgran and Höjer, 2003). Welfare legislation in Sweden stipulates that services should be based on research knowledge.

Social work's professional project and knowledge production

While contributing to knowledge and informing practice, theory also plays a role in what the sociologist Magali Larson (1979) has called 'the professional project' of social work and other professions. Having jurisdiction over a body of knowledge is a necessary means to advance a profession in relation to other potential occupational competitors. Larson states (1979: 40):

> The structure of the professionalization process binds together two elements which can, and usually did, evolve independently of each other: a body of relatively abstract knowledge, susceptible of practical application, and a market – the structure of which is determined by economic and social development and also by the dominant ideological climate at a given time.

Social work exists in a highly competitive market, with other occupational entities (e.g. psychology, counseling, nursing) laying claim to serve some of the same clientele. Since its emergence as a profession in the early 1900s, social work has continually sought new knowledge both to inform practice as well as to maintain and enhance its standing as a profession (Wenocur and Reisch, 2001). The development of social work doctoral programs, and their proliferation after World War II, has played a significant role in advancing social

work as a profession. As of 1984, there were 47 social work doctoral programs in the US, 42 of which had been established since 1950 (Orcutt, 1990: 183). Within academe, having a doctoral program brings prestige, status and resources to a discipline. In today's academic marketplace, university and departmental rankings figure prominently in attracting the best students and faculty, as well as external funding. Publications in peer reviewed scientific journals are a prime determinant of one's place in the rankings, giving added impetus to the production of published research.

One consequence of the expansion of social work doctoral programs has been a marked increase in social work scholars who are producing research, and generating new theories. While social work continues to look to other disciplines for theoretical insights, it is increasingly producing its own theoretical perspectives.

The theory–practice nexus

While discussions of theory in social work research are somewhat limited, there is an abundance of literature on the theory–practice relationship and on theories underlying the helping process. The typical social work textbook usage of the term 'theorizing' tells us about theories used in practice rather than research. Social work academia has been criticized as being anti-intellectual and hostile to the social sciences (Jones, 1996: 190). Jones asserts that the social work establishment approaches social science selectively. Theories, perspectives and research findings are 'plundered and adopted' to support social work, while theories critical of the profession are pushed aside and neglected (Jones, 1996: 194–5).

Zofia Butrym stated that social workers 'have a not wholly undeserved reputation for lacking sophistication in their use of theoretical constructs' (Butrym, 1976: 67). It is true that social workers have sometimes been hesitant to accept theories from sociology, psychology or medicine. At the same time, social workers have on occasion also been too eager to adopt theories from other disciplines, without paying enough attention to the difficulties in integrating and applying them (Butrym, 1976: 68).

A central question in the social work literature has been whether theory and practice cohabit as a unity, or do they exist in different realms? Noel Timms has argued that there is an intimate connection between the two. 'We cannot conceive of practice without employing some kind of theory about what constitutes … good or bad practice …' (Timms, 1968: 23–4).

But which one comes first? Fargion (2007) describes two opposing views. One holds that good practice should be driven by theory and *practice* is the problem here. This approach poses a somewhat negative view of the practitioners' capacity to apply theory. The other position finds fault with the theorists and theories. It considers theories, and the output of academic work in general, as less relevant than other forms of knowledge social workers rely on. It regards practice itself as an ongoing research process. However, the two sides define the central concepts, 'theory' and 'practice' differently. When social workers use a concept like 'task-centered social work', they use it in a way that is different from its use in the research literature. Their use is not wrong, it is only different. Fargion, drawing upon the language-philosophy of Wittgenstein, offers an alternative way of thinking about the theory–practice conundrum. She suggests that theory and practice play different language games wherein the same concepts can have different meanings when the rules of the game differ (Fargion, 2003).

We may differentiate 'theories *of* social work' and 'theories *for* social work'. Moreover, social work theories can be normative (suggesting how social work should be done) or descriptive (focusing on what social workers do). Yet no matter how one chooses to define theory and practice, the two are inextricably linked.

THE HISTORICAL CONTEXT OF THEORIZING IN SOCIAL WORK RESEARCH

While the development of the social work profession, its value base and methods are similar in different countries, theoretical discussions have developed along different lines, reflecting unique political and cultural conditions. In the US, having a highly individualistic culture and lacking a viable socialist perspective, social work has been more oriented toward helping individuals adjust to their circumstances. In Europe, with strong social-democratic political movements, there has been much greater emphasis on social policy and the structural conditions that promote or impede individual well-being. The contrasts stand out starkly in comparing European and US approaches to social provision. The US, among industrialized nations, ranks at or near the bottom of most social and health indicators, as well as inequality (see, e.g. Sierminska et al., 2006: 17).

Theorizing in social work is closely related to the development of social work education. Here we consider the development of social work education and its intellectual roots in the US, UK, Germany, Sweden and Finland. The emerging influence of the Asia-Pacific region, Africa and Latin America is discussed below.

Social casework in the US

The history of theorizing in social work is to a large extent the history of social work theories in the US. That history has seen an early concern with establishing social work as a profession and an emphasis on social reform until the 1920s, followed by the ascendancy of psychiatric social work. Except for a brief resurgence of reform activism in the Depression era, social work in the US remained focused on professionalism and clinical practice through the 1950s. The Civil Rights Movement and various liberation movements of the 1960s (on behalf of women,

Mexican Americans, Native Americans, persons with disabilities, gay men and lesbians, transsexuals and bisexuals (GLBT)), concurrent with a major expansion of social work doctoral education contributed to the opening of the discipline to a much broader range of theoretical perspectives and research concerns (Ehrenreich, 1985; Orcutt, 1990; Wenocur and Reisch, 2001).

The development of social work as a profession started in the latter part of the nineteenth century. The Chicago School of Civics and Philanthropy, founded in 1903, offered the first year-long educational program for social workers. By 1919, there were 17 schools of social work in the US and Canada. In 1920, the Chicago School of Civics and Philanthropy was incorporated into the University of Chicago as the School of Social Service Administration (SSA). Its dean from 1924 to 1943, Edith Abbott, an economics PhD with post doctoral training from the London School of Economics, is credited with establishing the structure of modern social work education – university affiliation, a master's degree for practice and a research doctorate (Ehrenreich, 1985; Wenocur and Reisch, 2001).

As the profession developed, it drew in varying degrees from several disciplines and intellectual traditions: economics, psychology, sociology, education, philosophic pragmatism, expounded by John Dewey and William James, and the symbolic interactionism of George Herbert Mead.

A touchstone in the development of social work as a profession is the presentation to the 1915 National Conference of Charities and Corrections by the prominent educator, Abraham Flexner. Flexner had earlier conducted an extensive review of medical education and had outlined a standardized medical training curriculum that remains in effect in the US and Europe today.

Flexner (2001 [1915]) concluded that social work lacked some of the essential conditions of a profession. His assessment has served as a kind of Rorschach test for those debating the knowledge base of the profession

(Morris, 2008). Morris states that the view attributed to Flexner, that social work lacked a knowledge base, was actually put forth by Porter Lee, a New York School of Philanthropy professor who had also presented at the 1915 Conference. She points out that Flexner's failure to accord social work professional status was based primarily on his concern, reflecting his functionalist perspective, that social work was too diffuse, that it lacked a definite purpose and a clear line of demarcation distinguishing it from other fields (Morris, 2008). The field could never have 'a technique capable of communication through an orderly and specialized educational discipline' (Flexner, 2001 [1915]: 155; Morris, 2008: 42). We would argue that, paradoxically, it is this very diversity and lack of specificity that has given the field its vibrancy and a richness of research, theoretical perspectives and methodologies focusing on the human condition in all its various aspects.

From the outset, the emerging field of social work and the more reform-oriented settlement house movement developed along divergent paths as represented in the work of two central figures, Mary Richmond and Jane Addams (Morris, 2008; Staub-Bernasconi, 2007). Richmond had worked in the Philadelphia Charity Organization Society, had developed teaching materials for Societies nationwide, and from 1910 through 1922 taught at the New York School of Philanthropy (later to become the Columbia University School of Social Work). She considered it her mission to formulate a basis in theory and practice for the profession of social work (Brettschneider, 1989). Her highly influential book, *Social Diagnosis* (1917), was in a sense an answer to Flexner (and Lee) by setting forth a clear methodology for social work professionals. According to Karen Healy, Richmond was 'mirroring' the medical profession when she developed her idea of social diagnosis (Healy, 2005: 19–20).

Analytical thinking was for Richmond central to the helping process. She drew a distinction between social study, where the social worker is observing, and social diagnosis where she is closing her eyes and thinking (Munro, 2002a; Richmond, 1917: 347).

Richmond focused on the individual, his or her personality and unmet needs and the social environment upon which the individual depends for need satisfaction. Locating the causes of social problems within the individual, her change program is therefore oriented to the individual – through professional casework – in order to remedy social problems (Staub-Bernasconi, 2007a).

Richmond's conception of social diagnosis was based on her readings in history, law, sociology and psychology, as well as her knowledge of medical social work clinical practice. She also acknowledges her debt to her contemporary, George Herbert Mead, philosopher and sociologist at the University of Chicago, a cofounder of pragmatism, and originator of the symbolic interactionist school of sociology. Richmond's central theoretical idea, at the core of her conception of social casework, was 'the theory of the wider self', that everyone has two sides to her personality: a social and individual self (Richmond, 1917: 368; 1922: 93). This clearly shows Mead's influence (Toikko, 2001: 389).

In contrast to Richmond, Jane Addams (1860–1935), social reformer, feminist, peace activist and founder of the Hull House settlement in Chicago, focused on social structure and culture and their influences on the individual. The first woman 'public philosopher' in America (Hamington, 2008), she was a significant contributor to the Chicago School of Sociology, with ideas that combined symbolic interactionism, pragmatism and cultural feminism (Deegan, 1988). Hers was an applied sociology grounded in action, and especially social reform, taking the philosophy of pragmatism to its logical conclusion (Hamington, 2008).

Although Addams was successful in helping launch the settlement house movement and in bringing an end to child labor, the community-oriented, reform social work tradition lost out against supporters of social

casework and professionalism (Addams, 1999; Staub-Bernasconi, 2007; Sennett, 2003). In the US, the profession has continued to maintain, at best, an ambivalent stance toward social change, with social action remaining outside or at the margins.

During the 'psychiatric deluge that took hold in the 1920s, social work theorizing was strongly influenced by the psychoanalytic tradition (Wenocur and Reisch, 2001). The rise and ascendancy of psychiatric social work through the 1950s was sustained by a confluence of circumstances: market demand, an available knowledge base, a supply of trained professionals and a political climate favoring individual adjustment over social reform. America's participation in World war I had yielded an abundance of problems among service men and women and their families that fell within the purview of psychiatry and social work. A linkage with the prestigious fields of medicine and psychiatry was an attractive lure to an emerging field seeking to solidify its professional standing. As stated by Wenocur and Reisch (2001: 103), a focus on individual adjustment '…was congruent with the "return to normalcy" engineered by successive Republican administrations, which meant adjusting individual and family behavior to the corporate-inspired norms of mass materialism'.

European traditions

The European traditions in social work theory and research varied widely. Here we consider just three, the British, Nordic and German traditions, with apologies to those whose countries we left out. While sharing much in common, they illustrate the diversity in the pace of development, intellectual contexts, and welfare traditions.

The scientific basis of social welfare provision was established concurrently in several European countries at end of the nineteenth century as poor relief legislation was adopted to deal with the dislocations of the industrial revolution. The first social work education program was started in Amsterdam in 1899 (Brettschneider, 1989: 18). Catholic and Protestant traditions of care giving (and their Jewish precursors), labor and socialist movements, and the First Women's Movement contributed to the ethical and political foundation of European social work (Lorenz, 1994). In the US, Great Britain and the British colonies, social work was strongly influenced by the medical model that viewed its clients through a lens of pathology. In northern Europe, however, social work was closely linked to the establishment of national welfare states and was based on a social policy and social pedagogy knowledge base (Lyons, 1999; Satka, 1995).

United Kingdom

The development of social work in Britain and the US shared common roots in the Charity Organization Society and settlement house movements in the two countries, and in the Protestant social gospel movement that inspired them (Shaw, 2008a). The first two-year-long courses for social workers started in London in 1903 with the founding of a 'School of Sociology' (Brettschneider, 1989: 18).

A leading figure in British social policy and social work was Fabian socialist Beatrice Webb (1858–1943). Together with her husband, Sidney, she founded the London School of Economics (LSE) which was to play a significant role in social work and social welfare policy in Britain and in other European countries (Kaskisaari, 1991). The tradition of social administration, combining social research, policy advocacy and a concern for social provision, had its roots in the LSE, and was closely associated with the development of the welfare state (Powell, 2002: 17). Social administration applied insights from sociology, economics and administrative sciences to the study of social welfare. Richard M. Titmuss (1907–1973), one of the truly great names in the history of social policy, was professor of social administration at LSE from 1950 to 1973. Titmuss saw social administration, together with casework theories, as providing a scientific foundation for social work (Titmuss, 1973: 15).

Social administration has had a significant influence on research in the Nordic countries that continues today (Swedner, 1983; Mäntysaari, 2005a). However, sociological theories and social policy concerns fell from favor in British social work during the 1950s and 1960s, giving way to Freudian psychology. British social work embraced psychoanalysis as it offered a theoretical coherence that the field had been lacking (Jones, 1996: 195).

Debates about effectiveness research and the role of research-based knowledge in social work figured prominently from the 1970s until recently in both the UK and the US. Advocates proposed cognitive-behavioral practice and research models in response to outcome studies showing modest results from counseling (Sheldon, 1995). Empirically based practice has been challenged by post-modernists and constructivists. Parton (1999), for example, points out that 'uncertainty, confusion and doubt' are integral to social work. Researchers should accept this and not to try to introduce scientized approaches.

Recent social work scholarship in the UK has developed in two directions. One looks toward postmodern theories for analyses of society and the role of social work, and frameworks for social work practice. The other has sought to generate intra-professional consensus about the importance of social theory in social work education (Cox and Hardwick, 2002: 35; Parton, 1996, 2000). Lyons (1999) notes a recent shift in social work research (also evident in the US) toward the increasing use of interpretative and feminist methodologies – ethnographic, narrative, biographical – and empowerment strategies such as action research that engage participants in designing and carrying out research.

Germany

Social work in Germany can trace its origins to the concept of social pedagogy as espoused by the Prussian educator Friedrich Diesterweg (1790–1866). Diesterweg is credited by some as the originator of the maxim, 'learn by doing', which later became an adage of the American pragmatists. Social pedagogy meant education to prepare adults to live socially within and contribute to the community (Smith, 1999, 2007). The concept has evolved to encompass a wide range of activities such as working with youth and ex-offenders, operating nurseries and day care centers, as well as crisis intervention and programs addressing various social problems. Along with casework, social pedagogy is today a coequal branch of social work with students sharing a common first year of training. Social pedagogy has also been a significant influence in social work throughout European, including Russia (Hämäläinen, 2003; Smith, 1999, 2007).

Germany's first social work school was established in 1908 by Alice Salomon (1872–1948). Salomon was also instrumental in establishing the International Association of Schools of Social Work and served as its first president. Her influence on the professionalization of social work can be compared to that of Mary Richmond. Salomon received a PhD in economics in 1906 having entered university by special permission, as women were barred from graduate study. Salomon was a friend of Marianne and Max Weber, and her economics professor was Max's brother Alfred (Radkau, 2005).

In Salomon's formulation, poverty was a consequence of the industrial revolution and the dissolution of extended families. Free-market principles led to the exploitation of those who had only their labor to sell. As a feminist, she called attention to the deplorable conditions of women. Young women were either pregnant or nursing, and their husbands' wages were insufficient to meet the families' basic needs (Kuhlmann, 2003: 100–1).

The Nazis closed the social work schools and exterminated many of those who had been cared for by social workers. Salomon, who was Jewish, came to the US in 1937 where she died in 1948.

The Nazi regime used techniques of social pedagogy to further its Aryan family policy, and to indoctrinate youth in the ideology of the fascist state. Not surprisingly, social pedagogy fell out of favor in the immediate post-war years having been associated with the aims of the totalitarian state. It was revived under the influence of social psychologist, Kurt Lewin, a German who had immigrated to the US, and Eduard Lindeman, an American educator who had developed the social work field of community organization. Lewin's theories of group dynamics and action research, and Lindeman's ideas about community organizing, both strongly infused with democratic values, helped refocus social pedagogy toward more individual and group interventions (Smith, 1999, 2007). Lewin, a firm believer in the integration of theory and practice, famously wrote, 'There is nothing so practical as a good theory' (1951: 169; as cited by Smith, M.K. 2001).

Nordic countries

Both the Swedish and Finnish cases show how social work developed from the practical training of social welfare workers, to providing professional social work education and generating social work research. The dominant theoretical perspective has been that of sociology, with research largely focusing on social policy issues. As more and more social work PhDs enter academia, social work research is, however, increasingly focusing on social work practice.

Social work in the Nordic countries developed within the poor relief system administered by local municipalities. Formal social work education began in Sweden in 1920 and in Finland in 1925. The curricula in both countries initially stressed social policy, social welfare and legal issues. Casework and community work did not appear in the curricula until the 1950s and 1960s (Brettschneider, 1989: 19; Toikko, 2001). This did not occur, however, without contradictions. There has been a gender-based difference in orientation in Finnish universities, with professors, mostly male, stressing social policy and social administration, and university teachers, mostly female, striving to introduce casework methods, sometimes against the orders of their superiors (Satka, 1995).

Sweden's first social work professor, Harald Swedner (1925–2004) was appointed in 1979. His influence on Nordic social work research has been enormous. His text (Swedner, 1983), a cornerstone of Nordic social work theory and practice, envisioned social work as an applied sociology tempered with a strong measure of phenomenology. Swedner was the son of missionaries, and spent his childhood in China. He received a sociology PhD in 1960 with a socio-ecological dissertation. Swedner was a sociologist who lost confidence in sociology's relevance for remedying the inequalities of society. He abandoned sociological research to develop a new discipline, social work, at University of Gothenburg. Instead of Marxism, he became interested in American grass-root activist Saul Alinsky and theories of Paulo Freire. His philosophical ideas were influenced by pragmatist John Dewey (Sunesson, 2003: 98).

The expansion of Swedish social work education and research since the 1980s has been impressive. There are presently five universities and two colleges that collectively confer Bachelor of Social Work (BSW) degrees to about 1000 graduates each year. The five universities also have social work PhD programs. There are currently ten full professors, three with degrees in social work, six in sociology and one in psychology (Dellgran and Höjer, 2003). From 1980 to 2006, 206 social work PhD dissertations were accepted (Brunnberg, 2006: 3).

Sociological theory has a very strong position in Swedish social work research, and psychology somewhat less so. Most PhD theses draw on a combination of theoretical perspectives from sociology, psychology and social work. It was not until 1998 that there was a PhD dissertation drawing mainly on social work sources (Dellgran and Höjer, 2003: 571).

As in Sweden, Finnish social work education expanded considerably in the 1980s, contributing to an increase in the scope and quality of social work research. Seventy-nine social work PhDs were conferred from 1982 to 2006 (Mäntysaari and Haaki, 2007). Social constructivism remains the dominant theoretical perspective in Finnish social work research. While most of the research is published in Finnish, the number of articles and books in international languages is growing (Karvinen et al., 1999).

International trends in social work theorizing

There is a widely held view that Western theories, concepts and practice models in social work, especially from the US, have dominated the field ('professional imperialism'; see Midgley, 1983). Although the profession has made great efforts to develop more culturally competent sensitive approaches, it remains a modernist Western invention with a history of silencing marginal voices and disseminating Western models of thought to the rest of the world (Gray et al., 2008).

The influences, however, have not been entirely one way, and there has always been resistance to Western domination (Payne, 2005: 14). Social work is, without question, developing as an international discipline. This is evidenced by the increasing numbers of international journals and conferences featuring research reports from throughout the world, and the emergence of international social work as a field of practice and research. Issues such as world poverty and disease, forced migration, the impact of armed conflict, and natural disasters have global, cross-border dimensions with world-wide implications. Efforts toward achieving world consensus on human rights, the rights of women, children and the disabled have also given impetus to the development of social work internationally.

Social work has in a sense been international from the beginning. Jane Addams,

Mary Richmond, Beatrice Webb and Alice Salomon exchanged ideas at international conferences. Two examples, one old and one recent, illustrate the flow of theories and perspectives internationally.

Exemplar: International circulation of theories and theoretical perspectives

Paulo Freire (1921–1997)

Pedagogy of the Oppressed (2007). First published in Portuguese in 1968, and in English in 1970.

Contribution: Sets forth a *critical pedagogy*, applying concepts of praxis, dialogic and conscientization in furtherance of the liberation of the poor and oppressed. His ideas remain influential, and especially among those espousing radical social work.

Education: Faculty of Law, University of Recife, Brazil.

Intellectual influences: Phenomenology; Marxism; liberation theology; and the writings of Franz Fanon, philosopher, psychiatrist and anti-colonial revolutionary from Martinique.

Practice experience: Grew up in Brazil during the Depression; worked as a secondary school teacher; was responsible for adult literacy campaigns among impoverished workers in Brazil.

Ling How Kee

Indigenizing Social Work: Research and Practice in Sarawak (2007).

Contribution: Proposes decolonized research methodologies that give voice to indigenous peoples and their ways of knowing; enhances our understand of social work in multicultural settings.

Education: PhD from the Department of Social Work and Social Policy, University of Queensland, Australia.

Intellectual influences: Radical social work; multiculturalism; non-Western practice models and perspectives, especially from Asia and Africa.

Practice experience: Social work practice and research in Sarawak, one of Malaysia's most ethnically diverse states, located in the northwestern part of Borneo.

While an international community in the natural sciences is well established, this is not so much the case in the social sciences and social work. Language is often a barrier hindering the dissemination of research findings internationally. Publishing in English has become a necessity. Prior to World War II, the social science research community was solely European and American. The social sciences were overwhelmingly located in just five countries – France, Great Britain, Germany, Italy, and the US (Wallerstein, 1997: 93). Wallerstein argues that even today, social sciences are Eurocentric by nature, a dominant feature of which is the idea that sociopolitical values can and should held as separate and apart from scientific research (Wallerstein, 1997: 96).

Peter V. Zima questions the international character of sociological theory. His analysis shows that German sociologists rely on English-speaking theorists like Giddens and Bauman, but rarely on French theorists like Foucault or Touraine. French sociologists focus on French concerns, English researchers on English preoccupations. French, English or German speaking researchers seldom cite Russian or non-European research or theories. Zima concludes that theorizing is always culture dependent and closely connected to the language. This is not new: Durkheim and Weber, leading theorists in their own neighboring countries did not comment on each other's work (Zima, 2004: 34–45).

The international exchange of ideas and influences in social work may be even more limited than in other social science disciplines. Few North American social workers read the international literature (Gray et al., 2008: 8).

The Nordic countries serve as an example of non-English national parochialism. Nordic researchers are able to read each other's journals and research reports, but the Finnish, Danish, Norwegian and Swedish researchers tend to relate to the discourse within their own countries. References to research from other Nordic countries are rare.

CONCLUSION: WHERE ARE WE NOW? WHERE ARE WE HEADING?

Our review of theory and theorizing yields several generalizations. First, there have always been tensions between individual, psychological theories and structural theories of human and social behavior. These theories seek alternatively to locate responsibility for problems and their solutions in individuals, or in social conditions and political arrangements. There are tensions too between the alternative priorities of practice and research, academia and the field.

Second, knowledge production and theorizing in social work (and elsewhere) have decidedly political dimensions that operate on several levels. There has been a lively competition among contending interest groups and theoretical perspectives to define what social work is all about (Payne, 2005: 8). The 'professional project' makes use of knowledge production to advance the standing of social work, as a profession and as an academic endeavor (Larson, 1977). Alternative theories and theoretical perspectives support or challenge extant political arrangements, implicitly, as with psychoanalytic theories, or overtly as with Marxist theories. Theoretical perspectives that find favor are those most compatible with extant social arrangements. Brief therapies were compatible with the cutbacks invoked by conservative governments. And finally, Marxist and some postmodern theories hold that social work is itself an integral part of regime maintenance and social control.

Third, social work will always look to other disciplines for theoretical insights, but will increasingly be able to draw upon theory and research findings generated within the growing community of social work scholars. Many theoretical contributions have been, and will be, derived from clinical observations. If one look back retrospectively, it seems clear that theory development in social work has proceeded incrementally, building upon or in opposition to prior theories, and this seems likely to continue.

Fourth, there are opposing forces operating both for and against the convergence, internationally, of social work practice, theory and theorizing. On the one hand, the forces of globalization, political integration as with the European Union, and the mandates of the UN and other international bodies push the field toward consensus and standardization. At the same time, as social work becomes more international, it also becomes more diverse, open to alternative world views and to a broader range of concerns.

Finally, theory development and theorizing will always be responsive to changes in social conditions. The AIDS epidemic, for example, spawned an interest within social work in prevention theory. Parton (2008) considers the implications for social work theory of information age technical innovations. Social workers increasing interact with data about people rather than with people themselves. In this 'database culture' social work becomes more circumscribed, routine and standardized in ways that limit social workers' discretion. The 'social' aspect of social work is replaced by the 'informational'. How does theory, by its nature, slow, reflective and detached, keep up with the accelerating pace of society – or should it? Parton (2008: 14) argues that theory should both speed up, to 'provide methods and techniques to allow social workers to think and act within the timescales expected of them', and slow down and engage in critical reflection about how practitioners can retain some aspect of interpersonal relatedness in an informational environment.

We would add that information technology is also changing everything from dating and courtship rituals, to social networks, pornography, shopping, child exploitation and bullying. It provides new opportunities for surveillance by governments and corporations, and erodes the boundaries between public and private space. The implications for social work theory and practice are profound.

We conclude where we started, calling attention to the nature of theory as a reflective, participatory activity, and to the example of the founders of social work who sought to apply theory for the betterment of the human condition. In this changing world, we have no lack of challenging issues to theorize about, to reflect and to act upon.

ACKNOWLEDGMENTS

We would like to thank Dr. Mark Schroeder of the University of Bielefeld for his helpful comments during the initial phase of writing this chapter.

The Uses of Social Work Research

Roy Ruckdeschel and Adrienne Chambon

INTRODUCTION

In this chapter we tackle the issue of the uses of research. This is a complex yet pressing problem for social work researchers. In one way or another, virtually all the chapters in the *Handbook* deal with issues of use. Since the term use is potentially ambiguous we prefer the term utilization. What than do we mean by research utilization? We begin by identifying three aspects of use. These are knowledge development, 'use' in the sense of how knowledge is incorporated into social work practice, and lastly the issue of how knowledge is disseminated to social workers at various levels of practice.

A number of additional clarifications are in order. First, as Orme (2006) points out, there is a difference between knowledge and information. Orme notes the work of Marsh and Fisher (2005) who suggest that social work knowledge combines evidence with practice wisdom and the views of practitioners and service consumers. As such, knowledge is potentially transformative (Chambon, 1999). What counts as evidence is itself problematic and contentious. Orme also maintains that there are negative and positive imperatives that facilitate or hinder acceptance of

knowledge in social work (Orme, 2006). We will build on these definitions of use. Our intent is not to replicate other chapters in the *Handbook* which deal more in depth with knowledge development but rather to focus on the relationship between knowledge development, use and dissemination. In the chapter we explore utilization through exemplars involving social work professionals and service users. Three Canadian exemplars are presented to demonstrate how knowledge development is influenced when concerns about application or actual use are the driving force. The exemplars also highlight the role of activism in the development and use of knowledge.

THE RELATIONSHIP BETWEEN SCIENCE AND USE

The role of science in the development of knowledge has already been acknowledged in the *Handbook*. In Chapter 1 Parton and Kirk make the distinction between science as a model of practice and science as a source of knowledge. In the first case, science serves as a systematic approach that embodies scientific techniques that should be incorporated into practice. Parton and Kirk go on to claim that the single subject design model reflects this logic. This so-called 'practice as science' view suggests that practice has to be informed by such issues as measurement and the operationalization of desired outcomes as well as precise specification of practice interventions. Joel Fischer and Walter Hudson were key figures in this movement (Fischer, 1973; Hudson, 1978). Fisher suggested that there was a paradigm shift taking place in social work from unsystematic loose conception of practice to a more scientifically based model of social work practice. The elements of this involved a combination of homothetic and single subject or single system designs (Fischer, 1981). The latter, which also came to be called the $N=1$ design, represented the application of a quasi-experimental design to mostly clinical practice. The claim was that the client or subject was her/his own control and as such would approximate the control possible only in experimental design. In a similar vein, Walter Hudson called for the application of measurement logic to social work practice. His foundational proposition was 'If you can't measure it, it doesn't exist, and if it doesn't exist you can't treat it' (Hudson, 1978). The practice as science trend was in turn resisted by some like Hartman and Meyer (Hartman, 1992, 1994; Meyer, 1984) who tended to view the kinds of research methods advocated by Fischer and Hudson as intrusions rather than aids to practice. Activists in social work (see Hartman for example) also argued for the importance of incorporating wisdom from indigenous movements (Hartman, 1992).

The second way of conceptualizing the role of science is to see science, including the social sciences, as a source of knowledge. In such case, social work needs to build the infrastructure that will facilitate the accumulation and translation of knowledge. Parton and Kirk maintain the research utilization movement in social work reflects this kind of logic (Chapter 1). The task becomes one of evaluating outcomes, deciding which of these have relevance for social work practice and developing guidelines for application. Parton and Kirk also suggest that this is the basis of evidence based practice (EBP) approaches.

Models of knowledge application

An important development in knowledge utilization in recent decades is the rise of research institutes or centers that evaluate existing research for possible knowledge applications in social work. Perhaps the most ambitious effort at the framing of research use comes from the Social Care Institute for Excellence (SCIE) from the United Kingdom. A SCIE report on improving the use of research in social care practice (Walter et al., 2004) addresses the status of research use in social care and social work in the UK and focuses on furthering efforts in this regard. The report provides an insight into how an important research institute approaches the issue of use. As part of the process, SCIE investigators decided to look at the empirical evidence on research use and how it has been discussed in the social work literature, restricting their search for such literature to the UK. The initial search resulted in over 3000 possible references. Of these 191 were selected as empirically based and potentially relevant. However, only 28 passed muster as having adequate methodological grounding to be incorporated in the survey. These 28 were in turn divided into those that were identified as of good quality (14) and those that were somewhat less robust (14). The 28 studies were than assessed for empirical evidence on usage (Walter et al., 2004).

For our purposes, two points stand out from this attempt to provide empirical grounding on how research is actually used in social work and social care. The first is the obvious one. If only 28 studies of 3000 articles met minimal criteria, we seem at an early stage in empirically addressing research usage. We might in fact conclude that while there is much concern about the role of evidence on research usage, there is actually relatively little empirical data that bears on the matter.

A second point that emerges is the need to clarify usage terminology and implications of such terminology. In the United States, Canada and the UK, the dominant mode of discussing the application of research is that of EBP. Other chapters in the *Handbook* will more directly address the utility of EBP as a methodology as well as examining its philosophical underpinnings and the implications it has for social work research. The SCIE prefers to use the term research informed practice rather than EBP. The rationale being that their studies suggest the need to have a more inclusive way of thinking about the application of research.

While not prescribing or endorsing any particular research methodology, the report went on to conclude that there are three distinct models of research use in social care. The first is that of the research based practitioner. In such case it is the role of the autonomous practitioner to stay current with and apply research findings to their practice (Walter et al., 2004). This is fairly similar to the previous discussion about the single subject design and the scientifically based practitioner (Fischer, 1981; Hudson, 1978).

The second model is that of the embedded research model. In this approach, research is to be embedded within systems of social work and social care. Responsibility for seeing that research informs practice in such settings is the task of managers, policy makers and research specialists. There is not an expectation that individual practitioners will be directly involved in research or decide how empirical data is to be used (Walter et al., 2004). In such settings there is the potential danger of managerial control of the research agenda.

The third approach is the organizational excellence model which suggests that research use requires the development of a research-oriented culture within social care organizations. Research adaptation is by necessity local (contextual) and implies differing kinds of knowledge and a commitment by all to be involved in research practice. As with the previous model, there is a risk of managerial control of the research agenda.

The report notes that the first two models imply a linear view of research (Walter et al., 2004). This suggests that research is an instrumental activity and that the major task for social work researchers is to apply the data that comes from research to practice. It also implies a degree of separation between the researcher and the practitioner. By way of contrast, the organizational excellence model is non-linear in that it views research development, use and roles in a more circular or dialectic fashion. While noting there is relatively little evidence about the effectiveness of any of these approaches, the report also suggests that the greatest resistance in social work/social care is to the first approach. In this chapter, our discussion of usage tends to build primarily on non-linear approaches. This is particularly the case in our discussion of the exemplars and the role of activism.

An important conclusion of the SCIE report is that no matter which model is employed, major gaps remain. The report noted two such ongoing and major gaps. These being the disconnect between the above models and effectively engaging the funders of research (Walter et al., 2004: xviii) and 'the lack of a core role for service users (practitioners) in supporting the use of research'.

In the United States, The Society for Social Work and Research (SSWR) and the corresponding listserv (one of several such partners) the Institute for the Advancement of Social Work Research (IASWR) function in a somewhat similar way as SCIE. The IASWR listserv reports, via the internet, on upcoming conferences, workshops and training opportunities, sources of funding, online recourses, relevant publications and research findings. SSWR through annual conferences mainly addresses the academic social work community in the US and is particularly influential in doctoral education. It has no particular unified model or approach to research usage but recent conferences have been dominated by presentations on evidenced based practice. Following the logic of the SCIE framework, we suggest that SSWR seems to implicitly embrace the view of science as a source of knowledge. While qualitative methods are included in conference reports and presentations, quantitative approaches dominate.

In the next part of this chapter we present the exemplars involving social work professionals and service users. The exemplars also highlight the role of activism in the development and use of knowledge.

RESEARCH UTILIZATION AND WHAT COUNTS AS KNOWLEDGE: INCORPORATING UTILIZATION FROM THE START

Our discussion raises the continuing issue of who contributes to and who produces the research and under what set of circumstances. Commissioned research can be instigated by various different players; policy makers within and outside of government, academics or social work practitioners and service users.

Commissioned research

For example, in Canada, the development of the welfare state was fostered, in a large extent, by social scientists that launched wide-ranging social urban programs of research and intended to foster social policies that would be responsive to the changing social conditions. This reflects one of our starting distinctions, namely science in general and the social sciences in particular as sources of knowledge.

The 1930s was a period of tremendous social transformation, with growing industrialization and swift urbanization. New social policy frameworks were needed to accommodate these profound changes. There was

public concern and agitation and political parties were looking for programs and ready to develop wide-ranging policies. A pivotal research project was led in the 1930s in Canada by Leonard Marsh, who had joined McGill University from the London School of Economics. Marsh had been invited to lead a major social science survey on poverty and unemployment that was to replicate a London study (Irving, 1986).

The intent was to draw on scientific research as above to inform government policy. A form of expert activism that is meant to set standards of research and of direct use (Irving, 1992). Expert knowledge was to be used as a tool of social policy in the service of social reform to pioneer a new direction for society. The social survey of the time consisted in a much broader array of methods than what is meant by survey today (Hughes, 1984b).

The Marsh Report on Social Assistance (1943) was one of the structural architects of social welfare arrangements in Canada post-war. Following upon the Beveridge Report in the UK, it denounced a state of affairs and formulated general principles and orientation that were implemented at the end of World War II. It had received huge coverage and was hailed as a pivotal document. A comment is needed here: though the questions of unemployment and poverty are core social work issues, they were addressed as a 'social science' research endeavor. And though social work academics were involved, social work as a discipline did not receive funding at the time, unlike sociology – reflecting the former's tentative status as a scientific discipline.

In any case, the importance of such research cannot be stressed enough. It defined the terms of what counted as 'problems' and 'needs' and set the parameters for the types of solutions, i.e., resources and interventions needed (Edelman, 1988), ushering an explicit social agenda. It is also clear from this example that the economic, social and political context of the time created opportunities for advancing social reform, what Orme refers to as a positive imperative (Orme, 2006), based on research. At other times, such support is lacking (a negative imperative).

Practitioner generated research

As a contrast in research use, a similarly important social issue has been the social gap between the income, health conditions and social participation of the general Canadian public and those of Aboriginal populations. This historically rooted problem continues to plague society. In 1996, the Royal Commission on Aboriginal Peoples that had academics on its panels, reiterated the crisis that represented the invisibility of this structural oppression.

In this instance, Hugh Shewell, a social worker who studied the history of social welfare in Aboriginal communities' had worked for many years as a policy staff in the Department of Indian and Northern Affairs in Canada. Painfully aware of the policy inadequacies, he chose to study the origins and development of Native welfare policy inequities. Interestingly enough, while the question of poverty had been discussed repeatedly no one had examined the actual policies of social assistance and their implementation: specific set of policies, regulations and practices. He used a social work and combined social policy approach to examine the arrangements and their consequences on people's lives, on children, women, families and communities. Initially intending to conduct a time-limited history, Shewell later expanded the study to cover the period from 'contact' between Colonizers and First Nations up to the mid-1960s.

This approach relied on a vast amount of primary archives, along with interviews, and theoretical considerations on colonialism. It opened up a new vista onto the construction of the state and the logic of social relations that have oppressed Aboriginal peoples. Initiated by the researcher himself, this study was conducted without a prior utilization plan. The published work, well documented, well grounded in everyday life, scope, quotes and accessibility of the study (Shewell, 2000) has become a major reference text in the history of the nation; a social history of Aboriginal communities in Canada and a leading text in undergraduate and graduate education used beyond the field of social work.

Trends in commissioned research

What are the trends about commissioned research? Asked another way, what are the incentives or positive imperatives that result in commissioned research?

Over the years, the major academic funding body for the social sciences in Canada, government sponsored SSHRC, created a Standard Research Grants yearly competition that has supported a range of research. The agendas were first open, to be defined by the researchers (see Orme (2006) for similar developments in the UK). The adjudication committees were organized by discipline, and projects continue to be adjudicated through peer-review, thus by academics, rather than by policy makers or politicians. However, with the creation of its 'strategic grant' program in the 1980s, whose funds were drawn from the same pool as the standard grants, SSHRC started to prioritize areas and problem-oriented topics of research, such as women and work; the new economy; homelessness. In the last few years, these agendas have become narrower with an identified focus and objectives – indicating, if not dictating the kind of study they would like to see. This in turn has implications for their actual use.

Alongside these longer-term research projects, provincial Ministries and federal government offices routinely commission research projects that are usually short-term. These come with directives and resemble, if not take the form of, program evaluations. They can also be commissioned by foundations, agencies or networks of agencies: for example, sponsorship of immigrant families, costs and breakdowns; health and homelessness.

A caveat is in order. Not all commissioned research will exert an influence in daily affairs. Research is sometimes invited as a way of appeasing the public, a promise to look into an issue of concern. A form of negative utilization is when results are dismissed or play no significant role in the actual policies that are put in place.

Exemplars of utilization

Below are three exemplars of mixed researcher–community involvement that illustrate different aspects of utilization. The first brings out the importance of local citizen involvement in research, and the significance of social movements. The second case brings out a critical dilemma between indigenous culture, indigenous voice and the kinds of research methods that typically 'speak' to, are deemed relevant to, policy makers. The third case illustrates the new audiences reached by research that addresses public culture and stigma through the social images (representations) of vulnerable populations that commonly circulate and are internalized in common sense and by professionals. This type of research broadens the audience of the research and engages emotions through embodied and aesthetic materials.

Exemplar 1: A case of innovative social planning with local input

In the 1960s, an exemplar of activist research was led by a social worker and a faculty member at the University of Toronto School of Social Work. Albert Rose led research on an experiment of social housing. It was the largest and most innovative initiative in social housing in the country. For several years prior to the research, Rose had been a leading proponent in local citizen groups advocating for the development of social housing by the city of Toronto (Finkel, 2006). His community

involvement combined with his faculty position made him a leader in the field. He was commissioned by the City of Toronto (with funding from the Central Mortgage Housing Corporation, the government arm of a burgeoning housing policy) to study the implementation of the project. Over a ten-year period this led to a number of studies by actively involving faculty and graduate students. The study included a critique of the implementation of the program, which by postponing the development of community institutions would have the result of cutting off a group and leading to its marginalization and lack of social integration. The author expressed the urgency to act upon the attitudes of the public that stigmatized this population. The intended audience was broad. In the preface to the volume on Regent Park, Rose states:

> In preparing this record I have attempted to write for the non-expert (as well as the expert) and in particular I have had in mind the citizen who is taking some responsibility in his community as a member of a service group, a home and school association, a women electors' association, a board of directors of a social agency or a welfare organization; this is the audience I hope this book will reach ... I hope, of course, that the book will be of interest to a good many other persons as well, particularly to those who serve the community as public officials, appointed or elected, and to members of the relevant professions – medicine, public health, social work, architecture and community planning. (Finkel, 2006: viii–ix)

The position and voice of the author are that of an engaged activist combined with a systematic approach to communication of results to give this position legitimacy. He did not shun taking an engaged position and making 'I' statements in an attempt to influence policy. At the same time, the City of Toronto Planning Board saw the project as a model of urbanization and housing for the country as a whole. In the introduction to the volume, we find their statement:

> We have now received his report setting out the findings. We believe that these will be of great

significance to the field or urban renewal and trust that the conclusions drawn will be fully reflected in future legislation and programmes … In issuing the consultant's report we hope that it will prove to be of value not only in Toronto, but in other cities as well.

This example is quite typical of its time in North America. We can think of the community-based studies during the Johnson Administration in the US.

Exemplar 2: Utilization and the dilemmas of indigenous voice, method and target audience – research development from outside the field

Aboriginal-led research has on one hand focused on a historically shaped critique of institutional arrangements under which Aboriginal people have been oppressed, as the example above illustrates. Increasingly, the critique of imperialism has encompassed the methods of research, and what counts as relevant knowledge in an Indigenous perspective (Smith, 1999). In this more recent vein, it is important that social claims be made within culturally valued ways of telling. This has meant, generally, a turn to narrative, oral history and holistic paradigms, reflected equally in the actual writing that is highly evocative. These features are openly at odds with mainstream research as perceived in Canada. They are compatible however within the academia with critical theory and feminist anti-colonial research endeavors. Structural claims are made within an Indigenous paradigm and pitched in this manner, as a political and cultural tool of survival, empowerment.

Indigenous approaches are more relevant to Aboriginal peoples. However, these approaches are largely dismissed by politicians, policy makers and part of academia. A number of research studies that are qualitative are considered 'soft research'. One of the structural difficulties

is therefore that different audiences are clearly at odds in their interests in the type of knowledge that they value. Addressing one audience often means alienating the other, or leading to disinterest and continued invisibility and marginalization. The opposite risk is that conducting mainstream research smacks of assimilation and disregard. Voices and views matter, as do usage and impact of the research imperatives.

One strategy taken by the director of the First Nations Child and Family Caring Society of Canada, Cindy Blackstock, a status Aboriginal person, with front line child welfare experience and a long-term policy advocate at the federal (national) level, was to conduct research that is quantitative in nature. She has taken the lead in a secondary analysis of Aboriginal child data from of a large national child welfare data set. She has done so as part of a national strategy developed by Aboriginal leaders to raise the visibility of oppressive social conditions in Aboriginal communities. The state of child welfare in Aboriginal communities in Canada is woefully inadequate. The issues remain unaddressed in spite of the repeated statements and appeals.

The historical plight of Aboriginal families is now becoming part of the Reconciliation agenda that has recently been launched in conjunction with the Assembly of First Nations toward the Canadian government and the Canadian people. This intent is clearly formulated in a recent paper entitled 'Reconciliation means not saying sorry twice: Lessons from child welfare in Canada' (Blackstock, 2008).

In February of 2007, the Assembly of First Nations in partnership with the First Nations Child and Family Caring Society of Canada filed a complaint with the Canadian Human Rights Commission alleging that Canada's conscious under funding of First Nations child welfare was resulting in First Nations children receiving unequal benefit pursuant to child welfare legislation and the Charter of

Rights and Freedoms. This case is currently before the Human Rights Commission and a ruling is expected in the summer of 2008. (Blackstock, 2008: 10)

The author is aware of the discrepancy in knowledge expectations, and is determined to address the policy-oriented findings of the research within a framework of Indigenous knowledge and responsibility. In other words, the tenor of the message is meant to be challenging in its findings and intellectual content and in its spiritual and collective aim. From a holistic perspective, they cannot be separated. Mainstream society has much to be accountable for, and can learn from this endeavor. The objective is to bring about a different societal attitude and conduct. These initiatives are themselves part of a movement of Indigenous peoples worldwide. There are ongoing consultations between Australia, Canada and the US leaderships, as well as among the circumpolar network of peoples. This is the role of voice, of native involvement and indigenous peoples. It also raises questions about the role of professional social workers. A research paper articulating this point of view (Blackstock, 2007) recognizes the different approaches to knowledge by indigenous peoples based on spirituality:

> Indigenous ontology and research methods are often more appropriate for research purposes of exploring ancestral teaching and researching phenomena occurring over a long period of time or within a highly interconnected environments whereas western methods are most often used for the purpose of translating Indigenous knowledge so that it can be understood by westerners or to conduct entrepreneurial research exploring new, and time bracketed, phenomena affecting Indigenous people. (2007: 5)

It goes on to stress that while methodology might be a secondary issue, qualitative and quantitative research methods are equally viable for use with Indigenous peoples so long as they are appropriately enveloped in Indigenous knowledge and research protocols. The claim that 'Indigenous

peoples and their knowledge count. Not just for Indigenous peoples but for everyone' (2007: 20) is relevant to work in Australia and NZ on research involving Aboriginal and Maori communities.

Exemplar 3: Contesting cultural assumptions, a different audience, a different strategy

Parton and Kirk (Chapter 1) view social work as characterized by contested and ambiguous knowledge. This is certainly the case with cultural assumptions. In a similar vein, Norman Denzin (2000) invited social work to grapple with the question of social representations present in popular culture that recruit us as viewers without our deliberate agreement and perpetuate stereotypical, injurious, stigmatizing portraitures; alongside such explorations are those that engage with forms of opposition to these widely held images and beliefs about vulnerable groups.

The following exemplar is an illustration of a research project that confronts the personal biographies of persons with intellectual disability with widely circulating images of their group produced by social agencies, media and art sources. The study is an act of contestation of such cultural assumptions. It is an extension of social constructionist and reflexive approaches to social work knowledge (e.g. in the work of Fook [1996] and White [1997]) along with image-based research (Prosser, 1998) arts-informed inquiry (Knowles and Cole, 2007). Subjectivities and identities are promulgated through discursive and other representational means. Social workers are not exempt from such problematic assumptions about what constitutes knowledge. It suggests the necessity for ongoing dialogue between the various parties. It is a cultural studies form of social inquiry that extends the scope of the social science view of social construction and subjectivity, to examine the ways in which everyday culture, 'popular culture', visual representations as well as texts offer blueprints for identification (Chambon, 1999; Giroux, 2000; Hall, 1997; Hooks, 1990). By critically engaging with questions of esthetics alongside ethics, the project addresses the difficult question of a social unconscious more readily. How such representations implicate the viewer, whether as lay or as professional audience. More specifically, the project is theoretically framed by the philosophical ethics of Emmanuel Levinas and the respect to the Other (Moyb, 2005).

With an extensive background in child welfare and in advocacy, working with persons who have an intellectual disability, Ann Fudge-Schormans conducted a research project focusing on the unchanging nature of stereotypes about persons with intellectual disability (Stainton, 2004). The research was conducted with a group of persons who have an intellectual disability and are part of an advocacy network. The small group examined a number of public images created by charity organizations for the purpose of fund-raising, by photographers, images that appeared in the press. In an additional move, group members created alternative versions of the images, re-appropriating for themselves the source of representations with the help of a technology person assisted by Photoshop (see Karvinen et al., 1999 for an example of similar research in Europe).

This is a highly meaningful study involving a group of marginalized citizens (including a small number of service users) whose voices and views are not typically heard because of long-held assumptions that they are unable to develop arguments. More fundamentally they are deemed to lack a sense of personal history which would render their views meaningful.

A crucial step in the research dissemination consisted in engaging distinct audiences to respond to the group's reactions and counter-images. Research utilization was from the start an intrinsic part of the study itself. Three exhibit events took place in which the work of the group was shown for discussion. The audiences were: (a) a group of persons with intellectual disability; (b) a group of persons who have siblings with an intellectual disability or who are staff members working with this population; (c) a group of persons who do not have a direct familiarity with the issues encountered by persons with an intellectual disability.

Since then, the group has presented their work in university departments in disability, at an arts-centre, and in disability policy forums. This is a very broad exposure and diversity of audiences, which is linked to the very nature of the study and its aims. A major fund-raising organization has invited the group to act as consultants for the design of their next campaign. Further, the group launched a website, which they named 'What's wrong with this picture'. The visibility of the group's interventions led to a feature article written about them by a journalist covering disability questions who interviewed them about welfare income policies. The PI has also presented this research in the UK and is developing international linkages. The significance of such projects is that the involvement of the research participants in all the research activities has enhanced public debate and presented group members with opportunities for expressing and staging their views. This was previously considered impossible by them, and others. The next step being considered is linking the initiative with a powerful advocacy research institute.

In conclusion, the advocacy usage was deliberate and the research project has resulted in an advocacy movement. The focus on collective representations, esthetic and emotional impacts generate a much larger array of usages of the research and a diverse audience.

Research dissemination

It is our contention that dissemination has been a taken for granted part of the process when in fact it is an essential and rapidly changing aspect of utilization. Up to this point in the chapter the focus has been on production and use of research but throughout dissemination has been implied. However, issues of use are increasingly connected to modes of dissemination. This also relates to the question of audience or the consumers of research. Social work researchers have traditionally circulated their findings in academic and professional journals and through professional association meetings. In this section we explore the implications of conventional or traditional ways of disseminating research versus the evolution of newer forms and conclude the section with a discussion of Open Access Journals and their implications.

For the purposes of this analysis, we note three patterns of dissemination of social work research:

1. *Traditional means* which essentially rely on the print media. Professional journals would be the most prevalent example of this.
2. *Neo-traditional forms of dissemination*. This refers to patterns of dissemination that represent avenues for the distribution of research usage that incorporates the same kinds of content that are reflected in the more traditional means of distribution but with mode of distribution being that of the internet and related resources.
3. *Evolving forms of dissemination*. This refers to internet resources that change or alter the pattern of distribution and the nature of the content. This is in reference to such forms as blogs, YouTube, MySpace, Facebook, Twitter, etc. These can also be considered platforms for distribution, a point we take up in the subsequent section.

Traditional and variants of traditional forms of dissemination Traditional refers to the historically common forms of academic research distribution. By this we mean professional journals, academic and professional conferences and corresponding proceedings, workshops and funding reports. In this

respect, social work is no different in its patterns of dissemination than the social science disciplines. The content is classical and reflects what Witkin calls the scientific form of writing (Witkin, 2000).

Journals are the most obvious form of a traditional pattern of distribution. The assumed audience is professional and is socialized into traditional modes of research presentation. Some examples of such major journals would be Social Work and the Social Service Review in the US and the British Journal of Social Work in the UK.

Even within this pattern of distribution, there are a number of developing trends that impact the dissemination of social work research. One has been the development of international journals (such as the *International Review of Qualitative Research*). These journals still mainly appeal to a professional audience but have to also reflect cultural differences in the context of social work or social care services and in the kinds of issues confronting social workers in their respective countries. The increase in the number and types of specialized journals raises the question of whether this dilutes the impact of research journals and correspondingly the impact of research reported in such journals.

While the main audience for these traditional modes of dissemination is the professional masters level social worker the articles are mainly written by doctoral level academics. The editors of a recent issue of *Social Work* noted that a survey of readers indicated that they would like to see more articles written by non-academic professionals (Marsh et al., 2004). Their preference was for topics that are practical and less theoretically based. This has obvious implications for issues of use by practitioners. The style of writing, i.e. scientific writing, may also be a barrier. Some organizations such as the Joseph Rowntree Foundation insist on 'Briefings' that are written in non-technical language to appeal to a wider readership.

An extension of the traditional form of dissemination is the use of the internet to carry essentially the same content as the print media.

We might term this neo-traditional. Most journals now have on-line versions. Similar developments have occurred with professional associations and conferences utilizing websites to convey diverse information including the posting of available research results.

An interesting development in this regard is the advent of the open access journal. These are on-line journals which differ primarily in terms of fee structure and access. Professional journals, including the journals in social work are produced by publishing companies. The editors and the publishers of a given journal decide on the editorial policy and the manner in which manuscripts are reviewed or evaluated. This typically involves review of anonymized manuscript by assessors who should have no knowledge of or connection to the authors to ensure the review is not biased by any information about the author or possible connections to that author. These procedures are intended to reinforce the gatekeeper function of professional journals and by implication the development of the professional knowledgebase.

Periodic debates arise as to how well journals are performing this function. For example the Presidential Task Force on Publications of the Society for Social Work and Research (a US organization) was established to make recommendations to improve the quality of social work journals, in particular research-oriented journals. The report of the Task Force (Holden et al., 2008) mainly focuses on how to make journals more rigorous and standardized in the manuscript review process. The underlying logic represents the continuing concerns about objectivity and the potential negative impact of non-rigorous journals on the development and systematization of knowledge in social work (see Fischer, 1981 on the need for systematic knowledge development as part of what he terms the scientific revolution in social work). The report includes recommendations about the appropriate use of statistics and the need for monitoring the adequacy and quality of reviews and reviewers over time. Reviewers are to be selected on the basis of substantiated

expertise. Interestingly, the report concludes with the plea that creativity in knowledge development should not be unduly hampered by the move toward greater standardization, rigor and efficiency (Holden et al., 2008).

A contrasting approach is represented by the development of open access journals (for a listing of such journals in all fields consult the Directory of Open Access Journals, DOAJ, 2008). Open access journals are publications that do not charge readers or their institutions for access and assume the right of users to 'read, download, copy, distribute, print, search, or link to the full texts of these articles' (DOAJ, 2008). Examples of such journals in social work are *Studies in Social Justice*, the *Journal of Social Work Values and Ethics*, *Research on Social Work Practice* and the *Qualitative Report* (see bibliography for details).

The above implies that knowledge is not proprietary but is a common good available to all. Viewed thus, the journal is less the gatekeeper than it is the location where professional and scientific dialogue and disputation takes place. The actual impact is unclear at this point in time but this represents a challenge to the professional infrastructure of knowledge management and distribution. The role of such journals is likely to increase in the future and to continue to be focal point for debates about research usage.

Evolving forms and platforms for dissemination The issue of dissemination is increasingly tied to platforms for the presentation of data, evidence and disputation. Traditional modes of dissemination (the print media) and variants of same (internet and online sources) have historically been the taken for granted platforms or vehicles for the communication of research results. The marriage of the internet as platform with the typical products of research is the model that is perhaps most dominant today. The internet as platform represents an extension of the print media but does so without essentially changing the style of presentation and the appeal to legitimacy.

This is not necessarily the case with the evolving media platforms. By this we mean the evolution of new and different forms of dissemination that potentially alter the content or products of social work research. Here we are referring to such forms as blogs, YouTube, MySpace, Facebook, and Twitter. While challenging our ways of thinking about communication, these forms have the potential to reach a much larger and more varied audience. It has been suggested that we may be moving into an era of what some term platform agnosticism (Kohn and Amatucci, 2007). We live in an age where the relationship between the media and message is quite complex with a multitude of media and forms of expression. While a social work journal will reach only a very limited audience, MySpace, YouTube and blogs can reach millions. However, the newer platforms are in essence non-controllable. Platform agnosticism (Kohn and Amatucci, 2007) refers to the view that no form of media or platform is privileged. Platform agnosticism is predicated on new ways to package and take in information. This includes theatre, social networks, the arts, visual and ascetic forms. In this mode, it doesn't particularly matter whether the message is delivered via the three inch screen of a smart cell phone through an on-line internet source or over the airwaves on a 60 inch LCD TV set.

A note of caution is relevant here. We previously noted the distinction between information and knowledge discussed by Orme (2006). The discussion about platforms and means of distribution is essentially about the circulation of information. Information is not knowledge per se. It is the task of social work researchers to distinguish between knowledge that can be useful to social work practitioners or the direction of policy and information that does not necessarily contribute to the professional knowledge base. However, even here a case can be made for the circulation of information. The promulgation of relevant information might help the general public have a better understanding and appreciation of social work thus potentially positively impacting the political environment of the profession.

No doubt we will continue to dwell in a period of competing and overlapping platforms. However, as we peer into the future, we see the arrival of a new generation that is far less dependent on the traditional and conventional ways of doing things. The educators of a new generation of social workers will have to adapt to and perhaps take the lead in addressing the challenges posed by the emerging technologies and platforms for dissemination. Inevitably this will impact the ways in which social work research and the products of social work research are put to use.

The much discussed Millennial generation is upon us with all the implications this cohort has for education. Some have characterized this group as the *eye generation*, a generation that relates primarily to visual forms of representation (Weeks, 2007). How will this generation impact the form, presentation and dissemination of social work research? How much effort should go into the dissemination of social work research via the evolving forms? What level of training and research sophistication will be necessary? What will be the rules for the production of knowledge? How are we to assess the effectiveness of our use of various platforms? How can complex issues/research findings be presented in the age of sound bites? What expectations will we have of our graduates and of doctoral level social workers? How will this play out in the non-English speaking parts of the world where religious and political movements dominate? We view these important questions that remain to be answered or for that matter even engaged with.

Tying it together – a political economy view of research use

Throughout this chapter we have tried to do justice to various different aspects of research utilization, namely the production, use and dissemination of knowledge. We have also tried to take into account differing views of science and its role in the production of knowledge. However, we conclude by suggesting an additional and somewhat more inclusive way of framing the issues. Borrowing from the SCIE report, we find the concept of research informed practice more viable than the far more pervasive concept of EBP. Likewise we find it helpful to frame usage in both linear and non-linear fashion. We have tried to incorporate the role of activism in the discussion and have drawn a distinction between commissioned research and research which comes from the community or the practitioner social worker. This pushed us into thinking about the issue of use in a more systemic way. That is to say, that much of the discussion of research usage is premised on individualistic models of research. The emphasis implicitly, if not explicitly, is on the need to develop a cadre of research proficient social workers both as doers and consumers of research. Perhaps the key word is consumption. As such research is a commodity, a product. It is a product to be consumed and/or applied for the improvement of social work practice. Research can thus be viewed as a context free, objective instrumentality. Training in that instrumentality becomes crucial and is the hallmark of the professional. The extent and type of the training will depend on the level of education (Bachelors, Masters and PhD in the US) with a corresponding heightened research expectation at each stage.

While conceding that this indeed is an important framing of research usage, we believe it is also necessary to expand our vision of research and research usage. There needs to be a way to better incorporate community based, activist and multiple and contextual approaches to research. Here we have come to see utility in political and economic terms.

Political in the sense of bargaining, coalition building and conflict as factors that influence the setting of the research agenda. Economic in the sense that costs and benefits are inevitably part of the equation. Putting these together results in a political economy

view of the research enterprise. This is inherently a structural as opposed to individualistic perspective of social work research. Before dealing more directly with the implications of such a model, we present a brief history of how this approach has found its way into the social work literature.

The political economy of organizations The major movement of the political economy model into the social work literature is through its impact on organizational theory in the 1970s and 1980s. Hasenfeld argued that it was necessary to draw a distinction between conventional organizations and those in which social workers functioned. He referred to the latter as human service organizations and that such organizations differ in significant ways from business-oriented models of organizations (Hasenfeld, 1983). Business-oriented organizations tend to beget business-oriented organizational theories. Organizational theory when imported into social work tends to focus on models such as scientific management and human relations which take the point of view of management and assume a consensual model of organizational goals (Longres, 2000). While any model, including the political economy, may be used for managerial purposes, the political economy model incorporates multiple perspectives and does not privilege the managerial viewpoint.

Hasenfeld frames this as a rational model or view of organizations. It assumes a means–end relationship between organizational goals and the means to achieve those goals. In such case goals must be clear, identifiable and essentially measurable. In the world of business profit would be such a goal. On the other hand, Hasenfeld notes that goals in human service organization are more amorphous and abstract. In the rational model, the means to achieve those goals must likewise be widely understood, distinctive and effective. When such conditions exist, there should be a strain toward rationality that would be reflected in the organizational structure. In human service organizations, by way of contrast, the goals are abstract, multiple and often conflicting and the means indeterminate.

The political economy model suggests the need to pay attention to both the immediate organizational environment and the wider societal system and to potential conflicting interests in those environments. It also emphasizes the need to understand how political and economic factors influence organizational goal setting and behavior. Conventional quantitative and qualitative methods for measuring the extent to which the organizations achieve their goals can be seen as only one factor among many which influence that organizational behavior. In a previous article, one of the authors of this chapter argued against the posing of key research tasks such as evaluation and accountability in narrow instrumental terms (Ruckdeschel, 1994). By way of extension, it appears most conventional organizational theories assume a linear model of the application of research to practice. A non-instrumental view might reframe the question as less one of effectiveness and more a matter of evaluation for whom and for what purpose.

The political economy model represents a movement away from such consensual top down theories that ignore context (see the work of Mayer Zald, 1970, 1981 for example). Borrowing from Zald, the political economy model suggests a focus on these aspects of organizational environments: the external polity; the internal polity; the external economy; and the internal economy. The political economy thus focuses on both the internal system of the organization and the external environment in which the organization is operating.

The political economy of research usage

It is interesting that the current discussion employing a political economy perspective of research has taken place largely in the educational research and policy arenas. Despite the fact that this perspective would seem to offer much to social work researchers the debate in social work has tended to concentrate on methods and in particular the relative value of qualitative vs. quantitative methods. While EBP has seemingly given the quantitative methodologist the upper hand, the authors of this chapter, taking a political economy view of research, believe that the methods debate essentially misses the point. It ignores the issue of voice of audience and community based research.

A political economy approach allows us to focus on issues crucial to research use in social work. Drawing on scholars from a number of fields, the following kinds of issues can be raised from this perspective. Maxwell, for example, claims that if the applied social sciences and professions are to be scientific they should focus on how actually scientists use evidence (Maxwell, 2002). Maxwell further maintains context is crucial. Evidence depends on context and its meaning varies from case to case. This suggests that research usage has to take into account the immediate environment but not lose sight of broader systemic issues. It also implies that we should avoid thinking about singular approaches to usage, to methods, to evidence (see also Arnd-Caddigan and Pozzuto, 2006). As Schwandt (2002) points out, evidence is provisional and contextual.

Continuing with this theme, Frederick Erickson recently maintained that we should avoid the futile search for general knowledge. He suggests that you cannot substitute general knowledge for clinical judgment. Erickson fears there will be increasing competition for scarce resources. Because of this, research evidence of varying kinds will play an important part, for better or for worse, in the allocation of resources (Erickson, 2008; see also Erickson, 2005). Whether one agrees with Erickson or not, he raises the issue of the relationship between general knowledge and its application in clinical practice. He also puts research use into a broader economic context.

Harry Torrance suggests that utility or translational research is an emerging focus in education research in the UK and will become increasing important in the US in the funding process. The resulting emphasis on utilization shifts the debate away from methods to use. While quantitative research will remain important, there is in fact value in detailed qualitative research. Consequently we need a diverse view of policy research (Torrance, 2008). Taking a positive view of contemporary developments, Creswell (2007) notes the advance of mixed methods models and that designs are becoming more holistic. He further suggests that the paradigmatic methods debate has moved into the practice community and that there may in fact be a variety of paradigmatic communities each with its own specific concerns and interests.

As we see it, the implications of the political economy view of research use are:

1. The need to emphasize how our research translates into use; use does not have to be tied to particular approaches or even particular forms of evidence
2. That both linear and non-linear approaches to research use are available and viable
3. Use has to incorporate both immediate context and the wider societal system
4. Use has to be tied to practice communities
5. Use has to be tied to audience
6. Use has to be connected to modes of dissemination and platforms for doing so
7. Use has to be conceptualized in systematic and structural terms

We are not suggesting that such a perspective will solve all the problems addressed in this chapter. Indeed the *Handbook* itself symbolizes some of the challenges. What are our hopes for its impact? Is it only of value to academics and some professionals as well as students? What is its audience, its platform? What are our hopes for dissemination? What forms of writing do we implicitly and/or explicitly endorse? What impact will it have on the future of activism? These are the challenges for this and future projects. It remains to be seen whether social work is up to the task.

Our hope is that the application of this perspective will broaden the discussion about research utilization in social work research beyond debates over methods and the role of science.

Places in Time: Contextualizing Social Work Research

Ian Shaw

INTRODUCTION

Social work research takes place within temporal, social, relational, cultural, faith, governmental, political, institutional, ethical, intellectual, spatial and practice contexts. So much is a given for this section of the *Handbook*. It inhabits these contexts in ways that are, by and large, parallel to and reciprocal with research in other professions, disciplines and fields of study that share to a significant degree a commitment to comparable purposes of research. At any given period there usually will be sufficient common understanding and acceptance of the purposes of social work research to enable the social work community across different nations and cultures to engage in near-enough mutual understandings and practices. However, the character, purposeful priorities and uses of social work research will always be shaped – diversely – by the challenges of the places and times in which it occurs. Time and place are not only the contexts within which social work research 'happens' but also the 'character-makers' of research and the (unduly neglected) focus and concern of the research act. The chapter falls into five general phases.

- First, by way of preamble, and to avoid merely gathering bits and pieces, I acknowledge the influence of wider social theorizing for thinking and living in time and place, in the section on *placing context*. I will not detail, still less appraise, this work. My approach is more inductive, mapping and suggesting how important stances on and assumptions regarding time and place come to be embedded in social work research.
- Context as the focus and concern of *the research act* – both methodological and substantive – draws our subsequent attention. My interest is restricted to pursuing several strands of how a contextualizing focus has the potential to enrich social work research. I draw, for example, on ideas from cultural geography and network theory.
- Third, the ensuing part of the chapter has a wider angle, and aims to understand with as much coherence as I can muster the contexts within which the research act occurs. I consider *social work practice* as context for research.
- I then consider the varied elements of the social work and wider *academic communities*. I consider ideas of social work as a discipline, schools of thought and research, the act of doing science, writing, research teams and interdisciplinarity.
- In the final phase of the chapter I widen the angle of vision to consider the contextual relevance of the *state, city, rurality and the community* and include aspects of race and politics.

More generally this closing part of the chapter considers those contexts extrinsic to the immediate research act.

Like William James' description of philosophy, all this demands 'an unusually stubborn effort to think clearly' – an exigency I may not satisfy. Though taking general ideas as a framework, I aim to stay alert to the risk of replacing understanding with 'overstanding', and losing the work of the individual.

PLACING 'CONTEXT'

'Context' should not be treated as a taken for granted feature of social work or research. What are our assumptions of the meaning of 'social work context'? Possibly roughly the same as 'setting' or 'agency' and as something that is a 'given' of social work practice. Something we can 'touch, taste and handle' – that is relatively fixed and durable – social work's material culture. Maybe we distinguish in our minds the local from the extended setting. This extended setting may be spatial, or defined by membership. Service users may well appear in our image of the social work context, or the domains of nation, community, health and so on, that structure the final section of this *Handbook*. Possibly we envisage the extended context as including policy and managerial contexts. But what about the time dimension? Contexts are retrospective as well as prospective, and context cannot be restricted to spatial models. Professional and organizational discourses, and the almost endless deposit of written texts, also form core elements of social work contexts.

It will be clear from this that the frameworks of meaning within which social workers practice are not fixed and given. They are the result of mutual 'labour' on the part of actors. Such labour encompasses the methods that members engage in, for making their activities 'accountable' – visible, rational, and reportable. This underlines the central importance of both language and structure in grasping the significance of social work contexts. Thus, there is a risk that a too exclusive emphasis on 'constructivist' orientations neglects issues of power, space, place and time – context. This is particularly true when we slip into speaking of constructions as if they were merely mental constructs, as when Guba, for example, said that 'realities exist in the form of multiple mental constructions ... It is the mind that is to be transformed, not the real world' (Guba, 1990: 27). But reality is not simply and solely a mental product. It comprises social, collective acts, and these collective acts are material transactions with the world (Atkinson, 1995).

Time and place

'Time' and 'place' are high level concepts by which we structure and make sense of the world, and 'use effortlessly all the time ... yet are quite unable to define' (Fulford and Columbo, 2004: 131). Both 'time' and 'place' are verbs as well as nouns, and hence are actions as well as locations. They are shifting rather than fixed. Foucault, Bourdieu and Wittgenstein have filtered down and in a broad brush manner have left us oscillating between thinking of the meaning of words as being the thing they stand for (i.e. as representing states of affairs as they exist in the world) or as found in the use to which we put them. Distinctions between observer and subject or describing and explaining 'become blurred, and combine in the act of interpretation' (Thomas and Bracken, 2004: 364).

Pierre Bourdieu's theory of action – of practices, habitus and field – has gradually influenced the preoccupations of social scientists outside of sociology. 'To understand is to understand firstly the field with which and against which one was made' (Bourdieu, translated and quoted in Costa, 2006: 892). The 'field' is a system of positions and relationships among positions, with each position carrying diverse and antagonistic interests. How do we act as social agents?

Bourdieu understands this via the concept of 'habitus' – a system of relatively enduring though not unalterable ideas, values and preferences (dispositions) acquired from living in society (i.e. living in a social position). By field and habitus Bourdieu sees a correspondence between social and mental structures, between positions and dispositions.[1] It is common to speak of such relationships as embodied, and to regard the body as defining our spatiality and temporality, such that the body is placed somewhere between psychology and biology.

This view of things has of course been set against positivism – criticized as unable to deal with the complexity of social and cultural environments. 'Contexts provide grounds or reasons for human action, not causes of it' (Thomas and Bracken, 2004: 363). That is true, but for most purposes no longer centre-stage as positivism is for most a 'swearword by which nobody is swearing' (Williams, 1983). Either way, it would be unwise to suggest irrevocable disconnections between social theorizing of this kind and quantitative methodologies. Bourdieu's work has led, for example, to the utilization of logistic regression to map social spaces in measuring health inequalities (Gatrell et al., 2004) – though the best social work writing in this field rarely develops the same connections (Bywaters, 2007).

It would also be unwise to assume time, place, space and context in general are newly minted within French phenomenology. Symbolic interactionism, from Mead and Blumer onwards, has long recognized the inter-connections of mind, culture and society. Goffman's work has perhaps been the most directly influential on social work theory and research, and is rich in spatial and temporal conceptualization.

For Bourdieu, unlike Marx, habitus, though produced by history, is relatively detached from it. Yet social work research demands a historical scope of conception, where the historical is intrinsic to our understanding and not merely background (Mills, 1959).

Foucault's notion of 'history of the present', his ideas of genealogy and archaeology, and his work on the history of madness and psychiatry have only just begun to percolate social work research, primarily in Europe (e.g. Satka and Harrikari, 2008; Skehill, 2007).

To insist on the importance of history is not simply a point about methodology (although it *is* that – archives, documents, oral histories and so on are strangely undervalued in social work inquiry), but has regard to a way of thinking – of 'focusing "upstream" on the historical roots of contemporary relationships' (Mallinson et al., 2003: 773). Walter Lorenz has pressed this point effectively (Lorenz, 2007, 2008). He complains that it is as if we are 'too embarrassed to look seriously at our history, afraid of the disorder we might find, too eager to distance ourselves from the pre-professional beginnings' and are, in consequence, homeless and 'disembedded' (Lorenz, 2007: 598–9). He concludes that 'All social work practices are deeply embedded in historical and cultural habits from which we cannot detach ourselves at will', and aptly infers from this that we should be practising history 'in the dual sense of positioning ourselves in a historical context and of giving our interventions a historical dimension' (2007: 601).

Take, for instance, the early tales of sociology and social work at Chicago – ones of rich and complex inter-relationships. But the departmental and eventually disciplinary parting of the ways after 1920, with their associated shift of (women) sociology faculty into a new social work school, while welcomed to some extent on both sides, led to an eventual closure of conversation that worked against the interests of both fields of study. In universities across the world, this continues to hobble both sociology and social work. I have suggested elsewhere that this may not need to be so (Shaw, 2009, see Exemplar 1). 'There has always been a danger of ignoring the otherness of history ... to not engage with history as the totally other, a disturbing encounter that might make us see the things we do not want to see' (Lorenz, 2007: 603).

Exemplar 1: Ernest Burgess and an unfinished conversation with social work

The School of Social Service Administration (SSSA) was set up at Chicago in 1920. Thereafter social work and sociology are assumed to have gone their separate ways. Apart from brief accounts of sociology's methodological indebtedness to social work there are no hints in the literature of any significant intellectual interaction after the 1920 divide. Yet the writing and work of the Chicago sociologist, Ernest Burgess, in the decade following the establishment of the SSSA help open up a different history and an alternative view of the possible promise of reciprocal work between sociology and social work.

Throughout the 1920s Burgess pursued a creative preoccupation with the identity and historical development of sociology and social work in relation to one another. This led him to an early position (Burgess, 1923) that there is an essential interdependence between the two, and that their separate disciplinary developments had converged on a mutual while still distinguishable set of linked research interests. This essentially egalitarian view of their relationship prompted him to a view that there are reciprocal gains to be had, the one from the other. It also enabled him to voice positive criticisms of his own discipline and of social work. In the earlier part of this period he expounded the primary contribution of sociology to social work in terms of emerging conceptualizations of the city and community from leading sociologists across North America. In the later years of the decade he gave closer attention to spelling out the benefits for social work of empirical work carried out in Chicago. His primary application of the

contribution social work could make to sociology was in seeing agency records as a radical resource for sociology, and, to a less developed degree, reflecting on the implications of seeing social work as a 'concrete experiment' that gradually focused his mind on the potential for what today we would call 'outcomes research' and on the possibility of predictive judgements.

To suggest but one example from his arguments regarding how social work potentially contributes to the field of sociology he complained that:

> Existing case records seldom, or never, picture people in the language of Octavia Hill, with their 'passions, hopes, and history' or their 'temptations', or 'the little scheme they have made of their lives, or would make if they had encouragement'. The characters in case records do not move, and act, and have their being as persons. They are depersonalized, they become Robots, or mere cases undifferentiated except by the recurring problems they present (Burgess, 1928: 526–7; cf. Burgess, 1927).

He reflects that 'characters ... do not speak for themselves. They obtain a hearing only in the translation provided by the language of the social worker' (1927: 527). He sets the choice as one between a legalistic conception of the interview and a personal one.

> To enter the interview in the words of the person signifies a revolutionary change. It is a change from the interview conceived in legal terms to the interview as an opportunity to participate in the life history of the person, in his memories, in his hopes, in his attitudes, in his own plans, in his philosophy of life (Burgess, 1928: 527).

RESEARCHING CONTEXTS AND CONTEXTUALIZATION

Once we give more nuanced attention to theorizing, a contextualizing focus has the potential to enrich social work research, both methodologically and substantively.

Gunaratnam (2003) highlights the spatial dimensions of qualitative research interactions, but this seems unduly restrictive. Spatial and temporal assumptions are deeply embedded in *all* research methods, whether these are the formalized face to face of the interview and the focus group, the temporal and spatial attenuation of survey methods, the varied significance of place as well as space in ethnography and case studies, or the profoundly temporally structured contexts of randomized control trails. Cross-cutting concerns such as reflexivity and insider/outsider roles have dimensions of place (cf. Al-Makhamreh and Lewando-Hundt, 2008), as also do older debates about research quality. Take, for example, the language of the terms 'internal' and 'external' validity in accountability models of evaluation, with their tacit assumptions about what is located 'inside' and 'outside' research. Lee Cronbach and colleagues took issue with Donald Campbell on precisely this issue. In his 'brilliant *tour de force*' (Shadish et al., 1990: 375), that sets going an intellectual tingle to this day, the core of Cronbach's position is the claim that '"external validity" – validity of inferences that go beyond the data – is the crux of social action, not "internal validity"' (Cronbach et al., 1980: 231). Cronbach unequivocally rejects Campbell's influential position. 'Campbell's writings make internal validity a property of trivial, past tense, and local statements' (Cronbach, 1982: 137). Cronbach prioritizes the understanding and explanation of mechanisms operating in a local context, in order that plausible inferences can be drawn regarding other settings, people and interventions that are of interest to policy makers.[2]

Social work research gives too little attention to spacing and placing in research methodology. A comparison of current journals with, for example, a scan of the early books and journals in anthropology (e.g. Malinowski) and sociology (e.g. W. I. Thomas) shows how little the methodological interest in visual methods has percolated through to research practice, compared with the almost routine use of visual images in early work. Brian Roberts nicely refers to 'moving stories' and the emotionality of disjuncture in Thomas and Znaniecki's classic *Polish Peasant* study, where hidden accounts of the oppressed are disclosed through experiences of moving between spaces (Roberts, 2002).

Cultural geography and networks

Social work research could make significant gains from work done in the intellectually lively fields of cultural and social geography. While this lies primarily in theorizing and substantive concerns, there are also possibilities for imaginative method work. Bingley and Milligan (2007) discuss the advantages of using multi-sensory methodologies in their study into the long-term mental health effects of different kinds of childhood play space. Working with a small group of young people aged 16–21 years, they used a multi-method approach including practical workshops where the young people took part in a day of woodland activities and artwork sessions. The cross-over with ethnography, and the challenges posed by research with children and young people feed into these developments (cf. Mandell, 1988 for both these influences).

Geographic perspectives have also developed the fruitful idea of therapeutic landscapes (e.g. Milligan et al., 2004; Williams, 2007). Social work has taken interest in ecological practice models, but has made too little connection to the ecological research heritage dating from Robert Park's human ecology research at Chicago – so much so that the appearance of Megan Martin's delightful paper on 'Crossing the line' (Martin, 2007) strikes the reader almost as a novelty.

Network theory bridges method, theory and substance. In its more formal manifestations it involves 'collecting information on relationships among members of a social setting, mapping these relationships using visual graphs, (and) clustering members in different sub-sets along different criteria' (Lazega, 1997: 119). It carries echoes of older sociological work as in Robert Lynd's classic studies on *Middletown*, and Stacey's studies in the UK of the town of Banbury. 'The main contribution of this method to theory-building is its capacity to contextualize behaviour by describing relational structures in a way that bridges the individual, relational and structural levels of analysis' (1997: 120). This more structured stance on symbolic interactionism poses a challenge to naïve postmodern perspectives in that, consistent with Bourdieu, there is typically a contextual availability of meaning.

An illuminating example of network analysis within organizational research can be found in a substantial national evaluation of a UK government initiative, the Children's Fund (University of Birmingham and Institute of Education, 2006). The Children's Fund was launched in November 2000 as part of the government's commitment to tackle disadvantage among children and young people. The programme aims to identify at an early stage children and young people at risk of social exclusion, and make sure they receive the help and support they need to achieve their potential. It encourages voluntary organizations, community and faith groups to work in partnership with local statutory agencies, and children, young people and their families, to deliver high-quality preventative services to meet the needs of communities.[3]

The authors pose the question, how does knowledge 'move around', upstream and downstream, within an organisation? For example, between *levels*, between *strategy and practice*, and between different 'spaces' or 'fields' within an organization – e.g. between child protection teams and teams working with children with a disability? Sustaining a sense of place and movement, they suggest that three types of informal networks among practitioners were evident:

- New trails trodden for the first time between individual practitioners who recognized the benefits of a collaborative response to the social exclusion of a child.
- Networks which built on old networks and relationships but where there was evidence of

the impact of the preventative intentions of the Children's Fund.
- Old established networks which were continued or resuscitated and where there was little evidence of the impact of the Children's Fund (University of Birmingham and Institute of Education, 2006: 193).

They describe the first of these as 'light etchings or traces on a local landscape' (2006: 193). They conclude that:

> Systems for moving knowledge from practice to strategy within the Fund rarely existed. More commonly partnerships relied on individuals to broker knowledge up the system. Consequently knowledge from practice sometimes did not inform strategic work ... Where there were no meetings to enable practitioners to look beyond the boundaries of their own services there was the danger of reliance on old networks, and either a lack of collaboration or misunderstandings when practitioners needed to collaborate. (2006: 218)

This gives a sense of what they call 'boundary zones' – organizational 'spaces between services where practitioners could meet' (2006: 193) but of limited space where strategy players and practice players could engage. 'Places where Board members and practitioners met to share ideas were relatively rare' (2006: 202). In addition, 'Changes in social contexts were so complex and often so fast moving that keeping up was beyond the capabilities of individuals' (2006: 215).

Social geographers have found a kinship with network analysis. In an illuminating study of voluntary care, Milligan takes care of the elderly as an example, on the premise that 'little attention has been given to the *inter*-agency relationships between informal and state providers. Still less attention has been given to any detailed examination of how these relationships vary across space and how this impacts on care outcomes for service users' (Milligan, 2001: 54). Milligan argues for and develops 'a multi-levelled analysis of the socio-spatial and structural impacts of care' that should 'enable the positioning of actors to be defined ... and allow interactions between them to be mapped out'. She develops a network analysis where 'space is seen to be bound into networks and any assessment of spatial qualities is an assessment of network relations' (2001: 54). She uses the idea of 'dependency networks' as a framework for 'exploring how the inter-relationships between actors operating across space and at differing levels of the care proc-ess contribute to local variations in care out-comes' (2001: 55). This work is grounded in the argument that 'geographical approaches to voluntarism are important for social policy as such approaches argue that *where* events occur matter (for) both their form and out-come' (Milligan and Fyfe, 2004: 73).[4]

Yet while research in this field offers fruit-ful perspectives, the NECF research offers a caution against wholesale embracing of net-works as a model for organizational change. Hudson may be unduly sanguine when he suggests that:

> It is within networks that ... the 'entangling strings' of reputation, friendship, inter-dependence and altruism become an integral part of the rela-tionship. Accordingly the information communi-cated is 'thicker' than that in the market and 'freer' than that in a hierarchy – a prerequisite to addressing issues with uncertain solutions, and a factor likely to encourage mutual learning and innovation. (Hudson, 2004: 79)

But social work research on contexts and contextualization does demand 'socially shared understandings of the normative con-tours of "proper places" which shape the way people respond to the everyday lived reality of places' (Popay et al., 2003: 55). The inter-twined methodological and substantive dimensions of such commitments are cogently illustrated and exemplified in work on homelessness where people are 'out of place' (Flick and Röhnsch, 2007; Hodgetts et al., 2007). For example, by taking a con-textual orientation to the psychology of the embodied experience of homeless people, Hodgetts and colleagues seek to materialize 'psychosocial processes in a combination of expressions, gestures, clothing, locations and relations that typify the positioning of home-less people' (Hodgetts et al., 2007: 710).

> Materially and spatially located experiences remind homeless people of who they are, who they want to be, whether they belong and how

they are connected or dislocated from others. (2007: 711)

There are fast-developing opportunities in this field. Geographic Information Systems (GIS), for example, provide a technology to enable the investigation of a problem's spa-tial context. Put at its simplest, GIS supports the production of maps from spatially arranged data. Yet the technology required for this supports a sophisticated environment for the management, manipulation and anal-ysis of spatial information, providing the means for the integration of disparate sources and types of information on the basis of their spatial content and the extraction and inter-pretation of spatial interrelationships. GIS have a promising potential to support social work researchers seeking to include a spatial component in their research.

Such research orientations are particularly pertinent to understanding the geographies of social exclusion from public life. But they also illustrate the gains in methodological enrichment. Homelessness entails research that takes place in open spaces. Hodgetts and colleagues undertook semi-structured inter-views based upon participant photovoice projects, where homeless participants were 'initially interviewed about their homeless biographies, social networks and health, and then given disposable cameras and asked to image homelessness, their social relation-ships and use of public spaces'. Although many important issues raised by the partici-pants in discussion were not pictured, the authors argue that 'image-based methods are particularly suited where respondents are spatially dispersed and mobile, and where the research requires a narrative that retains a strong sense of personal and social context' (Hodgetts et al., 2007: 712).[5]

THE CONTEXTS OF THE RESEARCH ACT

Taking social work research as an applied discipline, I briefly consider social work practice as context for research. Then I shift to consider the varied elements of the social work academic community and thereafter the wider academic community. I understand the research act broadly to encompass the career of research from its first social manifestations to the eventual more or less enduring responses of the wider community.

Practice contexts

Social work practice is slippery – more so the nearer one tries to come to pinning it down. Readers of this *Handbook* in Southern Africa, the Baltic States, France and the USA will each have deeply divergent assumptions regarding the defining qualities and characteristics of social work and its practice. Casework in its various manifestations, community development, and social pedagogy all have traditions within which priorities for knowledge and research vary. Science and social work – each conceived in various ways at different times – stand in a relationship of constant and perhaps inevitable tension. In the early history of social work it is fairly easy to detect instances of optimism and hope for the gains social work would obtain from science.[6] Charles Loch (founder of the London-based Charity Organization Society in the 1860s) argued that charity 'is not spasmodic, casual and emotional, but, like science, an all-observing, all-comprising intelligence. It is not antagonistic to science: it is science – the science of life – in operation – knowledge doing its perfect work' (quoted in Timms, 1968: 59). Early social work writing tended to exhibit confidence in science as displaying laws of human behaviour, and to refer to behaviour being 'determined', and to faith in the model of the natural sciences – the only model familiar to the social work community.

This optimism continues as a persisting thread throughout the subsequent history of social work, surfacing from time to time in the relatively absolutist form to which Loch adhered. Take, for instance, Joel Fischer's only slightly hedged prophecy of the end of ideology, with his prediction as recently as 1993 that 'by the year 2000, empirically based practice – the new social work – may be the norm or well on the way to becoming so' (Fischer, 1993: 55).

This suggests there is – or at least ought to be – a natural congruence between research and practice. 'Is – or ... ought' – there lies the rub. Often the perceived failure of social work practitioners to adhere to a particular variety of science-ruled practice attracts severe complaints from the adherents of research whose work apparently has been spurned. The identity of social work is, of course, nowhere near so uniform. For example, there was a tension from the first between scholarly aspirations and employer demands for training, specialisms and practical curricula – this remains social work's 'troublesome legacy' (Lubove, 1965: 143) to the present, as evidenced in the following remarks from different stakeholders in the knowledge business:

> I have a problem thinking about research from any university ... I don't know what is taking place ... Rigorous methodology ... doesn't stimulate lots for me ... People like me look out for good ideas ... Usefulness is my alternative to methodology ... If it works that interests me ... I'm interested in cost-effectiveness and outcomes for customers (Senior Manager).

> Policy makers and practitioners are usually untrained in research methods and so often cannot assess the quality of the evidence from a methodological perspective. Indeed, they are not particularly interested in doing so ... Those responsible for policy and practice will never depend on research evidence alone. Research always competes with 'common-sense' views of the world. (Yet) Unless we understand the different natures of these two worlds, we risk forever misunderstanding each other and failing to draw on joint strengths (Policy research commissioners).

> It's only theory (User researcher).[7]

Legitimating practice So how do frameworks of ideas and practice come to be accepted with a good-enough consensus for shared action to take place? Within any field or discipline certain knowledge claims and their associated discourses come to gain predominant positions. Platt remarks on this process that 'the treatment of a theory as important depends not only on its content in isolation, but also on the fit between the work and a structured cultural and institutional system' (Platt, 1996: 242). Within social work, evidence based practice is a case in point. How has evidence based practice become legitimized? I suggest the following, although little has been done within social work to develop or test such legitimation accounts.

1. It offers a link to medicine through the key definition by Sackett et al. (1996) and therefore offers borrowed status.
2. It is readily transferable to and from other fields of applied study (education, health, social work) so has become embedded within a bigger picture large than any one field.
3. It ties in to the work of the Cochrane and Campbell Collaborations which gives it an infrastructure for development and diffusion.
4. It seems to offer a bridge between academic and 'applied' work and seems to promise a way to avoid theory/practice tensions. It thus has the potential to interest policy and practice fields.
5. It is capable of varied interpretations and applications so captures a number of issues. It takes on the flexibility – and imprecision – of a 'bucket' category.[8]
6. It links readily to related discourses, e.g. the advocacy of the need for 'scientific practice' in American social work.
7. It is offered by its advocates as atheoretical so requires less intellectual sophistication to grasp the basic *motifs*. As a consequence it is more easily taught on social work and professional programmes.
8. It seems to travel well through *time* (a rhetorically plausible case can be made for historical pedigree from as early as the Charity Organization movement, Mary Richmond, and the 1960s 'What Works?' debates) and *place* (it is presented as culture-free).
9. Its weaknesses of argument are clear so it invites those 'outside' to react to it by way of 'correction' and thus stay within the frame of reference.

The abrasive tendencies in the research/practice context are, for me, simply as they should be. They are not at all special to social work. Schwandt and Dahler-Larsen engage in an illuminating conversation regarding their encounters with resistance to evaluation programmes (Schwandt and Dahler-Larsen, 2006). Dahler-Larsen reflects on an attempted evaluation of a free school with a Christian tradition in Denmark. He suggests that some communities may be characterized by 'a substantive value … which cannot be made the object of reform'.

> My proposition is … that there are some basic ingredients in communities that define themselves in a particular way which make these communities incompatible with the idea of evaluation, at least at some level or for some issues some of the time … I think that perhaps the reason why some communities resist evaluation is that they have sensed that evaluation is the capacity of asking exactly those questions that may threaten the very existence of the community. (2006: 499)

The possible lines of connection to social work are easily read. But in response Schwandt suggests a different interpretation, when drawing on a study of rehabilitation in a cardiology hospital. He poses what he views as 'the basic question of the justification for the evaluator's role to challenge and engage in critique' and says 'I am continually perplexed by this problem' (2006: 502). He reflects on the metaphor of 'rough ground' as 'signifying that evaluation cannot always smooth out the creases in the intricate, uneven fabric of social practices or iron out difficulties in the appraisal of the value of those undertakings' (2006: 503). Practice is rough ground because 'different ideas of what constitutes good practice and a good practitioner always compete for attention and because the moral, the political and the instrumental are always intertwined', and the very idea of critically engaging tradition is 'placing oneself in a place of being vulnerable to changing one's own ways of thinking' (2006: 504). Schwandt concludes in constructive terms (in both the moral and intellectual sense):

> Perhaps evaluators should listen more carefully and respond more prudently to voices in communities that are hesitant or sceptical about evaluation … Perhaps beneath their apparent 'resistance' to evaluation, communities … are saying that they do not regard evaluation as smoothing and fixing things but rather as an activity that touches the

rough ground of their lives, values and practices that constitute the world as they know it, and live in it, in other words, their *community*. (2006: 504)

Social work in the academic community

Social work's domicile within higher education has shifted over time. Indeed, it has sometimes been suggested that social work is ill-fitted for university culture, although with the growth of higher education rates in many western countries there has been a corresponding expansion of subjects thought acceptable for university level study. Not that the reluctance has always been on the part of the university. For example, in the UK the government withdrew probation officer training from universities in the 1990s.

The tensions were tautly exemplified early in the history of social work at the time of establishment of the social work programmes at Chicago. Edith Abbott complained that 'some of our social science friends are afraid that we cannot be scientific because we really care about what we are doing ...' (Diner, 1977: 11). Abbott and her colleague Sophonisba Breckinridge came under fire from both 'sides'. In addition to the doubts of their 'social science friends' they famously referred to 'our eastern colleagues' (the social work programmes at Boston and New York) who 'told us we could not have casework and fieldwork in a university' (Diner, 1977: 7; c.f. Lubove, 1965: 265).

But 'university' as a category covers extreme diversity, such that it is rarely straightforward for a colleague from one country to understand the arrangements in another. For example, in the USA most social work schools are free standing, single discipline schools. In the UK that is rare – there is either a broadly professional (often health, rarely education) or social science link (often social policy, sometimes sociology). This is important in that the one may orient faculty towards the practice task as the lynch pin and

the other may lead to a broader social science orientation – though this is at best a tendency rather than a direct association.

Disciplines and schools I have used the term 'discipline' with invisible quotation marks. To persist with Chicago, 'it is ... often not easy to distinguish between the "sociologists" and the rest ... the two groups were so intertwined that it might be more appropriate to regard them as one' (Platt, 1996: 263).[9] Platt goes on to criticize histories of sociology from within:

> Accounts written from within sociology ... generally treat both other disciplines and groups outside the academy as part of the background. They are seen as instrumental to the main aims of sociologists or as introducing distortion into the natural or appropriate course of pure sociological development. (1996: 264)

For Chicago this is 'singularly inappropriate'. The boundaries were not sharp and other disciplines and groups were not subsidiary. Now, as then, disciplines are not intrinsic entities but emerge as a consequence of negotiation and territorial claims – and this is as true of social work as of any other discipline (Shaw et al., 2006). If disciplines are not intrinsic entities then neither are they homogenous or self contained fields of work.

Indeed, disciplines are often thought to develop through the emergence of 'schools' of research or thought. But confidence of definition is as hazardous here as for disciplines themselves. Are schools relatively uncommon or does everyone belong to one? Does someone know if they belong to a school? There are doubtless numerous affinities and propensities within social work research – those who are committed to and largely confident in the value of empirical evidence; those who hold a constructivist stance; those who are driven by a political, justice-based agenda. There are also more clearly defined communities of interest – the disability movements, aficionados of Cochrane or Campbell, and so forth. Though are these 'schools'? In social work this has often as not been about practice 'schools', e.g. functionalist, psychodynamic and so on. But 'being influenced by a tendency is not the same as belonging to a school' (Platt, 1996: 236). Platt goes on to suggest that 'school' is used in three ways:

- school of current social membership;
- school of retrospective identification; and
- school of imputation.

This is helpful. For example it distinguishes between categories that refer to the sphere of ideas and those that refer to social relationships. Yet the concept and its reference points remain elusive. It is unlikely that temporal and geographical centres of research work capture even the best work. Jennifer Platt's comments on Stuart Chapin at Minnesota are very interesting. His work, she suggests, was both meritorious (methodologically sophisticated) and fairly extensive but he never became key in sociology history. Of equal interest is that he never became at all known in social work history. Yet he wrote work that was acutely relevant to social work (Chapin, 1920, 1947; Chapin and Queen, 1937). Indeed, he was probably 'caught' from both sides in that his social work focus was a reason why sociologists did not recognise him – along with the fact that he was not at either Chicago or Columbia, then the corporate *doyens* of social work research.

Debates surrounding the nature of evidence are sometimes fierce enough to imply that deeply held allegiances are at stake. But one is still left hesitating as to whether social work has or has had 'schools'. Perhaps this is explainable in part from the nature of social work as drawing on other disciplines for its inspiration – psychology, sociology, policy analysis and so on – and arising from the relationship between the applied, the ameliorative, and what Mills et al. (2006) have, in a somewhat invidious comparison, contrasted as 'practice oriented' and 'research-based' social science disciplines.[10]

Doing science All this raises the question of the nature of science work in social work. Weber located science within his ideal type constructions of work and organizations.

This reminds us that we need to place science in the context of work if we are to understand why it is that 'scientists' produce knowledge in the way that they do. Inward conditions motivate and external conditions constrain the work of science (Weber, 1948). Weber was thinking of the traditional sciences, but his general argument makes good sense for social work. How should academic discourse be taken forward in this kind of setting? As with most of these issues, the answer is likely to be contentious. Hammersley has outlined his views of how disputes about research should be conducted, grounded on a set of rules that deliberately exclude both relativist and strong activist/emancipatory conceptions of research, and as such they will not find universal favour. His conception of discourse is:

- The over-riding concern should be the truth of claims, and not their political or practical consequences.
- Arguments should be judged solely on the grounds of their credibility and plausibility, and not on the grounds of the personal characteristics of those advancing the argument.
- Researchers should be willing to change their views, and should behave as if other researchers are also so willing, at least until there is strong counter evidence.
- Where agreement does not result the researcher should accept there is some reasonable doubt regarding the argument they are advancing.
- There should be no restriction on participation in such discourse on grounds of political or religious attitude. (Hammersley, 1995: Ch. 4)

This will likely not satisfy those who have experience of the way power shapes relations in the university and scholarly community. In a recent example, Staller sets out transparently the process of editorial review and decision making regarding one of her publications, and argues for further examples of such a 'metalogue' (Staller, 2007).

Writing Staller is raising a related important consideration in understanding the cultural dynamics of communities, contexts and places in social work – the role of *writing*. The growth of metric measures of research quality is also part of shifts in discipline culture. Concerns can be heard about marketing research 'products', maximizing numbers of 'salami sliced' outputs, and so on, and all threaten the centrality of research excellence. Wolfgang Pauli's aphorism is well taken – 'I don't mind that you think slowly but I do mind that you are publishing faster than you think'.[11] Writing is indeed central to the location and context of research.

> When you're inside the possible world of a new book, tapping the walls, opening the cupboards, testing the slope of the floor, then that is where you are – inside it. Sometimes, with a different part of your brain, you wonder, 'Will it play?' Is it the right book for this moment – in the culture/my career/my writing life? You do, in other words, worry about location, but only once you have left the space itself. (Anne Enright)[12]

It is not easy to agree a list of classic texts in the social work 'canon'. Indeed, the diffuseness of social work makes the idea of the canonical contentious. Mary Richmond's *Social Diagnosis* may have some general claim, but even then it is often referenced as a point of departure rather than arrival. Classics are invoked in ways akin to disciplinary social rituals to reaffirm collective identity. But compared to other fields, social work citations as proxies for classic reputations are very low on visibility. The main citations are of textbooks, and the work of leading research scholars is lowly cited. For example, the late Bill Reid was perhaps the most important social work researcher of his generation (Shaw, 2004) but his citation levels are only a tenth of those for textbooks by well known writers for the student market.

Research teams and interdisciplinarity Writing is sometimes a solitary (pre)occupation, sometimes part of a team or shared product. The *research team* is itself a significant, perhaps fundamental, manifestation of research practice and careers. It offers the most ready form for developing interdisciplinary research. The growth of the Internet has also facilitated new forms of collaboration of 'distributed intelligence'. However, a recent

study of scientists and engineers where the principal investigators (PIs) came from multiple universities suggests that they did not use technology or travel more than principal investigators who were on the same research site. More worryingly, 'Having more PI universities on a project was significantly negatively associated with the generation of new ideas and knowledge, and it is also negatively associated with student training …' (Cummings and Kiesler, 2005: 711). Technology did not overcome distance. 'Despite widespread excitement about dispersed collaboration reflected in terms like "virtual team", "eScience", and "cyberinfrastructure", there appear to remain a number of challenges that scientists encounter when they work across organizational boundaries' (2005: 714).

Team research poses questions close to the central themes of this chapter, because of the spatial dimension, and the development of embodied knowledge within teams. Goodwin's observant study of anesthetic practice makes the empirical point convincingly (Goodwin, 2007). But we know little or nothing about the practice of team-work in social work research.

Exemplar 2: Contexts for a national research strategy[13]

The first decade of the twenty-first century saw a shift in the national leadership of social work research in the UK into the hands of people with a less substantive focus and a strong interest in generic methodological rigour, a growing active international network, and a value-led approach to research. The leading role of substantive research at universities like Bristol and York continued, but the rise of social work research at universities like Huddersfield, Southampton, Lancaster and Cardiff – all known not only for substantive specialism but for discipline interest and strong social science links, especially to sociology – helped foster a greater sense of a national disciplinary community of scholarly work. This trend was enhanced by a growing influence of networks like the Research Committee of the Social Work Education Committee (SWEC)[14] and to some degree the Association of Professors of Social Work, which operated as a national voice, whether or not they were entirely representative of the community. SWEC members were instrumental in securing Economic and Social Research Council (ESRC) funding for a research seminar series entitled 'Theorising social work research' (the papers at the time of writing are all still available at www.scie.org.uk/publications/misc/tswr/index.asp), leading, amongst other things, to the production of a code of ethics for social work research (Butler, 2002), and to the sharpening of an informal agenda of unresolved issues.

SWEC members played a key part in a growing and to some degree successful pressure for social work to be treated as a discipline. The ESRC – for reasons not entirely clear from the outside – proved amenable to lobbying from this grouping, and to the case made through a national research strategy (JUC SWEC, 2006). This was developed through the Research Committee of SWEC, and acted as a fulcrum for action by the social work academic community. It included the development of a case for resourcing capacity and competence strengthening in social work. Paul Bywaters, the lead facilitator of this work, reflects as follows on this process. 'It was believed that, if successful, the process of producing the Strategy would have a number of potential benefits in addition to any direct outcomes of the Strategy itself:

- It would give direction to the work of the Sub-committee and enable it to move from being largely reactive to being pro-active.
- It would enable the committee to address some potential conflicts of interest, for example,

between more established and recently formed universities.
- It would enable the committee to continue to promote a UK-wide approach to social work research despite the different directions which social work legislation and practice were taking in the four countries of England, Northern Ireland, Scotland and Wales.
- In itself, it would help to raise the profile of social work research in the UK'. (Bywaters, 2008)

Social work academics had key institutional support outside universities, particularly from the relatively newly established Social Care Institute for Excellence (SCIE), which had a core interest in developing the evidence base for social work and social care across the UK as a whole, and was reinforced in Scotland by the Scottish Institute for Excellence in Social Work Education (SIESWE)[15]. This parallel work had begun to provide a bridge between academic work and knowledge utilization.

A further focus for the development of a research agenda emerged with pressure for a national social work research conference in the UK. The influence of the Research Assessment Exercise (RAE)[16] also proved relevant, leading to a greater transparency of research effort and publishing outputs. The growth of numbers and perhaps standards of UK social work journals was doubtless also pushed forward by the RAE. The establishment of the new degree structure for social work education was raising the expectations of the quality of qualified social workers and bringing with it new discussions about the place of research and research literacy in social work education.

There may have been something of a pattern as well as elements of serendipity in these developments. There was a confidence in the academic community, and a sense of discipline identity, that both led to and fed upon the specification of subject-specific research training requirements for social work doctoral students, along with dedicated studentships monies.

STATE, CITY AND COMMUNITY

Platt concludes of sociology that 'though departments have undoubtedly sometimes been very important units, their importance has varied; they have contained major internal differences, there have been affiliations which cross-cut them, and non-academic units have been equally or more significant' (Platt, 1996: 230).

For social work, the non-university world is especially important. I write from inside just one small country, but in the UK there are key networks such as INVOLVE, DANASWAC, Making Research Count, Research in Practice, the Social Care Institute for Excellence and IRISS – its partner institute in Scotland. The 'What Works?' movement for the network of people working in and researching the Probation Service also brought together a mix of academics, senior officers, probation staff, and figures from central government (Home Office) and has become part of the language of practice.[17]

To see and to help see express both foundations and responsibility for the social work researcher, and in doing so pose the problem, in Bourdieu's terms, of understanding 'the relationship between position, disposition and the taking of a position' (Costa, 2006: 875). In a study of social work research in UK universities (Shaw and Norton, 2007), perhaps the least won of all positions was over differences regarding the response that social work should give to the various arguments for democratizing the research process. To put the issue candidly, are participatory, user-led, emancipatory and other responsive modes of research generally superior to and/or more in tune with social work values than more traditional modes of research relationship? Sharply contrasting positions emerged among academic faculty. The involvement of users as partners and co-producers in the research process was often seen as the litmus test of distinctively social work research.

> ... It wasn't just about writing, it was about actually involving people in what the writing was going to say

However, the standing of this as a fundamental mark of quality was not universally shared:

> I think we're beginning to make user involvement a kind of, a test for quality and I think that is extremely poor methodology. I think what you have to do, just as with anything else, is justify user involvement as part of the methodology

The first of these views was frequently expressed – that while intrinsic quality within the research is important, without a strong emphasis on value, user-engagement or impact, a framework of research quality that rested solely on inner-science criteria would undermine the practice-led, social justice principles of social work. This was one of the areas where more deep-seated debates emerged, ranging from those who would probably place 'value-for-people' and 'value-for-use'[18] above strictly epistemological and knowledge-building standards, to those who believed that such extrinsic, outer-science quality criteria may not always be appropriate for a particular piece of research, especially studies which focus on less applied aspects of social work.

Justice-based positions are plural, and not restricted to emancipatory and user-led research images. They also include Fabian research linked to the welfare state; Marxist positions that decline to take a direct and explicit involvement in transformative action through their research; Reformist positions, such as that held by Ernest House within the USA evaluation community; and positions that draw on older traditions. By way of illustration of this last stance Dingwall discusses the moral discourse of interactionism and draws on the eighteenth century Scottish philosopher and economist, Adam Smith, for how the moral and the empirical plug together. Dingwall suggests that 'If we have a mission for our discipline, it may be to show the timeless virtues of compromise and civility, of patient change and human decency, of a community bound by obligations rather than rights' (Miller and Dingwall, 1997: 204).

The city

We have noticed (Exemplar 1) how Ernest Burgess explored connections between sociology and social work. He, like most of his colleagues, played Chicago against Chicago – the city against the university.[19] He suggests the kind of ecological application of theory and research to practice he has in mind when he asks:

> ... if the city has, like an organism, a structure that is closely correlated with its functioning, why should this not be taken into account in any plan of districting by social agencies? What is the justification of treating the city not as a living organism, but as if it were a corpse which can be cut up arbitrarily into unrelated parts? (Burgess, 1930: 486)

His reflections on the importance of social data stem largely from the Chicago study of local communities, funded in part by the Chicago Council of Social Agencies. In accord with Chicago theorizing, he advocates gaining community level material on the social forces and trends of local community life, and draws on his colleague Vivien Palmer's work, in which she placed special reliance on interviewing older community residents and real estate men, in addition to more conventional small-area data from the Census. He pleads the relevance for social work, and the value of such data to enable social agencies to 'check the effectiveness of their case work processes' (Burgess, 1930: 488).

Community is not solely an urban category. Pugh has voiced concerns that social work suffers from a gap in middle level theory and research. In much writing on racism, poverty and sexism he detects a switch of focus 'between larger perspectives on social life and society and smaller scale accounts of individual action and practice. One consequence is that local context tends to be ignored' (Pugh, 2006). He complains that 'the history of social work shows an uneven and episodic engagement with notions of context and community', and proceeds to indicate how ideas of rurality and rural social work enrich a critique of work on local context.

He points up 'the personal and professional boundary problems facing workers who live and work in the same place, and who cannot operate as if they float free of the local context'. This takes on pointed relevance when we consider the forms of social work and social work research in countries that have interacted with dominant western traditions from their own cultural standpoints. For example, in Finland there was a very strong dispute regarding method in social work in the 1950s until the 1970s directed primarily against imported American social case work. It was opposed by some representatives of traditional Finnish welfare work. In predominantly agrarian Finland the time and place for social case work discourse and practice (the social context) was very different from that in the USA.

Politics and race

Social work's links to mainstream political parties have been part of a partly submerged agenda in the history of social work. Associated with the Progressive movement in the early twentieth century, early social work and sociology were embedded in the ameliorative mission of Chicago University from its founding in the last decade of the nineteenth century. 'Fundamental scientific understanding of immediately present events, directly observed, and all on behalf of the improvement of society' (Diner, 1997: 55) lay at the heart of Albion Small's programme as head of department. There is much evidence that early sociology or social work did not view theorizing and an ameliorative mission in dualist terms. For Small, 'scientism and moralism were integrally connected' (Bulmer, 1984: 35).

In preparing this chapter I spoke to a number of UK colleagues, and include their comments with their permission. UK social work academics have tended to be left-leaning in their political position. This sometimes led to commitment to community-based practice interests – 'as a social work trainee my political affiliations strongly orientated me towards community social work'. But the relation between this and their research is not direct or paradigmatic. The same person went on to admit, 'I have not particularly carried this interest forward in research, except perhaps current research and writings on participatory methods'. Someone expressed it as follows:

… not sure there was anything more noble and intellectually foundational going on other than a sort of Fabianesque view of our professional obligations, but with a fairly keen … eye to institutional demands/personal career interests

The following is a more elaborated expression of the first part of this response.

My take on this … is that Labour Party membership is part of a pragmatic political engagement and I would see a connection here to social work research. In social work and in the critical social sciences as a whole I come across a lot of people who talk a radical talk and see themselves as very much on the left, but they aren't politically active – aren't involved in any local or national political organisation but channel their supposed radicalism solely into academic work … I prefer the idea of mundane pragmatic political involvement to try and improve a few things in small ways. The same would go for social work research. I think the rhetoric of radicalism has its place but is usually less effective than getting your hands dirty – doing research commissioned by government for example, commissioned evaluations and so on. There's a common position here I think of pragmatic ameliorative politics.

This may account for why academic staff tended 'to look at a more local market of funders … and in doing so developed a more localist orientation to social and political issues'.

Politics and race have intertwined in the social contexts of research. One American commentator, who wished to remain anonymous, remarked that in the early twentieth century:

… even in the settlement house movement that we look to with esteem and honor in the field of Social Work, (people) did not highlight how discrimination was continued. We often think of that as a time when all groups were helped. Although there is some truth to it, groups like African Americans, Asians, Native Americans (Indians), and

Latino's (Mexicans in particular) were left behind, and were continually discriminated against in national, State and local laws and policy. The mood and attitude of the country contributed to this.

That is why informal and formal social supports in social services, community and education within these culturally specific communities were important for community survival.[20]

The identity, direction and force of social work research have suffered from unduly narrow understandings of its nature and domicile. To locate social work research as an 'applied' discipline or field is not – as too often assumed – to privilege other supposedly 'applied' disciplines, nor to exclude less overtly applied disciplines. It only sets the complex, diverse and hugely demanding agenda of intelligent eclecticism that follows. This demands not a mere 'pick and mix' approach. The contexts of time, place and space are trans-disciplinary categories that helpfully destabilize and open up conventional assumptions regarding the practice and substance of the research enterprise, and of the nature of the social work research community.

A focus on matters of context also attunes social work research to ways that structural and relational contexts talk back to research, and are not simply static domestic 'settings'.[21] This is true from our understanding of social work practice contexts, as well as those contexts of nation, state, city and community that are relatively extrinsic to the research act. The more direct implications of this paper may include the following:

1. Once we give more nuanced attention to theorizing, a contextualizing focus has the potential to offer coherence to social work research, both methodologically and substantively.
2. There are unrealized opportunities to capitalize on the temporal and spatial dimensions of common research methods.
3. Social work research has given too little attention to the opportunities arising from methodological developments that permit greater understanding of social work practice.

4. Understanding of social work will be impoverished if social work research operates within unduly narrow disciplinary and theoretical frameworks. I offered brief examples of how this can be addressed via social network theory and work in cultural and social geography.

5. Broad frameworks of practice within social work and the academic community stem from processes of social legitimization and not only rational decisions. Mainstream forms of research, such as accountability evaluation, are unlikely to produce straightforward prescriptions for best practice unless this often complex social context is understood and taken into account.

6. Tom Schwandt's conclusion will stand as an implication for social work evaluation researchers in their engagement with participants in the research act. To repeat:

   Perhaps evaluators should listen more carefully and respond more prudently to voices in communities that are hesitant or sceptical about evaluation ... Perhaps beneath their apparent 'resistance' to evaluation, communities ... are saying that they do not regard evaluation as smoothing and fixing things but rather as an activity that touches the rough ground of their lives, values and practices that constitute the world as they know it, and live in it, in other words, their *community* (Schwandt and Dahler-Larsen, 2006: 504).

7. Understanding the likely responses of the social work community to research and evaluation will be enriched insofar as there is a mutually shared view of the way science-work is and ought to be carried out.

8. Social work practice is often a more or less adequate response to urban life, and part of 'the pathos of modernity' (Plummer, 1997: 7).

9. It is easy to lose a constant alertness to a realistic, textured understanding of the relationship of politics and race (and other matters not discussed in this paper such as gender) to both research and practice.

What would research look like in the light of these realizations? It would be less disciplinarily restricted, though none the less interested in disciplinarity. It would recognize as part and parcel of social work research the sometimes profound differences of commitment that distinguish parts of the social work community. Commitment to working across boundaries, in the way that many chapters in this *Handbook* exemplify, would be a more enduring feature. And it would be a more modest enterprise, where social work researchers are 'merely experts'. Finally, it would take on board the implications of the recognition that contexts are not the surroundings within which social work research 'happens', but the dynamics and 'character-makers' of research.

ACKNOWLEDGEMENTS

I am grateful to Uwe Flick and Mirja Satka for comments on a first draft of this chapter, which helped clarify and elaborate parts of the framework, and hopefully do slightly better justice to valuable work and experience elsewhere in Europe.

NOTES

1 And, as we will see subsequently, the taking of a position.

2 I realize that this does not begin to do justice to arguments regarding external and internal validity, and the inconclusive debates about how far developments in relation to multi-site designs, meta-analyses and other design trade-offs offer solutions. But I do doubt the adequacy of responses that assume that the problems/issues can be resolved through methodological prescription. This is a form of response that sees problems in a modernizing perspective where better science practice will resolve them.

3 This statement was taken from the UK government website at http://www.everychildmatters.gov.uk/strategy/childrensfund/. Accessed 17 July 2008.

4 This emphasis has not been entirely absent in social work. As early as 1973 Michael Bayley identified those 'structures of coping' which carers of children living at home with serious learning disabilities crafted and on which they depended. But the relevant sociological work in the 1980s on neighbouring by Bulmer, Finch and Abrams has been little assimilated by social work.

5 I pick up a further example of researching context in my later remarks about the urban and rural contexts of social work research.

6 I have sketched some details of this history in Shaw, 2008.

7 These quotations are from Shaw and Norton, 2007.

8   The term is Karl Popper's.

9   I acknowledge my debt to Jennifer Platt's work in the following paragraphs.

10   Within the wider context of government monitoring of university performance, there has been a recent shift to the use of different forms of metrics for measuring research quality. I have suggested some problems with this development in the Joint Universities Council Social Work Education Committee's submission to the UK consultation on a planned Research Excellence Framework, at http://jucuk.files.wordpress.com/2008/05/jucswec-refresponse0208.pdf. Accessed 15 August 2008.

11   Wolfgang Ernst Pauli was an Austrian theoretical physicist. The Wikipedia entry is a fairly comprehensive starting point.

12   Anne Enright was the Booker prize winner in 2007 for her novel *The Gathering*. This is taken from an article by her in *The Guardian* newspaper, 31 May, 2008.

13   I am heavily indebted to Paul Bywaters' thoughtful reflections on this process in Bywaters (2008).

14   There is a deliberate local context of allusions in this exemplar. However, almost all the networks and organizations listed in the exemplar can be traced by a Google search.

15   This is now the Institute for Research and Innovation in Social Services (IRISS), at http://www.iriss.ac.uk

16   For 2001 results – the primary influence on this process - see http://www.hero.ac.uk/rae/ For the 2008 exercise see http://www.rae.ac.uk/ The results were scheduled for public access from May 2009.

17   A Google search will yield the key URLs for each of these networks.

18   The terms are those of John Furlong and Alis Oancea in an influential study of applied research in the field of education (Furlong and Oancea, 2005).

19   The phrase is the title of a 2007 conference paper by Daniel Cefaï, Louis Quéré and Cédric Terzi, 'Playing Chicago against Chicago', presented at a conference on 'The Legacy of the Chicago School', Manchester, England.

20   From a private email communication.

21   I have tried to make this argument in relation to research undertaken by practitioners (Shaw, 2005).

The Practice of Social Work Research

The Practice of Social Work Research

Jackie Powell and Blanca Ramos

INTRODUCTION

Research involves finding out about the world and is therefore unavoidably about making knowledge claims. Put slightly differently, research can be seen as a form of systematic enquiry in the pursuit of knowledge. Underlying such apparently simple statements are bigger questions and matters of dispute. These involve claims and counter-claims concerning how the knowledge has been or should be produced and by whom; what counts as knowledge and on what grounds such claims are being made. Social work research as a broadly based field of study seeks to be inclusive in its acknowledgement of different ways of knowing and the range and diversity of methodologies and methods that might be employed. Thus, research as a process of knowledge generation is inescapably a value laden activity within which the researcher plays a significant role in this process of knowledge creation.

Central to this approach is a commitment to the need for reflexivity on the part of the researcher and an understanding of research as a process within which the researcher is located. Ignoring reflexivity and maintaining an exclusive focus on methods and outcomes leads to seeing research as a technicized process limited to matters of technique and application of methods. This denies the practical–moral nature of research and the way in which moral and political issues are central to the conduct of research and the role of the researcher (Butler and Pugh, 2004; Humphries, 2004b).

Current approaches within social work research reveal tensions between what might be broadly conceived as relevance to practice, scientific or methodological rigour and social work as an emancipatory project. These tensions reflect the diverse nature of social work research exemplified by its many purposes and contexts. This diversity and variety is inevitably mirrored in the broad range of methods adopted within social work research where the emphasis on 'fit for purpose' becomes a central concern. How these tensions get played out in the day-to-day practice of the researcher are shaped by both the purpose(s) and context(s) of the particular research situation and how these are negotiated and managed by the researcher, whether a practitioner, service user or academic researcher. This underlines the complex nature of the researchers' role and tasks, not least how they understand their role within this process of knowledge creation.

These tensions in social work research are often presented as either hierarchically structured or rigid binary oppositions between theory and practice, pure and applied, or between rigour and relevance, and are evident in debates about the nature and purpose of social science research and the role of the social scientist as researcher. To what extent social work research might wish to align itself with social science research or whether it is largely inseparable from social work practice itself is also a matter of continuing debate and forms an underlying theme in this chapter.

This chapter has a focus on how the researcher manages the tensions arising from different and often competing interests within the research process in the pursuit of generating knowledge that is both rigorous and relevant, and conducted in ways that seek to make the research process both transparent and inclusive. An appreciation of the competing values, ideologies and commitments of the various interests involved in research serves to underline the multiple obligations of the researcher and the complex issue of accountability.

ACCOUNTABILITY WITHIN THE RESEARCH PROCESS

Social work research, like social work practice, involves multiple accountabilities where professional, academic or disciplinary, financial, political and user concerns compete in their demands for recognition and primacy. For the researcher, this necessitates attention to theoretical and methodological issues underpinning the research, alongside the pursuit of an approach congruent with social work's commitment to participation and empowering forms of practice. Accountability to the research community, more appropriately regarded as a diversity of academic interests, is only one dimension of accountability which has to be taken into account

throughout the research process (Powell, 2002). This is our starting point for an exploration of researcher accountability.

To what extent it should take primacy over other interests remains a highly contested issue within the academic social science community. Hammersley (1997) has made the claim that the very legitimacy of research is undermined if it is '… immediately directed towards achieving some practical or political goal rather than the production of knowledge' (1997: para 1.12).

This view has been contested by Romm (1997) who has argued for the inclusion of 'alternative epistemological orientations', and has subsequently explored the notion of accountability across a range of theoretical orientations (Romm, 2000). As a member of the UK social work academic community, Humphries (1998) has also drawn attention to the way in which academic debate, often conducted in an adversarial mode, may lose sight of 'the lived realities which constitute the substance of the theoretical argument' (1998: para 1.2). Those engaged in participatory research approaches, she argues, need to be responsive to their multiple constituencies and make themselves explicitly accountable to other than the academic or research community.

A useful contribution to this debate from outside of the academic research community has been made by the UK Social Research Association (Social Research Association, 2003). These ethical guidelines offer a framework within which the 'conscientious social researcher' should be able to work responsibly. The value of this framework is the way in which it seeks to address the competing obligations faced by the professional researcher irrespective of location (government: central and local, academic and voluntary and 'not for profit' settings are identified) and disciplinary commitment of its diverse membership. Alongside obligations to society in relation to scope of enquiry and dissemination, and to colleagues where issues of choice and transparency of methods are addressed, obligations to funders and employers, and research subjects are identified and explored. These various obligations identified here for the professional researcher resonate with those that the researcher drawn from any sector within the social work community might consider a useful starting point for further consideration.

By framing these guidelines in terms of the consequences of the researcher's actions on others, they seek to provide a standard setting point of reference that avoids the privileging of one position or interest over another. Rather than perceiving funders as a threat to undertaking 'good' social science research, the guidelines acknowledge the need to attend to their interests and concerns. The extent to which funders of research require attention to issues of value for money, which include both effective use of resources and potential knowledge utilization, varies in relation to the aims and commitments of the particular organization. However, funding bodies that draw on public monies have become increasingly concerned with issues of wider use and relevance. For example the Economic Social Research Council (ESRC), which is the largest single UK funder of social science research, has extended its brief in recent years to underline its role in making a social science contribution to evidence-based policy and practice. A review of the coverage of social work and social care research funded under the auspices of this key funding body (Shaw et al., 2004) made two specific recommendations that are pertinent here. Firstly, all ESRC applications should provide evidence that active utilization strategies have been considered and appropriately costed; secondly, that a broader concept of the research user be developed; one that goes beyond a recognition of policy relevance and adequately recognizes the contribution of service user and carer stakeholder interests, alongside those of practitioners in all fields of social work research. These recommendations signal important messages for the social work community as a whole and for researchers, in particular, in underlining the need to acknowledge a diverse range of stakeholder interests and the different ways in which

these various members of the social work community might make use of research.

Employers, as either funders of research or providers of other forms of support, may be less concerned with more abstract forms of knowledge and specify requirements that directly relate to 'problem solving' or information needs for policy planning and implementation. Here the researcher may be more aware of organizational needs expressed primarily in terms of management interests with limited recognition (implicit or explicit) of other interests, most notably practitioners and those (potential) users of their services. Practitioners undertaking research into their own practice may experience a conflict of interests within their particular organizational setting unless prior research agreements are established (Shaw, 2005).

Having noted the researcher's obligations to the academic community and wider society, briefly explored in terms of 'value for use' rather than cost-effectiveness, we need to give further consideration to more specific concerns in relation to relevance for social work practice. This goes beyond issues of accountability to funders and employers and addresses the concern of relevance for those engaged in planning, managing and providing social work services, alongside both service users and carers. Such interest groups might be the focus of study and/or potential users of research. They may be identified as research subjects, respondents, participants or partners in the research process. In the following two sections we examine the ways in which social work research has sought to become more relevant to practice, primarily through increased inclusion of the perspectives of practitioners and services users, and their engagement in the research process.

EVIDENCE FOR PRACTICE

Whilst there are many different approaches to social work research, there is a widely held view that the primary purpose of any research is to promote the development and improvement of social work practice and ultimately make a difference to the lives and well-being of people who come into contact with social workers and social care services (see, for example for the UK, JUC SWEC, 2006). However, how this commitment to practice is addressed will be influenced by the different conceptions of social work itself and how the relationships between social work theory, practice and research are understood. These issues will be taken up later in the chapter. At this stage it is sufficient to state that whilst the focus here is on exploring relevance for practice, there is no intention to privilege practice over theory or indeed the reverse. Rather, our emphasis here is on exploring the different ways in which social work research has addressed this issue of relevance for practice alongside the pursuit of 'good' social scientific research. Our starting point here is the direct involvement of practitioners in research and the long tradition in empirical and evidence-based practice.

Empirical practice movement

In the US the 'empirical–clinical practice' movement (Reid, 1994), a trend towards bridging and augmenting social work practice with scientific research inquiry, has had a major impact on social work knowledge development since the late twentieth century (Briar, 1979; Bloom and Fischer, 1982; Garvin, 1981; Kirk, 1979; Roberts et al., 2006). Here, research is viewed as an integral part of practice, and most social work research aims to generate the practical knowledge needed to inform social work practice with the ultimate goal of alleviating human suffering and promoting social welfare (Kirk, 1979; Rubin and Babbie, 2008; Yegedis and Weinbach, 2002). For example Bloom and Fischer (1982) referred to helping professionals who have the ability to assess whether their intervention is successful as 'scientific practitioners'.

Within the empirical practice movement such approaches have tended to make use of systematized, objective methods of research that can be replicated. This is consistent with the 'science of practice' as defined by Bloom and Fischer (1982) and underlines the need for technical expertise in traditional social science research skills. These include outcome-orientated methodologies that draw upon quantitative methods and experimental, quasi-experimental, and nonexperimental research designs. Within the context of social work practice Kreuger and Neuman (2006) discuss the advantages and shortcomings of each of these methods.

A key element in the 'empirical–clinical practice' movement is single-system design methodology (Whittaker, 1994). This approach to understanding causal relationships in individual systems rather than in groups is a useful research tool to evaluate individual practice effectiveness (Salkind, 2006; Yegedis and Weinbach, 2002). Although this methodology differs from traditional group research designs with regard to the unit of analysis both aim to determine the effects of an independent variable on behaviour (Salkind, 2006). It also employs repeated measures of the same variable over time; graphics and pattern or statistical analyses; and a variation of control group (Salkind, 2006; Tripodi, 1994; Yegedis and Weinbach, 2002). The highly sophisticated single-subject designs developed during the past few decades have made this methodology applicable to a wide range of practice situations (Tripodi, 1994; Whittaker, 1994). Authors such as Bloom and Fischer (1982) argue for the use of this methodology because it can be built into a social worker's practice without disruption and captures variations from one client system to another, although Tripodi (1994) identifies several concerns inherent in this methodology.

Qualitative methods offer an alternative research tool to support social workers in their quest to produce generalized professional knowledge and to evaluate practice effectiveness. Here, researchers assume the role of learners, and data collection occurs primarily through observation and interviewing within environmental contexts marked by trust and sensitivity (Yegedis and Weinbach, 2002). Qualitative practitioners may find these methods especially suitable given their effectiveness in tapping the deeper meanings of human experience and for examining social processes over time (Rubin and Babbie, 2008). Further, the flexible nature of qualitative methodology can facilitate practitioners' research efforts in multicultural practice situations. Some of the methodological challenges encountered by traditional quantitative multicultural research such as definitions of theoretical constructs and their valid measurement are not present (Yegedis and Weinbach, 2002).

Evidence-based practitioner research

Efforts to apply the scientific method to social work practice go back to one of the profession's best known pioneers, Mary Richmond, who in her seminal text *Social Diagnosis* (Richmond, 1917) discussed the use of research-generated knowledge to guide direct practice and social reform (Rubin and Babbie, 2008). Several models, mostly based on theoretical notions, have been proposed over the years. More recently, concerns over the use of practice methods that were not effective or were potentially harmful to clients added to the growing sentiment for a more empirically grounded social work practice (Gambrill, 2003). Subsequently, the evidence-based practice model was introduced as one of the major advancements in human services (Mullen and Streiner, 2002). Today, the development of evidence-based practice is not limited to the United Kingdom and the United States. Initiatives are extending to other countries, for example, Australia and Canada, and also Northern Europe including Finland, Norway, Sweden, Denmark and the Netherlands (Crisp, 2000; MacDonald, 1999; Mäntysaari, 2005c; Mullen and Streiner, 2002; Thyer and Kazi, 2004).

Although evidence-based approaches have made important contributions towards bridging social work practice with scientific inquiry, it has also generated serious tensions in the profession. While practitioners strongly resist these approaches, academics are split, with some promoting them and others referring to them as reductionistic and mindless empiricism (Roberts et al., 2006). A major criticism revolves around the evidence-based practice research hierarchy, which many believe devalues qualitative methodologies and non-positivistic paradigms (Rubin and Babbie, 2008). Straus and McAlister (2000) provide a comprehensive discussion of arguments against evidence-based approaches.

Current efforts to engage practitioners in evidence-based research increasingly underscore the client-centered nature of social work practice (Gambrill, 2001). According to Rubin and Babbie (2008) practitioners must take into account the clients' values and expectations, and involve them as informed participants throughout the helping process. Practitioners are encouraged to use critical thinking skills, integrate scientific information with their professional knowledge and expertise, actively search for the best research evidence available, and evaluate the effectiveness of their practice (Rubin and Babbie, 2008). While in the US evidence-based practice usually refers to clinical practice, it also applies to social policies and other levels of practice. For example, in the UK, it refers to both evidence-based policy and practice (Mullen and Streiner, 2006). Furthermore, much of the unease with this approach in the UK (and elsewhere) stems from its close association with managerial agendas and an emphasis on cost-effectiveness and performance measurement at the expense of other equally legitimate interests, most notably those of service users (Trinder, 2000a).

PROMOTING INCLUSION

Multiple perspectives

In this section the theme of relevance to practice is continued, although the focus is more on addressing the complexities of practice with greater attention to process and plurality of views and the use of qualitative approaches. The longstanding tradition of qualitative research in both the US and UK has been well documented (e.g. Shaw and Gould, 2001d). For example, practitioner research studies in the UK have tended to focus less on outcome and more on developing knowledge and understanding of the processes involved in social work practice drawing primarily on qualitative methods. What might be described as a 'strongly pragmatic approach' characterizes much of the research undertaken in this context (Trinder, 2000a). This more pragmatic approach is supported by the long-held and widely shared view that social work research should be seen as both methodologically robust and relevant to practitioners. While not ignoring the underlying epistemological and methodological issues, the focus is on the use of an appropriate choice of method in any given context. Every effort is made to take account of differences of view and the need to work in ways which facilitate partnership rather than patronage on the part of the researcher. Engagement with a diversity of perspectives may not necessarily involve practitioners or service users as research producers, but it does provide an opportunity for generating new understandings and alternative forms of knowing about social work (Fuller and Petch, 1995).

Exploring the various accounts of those involved in social work from the practitioners' perspective has contributed to a more informed understanding of the dynamics of social work relations and the delivery of services in the wider organizational and policy context (Williams et al., 2007a). Other studies have sought to explore service users' accounts alongside those of social work practitioners and setting these various perceptions alongside each other has created many rich descriptions of social work practice (Juhila and Pösö, 1999; Anis, 2005). Thus, recognizing the diversity of interests of those involved in the process and valuing personal accounts of the experience provide a means of visualizing and exploring the complexity of social work and the contradictions and tensions inherent within it.

An acknowledgement of this diversity of experiences and interests confronts the researcher with issues about appropriate ways of attending to these many, often competing voices within the research process and in the production of knowledge. Whilst attractive in its desire not to give primacy to any one approach or single perspective, this strategy risks an uncritical or unprincipled approach that has raised criticisms from both within and out-with the social work community. What becomes of the role of researcher in the production of knowledge? Is it sufficient for the researcher to adopt 'a relativist view from everywhere' rather than maintain the 'objectifying view from nowhere' or is there, as Humphries (2004b) suggests, a need to acknowledge the inevitability of 'taking sides' in some form or other. These issues were evident in a study undertaken by Powell and Goddard (1996) that sought to combine cost and stakeholder views in evaluating services for older people and underlined the complexities of researcher accountability. A further concern in this context is the way in which the diversity and fluidity of interests within these defined groups can fail to be acknowledged in the pursuit of emphasizing a collective concern (Fawcett and Featherstone, 1998). It is often in this way that positions or interests become fixed or entrenched and the opportunity for exploring 'sameness alongside difference' is lost.

Engagement with service users' and carers' perspectives

In this section we examine the ways in which social work research has sought to become more relevant to practice, primarily through recognition of the least powerful, marginalized voices: service users. Although there is wide recognition of the need to attend to service users' views and experiences, the way in which social work's espoused commitment to the empowerment of service users should be reflected in research practice remains a highly contested issue.

Client studies which facilitate the service user or client to 'tell their story' explicitly, place the person at the center of the activity rather than at the margins (Fisher, 2002a). In the UK context, much of this work builds on the seminal work of Mayer and Timms (1970) and has offered ways of understanding more about the complexities of practice alongside the generation of new forms of knowledge. However, promoting wider participation is not necessarily sufficient in itself to confront the built-in inequalities of power amongst the various research participants. The work initiated by the Research as Empowerment – Toronto Group, set up following the fourth International Empowerment Conference held in Toronto in 1997, has made an important contribution to this debate (Hanley, 2005). In tracing the origins of this 'new paradigm' of collaborative research, Beresford and Evans (1999) point to a range of sources, including the significant contributions arising from disability and feminist research and other emancipatory movements in both the US and UK. Action is integral to the research process as is the generation of new knowledge or alternative ways of knowing that can be used to question more dominant or privileged forms of knowledge held by politicians, policy makers or professionals as a means of achieving change, generally at a local level (Beresford, 2007c). Where the researcher takes on this more active advocacy role in promoting the interests of the least powerful, the status of the researcher and their role as expert with overall control of research methodology is challenged.

Arguably, approaches which seek ways of taking account of a diversity of perspectives and interests within the research process are consistent with the social work researcher's commitment to produce knowledge relevant to practice and to promoting inclusion and participation in the processes of knowledge production. However, the extent to which an explicitly emancipatory stance is or should be adopted remains contested. Whatever the researcher's commitment to addressing the diverse interests within social work, there are tensions arising from the need to balance concerns for both relevance, explored here in terms of multiple constituencies, and ensuring methodological credibility or rigour.

The changing role and relations of the researcher brought about via greater attention to the diverse interests, perspectives and claims involved in addressing issues of relevance may vary depending on both the purpose and context of the research and how these are negotiated by the individual researcher. However, the exploration of alternative ways of thinking about our practices encourages the possibility of acting differently and changing our ways of 'going on'. Whilst the role of the researcher as negotiator and facilitator is taken up again in the latter part of this chapter, in the context of pursuing systematic and rigorous research, in the following section the role of the researcher as a critically reflective practitioner in the research process is more closely examined.

CRITICAL REFLECTION

The focus so far in this chapter has been on the relevance of research to practice and the need for the researcher to remain open and responsive to the multiple constituencies identified here. This inevitably raises issues concerned with both the methodological rigour of the research and the kinds of knowledge or knowledges that might be produced. As we have suggested earlier, the researcher's practice is not fixed, pre-determined or entirely predictable. Irrespective of the purpose, context or chosen method(s), it involves a degree of uncertainty and negotiation throughout the process. This creates challenges to established boundaries of research and the traditional role of the researcher. Developing the capacity to be reflective assists the researcher in managing her role in ways that are responsive and potentially creative. This requires professional expertise similar in many respects to that associated with social work practice, where skills of reflexivity are seen as integral to the task. Fook (2000b) usefully distinguishes this form of reflexivity as:

> ... the ability to locate oneself squarely within a situation, to know and take into account the influence of personal interpretation, position and action within a specific context. Expert practitioners are reflexive in that they are self-knowing and responsible actors, rather than detached observers (2000b: 117).

In the research context, this continual process of reflexivity is central to the conduct of the activity and to the ways in which data are generated and analysed. Reflexivity is regarded as a resource to be acknowledged and valued (Fook and Askeland, 2007). Power relationships can be examined and built-in inequalities challenged rather than re-enforced. A multiplicity of interests and accountabilities can be foregrounded rather than ignored and continuously scrutinized and (re)negotiated.

Managing the complexity of the research process in ways which facilitate a more inclusive approach underlines the centrality of self-reflexivity on the part of the researcher. Certain groups can be supported or privileged, not least those whose interests have received insufficient attention or ignored. However, as Humphries (1998) highlights, there is a need for critical awareness and an acknowledgement of the researcher's role in the making or promoting of particular knowledge claims. Adopting an empowering stance can be seen as pursuing a commitment to social justice through the inclusion of a particular group previously excluded or unheard. At the same time, identifying various categorized groupings and privileging one against the other does not always adequately address the ways in which different constituent groups pursue their interests and at what costs to other groups. As noted earlier, Humphries (2004b)

argues that 'taking sides' is inevitable. What is important for the social work researcher is a commitment to values rather than 'to either a flag or a faction' (2004: 127). She challenges the claims of some social work researchers to be on the side of 'the oppressed' and advocates taking sides against oppression, articulated as 'forces that contradict social work's expressed values', by critically reflecting on the structures and processes that impact on service users thereby exposing their underlying oppressive nature. (Re)presenting data in an uncritical way devoid of its context is also to take sides and fails to address social work's commitment to social justice. She is careful, however, to avoid any sense of complacency or assumptions that the values we espouse are good enough or 'set in stone'.

In another sense, reflexivity is linked with knowledge and theory creation. Critical reflection and reflexivity are required in order to make sense of the particular social situation and to use that analysis and understanding to create new knowledge. Knowledge is not conceived abstractly but is viewed as a dynamic process in which theory and practice are interrelated. The researcher, like the expert social work practitioner, develops the ability to generate – or participate in the generation of – knowledge (Fook, 2000b; Fook and Askeland, 2007).

In this section we have looked at the role of critical reflection in the research process and how reflexivity on the part of the researcher can be a resource in addressing social work's commitment to multiple stakeholders and to a wider ownership of the research process consistent with social work's espoused commitment to promoting social justice. In the second part of this chapter, the contribution of critical reflection to research practice that is both systematic and rigorous forms an underlying theme.

METHODOLOGICAL CHOICES

Acknowledging the different kinds of knowledge associated with social work research reinforces rather than undermines the role of the social work researcher as one that remains focused on the goal of knowledge creation pursued in ways that reflect the complexity of social work practice. This suggests that methodological diversity is important in addressing the multiplicity of interests within the social work (research) community. Nevertheless, it is important that we recognize how different ways of knowing the world may influence how we explore it through the choices we make at every stage throughout the research process.

The task for the researcher is to consider what methods and activities are most likely to meet the purpose(s) of the research, and in what ways the purpose(s) of the research will impinge on those methods. In this second part of our chapter, we examine how the researcher sustains a critical approach to what constitutes appropriate attention to social work's multiple constituencies and interests in the research process alongside continuous attention to issues of methodological rigour. Our approach here is to examine the process of research emphasizing the role of the researcher in carrying out a research project. This enables us to explore the process from its initial conception through the implementation stages to completion. At all stages choices have to be made in the specific context of time and place and there are inevitably 'trade offs' that have to been negotiated throughout.

Establishing a research strategy

At the outset of any study choices have to be made regarding the relative merits of different methods and techniques as 'fit for purpose' broadly conceived. This approach is a useful one as it offers scope to encompass both methodological pluralism and diversity in the use of methods. At the same time this eclectic approach presents risks if seen exclusively as a consideration of technical issues. Attention to the embedded nature of these choices and the inter-relationship between our epistemological and methodological commitments and use of methods is also required. Being aware of our own commitments and interests and making these explicit helps us to better manage the inevitable choices that have to be made throughout the process. There are different approaches to managing these issues and dilemmas. For example, Hammersley (2003) argues the need to distinguish between different forms of inquiry: academic inquiry and practical inquiry as a means of guiding researchers in their activities. Within this framework he identifies different sub-types of inquiry arguing that no one form is privileged over another. His primary concern is to 'preserve the quality of research in a context where there are many forces operating that have a capacity to erode it'.

Rather than making a clear distinction between different types of research, others have argued the need for developing strategies that embrace different forms of knowledge as complementary and interconnected. Thus, research can make a contribution to both informing practice and the generation of theory (Fook, 2002b). In pursuit of more inclusive approaches to research that value the heterogeneous nature of knowledge, Martinez-Brawley (2001) argues that all searching and knowing in social work opens up valuable avenues for action. The more inclusive these searches are the more avenues they will open up. She advocates a commitment to 'exploration of avenues to knowing' rather than being wedded to any one method or approach. A key task is one of encouraging adequate discussion of the purpose(s) of the research – knowledge for what – and the ways in which these are most likely to be met. Thus, issues of epistemology and methodology are inseparably linked to practice. Such an approach is exemplified in a collection of papers describing the complexities of contemporary social work in Finland (Karvinen et al., 1999). This relationship between research and the development of both knowledge and practice is explored further in the context of promoting the role of researcher as an integrated part of professional practice (Karvinen-Niinikoski, 2005).

Making these links between different ways of knowing, the chosen methodology and methods explicit at the outset can assist the researcher in clarifying the choices that have to be made, particularly as these are not necessarily choices made only in relation to fitness for purpose. Choices at the outset of a project are influenced by context, funding opportunities, the setting in which the researcher is located (academic or practice context), particular interest groups and so on. The point at which purpose and context interact is a site for negotiation and agreement about the purpose(s) of the research proposed and how it is to be undertaken. In developing a research strategy the researcher engages in negotiations with many different constituencies and interests. Here, the researcher can be seen as carrying obligations in relation to ensuring 'fitness for purpose' (what methods) and ethical considerations associated, at the very least, with 'potential for exploitation' (use of methods), alongside an adequate understanding of the nature of the topic or issue to be investigated.

While advocating methodological pluralism we are not explicitly or implicitly sliding into random eclecticism. Rather, we wish to reiterate the importance of critical reflection as a resource in developing and implementing a robust methodology (Fook, 2001). An integral part of this process is the way in which critical reflection can be used as a means of facilitating the researcher's explicit exploration of how their own biography, values and assumptions, and personal conduct are intrinsically bound up in the process of undertaking their research (see for example Scourfield, 2001).

During the initial stages of question formulation and consideration of possible research designs, there is a need for rigorous examination of alternative approaches and the opportunity for debate and dialogue, not least with those who may hold different views from one's own. Discussion with others from within and outside the social work research community, with practitioners and with (potential) service users can be illuminating

in developing alternative ways of thinking about the research question and design (Fisher, 2002b). Undertaking research as part of an interdisciplinary team can also offer creative opportunities for extending ways of 'thinking and doing' research, despite the challenges and potential pitfalls (Powell, 2007). This is where we encounter different approaches to addressing issues of relevance for practice and multiple interests, alongside possible access to other forms of experience and expertise.

Critical use of diverse methods

Research methods as distinct from methodologies can be characterized as processes and techniques designed for both data gathering and analysis. Methods can be used alone or in combination with others. For some, the possibility of combining qualitatively driven methods with quantitative ones rests on the (in)commensurability of two different ways of understanding the world. For others, it is a more pragmatic matter where such differences are put 'where they belong – very much on the sidelines' (Reid, 2002b: 292). The contentious issue of combining methods in a principled way is further discussed in Chapter 18. The position taken here is that the methods used in social work research are largely drawn from the social science research community and are not distinctively social work research methods. However, their use in any social work context may give them distinctive characteristics associated with the broader social work enterprise (Shaw et al., 2006). Choice of method necessitates a careful scrutiny of its potential use in meeting the purpose of the study within its particular methodological framework. The term 'use' is problematic here as it implies a clear unidimensional linkage between purpose and use. Although choice of method as 'fit for purpose' is an important reference point, this is not necessarily straightforward: for example, in circumstances where a research project has multiple purposes incorporated into the design of the overall research study. We shall return to this topic in our concluding discussion of issues of quality in research.

Explicit and systematic reporting of the choices made and the 'trade offs' negotiated in undertaking the research gives the research potential credence in terms of both methodological rigour and attention to multiple constituencies and interests throughout the research process (Lincoln and Guba, 2000). Reliable explanation and justification underlie the making of knowledge claims irrespective of the research approach or choice of method(s). The use of a reflective diary can be a useful adjunct to both making sense of the process and reporting this in an authentic and honest way.

In the context of making knowledge claims, the role of the researcher remains a contentious issue. For some researchers given their choice of methods, attention is focused on issues such as 'striving for objectivity' and the minimization of 'bias' where the researcher is seen as expert or privileged (on the basis of technical competence) in the process of knowledge creation. For those actively engaged in promoting the wider involvement of participants in the research process, the researcher plays a more facilitative role with expertise to share in the joint process of knowledge construction. When research is conceived in this way, it involves discussion not only about the relative merits of different research approaches and possible methods to be employed, but also the carrying out of data gathering and analysis. Where the researcher is working with a diverse range of participants to promote dialogue as a basis for generating knowledge claims, the task extends to facilitating the reflective and reflexive skills of those involved. All participants, including the researcher, have the potential to become engaged in reflection and learning (Fisher, 2002b; Smith, R., 2004c). Such an approach can offer the possibility of creating shared knowledge that, although locally negotiated, can be seen as having a wider conceptual relevance and a specific action-orientated focus (Fawcett,

2000). Conceived in this way, social work research remains focused on the goal of knowledge creation but in ways which are consistent with social work's commitment to participation and empowerment (Beresford, 2000).

Making choices about the methods to be used consistently requires careful consideration of any method's potential to exploit rather than enhance opportunities for engagement in the research process. All methods have the potential for exploitation. Value is often placed on the use of qualitative methods in promoting more inclusive practices. For example, Reissman and Quinney (2005) argue that qualitative approaches are consistent with social work's commitment to social justice and, in particular, narrative methods with their emphasis on 'human interaction in relationships – the daily stuff of social work' (2005: 392). However, they caution against what they identify as studies adopting reductionistic techniques where 'lengthy accounts of lives were abstracted from their contexts of production, stripped of language, and transformed into brief summaries' (2005: 398).

Equally relevant here is the use of large-scale surveys undertaken in ways which reflect the interests of the less powerful and still meet the demands of policy makers for relevance (Truman, 1999). The continuing development of mixed-methods approaches is worth noting here in addressing the complexity of interests within both policy and practice arenas, not least those related to funding, where the differing conceptions of what constitutes relevant research makes for valuing particular methods above others (Ungar, 2006).

There is a continuing need to make creative use of existing methods, alongside developing innovative approaches to data gathering and alternative ways of involving groups previously excluded from having 'a voice' (Sanders and Munford, 2005; Whitmore, 2001). Again we emphasize the need for critical reflection on the part of the researcher as a means of ensuring appropriate use of any particular method, old or new, in addressing the complexity of social work practice and its multiple constituencies. Relevant here is the development of approaches that promote inclusivity and participation of indigenous groups that include, for example Australian Aborigines (Fook, 2003) and New Zealand Maoris (Gibbs, 2001b), and attend to the colonizing functions of many traditional research designs and ways of generating knowledge (Smith, 1999; Ling, 2004). For further discussion see Chapter 20.

In today's world most societies are marked by multicultural heterogeneity and the need for cultural sensitivity on the part of the researcher (Uehara et al., 1996). The exemplar introduced here illustrates some of the challenges confronting the social work researcher that have been outlined above.

Exemplar: A psychoeducational intervention for Latino family caregivers

In the US, the multicultural experience is heavily influenced by the presence of the Latino ethnic group. Its members trace their heritage to Latin American countries. Some are recent arrivals; others trace their Latino ancestry to the seventeenth century. Latinos, whose cultural patterns are clearly distinct, are significant in numbers, exhibit a precarious socioeconomic profile, and historically have experienced multiple social disadvantages (Ramos, 2004).

This exemplar illustrates the complex nature of social work research with multicultural populations in the US context. It challenges social work researchers to incorporate a multicultural perspective that is consistent with both the unique nature of social work practice and rigorous, sound research. It draws from a study to evaluate the effectiveness of the Health Education Program intervention for Latinos (HEPL), providing care for frail ageing kin.

Study description and methodological procedures

This study was designed to assess the impact of HEPL on the health and well-being of caregivers and care recipients. HEPL is a modified version of the Health Education Program (HEP), a rigorously tested group intervention shown to be effective with non-Latino caregivers (Toseland et al., 2001a). HEP materials were translated into Spanish and its protocol was modified to strengthen its cultural relevance.

Participants ($N = 78$) were Spanish-speaking, primarily women of low socioeconomic status, in upstate New York. A randomized control group design with two levels of intervention (HEPL and control groups) and two levels of measurement (baseline, 8 weeks, 10 months) were used. Sessions were led by a social worker and held in community settings. Participants were administered standardized outcome measures on health status, social provision, burden and use of community services.

Incorporating a multicultural perspective

During the implementation, the researchers encountered several challenges that reflected the tensions between adhering to social work principles of respect, dignity and right to self-determination that are at the root of research designs that accommodate multicultural variations and the Western influence of traditional ways of ensuring methodological rigour. Some of these are posed here as inquiries to stimulate reflexivity and discussion.

Random sampling may not have been optimal given cultural and social justice issues pertinent to the Latino population. It can run counter to social work values, engendering ethical dilemmas. How could the intervention and its potential benefits be offered to some participants and not to others? Everyone had made a decision to participate and eagerly anticipated being selected for the intervention. How would turning away some caregivers affect group morale and attendance given Latino collectivistic cultural practices that promote a strong sense of community and loyalty? How could this ethical dilemma be managed particularly when evidence (Ramos, 2004) shows Latino caregivers underutilize social services?

The use of standardized instruments calls attention to issues of validity and reliability as the psychometric properties of some had not yet been assessed with Latinos. They measure Western constructs, such as caregiving and stress, that are often unknown or convey different meanings cross-culturally. Also, some items may not reflect cultural appropriateness and relevance. How can researchers attend to the need for research methods appropriate for specific multicultural situations while remaining faithful to their own research paradigm? A challenge for researchers undertaking multicultural research is to know what methods to use, when and why.

Concerns arose over issues of accountability and responsiveness to participants, their families and community stakeholders who were closely involved in various phases of the study. Due to random sampling and budgetary considerations some participants were denied the intervention and those left in the sample pool were rejected. How can this be justifiably communicated? How would issues of historical exclusion, discrimination, and disempowerment play out? How can the researchers reconcile conflicting accountability responsibilities to be transparent and inclusive to stakeholders and to maintain scientific or methodological rigour to the research community?

The need for a plan for sustainability became increasingly apparent. What role should researchers play in ensuring and developing such a plan as part of the research process?

Conclusion

This study attended to multicultural issues in the HEPL protocol and its implementation. Nonetheless, the researchers sought to maintain fidelity in the rigorous research design used in HEP. Their primary aim was to contribute to the field with a much needed evidence-based intervention for Latinos. As a result, a cultural perspective was not incorporated in the research design.

GENERATING QUALITY IN SOCIAL WORK RESEARCH

Throughout this chapter attention has been drawn to the importance of skills in negotiation and facilitation on the part of the researcher, alongside critical reflection. These, it is argued, are needed to manage the 'trade-offs' required in seeking wider acknowledgement of the diverse interests involved in social work research alongside maintaining careful attention to decisions of methodological choice, use of both existing and innovatory ways of collecting, analysing and presenting data as the basis for making knowledge claims. This exploration of the tensions inherent in undertaking research in the context of social work practice has implicitly touched on different conceptions of what constitutes relevant and rigorous research. In this concluding section, we consider key reference points in relation to issues of quality in social work research.

Our focus on the resolution of tensions and the trade offs negotiated in the context of both thinking about and undertaking research has been built on an understanding of the creative potential of such tensions in generating alternative forms or approaches to research in social work that establishes both its academic credibility as a discipline and its relevance to practice (Lorenz, 2003). Our exploration of relevance for practice reveals the need to attend to multiple constituencies that extend beyond the research community, itself a diverse group of interests. A key question here is, who benefits from the research either directly as a research user or indirectly as a beneficiary of potentially more effective practice? Of what value is the research for these intended users or beneficiaries? Who is the judge of quality in social work research? Recent work by Shaw and Norton (2007) identifies a number of potential criteria for judging the quality of research. These are discussed in the context of reviewing our own position(s) as outlined in this chapter but are more fully discussed elsewhere (see Chapter 19).

Much of our discussion on the need to consider ways of engaging with the diversity of interests that can be identified within social work practice addresses 'value for people'. Here, we are concerned not to advocate participation in the research process as the only approach but we do suggest that acknowledgement of, and attention to these multiple constituencies can be usefully considered in the development of any research project. What emerges from such a consideration will depend on both the purpose and context of the particular study and the choices made by the researcher in collaboration with others. Shaw and Norton's (2007) work draws attention, firstly, to the need to include 'receptiveness to service user and carers' viewpoints' alongside the practitioner's perspective, and secondly, 'to a wider distribution of individual and social justice' (2007: 19). This, they argue, is consistent with social work's commitment to empowering forms of practice and suggests a distinctive characteristic associated with social work research (see also Powell, 2005).

We noted earlier that 'fit for purpose' was a likely reference point for any research project. This issue is encompassed within the criterion of 'value for use' where research quality is assessed according to whether it has been designed and undertaken in ways that are consistent with the purpose and intended use of the research. These are primarily technological matters. Alongside 'fit for purpose', questions concerning the balance between aiming for long- and short-term benefits, and a concern for enabling or facilitating impact are raised in this context. The latter is a key concern within the social work community where knowledge utilization is regarded as a key component of effective practice. The need for both the identification of knowledge utilization strategies and their resourcing has been noted in the context of initial negotiations and, in particular, with funders. With adequate resources, there are opportunities for creative approaches to engaging (potential) users of research that make use of the researcher's interpersonal skills in the context of facilitating learning.

In the second part of this chapter we examined the notion of rigour within the research process, underlining in many respects the importance of good beginnings as a way of establishing some guiding principles with which to negotiate the implementation of the research study. We drew attention to the value of conceptual clarity in relation to the substantive topic, alongside the development of a robust methodology. Exploring epistemological commitments embedded in research practice and seeking to make these explicit, alongside adequate systematic reporting of the research process, is central to the development of robust and rigorous research. We have argued here the value of critical reflection as a resource in the production of quality research and its dissemination.

This discussion of key reference points for what might constitute 'good enough' research practice is presented in a way that is exploratory of our own practice and that of others. Dialogue has been an underlying theme within this chapter whether in the specific research context or in wider debates about the nature of social work research. The need for dialogue within the research process emphasizes the importance of skills in both negotiation and facilitation alongside reflexivity on the part of the researcher. This ensures adequate discussion of the research at all stages, from the initial idea to wider dissemination and an agenda for change. Dialogue offers the possibility of creating space within which many voices can not only be acknowledged but heard. In a world where Western ideas and initiatives continue to dominant in relation to both models of social work and research approaches, there is a pressing need for wider deliberation and dialogue – in the particular location where research is undertaken and across the social work community – concerning the different conceptions of what constitutes relevant and rigorous social work research. The researcher's engagement in research as a dialogic process facilitates this possibility. Rossiter and colleagues (Rossiter, 2000) acknowledge the problematic nature of 'unconstrained dialogue' and emphasize the importance of attending 'less to regulating methods of individual reflection and more to inter-subjective communication' as a possible way forward. A notion of dialogue that seeks shared understanding, although not necessarily agreement, has merit in opening up opportunities for 'thinking and acting differently' in our research endeavours. It is with this note of optimism that we conclude this chapter.

Logics, Qualities and Quality of Social Work Research

Ian Shaw

INTRODUCTION

The purposes of this chapter are twofold. First, to explore the nature of and requirements for good-enough reasons for thought and action in social work research. These are among the most deeply contested exchanges within the social work community (e.g. Shaw, 1999: Ch. 3 and 4; Thyer, 1989, 2008). This takes up the major part of the chapter. Second, to deliberate whether there are general criteria that provide a framework for reaching considered judgements regarding the quality of social work research. The approach I have adopted responds to the brief for the *Handbook* contributors, to stand against naïve pragmatism and avoid any tendency toward a lowest common denominator. I hope in doing so to resist ethnocentric tendencies through the cultivation of a critical (rather than polemical) and open stance, and to include reflexive assessments of positions with which I may be associated. Being able to locate the friends and critics of our available viewpoints is central to good 'intellectual craftsmanship'.[1] My position combines a strong version of the *fallible* realism of postpositivism, the *constructed* character of reality, and the central role of political and personal *interests*. I agree with Greene when she dissents from those who hold that epistemological purity does not get research done. Rather, 'epistemological integrity does get meaningful research done right' (Greene, 1990: 229).

The structure of the chapter has few surprises. I start with a fairly general discussion of what it means to reason and work scientifically. In other words, I will not treat logic in the precise sense of inference, scientific method and formal argument, but in a more general sense of good reasoning. I will move on to contextualize this in the broad field of the social sciences, and in the specific field of social work. I ask, albeit somewhat sceptically, whether there is a particular species of evidencing that characterizes social work, methodologically or substantively.

I gradually shift to a focus on logical aspects of the relationship between social work practice and research. My way into this is to look at the arguments about the relationship between scientific knowledge and what I will refer to, following others (c.f. Evans and Plows, 2007), as citizen knowledge. What is entailed in being 'expert', 'practical' or skilled at developing the interplay of 'theory' and 'practice', are all raised by this discussion.

I take service user expertise as a comparison with researcher expertise, and also glance at the question of whether the logic of practice is akin to the logic of research.

Questions of expertise are picked up again in the final part of the paper, where I touch on work on assessing the quality of research, and offer a solution that proposes the possibility of a common framework for quality judgements, that seeks agreement on quality dimensions at a middle range of generality, with the purpose of maximizing agreement between diverse epistemological positions while not requiring a unitary consensus on more specific quality criteria.

There is much that I will *not* attempt in this chapter. I will not expound and appraise positivism.[2] Neither will I elucidate and comment on hermeneutic or justice-based approaches to social work research. Nor do I intend to revisit the debates regarding scientific or evidence-based social work practice. In part, this is because these themes fall elsewhere in the *Handbook* – in Section 1 insofar as they are about the purposes of research and later in this section inasmuch as they pose methodological issues. They are largely a given of this chapter. Contrasting stances can be pursued elsewhere (Thyer, 2004, 2007; Shaw, 2006, 2008b).

SCIENCE, SOCIAL SCIENCE AND SOCIAL WORK

The language of science is incredibly interesting; it's a natural language under strain

So remarked the theoretical chemist, Roald Hoffmann (Wolpert and Richards, 1997: 24). Interviewed for a BBC radio programme, he said of chemistry, 'I love it. I like the subject, its position in between, its compromise between simplicity and complexity ... (B)eauty is in the reality of what's out there, residing at the tense edge where simplicity and complexity contend' (1997: 20–1). He welcomes the 'love and hate relationship' between theory and experiment (1997: 20).

In pursuing his discipline he opposes reductionism (e.g. that the concepts of chemistry are reducible to those of physics).

Hoffmann is also an established poet. He goes on to say:

I think poetry and a lot of science – theory building, the synthesis of molecules – are creation. They're acts of creation that are accomplished with craftsmanship, with an intensity, a concentration, a detachment, an economy of statement. All of these qualities matter in science and art. There's an aesthetic at work, there is a search for understanding. There is a valuation of complexity and simplicity, of symmetry and asymmetry. There is an act of communication, of speaking to others'. (1997: 23)

Along with the other interviews in Wolpert and Richard's book, Hoffmann's stance and motivation should disabuse the tendency of some social work writers to extol simplistic, homogenized caricatures of the many supposed virtues and contrasts of social work as against the natural sciences.

Yet we hear different voices. 'Science is a way of generating and testing the truth of statements about events in the world of human experience' (Wallace, 2004: 35). Wallace contrasts science with modes he calls 'authoritarian', 'mystical' and 'logico-rational'. Compared with each of these, 'the scientific mode combines a primary reliance on the observational effects of the statements in question, with a secondary reliance on the procedures (methods) used to generate them' (2004: 36). Reliance on observation – assumed to be at least partly independent of the observer – seeks 'the annihilation of individual bias and the achievement of a "universal" image of the way the world "really" is' (2004: 37). This is premised on an image of science as distinct, to a substantial degree, from the world observed. Michael Scriven, the evaluation theorist, seeks something of the same end when he concludes that 'Both distancing and objectivity remain correct and frequently achievable ideas for the external evaluator' (Scriven, 1997: 483). 'Distance has its price', he concedes, but involvement 'risks the whole capital', and 'so-called participatory design ... is about as sloppy as one can get' (Scriven, 1986: 488, 486).

'Pure' statements of this position are not easy to find. Even here, expressions like 'At least partly independent' and 'frequently achievable', and the presence of inverted commas, suggest hesitation. Donald Campbell, sometimes wrongly bracketed with this position, remarked towards the end of his career that:

> There may have been a past time in which our model of science confidently posited context-free, atomic, indubitable facts; timeless, context-free, unrestricted, covering laws and theories; and a possible language of unambiguous, monosemic, context-free words and grammars to describe these facts, laws and theories. If so, that time is well past. (Campbell, 1991: 587)

Yet it seems to suit critics of various hues to wish such a straw figure existed. Michael Billig, in pleading the merits of 'the traditional, ill-defined skills of scholarship' against 'rigorous, up-to-date methodology', characterizes the latter as involving rules of procedure that are 'impersonal, in that they are meant to apply equally to all researchers. It is assumed that any two researchers who approach the same problem should arrive at identical results ... (M)ethodology attempts to standardize the practice of the social sciences and eliminate quirkiness' (Billig, 2004: 13–14). Social work critics of alleged positivism sometimes favour the same rhetorical devices (Shaw, 1996: Ch 6).

The key epistemological players on the social work field are positivism, realist postpositivism of the kind associated, among many, with Phillips (1987, 1990) and Hammersley (1992),[3] critical inquiry and varieties of constructivism.[4] Each position carries major internal diversity over issues such as objectivity and subjectivity (positivism and realist postpositivism), the advocacy role of the researcher (critical inquiry) and relativism (constructivism). But the four positions do have general coherence and correspond closely to major developments in the philosophy of science.

Despite claims to the contrary from both advocates and critics (e.g. Everitt et al., 1992; Thyer, 2008), philosophically rigorous forms of *positivism* have been in decline for at least sixty years. Three developments have been crucial in creating near unanimity among social scientists that there are no absolute justifications of scientific assertions. First, the role of observation as the final arbiter has been re-valued. For example, the acceptance that some mechanisms are unobservable led to the rejection of the belief that concepts can be reduced to a set of operational, observational statements. Equally influential has been the rejection of the assumption that observation can be theoretically neutral. Second, the relationship between theory and observation was shown to be more complex than previously thought. It became clear that theories are 'underdetermined' by nature, such that we are never able to say that we have the best theory, and a variety of theories can be constructed that are equally compatible with the available evidence. This has led to the almost unanimous rejection of 'foundationalism' – the view that research findings of indisputable validity can be a foundation for action. Third, the view that there is a steady accumulation of findings and theories, and that science grows thus, has been effectively challenged by Kuhn, Popper, Lakatos and others.[5]

Critical inquiry is a catch-all term to include neo-Marxist research, some feminist positions, the work of Paolo Freire, and some forms of participatory inquiry. These approaches are 'critical' in the sense that problems are conceptualized as part of the social, political and cultural structures in which the research is formed. The form of critical inquiry focuses on the contradictions of practice. Hence the basic logic is not preoccupied solely with the formal organization of argument, 'but also particular forms of reasoning that give focus to scepticism towards social institutions' (Popkewitz, 1990: 49).

A *social constructionist* would respond to both postpositivists and critical researchers by saying that:

1. facts are socially constructions rather than being objects,

2. it is constitutive of a given fact that it is so constructed, and
3. the construction is contingent and not universal.

The interest lies in exposing constructions where none are thought to exist – 'where something constitutively social had come to masquerade as natural' (Boghossian, 2006: 18). To 'de-construct' is then thought to be potentially liberating. This is a strong version of social constructionism. Schwandt expresses his own species of constructivism as involving the positions:

> (1) that the social world ... can only be studied from a position of involvement 'within' it, instead of as an 'outsider'; (2) that knowledge of that world is practical–moral knowledge and does not depend upon justification or proof for its practical efficacy; (3) That we are not in an 'ownership' relation to such knowledge but we embody it as part of who and what we are. (Schwandt, 1997: 75)

The classical philosophical view is that it is sometimes possible for the evidence alone to explain why we come to believe something. Task-centred social work may be taken as a hypothetical case in point. The original experiment, *Brief and Extended Casework*, (Reid and Shyne, 1969) was carried out with the assumption that open-ended casework would prove more effective, given ideal circumstances. When the contrary was supported by the evidence it led to a prolonged programme of research to develop and test the effectiveness of the model. A strong constructivist, as described above by Boghossian, would respond by asserting the *descriptive dependence of the facts* in this experiment, and would be deeply sceptical of evidential truth claims based on Reid and Shyne's experimental data.[6] A moderate constructivist would respond by asserting the weaker position of the *social relativity of descriptions*. S/he would accept that evidence may exist independent of description and language, but hold that we cannot assert that something is true, or that our warrant is unchallengeable, or that it will forever be warranted – to quote the post-positivist writer, Phillips, '*nothing* can guarantee that we have reached the truth' (Phillips, 1990: 43).

Hence, even if – like me – you go for the weaker position, judgement about evidence still remains a hugely demanding task. Because we accept that there are some mind-independent facts, 'This argument ... does not tell us all by itself which facts obtain and which ones don't; nor does it tell us, of the facts that do obtain, which ones are mind-independent and which ones aren't' (Boghossian, 2006: 57).[7] Interestingly, Bill Reid seemed to reach a position something like this when, in a chastening and memorable metaphor, he remarked of effectiveness studies, his own and others', 'It is like trying to decide which horse won a race viewed at a bad angle from the grandstand during a cloudburst' (Reid, 1988: 48).

How do these seemingly abstract debates play out against everyday inferences from research? Are we left with a pick and choose pluralism? Even if we reject the hard-to-find forms of unreconstructed positivism and relativism,[8] how do we weight values of evidence, justice and understanding? I offer one response to this question when I discuss research quality.

Knowing and social work

We can get into the same general epistemological problems by starting from social work practice. There has been much (generally welcome) attention to diverse arguments for reflective learning and practice in social work. While Donald Schön has had little to say explicitly about social work, his distinction between reflecting *on* action and reflecting *in* action has entered the social work vocabulary. We can call this a strong version of 'internalist' approaches to giving an account of a belief. We assume that we can find out what we are justified in believing primarily by a process of learned reflection; that this process is internal to our mind (at least to a significant degree); and that it is a process we can consciously access. None of these three assumptions is without controversy. There is a frequent tension in social work between 'internalist' and 'externalist' ways of justifying what we believe. Reflective practice is clearly a different approach from evidence-based practice,[9] which is strongly externalist, and rests on the view that we can find an essential and probably primary basis for knowledge-for-practice from empirical evidence external to ourselves. Social work knowledge calls for more than simply having an opinion or even being correct, but needs some kind of justifying account. While some accounts are 'externalist' (e.g. evidence-based practice) and some are 'internalist' (e.g. reflective practice), and there are perhaps unavoidable tensions between the two, we should remember that the tensions are logical and philosophical and may not always be pragmatic. (This is an important reservation. Critics of evidence-based practice [EBP] sometimes write as if advocates of EBP believe research evidence is all that is needed to form a judgment for action. While I think EBP adherents do give insufficient attention to issues of discretion and judgement, such over-simplified criticisms are not fair or accurate, c.f. Shaw, 2006).

One more distinction may be useful as a route into elucidating the potential strength of evidence claims – that between knowledge by *acquaintance*, what we derive from our senses, and knowledge by *description*. When we express knowledge by acquaintance in language it becomes knowledge by description. The face-to-face interview between service user and social worker entails knowledge by acquaintance on both sides, but as soon as the social worker refers to that interview verbally or in writing (in a record, email or report), it becomes knowledge by description. Likewise with a research article or report. 'It is a deep question how we learn to name objects of common experience … from our private knowledge by acquaintance' (Gregory, 1987: 412).

While the distinction is not absolute, it has uses and may not be well enough observed. Take from the UK an influential and interesting account of kinds of knowledge in social work and social care. Pawson et al. (2003)

helpfully invite us to distinguish between knowledge held by practitioners, the policy community, service users and carers, researchers and organizations, and set out to develop provisional criteria for assessing knowledge through a common framework of quality criteria. Despite its innovative approach and value, one of the difficulties of this scheme is that there may be as much diversity of knowledge by acquaintance and description *within* each of these as there is *between* them. But the acquaintance/description distinction is shaky, and has limited purchase in practical terms, in that it is generally accepted that there is description within perception and experience, evident most obviously in constructionist understandings of the world.

An understandable response to the discussion thus far would be to infer that there is not one single way of scientific thinking but many – each with its own forms of reasoning. Assumptions that different kinds of science are, of course, part of our routine ways of talking – the 'natural' and 'social' sciences, the 'hard' and 'soft' sciences, the 'pure' and 'applied' sciences. None of these holds much water. An alternative line of approach to identifying the nature of social work research is to pursue an empirical, inductive exploration of the kinds and qualities of social work research activity. Exemplar 1 summarizes a development of dimensions on which kinds of social work research may be allocated. While this is not a definition of social work research, it may provide a less ideologically driven basis for developing such a definition.

Exemplar 1: Kinds of social work research

This exemplar outlines an ordering[10] of kinds of research according to two different dimensions:

- Dimension 1 – On whom is the *primary substantive focus* of the research?

- Dimension 2 – *What is the primary problem focus* of the research?

The progressive development of the scheme was carried out through a series of ratings and inter-rater reliability exercises. A sample of forty papers published in a consecutive run of issues of the *British Journal of Social Work* was used for initial development. Inter-rater agreement (and in some instances attribution) was difficult in five cases for the first dimension (87.5% agreement, *n* = 35) and four cases for the second dimension (90% agreement, *n* = 36). The test was in one respect fairly stringent in that the authors come from different disciplines.

Methods of choice? Should certain methods be first choice for specific research problems? This is not an issue as to whether research methods offer an enriching diversity of ways of releasing the inquiry imagination – they do so, and in ways that are a long way from being appreciated by social work researchers tempted to adopt instrumentalist strategies in the selection of methods. Mills may be talking to sociologists but it will count as well for social work. 'What method and theory properly amount to is clarity of conception and ingenuity of procedure, and most important … the release rather than the restriction of the sociological imagination. To have mastered "theory" and "method" in short means to have become a self conscious thinker … to be mastered by "method" and "theory" means simply to be kept from working' (Mills, 2004 [1959]: 20). The question is not therefore whether we should close down sharp colleaguely exchange about research methods, still less whether methodology is, in Billig's terms, a restrictive set of procedural rules. It is whether there are field-of-study distinctives about the range and nature of research methods that mark social work off from, say, sociology or psychology.

Qualitative methods are sometimes seen as a candidate for this. Should social work researchers sign up to a methodological version of the implications of the Irish poet, Patrick Kavanagh, when he wrote 'parochialism is universal. It deals with the fundamentals'.

All great civilisations are based on parochialism. To know fully even one field or one land is a lifetime's experience. In the world of poetic experience it is

On whom is the primary research focus?	
Actual or potential service user or carer groupings	1. Children, families, parents, foster carers
	2. Young people (not offenders)
	3. Young offenders/victims
	4. Adult offenders/victims
	5. People with mental health problems
	6. Older people
	7. People with health/disability problems (including learning disabilities)
	8. Drug/substance users
Citizen, user and community populations	9. People as members of communities
	10. Service user, citizen or carer populations
	11. Women/men
Professional and policy communities	12. Social work practitioners/managers
	13. Social work students/practice teachers/university social work staff
	14. Policy, regulatory or inspection community
	15. Members or students of other occupations
Not applicable	16. For example, theorizing that crosses categories; methodology

The first dimension is set out at two echelons, and thus permits analysis at two levels.

Figure 15.1   First dimension: primary research focus.

What is the primary issue or problem focus of the research?
1. Understand/explain issues related to risk, vulnerability, abuse, resilience, challenging behaviour, separation, attachment, loss, disability or trauma.
2. Understand/explain issues related equality, diversity, poverty and social exclusion.
3. Understand/assess/strengthen user/carer/citizen/community involvement in social work; partnership; empowerment
4. Understand/promote the nature and quality of informal care, carer activity, volunteering, and their relation to formal care.
5. Describe, understand, explain, or develop good practice in relation to social work beliefs, values, political positions, faith, or ethics.
6. Understand/develop/assess/evaluate social work practices, methods, or interventions.
7. Understand/evaluate/strengthen social work/social care services, including voluntary/independent sector.
8. Understand/explain/promote good practice in social work/social care organizations and management.
9. Understand/address issues of ethnicity, racism.
10. Understand/address issues of gender, sexism, the role of women, the role of men.
11. Demonstrate/assess the value of inter-disciplinary approaches to social work services.
12. Demonstrate/assess the value of comparative, cross-national research.
13. Develop theorizing
14. Understand/appraise/develop the practice and quality of social work research (including user/carer involvement in research; feminist research; anti-racist research methods).
15. Understand/promote learning and teaching about social work or related professions.

Further information is given in the main report regarding the conceptual development of the two dimensions, the information base necessary to apply the framework, guidance on category meanings, and requirements for subsequent development and utilization by other stakeholder groups and research communities in other cultures (Shaw and Norton, 2007).

Figure 15.2   Second dimension: primary issue/problem.

depth that counts, not width. A gap in a hedge, a smooth rock surfacing a narrow lane, a view of woody meadows, the stream at the junction of four small fields – these are as much as a man can fully experience.

Robert Macfarlane, from whose essay I have taken this quotation,[11] says that for Kavanagh, 'the parish was not the perimeter, but an aperture: a space through which the world could be seen'. Yet the parish, literally as well as symbolically, does not exclude the quantitative (for a rewarding example, c.f. Healy et al., 2005). Several commentators who have contributed much to qualitative thinking and practice caution against over-playing attempts to over-define qualitative research or claiming principled grounds for choosing

qualitative over quantitative approaches. 'The multiple logics of qualitative research emerge from their relationships with the general purposes of research projects' (Silverman, 1997: 25). Similar cautions have been expressed by some who have been associated with the development of high levels of quantitative research. For example, Cowger and Menon (2001: 473–4) state that:

Both quantitative and qualitative research methods have distinctive and important contributions to make to the development of new social work knowledge. Used together, they provide unique advantages in the advancement of our knowledge base ... The social work epistemological debates over qualitative versus quantitative paradigms during recent years, although interesting, are generally ignored as they are not informative for our purposes and do not give coherent direction for the development of new social work knowledge. Campbell (1978) is essentially correct when he comments on the quantitative versus qualitative debate by stating, 'Each pole is at its best in its criticism of the other, not in the invulnerability of its own claims'. (p. 204)

Another way to understand how different social science communities see their identities is to compare statements about the requirements for doctoral training. A clear example of this can be seen in the UK's Economic and Social Research Council's guidelines and requirements that regulated research degrees up to 2009,[12] and the part of the guidelines that sets out what each of the disciplines regards as essential 'specialist' research training requirements specific to that discipline (ESRC, 2005a).[13] There is a lot of similarity between disciplines, but differences of emphasis. One of the main differences is how far the nature of the area is described in terms of understanding/theorizing and how far it also includes some notion of 'application'. Some disciplines are weighted quite differently from others in that respect. There are differences also in how each subject sees the balance between generic research skills and subject-specific ones. Some of the subject-specific statements (social work included) are quite a lot longer than others, thus appearing to imply that they regard their distinctives as relatively more important than those subjects where briefer subject accounts are given. This is what is said about social work:

4.1 In addition to the generic research methods training, students undertaking research training in social work will be expected to demonstrate:

- awareness of and sensitivity to the ethical and governance aspects of their research,
- reflexivity about their own and others' roles in the research process,
- knowledge of the social and political contexts and uses of research, and
- knowledge of and sensitivity to conducting research in emancipatory ways.

Much of the content of the first three points could be found in any social science 'benchmark' description of research. But this list is

saying that these issues take special 'shape' in social work research. The fourth point is, beyond reasonable contradiction, an area that is stressed more heavily in social work than in any other discipline and indeed, in most disciplines it is mentioned not at all. The Guidelines go on to say that:

4.2 Students undertaking research in social work study and interact with people as individuals and as members of families, networks, communities and societies. Research training must therefore give students:

- a clear understanding of the ways in which inequality and diversity shape research questions, and the skills, understanding and sensitivity to understand, reflect and, where appropriate, challenge these issues at all stages of the research process,
- an understanding of the need to incorporate the perspectives of all research users in an appropriate manner, and an appreciation of the tensions this may produce within the research process, especially where it is developed within a participatory framework, and
- a critical awareness of the potential and limitations of multidisciplinary and interdisciplinary approaches to social work research, and how these may usefully be integrated to further research in social work and social care.

This emphasizes value issues and also the relevance of work in a range of other disciplines. When the Guidelines deal with the details of the research process they emphasize particular designs and data collection methods. For example, on *research design* the guidelines ask for:

Knowledge and skills in experimental and quasi-experimental designs, n = 1 designs (i.e. single case designs), longitudinal studies, case studies, applied ethnographies, action research, intervention research and development, and evaluation designs.

On *data collection* they set out:

Knowledge of the scope, value and utility as sources for social work research of archival, documentary, institutional and agency records, official statistics, and policy reports.

A particular social work research agenda can plausibly be detected. The example of a research design requirement reflects the centrality of broadly evaluative questions, and the data collection example derives from the significance of institutional settings in social work.

Does this mean that social work research has its own array of distinctive methods? Perhaps not. The implications of these requirements seem not to require a claim for any distinctive methods *per se*, but suggest how choice of methods will (and ought to) be connectable to the characteristic disciplinary (social work) purposes of the research.[14]

Discipline-specific knowledge? The profession has devoted considerable effort over the past century to develop what could be called discipline-specific knowledge – that is, knowledge unique and specific to our discipline. This has not been a very successful undertaking (see Thyer, 2002, for a variety of knotty issues that [sic] have eluded resolution). There are serious difficulties in defining the profession and the practice of social work using terms which are genuinely specific and not superficial. Many disciplines embrace a so-called person-in-environment perspective, and many fields are active in the areas of social justice, relieving oppression, and combating discrimination in its myriad forms. All the professionals have intricate codes of ethics, so none of these oft-touted distinctive features are truly unique to our field. There is no particular area of practice – child welfare, probation, domestic violence, human rights, mental health, social policy – whose practitioners are predominantly social workers. And there are no specific interventions – case management, counselling, ombudsmanship, linkage and referral, psychotherapy, behaviour analysis and therapy, agency administration – that are unique domains of social work. It can even be difficult to define the edges of who is a social worker versus who is not. Certainly someone with a social work undergraduate or graduate social work degree, and who is credentialed or qualified by their government, can be said to be a social worker, but what about someone with a degree in another field (e.g. psychology), who works

in government in a 'social worker' role? Many leading 'social work' scholars have no academic degrees in the field of social work.

There *are* grounds for developing the identity of social work as a distinctive field or discipline, but the pursuit of discipline-specific knowledge is not among the strongest. We should thus stay cautious about claims that social work research is and ought to be different from research in other social science disciplines. Neither the subject matter, nor the investigatory methods employed in the research enterprise are unique and specific to social work.

I have at least two problems with counter-arguments for the distinctive nature of social work. First, key terms tend to be treated as self-explanatory, and in need of no unpacking – as forms of sloganizing, 'a swearword by which no-one is swearing' (Williams, 1983) – and leave proponents vulnerable to being regarded as ill-informed, and as a consequence risk being ignored. Second, such claims tend to undermine a culture of reciprocal exchange and argument that should mark social work activity at all levels. Lying behind claims to social work's special character is, I suspect, an old heresy that for many years was prevalent – the belief that social work has a basic value position that has greater merit/human authenticity and is more whole-person oriented, etc. than other professions.

WHO IS THE EXPERT?

Social work and social work research will be the poorer if we over-emphasize the distinctives. It will make us disinclined to listen to the voices of colleagues in other disciplines and professions. If we espouse joined-up services, why not joined-up inter-disciplinary research? On most occasions the right question to ask is not what makes social work research distinctive, but what might make a given research enterprise of distinctively good quality.

Before we explore that question, we examine these issues from a different perspective. Thus far we have taken research and social work research as our starting point. How do questions of good-enough reasons for thought and action in social work research look from the position of the practitioner and service user? Mills continued his remarks about method and theory, saying:

> Method and theory are like the language of the country you live in; it is nothing to brag about that you can speak it, but it is a disgrace, as well as an inconvenience, if you cannot. (Mills, 2004 [1959]: 20)

As an undergraduate sociologist in the 1960s I recollect how Mills was recommended reading, but, as I recall, with a sense of the maverick whose work did not quite fit, and who was read as much for his witty paraphrasing of Talcott Parsons' grand theorizing than as a serious member of the mainstream. Yet his moderate scepticism about the expertise of social scientists has now become almost commonplace, led by the wave of work by sociologists of scientific knowledge where science became reconceptualized as a social activity, that has found affinity especially with constructivist social work researchers.

The field has been mapped both extensively and intensively, and has a special though not exclusive home in the journal *Social Studies of Science*. Campbell gave early expression to some of these ideas. Writing in 1974 he expounded his insistence that qualitative, common-sense knowing is the building block and test of quantitative knowing (Campbell, 1979).

Anthropologists have suggested several reasons why we should treat common sense as a cultural system – 'a relatively organized body of thought, rather than just what anyone clothed and in his right mind knows' (Geertz, 1983: 75). If it *is* a cultural system and not mere matter-of-fact apprehension of reality, then 'there is an ingenerate order to it, capable of being empirically uncovered and conceptually formulated' (1983: 92). Geertz undertakes this 'disaggregation of a half examined

concept' (1983: 93). He identifies properties of 'naturalness', 'practicalness', 'thinness', 'immethodicalness', and 'accessibleness' as those general attributes of common sense found everywhere as a cultural form. Social work research cannot ignore the common-sense ways in which practitioners endeavour to make evaluative sense of their practical activities. For example, Bill Reid with Stuart Kirk argued that we know little of the everyday epistemologies of practitioners (Kirk and Reid, 2002).

Common-sense knowledge will often be tacit knowledge. The notion that experts have tacit knowledge was first introduced by Michael Polanyi. The idea has been refined and applied to fields as diverse as medical practice and laser building, social work and the development of nuclear weapons. Tacit knowledge can be defined as knowledge or abilities that can be passed between experts by personal contact but cannot be, or has not been, set out or passed on in formal statements, diagrams, verbal descriptions, or instructions for action (Collins, 2000). The question arises whether tacit, implicit understanding is in tension with more explicit, planned research. Stake may seem to suggest as much when he and Trumbull argue that:

> For practitioners ... formal knowledge is not necessarily a stepping stone to improved practice ... We maintain that practice is guided far more by personal knowings (Stake and Trumbull, 1982: 5).

Although they do not dismiss formal knowledge, 'the leverage point for change too often neglected is the disciplined collection of experiential knowledge' (1982: 8–9).

Is tacitness inherent in our knowledge? Is it a part of how we are or is such a response best treated and resisted as a 'God of the gaps' kind of explanation, where we might conceivably be able to render our knowledge explicit? The question 'matters' when, for example, we are engaged in identifying the different forms of knowledge that are part of professional work. In an example of such an attempt in the case of social care knowledge, Pawson and colleagues devote effort to suggesting how tacit practitioner knowledge can be rendered explicit (Pawson et al., 2003). The aspiration may be wise, if only to avoid the alchemy of intuitionism and appeals to 'personal style' that beset some professional practice. So long as we do not deceive ourselves that the goal is fully achievable.

If it is no longer clear, as some claim, that scientists and technologists have special access to the truth, why should their advice be specially valued? There has certainly been some rowing back from a strong position on the relativity of scientific expertise (c.f. McClean and Shaw, 2005; Schmidt, 1993). Yet it remains much more difficult to separate the credentialized social work researcher/ scholar from the experienced practitioner or user than was once thought. In an influential, though controversial discussion paper on studies of expertise and experience, Collins and Evans (2002) aim to reinstate the distinction between the scientific community and the 'laity', but without making that boundary coterminous with the boundary marking the possession or absence of expertise. They offer a provisional classification of expertise that has value for social work, and which they claim helps understand 'the *pockets of expertise* among the citizenry' and 'help put citizens' expertise in proper perspective alongside scientists' expertise' (2002: 250–1). They adopt the term 'experience-based experts' that almost exactly mirrors the term 'experts-by-experience' that is often adopted by service user researchers. They 'abandon the oxymoron "lay expertise" … (T)hose referred to by some … as "lay experts" are just plain "experts" – albeit their expertise has not been recognized by certification; crucially they are not spread throughout the population, but are found in small specialist groups' (2002: 238). Collins and Evans caution that though the phrase 'experience-based experts' shows the importance of experience, 'Experience, however, cannot be the defining criterion of expertise. It may be necessary to have experience in order to have experience-based expertise, but it is not sufficient' (Collins and Evans, 2002: 252). While this leaves open the question of what kinds of experience are relevant, they offer a distinction between three levels of expertise (2002: 255):

- no expertise,
- interactional expertise – i.e. enough expertise to interact interestingly with expert participants and apply learned research practice, and
- contributory expertise, such that one can contribute to the field being analysed.

There are obvious boundary and definitional problems with this classification, though in Collins and Evans' view they do not have to be fatal. The thrust of their argument is that there are groups of different kinds of experts in both the scientific and the 'lay' communities. We provisionally consider the implications of this analysis for developing relations between user researchers and university-based faculty in the final part of the paper.

Service users: experts by experience?

The Mental Health Foundation (mhf.org.uk) sponsored a UK-wide 'Strategies for Living' Project whereby service users could bid for small grants to carry out research of their own choosing and direction. Just over twenty projects were funded, and were supported by Advisory Committees at country level (i.e. Wales, England, Scotland, and Northern Ireland). National facilitators were appointed for each of the home countries. In the case of Wales, with which I was particularly associated, the facilitator was also a mental health sufferer, and, as far as I know, all but one of the Advisory Group were also current mental health service users. A UK-wide meeting of all projects suggested it was possible to draw the following inferences.

First, user-led research and evaluation shifts the focus from what practitioners think are *key questions for research* to those that sufferers and survivors think are central. The key themes raised by service users were:

- coping,
- identity,
- information needs,

- support needs,
- self-help,
- carers,
- women's issues, and
- rights and opportunities.

This list carries a quite different emphasis from the focus on service delivery and direct practice in a practitioner research study where the central focus of all but one of the topics was classified as either 'service delivery' (29) or 'direct practice' (12). A very small number were linked in secondary or 'accidental' ways to service user concerns and one was related to training (Shaw, 2005).

Second, user-led researchers shift the focus of what is regarded as *good research intervention*. They prioritize:

- an emphasis on telling stories (hence narrative).
- 'research from the underside' (Holman, 1987). A participant in the UK meeting of user researchers quoted in this connection what she believed to be a Ghana proverb – 'A person who rides a donkey does not know the ground is hot'.
- experience. Someone cited Paulo Freire, 'Reading the world always precedes reading the word'.

Third, user-led research provides *a powerful sense of what is stigmatizing*, for example through users' experience of language. They may reject the liberal term 'service user' because it feels to them to imply the very passivity and powerlessness that its proponents seek to avoid (the service user as engaging in one way consumption). The term 'victim', as in 'Victim Support Schemes', may be rejected for the same reason. People are also likely to be uncomfortable with terms that define the whole person in terms of the role – e.g. 'carer'. They may prefer 'sufferer' – 'because I *have* suffered' as one woman said to me – and 'survivor'.

A review of users and research emerged from a series of seminars sponsored by The Toronto Group – a network of user researchers and interested people (Hanley, 2005). This report is generally free from the stereotyping that sometimes marks such writing, and one that helpfully elaborates the issues.

My reservations are threefold. First, some user researchers tend to assume that direct change is a requirement of all good research and perhaps the sole criterion by which research should be judged.

> When academics are doing things it's just lip service. Black people don't want lip service without construction. We need to look at how we make things better for people. (Volunteer researcher, 2005: 35)

> Service users are sick of being asked the same questions over and over again ... They want payback, a product from all this research, something that would benefit them. (Seminar participant, 2005: 40)

Second, service users sometimes give insufficient weight to concerns expressed by some academic researchers, that user-led research is on occasion insufficiently rigorous. In this regard, moral and science arguments sometimes are not distinguished. Criticisms of 'institutional conservatism', elitism, etc. are important and challenging but not every reluctance on the part of academic researchers is due to these factors.

Finally, there is a tendency to caricature mainstream research. The criteria offered in the report for 'What do we mean by traditional or mainstream research?' (2005: 14) are limited to a view of research very few academics hold. In addition, the use of the term 'traditional' underplays the extent to which there is innovatory work. However these reservations do not detract fundamentally from the value of this review.

Practice and research logics

We have considered earlier whether there are areas of congruity and consonance between social work and the research enterprise, and return at this point to a question we have so far left in the sidelines – whether the logics of research methods are akin to those of practice intervention methods. Bill Reid made the key distinction as follows:

> Historically, the influence of science on direct social work practice has taken two forms. One is the use of the scientific method to shape practice

activities, for example, gathering evidence and forming hypotheses about a client's problem. The other form is the provision of scientific knowledge about human beings, their problems and ways of resolving them. (Reid, 1998: 3)

It is the first of Reid's influence forms that is captured at this point. We may label this the difference between research as a 'source' for practice and research as a 'model' for practice. Sue White and Gerhard Riemann have elaborated a detailed form of this in their chapter in the first part of the *Handbook*. It is not difficult to find advocates at either extreme. Fortune (1994), for example, argues forcefully that research (in particular qualitative forms) fits ill with the demands and logics of social work. Contrary to this, Goldstein claimed a natural affinity between the two when he said 'the language of ethnography is the language of practice', and that 'both the qualitative researcher and the practitioner depend on similar talents' (Goldstein, 1994: 46, 48). Martin Bloom, albeit from a very different access point, also sees a correspondence between research and social work in his elaborated series of parallels between single system research and social work practice (Bloom, 1999).

Each of these positions carries unduly unproblematic assumptions regarding the practice–research relationship. A demanding set of skills is necessary to achieve Reid's shaping of practice – skills that can be conveyed through the use of metaphors such as 'translation' and 'inhabit' and through ideas of transfer of learning. To inhabit some place does not happen simply by being there. It involves actively making it our home over a period of time. This process also may be described as one of 'counter-colonizing'. Implicit in this metaphor is the recognition that social workers often face the dominance of social science and research 'experts' over practice 'beneficiaries'. As Schön has expressed it:

Research and practice are presumed to be linked by an exchange in which researchers offer theories and techniques applicable to practice problems, and practitioners, in return, give researchers new

problems to work on and practical tests of the utility of research results. (Schön, 1992: 53)

Contrary to this, research and practice need linking in ways that release the potential for practice to challenge social work science, and in so doing contest conventional hierarchical ways of seeing expert/beneficiary relationships. To translate and communicate are equally demanding. Film often illustrates this, in ways comedic (e.g. *Lost in Translation*) or dramatic (e.g. *Babel*). The tasks of translating and inhabiting exemplify that the relationship between the logics of doing social work and doing research is one of conjunction but difference. These complex processes are explored elsewhere in this *Handbook* in Chapter 12 on uses of research, and in Chapter 5 on 'researching our own domains'.

There are consequences from this, for the way that the relationship between theory and practice should be understood.[15] There has been a renewed influence of Aristotelian views of theory and practice on writers in diverse fields such as ethnography, constructivism, and critical evaluation. The main effects of this have been twofold. First, it has led to a welcome reinstatement of the ethical dimension of reasoning and practice. Second, it has rescued notions of the practical from its status as second tier, derivative, and derived prescriptively from formal theory (Fahl and Markand, 1999; Polkinghorne, 2000; Schwab, 1969; Shaw, 2005).

I like the way Sheila Spong seeks to resolve the theory/practice dualism in her helpful reflections on counselling (Spong, 2007). She argues that effective relationship-based practice requires what she calls pragmatic belief, which obliges the practitioner 'to hold in tension the belief needed for therapy to be effective and the scepticism required to maintain openness to alternative interpretations' (2007: 55). This entails an ability to retain 'an "as-if" position: ... immersed but not absorbed; ... utterly present and to have a meta-view, understanding that there are other possibilities and perspectives' (2007: 62).

JUDGEMENTS OF QUALITY

... changes in the relationship between research and society and the changing role of research in knowledge production and use mean that there is a need to rethink and adapt the concept of quality as it is employed in current research evaluation procedures. (Furlong and Oancea, 2005)

I remarked earlier that on most occasions the right question to ask is not what makes social work research distinctive, but what might make it distinctively good? Offered as much as a proposal for debate than a formal statement, I suggest that social work research will be distinctively good when it:

- aims for methodological excellence in whatever it does,
- promotes social work inquiry marked by rigour, range, variety, depth and progression,
- sustains an active conversation with the social science community,
- achieves a thoroughgoing consistency with broader social work purposes,
- gives serious attention to aspects of the research enterprise that are close to social work, and
- aims to unsettle its preconceptions by taking seriously aspects of the research enterprise that seem on the face of it far from social work.

Good social work research has always done this to varying degrees. Take the final point. Ideas of knowledge, theory, and practice open up linked themes of evidence, learning, reflection, and expertise. Welfare and well-being – on which much work is being done across the social sciences – turn our attention in new ways to professional practice, risk, attachment, resilience, and power. New thinking about technology, as not solely about machines and hardware, but as a social manifestation, takes social work to developments in health, the biosciences, sociology, social policy, management, and business. Social work has made rich contributions to thinking about social justice.

This could be taken further through engaging with work done in disciplines such as philosophy, law and jurisprudence, political science, international development, social policy, criminology, and socio-legal studies. Language, culture, and communication open up allied themes of globalization, expertise, and practical knowledge. Finally, concepts of time, place and community – explored earlier in this *Handbook* in the previous section and by Staller and Mafile'o in Chapter 22 – suggest the potential fruitfulness of collaboration with colleagues in social geography, area studies, transport studies, sociology, environmental planning, and social anthropology.

But this list of proposals seems to imply a stance and position, whereas discussion of research quality immediately poses a succession of questions. Are some dimensions of quality judgements more important than others? How far is the social work community agreed on particular qualities of research deemed valuable? Is research that incorporates user involvement more valuable than traditional forms of research? Are perspectives, contexts and standards relative to local contexts or transferable? Should the quality of research methodology be judged pragmatically in the context of the particular piece of research, or are certain principles universal?

In the limited scope of this chapter, I refer to just one strand of work on research quality.[16] Brackstone, in work accepted as normative by Canada Statistics, has identified the quality dimensions of relevance, accuracy, timeliness, accessibility, interpretability and coherence (Brackstone, 1999, 2001), thus illustrating how the recognition that the quality of data involves more than just accuracy has entered the quantitative research literature. Once a multi-dimensional concept of quality is adopted, it immediately poses the question of the relationships between the different dimensions, and whether one dimension is more or less important than another.

'Implicit in the multi-dimensional definition of quality is that failure in any one dimension can cause ... the data not to be useful. The dimensions are in series, not in parallel. In that sense, all dimensions appear equally important' (Brackstone, 2001). Any single dimension is a necessary but not sufficient requirement for quality (defined here as value) to be ascribed. Brackstone adopts a hierarchical view of the dimensions of quality, where relevance is given priority. His argument has three aspects:

- Without relevance, the other dimensions are unimportant – perfect information on the wrong topics is not useful.
- Given relevance, without timeliness and accessibility the data are not available when they are needed.

And so:

- Only when relevance, timeliness and accessibility are satisfied do accuracy, interpretability and coherence become important.

His stance echoes the pungent position developed by Lee Cronbach and colleagues – equally astute statisticians – some years ago, when they argued that information that is correct and comprehensive is no use if it is not credible and comprehensible (Cronbach et al., 1980). A limitation of this line of argument is that it assumes all research is at the least use-inspired. 'Relevance' is less tangible in cases of research where this does not apply. Brackstone continues in his 2001 paper to articulate the relationship between judgements of quality and the stage the research programme has reached, thus helpfully embedding quality issues at each stage of any disciplined inquiry.

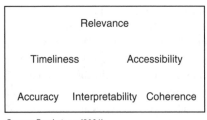

Source: Brackstone (2001).

Figure 15.3 Hierarchy of quality dimensions.

Exemplar 2: Quality of research

Black and Asian offenders

A multi-authored published report drew on a survey of almost 500 black and Asian probationers. It was carried out by an ethnically diverse research team. It reported lower scores on crime-prone attitudes and self-reported problems than the white comparison group, and questions some views of what respecting diversity will mean.

The interviewed researcher ascribed any quality it possessed to a range of factors. In this case, the peer-review response had been positive; the findings were seen as important; and the methodology had been well crafted.

More unusually – but by no means uniquely so – the output had been chosen by the interviewee because it raised interesting questions about where social work as a field of research stops and starts.

The methodological quality was contextualized in an interesting way. In summary, the researcher described 'the sheer difficulty of bringing it to conclusion'. This sense of triumph over adversity is present in the report as well. Records did not accurately reflect ethnicity; there were difficulties in setting up interviews; and some probation staff had negative views about the research. In all progress was 'slower and more fraught than had been envisaged'. Thus the epistemic (methodological) value of the research gained plausibility partly because it yielded well-founded data that challenged expectations, and partly because an impressive final sample had been achieved despite the problems encountered.

The researcher also claimed quality as reflected in the way team members acquired methodology skills. What seems a straightforward epistemic criterion is in fact presented as team learning – a species of value for people.

This illustrates how quality claims about research are typically made by conjoining dimensions of quality.

Social work researchers who undertake randomized control trials would have a different take and adopt standards such as the Oxford Levels of Evidence (http://www.cebm.net/), the CONSORT standards for reporting RCTs (http://www.consort-statement.org/?o=1011), and comparable approaches to judging evidence. However, most of these frameworks do not address the quality of research, but only the dimensions we need to know about to inform a judgement of quality. The judgement remains the responsibility of the appraiser.

Exemplar 2 depicts researchers in the process of making judgements about the quality of their work. I would propose for further consideration a stance on research quality that has several hallmarks. First, quality judgements for a given research output are likely to stem from several *different criteria* rather than from a single criterion. Hence, it seems reasonable to suggest that research quality should usually be assessed against a principle that good research ought to be 'good' on more than one dimension. For example, it will not be good *only* because it has been useful, or rigorous, or emancipatory. In this process, 'inner' and 'outer' science criteria of quality are both essential, and they should be brought to bear on any given research project or output. While the weight given to different criteria will vary for different stakeholders (Shaw and Norton, 2007), this requirement is more demanding than a simple plea for mutual respect and tolerance. Quality should not be applied through a framework of operationalized 'criteriology' (Stake, 2004). I regard this as perhaps the single most important point in the present context of social work research, and as the best way I perceive for maintaining ongoing conversations across thoughtfully held divergent positions.

Second, quality has a *temporal context*. Research work will sometimes – though not always – be seen as possessing quality because it is cumulative and builds on previous work. Quality judgements also have an unknown future life. A research project or output may not be viewed as 'good research' at the time of project completion, but will later be seen to possess quality when it leads to good later work. There is also the temporal issue of 'right research, wrong time' (or even 'wrong research, right time'), whereby research on a topic or theme is neglected, only to be 'discovered' at a time when the theme has topicality and currency.

Third, quality judgements about *research* connect to how social workers are likely to estimate the quality of their own *practice*. Consequent on our understanding of the nature of the relationship between the logics of practice and those of research, the connection will be neither straightforward nor easily anticipated. For example, researchers and practitioners both seem to draw on evidence partly grounded in the emotions in deciding whether work has gone well or not (see Shaw and Shaw, 1997 for the case made in relation to practitioners). Thus one university researcher described the tracing of cumulativeness as being 'fun'; the fieldwork also as 'fun'; and the fact that people were 'really interested' as part of her quality judgement (Shaw and Norton, 2007). Insofar as this conclusion holds good, it may provide a partial basis for making a case that fruitful comparisons can be drawn between how we evaluate different kinds of knowledge (c.f. Pawson et al., 2003).

Fourth, judgements of quality are about far more than what is enshrined in the written text. Judgements based on the quality of a text output will always be incomplete and not fully exhaustive or representative of quality dimensions. Linked to this, and to the temporal nature of quality judgements, they are always 'in-the-making'. To take a simple and uncontroversial example, community responses to research tend to be more extensive the more a project moves into the public arena. Furthermore, as people tell stories of the quality of their and others' research, those to whom they are told are more than neutral hearers. They are audience. All this suggests the dynamic character of quality, such that 'we never establish quality once and for all' (Stake and Schwandt, 2006: 405).

Finally, there will be diversity in how criteria are utilized from one project to another. It fits well with support for Furlong and Oancea's argument for setting criteria at a 'middle-range' of generality, whereby differences of approach can be acknowledged, without requiring an abandonment of the quest for collective assessment of quality.

For some, this may seem a betrayal, where profound philosophical differences are glossed over. If not a betrayal, then at best a nuisance-and-nonsense that unhelpfully dilutes the focus from local context[17] (for strong constructivists) or imports dubious pluralism (for those committed to strong realist stances on evidence or to critical theory stances on justice). I do not say this position is easy – it is neither comfortable nor amenable to manualized logic or judgement rules. But jaw-jaw is better than war-war.

ACKNOWLEDGEMENTS

Thanks are due to Bruce Thyer for comprehensive comments on the first draft of this chapter. He and I have been associated with quite different stances in relation to the issues explored in this chapter. I hope I have not unduly misrepresented those positions with which he and others are associated. I have aimed in parts of this chapter to suggest approaches to these issues that may enable continued scholarly conversations to take place between those who represent such differences, while not requiring concessions that dilute reputations or threaten participants' intellectual comfort. Thanks also to Geraldine Macdonald for her detailed attention to and generous comments on a previous draft.

NOTES

1 The phrase is C. Wright Mills' in his *Sociological Imagination*.

2 Bruce Thyer (e.g. 2008) argues that to talk of 'logical positivism' is a red herring, in that virtually no

one espouses this as a viable philosophy of science for social work. He claims that positivism, on the other hand, has been and remains the dominant philosophy of science for social work, and indeed, for all science. While this is helpful as a reminder that 'positivism' covers a whole family of positions its roots in from Hume onwards, via Auguste Comte, debates about 'positivism' in social work need further differentiation. Any claim that we are 'all' consciously or not, adherents of a certain position are of doubtful value.

3 The prefix 'post' is used in different and potentially confusing ways in the literature. For example, in the term *postpositivism*, 'post' is used to convey that this is a position that keeps some of the key ontological/epistemological premises of positivism, with some more or less radical changes to doctrines of realism and subjectivity. Thus, 'post' serves to signal a greater or lesser element of *continuity* with the position it conditions. However, in the term *postmodernism*, 'post' is used to convey that the key motives and *motifs* of the modernist enterprise are challenged. What unites adherents to this position is what is challenged. 'Post' in this context serves to signal the element of *discontinuity* with the position it conditions.

4 Schwandt elaborates these varieties as interpretivism, hermeneutics and social constructionism, in his essay on epistemological stances for qualitative inquiry (Schwandt, 2000).

5 Even the half-alert reader will detect that we do not discuss the place of postmodernism. This is not from an Anglo-Saxon disdain for Continental philosophy. Rather, postmodernist rhetoric has been taken up in social work more in the language of practice than research. While theoretically important, we concur with Matthewman and Hoey's remark that 'it is almost as if postmodernism never occurred' (2006: 530). We also agree that 'many of the questions posed by postmodernism will rise again... agency versus structure, Enlightenment versus Romanticism, humanism versus science, relativism versus realism, who can speak and what can be said' (2006: 542).

6 It is curious that no such critique seems to have been attempted.

7 For a fuller discussion of these three paradigm-like perspectives see Shaw (1999: 43–53).

8 For a critique of relativist research and evaluation commitments, see Shaw (1999: 54–8).

9 Some adherents of evidence-based practice would make the point that they are not entirely discontinuous from each other. Granted, but I am dealing here in ideal types.

10 In some places I have described this as a classification, but that protests too much.

11 In an essay in *The Guardian* newspaper, 30 July 2005.

12   This is a rather parochial UK source. New guidelines were announced during 2009, linked from http://www.esrcsocietytoday.ac.uk/ESRCInfoCentre/index_academic.aspx. Developments from the Bologna process have led to Europe-wide deliberations regarding all levels of university education. http://ec.europa.eu/education/policies/educ/bologna/bologna_en.html. Accessed 17 September 2008

13   This is not the only way to open up this question. Its limitation is that it tends to be partly aspirational. A different way would be to do empirical work on the methods and methodology actually used by different social science communities. Yet aspirational claims-making sheds light on how communities see their identities.

14   I have argued in a directly parallel way for the relationship between methods for research compared with methods for evaluation (Shaw, 1999: Ch. 8). The wider argument about whether social work research is distinctive is pursued in Shaw (2007).

15   There are also important consequences for how we understand 'practical' work. These fall outside the scope of this chapter.

16   For reviews of the literature of research quality see Shaw and Norton (2007) and Coryn and Scriven (2008).

17   I have set out a strong position on research context elsewhere in this *Handbook*.

Evidence and Practice: The Knowledge Challenge for Social Work

Geraldine Macdonald and Jennie Popay

INTRODUCTION

In this chapter we consider the prerequisites of providing evidence of the effects of social work and what it takes to improve practice. We focus on 'effects', rather than its effectiveness, because history affirms that we cannot take the latter for granted. Even well-supported, well-resourced and well-intentioned practitioners can do harm whilst convinced they are doing good (Mullen and Dumpson, 1972; Fischer, 1976; Petrosino et al., 2002). History also highlights the importance of drawing on a range of data and perspectives in order to understand the effects of professional practice on people's lives. For example, it may be important to know 'what works' in stopping a parent physically abusing their child, but, in the context of loveless relationships, attending only to this may serve to mask more pervasive and cumulative damage. Also important are data that shed light on why and how an intervention works; what sense recipients make of it; what facilitates or impedes effectiveness; what it costs and whether it has unintended consequences. Something may 'work' but not be affordable

or impossible to deliver in 'real world' circumstances. Assessing the effects of social work is, like social work itself, complex and costly. At the heart of complexity of outcome research (also called impact evaluation and evaluation research) is the challenge of demonstrating 'cause and effect'.

Knowing what causes what

Ascertaining cause and effect is not easy, particularly when the effects are less than dramatic. Suppose you have a psychological problem for which you seek professional help and the problem attenuates or disappears over a period of weeks. Should you conclude that the help was responsible? There are many other possible explanations: you may have fallen in love, won the lottery, got a new job, or taken medication which had unintended beneficial effects. The inter-relationship of such factors makes causal attributions particularly challenging in the field of psychological and social problems. If only in this respect, physicians and surgeons have it relatively easy, although nowhere near as easy as most social workers assume (see Maynard and Chalmers, 1997; MRC, 2000). Alternatively, you may just cease to be troubled – roughly two-thirds of most psychological troubles spontaneously remit (Rachman and Wilson, 1980). Consider the following scenario:

> A family centre wishes to evaluate a discussion/ educational group aimed at improving the parenting of a group of people whose children have been placed on the Child Protection Register because of neglect. The programme runs for 8 weekly sessions. It is considered by the workers and parents to have been a success for those who did not drop out. Their judgements are based on i) self reports of parents; ii) the workers' observations of parents' increasing self-esteem, and iii) improvements in the apparent well-being of the children (who have been cared for in a crèche whilst the parents met).

Was the group effective? When presented with this scenario, most student social workers say 'no'. They point out the following problems and possibilities:

- These parents might simply have improved with the passage of time;
- The social support, rather than the 'programme', might be the 'active ingredient';
- The children might have benefited from the crèche, providing parents with an opportunity for more positive interactions with them;
- Other things might have happened outside the group (for example, an increase in welfare benefits);
- Workers may have selectively perceived positive changes;
- The parents who stayed (unlike those who dropped out) might have been more motivated and therefore more likely to have improved anyway;
- Parents who dropped out may have done just as well – we don't know;
- After meeting with social workers on a weekly basis, people may simply have learned the right things to say (social workers are subject to influence too); and of course:
- The social workers have not directly assessed the impact of the programme on parenting, having relied on self-report and 'atypical' observational data.

So, even without training in research methods, students (and indeed practitioners) have an intuitive grasp of the problems of establishing causality. However, these intuitions are difficult to hold on to when conducting or appraising one's own research, or research into an intervention in which one has already invested.

Clearing the undergrowth: understanding the problem to be addressed

Effectiveness research often starts with questions such as 'How effective is intervention X in addressing condition Y?' Before asking these questions, however, there are important matters to be resolved 'upstream', that require familiarity with other research and explicitness about the assumptions being brought to the evaluation table.

Despite the complexity of the phenomena with which social work is concerned, these often attract misleading, single-category nomenclatures, e.g. 'child abuse', 'delinquency'. These 'things' manifest themselves in very different ways. Neglect is different from sexual abuse: both are 'child abuse' or 'child maltreatment'. Young people who steal, or misuse drugs, or cause bodily harm, may all be adjudicated 'delinquent'. Too often, we adopt equally oversimplified notions of causes, sometimes driven by an uncritical adoption of single theories of human development, e.g. particular psychological or sociological theories (see Williams et al., 1999), when the reality is more complex. For example, child maltreatment and 'delinquency', in their various forms, are the result of the interaction over time of biological, psychological and social factors (Rutter, 2006b). These interact in different ways for different people, producing multiple causal pathways, such that two people sharing broadly similar histories do not necessarily arrive at the same endpoint (Rutter, 2007b).

Our ability to design effective interventions is in part a function of how well we understand the problems we are seeking to address. This should include not only what makes individuals vulnerable – historically the focus of much research endeavour – but also what makes them resilient (see Williams et al., 1999; Titterton, 1992; Bartley, 2006). Longitudinal research is critical in mapping and understanding the interplay between the person and their environment, and highlighting potentially promising opportunities for intervention (see Rutter and Sroufe, 2000), but this 'broad canvas' research needs to be complemented with an understanding of situations from the perspective of the actors themselves and more in-depth understanding of the interaction between individual behaviour (agency) and environment (social structure) (see Bartley, 2006). Knowing what gang membership means, what life in care is like, and the explanations people give for their own behaviour, provides essential information to those seeking to develop effective methods of intervention. They may also generate hypotheses that larger scale research can subsequently test.

People's lay knowledge – the knowledge they acquire through their everyday experiences – provides unique insights into effective action for change. Without awareness of the 'knowing subject' (Williams, 2002) social work 'clients' are too easily reduced to unthinking bearers of deficits and risks. Simon Williams et al. (2007b) argue that lay knowledge provides '… a lived as well as a theoretical bridge between structure and agency, people and places, composition and context' opening a unique window on 'structuration': the processes that inflict the 'hidden injuries of class' (2007b: xx). In relation to health inequalities, Popay and colleagues have argued that attention to the articulation of 'lay knowledge' and how these meanings shape individual and collective action could provide a missing link in our understanding of the causes of common social problems and particular insights into the dynamic relationships between human agency and wider social structures (Popay et al., 1998: 6; see also Williams, 2002). More recently, Popay et al. (2003) have demonstrated the complex ways in which people construct an understanding

of health inequalities that acknowledges the differential impact of social and economic circumstances, but resists the moral judgements implied by dominant ideas about failure to cope and unhealthy behaviours and hence to some extent protects them from the consequences of these judgements.

We do not always do this preparatory work or do it well; in research or in practice. Sometimes we lack the necessary information; and our best understanding of something today will not be our best tomorrow. But the most effective interventions will be those that address dimensions of problems or situations that a wide range of research suggests may provide levers for change. Exemplar 1 contains an example of the development of resilience theory, based on a commentary by Rutter on four new studies (Rutter, 2007). Studies universally find differences in how individuals respond to social and psychological adversity or stress. Resilience theory is still relatively 'young', but for those in social work it represents a promising area of research and theory. The better we understand why it is that such variation exists and what underpins it, the more likely we are to be better able to use this knowledge to promote resilience, both in terms of primary prevention, but also by way of helping those who have been adversely affected by child abuse or other trauma.

Exemplar 2: Theory in the making

Resilience provides a good example of the interplay between theory and research. Resilience refers to the variation that exists in the way that people respond to physical and psychosocial adversity (Rutter, 2006a; 2006b). People can be resilient in the face of certain kinds of adversity but not others. Some are resilient to some kinds of outcomes but not others.

Rutter (2007a) argues that the concept of reliance differs both from social competence (Masten et al., 2006) and positive mental health (Layard, 2005). Resilience can't be 'seen': it is something we infer from studies of individual variation. In reviewing the literature, Rutter argues that three other considerations are needed to study the phenomenon of resilience:

i) Because how we cope depends importantly on our experiences after we have been exposed to risk or stress, a life span perspective is necessary.
ii) Although resilience is not the same as individual psychological traits, genetic effects on our susceptibility to environmental stress or change and/or the responses we make may be significant.
iii) Mediating mechanisms underpinning resilience may lie in personal agency or in the coping strategies people use, i.e. what they *do* in order to 'rise to the challenge'.

> ... the most exciting, and potentially important, aspect of the shift from risk/protective concepts to resilience is that the latter requires a move from *variables* to *processes* or mechanisms. (Rutter, 2007a: 205)

As our understanding of resilience improves, the opportunities for intervening to help people better to weather the storms that life throws at them will also improve.

Acceptability, accessibility and relevance/appropriateness

Perhaps, because social work is concerned largely with marginalized groups, part of its 'history of harms' includes the many ways it has adopted majority discourses in thinking about those in whose lives it intervenes, whether voluntarily or involuntarily. Other chapters in this book examine this legacy in depth, but it is important to note that those interested in identifying effective means of intervention have to attend carefully to the ways in which they frame issues. We have already touched on this in emphasizing the need to develop a knowledge base that incorporates the subjective understandings that people have of their experiences and situations. The argument here is that the requirement goes beyond this. Questions of

acceptability and accessibility highlight professional control over the *way* problems are to be addressed. In contrast, questions of relevance/appropriateness challenge professional control over the definition of problems addressed in the first place.

Acceptability means taking care to develop and evaluate interventions that are anchored in what people say they want or find acceptable. Social work with disabled people has largely reflected the ways that disabled people have historically been viewed by society as a whole, as people whose lives are marked by personal tragedy; who find it difficult or impossible fully to participate in society because of their impairments; dependent on others, in need of care:

> The very language of welfare provision continues to deny disabled people the right to be treated as fully competent, autonomous individuals. Care in the community, caring for people, providing services through care managers, case managers or even care attendants all structure the welfare discourse in particular ways and imply a particular view of disabled people. (Swain et al., 1993: 268)

Professionals operating within such an individual ('medical') model of disability will likely approach work with disabled people in ways that reinforce their experiences of inequality and oppression (Oliver and Sapey, 2006). Disabled people want interventions developed on a social model of disability, emphasizing citizenship and the removal of barriers to social inclusion. This requires a collaborative approach between disabled people, service developers and evaluators, recognizing that these groups are not mutually exclusive.

For the most part, social work services for disabled people will not be appropriate candidates for experimental research designs, but this underlines the importance of finding out how people see their worlds, what they want and don't want; what is acceptable and what unacceptable – something most of us routinely expect from services, but which is often not built into provision for people using social work services. Evaluation can itself provide an opportunity to surface these mismatches between provision and aspiration, and locate more general dissatisfaction, but learning this 'incidentally' is a waste of resources. Better to embed controlled trials, and other evaluation designs, in qualitative research that can shed light on potential participants understanding, and to help shape interventions that people can use, for example, exploring the barriers to attending a family centre, or involving fathers in a parenting programme. Qualitative research can also help maximise the chances of people participating in a study, particularly a trial, by exploring what their understanding of experimental designs, how they feel about the various groups, why some people would not participate, and so on (see Donovan et al., 2002).

Accessibility As well as being relevant to people (e.g. culturally sensitive) interventions need, quite literally, to be available to them. Too often researchers establish eligibility criteria that exclude groups of participants who comprise a major focus of health and social care practice. Exclusions appear to rest on assumptions that certain groups would be unlikely to benefit from the intervention on offer (or make the data difficult to interpret). This may sometimes be defensible. In tackling alcohol-induced aggression, for example, it is probably more sensible to target the alcohol misuse than the aggression. Further, not to exclude them makes it difficult to identify the impact of the intervention on those whose aggression is hypothesized to have a different causal pathway. But this tendency to 'tidy up' designs in evaluation research can undermine the relevance and generalizability of findings. Rossi, for example, argued that researchers evaluating intensive family preservation services provided few convincing rationales for their exclusions, which ranged from homeless or likely to become homeless, to 'serious cases with substance-abusing families' (Rossi, 1992: 176). He advocated a general rule that if there is any doubt about exclusions 'the decision should tip in favour of including' (1992: 176) unless there is clear danger to the child. Disinterring the mediating effects of 'additional' factors to that centrally targeted

can be explored using multivariate analysis; concerns about the differential effectiveness of an intervention can be used to identify a priori issues for subgroup analyses.

Appropriateness In order to improve social work intervention we must find out what matters to people and ensure that service development and evaluation does not just stem from the interests of professionals, policy makers and researchers. Though closely related, this is more than acceptability. In a meeting of agencies convened to identify research relevant and useful for disabled children in Northern Ireland, a group of young disabled people presented *their* priority topic, namely the emotional well-being of disabled children. None of the thirty people already canvassed, including advocacy groups, parents' organizations, policy makers had raised this. One of their basic needs has been overlooked by both services and researchers, even though the UK government has 'well-being' as one of the five outcomes for children underpinning child welfare policy (*Every Child Matters*) and even though UK child care legislation affirms that disabled children are children first, and children in need as a result of their disabilities second.

EVALUATION RESEARCH

We have argued that sound evaluation starts 'upstream' of questions of effectiveness, encompassing a range of issues other than simply whether a particular intervention X causes a particular outcome Y. But the issue of cause and effect is central to the enterprise. We now consider how impact research can best do this. It requires the introduction of some technical terms and concepts; not especially engaging, but important nonetheless. We have tried to keep this to a minimum. Readers wishing to know more about the theory and practice of evaluation are recommended to read Rossi et al., 2004; Campbell and Stanley, 1973; Datta, 2000.

External and internal validity are important concepts in evaluation research. Internal validity refers to the extent to which an outcome (effect) can confidently be attributed to an intervention (cause). External validity describes the extent to which the findings from a study can be generalized to other groups of the target population (e.g. delinquents), in other contexts, with other staff, and so on. There is usually a tension between achieving these two things in evaluation research.

In the parent group example above, the problems identified by students as preventing the drawing of conclusions about its effectiveness are 'threats to internal validity', or the extent to which an outcome (effect) can confidently be attributed to an intervention (cause). Threats to internal validity can both exaggerate or mask the effectiveness of any given intervention. The technical terms, and brief descriptions, for eight key threats to internal validity in effectiveness research are set out in Box 16.1.

How can one be sure that an intervention has caused any outcome that followed it rather than these competing explanations or 'confounders'? The answer lies in designing evaluation studies in ways that enable us to estimate the likely effects of any competing explanations and thereby control for them. This can be done by establishing two groups that are comparable in i) their composition (e.g. age, gender, and ethnicity), ii) their general experiences across the duration of the intervention (e.g. experiences of maturation, exposure to other influences), and iii) their attitude to participation in the study. We then provide only one group with the intervention in question. In this way, the only difference between the two groups will be in their exposure to the intervention. Some evaluation study designs – reflecting different combinations of these approaches – are briefly described below.

Randomised controlled trials (RCTs) are studies in which participants are randomly assigned to one of at least two groups: an

---

Box 16.1   Threats to internal validity

Selection People   Who volunteer or agree to participate in an evaluation study may be different from the general population and are almost certainly different from those that refuse to participate. They may, for example, be more motivated to change.

History Changes   These may be due to things that happened during the intervention period (of which researchers may be unaware) rather than the intervention. An intervention designed to help young offenders find employment may appear to be effective, whereas their employment may be attributable to an increase in employment opportunities.

Maturation   A range of things can happen to research participants in the course of a study which can have a bearing on the outcome. The maturing of participants (through age or experience) is an obvious example.

Testing   When participants are asked to complete a measure at different points over time, improvements in scores may reflect familiarity with the assessment measure and what is being looked for rather than a 'true' change.

Statistical regression   There is a natural variation in data. Study participants who initially have very large or very small 'scores' are likely over time to move closer to the average score for the population as a whole irrespective of any intervention. This is known as 'regression to the mean'.

Instrumentation   Problems can arise when those collecting study data (particularly observational data) change, or when measures become inappropriate (psychological tests, for example, would normally be revised or 're-normed' every ten years or so).

Attrition   Most studies 'lose' participants over time. Normally we would not know how the group that completed the study differed from the group that started it. Observed changes may be attributable not to the intervention, but to the characteristics of those that stayed.

Selection interactions   'Selection' can combine with other threats to internal validity to influence outcomes independently of the intervention.

intervention or experimental group and a control group. Randomly, in this context, means 'unpredictable': each participant has 'an equal chance' of being allocated to either group (rather than being allocated carelessly). Randomization is something that would-be recipients of an intervention often recognize as a more equitable means of distributing a scarce resource (Toroyan et al., 2000). Studies can involve the randomization of individuals or groups, institutions or communities. The latter are known as cluster-randomized trials and require different methods of analysis to those in which individuals are the unit of analysis. Methods of randomisation include the toss of a coin or computer-generated randomization tables. In RCTs with two 'arms', those in the experimental group receive the intervention, for example, restorative justice, financial assistance or anger management. Those in the control group might get nothing (a 'no-treatment' control); they might receive the intervention later on (a 'wait-list' control) or they might receive the services usually on offer (a 'management as usual' control). Randomization ensures that, if other factors are at work, they would be expected to operate in both groups: we have controlled for them. It does not guarantee that groups are precisely comparable on every dimension, particularly when samples are small. For example, one group might have a majority of girls, whereas the control group may have 50–50 boys and girls. What it does ensure is that any differences that arise in the composition of groups does so as the result of chance. In these circumstances, researchers can use statistical procedures to estimate the likelihood that any specific differences in outcome is due to chance (the result of randomization) or to the intervention. RCTs can also be used to assess the relative effectiveness of one intervention compared with another ('other treatment' controls) or to compare the relative contribution of different aspects of an intervention, for example, comparing the effectiveness of a group-based intervention for abused children with that intervention augmented by one-to-one counselling, or comparing an intensive intervention with a less intensive one.

The internal validity of a study is undermined when researchers or practitioners seek to influence the allocation of participants to different arms of the evaluation, or the measurement of effects: something they may do intentionally or unconsciously. Practitioners might want to ensure that those they consider most needy or who might most benefit are allocated to the intervention group. Researchers might want to ensure that the intervention group does not have too many people who are so difficult that they might make it harder to show the benefit. Randomization has therefore to be done in ways that ensure that those responsible for allocation cannot influence the process. Studies in which randomization is inadequately concealed are particularly prone to bias (Schultz et al., 1995).

Bias can also arise in data collection. Wherever possible it is desirable for those collecting information on the effects of the intervention not to know to which group participants have been allocated. Knowing a respondent's allocation may influence the observations made, and the way answers are recorded and subsequently interpreted. For most social interventions it is nigh impossible to mask assessors as to which group the person they are interviewing was allocated. In these circumstances, having independent researchers collect the data becomes very important. Incorporating administrative data where relevant, e.g. offending, or using well-tested self-report instruments, e.g. Achenbach's Child Behavior Checklist) can help (Achenbach, 1991).

Quasi-randomized designs have an element of randomness in their allocation, but this falls short of being unpredictable. One example is allocation to different arms on alternate days of the week. Such approaches are open to manipulation, and there may be systematic differences in groups using services on different days.

Quasi-experimental designs are common in social work research, particularly designs in which researchers establish two comparable groups by matching individuals (or institutions, communities, etc.) on variables of known importance. Matching can be done at the level of groups (aggregately) or at the level of individuals. In an evaluation of a therapeutic group for children who have been physically abused, children receiving the intervention might be matched (on age, gender, ethnicity, and history of abuse) with children who are not receiving the intervention. This is referred to as 'group matching'. Alternatively, any child receiving the therapy might be individually 'paired' with another child referred to the clinic (perhaps on the basis of gender, age, and history of abuse) who would act as the 'matched' comparison.

The business of matching is complex. It should be done on the basis of criteria such as individual, family, and community characteristics and not on the basis of the results of pre-intervention measures of the outcomes to be assessed (see Campbell and Boruch, 1975). Even those who recommend the virtues of quasi-experiments advocate caution. Samples need to be selected from larger pools of people. We cannot match on *unknown* factors that might influence group outcomes. Matched groups may therefore be different in important respects that we are unaware of. Researchers use statistical techniques to control for between group variations but these are only as good as the researchers' ability to identify what is relevant.

Other quasi-experimental designs use a series of measures before and after the intervention. An example is the 'interrupted time-series' study. These studies use a group as its own, historical, control. A non-social-work example would be the impact of introducing speed cameras on speeding offences and accidents, where data are often routinely collected, providing us with a clear picture of the rate of each over time, i.e. their trajectory (increasing, decreasing, stable, or chaotic). Knowing this pattern means that when speed cameras are introduced and we continue to collect data, we can estimate their likely impact. When the pre-camera accident trend is stable, or shows a clear upward trajectory,

and post-camera the data evidence a drop in accidents, then we can be relatively confident that it is the impact of the camera, particularly if the pattern repeats itself in different areas. Where the pre-camera trend is already downwards or unstable, then life is more challenging (see Glass, 1997). Generally, the longer the periods of measurements before and after, the more secure the evidence. In social work, the impact of a change in adoption legislation might be assessed by simply comparing rates and patterns of adoption before and after the legislative change. Such designs can involve advanced statistical modelling techniques. In the traffic camera example, for instance, the analyses might control for weather conditions, seasonality, traffic volume, and so on (Glass, 1997). Interrupted time-series designs are unsuitable for circumstances in which other changes might be occurring over time, such as changes that might be attributable to the maturation of participants. Single case designs, so often used in cognitive-behavioural therapy, are essentially time-series designs, but can be particularly misleading given the relatively short baseline period and lack of statistical checks (Kazi, 1998).

Non-experimental designs use neither multiple measures nor a control group. These research designs are appropriate for finding out what people think of a service, or to determine the effects on people of a flood or a change in income support. They are not good at assessing the extent to which an intervention is effective in bringing about intended changes.

Scarcity of RCTs

Although RCTs provide the most secure way of testing an intervention's effectiveness, they are rarely used, for several reasons. First, randomization causes disquiet that help is being withheld from people who need it. Certainly, if we know that something is effective then, all things being equal, it would be unethical to withhold it. Indeed it would be unethical to involve people in any study that seeks to answer a question that has already been answered satisfactorily. If, however, we do not know the answer, then it is unethical to impose it on everyone without determining its effectiveness. There is an irony here. Social workers can often decide what intervention to provide, irrespective of whether or not it has been shown to be effective. No ethical police descend on us. Yet if we decide to explore the effectiveness of what we do, in the absence of an existing evidence base, we may be accused of behaving unethically.

RCTs are also difficult to conduct and in some circumstances are not possible:

1. Wholesale policy changes and universal provision make RCTs difficult.
2. It is difficult to introduce two different policies in one institution or system. Even if we randomize groups rather than individuals, some circumstances make it difficult to control 'contamination effects', such as members of one group sharing their experiences with another.
3. We cannot, for example, randomize children to either kinship care or foster care by strangers.
4. In some circumstances we cannot *not* intervene, e.g. when people are suicidal or when children are being abused.

RCTs are expensive, requiring considerable commitment from a range of stakeholders over a considerable period. The retention of participants becomes increasingly challenging, with those in the control group particularly likely to drop out, having little incentive to contribute time and data for no obvious benefit. Those who commissioned the research may find the wait for results too long. But these difficulties beset all outcome studies. When obliged to use other research designs, their findings must be interpreted in ways that recognize their limitations in controlling for confounders.

Establishing causality: not the only question and not the answer to everything

RCTs provide the most secure basis for establishing causal links between outcomes and interventions, and for that reason alone they should occupy a more important place in social work outcome research than hitherto. This is not to say they are the *only* method relevant to providing evidence of the effects of social work. Their very strength in establishing causation means they are weak in other important respects. The steps taken to maximize internal validity can limit the generalizability of results to more diverse populations, i.e. RCTs often score low on external validity. Strategies to enhance the transferability of findings to 'real life' settings include replicating studies in different settings, with different samples and different staff, and running trials across a number of sites. Observational studies can monitor the pattern of results and factors influencing implementation in the roll out of an experimentally tested intervention. Qualitative research can help 'unpack' the processes whereby interventions make their impact, and what factors influence this. RCTs are a necessary, but not sufficient, tool in building a knowledge base of the effects of social work. Those advocating their use do so because they have particular strengths that are so rarely deployed – not because they are seen as a panacea (Macdonald, 1997, 2003, 2004).

Putting theory back into effectiveness research: developing better interventions

A prerequisite to providing evidence of the effects of social work is a structured approach to the development and piloting of interventions before embarking on expensive evaluations that ask much of participants. The failure to do so too frequently results in evaluations that are unable to provide a basis for decision-making. It is both unethical and inefficient to involve people in intervention studies whose design or conduct is such that they cannot answer the questions they are intended to address.

We earlier referred to the importance of theories about the causes of social problems in guiding the development of interventions. Another important category of theory is 'intervention' or 'treatment' theory: theories about the mechanisms whereby we expect an intervention to exert its influence and bring about change. Chen and Rossi put the case as follows:

> What we are strongly advocating is the necessity for theorizing, for constructing plausible and defensible models of how programs can be expected to work before evaluating them. (Chen and Rossi, 1983: 285)

Lipsey (1993) identifies the following as minimal elements of an intervention theory:

1. A clearly articulated problem definition, spelling out what the problem is, its aetiology (if possible), those it affects and the likely consequences in the absence of intervention;
2. Specification of the essential components of the intervention; the frequency, duration, and 'quantum' thought necessary to bring about change, and how this can be delivered;
3. The means whereby the intervention brings about change, including any important sequencing of events or relationships between component parts, any mediating variables that might explain differential responses to the intervention, such as individual differences, timing, method of delivery; and
4. Specification of expected outputs and outcomes, and the interrelationships between them.

An intervention theory should also seek to specify the likely influence of i) environmental factors (exogenous factors) – such as social conditions or facilities; ii) implementation issues – such as the ways in which the delivery of an intervention might influence its impact, for example staff skill levels, and iii) chance variations that occur in any research programme, including variability in staffing, external events, and measurement (so-called 'stochastic factors). In any one project there may be more than one intervention theory; after all, there are competing theories of the potential impact of an intervention amongst different disciplines. The aim is to 'theorise about change', not provide definitive templates of change. What is important is to be explicit about the theories

of change being used or hypothesized, so that they can be incorporated into the design of an evaluation and the analysis of results. In 1985 Lipsey and colleagues examined a representative sample of published outcomes studies and found that only 10% sought to integrate theory linking programme elements, rationale and the intervention processes. Some 70% offered no theory or only very general statements of the intervention strategy (Lipsey, 1993; Lipsey et al., 1985). Whilst the situation has improved in some areas, this is still a characteristic weakness in social work effectiveness research.

Sometimes it is possible to make use of well-articulated theories from other disciplines. Patterson, Chamberlain and Reid at the Oregon Social Learning Center and Henggeller and colleagues have used social learning theory and family systems theory to develop interventions for children and young people with antisocial behaviour (see Exemplar 2). Theorizing about interventions is an iterative process. Chamberlain and colleagues have incorporated theories about gender differences in the aetiology of juvenile offending to incorporate additional social–relational components to their programme (Chamberlain et al., 2007). However, ready-made theories are not always available, or do not lend themselves to easy adoption. In this context, Lipsey suggests that a good starting point might be to undertake qualitative research in order to identify what might be important and to ground one's theories in observation (Glaser and Strauss, 1967). Additionally, there is always more extant research than people realize and a review of the findings of existing qualitative and other types of research can help to develop programme theory. This is both less expensive and less time consuming than unnecessarily reproducing primary research.

Exemplar 2: Tackling delinquency

This extract is from one of the programme developers responsible for Multisystemic Therapy (MST), designed to tackle antisocial behaviour by targeting the many sources of influences maintaining it. It draws on a range of theoretical frameworks, but predominantly on systems and social learning theory.

Given the multifaceted nature of the influences on antisocial behaviour (Rutter, 2007b; Farrington, 2008) MST specifically targets the range of influences that operate across key social systems and which influence both antisocial and prosocial behavior. The programme theory is that since the influences on antisocial behaviour are multifaceted then an effective intervention must also be multifaceted.

MST is structured around a set of principles that 'offer general guidelines that direct case conceptualization, treatment specification, and prioritization of interventions' rather than a prescription for each session (Henggeler et al., 1998).

MST specifically aims to tackle factors contributing to young people's behaviour problems and poor family functioning through a range of formal and informal support in relevant social systems, including:

- improving discipline and supervision practices among parents and carers;
- promoting better family relationships and communications;
- reducing young people's involvement with delinquent peers, and increase their association with pro-social peers;
- improving young people's performance in school;
- increasing young people's participation in positive, pro-social leisure activities;
- strengthening parents' sense of efficacy by enabling them to identify their own strengths;
- strengthening parents' informal support networks; and
- removing the barriers that prevent families from accessing services.

(Henggeler, 1998; 2001)

How theory can help   Theory can help improve evaluation research in a number of ways (see Lipsey, 1993 for a detailed discussion). It can improve the research question

being asked, by helping to articulate the assumptions, constructs and relationships that underpin arguments for the effectiveness of an intervention. Theorizing at this stage can flush out implausible aims and unlikely mechanisms. Making explicit different theoretical perspectives can help refine and advance our understanding of how interventions work (or do not work) and guide future evaluations. Theorizing about how the intervention will work will focus attention on the component parts of an intervention, the factors likely to shape implementation (Bickman, 1985) and the dimensions on which an intervention might vary in delivery (e.g. exposure, duration, etc.). This is particularly important in social work where interventions are often complex and have a number of components – the person or team, the intervention (e.g. CBT), the method of delivery (e.g. group or individual), the setting (e.g. home, clinic or family centre), frequency (e.g. daily or weekly) or duration (e.g. one hour session, two hour; over twelve weeks or six months) to name but a few.

Theorizing about how an intervention might work (or not) also draws attention to the ways in which it might interact with the system of delivery, e.g. who delivers it, where, how? For example, how will the intervention be affected by the motivation of staff and how would one tell if this was a problem? More attention is now given to issues of 'treatment integrity' – the extent to which an intervention is delivered as designed and intended to be implemented. Assuring treatment or programme integrity requires the intervention to be clearly specified and operationalized in ways that can be monitored. This is primarily a technical issue, but doing it well depends on understanding the mechanisms whereby one thinks the intervention will exert an influence. Social work interventions are rarely 'cookie cutter' interventions: replicated precisely on all occasions: 'family therapy', 'cognitive-behavioural therapy' and 'task-centred casework' will look different in each application. The challenge is to specify – in ways that can be reliably monitored – what an intervention would have to include if it is to count as multi-systemic therapy, intensive family support, or treatment foster care, rather than that practitioners 'do' exactly the same thing with every young person or family.

Sometimes the identification of the target population (and their recruitment into a study) can be challenging. Without a clear understanding of those for whom the intervention is designed to help – and those it is not – its potential efficacy can be 'masked'. Finally, in relation to research design, it is important, a priori, to select outcomes that can reasonably be expected to change as a result of the intervention. This means not merely choosing indicators that are easy to measure, as this can result in a lack of ambition or 'easy' (irrelevant) targets. Measures need to capture 'ultimate outcomes'. Social work's early forays into evaluation studies embraced impressively ambitious and significant goals, such as preventing delinquency (Powers and Witmer, 1951). Although the intervention theories were reasonable, the aetiological theories on which they were based (e.g. how boys become delinquent) were weak, and their disappointing results were, in no small part, attributed to this. However, rather than revisit the aetiological and intervention theories that informed the interventions, the initial response was to reject the methodology and chosen outcomes. The next 'wave' of effectiveness studies opted for targets it would be hard to miss, for example, changes in attitude scores, and 'softer' study designs (Fischer, 1976). These do not help improve practice at the sharp end.

Lipsey highlights the importance of drawing on theory not only in identifying outcome domains, but in selecting the measures used to assess them. Too often researchers choose measures for ease of use or availability, rather than relevance. They may choose measures that bear only a tenuous relationship to the construct in question. For example, most evaluations of interventions aimed at preventing child physical abuse rely on indirect measures of attitude change, or enhancing parental knowledge (see Macdonald, 2001; Oates and Bross, 1995).

Theory can also help identify statistically significant effects, and their attribution to the intervention. It can help with the interpretation of results in terms of understanding why interventions work (or not). Small sample sizes often mean that evaluation studies are statistically underpowered, sometimes giving null results when an intervention is, in fact, effective (Rossi and Wright, 1984; Lipsey et al., 1985). There may be little one can do to increase sample size, and there is often a problem of attrition, and other difficulties in implementation and data collection that take their toll. In these circumstances, Lipsey argues that explicit theorizing about the change mechanisms thought to underpin an intervention, and participants' responses to it, can be used to increase statistical power. For example, researchers can use theory to identify the measures that can be expected to be most sensitive to differences between intervention and control groups, for example, choosing a measure of aggression rather than arrest in evaluating the effectiveness of an intervention designed to reduce aggression. Another example is when characteristics of participants that might be expected to mediate an intervention's effects are identified and used in a statistical model. For example, a home visiting programme for disadvantaged mothers might appear to have had no impact on improved parenting, but it might be that such a programme has an impact on *some* disadvantaged mothers. An appropriate intervention theory (e.g. that first-time mothers might be expected to be more receptive to such intervention; Olds et al., 1994) could aid the detection of differential intervention effects across sub-groups.

Theories about how an intervention will work can bolster our confidence in results when the internal validity of a study is weak. For example, when constrained to use a quasi-experimental design or when a randomized controlled trial has been weakened by breaches in the randomization, e.g. through high rates of attrition, we have the challenge of ruling out competing explanations for any effects identified, e.g. that those who dropped out of the intervention group and control group were different, resulting in 'incomparable' groups. The only way to assess the likelihood of this is by having identified 'relevant' characteristics at the outset (prior to attrition) and measured them appropriately. Researchers have also to argue why certain processes are more likely than others to account for observed differences. This means being aware of the theoretical claims of competing explanations and their relative strengths and weakness.

Finally, theories help to interpret data, whether positive or negative. When negative, they assist in the systematic exploration of reasons that might explain a null result, including weaknesses in the research design, which Lipsey argues should be the first port of call. That is to say, before deciding that the intervention was unsuccessful, we should first check whether the study was statistically underpowered. If not, we should check whether the outcomes were poorly specified or inappropriate? If not that, then we should ask whether anything else has interfered with the intervention's effect. Next, we should consider whether the statistical adjustments made to make comparable non-randomized groups were appropriate (which depends on clarity about the nature of the intervention). Finally, if 'none of the above', we should ask if the study was beset by other problems that all too often undermine effectiveness research, such as missing data, or whether the intervention was delivered as intended? Only when all of these methodological problems have been 'rejected' as potential explanations of the 'nil' results, should the spotlight fall on the intervention itself. In Lipsey's words 'null results should not be accepted unless the research circumstances are sufficient to make them credible' (Lipsey, 1993: 31). Positive outcomes require comparably rigorous scrutiny, this time with a focus on what appeared to account for the success (the 'active ingredients') and its generalizability. Theory-driven approaches do not make evaluation easier, but they should make it more profitable.

The importance of process and implementation

We earlier flagged the importance of embedding trials in explorations of how people respond to interventions and what problems might arise in implementing them. These pilot or feasibility studies are, essentially, examining process issues, but *process evaluation* is also an important dimension of impact studies themselves.

As well as predicting how an intervention *should* work, theory can help us to understand i) why, in some circumstances it has not worked (e.g. in some settings but not others; with some individuals but not others) and ii) how it could be improved. Multi-site RCTs in which the intervention is tested in a range of settings, can be organized so that they systematically vary aspects of the intervention package (such as composition, frequency, and duration of 'exposure', format) in order to shed light on the contribution of each to the intervention's effectiveness. But any attempt to understand how something works, to assess the impact of varying its key components, or determine how it might be improved, depends upon detailed information about how it was delivered, how it was perceived, how it was received, how people responded to it and how the context influenced all of these.

Studies providing this kind of information are referred to as implementation or process evaluations. Contrary to some stereotypes, they do not represent the 'qualitative' end of evaluation research: process data can be gathered in a variety of formats (Oakley et al., 2006), though qualitative data are often particularly useful in exploring both lay and professional perceptions and theories about what is happening (see Arai et al., 2007). Ideally, process evaluations form an integral part of outcomes studies. These data then provide the basis for generating a priori hypotheses about the patterns of outcome one might expect, which can be tested using both process and outcome data (Oakley et al., 2006). Oakley and colleagues argue that the additional cost (which need not be great) can significantly enhance the explanatory power and generalizability of an intervention. Process evaluations also provide invaluable evidence to inform the roll out of interventions found to be effective in experimental settings.

Improving social work practice

Evidence-based social work entails making decisions based upon the current best evidence of what works (Macdonald, 2008). Keeping abreast of the knowledge base in even one area of social work can be challenging, particularly given the variable quality of research. We have argued that experimental designs are the most suited to establishing causality because of their internal validity, but not all trials are well designed or well implemented. Things go wrong and experimental studies can easily become 'quasi-experimental'. Some studies result in differing patterns of results, some positive, others negative. How are we to make sense of this mosaic of evidence?

Literature reviews

One approach to keeping abreast of the literature has been to undertake (or find) a literature review, in which someone, with or without colleagues, summarizes a body of research. However, literature reviews can themselves be subject to a variety of errors and sources of bias. In this section we discuss some common pitfalls in undertaking a literature review, and make the case for prioritizing systematic reviews as the preferred approach to research synthesis (see Macdonald, 2000).

Bias can invalidate attempts to summarize research in a number of ways. The tendency to limit searches to English language sources or rely on a single method of searching (for example, electronic searching) may result in relevant evidence being omitted (Dickersin

et al., 1994). If only three-quarters of relevant studies are included in a review, one can't be sure that the conclusions would not be overturned, or otherwise influenced, by the other quarter. Then there is publication bias. Studies with significant results are more likely to be published than studies with inconclusive or negative results (Egger et al., 1998). This may be due to the selective *submission* of papers (Stern and Simes, 1997) or the selective *acceptance* of papers (see, e.g. Manuscript Guidance, 25; 4A, *Diabetologia* 1994).

Bias in databases and citations can lead to a failure to locate relevant studies (see Egger et al., 1998). Bias can influence decisions regarding which studies to include or exclude in a review. As practitioners we can all find, or favour, a single study that supports our preferred *modus operandi*. The same applies to reviews. Those who undertake the chore of reviewing the literature often do so because they have a particular interest in a given answer. Further, in assessing the relative merits of studies there is a natural, human tendency to be more forgiving of the methodology of studies that support a preferred or favoured view than of those which do not.

Even when reviewers have sought to minimize bias, different groups of reviewers will likely draw different conclusions because i) we all make mistakes, and ii) it is not possible to eliminate judgement from the process of research synthesis. Two reviewers conducting a review of day care for preschool children may have very different views of what day care is. Some may not regard child minders as 'day care'; other will. Different policy contexts may result in different age definitions of 'preschool' children. And so on. Unless authors are transparent and explicit about how they have defined core aspects of the subject matter, comparison across reviews (which may draw different conclusions) is difficult. The challenge for a reader (perhaps seeking a 'definitive answer') is that s/he may be faced with two different sets of conclusions without knowing how they were reached.

Systematic reviews of effectiveness research

Explicitness and transparency are the hallmarks of a systematic approach to the synthesis of studies of the effectiveness of interventions. Reviewers *may* use statistical tools to combine data from individual studies included within a review, known as meta-analysis. Meta-analysis can overcome some of the problems associated with underpowered, small studies. There are academic cultural differences in whether and when to seek to combine data in this way, with health reviewers (e.g. Cochrane) being generally less inclined statistically to combine data from very diverse studies than social scientists (e.g. Campbell). These differences reflect different histories, in which social sciences have a longer history of research synthesis, dating from Smith and Glass (1977). Those interested in pursing the science of systematic reviews and meta-analysis should consult the Cochrane Handbook (2008), Lipsey and Wilson (2000), Littell et al. (2008), Oakley (2000), and Roberts and Petticrew (2006). In this section we concentrate on the principles underlying systematic reviews of effectiveness research, of which meta-analyses may sometimes, but not always, form a part.

In undertaking a systematic effectiveness review important decisions about a range of issues that might introduce bias are made *before* the review is undertaken. Examples include:

- How to define essential characteristics, for example how to define 'day care' or 'older person'?
- How to manage methodological problems in studies such as differential drop out?
- How best to assess methodological adequacy?
- What statistical approaches are most appropriate? (see Higgins and Green, 2008)

The Cochrane and Campbell Collaborations are international organizations producing, maintaining, and making available systematic reviews of the effectiveness of health and social interventions (see Higgins and Green, 2008).

The decision points covered by systematic reviews within these organizations are listed in Box 16.2. Different people will make different decisions. This is fine. Such explicitness and transparency make clear what decisions have been made. The reader can then: i) make an informed decision about the relevance of a review to their circumstances and ii) if they disagree with a particular decision, they can consider what the implications are. In principle, they could 'redo' the review taking different decisions. Decisions about the conduct of a systematic review are set a priori in a published protocol.

The protocol provides a means of 'keeping reviewers honest' by requiring them to 'pin their colours to the methodological mast'. An example: suppose you want to undertake a review of the effectiveness of an intervention for child sex abusers. You think that only RCTs provide adequate evidence in this particular area. However, when you come to look for studies, you can't find any RCTs. What do

---

Box 16.2   Decision-points in a protocol

- Objectives
- Criteria for considering studies for this review
  - Types of studies
  - Types of participants
  - Types of intervention
  - Types of outcome measures
- Search strategy for the identification of studies
- Methods of the review
  - Selection of studies
  - Assessment of methodological quality
  - Data management
  - Data synthesis, e.g.:
    - How to deal with incomplete data
    - How to analyse binary data
    - How to analyse continuous data
- Whether and when to undertake a meta-analysis, and if so, what kind

you do? Most of us – concerned to produce 'something' of use to up-against it practitioners (or very demanding policy makers) – will be inclined to 'relax' our standard and produce a review based on the available evidence which may be non-experimental studies. In these circumstances, most non-systematic reviewers will either not mention their earlier views about what they regarded as adequate evidence, or will justify their change of mind 'post hoc' (after the event). Practitioners, eager for guidance on 'what works', are unlikely to be bothered by such 'academic niceties'. But they are not 'niceties'. Unsystematic reviews of evidence can mislead. Ironically, relying on experts in a particular area can pose a particular risk. Those recognized as experts may be less objective than those without national or international reputations: they may overweight research they themselves have undertaken relative to research done by others. And like their disciples, experts can have strong opinions about the focus of their work, which can lead them to judge evidence differently according to whether or not it supports their beliefs.

Finally, making mistakes is not uncommon in any activity involving the cerebral cortex (Kahneman and Tversky, 1972). Errors made in the process of research synthesis can seriously undermine the validity of its conclusions. Whilst a systematic approach to research synthesis does not guarantee accuracy, or entirely remove subjectivity from the review process (points too often ignored by ardent fans), a well-conducted systematic review can minimize common sources of bias and error, generally improve the quality of research syntheses, and provide to those with sufficient technical skill, the information needed to assess its value.

Systematic reviews of research on effectiveness are only one type of evidence synthesis. Dixon Woods and colleagues (2006) have argued that different types of evidence synthesis can be located along a continuum from quantitative approaches, which involve the pooling of findings from multiple studies (e.g. meta-analysis), to qualitative approaches, which involve an interpretative approach

(e.g. meta-ethnography). Syntheses of qualitative research, or mixed method research, may ask questions about the meanings people give to their experiences (e.g. Campbell et al., 2003), the factors shaping help-seeking behaviours (e.g. Noyes and Popay, 2007) or the barriers and/or enablers to implementing effective interventions (e.g. Arai et al., 2005; Roen et al., 2006). There are some key differences between these approaches to evidence synthesis and effectiveness reviews. For example, the synthesis process is often more fluid and iterative with the review protocol operating as a guide rather than a template for decision-making, the review question may change as the review proceeds, studies might be purposively selected for inclusion rather than on the basis of an exhaustive search and study quality may not determine inclusion/exclusion. These differences reflect the different types of research being reviewed but all approaches to evidence synthesis should ensure that the process is transparent so that users can clearly see how conclusions were reached and form a judgement about the validity of these decisions.

FINAL OBSERVATIONS

Evaluation research is hard. If the technical challenges were not enough, the would-be evaluator has to contend with the fact that policy makers or other funders of research are rarely minded to support the cost of well-designed trials of social interventions, let alone the additional costs of co-locating these with well designed process evaluations and studies of the experience of interventions. It is this, rather than the challenges associated with trials, that have constrained the flow of such evaluations. Not only that, but it is policy makers and not academics who drive the research process, who are often not minded to wait for results, and may not like the results when they come. If a topic falls out of political fashion, the development of a knowledge base may be effectively put 'on hold' until it again comes centre stage. Perhaps this explains the more consistent investment of funding into fields such as delinquency and substance misuse, as these impact more widely on society than, say, child abuse. The following should be read with that in mind.

Improving social work practice requires a sound basis for making choices between interventions and indeed, in some circumstances, whether to intervene at all. This requires good quality primary research *and* regularly updated systematic reviews of the best evidence available. Arguably, primary research should not be commissioned in the absence of a systematic review that sets out what is already know and how securely it is known. Evaluation research should, ideally, be developed in a more step-wise fashion than has hitherto been the case, and attend to issues of experience, process and outcome, preferably in the same study. This requires setting aside the social construction of 'qualitative and quantitative' methods, and capitalizing on the synergies between the two in developing potentially useful interventions, designing evaluations that will work well, and improving our understanding of what works, for whom, in what circumstances.

Methods for Enhancing Theory and Knowledge about Problems, Policies, and Practice

Jane F. Gilgun

INTRODUCTION

Anyone looking for examples of methods that enhance theory and knowledge about problems, policies, and practices need look no further than the work of Selma Fraiberg, a US social worker who is the founding figure in the infant mental health movement (Shapiro, 2009), and John Bowlby, a British psychoanalyst, who is a prime figure in the development of attachment theory (Bretherton, 1992). Both did their seminal work in the mid to late twentieth century. Both translated their theory and knowledge into programs, policies, and practices. Their work is carried out today in a wide range of researcher projects, policy initiatives, and prevention and intervention programs (see Lederman et al., 2007; Lieberman, 2007; Shirilla and Weatherson, 2002; Sroufe et al., 2005).

Their methods were roughly similar, based primarily upon observations of infants and young children in interactions with their parents that they often filmed for further study, in conjunction with interviews with parents and creative thinking about their observations. They advanced their thinking through on-going reading and consultation with researchers, theorists, and practitioners from many different disciplines.

The theory, research, and knowledge on which Fraiberg and Bowlby both drew included psychoanalytic theory, cognitive psychology, and the work of Renee Spitz (Bretherton, 1992; Shirilla and Weatherston, 2002; Sroufe et al., 2005). In addition, Bowlby incorporated ideas from ethological theory and Fraiberg used attachment theory as Bowlby developed it and as others elaborated upon it.

John Roberston, a social worker, made an enormous contribution to attachment theory, when, as part of Bowlby's research team, he filmed his observations of parent–child interactions, a method that transformed understandings of the significance of early attachment relationships for human development (Bretherton, 1992). Observation remains the key method in infant mental health and attachment-based research and applied programs to this day (Shapiro, 2008;

Shirilla and Weatherston, 2002; Sroufe et al., 2005).

These research programs contrast with some contemporary thinking on what constitutes good research for social work and allied disciplines. Rather than focusing only on randomized clinical trials (RCTs) and causal explanations, these outstanding researchers sought to understand the phenomena that they hoped to change through prolonged field observations and interviews. They developed their understandings and interventions over many years, collaborated with members of many disciplines, and incorporated relevant research and theory in order to influence policy and practice.

Exemplars such as these deserve wide attention for their generativity and the models of research that they demonstrate. Interestingly, these research programs have much in common with perspectives that combine what Otto and Ziegler (2008) have called 'empirically grounded social and cultural science aiming at both causal explanation and interpretive understanding'. These German researchers believe that research conducted without understanding (*verstehen*) has problems with its adequacy in accounting for the 'irreducibly open ... nature of the social world' (2008: 273). This chapter demonstrates that useful social work research requires both understanding of the social issues into which we intervene and the specification of what works, for whom, under what conditions.

PURPOSE AND DEFINITIONS

The purpose of this chapter is to describe and illustrate methods that generate theory and knowledge about problems, policies, and practices. By 'methods' I mean the actual procedures in which social workers and members of allied disciplines engage as they produce theory and knowledge. I will not discuss methodology to any degree. Methodologies are concerned with the epistemologies and ontologies of perspectives on social phenomena such as feminism, phenomenology, and constructivism. These perspectives fit social work well, but these topics are not part of the present chapter.

By 'problems' I mean the multiple, complicated social issues that social workers encounter in their everyday practice, which can be direct practice, program development, administration, advocacy, and policy formulation and implementation. I use 'social issues' interchangeably with 'problems'. By 'policies' I mean strategies and principles that guide the development of social interventions. By 'practice', I mean strategies used in intervention programs, which can be structured formal protocols, a more loosely defined set of interventions that particular programs implement, and the one-on-one interactions that occur between service providers, collaborators, and service users.

Theories are sets of transportable ideas that social workers can apply to particular cases or situations, whether these situations involve individuals, families, groups, or advocacy efforts. Concepts and their relationship compose theory. Theories illuminate social processes and help observers notice aspects of phenomena they might otherwise have overlooked.

'Knowledge' in this chapter refers to information and understandings that researchers and practitioners develop from their professional practices as well as from their personal and professional values and personal experiences. This store of information from which social workers draw includes the contributions of advocates of various sorts, service user perspectives, and the personal testimonies and narratives of individuals throughout the world who also contribute to social work's base of information. These sources are inextricable parts of social work's store of information. Along similar lines, Marsh et al. (2005) define knowledge as the combination of research evidence, practice wisdom, and the experiences of service users and carers. They define evidence as research findings and the interpretations of these findings.

These views on the multiple sources of knowledge contrasts with the idea that knowledge is composed of material developed through research and often called 'best research evidence'.

In my efforts to describe research methods that generate theory and knowledge, I will present examples of methods that social workers use to understand the multiple domains of social work. These examples will demonstrate methods that contribute to understanding social issues (problems), provide direction for social change (policy, programs, and interventions), and contribute to the process and outcome evaluations of interventions. I intend to highlight knowledge and theory that I believe direct practitioners, program developers, and policy makers find useful. Occasionally I use examples from allied disciplines, but for the most part the examples are from social work.

In addition, I will address other methods that generate knowledge besides formal research methods. These methods include the collective wisdom of practitioners and the testimony and knowledge claims of people involved in social movements, including knowledge that the International Federation of Social Workers calls *indigenous* (IFSW, 2008). Such knowledge becomes part of practice and policy through oral transmission and narratives on practice. Some researchers and policy makers believe that these are not legitimate sources of knowledge because they do not adhere to their idea of what constitutes knowledge and science. From a pragmatic point of view, these sources of knowledge are a major and inextricable part of social work practice and therefore any review of methods for theory and knowledge building would be incomplete if they are ignored.

Besides common sense and pragmatism, the rationale for the inclusion of these diverse sources of knowledge as contributors to the social work knowledge base is the view that the evidence base of practice is composed of four cornerstones. These cornerstones are research and theory, practice wisdom, service users' perspectives, and practitioners' personal experiences and personal and professional values (Gilgun, 2005c). The ideas of reflective practice are infused in this understanding of evidence-based practice. The implications of this definition of evidence-based practice are only at their beginning stages of exploration. This present chapter is a contribution to that process.

A COMPLICATED ENTERPRISE

The practice of social work is complicated, characterized not only by multiple domains in which social workers operate, but also by ecological perspectives that direct attention to persons, environments of all sorts, and the interactions between them. In addition, a set of core values and ethical principles guide social work and social work has a role in almost any setting where problematic human situations exist (IFSW, 2008). Because social work is an action-based discipline, social workers are supposed to do something to improve problematic situations through one-on-one work, program development, community development, advocacy, and policy formulation. Given these ecological perspectives and multiple roles, social workers must understand and intervene on a wide range of systems, from the individual level to families, groups, neighborhoods, states, counties, provinces, and countries.

Values that social work espouses include social and economic justice, autonomy or freedom of choice, and freedom to pursue personal goals without interference as long as actions meant to achieve these goals do not infringe on the rights of others. Social workers see a clear ethical, empowerment, and anti-oppression agenda in these values (c.f. IFSW, 2008).

If social work research is to be consistent with what social work claims to be, then social work researchers will create theory and knowledge that covers complex sets of domain, that is based on values, and that respects ethical dimensions of knowledge generation.

No one research method and no one research project can respond to these complex knowledge demands. Instead, social work by its nature requires a division of tasks in its approaches to knowledge development. Methodological pluralism is key to social work's effective response to demands for many types of knowledge. This means that social work knowledge can come from many different sources that use a variety of methods.

Further complicating the social work theory and knowledge-building enterprise are competing perspectives on what constitutes acceptable knowledge about problems, policies, and programs. Controversies within the evidence-based practice movement color and shape what constitutes 'evidence' and 'best research evidence' and which methods contribute the best evidence for practice. Some researchers and funders appear to believe that RCTs are at the top of a research hierarchy and constitute a 'gold standard', while qualitative research such as case studies are at the bottom (Soydan, 2008c; Strauss et al., 2005).

Those who place testing of interventions at the top of a hierarchy are focused only on intervention, and they are inattentive to the knowledge needed to understand social problems that include service users' situations, the knowledge required to build interventions in the first place, the knowledge needed to understand how applied programs work, and the knowledge needed to develop policies responsive to social problems as they affect quality of life.

Descriptive research is an essential component of social work's knowledge base, in addition to results of controlled experiments that test the efficacy and effectiveness of intervention programs (Gilgun, 2005a). Knowledge of social issues is required to inform social action, whether these actions are interventions, programs, advocacy, or policies. This includes theoretical knowledge in the sense of principles that describe social life and that can be transported from one setting to another, as defined earlier.

Finally, social work researchers, practitioners, policy makers, and program developers use research and theory that other disciplines generate. Although some believe this undermines social work's status, identity, and mission, others find that multi-disciplinary perspectives enrich social work's knowledge base (Cnaan and Dichter, 2008). For example, research on resilience, attachment, cognitive science, and cognitive-behavioral therapy are examples of research and practice theory developed in other disciplines that social workers have adapted for their own use.

As applied research, social work research and knowledge are meant to be *used*. In fact, some argue that the usefulness of research is one of the indicators of the quality of social work research (Gilgun, 2004b; c.f. Chapter 12). In order to produce such research, social workers who do research must know what kinds of research are useful to policy and practice. This requires that researchers take potential users' perspectives into account when doing their work. These potential users include practitioners in the field, administrators, policy makers, and, at times, the general public.

As is widely recognized, practitioners often express their practice knowledge in terms of stories, examples, metaphors, and principles that appear to be amalgamations of research and theory and practice experience (Osmond and O'Connor, 2004). Research findings that practitioners use would logically have to have some compatibility with such discursive and divergent ways of knowing.

ORGANIZING FRAMEWORKS

I begin this discussion of methods with the presentation of a conceptual framework that describes four general ways of generating and testing theory. I then discuss a series of methods and provide examples of how they operate in the generation of descriptive information and information for intervention effectiveness and efficacy. Finally, I give examples of methods for creating interventions and assessment and evaluation tools for practice. Such efforts require theory and knowledge on problems, policies, and effective interventions.

I will not spend much if any time on well-known methods, such as telephone surveys, but will focus on those methods that have great promise but are not widely used in social work. Some of these methods may be controversial.

The variety of methods that researchers use to generate theory and knowledge for social work probably cannot be pinned down definitively. Knowledge requirements change depending upon individual and shared perspectives and the kinds of social issues that are prominent at any given time.

Methods for theory development

In the development of theory, researchers have four broad choices.[1] They can enter the field with no preformulated theories or hypotheses to test, and with the goal of developing them; they can enter the field with preformulated theories to test, with the goal of reformulating them to better fit what they see; they can do a combination of the first two; or they can engage in theory-guided research and direct practice that may result in descriptions or in theoretical statements and categories (Gilgun, 2005b, 2007).

Glaser and Strauss (1967) named the first approach *grounded theory*, which in reality is a fundamental way of thinking that individuals have always done and will continue to do so. Researchers from the Chicago School of Sociology named the second approach *analytic induction* (Becker et al., 1961; Gilgun, 1995, 2005c, 2007). Like grounded theory, the term *analytic induction* simply names a process that is fundamental to human judgment and thinking. The third approach, *deductive qualitative analysis* (DQA) (Gilgun, 2005b, 2007), is yet another way of

thinking about the world that human beings have always done and will continue to do.

The fourth approach, *theory-guided research*, means that researchers and practitioners use theory to help them to focus and manage their inquiries. Their goals are not necessarily to develop theory further, but to develop deeper understandings of social issues and problems. Their products can be descriptions of social issues and/or interventions, as well as theoretical statements and categories.

In grounded theory, individuals enter the field in order to understand basic social processes. They have no hypotheses to test, but after deep immersion that comes about through observations, interviews, and/or document analysis, they begin to formulate concepts and ideas that fit their observations. Theoretical sensitivity and sensitizing concepts are important to doing grounded theory because researchers' knowledge base influences what they notice and how they interpret what they notice (Bryant and Charmaz, 2007).

In analytic induction, researchers enter the field with hypotheses to test. These hypotheses can come from research, theory, and personal and professional experience. Typically, the hypotheses are relatively informal and the concepts that compose the hypotheses are defined in open-ended ways. Individuals test these hypotheses explicitly, whether in direct practice, in formal research projects, or in everyday life. Flexible thinkers use explicit prior theories to alert them to what is significant in their observations and thus the research is theory-guided, but they also look for data that contradict their initial theorizing. In fact, in analytic induction, researchers' purpose is to find contradictory evidence, or negative cases, in order to elaborate upon or even refute their initial hypotheses (Cressey, 1953; Gilgun, 2005b, 2007).

The originators and users of this approach considered these procedures inductive. I did, too, for a long time (see Gilgun, 2005b, 2007), but I have changed my mind for two reasons. First, research that begins with hypotheses is automatically deductive because deduction begins with a premise, which theory and hypotheses are. (By 'premise' I mean an idea and no technical meanings are attached. By 'deduction', I do not mean deductive logic but simply approaching something with an idea in mind. Within the grounded theory and analytic induction tradition, hypotheses are simply statements of relationships among concepts.) Second, I now believe that induction is impossible, simply because no one is a blank slate. We bring prior conceptions with us, whether or not we have formally stated theories and assumptions. These prior understandings influence what we notice and how we interpret what we notice.

In the third approach, which is DQA, individuals construct hypotheses from multiple sources, including related research and theory and personal and professional experience and values (Gilgun, 2005b; 2007). Like analytic induction, deductive qualitative analysis requires a continual effort to modify, undermine, and refute initial and emerging theoretical understandings. DQA is an updating of analytic induction. DQA makes no claims to producing findings that are universal, which some analytic inductionists claimed, and requires a formal conceptual framework. The conceptual framework builds from a literature review and, when applicable, from a description of researchers' personal and professional experience as well as results of any preliminary research.

Examples of studies that label themselves DQA and analytic induction (AI) are rare, but increasingly qualitative researchers who do not label their work 'analytic induction' or 'deductive qualitative analysis' begin their studies with a review of the literature and are straightforward about the professional and personal experience, as well as values, that influence their world view and consequently their research and how they interpret their observations.

In the fourth approach, which is theory-guided research, researchers and practitioners develop research questions informed typically by research and theory and by personal and professional experience and values. The questions focus their research, and their goal, logically enough, is to answer the research questions. There are many examples of this kind of research, including Keeling's and Piercy's (2007) qualitative internet-based survey on the views of an international group of family therapists on power, gender, and culture in marriage. Keeling and Piercy call their work analytic induction, as do a few other researchers, but since they do not have stated hypotheses to test, their studies do not qualify as analytic induction. They end with a set of conceptual categories and statements that qualify as theoretical statements or hypotheses that can be transported for use and tested for fit in other situations.

For all four approaches, individuals who are flexible thinkers change their theories when their interpretations warrant change. Inflexible thinkers do not change their ideas, and they are at risk of misinterpreting phenomena, overlooking important dimensions of the phenomena of interest, and forcing data into categories that are inappropriate rather than creating new categories.

These four broad approaches to theory building and testing are applicable to theorizing on data from direct practice, from formal research projects, and from informal everyday interactions. Individuals who theorize are not blank slates, but bring with them a whole host of ideas, assumptions, and biases based upon their personal and professional experience and their formal education. Glaser (1978) used the term *theoretical sensitivity* to describe capacities to use theory effectively in the interpretation of data. Whatever 'theories' and other assumptions that we carry with us help us to make sense of whatever data we consider. In this kind of theorizing then, theory is the formulation of ideas about what data connote.

At their best, all four approaches recognize that individuals have blind spots and biases that shape what they notice and how they interpret what they notice. It makes sense, then, that individuals who engage in theory development and testing do a kind of reflective practice, which some researchers call reflexivity. Keeling and Piercy (2007) included a brief reflexivity statement in their article. This may involve engagement in on-going discussions with others on their emerging interpretations and on personal meanings and emotions. Reflexivity or reflective practice in research can also involve journal keeping and memo writing that involves reflections on personal and professional meanings.

These four approaches to theory building are typically used for the analysis of qualitative data (words and other texts), but researchers can develop grounded theory from numerical, quantitative data as well (Glaser, 2007; Glaser and Strauss, 1967).

I will use these four approaches to theory enhancement and development in the discussion to follow on methods that enhance theory and knowledge about problems, policies, and practices. I make copious use of examples to show how researchers and practitioners use these methods.

SURVEYS AND QUESTIONNAIRES

Surveys are a form of questionnaire that may be administered in-person, by phone, or via the internet. Samples typically are large, totaling hundreds if not thousands of respondents, selected through a random process. Surveys can provide information about the incidence, prevalence, and correlates of social problems. Questionnaires are used in direct practice in program development and evaluation. They are a relatively easy way to tap into perspectives of potential and actual service users and can, therefore, contribute information that becomes important building blocks of assessments and interventions. They can be helpful in needs assessments and participatory action research (PAR) when researchers and advocates want to understand social issues from multiple points of

view and possible ways to deal effectively with these issues (McTaggart, 1997; Sung-Chang and Yeung-Tsang, 2008). In evaluation of programs and direct practice interventions, questionnaires can provide information about effects and meanings of these interventions.

Surveys

Phone, internet, and in-person surveys provide information on social issues and interventions. Governmental agencies and local authorities often commission surveys that establish the prevalence of social issues that are archived in large data bases. For example, the Office of National Statistics in the United Kingdom commissioned a survey on the mental health issues of young people between the ages of five and 17 under the care of local authorities. They found that 45% of these young people had mental disorders (Office of National Statistics, 2003). The federal government in the United States commissions many studies, such as the survey research of Straus and associates (Straus et al., 2006 [1980]) to establish the incidence and correlates of family violence, research that has a major impact on the provision of social services in many countries.

Internationally, in a study of violence against children, the United Nations compiled administrative data, surveyed 138 countries on their approaches to violence against children, did field visits to 18 different countries, and convened nine regional conferences that included all parts of the world. An average of 350 people attended these conferences that heard testimony from a range of knowledgeable persons, including children, practitioners, and policy makers. This multi-method approach to establishing the prevalence, correlates, and responses to violence against children resulted in a report that has had wide-circulation (Penheiro, 2005) and has a world-wide influence on prevention programs and services to children and families.

Survey research centers often conduct large-scale studies and then make their data available for secondary data analysis. One example of many is the International Social Survey Program module on Family and Changing Gender Roles that has data on married and cohabiting women from 25 countries (Zentralarchiv für Empirische Sozialforschung, 2004). Universities throughout the world provide internet survey software to faculty and increasing numbers of researchers rely upon internet-based surveys.

An example is the work of Tower and Krasner (2006) who conducted an internet-based survey on more than 1100 couples to study the relationship between marital closeness and symptoms of depression. Respondents were predominantly white and middle or upper middle class from all over the United States. Research using a translated version of the survey instrument was done in French and Vietnamese, and Spanish, Hebrew, and Korean versions are available.

Internet-based surveys are of recent vintage. Other innovations in survey research are in approaches to data analysis. Jenson (2008) pointed out what he considers to be advances in quantitative techniques for the analysis of complex data. He highlighted multi-level and hierarchical techniques as well as new approaches to handling missing data and for estimating statistical power. He stated that funding for research may depend upon the level of sophistication of researchers' proposed analysis plan. He does not discuss, however, how research using these complex analytic strategies is translated into findings that front-line service providers, program managers, and policy makers find useful. Since the usefulness of knowledge relevant to social work is of high concern, the benefits of quantitative advances could be weighed against how the findings can be used.

Keeling's and Piercy's (2007) internet-based qualitative survey, for example, developed theories on how therapists in several different countries viewed and worked with issues related to gender, power, and culture. Edleson's (1999) review of 35 primarily survey research studies published in a recent 25-year period on the overlap between child maltreatment and woman battering is a highly influential piece of scholarship. He found that service providers from the two sectors have difficulties in collaboration. Child welfare agencies were not attending well to issues related to women battering, and services to women who were survivors of intimate partner violence often overlooked effects on children. This review article alerted policy makers, program developers, and direct practitioners about a serious defect in the provision of services to families where violence has occurred. This one review article has influenced policies and programs internationally.

Through his analysis of the survey research of others and his own research and professional knowledge, Edleson (1999) developed theory about gaps in services, although he did not call his conclusions theory. If theory can be defined as abstractions from more concrete indicators and also as abstract statements of relationships that can be transported from one setting to another, then this finding qualifies as a theoretical statement. Furthermore, his work can be classified as theory-guided because he had extensive practice and research experience in the field of family violence and had already observed and documented the gaps in services he investigated in his review article. His conclusion that indeed the gap exists and has serious consequences qualifies as a theory because he extracted higher order concepts from lower order data.

Analysis of survey data as a means of developing theory

Surveys can also provide information about the workings of social policy and programs.

Questionnaires

Questionnaires increase knowledge of social issues and can foster the development and evaluation of policies and programs and contribute to the evaluation of one-on-one interactions. Needs assessments, often done within PAR framework, are particularly helpful in policy formulation and program development. PAR collects survey and questionnaire information – and observational and archival information typically – for the purpose of understanding social issues typically from the points of view of those affected and for advocacy and program development.

This approach includes potential service users in the design, analysis, and interpretation of the survey, in advocacy efforts, and then in program development. By design, PAR integrates the perspectives of potential users of services into their efforts (McTaggart, 1997). As Denzin (1989) pointed out many years ago, applied programs are doomed to fail if the perspectives of potential services users are not taken into account. Shaw (2005) found that service user involvement in research is rare, but an important challenge for researchers.

In an action research project, Sung-Chang and Yeung-Tsang (2008) showed how service users and members of communities can be integral to a project's success. After extensive interviews that community members and service users themselves conducted, they chose to establish a summer camp for migrant children so as to provide a kind of child care for families where parents worked. Learning about community needs empowered and emboldened them and they managed the difficult tasks of finding funding for this service.

Questionnaires can be helpful in generating knowledge about direct practice, such as how services users experience the intervention and the suggestions they have for improving services. The Criminal Justice Client Evaluation of Self and Treatment (CJ CEST) (Garner et al., 2007) is an example of a questionnaire that seeks to understand service users' perceptions of their own treatment issues and of their own processes as they experience a prison-based treatment program. Questionnaires are important in the evaluation of interventions.

Mokuau et al. (2008) used a variety of methods including questionnaires to do a formative evaluation of a program for Hawaiian families of women with breast cancer. Other methods included informal interviews with service users and standardized instruments. Formative evaluations are done in order to understand how programs work and what might help them to work better.

The findings from such questionnaires become part of a knowledge base that documents what policies and programs might serve the social good, what can be done to improve them, and what new polices and programs are needed.

In-depth, open-ended interviews

In-depth, open-ended interviews can provide detailed information about the development, course, and present circumstances of problematic situations that human beings experience, as well as build knowledge about service users' and practitioners' experiences of policies, programs, and one-on-one interactions. Such information offers a solid foundation for policy initiatives and for the development and re-design of intervention projects. Material from open-ended interviews also can be a basis for theorizing.

Coy (2008) conducted unstructured life history interviews with young women with a history of local authority care and who engaged in prostitution. Her review of available research showed that findings of surveys and ethnographies suggest an association between young women being in care and engaging in prostitution. She had observed this association while in practice. She also found that available research and theory did not provide knowledge on which to base day-to-day therapeutic social service activities with these young women. Services to these young women were largely ineffective.

Coy (2008) reasoned that in-depth interviews would provide information on why these young women are vulnerable to selling sex and how their involvement in this work might be prevented. The impetus for her research was her realization that she and her co-workers at a residential facility had very little knowledge on which to base their work with vulnerable girls.

Coy's (2008) work has many of the characteristics of an ideal social work research project because she used theory, previous research findings, and prior knowledge, including her own practice experience, to design her research and to interpret findings. She conducted the interviews in an open-ended way in order to allow the respondents to tell their stories in their own ways. They described their lives before going into care, their lives in care, and then their lives as sex workers. Coy (2008) did not test hypotheses in her research, nor did she state that she was seeking to develop theory, but she did. She also used theory that others had formulated and her own theory based on her practice experience to both guide and interpret her findings. Her methods fit into a loose definition of deductive research because of her use of prior theory. Because she did qualitative research, her method can be described as deductive qualitative analysis, as discussed earlier (see Gilgun, 2005b).

Studies such as Coy's (2008) not only theorize about a significant social issue, but also provide in-depth descriptions of how individuals interpret their own lives as well as show the effects of social policies and programs on service users. With such information, policy makers and program developers can build more effective policies and programs. In addition, front-line service providers will be more informed. Unfortunately, policies, programs, and their implementation result from a confluence of many sources of information. Findings based upon the experiences of service users deserve a much bigger part to play in these efforts.

Mancini's (2007) semi-structured interviews with persons with psychiatric illnesses is an excellent example of theory-building research that has strong implications for policy and practice. Through his analysis, Mancini developed a theory of recovery from serious psychiatric disability based on the notion of

self-efficacy. The dimensions of this theory include supportive relationships that were collaborative partnerships, peer support from other persons with histories of psychiatric disabilities and who were in recovery, experiences of mastery of difficult tasks and situations, and a variety of ways to maintain emotional equilibrium, including exercise, hobbies, and a healthy life style. Mancini showed how his findings are linked to Bandura's theory of self-efficacy and theory about informed choice and self-determination.

Mancini (2007) engaged in a long discussion about how this theory could be applied to work with persons with psychiatric disabilities. In its clarity and clear support not only in the stories of the persons he interviewed but also in the theory he applied to help interpret his findings, Mancini's theory of self-efficacy in work with psychiatric patients is a model for theory-building practice research.

A final note on open-ended interviews is their potential importance in RCTs. As Floersch (2003) points out, the subjective experiences and perspectives of youth must be taken into account when they take psychotropic medications. If not, practitioners and researchers not only violate values such as social justice, self-determination, and starting where clients are, but they also miss opportunities to understand what works with whom under what conditions. RCTs only provide information on groups of persons, and without open-ended interviews cannot provide information on the differing effects of medications on individuals. The combination of RCTs and in-depth interviews provides information that enhances the usefulness of research to practice and to policy.

Focus groups

Focus groups have for some time been a popular way of generating information. They are a form of interviewing. At their best, they delve deeply into social issues and contribute to a knowledge base that influences policy and programs. Examples are plentiful, but one that is particularly relevant to the purpose of this chapter is Kohli's (2005) review of the literature and focus group research on the experiences of unaccompanied refugee children. Kohli shows the complexity of issues that might be at play in children's silences. Silence can have many meanings, including indicators of resilience, attempts to manage trauma, inability to cope with trauma, and mistrust of governmental officials and social workers. Stories the children tell may be rehearsed because parents and others have taught children what to say in order to increase the chances that officials will accept the children as refugees.

Knowledge of the personal circumstances of the children before they left their countries of origin and the nature of the catastrophes that led them to seek asylum are essential. Without in-depth knowledge of the circumstances of unaccompanied children, effective interventions are impossible.

Focus groups are also helpful in understanding policies and their effects. Clements and Rosenwald (2008), for example, conducted focus groups with foster parents in order to understand foster parents' experiences with and concerns about fostering gay, lesbian, or bisexual (GLB) youth in their homes. (They did not include transsexual youth in their research.) They found that foster parents are fearful of caring for GLB children. They recommended that social workers help foster parents understand the issues of GLB children and that social workers themselves become better educated about the issues.

Crawford and Tilbury (2007) conducted focus groups with child welfare case managers using an interview guide in order to understand issues related to services for young people about to leave care. The researchers found that case managers were so preoccupied with finding and helping to stabilize placements that they had little time to work with youth on obtaining resources and otherwise helping them prepare to make the transition from foster care to the work force. They also found that there are few treatment options available for those youth with mental health issues or who had learning and behavioral issues that impeded their progress in school. These issues affected their capacities to find employment. School personnel were unprepared to deal with the learning and behavioral issues that youth in care often presented. Many also did not have knowledge of the vocational and educational options that young people have access to. Such findings have important implications for policy and also generated practice theory that practitioners can apply to their work with young people in other settings.

Personal and professional testimonies

Personal and professional experiences are part of social work's knowledge base and can contribute to the understanding of social problems. They also can inform policy and practice. Practitioners and policy makers often use their personal experience in their work. For example, besides exemplifying the use of questionnaires in formative program evaluation, as discussed earlier, the Mokuau et al. (2007) study is also an example of how personal and professional knowledge contributes to program development. In this case, three of the four program developers were native Hawaiians who drew upon their own experience to ensure that the program was culturally appropriate and sensitive.

Personal narratives and creative non-fiction

Personal narratives by both professionals and lay persons with compelling personal stories inform both policy and practice. A few social work researchers and practitioners have written fictionalized cases with which they have worked in order to make social issues prominent in the minds of the general public.

In general, personal narratives and creative non-fiction not only facilitate self-understanding, but when they are shared they can enlighten others. The following brief discussion provides examples.

Personal narratives are oral (as in tape recordings, videotapes, and performances) or written accounts of individuals' life experiences that, at their best, involve minimal or no involvement of researchers in their construction. Within social work's knowledge base are narratives that survivors of harsh circumstances compose as well as narratives that service providers themselves compose. These narratives inform and enhance social policy and intervention. Personal narratives can be thought of as forms of autoethnographies, whose goals are to invite audiences into the experiences of narrators and in so doing to deepen understanding and to bring about social change (Jones, 2005).

Kumsa's (2007) personal narrative about her relationship with her younger brother during the Ethiopian civil war digs deep into her heart and mind and deep into the hearts and minds of readers. She powerfully conveyed what it means to survive a national catastrophe and the loss of family, home, country, and the sense of identity and belonging that is bound up in these losses. Narratives such as these contribute enormously to social work's knowledge base. Understandings such as these truly start where clients are and are the foundations for effective policies, programs, and direct practice. They also can be the basis of theorizing. Practitioners and researchers can extract working hypotheses from this one narrative and use the hypotheses to illuminate other similar situation. Such hypotheses, as discussed previously, would have to be used in a flexible way, meaning that they are used to illuminate poorly understood situations, but must be modified when observations warrant this and also but must be modified when observations warrant this. They also cannot be imposed but must be tested for fit in new situations.

Personal narratives can be the foundation for PAR. Sung-Chang and Yeung-Tsang (2008) began their action research with unemployed women in China by having the women collect oral histories with other unemployed women. Oral histories are a form of narrative research where those who collect oral histories create situations where participants tell their stories in their own ways. They thus are minimally intrusive. The women also told their own stories and developed insight into their situations and the situations of other women.

Through this work, the women developed new theories of unemployed women that rejected the dominant discourse and that involved seeing other women as active agents who can bring about changes in their own lives through collective action. They applied this new theory of unemployed women to themselves that gave them a framework for new actions and the development of an income-generating business.

Oral histories, a form of narrative, were the foundation of Sung-Chang's and Yeung-Tsang's (2008) action research that empowered participants to engage in advocacy on behalf of themselves and an unmet community need. Similarly, personal narratives about social work practice itself have great promise as an advocacy tool (Craig, 2007; Weick, 2000) that can educate the general public about social work's day to day work.

As a profession that women largely shaped, social work does its daily tasks out of view of the public. Weick (2000) noted that the status of social work parallels the status of women in society. The private domain of social work replicates the work women have traditionally done in the private domains of families, also out of public sight. This results in misunderstandings about the nature of social work, including the nature of social problems, policies required to address these problems, and the money needed to run them. In the United States, myths of 'the welfare Queen' stand for such misunderstandings and have had long-term negative effects on knowledge and theory development about policies and programs.

Creative non-fiction

Sometimes social workers experience power-ful stories that they want to convey to a wider audience, and they write the stories as crea-tive non-fiction. This means that they use the techniques of fiction and change some of the facts so that the privacy of the service users is protected. Ungar (2003a) wrote a short story called Stale based on his experiences as a child and family social worker.

I was so taken by a story that one of my research informants told me and so much wanted the real-life story to have a different ending that I wrote a novel where the inform-ant lived up to his potential and turned his life around instead of becoming a person who beats his wife and molests boys. I published an excerpt from the novel (Gilgun, 2004a) where I described the sexual assault of the informant as a boy and its immediate aftermath. Both Ungar and I decided that the stories needed to be told in the fullest manner possible. The techniques of fiction-writing helped us to accomplish our goals.

Such stories add to social work's knowl-edge base on problematic human situations. Like personal narratives, they also reach a broad audience and have promise of influ-encing public opinion, which can in turn influence policy and programs. They there-fore can be tools of advocacy.

Critical discourse analysis

Critical discourse analysis (CDA) can pro-vide an in-depth view of issues with which client contend and by definition involves person–environment interactions, making it suitable for social work policy, programs, and interventions. CDA examines language and other texts for its implications for power, privilege and prestige as well as resistance to them (Fairclough, 2001; Wodak, 2001). Language and text are full of meanings on both the individual levels and the cultural levels. Indeed, individual gestures and speech acts only have meaning as they connect to shared meanings within particular cultural groups. A critical discourse analysis can reveal what otherwise may have been hidden meanings in language, gestures, clothing, and other texts.

For example, the discourse of 'cool pose' (Majors and Billson, 1992) for young African American men involves clothing, hair style, body language, speech acts, attitudes toward women, and a multitude of other qualities that create identities that may in fact be a form of resistance to a larger culture that continually threatens to marginalize them.

Valandra et al. (2008) used CDA and criti-cal race theory (CRT), which highlights the contemporary and historical contexts of race relations and racist practices (Decuir and Dixson, 2004; Dunbar, 2008), to analyze the discourse of a young black man on the brink of puberty and his white upper class case manager. Dueling discourses ensued when the young man expressed sexual interests in girls. The young man drew upon gendered and racialized discourses of cool pose to con-struct his version of how he wanted to relate to girls and the white case manager drew on a very different discourse to reprimand him. This analysis showed the importance of understanding the discourses of clients – in other words, to first understand where serv-ice users are coming from before making decisions about how to respond.

Another example of critical discourse analysis is the work of Sung-Chang and Yeung-Tsang (2008), discussed earlier, who embedded a critical discourse analysis in their interpretations of the oral histories of unemployed women in China. Within the women's oral histories, they identified the voices or discourses of the government that not only has a deficit model of unemploy-ment but paternalistic solutions. In response, the researchers took a more active role and invited the participants to reflect on the implications of these discourses and engaged them in a search for alternatives that empow-ered them to take actions based on their own competencies and agency. Critical discourse analysis is under-used in social work research, but has great potential for identifying social problems and issues that disempower service users and that also can render social interventions ineffective because of unexamined assumptions.

Ethnographies

Ethnographies are of several different types, such as more traditional written ethnographies, autoethnographies, and performance ethnographies. Ethnographies describe or portray persons in their environments that result from researchers' prolonged engagements in these environments. They are particularly useful for highlighting aspects of culture that persons who create and live the culture take for granted. There are many issues related to how researchers represent the persons and cultures they observe, and researchers therefore have to monitor their own assumptions and reactivity to the situations and person they observed.

Some social work researchers believe that the tasks of ethnographers are similar to those of service providers, who observe service users in various contexts, including in homes, group residential settings, and in the office. Those who make home visits observe the communities and neighborhoods in which service users live. They make case notes of their interactions and may review reports and other documents that are relevant to their work. When applied to social work practice, ethnographies can result in many different products, such as descriptions of social phenomena, descriptions of program activities, descriptions of what works for whom under what conditions, and assessment and evaluation tools.

Findings from ethnographic approaches are immediately useful to direct practitioners. The rich and complex details of ethnographies match the rich and complex detail of social work direct practice. For example, Britton's (2008) street-level ethnography

of race relations on a Chicago, USA street, would make a lot of sense to service providers and policy makers alike because what Britton reported is an in-depth look at a readily identifiable pattern on use of public places based on race and social class.

Performance ethnographies

Sometimes researchers chose to present their ethnographies as performances, borrowing from the humanities, such as cultural studies, theatre, and creative writing, to do so. Performance ethnographies can be intensely personal or they can represent a significant event in the life of a culture. It can be difficult to distinguish between ethnographies that are performances of personal experiences and autoethnography and personal narratives as discussed earlier.

Performance ethnographies can involve an ensemble of actors who use the words of informants to portray in as full a manner as possible the lived experienced of the informants. The goal is to raise the audience's critical awareness of significant social issues. Five students in Alexander's (2005) undergraduate course in performance studies did ethnographic interviews and participant observation with immigrant Mexican street vendors in Los Angeles. By the performance's end, the students had conveyed the multiple meanings and issues that Mexican immigrant street vending represents.

The potential of performance ethnography for social work advocacy is huge. Not only can various groups tap into their own experiences and creativity to inform audiences in their communities, but they could videotape these performances and put them on YouTube or other internet sites. Such information would be an important tool for informing the general public world-wide about the every-day issues that service users confront. As stated earlier, an informed public is required in order for social policies to be responsive to social needs.

How case managers use practice theory

How applied programs actually work is one of the 'black boxes' in social work, meaning that there is little information about what goes on day to day in social service agencies. Such information is of high importance because it provides a front-row view of 'street-level bureaucracy' (Ellis, 2007; Lipsky, 1980), or how social policies are implemented in programs and in one-on-one interactions. With such knowledge, policy makers, administrators, program planners, and direct service providers can reflect on what is going on and make judgments about what is working and what is not, what resources are available and which are lacking, among many other policy and program issues.

Floersch (2002) did an ethnographic study of strengths-based case management in a mental health center in the Midwestern United States. His purpose was to understand how case managers used strengths-based practice theory to respond to the policy of deinstitutionalization of mental health patients from hospitals to the community. For more than seven months, Floersch, as a researcher, joined one of four treatment teams and was given entrée into all of the settings in which team members did their work.

His findings included an analysis of the strengths and short-comings of the strengths-based practice model and made suggestions for how to develop a more comprehension model. In particular, he recommended that strengths-based case management develop a theory of the self that could account for self-monitoring, self-observing, and self-regulation. His observations, interviews, and case record reviews revealed repeated instances where service users were unable to perform these essential human functions and that strengths-base theory did not account for these issues.

Change process research

In practice disciplines such as social work, where changes of various sorts are at the core of their missions, an understanding of how change comes about appears to be foundational. Change process research (CPR), which originated in psychology, provides a set of procedures for identifying factors associated with change (Reid, 1990), whether this change is at the level of individuals, families, groups, communities, or nation-states. CPR involves the development and testing of practice theories and thus can be considered a form of process evaluation. CPR seeks to respond to enduring questions of what works, with whom, under what conditions.

Testing practice theories: task analysis

The formal use of task analysis is rare in social work and in other practice discipline, but I believe such an analysis is routine informally. Briefly, task analysis involves the formulation and testing of a theory of change that practitioners hold about a particular field of practice (Berlin et al., 1991; Heatherington et al., 2005). Researchers (or direct practitioners) first specify the elements and processes of client change and then observe how these elements lead or do not lead to change. Researchers continually revise their practice theories as their observations warrant revision. Berlin et al. tested a cognitive behavior theory of client change in group work with women with histories of depression. Their approach was a form of deductive qualitative analysis as discussed earlier. Their product was an enhanced theory of client change that is immediately useful to practitioners.

In their review article for a special issue on change processes in psychotherapy, Heatherington et al. (2005: 18) pointed out 'the glaring lack of published empirical evidence for the efficacy of some widely used approaches', a concern replicated in social work for many years (Berlin et al., 1991; Gilgun, 2005c; Marsh et al., 2005; Reid, 1990; Soydan, 2007; Thyer, 2008). Direct practitioners and policy makers have obvious needs for descriptions of what works, with whom, and under what conditions. Task analysis and change process research in general provide sets of procedures to respond to these issues.

Theories of change for program evaluation

Theories of change provide a kind of 'road map' that describes the operations of applied programs and is one of many types of program evaluations (Patton, 2002). These operations take place within specific types of situations, persons, and impinging conditions. Typically, theories of change identify the antecedents, processes, and conditions associated with problematic situations, the activities and interventions that programs initiate in order to ameliorate the problematic situations, and the persons, the activities, the conditions, and the interactions among them associated with favorable and unfavorable outcomes. Approaches to theories of change vary according to the perspectives of those who develop them. The descriptions of change processes promote the replication of successful programs.

An example of a theory of change project is my work with EXCEL (not the real name of the agency), a program that provides services to children under ten who commit acts that could be charged as felonies if the children were ten or older. By law, only children ten and older can be charged. The intended product is a detailed description of the program in terms of activities, the environments in which the activities take place, the clients and their historical and present

circumstances, and the case managers and their practice theories.

Quantitative outcome studies have shown the program to be effective. My task is to develop a theory of change that describes the change processes associated with 'good' and 'poor' outcomes, to document how the program works in general and to produce a program description that is replicable. Methods are participant observation, interviews, and case record reviews and the approach is grounded theory, as discussed earlier, meaning I and other researchers did not have a prior theory of change to test. Instead, we believed we had some theoretical sensitivity based on our knowledge of existing research and theory and our own practice experiences.

Intervention research

The kinds of research discussed above provide the theory and knowledge about policies, problems, and practices that are required for the development of interventions. Intervention research involves a detailed description of the target population based upon research and theory and practice experience, the interventions to be implemented, how the processes and outcomes are to be evaluated. Furthermore, intervention research involves the on-going modifications when observations warrant them (Rothman and Thomas, 1994b). Intervention research is a central task of social work (Fraser, 2004) for the obvious reason that social work is involved in interventions. Change process research, as discussed earlier, is a form of intervention research as are ethnographies of intervention programs.

The Mokuau et al. (2008) account, discussed earlier, is one of many examples of intervention research. The developers specified the population to be served, incorporated relevant research and theory, the practice and personal experiences of the program developers, as well as the various evaluation approaches discussed earlier. Furthermore, true to the tenets of intervention research, the developers also did a careful evaluation of process and outcome for the purposes of improving their program (c.f. Rothman and Thomas, 1994).

Hawkins and Catalano (Catalano et al., 2004; Hawkins et al., 1992) provide a model of intervention research in social work. For more than 20 years, they have applied research and theory on risk and protective factors to develop prevention programs intended to promote positive youth development and decrease violence and drug use. A theory-guided longitudinal intervention, the program involved multiple systems including families, schools, and communities and on-going evaluations that built in program modifications as warranted by observational evidence. Outcome evaluations of program participants in early adulthood indicate program effectiveness as measured by various indicators of physical and mental health, drug use, and criminal behaviors.

DISCUSSION

Social work is a complicated endeavor that requires a wide range of methods that generate knowledge about policies, problems, and practices. I premised this chapter on the principle that effective programs, policies, and practices are built upon 1) understanding the social problems into which we want to intervene, and 2) the specification of what works, for whom, under what conditions. The scope of social work is vast, covering different types of efforts whose goal, in general, is to ameliorate personal and social conditions and problems in the name of social justice.

Many of the areas in which social workers practice are under-researched and therefore not well understood. Furthermore, as is widely recognized, social work is in great need of tested, reliable interventions that can be tailored to fit particular situations. The present chapter is an attempt to outline some of the methods that can be responsive to these issues.

Social work practice takes place over time, typically with a beginning, middle, and end. Practice begins with the recognition of the existence of a social justice issue or problem, continues with a decision to respond to the issue, which in turn leads to assembling and developing theory and knowledge about the issue, followed by the development, testing, and implementation of the intervention, and concludes with evaluations of the effectiveness of the intervention. These time-ordered segments can be thought of as phases of practice. In the real world of policy and practice, there are varying degrees of fidelity in each of these phases and sometimes biases and even suspect sources of theory and knowledge, but overall these phases are quite stable across fields of practice.

Each phase of practice requires its own type of knowledge and requires research methods best suited to generate this knowledge. When social work researchers design their studies, they could specify the phase or phases of practice to which they hope their findings contribute. When they write up their results, they could show how what they found contributes to which phases of practice.

In the end, the core of any research method meant to ameliorate social problems and that contributes to policy, programs, and practices must add to understandings of populations to be served, must describe interventions and the change processes involved, and must evaluate both processes and outcomes. How researchers do this varies as functions of their assumptions and worldviews. Such variations are consistent with the wide scope of social work, which accommodates and requires this pluralism.

NOTES

1 Chapter 11 should be read as part of the context for this discussion.

Methods for Understanding, Learning and Social Justice

Carmen Lavoie, Judy MacDonald and Elizabeth Whitmore

Tell me and I'll forget

Show me and I may remember

Involve me and I'll understand

(Chinese proverb)

INTRODUCTION

If the goal for social work research is to gain a deeper understanding of social work practice, we must ask ourselves, 'Understanding for whom?' Is it the university researcher or is it also those who are implicated in social work practice, such as social workers, policy-makers and service-users? If one purpose of research is to build understanding beyond the walls of academia, then we may well depart from traditional approaches that limit involvement in social work research to academics and trained experts. When ordinary people become involved as researchers and decision-makers, their interests and interpretations are reflected in every aspect of the endeavor. Research involving social workers has the capacity to explore the deeper meaning in their practice and to bring about change that reflects their day to day concerns.

For social workers, however, there is often a divide between research and practice.[1]

Social workers often think of research as an abstract process carried out by experts who are detached from the day to day challenges of social work and the reality of those they work with (Potts and Brown, 2005). This perception is reinforced by traditional research approaches that tend to respond to social workers and service-users as objects of study rather than as potential collaborators and benefactors of the research (Shaw and Gould, 2001b). Social work education may also compound this perception by emphasizing statistical analysis and positivist approaches to research without opportunities to apply classroom content to actual social work intervention. For many social workers, this approach to research has little resonance with their own value system and little bearing on the issues of injustice that are evident in their work.

A growing literature in the health and social sciences concerned with injustice and inequality argues that it is necessary to reformulate research to ensure participants are involved throughout the research process (Beresford and Evans, 1999; Bradbury and Reason, 2003a; Hall, 2001). Such approaches, referred to here as participatory approaches, challenge the exclusion of research participants from decision-making and the traditional abstraction from local context in order to discover, and change, local relationships of oppression and inequality. There is an extensive literature on participatory approaches to research and that appear under various names (community-based participatory research, empowerment research, participatory action research, emancipatory research, feminist action research, etc.). All share a commitment to the active engagement of participants in the research process and to greater equality and justice in their lives.

This chapter explores participatory approaches to research and their relevance to social work. Although not all participatory approaches are concerned with social justice (nor, conversely, are all social justice methodologies participatory), this chapter takes this focus to address practitioners who are skeptical about the usefulness of research and who seek social justice in their practice. In particular, we aim to demonstrate the capacity of participatory approaches to create change in social work by serving as a bridge between research and practice. In order to do this, we first review the ways participatory approaches to research strive to democratize knowledge production (understanding), raise awareness of processes of oppression (learning) and engage in social change (social justice). We then consider the compatibility of participatory approaches with social work by examining the characteristics of participatory approaches in light of social work concerns. This includes an analysis of the research goals, process and skills of the researcher that parallel social work practice.

Two exemplars demonstrate the links between participatory approaches and social work practice. A third exemplar describes a social work research methods course that uses a community-based participatory research approach. The chapter concludes with a brief examination of the suitability of participatory approaches to different contexts and two key issues, diversity and ethics, that researchers will encounter as they grapple with the complexity of working in this way.

PARTICIPATORY APPROACHES TO RESEARCH

In traditional approaches to research, people who are the 'subjects' of the research normally lack control over the research process. Generally, control over the research process resides with a lone, external researcher who is valorized for their 'objective' distance and detachment from the matter being studied (Brown and Strega, 2005). Many times this approach to research has led to a misrepresentation of participants' experiences (Stoecker, 2005). There is a long history of research in indigenous communities in which the researcher 'helicopters' into a community, collects data and then disappears (Flicker et al., 2007). This research may elevate the status and social power of the researcher but at the same time fuel misrepresentations and stereotypes that compound community marginalization (Smith, 1999).

Those involved in participatory approaches recognize that knowledge production takes place amid unequal power relations (Gaventa and Cornwall, 2001). By ensuring that participants have control over the research process, participatory approaches aim to foreground the experiences and interpretations of marginalized groups and to bring about change that reflects their interests in terms of empowerment and liberation (Greenwood and Levin, 2004). A combined process of understanding, learning and social justice in research changes relationships of power that contribute to experiences of injustice.

Understanding: democratizing knowledge production

Academic training, and its attendant 'expert' status, legitimizes research by privileged groups into the lives of others (Ansley and Gaventa, 1997). Ordinary people are excluded at the outset by specialized language and techniques used in the research process. This monopoly on knowledge production favours the interests of the elite and more powerful in society by transforming the lived experiences of marginalized groups into categories that can be analyzed and controlled (Smith, 1987). 'Expert' versions of the social world so dominate our understanding that people internalize these constructions and discount their own interpretations (Sohng, 1996).

In order to diffuse dominant constructions of the social world and reveal processes otherwise subordinated by power relations, participatory approaches seek to democratize knowledge production (Bradbury and Reason, 2003b; Greenwood and Levin, 2004; Park, 2001). By sharing control over knowledge production, the voices and experiences of oppressed people rise to the surface and yield interpretations that undermine the preferred versions of more powerful groups. Research that is 'democratically steered by people' (Shaw and Gould, 2001b: 39) reflects a belief in 'the legitimacy of the knowledge [ordinary people] are capable of producing through their own verification systems' (Fals-Borda and Mohammed, 1991: 15) and a commitment to understanding our social world as it is experienced by those who live it (Maguire, 2001).

A democratic research process is one in which the participant is co-researcher and decision-maker so that, at all stages of the research including the problem definition, research design and analysis, control over the process is shared (Greenwood and Levin, 2004). A research coordinating committee is one example of an egalitarian forum for decision-making that takes account of peoples' interests and skills and will likely precipitate additional participatory mechanisms as people realize the understanding and change that is possible by involving others in the research process (DePoy et al., 1999). The researcher must also anticipate barriers to participation, such as family responsibilities and mistrust of the researcher, that might undermine democratic claims.

A constant tension exists between democratic principles and centralized decision-making when dealing with practical questions of time, resources and ability in participatory approaches. This tension may be exploited by powerful groups whose claims of participation legitimize practices that further their own interests (Wallerstein and Duran, 2003). Gaventa and Cornwall (2001) suggest 'enabling factors', such as ongoing evaluation and linking to social movements, to ensure participatory strategies are meaningful and reinforce social justice goals. At the very least, research must reveal the interests served by the study and provide explicit details about the research methodology to substantiate claims of authentic participation (Ristock and Pennell, 1996).

Learning: raising awareness of the processes of oppression

Much of the literature concerned with participatory approaches to research refers to the work of the Brazilian educator and philosopher, Paulo Freire. His theories on learning suggest that social change comes about when people realize that their personal experiences are politically constituted (Freire, 1970). For Freire, self-questioning and group dialogue are central ingredients to developing such critical awareness.

Self-questioning is the basis for awareness-raising and discovering the relations of power that bring about inequality. Using such strategies as journaling (Williams and Harris, 2001) and photography (Molloy, 2007), participants begin to question their experiences and draw connections between their daily lives and broader social forces. Researchers and social workers, who are often more powerful than the individuals with whom they work, discover how their routine practices, beliefs and assumptions unwittingly contribute to existing inequalities (Gaventa and Cornwall, 2001). For example, students in a graduate research course reflected on their assumptions about research and its relevance to practice. One commented:

> I have learned through this research experience that imposing order too soon, or in an inflexible way, limits discovery ... Being flexible enough to allow for a little 'chaos', revision and uncertainty will lead to a richer, more valid picture in the end.

It is interesting that this approach to research (which I initially resisted) actually reflects how I try to work with clients. The fact that I did not see a parallel between these two activities, reveals my assumption that social work research and practice are separate and distinct sphere. (Stuart and Whitmore, 2006: 160)

People also learn about oppression through opportunities for group dialogue. By listening and talking to others, people can identify the connections to their own life and create a picture of the social world that accounts for common experiences. Group techniques, such as theatre (Fals-Borda and Mohammed, 1991), story telling (Blakeslee et al., 1996), quilting (Etowa et al., 2007) and mapping (Chambers, 1994), deepening their self-awareness and their understanding of the wider forces that constrain daily life. Through a shared process of learning and teaching, participants can collectively 'name the world' (Freire, 1970: 61).

Social justice: engaging in social change

Changing relations of power that contribute to injustice is a central goal of participatory approaches to research (Bradbury and Reason, 2003b; Hall, 2001). Freire (1970) tells us that in order for such change to occur, people must be engaged in an iterative process of reflection and action: reflection is necessary to understand power relations and our positioning within those relations, and action is necessary to put those ideas into practice. In a synergistic relationship between reflection and action (commonly referred to as *praxis*), actions are analyzed in order to understand their implications before undertaking new actions. This process then repeats itself in order to deepen understanding and bring about appropriate change.

When research is integrated into practice, it follows that the kind of actions taken to bring about change would vary widely. Some groups rely on explicit tactics, such as awareness campaigns (information sessions, publicity) and public pressure (petitions, letters, protest, and boycott) to expose and disrupt existing

relationships of power. Individuals may also take action in their own daily interactions as they realize their contribution or complacency to injustice and the potential for change (Chapter 6). Ultimately, continuous movement through action and reflection in research means participants are able to test the impact of different actions in their real context and to reflect on the degree to which the outcomes match their intentions before they embark on further change.

A commitment to equality and justice in participatory approaches results in actions that not only confront relations of power but also empower participants (Park, 1993: 2). This begins by confronting asymmetries of power in the research process. As coproducers of knowledge, participants experience external validation and recognition of their expertise on issues important to the progress of the study. Through their accomplishments and responsibilities in the research process, 'people strengthen their awareness of, and belief in, their abilities and resources for organizing' (Maguire, 1987: 30).

Although the concept of empowerment is central to participatory approaches to research (Dullea and Mullender, 1999; Evans and Fisher, 1999), the term is applied inconsistently. At times, empowerment has been used to describe behavioral changes amongst participants that more accurately reflect the interests of powerful groups than the aspirations of research participants (Cahill, 2007). Overuse of the term has led researchers to identify a range of 'empowering' factors, such as training in research (Titterton and Smart, 2008), researcher accountability (Beresford and Evans, 1999) and emotional support for research participants (Linhorst, 2006).

Linking research to practice

Researchers have used participatory approaches to evaluate social services (Baldwin, 1997; Croft et al., 2005; Titterton and Smart, 2008; Whitmore, 1994, 2001; Whitmore and Mckee, 2001) and examine access to them, particularly for ethnocultural communities (Doyle,

1996; Sin, 2007). Studies have examined the experiences of marginalized groups, such as female sex workers (Wahab, 2004), people with learning difficulties (Redmond, 2005; Smith, 2004c), people with mental health issues (Linhorst, 2006), youth (Fahmi, 2004; Rutman et al., 2005; Smith et al., 2002) and indigenous groups (Brown, 2005; Potvin et al., 2003), drawing attention to their health and social service needs. The spectrum of participatory studies also includes social workers as research participants in studies of social work practice (Ingamells, 1996; Schuldberg, 2005).

In this section of the chapter, we outline a practice framework for participatory approaches that parallels social work practice. We summarize the goals of participatory approaches, pinpointing the similarities to social work, and then examine the characteristics of a participatory research process that makes such approaches interesting and feasible for social workers. We also include a discussion of the role of the researcher, with particular attention to the specific skills that overlap with social justice-based social work practice. By demonstrating the parallels between social work and participatory approaches to research, we are not suggesting they are one and the same, but rather that

participatory approaches allow the social work researcher to address the concerns, commitments and skills that they bring to social work practice.

The goals of participatory approaches to research

The goals of participatory approaches to research extend beyond that of *understanding*. There is overarching commitment to learning about peoples' lives and their experiences of oppression and to bringing about social justice through social change efforts. In Box 18.1, we summarize each of these goals using terms most commonly associated with social work in order to highlight the parallels between participatory approaches and social work.

The process of participatory approaches to research

Five characteristics of participatory approaches described below highlight different aspects of the research process and their relevance to social work.

Box 18.1   Goals

Social justice   Participatory approaches and social work share an ethical commitment to social justice[2] and changing existing power relations (Healy, 2001; Hick, 1997). Participatory approaches seek social justice by creating space for marginalized voices, by increasing awareness of oppression and through actions that bring about social change.

Empowerment   Empowerment is a central goal of social work and participatory approaches to research (Finn et al., 2004). Through collective learning and decision-making about the research problem, participants experience control over their lives and gain an increased sense of agency (Maguire, 2001).

Service-user involvement   Participation in research is comparable to service-user involvement in social work treatment planning and program administration (Baines, 2007b). Such an approach to research enhances understanding of the problem and strengthens outcomes by identifying appropriate and sustainable solutions (Beresford and Croft, 2004). It also puts democratic principles into practice (Altpeter et al., 1999).

Strengths-based   Participatory approaches place an emphasis on the skills and insights that community members bring to the process (Dullea and Mullender, 1999). As in social work, this is an attempt to draw attention to knowledge and abilities that are typically undervalued and to balance the power between community members and professionals (Staples, 1999).

Capacity building   Participatory approaches to research, like social work, aim to increase individual and collective capacity (Chow and Crowe, 2005). By enhancing skills, understanding (of research as well as the social and political context), resources and community connections, there is greater capacity for local control, decision-making and social change (Reason, 1994).

Research that is people-centered Participatory approaches to research and social work have corresponding ways of working with people, one that is people-centered. Unlike other research methods, a major point of departure for participatory approaches is people's own lives. The process of inquiry begins 'where people are at' and explores problems from people's own perspective (Israel et al., 2003). As in social work, individual experiences form the basis of any relationship and the focal point from which all subsequent interventions/actions evolve.

Research that is grounded Research that is grounded in social work practice goes a long way in bridging the divide between knowing and doing. In participatory research approaches, the research process is not a distinct moment in time removed from practice but is in fact entwined with it. From the identification of the research topic to the research results, the process reflects 'the real, material, concrete, and particular practices of particular people in particular places' (Kemmis and McTaggart, 2005: 564). The research findings thus emerge from a process figured into the context and interactions in which the problems arise. This allows the capture of tacit knowledge (or 'experiential knowledge') (Heron, 1996), such as judgment and intuition that are apparent through the context and interactions that it serves. Research that is located in the actualities of social work practice and that captures the complexity of social work knowledge provides practitioners with a direct connection to their work and a sense of ownership over the research process.

Research that is interactive Participatory approaches allow for the type of relationships that social workers generally prefer. Unlike some other approaches to research, participatory approaches involve ongoing interaction with research participants, often in different contexts. Interactions are thus dynamic, flexible and responsive to participants' needs and interests. Interactions are also non-hierarchical so that, rather than a one-way flow of information from the participant to the researcher, there is a exchange of information (Stringer, 2007). Each participant, including the researcher, is learner and teacher in the research process.

Research that combines conventional and creative methods As in contemporary social work, participatory approaches to research are concerned with the inclusion of people with varying backgrounds, abilities, languages and skills (Maguire, 2001). As such, the research process includes 'a diversity of methods that facilitate engagement among all' (Lykes and Coquillon, 2007: 301). Arts-based methods, such as theatre, mapping, drawing, photography, poetry, quilting, music and so on are now commonplace in participatory studies, occurring alongside more conventional methods such as surveys, interviews, focus groups and statistical analysis. Arts-based methods overcome some of the practical barriers to expression (such as literacy and technical support) in the research process while at the same time allowing people to convey the complexity of their lives in ways that can capture often subtle cultural differences.

Research that is change-oriented In participatory approaches, change is an outcome of the dialectic relationship between reflection and action. The process of change emerges through participants' engagement with ideas, their analysis of those ideas and their measure of success. The result is a steady evolution of practice that is specific to the context, its possibilities, contradictions and constraints (Kemmis and McTaggart, 2005). The changes that result are practical and deeply tied to participants' concerns. Researchers have noted the possibility of change in social work practice (Whitmore, 2001), organizational activities (Gardner and Nunan, 2007), social policy (Bradbury and Reason, 2003a) and the lives of service-users (Finn et al., 2004) using participatory approaches.

The role of the researcher

There are two aspects of the researcher's role in participatory approaches that make it distinct from traditional research but quite similar to social work. First, to achieve empowerment and social justice, participatory researchers must *share power* with research participants (Maguire, 2001). Using a combination of skills, such as critical reflection, advocacy and ally work, researchers share power over decision-making and ensure that participants benefit from the research.

Second, the researcher is fully *engaged* in the research context (Potts and Brown, 2005). In order to understand the actualities of day-to-day life and to support a process of change, the researcher is embedded in, and involved with, the research context. This close contact between the researcher and the research participants may lead to complicated interactions and bring about feelings in the researcher that are difficult to resolve (Redmond, 2005).

To build relationships with research participants that are healthy and that share power requires a set of new and different skills for the researcher that are not new to social work. In Box 18.2, we present practice skills that are common to both. It is not our intention to portray social work skills and the skills of the participatory researcher as one in the same, but rather to show the (substantial) areas where they overlap.

EXEMPLARS

In this section we present two exemplars that describe our experiences with participatory approaches with a further example that brings community research needs into the classroom.

Exemplar 1: Untold stories – women, in the helping professions, as sufferers of chronic pain (Re) Storying (dis)Ability

By Judy MacDonald

No more about us, without us (Charlton, 2000)

Throughout my social work career I have used a personal–political lens to my practice; my doctoral dissertation (MacDonald, 2008a) would be no different. Having

---

Box 18.2   Skills

Active listening   By taking the time to 'tune in' to peoples' daily struggles (Shulman, 2006), the researcher can learn about the role of family, culture, history and politics in individuals' lives (Lundy, 2004). This helps researchers identify the potential barriers to participation as well as those features of daily life that constrain and empower research participants.

Relationship-building   Relationships based on respect, clear boundaries and power-sharing are necessary in order for people to work together in an egalitarian way and to sustain the research process (Redmond, 2005). Communication skills, including clarifying, summarizing, questioning, and empathy, help to make this possible (Carniol, 2003).

Facilitation   Like social work, the research moves forward by facilitating a process of decision-making, group sharing, learning, and collective action (Finn et al., 2004). The goal of facilitation is a space for self-expression and dialogue that considers power differentials in the group and ensures that all voices are heard (Mullaly, 2002).

Critical reflection   Critical reflection is necessary to understand how judgments and preconceptions reproduce relations of power (Chiu, 2006). This includes an awareness of our own positioning along the lines of ability, sexual orientation, gender, class, race and other social divisions in order to understand and confront the power relations intrinsic to practice (Fook, 2002a).

Advocacy   Ideally, the researcher accompanies participants who advocate for themselves. If participants are unable to represent themselves, however, a participatory researcher may act as advocate on behalf of community members with service delivery organizations and policy makers for access to better services, for example (Ristock and Pennell, 1996).

Being an ally   The researcher serves as an ally to oppressed groups by taking a stand against injustice (Dullea, 2006). As in social work practice (Bishop, 1994), this includes putting personal power at the disposal of the group, engaging in social action in support of research participants and building solidarity amongst groups that share social justice concerns.

lived with chronic pain for over twenty years and having worked with sufferers as a medical social worker, I chose to focus upon women in the helping professions who were sufferers of chronic pain.

The dominant intervention for chronic pain has followed a rehabilitative behavioral science perspective, where the ultimate objective is to diminish sick-role behavior and avoid disability (Fordyce, 1990, 1996). Disability has been encompassed within the medicalization of illness and impairment, hence representing a personal tragedy model that is individualistic and reductionist, and relies upon the knowledge and expertise of medical personnel (Linton, 1998). Further, people with (dis) Abilities have been excluded from the decision-making components of research processes (Rioux and Bach, 1994). The chronic pain sufferer[3], the person living with the (dis)Ability[4], has the personal 'knowledge of her body and life silenced in discourses of objectification' (Greenhalgh, 2001: 320).

Researcher's reflection on self Recognizing my experience and self-knowledge in relation to the research topic it was paramount that I be transparent. Reflections of self were integrated into the research in the following ways:

- shared similar identification re: (dis)ability and chronic pain with participants and where appropriate self-disclosed aspects of my own story,
- highlighted 'researcher's reflection' at the beginning of each illness story – relaying the emotional and intellectual impact of listening to and hearing the participant's story,
- followed participants' case examples of working with sufferers with learnings derived from this collaborative process, and
- concluding remarks incorporated a reflection on my insights prior to, during and following the research.

Using oneself in the research process helps address power relations, minimizing the distance between the researcher and those being researched, and contributes to understandings/interpretations of locating knowledge through dialogue (Becker, 1999).

Methodology The methodology needed to invite the voices of sufferers' forward, for 'the vulnerability of our work, our identities, and our voices [sic] need to be heard' (Tierney, 2000: 249). Therefore, I selected a narrative testimonio methodology, embracing an autoethnographic component where sufferers were invited to share a personal expression of their 'life in pain'.

Testimonio is a research process focused on finding voice for those who have been silenced, oppressed and marginalized within a dominant social structure, bringing change to an oppressive structure or practice, putting a political, social justice location onto a narrative form of inquiry (Beverley, 2000; Tierney, 2000). Testimonials were gathered through the interview process, where sufferers were asked in the first interview to tell their own illness story and in the second interview to share their experiences as a helping professional working with pain sufferers. Two social workers, two nurses and two physicians participated. They had lived with chronic pain between seven and twenty-five years, with the combined experience of 92 years. Through this process participants' stories were respected, appreciated and honored.

Segments from pain narratives
Part of bendy's story

After her accident, bendy's partner had her out for a drive one day. She suggested they stop into their friend's shop to check on the framing of her cross stitch. Her partner said in a firm voice, 'Nobody wants a cripple in their establishment!' All bendy heard was 'nobody wants a cripple!' Instantly he tried to re-tract his statement, but the damage had been done. bendy reflected: 'nobody wants a cripple, … society doesn't want a cripple, your family doesn't want a cripple, the one you love doesn't want a cripple. That really altered my thinking from then on, accepting the fact that I have an impairment was much easier from that blunt harsh attitude.'

bendy's story challenges the societal and cultural constructs of normalcy. In our ablist society, anyone with differences in body shape or ability is disregarded and pushed aside (Titchkosky, 2001). As social workers we need to challenge those assumptions and advocate for the inclusion of persons with (dis)Abilities within society.

Part of Dawn's story

> The third visit to the rheumatologist proved to be emotionally charged, as Dawn recalled, 'I was basically told ... I had arthritis ... I had to learn to live with it, and I was wasting her time." She felt devastated, to be basically told that there was nothing wrong with her, yet her experiences and her body told her differently.

The 'Researcher's Reflection' that accompanied Dawn's story captures the distinct nuances involved with sufferer/physician communication.

> *Researcher's Reflection:* Dawn speaks eloquently about her coping strategies in negotiating a life in pain; she is not hesitant to name her fears and inhibitions created out of her struggle. As the researcher, on a personal level, I admire Dawn's location as a psychiatrist who not only believes the stories and struggles of sufferers, but, intimately knows the fight often necessary in communicating one's pain.

From Dawn's story, I formatted three knowledge claims; one, more education on chronic pain is needed, including the impact upon sufferers and various treatment modalities; two, helpers need to develop the capacity to hear sufferers' perspectives; and three, Medicare payments need to switch from a fee-per-visit formula to one based upon the depth of involvement, time and services provided, thus giving physicians time to deal with the complexities of chronic pain.

Participants were invited to share an autoethnographic contribution to the research, a self defined piece that would depict their life with pain. Five participants made a contribution, including poetry, academic paper presentation, paintings, doodles, dreams, visions and written narratives. As an extension to their personal stories, they add description, emotionality, and color to understanding of living in pain.

Helen's dramatic drawings vividly illustrate the power of artistic expression.

Autoethnographic illustration:

Evelyn used poetry to communicate her experience.

> In 1978, Evelyn was diagnosed with systemic rheumatoid arthritis. Evelyn's condition was so grave that she was instructed to stop work and to completely rest. Sitting in the rheumatologist's office, Evelyn noticed a fly trapped between the window panes, totally ensnared. She felt the fly's entrapment, trapped within her own body feeling exhausted and in pain.

> Without Wings
>   Like you Mr. Fly
> I am Trapped
>   You in the spider web
> So intrinsically woven
>   Me in my body
> So riddled in pain

>   You feel it too
> Your body
>   Screams
>   Throbs
>   Cries

>   You hang on
> I do too
>   You are almost dead
> I am too

> I try
>   I climb
>   I live

>   Unlike you Mr. Fly
> You were caught
>   By your enemy
> I am my enemy
>   I am the web

> Evelyn worried if she took the doctor's advice she would end up in a wheelchair. She feared that if she did not keep moving, no matter how painful and difficult that was, she would seize up. Besides, she was a single parent with three children who depended on her financially and emotionally, 'completely resting' was not an option.

Respect of sufferers

From the onset of this journey, I was determined to work with the participants

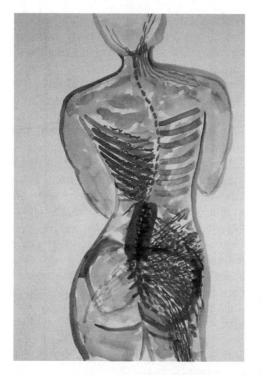

Figure 18.1 'Everything under control'. Helen is holding everything together in order to present a controlled picture to the outer world. In her words, 'Even though I am in pain and uncomfortable, I am able to hold it in and pretend it is not there to the public'.

Figure 18.2 'Losing control'. In this painting, Helen was trying to keep control but she could no longer maintain composure, everything was coming apart. In her mind she thought, 'Got to get home, out of the public'

in an equitable manner, respecting their voices, and, together, directing changes in working with pain sufferers. The following are strategies I enlisted to meet this goal:

- With concern for the participants' pain levels and not wanting to create undue stress, the following measures were applied: a pre-participation interview was conducted with potential participants, followed by a week to consider the risks vs. benefits; debriefing protocols were established (at the end of the interview, telephone follow-up two days later, and access to a professional counselor); approximately a year following the interviews, participants were contacted by telephone to discuss the impact of the research on them personally.
- Accommodation needs were met, for example, time, duration and location of interviews.

- The research was a 'working with' process, collaborating with sufferers at various stages, including verification of transcripts, proofing story chapter, teleconference on preliminary theme analysis, and review of findings. Further, they were invited to be involved in future research initiatives and writing opportunities.
- Participants were kept informed through all stages of the research, including conference presentations, preliminary drafts and defence.
- The research was designed to include an action component, for example, educating helping professionals on an anti-oppressive way of working with sufferers through the dissemination of findings to academic journals (MacDonald, 2008b) and conference presentations (MacDonald, 2005, 2006).

The research participants spoke to both personal experiences in living with chronic pain and professional experiences in working with pain sufferers. Until this opportunity arose, the sufferers' professional identity over-shadowed their pain experiences, as their helping roles positioned the focus of care upon others. Through politicizing their experiences as sufferers', they recognized their own voices as vehicles toward the empowerment of pain sufferers.

Exemplar 2: Research and community work in Maple Heights – discovering discrimination and resistance

By Carmen Lavoie

In 1999, after finishing my Masters of Social Work, I began working as a community worker in several low-income neighborhoods in a large Canadian city (Lavoie, 2006). At that time, the government was making drastic cuts to social welfare programs, including a 22% cut to social assistance. For residents of one neighborhood, Maple Heights, the stress due to government cutbacks was compounded by the public stigma of prostitution, drug-dealing and gangs. Maple Heights was a neighborhood of over 100 family-size social housing units. About half of the residents were Canadian-born and half were new immigrants (at least 19 different languages were spoken in the neighborhood). Despite the day-to-day pressures of living in poverty, many residents were also volunteers in the community. The community had won awards for their efforts, including a youth volunteer award. However, newspaper articles depicting crime in the neighborhood continued to mount. In 2003, with funds from a federal agency, the residents of Maple Heights, with my collaboration, launched a 15-month research project with a goal to understand residents' experiences and the impact of this media coverage. What follows is a brief description of that project.

Seeking justice

The first step in the research was the formation of a coordinating committee, consisting primarily of residents. The coordinating committee was responsible for deciding the overall focus and direction of the research and any actions that would be taken as a result. At one point, the committee decided to conduct interviews with residents in order to understand their experiences more in-depth. In the interview process, residents were asked to draw (using markers, crayons, etc.) their experiences of living in Maple Heights. Once completed, residents were able to interpret their own drawings and make links between their individual experiences and the broader forces that shaped their daily life. One thing we discovered was that many residents described close relationships with their neighbors and extensive volunteer activities in the community.

> People are well connected. It has developed into a trusting place. We are here for each other if someone is in need. If I see a familiar face in the community, I know I'm okay. If I see the guys volunteering on the skating rink, I know we are here for each other.

> People speak out. If things are not working, there is someone there to change it.

Residents' willingness to volunteer and support one another was not a surprise; the committee was well aware of the generosity and kindness between neighbors. However, it was striking that not a single person who participated in the research was concerned about criminal activity in the neighborhood. These results contrasted with the large number of media articles suggesting otherwise. A content analysis of newspaper articles was then conducted by a student volunteer from the local university. From 1993 to 2003, she found 17 newspaper articles that depicted the neighborhood in a negative light. An article in the city paper reported:

> Maple Heights is a bruised community. Fear of crime has made people angry and mistrustful.

In a local paper, Maple Heights was reported as an:

> ... area ruled by a gang or gangs ... drug dealing and prostitution.

Not surprisingly, these news articles all based their findings on the views of individuals who lived outside the community, rather than the residents themselves. In the interviews, many residents discussed the shame and upset the felt when they read media articles about their neighborhood.

> Sometimes you are ashamed to say where you live.

> When I say I live here, they think I'm bad and tough.

When the research coordinating committee began analyzing these results, they realized the importance of sharing the results of the research. The residents decided to create their own 'Good News' community newsletter to highlight community strengths and share information with other residents. The youth in the neighborhood worked with an artist to hone their artistic skills and create a large mural that contrasted their life in Maple Heights (sports, going to school, volunteering, fundraising) with the media portrayal (drugs, guns, violence). Residents also realized that, if they were going to bring about change, they needed to talk to the media. The project wrapped up with a large community potluck dinner and talent show to launch the research report and youth mural to the media. At this event, residents presented awards to those media outlets that provided 'fair and decent coverage' of their neighborhood.

> High class people and police think less of us but showing good things shows us differently.

Research as community work, community work as research

For me, this research project was in many ways like doing community work. In order to respond to people's interests and concerns, I relied on certain skills such as facilitation and trust-building that are standard in community work. Residents' interest in improving neighborhood quality of life and building community pride resulted in a number of activities that required a community development approach. Also, the relationships and connections that I had established as a result of community work expedited the research process. I knew many of the residents well and was closely linked to city-wide groups and coalitions that provided information and support for broader mobilization. Lastly, the physical resources and support available to me through my host agency matched many of resources necessary for research. Such basics as meeting space and computers were important to our progress as well as the availability of other agency staff to provide supportive counseling, advocacy and follow-up.

A participatory research process also strengthened my community work. Through ongoing dialogue with residents who were hired as co-researchers and through regular meetings of the research coordinating committee, I gained a deeper understanding of the complexity of neighborhood relationships and was able to recognize important ways of preventing or remediating power differences (Lavoie, 2005). Also, there was a deeper understanding of the role of media in reproducing discrimination, a greater awareness of the long history of residents' efforts to bring about change, and a series of actions that opposed injustice and raised the level of community engagement, resistance, and pride.

Exemplar 3: Research as if it mattered – bringing participatory approaches into the classroom

By Elizabeth Whitmore

I hate research!

Thus a student introduced herself in the first class of an MSW research methods class. It was clear that if we (both the students and I, as the instructor) were to survive this (required) course, we would have to do something quite different. So we redesigned it, using a community-based participatory research (CBPR) as our framework; that is, engaging the community actively in the process and directly linking research or evaluation to real issues in the field (Strand et al., 2003). In doing this, we wanted to create what Everitt et al. (1992) call 'research-minded practitioners'.[5]

We began by inviting a broad range of community agencies to send us proposals for a research or evaluation project, to be offered as an option for students in the course. The criteria for acceptance were twofold: usefulness to the agency and feasibility of the project within the six-month academic course timeframe. Community agencies responded with considerable enthusiasm, not least because this was free work for them, and was something they wanted to do but didn't have the time. Examples ranged from evaluations of specific programs (about half the proposals) to needs assessments and research with particular populations, such as street youth or seniors, to background research for policy development. The project then became the focus of the students' work in the course.

Though any one project would involve only a limited set of issues and methods, we assumed that the variety of projects selected by students would encompass the broad range of material needed to conduct systematic inquiry. We therefore built in a process of sharing methods and issues, in addition to basic content (e.g. a range of design possibilities, ethics, the role of culture, and data collection and analysis). Students raised questions, concerns and dilemmas that they were encountering in their work, and used their colleagues and ourselves as consultants. The student presentations, in the last month of the course, focused on teaching their peers about the methods they used and lessons learned in the process. In these ways, students became both teachers and learners, rather than assuming that the instructor is the only expert.

Getting Research Ethics Board (REB) approval could be an obstacle Nationally prescribed research ethics guidelines (Tri-Council guidelines) for all universities in Canada require that research on 'human subjects' be reviewed by a university-wide Ethics Committee.[6] This is done within a fairly rigid university-oriented time frame and does not easily fit with the more contingent timing of events in the community. The guidelines tend to reflect a medical model and positivist assumptions, including detachment, a we/they dichotomy separating researchers from the researched. This does not allow for the process needed to establish relationships and trust in participatory approaches. We spent considerable time working with the REB to make the process more flexible in meeting the needs of CBPR.

Higher workloads There are many tensions inherent in working in this way. For example, the workload was heavier than in a conventional course, as students had to rewrite their proposals, sometimes many times, since there was no point sending incomplete work to the REB. Yet it is here that the learning really took place, as they had many opportunities to 'get it right'. This was also true for their final reports to the agencies, as we insisted that the work be of sufficient quality that would not only be useful but reflect positively on the School of Social Work.

Dealing with uncertainty Inevitably, the design of this course meant some uncertainty. 'The relative tidiness of research design is usually replaced by the fuzziness and compromise of practice' (Hall and Hall, 1996: 268). We did not know about and could not control what happens in community agencies and internal political differences could result in staff or program changes which sidelined a student project. One year, for example, an agency board fired the Executive Director in the middle of the academic year. Clearly there were internal tensions that neither we nor the students knew anything about, and we were left to develop alternative plans. Nonetheless, such issues are part and parcel of doing applied research, and dealing with those obstacles when they occur becomes part of the students' (and instructors') learning.

Linking participatory approaches to pedagogy In the end, students understood that they were capable of conducting credible research (though not all were enthusiastic about doing so once they graduated). Our attempts to integrate participatory approaches to research into an academic course had limitations, of course, especially those related to operating within institutional constraints and the differences between community and university expectations and realities (Stuart and Whitmore, 2008). However, grounded in the community as it was, the research helped students make the connection between research and social action, emphasizing that these are not separate, but rather parts of the same thing.

At the same time, the process of collaboration with community organizations expanded student's understanding of who are the experts and the importance of engaging community people in the process of research. They recognized that without this, the lived experience of people can be obscured or even transformed into something entirely different (Campbell and Manicom, 1995; Smith, 1987). Students learned about the ups and downs of research through actually doing it, and were asked to think critically about their learning through reflexive journals (Stuart and Whitmore, 2006).

One final note: the student who had introduced herself by declaring 'I hate research' ended up becoming totally immersed in the project she chose. In the last class, during a round of comments and feedback, she jumped out of her seat and exclaimed 'I love research!' She received a standing ovation from her classmates (and her instructors).

SUITABILITY OF PARTICIPATORY APPROACHES

Clearly, research using a participatory approach takes place in varied contexts as a way to address a range of social issues. The suitability of this approach, however, rests upon three facets of the research process: the life circumstances of the participants, the research context and the skills of the researcher.

A participatory approach is sometimes ill suited to participants' life circumstances. The substantial time investment and long duration typical of this research approach may be unrealistic for participants who have more pressing life concerns (Alvarez and Gutierrez, 2001). Marginalized populations, such as street-involved youth, who sometimes move around depending on the availability of local services, might require extra incentives to remain involved in the research process (Whitmore, 2001). For some migrants, participation in a study may be associated with real or perceived risks to their migration status (Cooper et al., 2004). The relevance of such issues will vary across group members and have more or less of an impact at different times throughout the study (Guijt and Shaw, 1998).

There may also be pragmatic and political constraints on a participatory process due to the research context. For instance, without a space to gather or time allowance for group dialogue and problem solving, the participatory components of any study will likely be curtailed. Also, organizations that follow an authoritarian model of decision-making are likely to conflict with research that embraces principles of participatory democracy (Gaventa and Cornwall, 2001). Certainly, administrative delays or complications regarding compensation for participants may dilute efforts to establish an egalitarian research relationship between the researcher and the research participants (Alvarez and Gutierrez, 2001). The socio-political context may also exert subtle or overt pressures on the research process. Findings of a participatory process may be limited by political tensions or discriminatory practices in the research context that carry over into the research process (Greene, 2006) or by funders who set the parameters for the scope of the research findings (Bamberger, 1999). The hierarchy of power in some contexts may be so acute that participants lack the freedom to attend research activities (Busza, 2004) or their involvement is designed to appease powerful interests who are threatened by a research process geared toward change (Alvarez and Gutierrez, 2001).

Researchers who rely on skills in social justice-based social work practice are well positioned to recognize and address these challenges. Such situations point to the importance of working closely with the participants to assess their needs and the levels of vulnerability they experience in the participatory process. The researcher must be committed to individual check-ins and follow-up to support each participant in a process of finding their own voice and addressing barriers to participation (Whitmore and Mckee, 2001). The researcher must also draw on social work skills designed to challenge the systemic forces that erect obstacles to participation and sustain relationships of inequality.

FUTURE DIRECTIONS

In this subsection, we will focus on two issues, ethics and diversity, for further exploration.

Ethics

Ethical review procedures in research exist to protect the dignity and privacy of individuals, particularly those who are regarded as vulnerable or oppressed (Strand et al., 2003).

However, as Whitmore discovered in her research class, there are conflicting ethical frameworks between institutional ethics review procedures and participatory approaches to research. The forms and guidelines of North American institutional ethical review boards often reflect 'a biomedical framework privileging "knowledge production" as the exclusive right of academic researchers' (Flicker et al., 2007: 490). This power-over relationship positions the research participants as individuals in need of protection rather than as active, dynamic subjects of their own research (Boser, 2007). As a result, the ethics review process may thwart efforts to include democratic and power-sharing mechanisms in the research process (Lincoln and Tierney, 2004) while, on the flip side, failing to anticipate the ethical issues that arise in participatory studies (Leadbeater et al., 2006).

As practitioners and researchers become increasingly interested in community-based participatory approaches, it is important to find ways to address ethical concerns while also preserving a commitment to community control and social justice. Flicker et al. (2007) suggest that the ethics review include signed 'terms of reference' that delineate the participatory mechanisms in the research, such as decision-making procedures and the principles of partnership, rather than constraining the research to a fixed method at the outset. Boser (2007) argues that it is also contingent upon federal regulatory frameworks, professional associations, training programs and peer-review processes to enhance understanding and application of participatory ethics. Some communities have devised their own ethics review process to ensure research complies with their unique criteria and their goals for research participants and the community as a whole (Blumenthal, 2006; Family Health International, 2004; Macaulay et al., 1998; Quigley, 2006).

The participatory research process includes activities that are beyond the scope of the institutional ethics review process, such as activities at the pre-research stage intended to build relationships and develop trust. In instances where institutional ethical guidelines are inappropriate or inadequate, the social work code of ethics provides a de facto framework for ethical research. The code of ethics includes important principles related to human relationships and social justice that guide social work practice and equivalent activities in participatory approaches to research. It is also incumbent upon professional associations, schools of social work and community agencies to partner in providing training and guidelines in participatory ethics. This includes support for practitioners whose work falls outside the authority of institutional ethics review boards and who choose to conduct research in their own practice setting.

Diversity

Social justice in research necessitates efforts that challenge power relations along lines of social difference, including ability, race, class, gender and sexual orientation (Minkler and Wallerstein, 2003). Maguire, in writing about feminist participatory approaches, describes it as 'a commitment to expose and challenge the web of forces that cause and sustain all and any forms of oppression' (2001: 60). Unfortunately, the tendency in participatory studies is to highlight the commonalities amongst research participants and less attention is given to the social differences between them (Gaventa and Cornwall, 2001). In the pressure to forge consensus and create some common understanding of the issue being studied, the process can work to minimize diverging opinions and experiences. Thus, participatory approaches may inadvertently serve to disguise or diminish social differences and contribute to, rather than challenge, experiences of injustice (ibid).

The discourse of community in much of the literature can hinder an analysis of social difference. Few participatory researchers describe what they mean by community and who is and who isn't included in its formation (Lykes and Coquillon, 2007). 'The community' gets romanticized, and assumed to be homogeneous, wise and consistent in its decisions while the inevitable tensions, conflicts and threats to power that exist in any group are overlooked. Few groups are homogeneous, however, beyond some superficial characteristics, such as race or gender. Communities generally consist of a diverse group of individuals who, in the face of outside pressure, coalesce around a single issue.

The challenge is then to address an individual member's particular experiences of oppression while also fostering solidarity in the group. In their discussion of 'inclusive communities', Ristock and Pennell argue, '[t]he goal is not to discard communal connections but to make room for the differences that separate us' (1996: 18). We need to create spaces for diverging opinions and unique experiences so that these are not trumped by efforts aimed at building group solidarity.

As the exemplars in this chapter demonstrate, researchers must also stay committed to the central principles of participatory approaches that provoke analysis of power relations and one's own role in bringing about change (Healy, 2001; Maguire, 2001). The challenge for researchers remains to enable the participation of those often excluded from knowledge production while simultaneously confronting the dominance of their own practices and interpretations.

CONCLUSION

Our interest in participatory approaches to research in social work is due, in part, to our belief in the importance of practitioner-based research. Participatory approaches to research in social work are not only facilitated by a common practice framework but also by the unique position of social work practitioners to engage in participatory studies. Working on the front lines of social service delivery, practitioners gain the trust of community members and share in their everyday joys and struggles. This allows them to recognize recurring themes in their work and capture tacit forms of knowledge in the research process. Practitioners have a unique position, one that allows them to witness the impact of social policy changes on people's daily lives and to connect theory and practice in ways that few outside academics can match.

The possibility of practitioner-based research and research-minded practice often begins with social work education. Adding participatory approaches to the research curriculum will help students understand the relevance of research to their practice and more likely produce 'research-minded practitioners' (Everitt et al., 1992). Bringing participatory approaches into the classroom demonstrates to students the connections between research and practice, so that research is seen as a vital and important part of what we do.

We have described an approach to research that combines knowledge production, social work practice and social change. Our own experiences demonstrate this point. MacDonald's participatory study with a group of women with chronic pain led to new understanding of their identity as (dis)Abled and their work as caregivers. In Lavoie's example, we see how a low-income neighborhood found dignity and solidarity in a victory against media bias. And in Whitmore's graduate research class, students learning research methods found a means to work with practitioners as allies in investigating concerns/issues identified by the community. Such acts give new meaning to participants' daily lives and together form part of social work's contribution to a broader movement of social justice and social change.

NOTES

1   The Southampton Practice Research Initiative Network Group (SPRING) is actively working on this issue. See www.soton.ac.uk/spring.

2   Examples include the code of ethics for the International Federation of Social Work (IFSW), the National Association of Social Work (NASW) and the Canadian Association of Social Workers (CASW).

3   'Sufferer' was consciously chosen to represent participants through validating their pain.

4   Disability is written as (dis)Ability when referencing my own knowledges and in relation to the sufferers' storied experiences of living with chronic pain. An alternative reading of ability is created, recognizing the varied skills and abilities of people with (dis)Abilities, while not denying the social and physical connection with disability.

5   I refer to 'we' in this discussion, as I was later joined by a colleague, Colin Stuart, who co-taught the course with me for a number of years.

6   For further details, see http://www.ncehr-cnerh.org/english/code_2/.

Mixing Methods in Social Work Research

Jennifer C. Greene, Peter Sommerfeld
and Wendy L. Haight

Box 19.1

Mark is an eight-year-old, North American boy whose family recently moved from the countryside to a small urban community. Mark's father was disabled in a farming accident last year, and his mother is now seeking work. Mark and his two younger siblings are enrolled in the same school. They all ride the school bus together, and Mark likes that time of day with his brother and sister. The two younger children are doing well in their new school, but Mark is having increasing difficulties in his interactions with his peers – difficulties that are beginning to negatively affect his heretofore adequate academic performance. Despite his quick wit and better-than-average athletic abilities, Mark remains socially isolated in the classroom. Over the past month or so, he has started to react to particular comments and actions by his classmates with anger and withdrawal. For example, last week when the children were gathering in the classroom, one of the other boys in his class asked his classmates if they had seen a particular television program the night before, 'Did you see Sam on the soccer field? Weren't his shoes *so* cool?' Upon hearing this, Mark slammed his backpack on the floor and angrily sat down at his desk, crossed his arms, and remained sullen and silent for the rest of the morning. The school's social worker has been called in to work with Mark to understand what is troubling him, and help him to express his anger more constructively and become a part of the social life of the classroom.

Box 19.2

On the other side of the world, social workers in southeast Asia have come together for a working meeting, convened to give them opportunities to share experiences and ideas about how to counsel girls and young women who have been victims of the sex trade still active in that part of the world. Most of these girls and young women have experienced multiple traumas, including being sold by or forcibly taken from their families, transported to places unfamiliar and unknown, and forced to serve as prostitutes for countless strangers, few of them kind. The roots of this sex trade are economic, political, and cultural. Although recognized as exploitative, the sex trade generates economic benefits for many, including people in regions of grueling poverty. The social workers who work with these girls and young women after they have left or escaped from their near enslavement as prostitutes respect their strength to survive, even as they find the magnitude of their emotional trauma overwhelming and their real-life options almost unbearably limited.

These and other stories of human tragedy, suffering, and struggle are the highly complex problems of social work practice. They are multi-layered, dynamic, and particular, even as they embody universal strands of human drama. These problems involve unique constellations of human beings in dynamic interaction with one another within multi-layered contexts that are also unique, dynamic, and contingent. These contexts for social work practice include both the micro levels of the specific individual and setting, and the macro socio-political, economic, and cultural contexts within which the specific is located. Mark's classroom is a unique microcosm within which he is struggling for a sense of place and belonging. This classroom is also part of a larger community with its own political, economic, and cultural struggles for self-sufficiency, safety, and stability. The girls and young women who are caught in the snare of the sex trade each has her own individual story of trauma and resilience to tell, even as these individual stories together weave a larger web of economic and political exploitation.

Understanding the complexities of social work practice, especially their micro and macro dimensions, can only be realized by the use of our full social scientific methodological repertoire. The combined use of multiple methods and methodologies in social inquiry has come to be known as mixed methods social inquiry. (See Johnson et al., 2007 for a definitional statement on mixed methods inquiry.) This genre of social inquiry has seen an explosion of interest and development over the past 15 to 20 years (Brewer and Hunter, 2005; Bryman, 1988; Creswell and Plano Clark, 2006; Greene, J.C., 2007; Greene and Caracelli, 1997; Tashakkori and Teddlie, 2003). At the conceptual level, various typologies of mixed methods designs have been offered (notably, Creswell et al., 2003; Teddlie and Tashakkori, 2006), as have integrative data analysis strategies (Bazeley, 2003). The knotty problem of developing quality criteria for judging the warrant of inferences derived from mixed methods inquiry has also been

engaged (Onwuegbuzie and Johnson, 2006), alongside the challenges of writing up mixed methods findings (Sandelowski, 2003). And threaded throughout many of these conceptual conversations is the question of, 'just what is being mixed in a mixed methods study – forms of data, data collection instruments, design parameters, underlying philosophical assumptions, value commitments?' (Greene, J.C., 2007).

At the level of practice, many creative and thoughtful social inquirers in many different domains are conducting mixed methods studies, some using the guidance of the emerging conceptual frameworks for mixed methods inquiry, and some using only their own ingenuity and responsiveness to context. In highly practical fields like education, social work, nursing, and evaluation, the development of the mixed methods field has involved a respectful conversation between practice and theory, with practice often leading the way.

This chapter first provides an overview of selected conceptual ideas in mixed methods social inquiry, followed by two extended empirical exemplars that highlight the potentialities of mixed methods ideas for social work research. The first exemplar is a study, conducted in Switzerland, of the psychosocial dynamics of individuals' social reintegration processes following a period of time in prison or a psychiatric clinic. This complex study involved several mixes of methods aiming on three different time periods: before entry into the prison or psychiatric clinic, during the period of institutionalization, and during the post-institutional reintegration process. The mix to be showcased in this chapter took place after institutionalization. The researchers asked participants to record responses to 23 standard questions on a daily basis, using an instrument they called 'real time monitoring'. Then, the data from these records were incorporated into bi-monthly clinical interviews, which addressed participants' progress, goals, and reflections on their personal progress during the previous two months as documented in the monitoring data.

The inclusion of these monitoring data in the clinical interviews revealed a strong and direct link between the psychic dynamics of individuals' progress and social events.

The second exemplar involves a program of research in the United States on children from methamphetamine-involved families who are in foster care. These children face both psychological and physical trauma and a mixed methods approach enables the study of both structural factors and individual narratives. The presentation in this chapter showcases a mix of four different methods in the first phase of this research program, designed to develop a better understanding of the sociocultural context and the psychological challenges encountered by children from methamphetamine-involved families – an understanding that was grounded in both relevant theory and the particularities of rural poverty in the United States Midwest. The chapter concludes with a reprise of the two exemplars in terms of key mixed methods concepts, and a brief commentary on how a mixed methods approach engages the politics of methodology.

KEY CONCEPTS IN MIXED METHODS SOCIAL INQUIRY

This conceptual overview of key concepts in the mixed methods field begins with the most abstract level involving issues related to mixing philosophical stances and overall inquiry purposes, then moves to the broad level of mixed methods inquiry design, and then to a critical issue in mixed methods practice, data analysis. This discussion is necessarily illustrative rather than comprehensive.

Mixing at the paradigmatic level

Social research takes multiple forms and serves multiple purposes, including explanation, discovery, understanding, and action. This variation is connected to different assumptive traditions within the philosophy of science regarding the nature of the social world and our knowledge of it.

Is it possible to combine in the same social inquiry study assumptions that the social world is real and exists independently of our knowing it, with assumptions that the social world is constructed via interactions with others in context? Is it possible to combine in the same study an inquirer stance of distance and detachment as a vehicle for minimizing bias and enhancing objectivity, with an inquirer stance of closeness and engagement, or even advocacy or social critique, as expressions of inevitable inquirer subjectivity? Is it possible to combine in the same study analyses that seek to identify cross-context patterns of relational regularity in social phenomena, with analyses that intentionally generate contextualized portraits of the meaningfulness of human action? And if possible, is it desirable? What can be accomplished by such a mix that cannot be accomplished with social inquiry conducted within just one tradition of the philosophy of science?

These issues have challenged many contributors to the mixed methods conversation and, to date, they remain highly contested. The issues are also of considerable consequence, as they directly involve the question of just what is being mixed in a mixed methods study and with what intentions. The substance of the arguments revolves around several critical questions (see more elaborated discussions of these issues in Greene, J.C., 2007; Greene et al., 2001; and Greene and Caracelli, 1997):

1. Are the assumptions of traditional paradigms necessarily incompatible or incommensurable with one other? For example, do the assumptions of postpositivism (that the social world is real; objective and unbiased knowledge of this world is possible; and sophisticated, quantitative methods can best generate this knowledge) fundamentally conflict with those of social constructionism (that the social world is constructed, social knowledge inevitably subjective, and qualitative methods most defensible)?

2. Are traditional paradigms still useful in informing social inquiry practice? Or are there alternative

paradigms – such as transformation, critical social science, feminism, and especially American pragmatism – that embrace traditionally different philosophical stances unproblematically?

3. And finally, do philosophical assumptions actually guide methodological decisions in practice, or are such practical decisions more importantly guided by the requirements of the substantive theory, by the demands of the particular inquiry contexts at hand, or by a political imperative such as social change?

Varied positions on these critical questions intersect to form a set of 'mixed methods paradigm stances' in the literature. These stances form two rough clusters, one opposing and one favoring the mixing of paradigmatic assumptions in mixed methods inquiry. Examples of the arguments within each cluster follow next.

In opposition to mixing traditional paradigmatic assumptions Some advocates of the stances in this cluster maintain that mixing can happen at the level of inquiry design, method, analysis, and reporting, but not at the level of philosophical assumptions within a single study. Different sets of assumptions may be adopted across studies in a *program* of research, but within any single study, just one set of assumptions may be justifiably adopted. This is because, argue these advocates, different paradigm assumptions are incompatible, even contradictory, and moreover, a given social inquiry study should just have one primary thrust or purpose (e.g. exploration or explanation).

Or, as other advocates in this cluster maintain, paradigms inform our thinking and our understanding of the character of social inquiry, but they do not play an important role in guiding our inquiry practice. Rather, what matters more in making methodological decisions are the characteristics of the concepts being measured or the exigencies of the contexts in which the study is being conducted. So, the possible tensions or incommensurabilities among the assumptions of different paradigms simply do not surface when the inquiry is steered more by theoretical or contextual considerations.

Further, possible tensions and incommensurabilities among assumptions of traditional paradigms do not surface when an alternative paradigm is adopted for a given study. In particular, the alternative paradigm of American pragmatism is presented as a possible 'mixed methods philosophical framework' that itself resolves historic dualisms, for example, between realist and constructionist assumptions (Johnson and Onwuegbuzie, 2004). In this instance, Deweyian pragmatism maintains that human behavior involves interactions between a real social world and our interpretive constructions of meaning of the consequences of these actions. That is, Deweyian pragmatism is *both* realist and constructionist. Another alternative paradigm in the mixed methods literature, promoted by Donna Mertens (2003), is that of emancipation or transformation. Mertens argues that the socio-political imperative of conducting social inquiry that helps to redress past injustices in society trumps all other possible influences on practical inquiry decisions. So, again, possible tensions among philosophical assumptions are overridden by this political agenda.

In favor of mixing traditional paradigmatic assumptions Proponents of intentionally engaging with a mix of paradigmatic assumptions as part of mixed methods social inquiry primarily promote the possible contributions of different perspectives and different ways of knowing to the comprehensiveness of inquiry findings and interpretations. It is precisely *because* different social inquiry traditions have different assumptions that each offers a distinctive lens on complex social phenomena. Thus, the use of multiple lenses can afford an enriched portrait and understanding of the social phenomena under study. Moreover, although different, traditional paradigmatic assumptions are not necessarily or inherently so radically incompatible that they cannot usefully co-exist in a single study (Howe, 1988; 2003). This is especially so when attention is focused on the more concrete features of paradigms. To illustrate this point, consider the following contrasting but not contradictory features of postpositivism and constructionism, respectively – outsider and insider perspective, the expertise of social science and the expertise of lived experience, the general and the particular, patterned regularities and contextual meaningfulness.

Within this cluster, there are variations in views about how different paradigmatic traditions can be justifiably mixed in a given study. Some argue that the different traditions need to be kept quite separate throughout the study until the point of inference, so that the integrity of each can be importantly maintained. These contributors to the mixed methods conversation worry that the fundamental character of a paradigm could be seriously undermined if data generated from that paradigm were somehow mingled with data from another paradigm. One can think of key assumptions of independence and the importance of minimizing bias, as well as the frequent importance of preserving samples that are representative as well as samples that are purposeful, as instances of this concern. Others in this cluster argue more actively for an ongoing dialogue among the various methods, types of data, and analytic strategies – that is, a mixing throughout the study – as the most generative of insight and deeper understanding.

Mixed methods design

How to envision and design a mixed methods study has been a central site of conceptual development in the mixed methods conversation, notably by contributors Abbas Tashakkori and Charles Teddlie (e.g. Teddlie and Tashakkori, 2006) and John Creswell and colleagues (e.g. Creswell and Plano Clark, 2006; Creswell et al., 2003). These contributors have formulated mixed methods design alternatives as typologies, along the following core dimensions:

- Stage of integration of the different methods used and data generated – does the mixing happen only at the end of the study or in some integrated fashion throughout the study?

- Priority of methodologies involved – is one methodology primary and the other secondary, or are they of equal importance and influence in the study?
- Sequence of implementation of the different methods – are the methods to be implemented sequentially or concurrently? Is there a plan to convert one data type into the other?

Teddlie and Tashakkori (2006) further highlight design dimensions and decisions involving (a) whether to do a mixed methods or a monomethod study to begin with, thus situating mixed methods inquiry within a larger framework of social inquiry, and (b) how many phases to include in a study. A study in which the results of an initial survey are used to design an interview guide and select an appropriate interview sample illustrates a two-phase study.

The work of the first author of this chapter has conceptualized mixed methods design using similar dimensions as those of Teddlie and Tashakkori and Creswell, but with a focus on the intended purposes for mixing. These are not the substantive purposes of the overall study, but rather the methodological purposes for designing and implementing a given mix of methods. These purposes for mixing originally arose in a review of a sample of empirical mixed methods evaluation studies (Greene et al., 1989), so they are well grounded in practice. And they appear to still be relevant today (Greene, J.C., 2007). These purposes are:

- Triangulation: the use of data from one method to corroborate data from a different method; the designed convergence of data from different methods, both assessing the same phenomenon, in order to enhance the validity of inferences.
- Complementarity: the use of data from different methods to generate a deeper, broader, and more comprehensive portrait of a complex phenomenon, as the different methods tap into different facets or dimensions of the phenomenon being studied.
- Development: the use of data from one method to inform the development of another method, where development is broadly construed to

include instrument design, sample selection, and data collection.

- Initiation: the use of data from different methods to evoke paradox, contradiction, dissonance, in service of fresh insights or new perspectives; the designed divergence of data from different methods, which assess overlapping facets of the same complex phenomenon, in order to initiate original understandings.
- Expansion: the use of different methods to assess different phenomena, as a way of expanding the scope and range of the study; the extension of the study design to methods from more than one methodological tradition, thus expanding the scope and reach of the study.

These different purposes for mixing invoke different combinations of key mixed methods design dimensions. For example, for a triangulation purpose, methods are optimally of equal influence, implemented concurrently, and not mixed until the very end of the study.

With this plethora of alternative ways of thinking about mixed methods design, mixed methods inquirers have a rich set of ideas to inform their own inquiry planning. A careful review of extant alternatives will enable mixed methods practitioners to select the design best suited to their inquiry context, or to contribute their own creative ideas to the continued development of the conceptual landscape of mixed methods social inquiry.

Mixed methods data analysis

The mixed methods field remains ripe for further conceptual work on the challenges of analyzing, in well-planned and meaningful ways, multiple data sets of different form, content, and character. These challenges are especially important for designs that intentionally incorporate a back-and-forth conversation among diverse methods and data sets. (The mixed methods field can also continue to benefit from the creative thinking of diverse social inquirers in the form in exemplars of empirical mixed methods analytic work; Greene, J.C., 2007: xiv.)

In this final conceptual section of this chapter, a brief overview of selected mixed methods data analysis strategies will be offered. These strategies have come largely from exemplary practice, as mixed methods data analysis remains conceptually underdeveloped.

- Data transformation or conversion: in a mixed methods study with two different types of methods, data of one type can be converted to data of the other type, permitting joint analyses of all data together. For qualitative and quantitative data, Teddlie and Tashakkori (2003) call this 'qualitizing' and 'quantitizing'. Clearly, a major benefit of this approach is the ability to conduct a joint analysis of data of different types. The loss or possible distortion of information remains a limitation of concern.
- Data consolidation: data consolidation is a variant of data transformation. It involves 'the joint review of both [or multiple] data types to create new or consolidated variables or data sets, which can be expressed in either quantitative or qualitative form [or a mix]. These consolidated variables or data sets are then typically used in further analyses' (Caracelli and Greene, 1993: 197).
- Data importation: this strategy involves the importation of mid-stream analytic results from one method and type of data into the analysis of a different type of method and data. For example, results from a factor analysis of questionnaire data could be imported into a qualitative analysis of interview data by considering the relevance and value of the factors as possible categories or themes for the qualitative data. Or qualitative themes from an interview data analysis could be imported into an analysis of administrative records by singling out and examining cases characterized by low-incidence themes. The core idea here is to invite a conversation among the various data sets by bringing mid-stream results from one into the analysis of another and asking, 'what can be learned from the use of this outside framework or set of concepts?'
- Integrated data displays: one final mixed methods data analysis strategy is that of the integrated data display or matrix, borrowing from the qualitative analytic insights of Matthew Miles and Michael Huberman (1994). In this strategy, the inquirer envisions an ordered presentation of data from multiple methods, all in one space and framework. Such a presentation can lead to important and meaningful substantive insights precisely because it offers a joint display of different kinds of data and invites analytic integration

and imagination. (See Lee and Greene, 2007, for one example of an integrated display.)

The discussion now turns to the presentation of two exemplars of mixed methods social work research.

EXEMPLAR 1: INTEGRATION AND EXCLUSION

The problem engaged in this research was one of reintegration of individuals into their social systems following a period of exclusion, in particular, how the psychological and social are dynamically interconnected during this process. There are two primary reasons individuals are legitimately – and usually only temporarily – excluded in western societies: criminal action and illness. Traditionally there are two institutions that execute exclusion (through hyper-inclusion): prisons and (psychiatric) hospitals. For significant numbers of people, reintegration following some time in prison or a psychiatric hospital is not successfully accomplished, leading to reincarceration in prison or readmission to a psychiatric hospital. Better understanding of the dynamics of the reintegration process can help address this problem.

Theoretical framework

The project featured here was part of a national research program on 'Integration and Exclusion', funded by the National Swiss Science Foundation.[1] Integration and exclusion are concepts that well capture the complex relationship between an individual and society. The goal of the project was to understand in depth the dynamics of reintegration processes, particularly, the complex interplay between psychic and social systems. The primary theoretical assumption was that this dynamic interplay can be conceived as one process that happens on two different but closely linked levels – the micro level of the

individual's psychic processing and behavior and the macro level of the social system. In this understanding, which is inspired by the theoretical approach of 'synergetics' (Haken, 1990), the dynamic relation between these levels is called 'circular causality', which means that each level dynamically structures and constitutes the other.

That is, the macro social order emerges out of the micro interactions among individuals and, in turn, orders or 'enslaves' individual action and psychic development in a process called 'integration of the social systems'. The process of production and reproduction of social order is done by 'integrating individuals into the system', into defined positions within the interactional patterns that constitute the social order. Reintegration means coming back into a social order after exclusion and involves the individual's dynamic re-adaptation into the family, the work place, the sports club, and so on. This reintegration process is decisive for the individual's social position and therefore has a strong influence on his/her development and the scope of available opportunities or 'life chances'. If social workers were able to use this theory to reconstruct the dynamics of reintegration processes, they could more effectively influence these processes with their interventions. The challenges for our research project were to provide empirical support for the theorized interplay of micro and macro processes and to reconstruct the concrete corresponding social and psychic patterns that lead to specific forms of integration, for example, in an individual's living conditions.

Mixed methods study design

The study involved 16 cases recruited from prisons and a psychiatric clinic. From the beginning, we determined that a longitudinal design was necessary to observe and systematically record important dynamic processes over the one-year post-institutionalization period of the study. But how is it possible to observe internal psychic processes, as well as the correlated dynamics of the integration processes over an entire year to illuminate the interplay between the psychic and social levels? The key solution to this methodological problem was 'real-time monitoring' (RTM), a method developed by Schiepek et al. (2003). RTM is designed to monitor psychic processes in real time, which in the present study meant daily. Participants were given handheld computers containing a questionnaire, much like a standardized diary, which they were asked to complete every evening. Participants were asked to rate intensities of responses on a seven-step Likert scale. The data were then transferred to our server and so constituted a dense time series on each of the questionnaire's 23 items for each participant, with up to 300 measures on each item. The questionnaire contained items on six dimensions: hope/meaning, change/progress, self/integrity (self-reliance, self-effectiveness), physical and psychic well-being, different emotions, and quality of social relations. It was derived from research on recovery processes (Onken et al., 2002), as well as from an existing RTM questionnaire developed for psychosomatic therapy (Schiepek et al., 2002).

With this instrument alone, the study would have served to describe the dynamics of selected psychic processes of people coming out of a prison or a psychiatric clinic, along with their judgments of the quality of their social relationships. Beyond these intrinsically important findings, the challenge was to explain *how* these dynamics and judgments are linked to the social processes of reintegration.

This methodological challenge was addressed via the qualitative or reconstructive paradigm of social sciences and the analytic framework of grounded theory (Strauss and Corbin, 1990), which combines respect for contextual meanings with analysis of systematic regularities. The qualitative part of the study began

with individual biographical interviews (conducted at the outset of the study), on the assumption that a reintegration process and its contingent conditions cannot be totally understood without the history of the case. The biographical interviews served to identify the main patterns of the relevant social systems as well as the main psychic patterns of study participants. Through this reconstruction work we achieved, among others, a deep understanding of the crisis leading to exclusion.

The second qualitative method focused on collecting longitudinal data about the social side of the reintegration processes (complementing the RTM data on the psychic side). Every two months during the one-year post-institutionalization study period, all participants were interviewed with what we called 'reflecting interviews'. In these interviews, participants were first asked to reflect on their lives over the past two months in a narrative, open way. Then, they were asked to review and analyze the RTM data they had produced during the preceding two months by reflecting on the significant peaks in that data – what happened at that time, how could this be understood, and what might this mean for themselves. In the third and final part of the reflecting interviews, participants set personal goals for the next two months and reflected on progress made toward the personal goals established during the preceding session.

Our analytic processes were intentionally integrative across these different instruments and data sets, toward the generation of not only a good description but also a worthy explanation of how psychic and social systems are interconnected and how reintegration processes work.

A short presentation of selected data and results

These sample results highlight the mixing of the quantitative time series RTM data with the qualitative interview data.

The presentation concentrates on data from one case that evinced success through professional intervention.

Brief case history

The alias name of the male participant is 'Sandra Bullock', chosen by the participant himself. He entered a psychiatric clinic after a suicide attempt. For Bullock, two social systems were most relevant to the suicide attempt – relations at work and his personal intimate relationship. At the workplace Bullock was feeling challenged in many ways, which triggered an old feeling of insecurity concerning his performance and his social recognition. He reacted to this insecurity with two strategies long-established and deeply entrenched in his psychic system: 'keep the façade' and 'retreat into safe zones'. Use of these strategies led Bullock into conflict with his partner. They were planning their wedding, and she perceived that there was something wrong with him, but he denied it. He kept everything to himself, which led to further conflicts with his partner and a deepening crisis in their relationship. At the same time Bullock's psychic system turned into a depressive circle, which meant that he felt even less competent and recognized at work. These feelings became fact as he started to act in unexpected and troubled ways. In both social systems, things got progressively worse. The depressive circle took him down to deep pain, senseless-ness, hopelessness, the feeling of loss of control, and finally to the suicide attempt as an 'act of liberation'.

Reintegration: quantitative analyses of critical instabilities

Moving now to the reintegration process for Bullock, sample RTM data are presented in Figure 1. Each chart represents one questionnaire item, rated across several months. On the right side are the raw data, that is, Bullock's ratings on the seven-step Likert scale, which display considerable variation across most of the time period. The question is, What is a 'normal' fluctuation and where does it begin to turn into a 'critical' one, signaling that the system has moved to a state of instability or crisis? In the method we used, the number of direction reversals in the raw data and the amplitude of those reversals were assessed as indicators of the complexity of the time series patterns. These complexity measures are presented on the left in Figure 19.1, where the lower horizontal line corresponds to a .05 significance level, the upper one to .01. (For a more detailed description of the calculation see Sommerfeld et al., 2005.)

Since the notion 'critical fluctuation' means that the whole system is in a state of instability, one significant level of fluctuation on a single item does not mean much. When the significant values from the complexity measures are placed into a matrix with all items on the vertical side and the time scale along the horizontal axis, the result is a 'Complexity-Resonance-Diagram'. The diagram makes visible the resonance among the complexity measures on single items. Figure 19.2 presents such a diagram for Sandra Bullock. Each column stands for one day. A white field means that for that item on that day there is no significant complexity measure. A gray field corresponds to the .05 level of significance and the black one to .01. The histogram on the top of the matrix shows the number of items with significant complexity measures for that day. Sandra Bullock's histogram for the first six months after release clearly shows four distinct phases of critical instability. Such phases of critical instability occurred in all 16 study cases after release and thus distinctively characterize the process of reintegration. This is one important finding of the study because it seems that we have identified a valid cross-case regularity.

Reintegration: qualitative explanations for critical instabilities

The quantitative RTM analyses demonstrated that phases of critical instability occur after release from an institution.

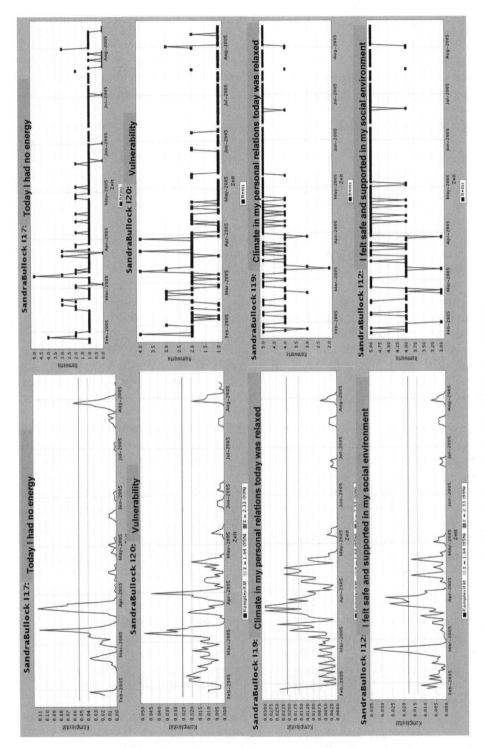

Figure 19.1   Raw data and complexity measures selected items, Sandra Bullock.

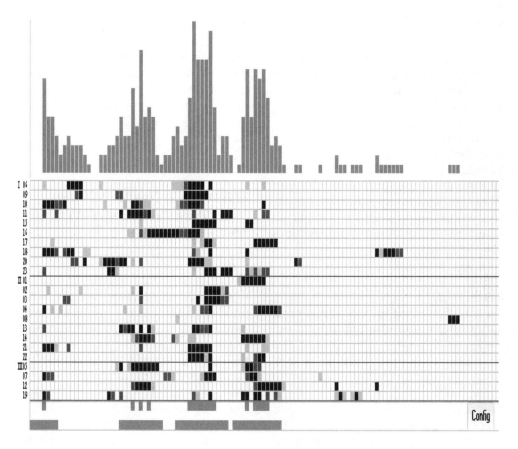

Figure 19.2   Complexity-resonance-diagram, Sandra Bullock, first 6 months.

But, neither the data nor the analyses provide clues as to why. For this, we turned to the qualitative data. When the RTM data were shown to study participants as part of the reflecting interviews, they always had clear answers to 'what happened' at the time of significant fluctuations. Sometimes they reported specific activities like searching for a job, but in all cases and in all explanations social dynamics were the primary point of reference in participants' reflective recollections. For example, searching for a job is the activity named, but this activity is embedded, framed, and accompanied by social processes. These processes include how you are treated as a job seeker, how you perceive the quality of your performance in a job interview situation, and how you are supported or not in your job search by your family, friends, and professionals.

In the case of 'Sandra Bullock', the first phase of critical fluctuations occurred when he went back to work half-time. At that same time his ex-partner, who had quit the relationship when he was at the clinic, moved out of their shared apartment. The second phase occurred when Bullock was first given full responsibility for a project at work (with coaching from his boss), and when he also had a final conversation with his ex-partner about their relationship. In the third phase, Bullock experienced a strong conflict with his parents (probably one of the first in his life) and massive back problems, accompanied by a beginning depressive crisis. And the fourth phase was triggered by

Bullock's return to a full-time work just as his boss announced that he was leaving the company, together with the start of new social contacts. These social events do not directly cause the critical instabilities; rather they interfere with the cognitive–emotional–behavioral patterns Bullock had developed through his social life history. Only the reconstruction of these individual patterns, together with their interference in the social system's order, reveal the systems dynamic in its totality and thereby offer a precise information base for 'synchronized' interventions directed toward improving integration on both social and psychic levels.

Key findings

The trajectory of the reintegration process begins in the past. Criminal activity and mental illness emerge in the context of a life history. The circular dynamic of individual and social processes leading to temporary exclusion can be called 'negative escalation', which occurred in all cases in both fields of mental illness and criminal behavior. The interference between different processes in different social systems leads to a phase of critical instability of the psychic system accompanied by unexpected and socially unacceptable behavior (for example a criminal act or suicide attempt), which finally leads to temporary exclusion through hyperinclusion in an institution.

Then, when people are released, they have to redefine their position within their various social systems. Social systems tend to resist change and so reintegrate their former members in the same position or lower (because of stigmatization), or exclude them definitively. This struggle for integration in a new form and eventually for sustainable personal development to solve one's problems causes the phases of critical instability. A successful reintegration process therefore implies rearrangements in both the social order and the individual's patterns. Bullock's case was a success because through the intervention

the 'negative escalation' was transformed into a supportive, 'positive' one. The transformation of the integration conditions at the workplace, for example, was as important as the therapy because together, through their interplay or 'synchronization', a new problem solving dynamic emerged.

EXEMPLAR 2: CHILDREN FROM METHAMPHETAMINE-INVOLVED PARENTS

During the opening years of the twenty-first century, the misuse of methamphetamine, a powerful central nervous system stimulant and neurotoxin, was a growing and urgent public health, criminal justice and child welfare problem across the United States. The problem was particularly acute in rural areas with limited law enforcement and social service resources. Many individuals who misuse methamphetamine experience long lasting psychiatric symptoms such as psychosis, depression, intense paranoia, visual and auditory hallucinations, and suicidal behavior; repetitive behavior; rapid mood changes; irritability; out-of-control rages and violent behavior (Anglin et al., 2000; Copeland and Sorensen, 2001; Cretzmeyer et al., 2003; Rawson et al., 2002; SAMHSA, 2002). Not surprisingly, rural law enforcement officers and health, mental health, and child welfare professionals increasingly encountered children living in homes where methamphetamine was produced and misused. Many of these children had been exposed to environmental toxins from the production of methamphetamine in Mom and Pop labs, violence, adult substance misuse, and child maltreatment. Despite the growing numbers of children who were referred to state child protective agencies because of parental methamphetamine misuse, there was a lack of evidence-based treatments to address the needs of these high-risk children. A research team from the University of Illinois initiated a mixed methods program of research to supply needed information.

Informed by our experience of child welfare practice in rural Illinois and the existing literature, we developed several general research questions: 1) What are the contexts in which rural children in foster care because of parents' methamphetamine misuse are reared? 2) What is their psychological functioning? 3) What are the basic components of a culturally appropriate mental health intervention for these children? 4) How effective is this customized intervention? To address these research questions, our interdisciplinary research team planned a three-phase, mixed methods research program that focused first on better understanding the impact of parental methamphetamine misuse on the development and well-being of school-aged children in foster care, and then on the design and evaluation of a culturally appropriate intervention for them. The research program is case-based and is being conducted in several rural counties in the Midwest experiencing large numbers of families entering the child protection system due to parent methamphetamine misuse.

Rationale for mixed methods approach

Our decision to use a mixed methods approach reflects our underlying theoretical interest in understanding human development as an outgrowth of cultural life (e.g. Corsaro, 1996; Lave and Wenger, 1991; Rogoff, 1990; Shweder et al., 2006) and in using such knowledge to inform the design and evaluation of interventions for vulnerable children. Thus, we approached the problem of parental methamphetamine misuse not as an isolated event, but as embedded within a complex sociocultural context. We considered that the impact of methamphetamine misuse on individuals,

families and communities results from a complex interaction of biological, psychological, social, and cultural factors. Methamphetamine misuse has certain biological effects on the human body, but how the resulting medical symptoms are understood, experienced, and responded to by the individual, family, and community also have strong cultural components. Moreover, cultural communities vary in their understanding of addiction, for example, as illness or moral failing, as well as child maltreatment, for example, the degree and type of supervision and physical resources deemed adequate (Agathonos-Georgopoulou, 2003; Bamba and Haight, 2007; Fullilove, 1996). These understandings have implications for culturally appropriate interventions for families affected by parental methamphetamine misuse.

Our mixed methods research strategy allows a context-specific conceptualization of the problem of parental methamphetamine misuse. It integrates developmental, ethnographic, case study, and clinical methods. The intent of such methodological pluralism is to strengthen each approach to characterize the complexities of community members' points of view and social practices in their sociocultural contexts. Developmental methods include the systematic, often microscopic, description of children's participation in various activities and changes over time. Ethnographic methods include the description and interpretation of social behavior and its meanings from participants' perspectives through analysis of the broader context of beliefs and practices. Clinical methods include the use of in-depth interviews and culturally appropriate assessments of psychological functioning. Case study methods allow in-depth, contextualized understanding of the lives of individuals with experiences of conceptual and practical significance. The intertwining of developmental, ethnographic, clinical, and case study methods allows identification of the regularities inherent in everyday life within particular communities, an interpretation of what such regularities may mean to the participants themselves (Gaskins et al., 1992; Sperry and Sperry, 1996), and a broader conceptualization of participants' psychological functioning.

Our mixed methods approach also reflects our commitment to culturally sensitive interventions, as respect for difference is intrinsic to mixing methods. Many mental health and child welfare interventions for children are based upon European American, middle-class preferences for child-centered, verbal, emotionally positive, stimulating, and sensitive adult–child interactions. Comparative research, however, indicates that adults in many other cultural communities exhibit these behaviors less frequently than middle-class, European Americans, and that such differences reflect a commitment to other socialization goals, values, and understandings of the world (Shweder et al., 2006). Understanding the socialization beliefs and practices of the community within which the child is being reared, as opposed to that of the social worker or researcher, is prerequisite to the design and implementation of an effective intervention that is comprehensible to and accepted as relevant by the child, the child's family, and community.

The remainder of this exemplar concentrates on the methods used for the first phase of this research program.

Understanding the contexts in which children from methamphetamine-involved families are reared and their psychological functioning

Phase 1 of the research program provided an in-depth description of the problem of parent methamphetamine misuse in the cultural context of rural Illinois (Haight et al., 2006, 2007), and a description of affected children's experiences and psychological functioning (Ostler et al., 2007). The site of our research was in the rural Midwest from about 2003–2006. The

extent to which these specific findings are transferable to other cultural contexts, for example, urban communities, is an open empirical question. The extent to which our specific findings are transferable to other historical contexts also is an open empirical question. For example, since approximately 2004, laws limiting access to the precursors for methamphetamine production have dramatically reduced small-scale methamphetamine manufacture (Office of National Drug Control Policy, 2006). Since the ongoing demand for methamphetamine remains, the control of the supply has shifted to organized, criminal groups (U.S. Drug Enforcement Agency, 2006), and these will introduce new and different risks to rural Midwestern children, families, and communities.

Our access to the community was made possible by our collaborator, a child protection worker with deep roots in the community and generally excellent relations with other professionals as well as clients. We began our study with extensive participant observation, including attendance at Illinois state methamphetamine task force meetings, drug court, and over 90 hours of shadowing child welfare investigators. Systematic field notes recorded our conversations, community reactions, and responses to the methamphetamine problem, as well as the living conditions of rural families involved with methamphetamine.

In addition, we conducted in-depth, audiotaped, individual interviews with participants occupying diverse social vantage points in relation to methamphetamine misuse. We interviewed 28 professionals who deal with the problem of methamphetamine on a regular basis (child welfare professionals, law enforcement professionals, educators, substance misuse treatment providers, and counselors), and seven foster caregivers of children from methamphetamine-involved families. They discussed their experiences with families involved with methamphetamine, beliefs about the effects of methamphetamine on school-aged children, and appropriate strategies for intervention.

We also conducted oral histories with four recovering mothers with children in foster care because of their methamphetamine misuse. Mothers described their experiences of methamphetamine addiction and recovery. They described their own experiences growing up, how they became involved with methamphetamine and its impact on their lives and children. Their discussions were the basis for a comparative case analysis (Haight et al., in press).

We also visited the children in and around their homes and communities. As part of a semi-structured interview, we engaged with children in a variety of leisure and play activities, or just talked, during which time we invited them to respond to several questions. We began with some fairly open-ended probes, for example, 'Who is in your family?', 'Tell me about a time in your family that was happy', 'Tell me about a time in your family that was sad or scary' before moving to more specific probes about methamphetamine, for example, 'Sometimes adults use meth. How does it make them act?' In addition, we conducted a variety of standardized assessments of children's development and mental health including the Peabody Picture Vocabulary Test (PPVT) (Dunn and Dunn, 1997), Childhood Behavior Checklist (CBCL) (Achenbach and Rescorla, 2001), the Trauma Symptom Checklist for Children (TSCC) (Briere, 1996), and the American Drug and Alcohol Survey.

A key challenge in this research program has been understanding participants' perspectives of a highly stigmatized, illegal activity, especially the perspectives of children, many of whom were experiencing symptoms of trauma and had been taught not to talk about their parents' drug use. A mixed methods approach was critical to addressing this challenge, as different methods provided different venues for children's responses (e.g. interviews and standardized assessments).

For example, the interviews were a generally rich source of narrative data. Once rapport had been established, many children were able to provide elaborate accounts of their lives including their experiences in their families of origin. Other children, however, had limited experience talking about their lives, and had had little support in making sense of confusing and traumatic events in their lives. They had a much more difficult time providing coherent accounts. In these cases, the standardized assessments were valuable in the identification of clinical symptoms of psychological distress such as post traumatic stress disorder, and in placing children's psychological functioning within a broader context, for example, of children living in foster care.

Such assessments, however, typically assume universalism in human development and can only be used with caution. We chose widely used assessments that can be administered individually and which allow children to provide narrative elaborations of responses to questions about basic emotional and behavioral responses (e.g. reporting on the presence of angry feelings or nightmares). Nonetheless, many children did not provide valid responses to one or more of the standardized assessments, perhaps primarily because many children had been strongly socialized not to discuss family matters with outsiders. Approximately one-third of children in our sample had invalid scores on the TSCC due to underreporting. For example, they simply denied ever having felt angry or sad. Similarly, the American Drug and Alcohol Survey was problematic for most of our children, some of whom refused to answer the questions, or simply responded in the negative to all items before they had been read. Given the limitations of any particular method for any individual child, we combined diverse methods to obtain a more complete understanding of each child's psychological functioning as well as interpretation of their experiences and perspectives.

Next steps: designing, implementing, and evaluating a culturally sensitive intervention

The aim of the second phase of the research program was to design a culturally sensitive intervention for rural children to harness potential protective factors to address risks to their mental health. We integrated findings from phase 1 with clinical research results and practice experience in a narrative- and relationship-based mental health intervention. We then drew upon rural professionals – specifically, child welfare workers, social workers, retired counselors, and educators – to implement the intervention with one or two children each in their own rural areas. We provided them with weekly supervision from experienced clinicians on our research team who were located in an adjacent urban area. In the ongoing, phase 3 of our research program we are evaluating the intervention using an experimental design and combination of qualitative and quantitative methods to describe children's functioning over a period of 12–18 months in relation to their participation in the six-month intervention.

REPRISE

These two exemplars of mixed methods social work research vividly illustrate the power of mixed methods inquiry to meaningfully engage with the rich and full complexity of human action and interaction at both micro and macro levels. This engagement is enabled precisely because mixed methods inquiry uses multiple methodological traditions, each with its own lens on human phenomena, and thus collectively affords multiple lenses and generates better, deeper understanding. Peter Sommerfeld's research study brilliantly connects *internal* psychological states with *external* social relationships, the individual's private mental pulses with the fabric of her or his socio-relational network. Wendy Haight's research insightfully situates

the tragedies of children of methamphetamine-involved parents within the *particular* tattered contexts of rural America, while also connecting these children's emotional profiles to *general* standards and norms. These connections enhance these studies, offering enriched understandings that would not have been attained with one methodology alone.

These studies also well illustrate the mixed methods conceptual ideas presented at the outset of this chapter. First, with respect to paradigm stances, both studies intentionally included methodologies representing different philosophical or paradigmatic traditions. Sommerfeld's research used a structured, self-report quantitative questionnaire – representing a realist and objectivist paradigm – along with qualitative biographical and reflective interviews – representing a 'reconstructive' or interpretive paradigm. For this research, the quantitative realist RTM methodology offered a detailed and accurate portrayal of *what* happened to participants' mental states over time, and the qualitative interviews helped understand participants' interpretations of the meanings of these changes. Jointly, the data from the different methods offer a more complete and complex portrayal of the process of reintegration than either method alone. In Haight's research, an understanding of the children's psychological and emotional status was garnered through both qualitative, narrative interviews – representing a constructivist framework – and standardized measures of children experiencing trauma – representing a postpositivist framework. Some of the children in this study had difficulty responding to the interviews; others had trouble with some of the questions on the standardized measures. These 'measurement' difficulties in and of themselves revealed important facets of the children's emotional status. Jointly, the different methods – and the different paradigmatic frameworks they represented – offered a more comprehensive window into these children's experiences than would either alone.

Second, the mixed methods designs used by these researchers are informative. Sommerfeld's mixed methods design involved two methods of relatively equal importance, implemented iteratively and interactively. Haight's research was more clearly dominated by the qualitative methods (interviewing and observation) but the standardized quantitative measures played a critical role in understanding the children's emotional well-being. The different methods were also implemented interactively in Haight's study. Both studies thus well illustrate the mixing of methods for the primary purpose of complementarity (generating a deeper, broader, and more comprehensive portrait of a complex phenomenon, as the different methods tap into different facets or dimensions of the phenomenon being studied), and for the secondary purpose of initiation (evoking paradox, contradiction, dissonance, in service of fresh insights or new perspectives).

Third, with respect to analysis, these mixed methods studies conceptually connected the results from one analysis with the results from the other analysis, but did not conduct any fully integrative analyses, thus perhaps missing opportunities for additional insights.

Finally, these two studies well illustrate the broad applicability of mixed methods frameworks in social work research. Peter Sommerfeld's research focused on theory building and theory testing, with strong implications for further practical development, Wendy Haight's on developing a practical therapeutic intervention for the children involved. Theory and practice can be equally well served by a mixed methods way of thinking.

FINAL COMMENTS

The contemporary popularity of mixed methods social inquiry is not without its critics, especially from the qualitative inquiry communities. Some express serious reservations that mixed methods inquiry is but a political 'cover' for a reclamation of the superiority of a traditional quantitative, postpositivist stance on knowledge and the role of social science in society.

Ideologically, mixed methods covers for the continuing hegemony of positivism, albeit in its more moderate, postpositivist form. Rather than the promotion of more cooperative and complex designs for increasingly complex social and health issues, economic and administrative pressures may lead to demands for the 'quick fix' that mixed methods appears to offer (Giddings, 2006: 195).

The excellent exemplars featured in this chapter clearly support the theoretical, practical, *and* political value of a mixed methods approach to social work research. Beyond the evident contributions to conceptual understanding and practical action, a mixed methods way of thinking politically embraces difference and diversity as generative of human compassion and tolerance. A turn to mixing methods is *not* an acquiescence to an objectivist, evidence-based, 'sound byte' framework for social inquiry of consequence, nor is it a celebration of the experiential eloquence or persuasive power of narratives. Neither does it champion the value commitments of any particular inquiry tradition. Rather, in its most generative form, a mixed methods approach to social work research offers space for respectful engagement with the multitude of human experiences and the diversity of human values and aspirations. At its most generative, a mixed methods approach offers deep and potentially inspirational opportunities to meaningfully engage with the differences that matter in today's troubled world, seeking not so much convergence and consensus as opportunities for respectful listening and understanding.

NOTES

1 A more detailed description of the project, its methodology, and its results only exists in German (see http://www.nfp51.ch/files/SchlussberichtProjekt-Sommerfeld.pdf). The book, in German as well, is expected to be published in 2009. Lea Hollenstein and Raphael Calzaferri were co-workers in this project.

Challenges and Directions in the Practice of Social Work Research

Katharine Briar-Lawson, Robyn Munford
and Jackie Sanders

INTRODUCTION

This chapter focuses on some of the current challenges and directions in the practice of social work research. Drawing on perspectives from the US and New Zealand, this chapter cites issues for the more global research community in social work.

We deal first with the relevance of research in the context of the 'engaged university'. This growing outreach and engagement agenda of universities positions social work to play a key role in promoting relevant research. Research productivity and funding is a challenge for social work investigators. We cite contextual developments in the US that attempt to augment research effectiveness and productivity. This includes infrastructure supports with more administrative and organizational research structures.

Given the paucity of evidence based interventions in social work, this chapter highlights the importance of several kinds of applied research to advance practice knowledge. Intervention, developmental and translational research strategies are cited. We frame this discussion in the context of the growing movement for evidence based practice (EBP). An exemplar is cited of developmental research.

Multiplism, or multiple methods, is required for knowledge building (Cook, 1987). Because of the growing need for both quantitative and qualitative research as methods for answering key research questions, we focus next on one example of qualitative research. We examine the centrality of Community Based Participatory Research (CBPR) as a promising twenty-first century research strategy. CBPR is seen as exemplifying empowerment based research practices as participants collaborate on most aspects of the research study. Using exemplars from New Zealand we highlight both CBPR and practitioner collaboration in research. We then examine international research innovations and cite systematic reviews which serve as one foundation for more cross-national research. Finally we argue that the social work knowledge base must be fortified with more empirical research that addresses diversity. This includes knowledge that is informed by both qualitative and quantitative research as well as studies that are culturally inclusive and relevant.

RELEVANCY AND RESPONSIVENESS: THE ENGAGED UNIVERSITY AND SOCIAL WORK RESEARCH

Multiple challenges persist in aligning social work research with the key social needs of the community or region, broadly defined, in which a university or college is located. If one were to assess the needs and perplexing problems and issues in and across our nations and compare this to the research studies that are undertaken, a deep discrepancy might be found.

Although discrepancy or alignment indices or metrics do not exist, it is apparent that over time a growing disparity has occurred. The focus of researchers and the social issues of the community may not be aligned. For example, in the US and in several other nations, the economy is currently the most perplexing issue facing many but few social work researchers study the effects of economic insecurity on individuals, families and communities or test or evaluate interventions that best address basic economic needs. Other examples could be cited. The point is, if there were a systematic inventory of the most complex and challenging problems facing communities to guide and inform relevant research agendas, there might be less discrepancy. By calculating the percentage of congruent research studies, derived, for example, from needs assessments of various stakeholders, it could then be possible to construct an alignment index for all schools and departments in a given region, state or nation. While we do not intend that research serve instrumental goals, we cite these alignment issues because they help to set the context for the future practice of some forms of social work research in general and university based research more specifically.

One major explanation for the presumed 'disconnect' involves the structural divides that persist between communities and institutions of higher education, research centers and public and private sector think tanks. While policy leaders and other stakeholders in communities may seek to hold universities more accountable for helpful and relevant research, there may be a clash in expectations. In many universities and colleges, it is expected that the prototypical researcher will have a career defined by a focused research agenda. Building on a sequential line of inquiry over time, this focused research should ultimately yield a high impact research program. The incentives and rewards for such a well demarcated and focused agenda often preclude a more diverse, adaptive and responsive community research program. Such community accountable research might be questioned by peers about the potential to create a diluted and fragmented research program thus weakening the profile of the faculty researcher. In some cases, at least in the US, this fragmentation might even jeopardize tenure and a post as a professor. Moreover there are key questions as to which 'communities' and needs should shape the research program – for example, community residents, the business community, the social service and non-profit or governmental sectors, interest groups, or local, national or international domains.

One might thus conclude that the disparity between the needs of the community, broadly defined, and the research that is undertaken is, in part, potentially structurally induced. In other words, while researchers have individual 'agency' based on their aspirations and socialization, tensions may arise with emerging norms governing relevance. We suggest this because there may be non-compatible and institutional constraints and expectations that shape the career of academic and related researchers. To remedy some of this, a growing movement in the US and elsewhere is fostering the 'engaged university' (Carnegie Foundation, 2008). This new 'engagement' movement promotes research that addresses questions that come from community led inquiry and relate to community needs. Attributes of the engaged university include serving the community with knowledge and solving problems.

Guiding visions for this growing movement in the US and internationally require ongoing community needs assessments and profiles which shape more responsive university research, education and service. These might involve door to door resident surveys regarding perceived needs and issues or routine surveys of different sectors and stakeholders of the community such as business, public and non-profit organizations, policy leaders, and media. At this time the Carnegie Foundation (2008) uses its recently developed 'engaged university' classification system in the US to grant universities and colleges new designations as an 'engaged campus'. Supported by an array of national bodies in the US, this more community accountable realignment work is underway across some universities. Not surprisingly, social work is often seen as an exemplar in some of these 'engaged' academic institutions. This is because more of social work research is seen as being linked to community needs and goals. In the US the relatively recent *Journal of Community Practice* (2004) and other works such as Soska and Butterfield (2004) focus on the engaged university and role of social work.

Engaged scholarship

Parallel initiatives are being developed in the US to support engaged scholars. New standards and evaluative criteria are also being promoted for tenure (Michigan State University, 1996). They build on Ernest Boyer's more expansive ideas about scholarship. He argued that scholarship comprises discovery, integration, application and teaching. Boyer's (1996) influential views involving his scholarship of engagement entail connecting the vast resources of the university to pressing civic, ethical or social problems in

communities. This strategy might compel university research and interventions to address the condition of children, failing schools or deteriorating cities (Boyer, 1996). In New Zealand these trends are prevalent in the guidelines of government funding agencies where there is an expectation that grant applications will provide evidence of partnerships with practitioner and policy stakeholders and detail end-user involvement in the formulation of the research. This includes being able to demonstrate how the research will have policy and practice relevance.

In the US the extent is unknown as to how widely adopted alternative forms of scholarship are as they relate to community engagement and more service oriented research. Even if not adopted wholesale in a college or university, some of these norms are used strategically as tenure arguments in support of the 'outreach scholar'. The case is often made that outreach scholarship qualifies as relevant and potentially rigorous as it is sought by and found helpful to community groups. Such research may not advance a faculty member's own research trajectory in terms of a focused line of sequential investigations that build a definable knowledge base but may exemplify institutional and community responsiveness and relevance by attempting to better understand or solve community problems. This observation is based on expectations especially in research universities. A similar situation occurs in the New Zealand context where community-based academics are encouraged to reach out and provide research leadership to communities of interest. Of particular significance is the work of indigenous scholars who are supported by their universities to assist indigenous communities to grow their research capability and capacity, and to develop culturally sensitive research methodologies and advance the utilization of cultural knowledge to inform research processes (Walker et al., 2006).

What does the engaged university mean for the practice of social work research? At a minimum the focus on service and relevant research positions social work to be at the forefront in community responsive research. Community might be defined in many ways ranging from local and regional residents, institutions, etc. Moreover on the horizon are opportunities for the integration of service, education and research. A faculty member serving as a liaison to a field agency where social work students are placed can then enjoin the students, field site supervisor and agency staff in relevant qualitative and quantitative research that advances more empirically based and evaluated practice. The field placement becomes then the site for mini pilots to ferret out what interventions are most effective, perhaps with group based experiments or ongoing single subject studies. Or the faculty researcher may help to foster agency relevant descriptive, survey, case study or qualitative research. This natural nexus of the university social work educator with the field agency and student field experience provides a platform for building new infrastructures in support of more social work research.

RESEARCH INFRASTRUCTURE IN SCHOOLS AND DEPARTMENTS OF SOCIAL WORK

To accelerate more research productivity and rigor, efforts have been mounted in some universities to build supports for faculty and entire schools to increase their research work and grant funded portfolio. In the US, there have been several developments to augment research supports for educational programs, faculty and doctoral students. At the national level such developments have resulted in capacity building workshops and expanded partnerships with federal funding agencies. The Institute for the Advancement of Social Work Research (IASWR) brokers much of this work and promotes social work research especially within the National Institutes of Health (NIH). The Society for Social Work and Research has emerged in the past decade

as a US body advancing and showcasing social work research through its conferences, awards and publications. Deans of research schools of social work with external research funds of over $3 million or more have organized as the 'St. Louis Group'. This group initiates focused research exchanges and meetings to share lessons learned on infrastructure developments, faculty supports and research grants. National Institute of Mental Health (NIMH) has funded research centers in 10 schools of social work and NIDA has funded research infrastructure development programs in seven schools of social work. These NIH investments advance pilot studies sometimes leading to NIH funded investigations. Such NIH funding has also provided for statistical consultation, interdisciplinary collaboration and the provision of scientific mentors.

Over the past decade, some progress has been made in the US and elsewhere in the development of research centers. Such research centers comprise one example of needed infrastructure supports because they may help faculty, doctoral and practitioners with research consultation and research participant access, literature reviews, research design and statistical supports, pilot funds and peer review of research proposals. Currently about half of US graduate schools of social work have research centers and some notable progress is being made to provide supports to faculty to advance their research (Briar-Lawson et al., 2008). In fact, an entire volume of *Social Work Research* is devoted to infrastructure developments and supports that advance research primarily in the US. This includes depictions of developmental progressions in academic units seeking to build quality research and expanded funded research portfolios over time.

Interdisciplinary research

The social work profession sits at the vortex of critical social issues. Because of this, social work can serve as a gathering point for interdisciplinary research. All too often, however, such interdisciplinary partnerships may emerge because social work has access to populations required by researchers in diverse disciplines rather than for the discerning research expertise social work researchers offer.

Social work researchers are positioned to be both collaborators as well as leaders forging cross-university and cross-disciplinary institutes and research agendas. Examples of social issues spanning interdisciplinary domains include poverty, addictions, discrimination and exclusion, mental health problems and resilience, health and minority health disparity issues including HIV/AIDs, aging, child abuse and neglect, juvenile delinquency, disabilities, challenges for migrant populations and displaced persons and so forth. Any one of these areas could be the focus of research centers that marshal interdisciplinary partners. Funders may concur that the cross-disciplinary research agenda will enhance problem solving effectiveness. Further, innovation transfer across the disciplines may also help with more coherent and integrative assessment and intervention strategies as well as new interdisciplinary PhD and graduate programs. Interdisciplinary research may add to the analytical and methodological tools that social workers require for effective research. These are also essential as the profession embraces or is challenged to increase rigor. Social work has historically been lagging in rigorous research advancing knowledge in many fields of service (Khinduka, 2007; Reid, 2002).

Evidence based practice and agency research

Demands for rigor are heightened in countries like the US as questions about accountability and EBP are raised by policy makers, public agencies and philanthropic funders. This is also increasingly the experience of countries like New Zealand that are strongly influenced by research and practice developments in the US and the UK. Pressures are building from outside the profession to accelerate research and to adopt EBP. In fact, in one high level social work meeting at the NIMH in the US, discussion focused on how to foster more adherence to evidentiary knowledge bases (IASWR, 2008).

This call for EBP and the creation of more practice based knowledge development is not new. It has been an ongoing tension in social work for over 40 years. Over the decades there have been a variety of attempts to build practice knowledge. Originally defined as a movement to build 'clinician scientists' or 'empirically based practitioners', it has more recently been reflected in the calls for 'agency based practice', 'practice research' or 'intervention research'. Practice is to be research informed and, where possible and desirable, research is to be practice driven (Wade and Newman, 2007).

Some schools of social work respond to this by requiring that students learn and apply single subject methods in their field placements. While superseding group designs in part due to ease of application, single subject methods are also seen as addressing individual variability. Yet, when graduated, few students employ single subject or any evaluative research methods (Rosen and Proctor, 2003).

No one model of the practice researcher or researcher practitioner model has had durability over the 40 years, at least in the US. This predictable challenge in fostering the research informed practitioner is now compelling new models of agency–school collaboration. Such models include agencies as research hubs, fostering translational research strategies and helping the practitioner to be research informed. This may entail research briefs prepared by the schools of social work on selected practice methods showing effectiveness for relevant populations being served. From such briefs, practice guidelines are generated (Rosen and Proctor, 2003). It may also entail training in new practices as well as the design of some evaluation measures.

Beginning consensus has been achieved in the US around the centrality of both client and practitioner judgments as composite contributions to the selection of relevant interventions. In fact in the US the EBP movement subscribes to client and practitioner determinations as to what interventions ultimately will be in the best interest of the client. Such focus on context and client culture helps to balance what some might see as the imposition of external dictates of the interventions to be employed (IASWR, 2008).

Debates continue if not accelerate about what is 'counted' as robust and sound evidence for determining the effectiveness of practice interventions. Fueling these debates is the ongoing concern that interventions that show effectiveness or promise may not have been tested across diverse populations. This is especially true of populations differentiated by age, gender, sexual preference, disabilities, ethnic, cultural, racial and socioeconomic status. Context matters greatly. Moreover the selection of interventions can be a complex process entailing attention to unique characteristics of the client and client system, their presenting problem or problems, their personalities, their treatment or outcome goals, their unique situations and the behaviors that need to be changed or that are required for the interventions to be utilized (Fraser, 2003). Attention is also focused on the barriers and necessary conditions that need to be addressed for certain interventions to be successful. For example, with jobless clients, do they have access to child care so that they can participate in job search and job club activities? Their age, as well as ethnicity and race, health status and service auspices are all germane to this decision making (Fraser, 2003). This adds to the importance of the client and practitioner's joint decision making as interventions are tailored, adapted and revised as appropriate. In other words, practice ethics and social work values regarding client self determination must be taken into account when implementing EBP.

Several US based clearinghouses have emerged featuring EBP, treatment and interventions. Groups such as the California Clearinghouse on Evidence Based Practice attempt to classify programs and practices in terms of the research evidence (Johnson and Austin, 2006). Classifications include practice which "1) is of concern, 2) fails to demonstrate effect, 3) lacks adequate research evidence, 4) exhibits promising research evidence, 5) is supported by research evidence and 6) is well supported by research evidence" (Johnson and Austin, 2006). Other groups such as Substance Abuse Mental Health Services Administration (SAMHSA) (2008) offer classifications as well. Together these varied sources provide the practitioner community with some beginning ratings of different practices and programs. Some of these developments in the US are paralleled in the UK with the Research Assessment Exercise in the promotion of new research standards (Shaw, 2007; 2008).

Currently there are insufficient taxonomies of treatment goals involving the outcomes to be achieved or intervention targets. Even with these national resources on EBP there are few sufficient inventories of interventions that show effectiveness. This is due to the relative paucity of intervention research in our field. Thus it is premature to expect that practitioners have reliable and useful intervention inventories based on assessments of differential effectiveness. Moreover, studies show that few social work practitioners are guided by research (Rosen and Proctor, 2003).

In the US the response to the pressing needs to advance EBP is taking many forms (IASWR, 2008). For example, to foster more EBP in universities, faculty are undertaking syllabi review to ensure that course content addresses critical thinking and an evidence base to the extent that it is available. This is often undertaken in a faculty driven consensus oriented environment.

Critical reflection in research

Reflexivity and critical thinking are key competencies of twenty-first century inquiry and components of EBP (Gambrill, 2000). Critical thinking is essential to evidence based field work internships as well (Thomlinson and Corcoran, 2008). Through an action and reflection cycle, the learning of practitioners and of organizations can be advanced.

The literature on qualitative research in social work has a major focus on reflexivity. Students are interested in understanding the connections between reflexive practice, in social work settings and in research practice (Schön, 1983; White et al., 2006). They are interested to understand the theoretical under-pinnings of these processes and the princi-ples that inform these processes in practice. They want to know how the commitment to engaging in reflexive research practice can be facilitated in research settings. The links between theory and practice are an essential part of this reflexive practice deeply impli-cating the involvement of practitioners in research practice.

Research partnerships are emerging with public and non-profit field work agencies. The design features of some of these partner-ships include literature reviews for practi-tioners, training of staff on EBPs as well as new research programs launched with faculty and field supervisors. In some cases the partnership includes researcher–practitioner collaboration assessing evidence and dis-cerning promising practices that might be tested or adapted for use with new popula-tions or risk factors. Of particular interest to researchers and social service agencies is learning how to incorporate consumer views into research processes and to facilitate opportunities for collaboration in the con-struction of research questions and design (Tregaskis and Goodley, 2005).

A survey of interventions used in social work agencies might show great variability in the adoption of EBP. For example, cogni-tive behavioral treatment is a well recognized evidence based intervention that can be used with a number of populations and risk fac-tors. Even so, its underutilization may be evident in many agencies. This is in part a result of the gap that exists in transferring research findings to practice communities. The structural divides that account for this include the absence of practice friendly research exchanges, the absence of computer as well as internet access in some agencies, lack of continuous learning and improvement systems in agencies, lack of continuing edu-cation courses that build on EBP and the relative inattention to or even discounting among some practitioners of research on treatment effectiveness.

Even so, growing numbers of public sector, governmental agencies that fund social work services in the US now require more inclu-sion of EBP in practice settings. This funder driven expectation that EBP will be utilized heightens the need for a practice based research movement (Wade and Neuman, 2007). To address some of the structural issues, future researchers may be more sys-tematically embedded in field agencies or serve in infomatics roles, mining large data systems to build continuous quality improve-ment programs to advance better outcomes. In fact, future academicians in social work may be more systematically embedded if not housed part time as agency researchers and capacity builders.

Critiques of EBP are also building. These range from concerns about the imposition of dictates for practice to debates over what is considered evidence and worries over the discounting of the expertise of the practi-tioner in favor of prescribed interventions (Gibbs and Gambrill, 2002).

PRACTICE RESEARCH STRATEGIES

Rigor in the profession has been affected by the relative paucity of research practices involving the design and testing of effective interventions. Historically, many social work investigations pursue explanatory research strategies found in traditional university disciplines. Certainly understanding the etiology, prevalence and incidence of a problem is of great concern. Thus explanatory research always needs to be a key facet of the research base for social work. Nonetheless, applied research is foundational to explanatory research as it moves understanding-oriented research to efficacy and effectiveness trials. To advance the need for more practice research we briefly profile several strategies involving intervention, developmental and translational research.

Even though social work is an intervention based discipline because it is first and foremost a practice oriented profession, few intervention studies are published each year (Fraser, 2004). Intervention research involves the design and successive testing of interventions building outcome improvements over time. Described as 'sequential experimentation' (Fraser and Jenson, 2007), intervention research is characterized by iterative testing, refinement and retesting of both interventions and 'doses'. Teams of practitioners may collaborate with researchers on the design and testing of interventions. In one research center, teams were formed. They included a design and measurement group, data collection team, intervention work group, data management and analysis subgroup (Schilling, 1997). While often the intervention is co-constructed with practitioners, faculty researchers can also be the intervention specialists.

Developmental research

As a variation of intervention research, Thomas (1978, 1984, 1994) introduced developmental research. This is an innovative framework for successive intervention design, testing, redesign and scale up. Developmental research strategies build on the iterative, sequential testing and retesting approaches of intervention research with ongoing refinement over successive months or years. Developmental research involves a series of studies to invent new, effective practices and programs.

Developmental research strategies may be useful for building twenty-first century solutions to seemingly intractable problems such as poor school and behavioral health outcomes for children in inner cities and recovery models for addicted parents losing their children to adoption. Setting goals for designing and discovering which practices are effective, developmental research is a relatively underdeveloped approach to intervention research. Both quantitative and qualitative research methods are used in such iterative work. Drawing on meta analyses, an array of knowledge utilization strategies, innovation adaptation, cost benefit analyses and interventive innovations are created (Thomas, 1978; 1984; 1994). Outcome evaluation, procedural guidelines and field testing are key elements in these effectiveness driven research missions. Research guides a continuous learning and improvement system, adapting and adjusting as knowledge and needs develop.

Thomas (1978; 1984; 1994) has delineated the phases of developmental research as analysis, development as well as design evaluation, diffusion and adoption. For example, in the analysis phase, a study is undertaken of the problem or condition to be addressed. This may entail research reviews on the problem or the solicitation of practice knowledge from practitioners. Development involves the creation of the intervention design through information gathering and evaluation of the literature, consultation with peers and practitioners, invention of strategies, translation of research into practice, construction of prototypes and statement of procedures. Evaluation comprises trial and error testing, the collection of evaluative data through single subject case study, group based research, qualitative case studies and ongoing data gathering with testing and retesting as the intervention changes. Through this phase, cost benefit and policy analyses may be undertaken. Diffusion may include materials development for promotional purposes, dissemination in articles, books, manuals and training materials. The adoption phase promotes broad use by fostering investments by public policy leaders (Thomas, 1978; 1984; 1994).

The historic role of the researcher has been one of intervention evaluator and not necessarily intervention developer, staff capacity builder (to ensure fidelity in intervention and in data collection), designer of more advanced intervention strategies, scaling up interventions to other sites, settings, evaluating, refining, adapting and then disseminating. Such ongoing design, development, testing and redesign work requires research partnerships that enable the testing of successive interventions over the years until the desired practices and programs are achieved. It also requires a commitment to continuous professional development of staff and ongoing review of resources so that effective interventions can be sustained over time. These requirements can present challenges to both researchers and community organizations. The nature of such research requires long term investment of funds. One shot evaluation funding, often derived from policy makers' sense of urgency for immediate results and outcome effectiveness, does not enable the development of mechanisms that will ensure that these programs and interventions can be redesigned and retested, then selectively and systematically transferred across settings and populations. This is a significant barrier as few public or private sector policy or program agendas systematically embrace design and development spanning successive years, nor do they facilitate long term inter-organizational research partnerships.

Exemplar 1: Interventions addressing positive youth outcomes

There are, however, examples of this iterative design, development, evaluation, redesign, evaluation and scale up work.

One exemplar is the research program of Hawkins and Catalano in the US (SDRG, 2008). Seeking to promote positive youth development and outcomes they have designed, tested and retested, scaled up, adapted and retested a rigorous set of interventions addressing positive youth outcomes. Through their Social Development Research Group they have been able to map risk and protective factors for positive youth development and to then build intervention programs that avert undesirable outcomes such as substance abuse, teen pregnancy, delinquency, dropping out of school and violence. Key interventions mobilized to reduce risk factors include parental engagement and capacity building (parenting supports and skill development), provision of meaningful social roles for youth along with skill building. These are accompanied by explicit recognition and affirmations (SDRG, 2008). Their multimodal strategies include community mobilization, data driven programs, progress charting of outcomes, strategic resource investments and specific interventions for youth and parents. Together these have been shown to increase protective factors and demonstrate positive results. Their work is applied in a variety of settings, such as schools, when drug use and related risk factors are assessed. Their work also spans community based research involving complex systems changes. Using comparison communities, multiple interventions are tested for differential outcomes (SDRG, 2008). The SDRG example exemplifies how developmental research agendas may be iterative with the intervention or intervention mixes evolving over time.

In some developmental research the intervention(s) may change as do the hypotheses (Springer and Phillips, 1994; Lawson, 1997). While randomized controlled trials remain the gold standard and thus the most desirable research practices, these may not be possible. In fact in some cases of complex systems change, there may be more of a reliance on theory driven evaluation models (Weiss, 2006). While the SDRG has exemplified more rigorous standards of experimental research, in many practice communities and among community change collaborations such research designs may not be as well formulated, feasible or funded as those of SDRG. For this reason the Aspen Institute developed recommendations to address research challenges. The Aspen Institute's work underscores the importance of theory and logic model driven research. In fact, Weiss (1995) has argued that theory and proposition driven research may suffice in those instances in which comparison and control groups are not accessible and especially if the predictive model demonstrates utility.

To that end intervention researchers at a minimum are expected to prepare logic models that depict the problem, theory, assumptions, target populations, interventions, proximal and distal outcomes. Such logic models are reminders that each time interventions are tested, propositions, assumptions and theory are also implicated and need to be made explicit. While there are some who may argue that theory driven research is unnecessary (Thyer, 2001), its utility is most evident in complex systems change research (Weiss, 1995). Moreover to advance practice research the micro-theories of practitioners need to be made explicit (Fraser, 2003).

Translational research

There is longstanding recognition that the transfer of empirically based practices from test sites to scale up sites and to widespread application and adoption may take up to 20 years (New Freedom Commission on Mental Health, 2003). Thus, an effective intervention might take two decades to be adopted in social work practice. This lag is seen by some as part of the ongoing disparity and disconnect between researchers and practitioners as well as consumers. To bridge the gap and time lag, translational research represents a relatively new domain for research practice. It involves systematizing the application and adoption of effective interventions. Translational research aims at more rapid diffusion of research findings as well as the testing of the interventions in new contexts (Brekke et al., 2007). The social work researcher can use information technology as a key resource to help with translational issues. Brekke et al. (2007) detail two phases to translational research. The first entails moving interventions from efficacy to effectiveness trials. The second phase promotes the adoption of a best or more efficacious practice in the community. Translational research is also a key mechanism for promoting more contextual as well as cultural adaptation and testing. One example is cited by Wethington et al. (2007) in the dissemination of EBPs evidence based practices in aging. Necessary conditions for the translational research processes include the provision of stipends for practitioners, along with training and capacity building. Incentives are sometimes provided to ensure that some of these effective approaches are piloted and then scaled up to other sites. Mentoring is also an essential component (Wethington et al., 2007).

EBP and the array of applied research strategies to build practice and programs require knowledge about why certain strategies work and for whom. Qualitative research methodologies ferret out answers to these questions and engage participants in the research in potentially effective ways. In fact, discussion of research on social work interventions from design, testing and translational practices has obscured the role of the study participant. To address this critical issue we turn now to CBPR as a promising form of inquiry for twenty-first century social work researchers as a tool for participant involvement in research. We see CBPR as a major contributor to knowledge building as it can advance action science while creating the conditions for the testing of interventions designed by participants.

CBPR responds to some of the criticisms about EPB research as it involves practitioners in developing research that is relevant to practice settings and, by involving external researchers, questions of rigor still can be addressed. The use of external researchers who research across settings also enables agencies to combine the results of research and develop the most effective interventions across populations and contexts.

COMMUNITY BASED PARTICIPATORY RESEARCH

Many of the ethics and goals of community based research intersect with community building and emancipatory goals. Capacity building, asset enhancing, social capital development values and objectives accompany community based research. The growing use of CBPR responds to the need for researchers to avoid reductionist, exclusionary practices and to provide methodologies for those, often members of oppressed groups, to be key partners. In traditional explanatory or evaluation research the traditional rules of the investigators may count, not those of the community. In community based research, the alliance is with participants who may collaborate on all aspects of the research. They help to define key questions and select the methods to be employed in data gathering, they help to define and interpret variables, and may co-develop and help select the instruments. Not only may they assist in stewarding the data collection, they may also undertake the data collection. When appropriate, they participate in the analysis and interpretation of the data. In addition, they may be co-authors as well as co-presenters of the findings while helping with the dissemination in a wide variety of circles.

Debates around inclusion of participants in research projects are reaching new levels of consensus with action and participatory research approaches (Dominelli, 2005; Humphries, 2005). The commitment to ensuring that participants' voices are heard is one aspect of such research but a major point of interest is also about how their interests are protected. While this can be viewed from the perspective of ethical practice in research it is much wider than the requirements of research ethics committees and includes an understanding of issues such as trust, reciprocity and representation of data (Munford et al., 2008). Moreover, the voices and perspectives of those studied may provide new insights into relevant variables, cogent research for the future and its effective impacts and its translation into other settings.

Exemplar 2: Participant voices

We present an example of CBPR, which depicts the asset enhancing benefits of research. The study utilized qualitative methods to explore the experiences of parents. It was located in three cities in New Zealand and involved nineteen parents with learning disabilities. The research was motivated by a growing awareness that increasing numbers of adults with learning disabilities are becoming parents. For a number of reasons, not only due to their primary disability in learning, these parents face some particular challenges in raising their children successfully. The research aimed to identify and understand the barriers that prevent services from adequately meeting the support needs of these parents. Accordingly, it focused on understanding the mix of complex formal and informal relationships that inform approaches to parenting and examined the way in which past engagement with both mandated and non-mandated care and support systems shaped their experiences. The three-year study recognized the need for longitudinal research in this area in order to understand the history of family and parental development over time. A major focus of the research was on parent–support person relationships from the perspectives of the parents. The data was collected through in-depth qualitative interviews over a period of 36 months. Data relating to support relationships, and legal, policy, funding and administrative factors were collected. We consulted with parents with a learning disability prior to developing the project and throughout the project we received unsolicited feedback from the parents about the research processes. Parents underlined how useful it was to tell their story in their own words and to know that the research had the potential to achieve positive change in support systems.

The project used qualitative methods to explore the meaning of the parents' experiences. The rich and thick descriptions generated in qualitative research enables researchers to explore the lived experiences of participants (Munford and Sanders, 2003) and to understand the complexities of social life including the ordinary and the mundane (Fine et al., 2003). This approach was particularly helpful in this project where the parents had, over many years, experienced complex relationships with service agencies and support systems.

While qualitative research opens up possibilities for insight into the meanings and nature of experience from the perspective of participants, researchers are constantly reminded of the need to be vigilant about the impact of the research on participants' lives (Humphries, 1999). Exploring the experiences of the participants in this study would likely reveal many painful stories but it would also generate many possibilities for new and more informed interpretations of the diverse realities of the participants. We knew we needed to balance the desire to find meaning in the narratives of participants, which once revealed could have positive outcomes for the participants and others (Munford and Sanders 2003), with the potential for disruption that qualitative research can have on the lives of participants. It was also important to ensure that the interpretations we drew from the participants' viewpoints were also checked out with them and that there were opportunities to hear a diverse range of perspectives.

Humphries (1999: 126) presents a constructive challenge to researchers and evaluators when she asks them to consider whether they have a praxis orientation to the research. This orientation alerts researchers to the possibilities for making visible negative practices. What is central to praxis-oriented research is for the researcher to critique their research intentions and practices (Humphries, 1997). It is not simply enough to state that one is engaged in emancipatory research for this research can also perpetuate disadvantage if the researcher does not understand how the knowledge of groups on the margins has been subjugated. Within this perspective researchers need to develop strategies for critical reflection on research processes and on the discourses that have functioned to marginalize some groups. In our experience it has been the world views of practitioners and service providers that have dominated the research stories of people with learning disabilities; these stories have been imbued with taken for granted assumptions of the experience of disability. As Humphries (2005) asserts in her critiques of research practice, a key challenge of critical research is to challenge normative assumptions and to also make the links between personal experience and wider social discourses. Through these practices researchers can challenge reductionist accounts of oppression which do not enable us to understand the nature of oppression as fluid where context is central and where resistance can also be understood.

Involvement of practitioners in research

One of the challenges we face in our research practice is how to involve practitioners as research partners. In participatory approaches practitioners have a strong involvement in all aspects of the research process but this can present challenges as they try to balance the demands of practice and of research. Some of these challenges include: dealing with pressures on time; relationship building; dissemination of research products and the transfer of learning from research outcomes into agency practices.

Often the opportunity to be a research leader will be sufficient for a practitioner who can then negotiate some flexible time from their practice role to undertake the research. More often than not, such research time may require some kind of an incentive or stipend or even require part of their time bought out. In some cases the data that need to be collected require a small addition to the case record, the management information system or quality assurance system and may be low demand for practitioners. Nonetheless, finding ways for them to be aligned with research questions remains a major challenge and is critical to stakeholder ownership of the research.

We cite below an example which depicts the benefits of capacity building to ensure that a practitioner–research facilitator plays a key role in all phases of the research. This facilitator may help to address ethical dilemmas involving protection of human subjects, recruitment of participants and barriers to their participation. Such collaborative practices are essential, as seen in the case below, to help navigate through agency concerns, addressing the contextual barriers for the data collection and helping to promote a safe environment for the participants and agency staff.

Exemplar 3: Practitioners engaged in research

Our research project was a community study of well-being and resilience among young people living in a small urban area in New Zealand (Sanders and Munford, in press). In this project we conceptualized young people as competent and able to effectively articulate their life experiences and to explore with us the many different types of factors that influenced their capacity to be resilient and to experience well-being. We drew on the works of writers such as Gordon (2000); Mayall (2001) and Ungar (2004; 2005) who with others highlight the key contribution research can make in providing vehicles through which youth can achieve greater voice, generating research findings and results grounded in these voices. Historically policy and practice have been developed within adult frames of reference, taking little account of the perspectives of young people. Youth have been seen as relatively passive recipients of adult attention and little effort has been invested in trying to establish how they come to the position where they manifest troubled and troubling behaviors.

Our project located itself within the new youth studies paradigm. As researchers we considered that we had much to learn from young people about their worlds and about how adults could support them to effectively confront adversity, to recognize and draw on their own resilience, and to develop their own capacities to experience well-being. Participatory action methods provided a powerful set of technologies but in using these approaches we confronted some important ethical and methodological challenges, particularly in relation to recruiting young people who were facing the most adversity and who daily needed to deal with significant challenges. In the study we were able to work with 15 young people, their families and key support people. As background information to the study we documented the work of the community agency and met with the support workers to learn about their work with young people. We used a variety of techniques for gathering information from the young people and while the interview was the primary data gathering tool, young people chose other mechanisms for telling their story including constructing life stories, drawing, writing and presenting music and writing their answers to interview questions rather than talking about these.

Researchers need to give very careful consideration to the processes used to collect essential information while protecting the right to privacy of young people who participate in research. From a methodological point of view, these young people can be quite hard to locate and recruit; they are not typically trusting of adults and will often be reluctant to tell strangers their stories (Munford and Sanders, 2004; Sanders and Munford, 2005). Navigating through these issues reinforced for us the value of building a collaborative relationship with a community based agency (Reid and Vianna, 2001). This approach meant that there was separation between us and the young people until they had agreed to participate. It also meant that youth had access to ongoing support throughout the project. Our approach to the community agency coincided with an approach from their community social worker to undertake her Masters' studies through our University. She wanted to use participatory research methods to develop her social work practice and to explore its potential for the development of her agency's overall approach to working with young people. What this allowed us to do was to employ a field-researcher who was known and trusted by the young people. This situation raised its own ethical issues. For instance, we needed to exercise considerable care to ensure that information she was privy to as a social worker did not become part of the research data. We also needed to ensure that youth did not feel compelled to participate because they were receiving support from the person who was our fieldworker. Resolving these issues took time as we worked with the agency and our University's Ethics Committee to develop protocols to protect

both the young people and the social worker.

The wider research team, including the community agency and the field-researcher, agreed on the protocols to be followed throughout the project. The community agency retained control of who would be approached to be in the study and talked with the young people about the research including what involvement in the research would require of them. The young people were informed of the ethical protocols that would enable them to retain control over what they shared with an interviewer and how this material was to be used. They knew that they could withdraw from a particular research situation at any time and from the study without any consequences for the support they would receive from the agency. It was important that the young people knew from the outset that receiving services from the agency was not contingent upon being involved in the research project.

During the project we used strategies to reinforce the difference between the research and social work practice. These included holding research interviews in locations chosen by the young people and clearly separating these from any social work support work. The field-researcher carefully explained the difference between the research interview schedule and the tools used to gather information for a social work intervention. The field-researcher had regular debriefs with the research team to ensure that research processes were not interrupting support work with young people and to raise any issues about the research and its impact on agency work.

The careful negotiations and decisions around research protocols produced benefits for the research, the social worker and the agency, as well as for the young people involved. It allowed us to learn significantly more about the practice of social work with young people, to gather a greater depth of information and to engage the young people and agency staff in the transfer of research learning into everyday life. This research project provided us with the opportunity to observe the ways in which research knowledge can contribute to the development of more effective practice with vulnerable young people.

CROSS-NATIONAL RESEARCH COLLABORATIVES

The world is a laboratory of innovation with marked opportunities for cross-national information and technology transfer. Discoveries of promising practices among indigenous peers in rural communities in one nation may inform inner city pilots in industrialized countries. For example, the work of New Zealand Maori (indigenous) social workers alongside their non-Maori counterparts in developing 'just therapy', a culturally inclusive intervention (Waldegrave, 2000) or the design of Family Group Conferencing (FGC) in New Zealand (Burford and Hudson, 2000) are reaching new levels of utilization in the US. In fact, FGC is commanding increasing attention among policy makers, practitioners and social work researchers in child welfare, juvenile justice and even adult services involving care coordination for the aging. The need for innovative solutions to social needs and problems makes the rapid diffusion of ideas most pressing. An innovation may emerge in one nation, such as FGC, and even without years of rigorous testing be quickly adopted elsewhere. In the US social work researchers have been attempting to keep pace with the demand for replication of the family group conferencing approach. In some states, FGC is required, despite only a handful of empirical studies currently available. Nonetheless, the rapid involvement of key family stakeholders and problem solvers demonstrate utility in practice and policy even though the rigorous research is lacking. The point is that many innovations crafted in one part of the world may offer the ingenuity and promise to solve problems elsewhere. Social work researchers play key roles in this innovation transfer and in testing effectiveness in a range of settings. One very discerning research enterprise involves the development of cross-national systematic studies.

Systematic studies and cross-national work

Promising directions for the practice of social work research are illustrated by the cross-national work of the Campbell and the Cochran Collaboratives. These are cross-national knowledge synthesis and evaluation networks involving research volunteers from such countries as the UK, Europe, Canada, the US, China and South Africa. Research syntheses help to inform efficacy questions and to foster more knowledge brokering involving research reviews for practitioners and policy makers. The Campbell Collaborative houses the social welfare research syntheses and systematic studies. As a cross-national work group, these research colleagues have established protocols for reviews, undertaken research syntheses and critiques, published reports and fostered wide dissemination and utilization of findings. Systematic reviews include the bibliographic search for studies of effectiveness and a re-analysis of the data, using standardized coding and protocols applied across studies. When the studies and findings are summarized, they are subjected to peer review and critique. A users group then distils the findings and prepares briefs for policy makers and practitioners. Such work also involves collaboration with economists on cost–benefit analyses so that the program costs can be calculated against the benefits. Single subject case studies are also being used for systematic review. These reviews have gained stature and have helped to inform public policy decisions.

For example, several years ago Julia Littell (2005) in the US led a Campbell Collaborative in a systematic review of Multisystemic Family Therapy (MFT). Popular among some US policy makers and social service programs in the US, MFT promotes services to high risk youth who are in and out of home placements and incarceration. Based on Littell's (2005) systematic review, the program that had claimed efficacy is now being questioned as her international research team has shown the need for more rigorous efficacy trials. In fact the re-analysis of prior published outcome findings suggests that there were no differential benefits of MFT over other programs. The data re-analysis and synthesis showed some of the weakness in prior studies and has helped to foster more discerning utilization practices. In fact, policy makers have been given tools now to both question investments in MFT and incentives to fund more rigorous studies of effectiveness.

In contrast to the MFT review, some data re-analyses can elevate programs that might have been dismissed in the past as having less than desirable effectiveness. One example is intensive family preservation programs (IFP) used to promote out of home placement prevention in child welfare. Helping families reduce risk factors and increase protective factors required a program of interventions that comprised development and research most effectively undertaken by Homebuilders in Washington State in the 1980s and 1990s. While Homebuilders showed promising success, the absence of fidelity when replicated and poor research conditions created less effective child welfare outcomes. Policy makers in states and counties in the US, instead of seeking to advance these innovations, dismantled and defunded them. The family preservation movement that emerged as the public policy framework for much child welfare practice in the US became quickly impeded when the necessary conditions for successful replication and adaptation were not in place. Recently, the Washington State Institute for Public Policy (2008) undertook a systematic review of intensive family preservation effectiveness

studies that adhered to the Homebuilders Model. They found that those with fidelity to Homebuilders reduced out of home placements and reoccurrence of abuse and neglect. Their re-analysis now suggests more promising outcomes than previously held which may help to foster a reinvestment by policy makers in the Homebuilders program. They further estimated that homebuilder-like programs produce $2.54 of benefits for each dollar of cost (Washington State Institute for Public Policy, 2008).

Other systematic reviews now underway with the Campbell Collaborative include Functional Family Therapy and the popular New Zealand Family Group Conferencing program, used widely in the US, Canada and New Zealand. While a major asset in cross-national consensus building around effectiveness questions, these systematic reviews and the data syntheses have been met with some scepticism (Fischer, 1990). Data syntheses and reanalyses involve published studies generally showing significance and positive results. This is a by-product of the peer review and publishing bias, favoring research showing positive rather than negative results.

INCLUSIONARY RESEARCH PRACTICES FOR THE TWENTY-FIRST CENTURY

The wide range of research practices comprising new century inquiry provide social work investigators with a broad tool kit for knowledge building, practice and policy research. Because many studies are enhanced by both qualitative and quantitative methods, it is expected that mixed methods will increasingly be the norm in many research practices. Such multiplism provides multidimensional data offering more discerning and sometimes more comprehensive answers to research questions.

While the gold standard in developing evidence involves randomized controlled trials, much of this is not possible in social work due to the ethical prohibitions involving leaving some populations untreated. Nonetheless, research rigor and relevance remain major concerns for the profession's future and status.

A key focus in research practice in all countries is the challenge to researchers to provide evidence that their research is culturally sensitive and that research approaches are informed by an understanding of the cultural norms of particular individuals and groups. While this inclusionary goal can apply to a diverse range of groups, a primary focus in New Zealand, for example, is on researchers' relationships with the indigenous population. The debates focus on both research processes and research outcomes and on defining the nature of the research and how researchers will incorporate cultural practices into their research practice (Walker et al., 2006). Culturally relevant research programs generally have an explicit goal of enhancing the influence of cultural knowledge in determining research questions, practices and outcomes including creating new opportunities for innovative research dissemination and uptake.

The growing diversity of the many research populations creates challenges for researchers and the research enterprise worldwide. Such diversity warrants great caution if not 'cultural humility' (Faller and Ortega, 2008) among researcher investigators. For example, while still needing to be validated empirically, it is believed that culturally competent research strategies and knowledge need to inform all facets of the research process. This includes the intervention to be designed and tested as well as the data collection and analysis. Ortega and Richey (1998) argue that promoting methodological diversity is also one facet to this culturally inclusive research.

Measures need to be validated across diverse populations. The variables to be studied also require culturally competent researchers (Ortega and Richey, 1998). Attention to the data gathering team members and their cultural congruence with the research participants may also be a critical attribute of cultural competence of the researcher. Despite what may be promising or even highly ranked for evidentiary rigor may, nonetheless, be subject to empirical questioning and cross-cultural adaptation in differing contexts and among different groups. Thus twenty-first century social work researchers are challenged to be equipped with diverse competencies including skills in mixed methods, and where appropriate intervention research and translational research along with culturally competent investigations.

Inclusionary research challenges for this new century also involve interdisciplinary and international research undertakings. For example, multisite and multinational studies of shared interventions such as Family Group Conferences might unite researchers in new ways while advancing practice knowledge.

Multinational research is an even more pressing and compelling agenda as globalization and its effects, both positive and negative, generate new areas for inquiry. Moreover, most of our nations are united by the human costs of exclusion and discriminatory practices along with the consequences of fluctuating market economies and underdeveloped welfare with insufficient employment or income guarantees. Thus, transnational research may be warranted as current paradigms for twenty-first century market economies and welfare states are affected by global recessions. This book may be one of the stepping stones in this quest for more inclusionary, cross-national collaboration and joint agenda setting for future research.

Domains of Social Work Research

21

Nation

Linda Briskman

INTRODUCTION

The concept of nation is elusive and its enactment in neo-conservative environments is interlinked with constructs of nationalism, monoculturalism, assimilation, control, 'superiority' and protectionism rather than embracing inclusivity. Definitions of research can be equally elusive and the relationship between the two is complex. This chapter argues that it may be necessary to move beyond traditional research paradigms to consider what research might look like if we wish to challenge 'evidence' presented to support policies antithetical to human rights. This may also necessitate challenging the normative 'gate-keeping' role that ethics bodies perform, creating pressure upon them to extend research hegemony for the greater good of communities, states and the international domain. It is also argued that research with politicized groups within nations may not follow a standard format (that is: including literature review, question posing, selecting methodology, collecting data and analysing results).

One reason for this is that, arguably, social work has an ethical and moral duty to move beyond the realm of everyday practice to explore critical issues that impact on the well-being of not only individuals and communities, but also the health of the nation and the world. How this can be achieved through research remains relatively unexplored. This chapter discusses the consequences of drawing on social work ethics, theories and expertise in research to challenge inequity and to advocate for social change by examining national and international issues that directly and indirectly impact on the profession. In so doing it proposes a broad view of research beyond established paradigms and posits that social workers can reposition themselves as active ethnographers in their endeavours. It is proposed that contemplating social workers as practice ethnographers could provide a means of legitimating entry into the political research realm. This integrates the cultural, practice and policy immersion that occurs within social work practice with vulnerable groups. Although outlining some exploratory research principles, this is not a 'how to' chapter, but rather one which challenges the hidden orthodoxies and paradigms of research and advocates for the overt recognition of the political nature of research, enabling social workers to more consciously engage with the political context of their work. As such it does not advocate a 'new methodology' but a rethinking of how such research might be a device for contributing to change in complex political times and how social workers may be able to draw on their knowledge base for this purpose.

In promoting this position the chapter extends the boundaries of conventional practice research, calling on both experienced and novice social work researchers to use social work ethics, practice wisdom and theoretical knowledge to investigate some of the most pressing questions facing nation states today, both domestically and internationally. Such research can, and should, complement existing research and practice endeavours. Three exemplars that are familiar to many social workers illustrate this call. These are:

1 people movements, asylum seekers and refugees;
2 indigenous peoples; and
3 development, world poverty and aid.

All three case studies broach issues relating to the human rights of all peoples and the obligation of social work to contribute to policies, practices and research that ensure that core human rights tenets are adhered to and not violated. They raise questions of 'race' and 'power', concepts that are familiar to social workers. In selecting these case studies the words of Oxfam (2007) resonate: that respect for human rights should be measured by a country's actions towards the most vulnerable, not the most fortunate. By the very nature of its mission, social work deals with the most vulnerable in society and hence has an obligation to assess the impact of the actions of governments in relation to excluded groups. This can be done in a range of ways but ethical change-focused research with a political basis is one significant contribution for social work and can complement less overtly political research activities.

Consistent with this approach, the adoption of the definition of research coined by Anthony Smith and Marian Pitts (2007) is utilized in this chapter particularly as it dispels the myth of research expertise as separate to practice expertise:

> ... we define research very broadly: research is purposive knowledge generation. That is, we set out explicitly to create knowledge in relation to a specific set of problems or challenges. Given such a broad definition of research, we consequently include in the pool of those we consider researchers: students, practitioners, academics and other gatherers of information (Smith and Pitts, 2007: 4).

This chapter adopts a critical stance by challenging the type of evidence-based practice that is dependent on positivist and behaviourist methods. These traditional methods may be more concerned with changing behaviour of those refusing to or unable to conform, rather than creating a critical understanding of people's circumstances (Humphries, 2004a: 37). This challenge is pivotal for research that aims to contribute to the overturn of dominant worldviews, political manoeuvrings and the community attitudes that endorse harmful policies and practices.

Within the existing power structures of societies, asylum seekers, Indigenous peoples and 'developing' nations are among those frequently conceptualized as being marginalized. Although using the term marginalized from time to time to reflect the literature, for the purpose of this chapter I prefer to adopt the concept of vulnerable groups or even 'politicized groups' as these terms avoid the vexed notion of 'centre' and 'margin' that reinforces uneven power relations. The groups referred to are also described in research terms as 'hard to reach' groups (Hurley, 2007: 160), and the challenge for social work here is for creative, context-driven approaches to reach such groups and frame sound research practice.

RATIONALE

Social work has a long-standing commitment to social justice and human rights and these are clearly articulated in codes of ethics and through the work of the International Federation of Social Workers. In devising a code of ethics for social work research, Butler (2002) argues for the ethics of social work research to be grounded in the ethics of social work and Hugman, in Chapter 9 of this volume, explores these issues.

Despite this, other professions more readily respond to researching complex political and social issues than social work, but such research should not be the mere preserve of social scientists, politics scholars, journalists, lawyers, psychologists and health professionals. Like other professions, social work has the value base and the expertise to undertake such research in its own right. It also has the networks to partner with a range of professional and advocacy groups, particularly those which have a shared value base and challenge the concept of research neutrality in order to contribute to social change.

Taking a human rights and common humanity perspective, it becomes clear that some of the most contested issues facing the world today are constructed by dominant national groups. Critical research endeavours can contribute to solutions through resistance to hegemonic paradigms and the production of emancipatory questions and methods. The liberatory potential of Foucault's notion of discourse underpins this thinking as it provides the possibility of creating alternative discourses and repositioning ourselves against dominant ones (Pease and Fook, 1999b: 15).

Social good arising from research must be to the forefront and political advocacy forms both the motivation and the desired outcome. The Australian historian Henry Reynolds (cited in McGrath, 1995: 371) speaks of how his research endeavours are motivated by a desire to change an ignorant, racist society. In enacting such a vision social work has an obligation and the knowledge and theoretical and policy expertise to play a part in social and structural change. Specifically, this can take place by attesting to how the status quo harms the most marginalized in society and erodes their civil, social, economic and collective rights (see e.g. British Association of Social Workers, 2007; Briskman et al., 2008).

In this sense, research that explores the concept of 'nation' pushes the boundaries of received wisdom on how research should be conducted both methodologically and

ethically. The voices of politicised groups which are intentionally shut out from decision-making should be at the forefront of data collection. This sometimes requires less predictable methods. For example, in order to conduct such research it may be nigh impossible to conduct research that fully adheres to accepted research ethics. These may require re-consideration and reframing because of the particular exclusionary context. This challenges one view of research ethics that suggests that morality can be reduced to generalizable rules that are applicable to all research situations (Ferdinand et al., 2007: 534). Refugee research requires a different approach because refugee voices are often hidden from the public domain through a long wait in camps or due to incarceration in immigration detention and access to information gatherers is restricted by a fear of speaking out (see for example the work of Harrell-Bond and Voutira, 2007).

There are similar issues in conducting research with Indigenous peoples. In addition to following now accepted universal and codified guidelines for conducting such research, the wisdom of both the elders and Indigenous academics and practitioners enables us to have some 'outsider' insight into how Indigenous peoples see the problems that have been created by colonizing nation states. In dealing with questions of development and world poverty, there is an argument to research-enable international aid workers at the front line to assist in documenting and exposing the impact of policies on the poorest peoples of the world. This may be a difficult area to negotiate in some contexts, for example where aid workers are involved in disaster relief or where pressing needs of survival in these countries may detract from less pressing research imperatives. There is hence increasing urgency to conduct research on nation for as will be demonstrated, governments and others with power are often quick to draw on shaky evidence to propose policies that may be antithetical to human rights and core social work principles.

UNRAVELLING NATION

As noted earlier in the chapter, in the twenty-first century the concept of nation is elusive; indeed it is also contested. Globalization is the catch-cry implying internationalism, cooperation and universality beyond nation states. At the same time that predominantly western nations cooperate on economic endeavours, the so-called 'war on terror' and, to varying degrees, humanitarian obligations, individual nations retreat into their territorial bunkers in a number of policy domains. These include border control to restrict movements of people, aid programmes that serve national donor interests, and resistance to Indigenous rights as a threat to national sovereignty.

Given this new world order in which social work is a player, the profession can no longer limit its research to the comfort zone of the mainstream. In the geopolitics of today, there is a pressing need for social work research to engage with the way in which dominant discourses that impact on the lives of the citizenry are discordant with the value base of social work. Despite difficulties arising in neo-conservative environments, many social workers find creative ways to integrate critical practice and advocacy, and examples of this are increasingly evident in the literature (see e.g. Pease and Fook, 1999b; Allan et al., 2003). Less explored is the application of political advocacy research in which social workers can contribute to policy debates, information flow and exposure of capricious practices. Sharing knowledge within nations and trans-nationally is an essential ingredient for political social research.

Research beyond the margins has the potential to expose the exclusionary nature of 'nation' and how this can be turned around so that those not part of the dominant structure of society can have their rights realized. In this, social work research needs to be critical and political in challenging mono-cultural dimensions of nationhood. Thinking on 'race' must underpin the analysis as this underlies much of the exclusionary basis of societies today. Furthermore, power relations evoke reactions in critical social workers in a range of fields of practice. Social workers need also to consider how power relations require careful consideration in the research domain. As noted by Smith and Pitts (2007: 10) there has been a challenge to researchers viewed as being in positions of authority over research participants, with more egalitarian frameworks emerging.

An added complicating dimension is that the ideology of nation becomes blurred with an increasing nationalism and nationalistic fervour that pervades states today, including western countries. As Spencer and Wollman (2007: 81) expound, substantial disagreement exists as to what makes a nation in the first place and with different emphases placed on issues of identity, culture, language, history, myth, memory and territory. At root, they suggest (2007: 81), the ideology of nationalism imagines the world in a particular way as made up of nations and communities in which people share a common national identity that involves a fundamental distinction between the national self and the other, variously conceived but generally in a negative light. This is evident in the way the leadership of various countries has conceived of 'nation'. Alaine Touraine (2000) speaks of how the ideal of the nation state has degenerated into an aggressive nationalism. Former Australian Prime Minister John Howard spoke with little public challenge of how all those who come to Australia are expected to make an overriding commitment to Australian democratic values and to enrich the country with their loyalty and patriotism (Howard, 2006). Similarly, in Britain, Kundnani (2007) speaks of the politics of a phoney Britishness rather than a genuine universalism. This is consistent with the thesis of Spencer and Wollman (2007: 82) that in the view of 'nationalists', national identity takes precedence over other identities. For social workers, who proclaim concepts of diversity, multiculturalism and acceptance, this form of nationalism contradicts the basic tenets of moral practice through the imposition of dominant meanings of identity and belonging that contradict the acclamation of difference. This is also played out in the Indigenous realm in many countries where governments, often insidiously, denigrate Indigenous lifeways and spirituality that is cast in moves that are reminiscent of earlier assimilation policies.

RESEARCH AS MORAL PRACTICE

The majority of social workers are employed in direct practice settings. Once leaving the academy few conduct research although the importance of practice research is becoming increasingly recognized in order to inform ways of working with vulnerable groups. Less explored is the potential, and indeed obligation, for social workers to draw on their social work skills, knowledge and practice experience to examine some of the broader problems facing the world which directly and indirectly impact upon their practice contexts. Humphries suggests that social work has choices to make about a new moral effort to engage its knowledge about sources of inequality with a new sense of imperative and urgency. Voices of resistance, she reassures, have never been silenced (2004a: 39).

The challenge for social work research and practice is how to critically interrogate pervading ideologies in order to move policy, political consciousness and practice into the ethical realm (Briskman and Babacan, 2008). By its very nature social work should always be moral practice but not all practitioners overtly subscribe to a moral practice imperative. If we propose the tenet of moral practice then our obligation to rigorously present issues of concern through research endeavours becomes more obvious. Although not pervasive in all countries, there are many contexts where social workers perceive a dichotomy in social work as either conventional or progressive (Mullaly, 1993) and this

distinction can restrict the integration of practice with political endeavour. Social work has always incorporated a more radical element but the dichotomy in the way social work may be practiced regrettably continues. This is partly due to resistance to melding an individual focus with a critical and structural approach (Briskman, 2007).

For many, social work is largely organizational practice and there is a wealth of literature that discusses how organizations can be sites of tension for social workers as their practice ideals are subsumed by the organizational mission (see for example Hough and Briskman, 2003; Lymbery and Butler, 2004). But social work needs to think beyond the constraints of genre, field, method and established policy in order to take on a leadership that necessitates both political positioning and critical reflection. If we accept this basic stance, social workers operating at the most micro-level can gather information that assists in the interrogation of policies and practices. In order to advance our research mission we can take heed from anthropologists who not only explore distant places but conduct research on cultural settings closer to home (Atkinson et al., 2001: 2). For example hospital social workers can question the cultural appropriateness of medical practices and can also create wider understandings by delving into the issues that may be facing those with whom they work arising from journeys of persecution, flight and resettlement. For those working in child and family settings with Indigenous people social workers can listen directly to their experiences and document what barriers their services present and how they might be overcome. This is consistent with an ethnography grounded in a commitment to the first-hand experience and exploration of a particular social or cultural setting based on participant observation (Atkinson et al., 2001: 4). It is a small step from direct practice experience and observation to the incorporation of a researcher lens in settings in which social workers are familiar.

In many societies the freedom to conduct research is neither automatic nor absolute (Harrell-Bond and Voutira, 2007: 285). In most western societies constraints are not imposed through government repression or fear of consequences for exposing perceived injustices. The constraints that do exist for most social workers in the west are primarily organizational, ethical or self imposed. With some creativity they are able to be navigated for the achievement of social justice.

There are obstacles to social workers ensuring that ethics and human rights are at the forefront of their research activities. Taking an overtly political stance, which implies taking the privatized world of practice into the public arena, directly challenges the notion of research 'objectivity' and asks social workers to be partisan. Although all social work research ideally has change as a focus much of this does not challenge dominant systems and structures. Research that is truly political upturns dominant accounts in a robust way. The desirability of overtly political research may be contested by more traditional researchers focusing on micro-practice and by those who reject the notion that activism is an inherent a part of social work. For example a study by the National Association of Scholars in the United States concluded that descriptions of social work education programs were 'chock full of ideological boilerplate and statements of political commitment' (NAS, 2007). Rather than trying to defend itself against such accusations, social work is well placed to argue that its value stance is important and that politics matter including in research. It is unrealistic to expect researchers to remain passive and objective in many of the situations in which they find themselves (Ferdinand et al., 2007: 521). Where research is politically inclined and sees 'the purpose of ethnography as being about emancipatory change, to help make the world a better place' the question of ethical responsibility is tackled directly with critical social workers subscribing to the view that it is not enough

to merely observe the world and to understand it, but to change it (Ferdinand et al., 2007: 531–2).

It is likely that some social work researchers will see a tension between ethical research and 'rigorous' research, particularly those who subscribe to established research conventions. It needs to be remembered that rigour is not achieved by unquestioning conformity to rules but rather a need to ensure that ethical principles are adhered to throughout a research process and that the best possible methods are applied to the research question (Smith and Pitts, 2007: 11). However this is not straightforward. Ferdinand et al. (2007: 540) warn that codes of ethics have the regrettable potential to silence voices that do not fit within the dominant views of ethical research standards. If we are complicit in this silencing, they say, we as researchers are behaving unethically.

Given the ethical stand of social work our research must be guided by a belief that it is in the public interest to expose the policies that undermine our value base and that it is indeed a professional responsibility. In taking such a stance the profession can become more visible in contexts where human rights are violated. There remains the question of moral responsibility and collective action, a question raised in relation to the silence occurring in countries where evil acts take place. If it is in our power as 'practice ethnographers' to expose harm, then it is only a small step to using this knowledge to help in preventing malevolent policies and to execute our moral responsibility when those being oppressed are effectively silenced through the political system or when their attempts to exercise resistance are quelled. Through in-depth research-generated knowledge of how oppression is imposed and maintained, social work researchers are well positioned to confront the social imposition of disadvantage, within the limits of their practice settings and own knowledge base, through integrating practice and research ethnography with other fields and methods of research activity.

THEORETICAL LEADS

There are a number of theoretical frameworks familiar to social workers that help push the boundaries of researching nation. These include the social construction of whiteness, colonialism, racism, human rights and citizenship.

Theories of 'whiteness', stemming from the work of Ruth Frankenburg in the United States, help understanding of the ways in which the dominant society inoculates us against difference (Barthes, cited in Sandoval, 1997: 88). Recognizing the power of whiteness and dominance enables us to see how the concept of race, for example, still has the power to generate hatred, oppression and violence (Quinn, 2003: 89). When 'whiteness' is the unquestioned norm against which everything else is measured we observe the power this invokes (Briskman, 2007: 26) and can begin to understand how those 'othered' in the interests of 'nation' are never truly accepted. This is evident in the examples given whereby Indigenous peoples are seen as never quite meeting the 'conditions' of being 'white', where the Muslim 'other' who represent a percentage of refugee populations, are represented as violent and fanatical (Perera, 2002: 28) and where those in the 'third world' are perceived as lacking in civilization and requiring democratizing and capitalist economic reform. Similar constructs are evident in a number of countries where we observe how notions of a hierarchy of 'race' cause suffering and discrimination. Understanding what is happening in national contexts in these domains is foundational to the conduct of research.

An understanding of colonialism is essential to development research and research with Indigenous populations. Colonialist constructs are linked back to the Enlightenment period of the eighteenth century and the associated belief in the superiority of those at a higher stage on the so-called journey of progress. These constructs provided justification for the domination of nations deemed inferior in order to absorb them into western ways of being (Ife, 2001: 64). The institutional

vestiges of colonialism may have vanished in most of the world, but the way aid is implemented and the manner in which Indigenous peoples are dominated demonstrates the pervasiveness of colonialism and the mythology that we are in a post-colonial era.

As already noted, race, domination and oppression still pervade the way in which contemporary society sees difference (Ratcliffe, 2004: 16). Racism is at the heart of the exclusion within and outside nation and although a social construct it raises questions of how beliefs, statements and acts make certain groups inferior on the basis that they do not belong to the culture of the dominant group within the state apparatus (Hollinsworth, 1997). Race is no longer seen as an explanatory construct but has been refocussed as racism based on an ideology of domination and exclusion (Torres et al., 1999: 2). Here people are classified according to a norm, setting up a symbolic boundary between acceptable and unacceptable, the normal and the deviant (Torres et al., 1999: 8). This can be applied to those excluded from the formal citizenry (refugees), for those included but never fully accepted (Indigenous peoples) and those outside the 'benevolent' nation (the developing world) where beliefs, values and cultural practices may be insidiously denigrated in order to impose western beliefs. Racism may be shrouded and unrecognized in organizations where social workers are employed and not contested. This institutional racism requires social workers to consider their ethnographic potential through gathering, analysing and disseminating information that is embedded in policy documents and procedural guidelines, or covert in organizational cultures. Failure to do so implies an uncritical and unquestioning acceptance of organizational norms. A critical approach to social work practice that goes alongside such data gathering has the power to influence the removal of harmful policies that impact on social work practice.

A human rights framework provides some lead for research that exposes policies that violate basic human rights tenets whether at the level of civil, political, economic, social or collective rights. Taking a human rights stance, that can be gleaned from social work codes of ethics and documents such as the Universal Declaration of Human Rights, can assist in providing social workers with what Ife (2001: viii) describes as a moral basis for their practice. Rethinking research within a human rights paradigm enables social work to recast the practices it observes. This is nowhere clearer than in the realm of asylum seekers and Indigenous rights where the capriciousness of government responses create the need for human rights vigilance and exposure of violations.

Social citizenship is another area that provides a basis for assessing who is included in the body politic and who is excluded. Ruth Lister in her work on feminist citizenship argues that inclusion and exclusion represent the two sides of the citizenship coin. She explains that while much of the citizenship literature focuses on inclusion, more radical approaches portray citizenship as a force of exclusion (Lister, 1997: 42). For social work researchers approaches to the provision of services can be documented and interrogated to evidence exclusion from citizenship in all its forms. For example in Australia, as we shall see, Indigenous people are subject to discriminatory policies that are not applied to other groups. In a number of countries refugees and particularly asylum seekers are excluded from the range of rights and benefits afforded to other people resident in a nation (Briskman et al., 2008). Social work research on such pressing issues confronting nations can help reframe 'difference' as a desirable trait and not a liability.

MELDING ETHICS, THEORIES AND POLITICS: TAKING THE RESEARCH LEAP

The three examples analysed later in this chapter demonstrate how a counter discourse is required to challenge dominant voices. The research of Iain Lygo provides some leads. Lygo analysed extracts of readers' comments in tabloid newspapers in Australia, which are a clear indication of the need to turn around populist sentiment. The following quote exemplifies the type of obtuse sentiment that requires challenging:

> I would like to know also why Muslims insist upon coming here hating our customs, our beliefs our lifestyle and our religion as they do? (cited in Lygo, 2004: 1)

This is mirrored in Britain where a prevailing ideology suggests that Muslims are inherently at odds with modern values, into which they need to be forcibly integrated (Kundnani, 2007). But prevailing views can be turned around. Asylum seeking can be perceived as a site of danger to national identity, security or wealth or it can be seen as part of the process for enriching the cultural life of a nation (Collett, 2004: 77). Similarly, for Australian Aboriginal people, Pedersen et al. (2005: 171) conducted research that exposed the widely held false beliefs about Indigenous Australians including excessive alcohol consumption and the receipt of benefits over and above other Australians. Such research is critical in exposing prejudices and hence providing leverage to challenge and overturn them, in affirming the special place of Indigenous peoples within nation states and valuing their cultures and in honouring aspirations for self-determination, sovereignty and retention of culture.

The exemplars below reveal how research in differing guises is worth persevering despite obstacles that may be presented by research communities or by ruling elites. Refugees are often so marginalized they are unable to be research participants and have their voices heard. This may mean a reconsideration of what constitutes research to work for a common good. In research in developing countries research can move from being an afterthought in a world where disadvantage reaps chaos in terms of poverty, AIDS, war and famine for example. Alongside their everyday practice, social workers by adopting research ethnography can integrate into practice a means of utilizing their knowledge for positive change. In the developing world, it could be argued that social workers, at the very least, have an obligation to inform the citizenry of donor countries of the impact of externally imposed dictates upon the people with whom they work. This is not to minimize the difficulties such research may confront, particularly normative research ethics standards and organizational privacy provisions to which many social workers are expected to adhere. However, the complexities can be dispelled. In terms of research ethics for example Ferdinand et al. (2007: 520) call upon researchers to assess the situation in which they conduct their research. In regard to advocacy and speaking out, many human services workers have openly breached such clauses for what they see as a greater good in exposing practices they have deemed immoral (Australian Council of Heads of Schools of Social Work, 2006).

How can social workers position themselves as research activists in these ways? From my own experience transformation to ethnographic political insights usually arises from hindsight and when one is removed from the context. For me there were some key past experiences that guide my research explorations today including living and working in a rural town where Indigenous people were denigrated and discriminated against; being part of the refugee movement and observing the tribulations of immigration detention through visits and friendships; and through the experience of living and working in Papua New Guinea where I directly observed the results of continuing colonial practices despite the formal independence that had been granted. Although critical reflection and the wisdom of hindsight is important, it is even more crucial for social workers to take a lead by working with foresight, vision and action that link with the exploratory principles that will be advocated later in the chapter.

The three exemplars that follow – people movements, indigenous peoples and

development – illustrate the prospects and limitations for research that focuses on concepts of nation.

Exemplar 1: People movements, asylum seekers and refugees

Through their training and direct practice, many social workers are familiar with the plight of refugees and sometimes less so with asylum seekers who are still awaiting determination of their refugee claims. Hannah Arendt (1986: 269) disturbingly but aptly tells us that refugees have been considered as the 'the scum of the earth'. Their human rights have been obfuscated (Gosden, 2007: 162). Officials at the United Nations speak of 'problems without passports' (Kundnani, 2007: 1). With asylum seekers a human rights discourse is turned upside down with the rights of asylum seekers violated in the name of sovereign rights as absolute and non-negotiable in order to control national borders (Every, 2006, cited in Gosden, 2007: 151).

Some creative and important research and advocacy has been conducted in this realm. A research project underway in Australia on Caring for Asylum Seekers in Australia: Bioethics and Human Rights[1] is conducting interviews with health professionals who have participated in the delivery of health care to asylum seekers in detention centres to explore the dilemmas and the ethics of such involvement. Pushing the boundaries further, the Australian Council of Heads of Schools of Social Work initiated a People's Inquiry into Detention (Briskman et al., 2008) in order to record the voices of those affected by immigration detention with the dual aims of influencing policy and placing the stories of detention on the public record. Although an inquiry is not traditional research, it had at its core the duty of social work to use its knowledge and skills to investigate a shameful period in

Australia's history. This endeavour was not entered by passive observers but those involved were civically and politically informed individuals with their own personal moral views and values (Ferdinand et al., 2007: 532). Social work knowledge and observation is also disseminated in other ways including newspaper opinion pieces (see for example Goddard, 2004).

In the United Kingdom, Steven Cohen (2004: 9) draws upon professional expertise to highlight the problems associated with the National Asylum Support Service (NASS) that he sees as a modern poor law for asylum seekers, as it is provision outside the welfare state based on forced dispersal into sub-standard accommodation with less income support than is granted to others. He suggests that local authorities and voluntary sector agencies are placing themselves in a politically impossible position by cooperating with NASS. Although such a viewpoint did not arise from the conduct of formal research it was the knowledge base of social work that enabled members of the profession to speak with confidence, consistent with an ethnographic approach.

Taking this further, The British Association of Social Workers (BASW) has derived policy from ethical considerations and knowledge of children to support members who do not collude in policies deemed unethical. In 2007 the BASW agreed to support members who found it necessary to refuse to co-operate with unethical practice by immigration authorities, which violated the rights of children and young people. The 'ethnography' of social work validates such a stance and shields social workers from political and organizational confrontations.

Exemplar 2: Indigenous peoples

The ongoing plight of Indigenous peoples throughout the world should be of deep concern to social workers. The denial of the status of Indigenous peoples is no more clearly emphasized than in the resistance of a number of western countries to endorse the United Nations Declaration on the Rights of Indigenous Peoples which was debated for two decades and only came into force in 2007.

Smith and Pitts (2007: 7) state that the marginalization of Indigenous communities is a worldwide phenomenon of a scale that dwarfs most other forms of marginalisation. This situation has resulted in a heightened research interest in Indigenous communities that has frequently led to some communities being severely over-researched, particularly using a method characterized as 'helicopter research' where researchers arrive, collect data and leave (Smith and Pitts, 2007: 7).

Unsurprisingly, for many of the world's Indigenous populations there exists an antipathy towards research as a legacy of the colonial era whereby colonial authorities were obsessed with documenting the exoticness of their captive populations or recording their failures to comply with or thrive under colonial rule (Willis and Saunders, 2007: 96). However, in the current era of ongoing oppression and discrimination social workers cannot be mere bystanders as governments enact policies antithetical to Indigenous rights, sovereignty and land justice. Nor can they ignore the resistance, activism and research endeavours of Indigenous peoples themselves and their calls for measured participation in their struggles by non-Indigenous colleagues and supporters. Moreover, there is existing research in the Indigenous sphere from which the activist social work researcher can derive their position. This includes clear evidence of ongoing socio-economic disadvantage that exposes the inadequacy of current approaches that are premised on practical reconciliation measures alone.

Ongoing policy impositions, with a dubious research base, were exemplified by the federal government of now deposed

Australian Prime Minister John Howard who, in June 2007, declared a national emergency in the Northern Territory. Ostensibly to deal with child abuse, the interventions announced by the federal government were monumental including sending in the military and Australian Federal Police, widespread alcohol restrictions, welfare changes, enforced school attendance, compulsory health checks for all Aboriginal children, acquisition of townships and increases in policing levels (Hinkson, 2007: 1).

The announcement was made just before a federal election in which the ruling conservative coalition was losing support. The National Coalition of Aboriginal and Torres Strait Islander Social Workers Association expressed grave concern about the intervention. This is not to deny problems that were occurring in communities but previous research based reports were gathering dust with recommendations not implemented. The sensationalist media reportage tended to garner more public attention than empirically based evidence. In these circumstances, social workers can protest, can refuse to collude with policies and can proclaim Indigenous rights. But what of research? We can present evidence of the moral wrong of discriminatory provision; we can draw on our practice experience to speak out on the range of issues facing Indigenous communities; and we can demonstrate experientially what works including cultural respect, meaningful consultation and partnership. From our work at the coalface and at a community level, we can expose the impact of policy imposition on the communities including the fear generated. Although we have no guarantees that this 'research' will not be ignored, to cease presenting information and policy ideas would be a dereliction of professional responsibility.

Research with Indigenous peoples is a matter that requires careful consideration of whether it should be undertaken by Indigenous people alone or whether there is a place for non-Indigenous researchers to participate. If participation is the outcome of such deliberations and negotiations, what then are the rules, goals and limits? Social workers are among those who critique the plight of Indigenous peoples but social workers have also been participants in the process of dispossession and oppression, albeit only by default (Gilbert, 2001: 15). Social work needs to be careful about jumping in as a means of reparation because the task of influencing policy change and producing emancipatory outcomes is fraught. The undertaking confronting social work and Indigenous peoples is to have research conducted that reflects the experience, expertise and concerns of those who have traditionally been marginalized in the research process and whose knowledge has been discounted (Brown and Strega, 2005: 6). It may mean a diversion of some resources from government-supported evidence-based research to research that acknowledges experiential knowledge (Briskman, 2007).

The forcible removal of Indigenous children from their families and communities occurred in many countries in different guises, including in the United States, Canada and Australia. In Australia the removal of Indigenous children is now referred to as the Stolen Generations and the practices occurred predominantly under the past policy of assimilation. This is one example of research endeavour with direct applicability to social workers as child and family welfare practice is commonplace. The conduct of such research is complex and politicized for a number of reasons. In Australia because of the advocacy of Indigenous organizations, the federal government conducted an inquiry into the removal of Indigenous children from their families (Human Rights and Equal Opportunity Commission, 1997) in order to expose the harmful policies and practices. Using oral testimony as the main method of information gathering, the work became controversial as dominant voices criticized Indigenous voices as being subject to failed memory rather than hard evidence. Indigenous organizations however, remained resolute in their determination to have their voices heard. In research commissioned by one Indigenous organization on the oral history of activists who had fought against the removal of children throughout Australia, it was demanded of the researcher that oral history be the methodology adopted (Briskman, 2003). This type of research contributes to reducing the invisibility of Indigenous people in the Australian nation including what anthropologist WEH Stanner refers to as the Great Australian Silence (cited in McGrath, 1995: 366). Restoring the rightful place of Indigenous peoples in nation states may be beyond the scope of the work of many social workers; nonetheless practice research that documents the ongoing impact through practice observations and Indigenous voice is critical in restoring well-being and enacting human rights and social justice.

Exemplar 3: Development, world poverty and aid

International social work engagement poses some dilemmas for social work in paving the way between universalistic and even imperialistic assumptions and the question of context and 'indigenization' (Gray, 2005: 231). Some social work organizations such as the International Federation of Social Workers and the International Association of Schools of Social Work have acted as champions and identifiers of social work at international and regional levels (Lyons et al., 2006: 3). For Lyons et al. (2006: 10–11) there was a time when social workers had a greater say in the policies of international bodies including the United Nations, but the increasing encroachment of economic development over social and environmental development lessened their role.

The UN Millennium Development Goals adopted by the General Assembly in 2000 are hard to contest and could be supported by social workers concerned about the plight of those who are invisible or ignored in 'the west'. They include the eradication of extreme poverty and hunger, the achievement of universal education, gender equality, a reduction in child mortality, improvements in maternal health and the combating of such diseases as HIV and malaria. Regrettably, these goals are still a long way from being realized. Moreover the way nations implement such goals through aid programmes is often conditional and non-participatory and also presents those seen as 'undeveloped' as inferior. As social worker Elisabeth Reichert (2006) states, 'one should never assume that your way of doing things is better than the local population's'. If we take this statement seriously social workers should be examining the policies of their own governments and helping formulate solutions in partnership with the recipient countries and communities. Basic to development research is exposure of policies and practices and the formulation in partnership with the recipient community of credible solution-focused alternatives.

Political engagement in this process of investigation and solution-seeking is crucial because with knowledge, political will, participation and adequate resources it is possible to bring about positive change and a different social order. Peter Singer, Professor of Ethics at Princetown University, comments (2007: 21) that 'it would be astonishingly easy for the rich to free the world's poorest from extreme misery'.

Taking this a step further, by adopting an anti-colonialist stance social workers can promote policies and practices that do not create or perpetuate dominance and dependence (Lyons et al., 2006: 185). This involves reviewing the needed knowledge, skills and approaches and appreciating the experiential knowledge which resides within social workers (Lyons et al., 2006: 187). It requires only a small step to utilize this knowledge for applied research.

In *The Road to Hell* Michael Maren (1997) speaks of how aid and charity is a self-serving system that sacrifices its own practitioners and intended beneficiaries in order that it may survive and grow. Researchers need to comprehend, question and challenge the conditions that are often put on aid recipients, for example, to strengthen the rule of law, to engage in public sector reform or to support private sector development. Loans from international institutions may be conditional on poor countries developing an open market economy, a measure that has benefits for rich western nations. In this social workers can readily adopt a staunch epistemological defence of alternative, but more appropriate ways, to generate knowledge. This is a necessary component to counter the dominance of the economic discourse of such powerful institutions as the World Bank and the International Monetary Fund and even to engage with and integrate the position of alter-globalization activists through such bodies as the World Social Forum. Part of the problem is that the language of humanitarian assistance is generally not couched in human rights terms and this should be of key concern to social workers. Humanitarianism is premised on inequality between benefactor and beneficiary that arises when someone is 'in need' (Every, 2006, cited in Gosden, 2007: 151). The current thrusts can be considered to be colonialist in nature. They fail to take into account struggles for the full self-determination of peoples to determine their own destinies even when the colonialists have formally left.

Consider the example of the Global Gag Rule in the United States. This occurred in 1984, when the Reagan Administration imposed restrictions on U.S. funding for international family planning. The so-called 'Mexico City Policy', also known as the Global Gag Rule, prohibited overseas NGOs from receiving U.S. funds if, with their own funds and in accordance with the laws of their own countries, they 'perform[ed]' or 'actively promote[d] abortion as a method of family planning'. Since 1995, U.S. congressional foes of family planning and abortion rights have sought to enact funding restrictions similar to the original Global Gag Rule (Center for Reproductive Rights, 2003). What can social work research do here? It can provide evidence of maternal and infant mortality; it can demonstrate limited access to education and can present examples of extreme poverty that counter the 'moral' and often religiously derived motives imposed from the outside.

As Hurley argues (2007: 182) 'The Third World "other" is often constructed and spoken about as though it bears no relation to the First World other than that of being less economically developed'. The way aid is portrayed is frequently unquestioned. Escobar's (1995) assertions still stand in that the western media portrays images of malnourished, helpless children in poor countries, as a striking symbol of the power of the aid donors over aid recipient countries. Social work's research endeavours can bring to bear a range of theoretical positions, advocacy measures and analytical approaches to 're-story' what is occurring for people on the ground as a counter to the propaganda generated. Social workers and community workers can adopt change rooted in small communities of poor people (Farmer, 2003). The notion that developing countries are incapable of finding their own models needs to be challenged (Gray, 2005: 235) or as James Midgely argues, 'it is time to challenge the one-way international flow of ideas and practices and to learn from the Third World' (Midgley, 1992: 300, cited in Gray, 2005: 235).

RESEARCH LEADS

To fully comprehend, explore and disseminate the question of nation, social work research needs to develop a set of core but adaptable guidelines to facilitate this prospect. The ideas below are tentative and exploratory and not intended to be prescriptive, but to provide a basis for ongoing discussion rather than ways to codify action. Drawing from the arguments presented above, I contemplate the guiding principles required, the questions to be asked, and ways in which research should be conducted and how the results might be disseminated.

Research principles for nation

1   An obligation to uphold social work ethical standards
2   A duty to understand, investigate and challenge policies that violate human rights standards
3   Advocacy and social change to be at the core
4   Research to be framed as political in nature
5   Recognition of the inherent contradictions of social research and recognition that creative responses are possible

Research questions for nation

1   In whose interests are the policies developed and implemented?
2   Who benefits from ongoing exclusion and who suffers?
3   How can social work and related theories help our understandings?
4   Who should take responsibility for change?

Research methods for nation

1   Adaptable, flexible, political and context driven
2   Putting the voices of the excluded to the forefront

3   Avoiding positivist evidence based data collection
4   Extending practice into the research arena particularly through adopting an ethnographic approach

Research dissemination

1   Moving beyond the academic comfort realm of journals and conferences
2   Ensuring that those with political and economic power receive results
3   Utilizing mediums that reach the public domain such as the media
4   Drawing on international social work and related networks

CONCLUSION

Considering the impact of the concept of nation on research means that in all our actions to counter dominant discourses and approaches we need to remember that social problems are made by people. They can therefore be solved by people and this includes social workers. It is only a small leap of courage for social workers to stretch their practice modalities to include research paradigms that are ethical, political and advocacy driven and derived from social work ethics, values and knowledge base.

NOTE

1 This research is being undertaken through an Australian Research Council grant by Deborah Zion, Linda Briskman and Bebe Loff.

Community

Karen M. Staller and Tracie Mafile'o

INTRODUCTION

The focus of this chapter is community as a domain of social work research. We consider the different ways in which community is conceptualized in social work practice and research. This leads to an overview of the historical unfolding of community-based research, including discussions of the settlement house movement, and developments in ethnographic practices, participatory action methods, feminist and standpoint theories, and indigenous/non-western research, each as part of the evolving landscape of research methods as they relate to community domain. Finally we consider future directions.

SOCIAL WORK AND COMMUNITY

From its formative days as a profession, social work and social workers have been particularly attentive to the notion of 'community'. Although the profession has been interested in the individual as target of intervention, it has also understood and tried to divert the focus of responsibility from the individual to institutions, policies, and social conditions that interfere with well-being. After all, individuals cannot be separated from the environments in which they live, work, play, and pray. Thus community has been infused into the social work lexicon such that we routinely speak of community organizing, community development, community-based practice, community outreach, community intervention, community empowerment, community education, community participation, community welfare, community change, and the like. Ife (1997; Ife and Tesoriero, 2006) has argued that a community discourse is the way forward for the profession. But how is community being defined, conceptualized, and employed for practice and research purposes?

In teasing out some of the various notions of community we offer several organizing features for consideration. First, community can relate to a geographic or political boundary and those boundaries may be constructed at any number of levels such as villages, towns, cities, states, provenances, governorates, confederacies, or nations. We may talk about urban or rural communities; domestic, international, or transnational. These might be considered communities of *place and space*. Second, we might organize the notion of community around *institutional or social structures* such as prisons, public housing, schools, or nursing home facilities. Third, community can also be organized around cultural, ethnic, racial, or religious identities or heritages. So we speak of Czech or Slovak, Pacific island, Asian or African, black, Caucasian, or Latino, and Muslim, Jewish or Catholic. Then again, each of these communities are made up of more specific embedded communities, for example, the Pacific islands is comprised of a number of nations and ethnic groups such as people of the Cook Islands, Samoa, and Tonga; or the Jewish community might be associated with orthodox, conservative or reform movements. These might be called *communities of culture*. Fourth, we might also define community by some sort of shared identifying characteristic such as a health or mental health feature (e.g. cancer survivors, AIDS, disability or ability status, mental illness), sexual orientation (e.g. gay, lesbian, bisexual) or gender identity (e.g. transgendered, intersex, and so on), or other organizing status such as homelessness, refugee, or special needs. In this aspect of community, the shared characteristic might serve to identify the population, target of intervention or be utilized to organize, empower, educate, or provide services. These might be communities of *identity or status*. Finally, communities might be organized as *communication networks* (Williams, 1958). New networks were made possible by telegraph, radio, cable, and telephone; more recently we are seeing communities organized in cyberspace. Obviously these very diverse conceptualizations of community will have different implications for social work practice, services, and research. Furthermore, researchers, service providers, and/or community members can define community. The perceived and constructed boundaries of membership may or may not overlap.

For social workers any of these 'communities' can be employed in a number of different ways. For example, community may provide the *context or environment* in which the practitioner works. So a social worker needs to be culturally competent to work in a particular community such as Muslim,

Vietnamese, or AIDS. Second, the community can provide the *population targeted for intervention*. So a social worker might seek to educate or empower a particular community about a particular social issue or problem such as dealing with domestic violence in the community of Asian immigrant women. Or a social worker might be engaged in street outreach efforts to reach the community of homeless youth or street prostitutes. Third, community can provide the *place or site of service delivery*. So community-based social service agencies attempt to meet the particular needs of the local constituents such as community-based mental health clinics, or community-based social welfare offices. Finally social workers may target communities for the purposes of *organizing and promoting* social justice issues. So social workers might seek to engage community members for improving housing conditions or neighborhood safety.

It should also be noted that the role of community in relation to social work varies according to the cultural context. In places where communally based cultures predominate, we might expect that community has a more prominent role in social work compared to those places where more individually based cultures and practice predominate. Where social work is less regulated or has not developed as a formal profession, community development tends to be more prominent as a focus of social work (Kaseke, 2001; Tiumalu-Faleseuga, 1993).

COMMUNITY AS A DOMAIN OF SOCIAL WORK RESEARCH

Given these complicated relationships between 'social work' and 'community', it is not surprising that there are also a number of issues to consider for research purposes. How is community defined? What are the researchers' relationships to the community of interest? What are the intended outcomes of the research relative to the community?

Not unlike social work practice, community can sit in a number of different locations in research design. For example it can provide the *context*. So the researcher might simply consider community as the environment in which inquiry would be occurring. According to Blumenthal and Yancey (2004), 'community-based research is scientific inquiry involving human subjects that takes place in the community – that is, outside of the laboratory, hospital, or clinic setting' (2004: 3). Second, it might be the actual *object of study* so a researcher may want to better understand the functioning of community itself. Third, community might be the *object of intervention* so researchers might be seeking to promote social justice through community change. Note that in each of these examples 'community' occupies a different spot in the study design. Community can be the unit of analysis, the location of the study, provide the sample, or be the object of intervention.

In addition to these various conceptualizations of community for research design purposes it is important to consider from whose perspective 'community' is being defined. While a researcher might conceptualize a community based on some imposed attribute, the individuals so labeled may or may not share a sense of community. For example, youth residing in a 'runaway shelter' may or may not consider themselves 'runaways' although researchers may study them as such. Or 'census' data may be utilized to examine community factors, however, when asked to identify neighborhood boundaries, residents may point to very different geographic borders than those drawn by the census bureau. Indigenous communities' tribal and geographical boundaries often differ from the nation-state, regional or city boundaries that have been defined by settler groups. So whether the notion of 'community' is shared and originates from the indigenous population itself or is imposed by the researcher as a matter of design can be an issue. Second, the researchers' relationship to the community is always significant. Are they

community insiders or outsiders? Are they utilizing indigenous community experts or not? Methods of research are not culturally neutral. If the focus of the research is a cultural community, then consideration must be given to methods appropriate to that cultural community (Health Research Council of New Zealand, 2003; Smith L.T., 1999).

Of course any number of different research methods might be employed in community-based or community-oriented research but there are some that are obvious candidates. For example, *case studies* which can use neighborhoods, networks, or institutions as objects of investigation; *evaluation studies* which look at the effectiveness of services or interventions; and *action research or participatory research* in which the methods employed may include organizing, educating, and promoting social justice or social reform. We discuss these community-based action methods further below. Community-based social work research may be particularly relevant within communal based cultural contexts and where community and social development is emphasized. Alternatively, some research methods where engagement of participants in the design or implementation is frowned upon and where strategies of inquiry rest on highly controlled experimental conditions might be less appropriate for use in community-based projects where variables are difficult, if not impossible, to control.

All types of community-based inquiry call into question the role of the researcher and his or her level of participation as well as the level of participation of the community. The researcher can be fully engaged as in some participatory methods or not at all as in some case-based methods. Similarly the community may be fully involved in the project or participate only minimally. Further in question is the ultimate goal of the project such as whether is it primarily descriptive, evaluative, or preventative, and whether it seeks to promote community change or not. Taken together this begins to illustrate the complicated landscape of community as a domain for social work research.

HISTORICAL PERSPECTIVES ON COMMUNITY AND RESEARCH

A number of different historical threads contribute to the tapestry of community-based inquiry as we know it today. We examine a few of these arguably important pieces of the narrative including the settlement house movement; early ethnography and studying the exotic 'other'; the rise of action-based research; the contribution of feminist and standpoint theorists; and indigenous and non-western critiques.

The methods we consider have appeared under a variety of different names. That said, however, they mostly vary on two major dimensions. The first is on a continuum of control allocated between researchers-as-experts on the one hand and community-members-as-experts on the other. The question of how control or power is allocated extends throughout the entire process and project. Thus, it can complicate each and every step from initial design to final reporting. The second major dimension has to do with the degree to which the inquiry itself seeks to change the community and community members as a result of the project.

Settlement house movement and social research

Perhaps there is no better starting place for considering the historical relationship between social work practice, social action, and community-related research in the western world than the Settlement House Movement of the late nineteenth century. The Settlement House idea originated in Great Britain where well to do and educated 'settlers' moved into poor areas in order to share community-living experiences and with an eye toward social reform. Among the earliest of these settlements were Toynbee Hall, located in the heart of London's Irish and Jewish immigrant communities and established by Church of England curate, Samuel Barnett and his wife in 1884 and the Mansfield

Settlement – one of the earliest university settlements – which was connected to Mansfield College (Oxford). Among other things these settlements were based on the idea that activists needed to have a rigorous and shared understanding of the needs and living conditions of the poor and that research and action were inextricably interconnected.

The Settlement House movement also took hold in the United States particularly in urban industrialized settings such as New York City and Chicago, where large immigrant populations resided. Fabricant and Fisher (2002) have argued that settlement houses workers' method was based on three key factors: '1) an integrated collaborative practice that intervened at the individual and the community level and sought to develop solidarity between settlement house workers and neighborhood residents; 2) a sense of the essential importance of community and community building, and 3) a willingness to organize and advocate for social, political, and economic justice' (2002: 25).

Community building and community reform were deeply intertwined. The Settlement mission was to engage community, promote larger social change and to tackle a number of social issues. In doing so they developed new institutions and advocated policy reform. Targeted concerns included health, sanitation, labor conditions, childcare, recreation, day care, early education, preserving ethnic cultural heritage, civil rights, housing, and juvenile justice.

Jane Addams (1860–1935) was an internationally touted social activist and co-founder, along with Ellen Gates Starr, of Hull House in Chicago. Addams and her Hull House associates contributed greatly to the scientific advancement within the applied philanthropy and charity work movements. The work was largely based on the assumption that researchers must be *of the community* in order to better understand its needs. One method employed was to generate social statistics through systematic, community-based data collection that could be used for social reform. For two years, between 1892 and 1894, Hull House residents collected data and drafted reports on community conditions that were first published in 1895 by Thomas Y. Crowell and titled, 'Hull-House Maps and Papers: A presentation of Nationalities and Wages in a Congested District of Chicago, Together with Comments and Essays on Problems Growing Out of Social Conditions'. Presented were detailed maps of data plotted block by city block on nationality and wages as well as a number of papers documenting social conditions and urging social change. Settlement house residents were, 'certain that publishing maps with explicit information about the wages and conditions of the working poor in the 19th Ward would educate the public and lead to much-needed reforms' (Schultz, 2005: 1). Thus the idea of generating community-based data (or social statistics) and utilizing these data for the benefit of that community came to the fore.

Edith Abbott (1876–1957) who was associated with Hull House but was also on the faculty of the University of Chicago's School of Social Service Administration, one of the first social work schools in the United States, sought to train students to administer – with increasing professionalization – social welfare service agencies and organizations. Therefore, like the work being done in London's Mansfield Settlement, Abbot's work linked community-based research or 'social investigation' with practice, theory and academic course work. So this community-based research model was intertwined with the earliest educational training for social workers and indistinguishable from the very essence of social work practice.

Ethnography and studying 'others'

In addition to the Settlement House movement there are other historical trends of note that impact the current conversation on community research. For example, in the sixteenth century onward, Europeans used 'knowledge gained from travel' as a basis of 'colonial power sustained by exploratory expeditions, practical sciences, missionary work, and territorial penetration of colonial civil services' (Hall, 2001: 12,613). In short, these excursions were utilized as a method of extending the power of European empires. Additionally, the knowledge gained was disseminated to those back home. Hall (2001) reports that, 'Sometimes authors combined traveling for a trading company or state with writing for a popular audience that wished to visit other lands vicariously' (2001: 12,613). These travelogues were associated with the earliest roots of anthropological ethnographic research. This research often involved visiting exotic locations, recording what was seen and reporting to those back home. This journalist reporting 'became increasingly systematic' and included 'inventorying the languages and practices of its peoples. Organizations such as the Smithsonian Institute (founded in 1846) coordinated efforts to gather data and circulated inventory questionnaires that could be filled out by non-professional travelers' (Hall, 2001: 12,613–14). In addition to the colonization of these places, there were other dangerous downsides, such as the fact the written accounts were 'often saturated with racist and ethnocentric assumptions' (Hall, 2001: 12,613–14).

A major advancement in cultural research credits anthropologist Bronislaw Malinowski with embracing 'participant observation' and encouraging sustained observation in his ethnographic work during WWI. His seminal work, *Argonauts of the Western Pacific* based on field work in the Trobriand Islands was pivotal in this regard. Nonetheless it retained the 'authoritative' voice and expert account 'aimed at an emic understanding of the "other's" point of view' (Hall, 2001: 12,614). Since then, however, anthropologists have engaged in an extensive critique of both the level of 'participation' of the researcher in the project and the 'representation' or authoritative voice used in describing or reporting on these communities to others. These critical discourses on position, voice, and representation have spilled over into the social work literature and scholarship as well.

Kurt Lewin and his followers: social action, research, and community

Kurt Lewin (1890–1947), a social psychologist interested in social change, is generally credited with coining the term *action research* as a way of combining his interest in group work with research activities. This fusion of interests had dramatic implications for community as a domain for social inquiry.

Lewin asked questions about both how to conceptualize social change and how to promote it (Greenwood and Levin, 1998). Prior to his death in 1947, Lewin's interest in social change, and ameliorating social problems coupled with an interest in group dynamics led to unique and long-lasting philosophical, epistemological, and methodological contributions to scientific inquiry. Lewin is credited with shifting the role of the researcher from 'being a distant observer to involvement in concrete problem solving' (Sabo, 2003: 2). This had two natural consequences. First, it 'involv[ed] people affected by a problem in practical problem solving' (Minkler and Wallerstein, 2003b: 6). Second, it assumed problem-solving occurred through 'a cyclical process of fact finding, action, and evaluation' (Minkler and Wallerstein, 2003b: 6).

Under this approach, provisional solutions were tested and modified as warranted until an effective intervention was developed which ameliorated the problem. So the project was always both provisional and subject to alteration but it was also practical and grounded. It was absolutely imperative to involve community or group stakeholders because their participation would 'limit the range trial solutions' to those which were practical, would 'illuminate the data', and would make 'the ultimate adoption of promising solutions more likely' (Gold, 1993: 253). Besides, concluded Gold (1993), 'the culture of action research includes a strong commitment to democracy and egalitarianism' (1993: 253).

Lewin's students and followers emphasize that action research is comprised of three basic elements *research, action, and participation* (Greenwood and Levin, 1998). This method is based on assumptions that knowledge is situated both in the hands of expert researchers but also in the hands of community-based participants. Action researchers are both 'deeply skeptical about the transcendence of professional knowledge over all other forms of knowing' but also 'weigh the knowledge of local people much more heavily than do orthodox researchers' (Greenwood and Levin, 1998: 95). Furthermore in order to be effective and sustainable, community-based problem solving requires active community endorsement. Finally unlike conventional social science research that prescribes a rigid research design in advance, action research is a method in which '... the goals of the process are constantly being redefined, refined, and even altered completely' (Greenwood and Levin, 1998: 94). It is a collaborative process and the research design needs to be flexible and responsive.

Like Malinowski's contribution to ethnography, this model directly challenged the relationship between researcher and community domain in which the research was taking place. It necessarily required a continually iterative and interactive procedure adjusting process, goals, and results based on community responses and needs. It required the engagement of community participants. In short action research is, 'a social process in which professional knowledge, local knowledge, process skills, research skills, and democratic values are the basis for co created knowledge and social change' (Greenwood and Levin, 1998: 93).

Feminist critique and influence: empowerment and action

Feminist critical methodologists and others have sought to engage and empower communities as part of an integrated social research and reform agenda. Critical methodologies gave voice to silenced communities. They continued to challenge the researcher-as-expert but also sought to build community and community capacity, social capital and promote reform.

Ristock and Pennell (1996) have considered the feminist movement and critique in the context of community-based research. In particular, they examine the role of *empowerment* and community. The primary method of empowerment during the 1970s feminist movement in the United States came from consciousness raising groups and thus the notion of giving voice to women though critical examination of their own stories, experiences, and realities. This approach challenged dominant patriarchal paradigms and existing political and social structures. When coupled with a research agenda, Ristock and Pennell (1996) note:

> Empowerment as an approach to community research means thinking consciously about power relations, cultural context, and social action. It is an approach to building knowledge that seeks to change the conditions of people's lives, both individually and collectively. It involves consulting or collaborating with diverse individuals, groups, and communities as part of the process of illuminating people's lives and social issues. Fundamentally, it is research that is 'committed to identifying, facilitating or creating contexts in which heretofore silent and isolated people, those who are "outsiders" in various settings, organizations and communities, gain understanding, voice and influence over decisions that affect their lives'. (1996: 2)

The idea of feminist empowerment has not gone without critique. In particular the solidarity of 'women' as a uniform and monolithic group has been challenged by 'women at the margins, for whom age, race, sexuality, disability, or some other aspect of their identity makes for an uneasy fit with a fixed category that specifies the "essential" properties or characteristics of all women' (Ristock and Pennell, 1996: 3). By extension an important conversation on 'intersectionalities' has emerged to try to incorporate and respect these multiple identities.

The net result was a feminist view that not only introduced the notion of empowerment as part of the research process but required a careful and critical examination of power relationships between and among the researchers and the researched. This analysis of power dynamics necessarily extended beyond just considering relationships between genders and included examining power dynamics more broadly. Furthermore it introduced the idea of considering power as part of an ethical imperative associated with the research process. In short, the 'feminist research agenda requires the critical analysis of power as well as its responsible use' (Ristock and Pennell, 1996: 9).

Thus feminist scholars contributed to the conversation on community-based research by calling into question the relative position and authority in the researcher–subject relationships of traditional social science and encouraged projects that sought to empower community members and promote social change. Furthermore, attention to intersectionalities challenged simplistic notions of community boundary-drawing. These conversations had implications for social work and its concern for community domains in practice and research. The role of privilege, oppression, empowerment, cultural competence, and attention to intersectionalities have become commonplace.

Indigenous and non-western critique and influence: community development, education, and action research

Minkler and Wallerstein (2003b) argue that in spite of a great deal of convergence in the principles and values of participatory and action-based approaches to inquiry, the two approaches really evolved from very different traditions. On the one hand was the action research of Kurt Lewin and his followers who sought to involve 'people affected by a problem in practical problem solving through a cyclical process of fact finding, action, and evaluation' discussed above; and on the other hand was the 'participatory research (PR), collaborative action research, and participatory action research (PAR) traditions, which have their roots in popular education and related work in the 1970s with and by oppressed peoples in Africa, Asia, and Latin America' (Minkler and Wallerstein, 2003b: 6).

So far, we have reviewed community as a domain of research as it has developed within western academia. While only recently being recognized within the academy, indigenous peoples have traditionally undertaken research within their own communities. Absolon and Willett (2004) state that 'traditionally, research has been conducted to seek, counsel and consult; to learn about medicines, plants and animals; to scout and scan the land; to educate and pass on knowledge; and to inquire into cosmology' (2004: 7). Recorded and recounted orally and in connection with nature, indigenous scholars have asserted the importance of story telling as a research tool which is consistent with indigenous cultures and their way of understanding the world they live in (Lekoko, 2007).

The centrality of community within indigenous worldviews, in contrast to individualism, suggests that the community domain will have particular importance when undertaking research. For indigenous researchers, research and writing must be done in connection to community, beyond the library, in context and based on current reality (Absolon and Willett, 2004). Indeed, it could be argued that in order for social work research to be anti-oppressive, and for research to be undertaken in a way that values the worldviews of diverse cultural groups, the community domain must be central to any social work research, particularly when there is an interest in culture and diversity. Questions about the involvement of community and the impact on community, the extent to which the research is in tune with the concerns and aspirations of a community must always be taken into consideration (see Exemplar 1).

Exemplar 1: Whaia te hauora o nga rangatahi (Maori youth well-being)

Background

In 1840, most of the indigenous tribes in New Zealand signed the Treaty of Waitangi with the British Crown, which guaranteed protection, participation, and partnership for Maori tribes. The Treaty, however, was not honored in the pursuant decades resulting in the widespread dispossession of Maori lands, language, and culture. Tribal groups continue to seek to reclaim their lands and regenerate their knowledges and ways. *Whaia te Hauora o nga Rangatahi* was research undertaken by Te Runanga o Raukawa Inc., an indigenous tribal organization within its own community from 2003 to 2005. Maori youth (12–24 years of age) in the geographic community or the tribal area of Ngati Raukawa (inclusive of Rangitane and Muaupoko) were the focus of the research.

Aim

The aim of the research was to consider hauora (health and well-being) of Maori rangatahi (youth). Specifically, the research set out to identify health and well-being issues that Maori youth face; to consider how they think these issues should be addressed; to include the youth voice by actively involving Maori youth as researchers in the project; to utilize kaupapa Maori (Bishop, 2005) and participatory action research methods; and to undertake a social audit of youth agencies in terms of their responsiveness to Maori youth.

Approach

All the researchers were Maori. The community were integrally involved in the research process from its inception. During the tender process meetings were called with key Maori social services working with youth. In addition to this, young peoples' contributions were sought regarding research design and the research questions.

The team utilized youth forums firstly to invite young people to be a part of the group as young researchers and secondly to ask what they thought should be the focus when looking at the hauora (well-being) of Maori rangatahi (youth) and to consult on how these issues would best be explored with rangatahi (individual or focus group). Throughout the research, over 20 rangatahi were recruited from Maori social service agencies, urban community-based agencies and by referrals directly from the young people. These young people received research training and worked alongside adult researchers to collect and analyze data. The youth researchers also assisted conference presentations and two youths were on the advisory group.

The theoretical perspective was informed by concepts of youth development, kaupapa Maori research (Bishop, 2005; Smith L.T., 1999) and action research – all of which aligned well with the community development principles of the Treaty of Waitangi, locating ourselves, self-determination, power, working alongside and collective decision making (Munford and Walsh-Tapiata, 2000).

Findings

Negotiating balance between a youth approach and a cultural approach was a significant challenge – particularly given that the research project was based in a tribal agency. At times there were divergent perspectives, as tribal members did not necessarily value the importance of hearing the youth voice as much as they upheld cultural values of respect for elders. Some elders expressed that too much focus was given to these young people. It was a challenge to finely balance these different perspectives. It was also a daily challenge for the adult researchers to see things from a youth perspective, and to progress at the pace of the young people rather than rushing ahead. Negotiating of roles between youth and adult researchers

and the 'voice' of the youth was ongoing throughout the research. (Personal communication, Wheturangi Walsh-Tapiata, 2008.)

Concerns have arisen from community development efforts in third world countries and from first nation peoples in the United States, Canada, Australia and New Zealand. Included in these critiques are that some cultural groups had been over-researched, that researchers had benefited from the research process with no benefits accrued to the researched communities, and that research findings had been interpreted primarily through western worldviews (Smith, 1999). Activists, scholars and others challenged the patriarchal and colonizing effect of western research models particularly those stemming from positivistic research traditions. These critiques called for participatory and libratory projects that recognized the oppressive and colonizing nature of western research and called for participation and involvement of community but also for social change in efforts that challenged oppressive practices and generated theories that led to human emancipation.

For example, in the 1970s western social science methods based on positivistic philosophical assumptions such as the importance of instrument construction, generalizability and replication were failing miserably in the context of research in Africa while community development workers who were working with indigenous populations seemed better able to provide and produce useful information. Furthermore, social scientists 'came to realize that their own conventional research methods, which privilege the experts who control the production and distribution of knowledge, served only to reproduce a model that was tied to the Western domination of the newly emerging African nations' (Strand et al., 2003: 7). Development workers and social scientists began 'to rely more and more on local knowledge for the technical solution of problems facing the people, who were encouraged to contribute their own experience, wisdom, and skills to the research' (Strand et al., 2003: 7).

Indigenous researchers critique the use of research as a tool of imperialism and colonization and are seeking to decolonize research (Smith, 1999) and to challenge the dominance of western epistemology and methodology in research (Absolon and Willett, 2004; Bennett and Blackstock, 2006). Indigenous research must also have tangible benefits in order to give back to indigenous communities. There is a developing body of literature which addresses research from the perspective of indigenous, first nations and non-western peoples that ought not be ignored by western social scientists and practitioners. Such researchers typically straddle western and indigenous perspectives and seek to re-invent indigenous ways of practicing research in a contemporary context, weaving together learning from both the western and indigenous worlds.

Dialogues that linked social change with liberation and emancipation practices are occurring in Latin America and Asia as well. Among the best known and most influential of these scholars was Paulo Freire. His book, *Pedagogy of the Oppressed*, first published in 1970 has influenced generations of researchers and activists and had a global impact. He believed that education could be used as a 'political tool for raising the consciousness of oppressed people at both the local and global levels' (Strand et al., 2003: 6). In doing so he linked education to 'an agenda of social change in which learning was to be coupled with the investigation of social conditions and then their transformation' (Strand et al., 2003: 6).

Participatory action research has continued to challenge the domination of the university as the site of primary knowledge production and western notions of knowledge and knowledge development. Building on these critiques and in furtherance of Freire's ideas, are new emergent research methods such as one growing in popularity known as photovoice (see Exemplar 2). Caroline C. Wang (2003) who developed the

method and has employed it in a number of projects notes that it, 'integrates Paulo Freire's (1970) approach to critical education, feminist theory, and a participatory approach to documentary photography' and that it 'builds on a commitment to social and intellectual change through community members' critical production and analysis of the visual image' (2003: 181). Of great significance is that community member participants – and not the researchers – are in control of capturing, recording, and promoting what is important to them. As Wang notes, 'this method confronts a fundamental disparity between what researchers think is important and what the community thinks is important' (Wang, 2003: 182). Critical discourse starts within the group but ultimately participants attempt to reach policy-makers or others in positions of power.

Exemplar 2: Photovoice in global context

Photovoice has been used in many diverse communities and cultural contexts. For example:

- *Village Works* engaged 62 women in China's Yunnan Province to record through photographs one year of their daily life, work, and health conditions. The women selected photographs for public exhibition and engaged health specialists around plans for village improvement (www.wellesley.edu/DavisMuseum/VillageWorks/index.html).
- Photovoice was used by feminist activists in Canada to engage women living in poverty to raise consciousness and identify the inadequacies of social policy (Willson, 2006).
- In Guatemala a group of Mayan Ixil women conducted a project in which they produced a book of their past and present struggles (Lykes et al., 2003).
- Working class women in Belfast, Northern Ireland were engaged in order to record the experiences of their everyday lives and ultimately explore the relationship between place and identity (McIntyre, 2003).

- Radley et al. (2005) worked with London's homeless women to record daily life in hostels and on the streets.
- Moyle Women's Forum in Northern Ireland using photovoice with Protestant and Catholic women through cross-community efforts 'developed personal skills, enriched the social environment and enhanced civic participation in their rural district' (Side, 2005).
- Mexican and South Asian immigrant communities of battered women worked to promote 'community education and action' (Frohmann, 2005).

Together these various photovoice, action-based and community-oriented projects can be seen as promoting critical thinking, community empowerment, grassroots activism and social change. (See http: //www.photovoice.org and http:// www.photovoice.com.)

So where are we?

Clearly there are a number of choices available to social work researchers who are interested in doing research in the community domain. This cursory history of ideas associated with community as a site of research raises questions about power, authority, participation, education, democracy, social change and social justice, and should be an integral part of the social work community research agendas.

Israel and colleagues (1998) identify nine critical characteristics of Community-Based Participatory Research (CBPR). They are that CBPR:

- recognizes community as a unit of identity;
- builds on strengths and resources within the community (1998: 57);
- facilitates collaborative, equitable partnership in all phases of the research, involving an empowering and power-sharing process that attends to social inequities (1998: 56);
- promotes co-learning and capacity building among all partners (1998: 56);
- integrates and achieves a balance between research and action for the mutual benefit of all partners (1998: 56);

- emphasizes local relevance of public health problems and ecological perspectives that recognize and attend to the multiple determinants of health and disease (1998: 57);
- involves systems development through a cyclical and iterative process (1998: 57);
- disseminates findings and knowledge gained to all partners and involves all partners in the dissemination process (1998: 57); and
- involves a long-term process and commitment (1998: 58).

This list, perhaps, provides some guidance as we move forward in our thinking about community as a domain for social work research. Community-based social work research should be cooperative and collaborative, thus involving co-learning, co-doing, and should rest heavily on the participation of community members. It should promote community development, capacity building and social justice. Problem definitions cannot be imposed on the community but should be generated with and by community members. Social work community-based research should foster critical awareness while recognizing and building on community strengths.

FUTURE DIRECTIONS

When contemplating community as a domain for social research, it seems critical to extract lessons from the past to help guide us forward. In this chapter we have conceptualized community in a number of different ways including as place and space, as institutional or social structures, as communities of culture, communities of personal identity or status, and communication networks. As we increasingly acknowledge our global interrelatedness, each of these community conceptualizations is being altered. Technology, in particular, is fundamentally changing our definitions of community. The World Wide Web altered limitations of place and space by breaking down barriers imposed by time and distance. It offers a new primary place to go for information challenging existing social institutions and structures. It has begun breaking down cultural barriers by creating shared virtual worlds. Language programs, such as Babel Fish Translation (http://babelfish.altavista.com) even allow people to transcend barriers that might otherwise isolate linguistic communities. It has provided a place for communities of identity or status to organize. Blogs and email have fundamentally changed our communication networks and shifted the boundaries of these communities. As our definitions of community evolve so too must our ideas about community as a domain for research.

In this chapter we also surveyed briefly some approaches to inquiry as they related to community as domain. These included: settlement house advocates' systematic collection of social statistics, their belief that reformers must be *of the community* and their linking of community-based work to the academy; early ethnographic ventures in exotic other cultures, the colonizing effect and its backlash; early discussions of action researcher which dislodged the notion of expert from the academy and placed it in the hands of community members thereby introducing more democratic and egalitarian methods to the process; feminist and other theorists who introduced conversations about power and empowerment to the discourse along with corresponding notions of exploitation and privilege; and finally the contributions of indigenous, non-western traditions which have fundamentally challenged the nature of accepted knowledge and knowledge production. In short, we have argued that many basic challenges to traditional research paradigms have arisen from community practice and community-based research. These challenges include resistance to the monopoly of university-based knowledge production; increasing respect for local or indigenous knowledge; questions about distribution of power and control throughout the research endeavor; and questions about the very essence of knowledge and knowledge development. Community researchers

have raised questions about who has the right to ask or define questions; who has the right and authority to answer those questions; and who should speak for a community. They have raised inter-related questions of power and power dynamics on a number of dimensions (gender, race, class, sexual orientation, sexual identity, culture, etc.). These lessons ought to inform us as we move forward.

Paradoxically, while there is increasing interconnectedness across diverse cultural groups, there is also a movement amongst non-western and indigenous cultural groups toward maintaining and advancing a centeredness in their particular worldviews and systems. In the realm of community-based research, this is most clearly evident in the articulation of epistemological approaches and methodologies that are culturally based. Absolon and Willet (2004) reflect on aboriginal epistemologies and their place in child and family research. They highlight the need to re-examine 'the process of seeking knowledge and knowledge creation' and state that, 'Aboriginal scholars are forging pathways and making positive contributions toward a reclaiming of our own knowledge production' (2004: 15). Although not directly in social work, Gegeo and Watson-Gegeo (2001) have demonstrated the value of employing indigenous epistemology on research on development of indigenous communities in the Solomon Islands. The future landscape of community-based social work research will increasingly contour according to diverse cultural paradigms that may stand in contrast with western scientific research approaches.

As we look forward it is useful for us to acknowledge the lessons learned by those who pioneered ideas about community-based research (both good and bad) and consider applying them wisely in new contexts. The challenges confronted by western world scholars must also be negotiated by indigenous researchers who inevitably occupy a difficult position, moving 'across the boundaries of indigenous and metropolitan, institution and community, politics and scholarship' (Smith, 1999: 71). We should be careful not to replicate subtle and not-so-subtle oppressive research practices as social workers seek to work with and among indigenous communities. However, we suggest that the basic struggles identified in this chapter relating to power, voice, representation, and the like must be continually revisited and will never fully disappear when thinking about communities as domains for social research in the future.

Children, Young People and Families

Mary C. Ruffolo, June Thoburn and
Paula Allen-Meares

INTRODUCTION

Over the past 20 years or so increased emphasis has been placed on improving outcomes for children, young people and families served by child welfare and their partner agencies. This is most apparent in jurisdictions with well developed child and family services but also the language of 'cost-effectiveness' (central to the globalization agenda) places evaluation to the fore as services change in the 'emerging economies' of Eastern Europe and in developing countries. With this renewed emphasis on outcomes and the increased pressure to intervene using best practices and best evidence, social work researchers are framing questions that can inform families, policy makers, practitioners and managers in the child serving systems and policy makers about 'what works'.

The characteristics of the research and evaluations differ from country to country as does the means of dissemination to policy makers, practitioners and those who use services. Some of these questions are best addressed through administrative data sources and national/cross-national surveys that address service access and use. Other questions are being examined using randomized controlled trials (RCTs), process and outcome evaluation studies, client data mining activities, and through qualitative methods. In addition, systematic reviews and syntheses of the evidence from a range of sources are helping policy makers and practitioners understand the conditions under which particular approaches to social work practice and specific interventions have the greatest chance of improving outcomes for children, young people and families.

By far the greater volume of publicly available research emanates from the USA (published mainly as refereed journal articles or government reports and statistical series) and the UK, where books, book chapters and research digests are also important sources. Given the authorship of this chapter, in the main we provide examples from these countries but draw attention to the growing body of epidemiological, process and outcome research, especially from Scandinavian countries, Australia, Canada and New Zealand. Exemplar 1 highlights the organizations and academic societies that are working to increase the quality and accessibility of child welfare research across national boundaries.

Exemplar 1

The International Association for Outcome-Based Evaluation and Research on Family and Children Services (IOBER) and the European Scientific Association for Residential and Foster Care for Children and Adolescents (EUSARF) are two organizations comprised of leading researchers and scientists that cross international and national boundaries to promote improved services for children, young people and families. IOBER promotes cross-national research and comparisons on theories, methods and techniques for outcome-based evaluation and research and dissemination of the findings to improve services (http://www.outcome-evaluation. org). EUSARF also advances knowledge in the field of residential care, foster care and their alternatives for children and youth within Europe (http://ppw.kuleuven.be/ ortho/Eusarf/Eusarf.html).

In most countries, researchers focusing on child and family social work issues (especially those who started their careers as social workers) are usually located in university schools of social work or research centres, but work closely with and are often funded by government departments and social services agencies which usually have their own monitoring and evaluation sections.

In this chapter, we will address primarily the unique contributions and limitations of research and evaluation within the primary service delivery systems where child and family social work takes place. We will explore the challenges of using research and evaluation to inform social work practice with families experiencing a range of difficulties. In doing so, we refer to some studies as exemplars in order to illustrate the different characteristics of the available research

by, for and about social workers and their practice with children and families.

By concentrating on the research and evaluation approaches specific to the provision of services to this population, we do not wish to underplay the importance of multidisciplinary sources of essential knowledge for effective social work practice. Research on the impact of poverty, inequality, disadvantage and discrimination from sociology and social policy; disabilities, mental health and addictions research; from the fields of anthropology, ethnography, psychology, child development and medicine; and research undertaken from a legal perspective come together to provide the foundation for much of the research and evaluation studies in the area of children, young people and families.

In reviewing the state of social work research and evaluation within the key service delivery systems, we will highlight a range of approaches in two key areas:

• studies designed to address access, organizational and service system issues, and pathways to services, and
• studies that examine effective and appropriate interventions for diverse populations of children, young people and families across different service systems.

In the UK the terms 'tiers' or 'levels' are used (Hardiker et al., 1991) with level 1 interventions being 'universal', i.e. for all families, level 2 being services available to geographical areas or groups known to be at risk of social exclusion or 'targeted' at individual families who refer themselves or are referred for a service; level 3 being services targeted at individual families because there are concerns about actual or likely impairment to a child's development or actual or likely significant harm, and level 4 being services to children who have been harmed, or are in the formal care system as a protective measure. In the UK, most social workers are employed at levels 3 and 4 and most research about specifically social work interventions concerns this level of service.

In the USA, a similar system is in place that addresses service needs from preventive, universal interventions to targeted interventions with children and families experiencing high levels of service needs.

We will conclude the chapter with a discussion of next steps for social work research and evaluation in the area of children, young people and families that hold implications for future research and evaluation efforts in the UK and the USA.

BACKGROUND, CURRENT STATE AND CONTEXT OF SOCIAL WORK RESEARCH AND EVALUATION

While the goals of the different child serving systems may vary in different countries, policy makers, researchers and evaluators continue to search for the most feasible and effective approaches to study what works for children, young people and families and how services can be organized to improve outcomes.

In the UK, the Children Act 2004 and the accompanying guidance (*Every Child Matters*, DfES, 2004) require that children's services be organized to improve the well-being of all children living in their area. They define five child well-being outcomes that need to be achieved in order to stimulate long-term improvement in children's health and well-being. The five outcomes are considered key to securing well-being in childhood and in later life (being healthy, staying safe, enjoying and achieving, making a positive contribution, and achieving economic well-being). However, these are too broad to be used by researchers as outcome dimensions for the more complex needs of children within the formal child protection and out-of-home care systems and instead they tend to use the seven dimensions of child well-being developed initially as a research tool and now incorporated into the assessment framework for all child welfare work (Parker et al., 1991). Much recent government funded research has focused less on child outcomes and more on evaluating changes aimed at bringing services closer together around the child, young person and family (DfES, 2004).

In the US, similar movements have occurred at the federal and state levels, and challenge child serving systems to demonstrate outcomes. For example, State Children's Cabinets and Councils were established to improve coordination and efficiency across state departments and non-profit and private sectors and to mobilize resources to facilitate the achievement of common outcomes to improve child well-being (Pittman et al., 2007). In Sweden (Socialstyrelsen, 2006) the Centre for Epidemiology of the National Board of Health and Welfare fulfils a similar function as do the *Observatoires* in France (ONED, 2008), Italy and a growing number of European countries.

In this chapter we take the stance that, while research and evaluation that focuses on outcomes are important, *understanding how* diverse groups of children, youth and families access and benefit from services and interventions must also be a focus of research and evaluation. One of the most critical tasks of social work researchers in the field of child and family welfare is to find effective ways of ensuring that their findings assist practitioners in deciding how best to intervene at a particular point in time with a particular child, young person or family.

In the USA and some countries in Europe current social work research and evaluation studies cross several service delivery systems in which social workers are employed, including but not limited to child welfare, schools, physical health, mental health/substance abuse, developmental disabilities, juvenile justice and general welfare. In the UK, the majority of child and family social workers are employed by local authority Children's Services Departments or by the not-for-profit agencies with whom they work closely. (See Thoburn, 2007, for a discussion of the contexts for child and family services in 14 'developed' countries.) These recently established departments have overall responsibility for promoting the well-being of all children in their area, including children with physical disabilities and emotional and behavioural problems, and sometimes also for children who become involved with the juvenile justice system. Most research by and about child and family social workers has therefore tended to focus on the family support, protective and out-of-home care services provided by these statutory agencies (and their predecessor social services departments). Research on local authority child welfare services increasingly looks at inter-agency or inter-disciplinary practice, and research teams have in recent years more frequently included researchers from the academic disciplines of psychology, medicine and education as well as social work and social policy. Examples are the large scale government funded studies of the setting up of the *Sure Start* initiative to provide a range of services to children under five and their families (Belsky et al., 2006) and the evaluation of the 'pathfinder' children's trusts which preceded the roll out of the programme for more integrated child and family services (O'Brien et al., 2006).

Services for children, young people and families are constantly changing as policies evolve and resources increase or diminish over time. These evolving systems create challenges for social work researchers and evaluators since many current research and evaluation methodologies do not effectively capture this movement or the complexity of the service systems. For example, in the USA the federal government is increasingly focusing on requiring states and local communities to demonstrate that the interventions used are supported by evidence (often taken to mean at least one set of positive findings from an RCT) in order to receive federal funding. The establishment of a common set of performance standards in the child welfare system, the juvenile justice system, the mental health system and the educational system has accompanied these funding requirements. Sweden, Denmark, Australia, Canada and New Zealand and the UK nations are amongst the other countries with this emphasis on determining what interventions improve outcomes for children and young people, and are recognizing the need for a range of research and evaluation approaches to answer these questions. Most reviews and syntheses of research in the broad area of child and family welfare reveal that while there is a growing body of relevant research, there are many unanswered questions especially as it relates to outcomes for diverse groups of children, young people and families. A majority of the research tends to be descriptive studies of populations of children and families needing and/or receiving services, or of the services provided. Some of these (mainly small scale) studies provide outcome data but very few are able to relate child or family outcomes to specific aspects of the service provided.

Evidence-based practice and best practice

While there is increased emphasis on evidence that demonstrates improved outcomes for children and young people, what constitutes 'best practice' or 'evidence-based practice' (EBP) varies based on definitions used in various service systems. Often a tension emerges between policy-makers and practitioners who report that particular interventions have been helpful in addressing the identified problems and researchers and evaluators who indicate that the evidence base for these interventions has not been well-established. This tension results in evolving policies and models of intervention based on principles, practice frameworks and interventions that may not have been rigorously demonstrated to lead to good outcomes although there may be some indications that the interventions being studied are 'promising'. EBP, 'knowledge-based practice' or 'empirically supported practice', in this chapter, will be defined as the integration of the best available research with practitioner expertise.

Several USA federal and national organizations have compiled lists that identify evidence-based or empirically supported or promising practices for work with children, young people and families in order to facilitate the use and further testing of interventions that have demonstrated success. One example is the Substance Abuse and Mental Health Services Administration (SAMHSA) that used an expert consensus review of published and unpublished evaluation and research intervention studies to develop a web-based listing of science-based prevention programmes that may be replicated and identified as models, effective interventions or promising practices. In the UK, the Social Care Institute for Excellence (SCIE) set up by government to assist in the dissemination of best evidence, started its work by commissioning a review of the 'types and quality of knowledge in social care' (Pawson et al., 2003) and regularly publishes 'knowledge reviews' aimed at practitioners (www.scie. org.uk). Best practices involve using practice wisdom, learning from other systems, expert consultation, professional guidelines and EBP (Kessler et al., 2005).

In keeping with a greater emphasis on the aspirations of people who use services to be involved in defining what they regard as satisfactory outcomes and the broader approach to research, the term 'knowledge-based' tends to be used by social work researchers alongside 'evidence-based', in part to establish the differences between the social and medical models of practice and research.

In a growing number of countries the current state of the evidence to support effective practice in work with children, young people and families has been improving as more work is done to understand not only the what, when, how, for what children and young people and under what circumstances interventions are effective but also the how and why services and supports make a difference (Maluccio et al., 2002; Zeira et al., 2008). Practice guidelines and intervention manuals have been developed to facilitate implementation of best practices. However, researchers in this field have also called attention to the weaknesses in research methodologies and reporting and to

the importance of challenging researchers if the weaknesses in the present level of evidence are to be addressed. Exemplar 2 summarizes the conclusions drawn from an edited volume on child and family welfare research by Pecora et al. (2006).

Exemplar 2

Pecora and colleagues (2006: 16–19) identified twenty-one methodological and other challenges to measuring effectiveness in child-serving systems and specific interventions or programmes. In summary these included:

- weaknesses in the theoretical frameworks guiding research or the interpretation of data;
- positive results in sheltered environments do not translate well to community settings;
- costs of evaluation often results in limited inclusion of outcome indicators;
- over-reliance on cross-section or exit data instead of longitudinal cohort data;
- limited focus on service usage and programme fidelity data;
- lack of use of standardized diagnostic measures that assess behaviour, educational functioning, satisfaction, self-esteem and other central dependent variables;
- youth, caregivers and front-line staff are often not involved in the study design and data interpretation;
- few qualitative studies have been conducted to better understand the programme model and dynamics;
- few replication studies being conducted; and
- some interventions are comprehensive but also individually tailored leading to variation within the treatment group on specific intervention components received.

Differences and similarities across jurisdictions/countries

To better understand how these challenges can be addressed it is important to briefly explore the context for interventions by identifying key practice frameworks that guide child serving system interventions. In the UK, as in much of Europe and New Zealand, the policy focus is increasingly on early intervention and universal services to prevent 'criminal activity, anti-social behaviour, under-achievement at school, and ensuring that all children fulfil their potential' (Munro and Parton, 2007: 9). The practice framework calls for improving outcomes for children and young people through integrating services across settings and enhancing the effectiveness of universal services, supplemented by targeted services for the most vulnerable or those who are already suffering maltreatment or impairment to their development. To improve communication and increase cooperation across child serving systems, the *Integrated Children's System* (ICS) and the *Common Assessment Framework* (Brandon et al., 2006) were introduced. Research to evaluate these system changes tends to take a social policy perspective rather than focusing on particular interventions for defined needs groups.

In the USA, and to a lesser extent some states in Australia and Canada, the intervention focus and funding streams continue to support a more problem-focused framework and can result in a more fragmented network of services for children and young people. The more universal approach to services and the integration of services across related systems adopted in the UK (DfES, 2004) has not been fully operationalized in the USA. The US Adoption and Safe Families Act of 1997 (ASFA Public Law 105-89), identified three national goals or outcomes for children: safety, permanency and child well-being. The focus of this act was more limited than similar UK legislation and the definitions of what these goals mean varies across states. In the USA, while each child service system has a commitment to improving child well-being, the universal and integrated focus of the UK is not supported in the USA current funding structures. While a larger proportion of the child population is served in the USA in the community, at schools, clinics and through outreach services in the home, the majority of expenditures on services for vulnerable children and young people remains invested in institutional-based services, such as residential treatment centres, juvenile justice facilities and hospitals (U.S. Department of Health and Human Services, 1999).

If we focus on approaches to *social work practice* with children and families, however, there is more commonality across national and jurisdictional boundaries. In most countries, the primary organizing framework for working with children, young people and families involves using an ecological, developmental, family-centred, resiliency-based, multi-systems perspective. The next sections will highlight key research and evaluation approaches used to measure effectiveness of, firstly, child serving systems and secondly, specific interventions and approaches to social work practice.

SOCIAL WORK RESEARCH AND EVALUATION APPROACHES THAT FOCUS ON ACCESS, ORGANIZATIONAL AND SERVICE SYSTEM ISSUES AND PATHWAYS TO SERVICES

In reviewing the social work research and evaluation methods used to address access, organizational and service system issues, and pathways to services, it is clear that the methods are influenced by the type of questions being asked.

Surveys and reanalysis of administrative data

Many studies have been conducted using administrative data and national data to better understand who is receiving services, what types of services are received, the intensity of the services, and the length of the service use for different groups of children, young people and families across child serving systems. The studies address a range of service settings (e.g. family, foster care, residential care, day treatment, specialized school settings hospital placement, juvenile justice placements, and community care) and organizational structures. Exemplar 3, from the USA, provides an example of a large scale survey building on routinely available administrative data.

Exemplar 3: The National Survey of Child and Adolescent Well-being (NSCAW) study

This federally funded study was the first longitudinal national representative study of youth (aged birth to 14 years) referred to child welfare system for maltreatment investigation. The NSCAW study used a national probability sampling strategy to select primary sampling units that were defined as geographic areas that one child welfare agency served. The NSCAW study included first hand reports from the caregivers, the case workers, the teachers and the youth over time. The study used state of the art assessment tools to measure several factors relevant to understanding child well-being. The survey methodology included over-sampling of under-represented groups. The initial NSCAW sample was obtained over a 15 month period and included 5501 children (NSCAW Research Group, 2002). Three rounds of follow-up data collection (12 months, 18 months and 36 months post baseline) have been completed and a fourth follow up began in 2005. The study addressed programme, practice and policy issues focusing on the child welfare system, and outcomes for children and families. The major research questions examined in the study included:

- Who are the children and families who come into contact with the child welfare system because of concerns about maltreatment?
- What pathways and services do children and families experience while in the child welfare system? and
- What are the short- and longer-term effects for these children and families?

(http://www.acf.hhs.gov/programs/opre/abuse_neglect/nscaw/nscaw_overview.html#overview.)

There is no similarly detailed study in the UK although three longitudinal studies of large cohorts of children born in 1958, 1970 and the recently started 'millennium cohort' study have provided opportunities for researchers to focus on different aspects of service provision (http://www.cls.ioe.ac.uk/). For example, the National Evaluation of Sure Start researchers have linked child data from the millennium cohort to improve understanding of which children are using *Sure Start* services for the under fives and have concluded that those at most risk of social exclusion are least likely to access these services (Belsky et al., 2006; Tunstill et al., 2005). Sinclair et al. (2007) used administrative data to identify a large sample of English children in out-of-home care. This cross-sectional study uses a range of quantitative and qualitative methods, and as well as reporting on the children's care careers and placement disruptions the researchers draw on their findings to explore the relative impact of the departmental organizational systems and social work and child placement teams. Swedish population data routinely updated on all children are analysed by Socialstyrensen including data on broad outcomes such as suicides, imprisonment, parental death, and basic data on services received (including foster care placement), although there is not the level of detail available from the NSCAW survey.

Using randomized trials and quasi-experimental designs to focus on service system changes

Few studies have used experimental designs in examining organizational practices. Resources for conducting randomized trials within real world settings and the complex, changing organizational structures that make up the child-serving systems has limited the use of true experimental designs. In addition, some of the questions that need to be addressed about service system access and pathways to services need to focus on understanding what happens, not just outcomes and this calls for more quasi-experimental or qualitative studies.

Exemplar 4 is an example of a randomized trial conducted in the USA focusing on the quality of child welfare services provided to youth and families and the qualification of the staff to provide needed services.

Exemplar 4

The study examined the effects of an organizational intervention strategy implemented in one state child welfare and juvenile justice system. The intervention, called the Availability, Responsiveness and Continuity (ARC) organizational intervention strategy, targeted caseworker turnover, organizational climate and organizational culture in both the child welfare and juvenile justice systems. They used a pre-post, randomized blocks, true experimental design to study this organization intervention strategy. The study hypothesized that case management teams that participated in the ARC organizational intervention would have lower levels of turnover, would develop healthier climates and develop more constructive cultures than those case management teams in the control group condition. The ARC organizational intervention, guided by five principles (mission-driven, results oriented, improvement directed, relationship centred and participation based), is delivered using a three stage process (collaboration, participation and innovation). The results of this study confirm that the ARC organizational intervention was more effective then the control group sites in reducing staff turnover by two-thirds and improved organizational climate by reducing role conflict. This study has provided the child serving systems with an effective intervention strategy to use to change organizational climate and culture, to

decrease turnover of staff and to improve child outcomes (Nunno, 2006; Glisson, 2007; Glisson et al., 2006).

It is more common for researchers and evaluators to use quasi-experimental methods to examine the effectiveness of service system changes. Quasi-experimental studies have been used to focus on the integration of service systems, the impact of providing enhanced services to children and families, and to compare costs and outcomes (O'Brien et al., 2006; Belsky et al., 2006; Berridge et al., 2008; Ryan et al., 2006).

Across jurisdictions researchers have identified that young people of colour and families and children from particular ethnic minority backgrounds are disproportionately represented in many of the key child serving systems, especially in both the child welfare and juvenile justice systems. In the USA, concepts such as over-representation, disproportionality and disparities have emerged to characterize the current state of affairs in the child welfare system and the juvenile justice system. (Disproportionality refers to a situation in which a particular racial or ethnic group of children is represented in foster care or restrictive residential or juvenile justice placements at a higher percentage than other racial or ethnic groups; Hill, 2005; Crane and Ellis, 2004; Pope and Snyder, 2003; Thoburn et al., 2005; Tilbury and Thoburn, 2008.) In addition, many researchers and evaluators are concerned with disproportionate treatment or disparities, and focus their studies on disparate or inequitable treatment or patterns of service utilization (e.g. in terms of types, quality, availability, and accessibility of services at various decision points). Using quasi-experimental and experimental studies, worker decision-making and worker turnover are some of the critical variables studied as it relates to these disparities. In addition, research and evaluation studies using administrative data and quasi-experimental methods have focused on system response concerns including placement of ethnic minority children and children of colour outside the home and in less desirable placements, differential length of stay while in out-of-home care, referral to inadequate public sector social services rather than private sector agencies, and lack of in-home or other support services.

Qualitative and mixed methods descriptive research has also been used to provide an understanding of the children and families referred for services, the helping and protective processes. The methods involve not only using administrative data and survey data, but also focus groups, in-depth interviews with children, young people and families, and other qualitative methods to better understand the context for effective service use. The government-funded *Messages from Research* series of research syntheses (for example, Quinton, 2004; Sinclair, 2005) contains many examples of UK research, some of which have a longitudinal cohort design, with data collected from records on a total cohort supplemented by detailed interviews with clients and/or workers.

In summary, a range of research and evaluation methods are currently being used to assess organizational and service system issues, access and pathways to services. Bringing the information from these evaluations and research studies to the world of policy-making and for administrators to use to improve current service delivery systems is an area where much more work needs to be done. The time lag from the study to publication often makes the information less relevant and timely for policy-makers and administrators.

STUDIES THAT EXAMINE EFFECTIVE AND APPROPRIATE INTERVENTIONS FOR DIVERSE POPULATIONS OF CHILDREN, YOUNG PEOPLE AND FAMILIES

The push to use evidence-based or empirically supported interventions in working directly with children, young people and their families has resulted in a number of evaluation and research studies that attempt to capture the key components of effective practice and to manualize interventions so that replication of these can be conducted. Many of the evidence-based or empirically supported interventions require that organizations provide significant training to ensure fidelity to the intervention model and changes in the organizational practice environment to support the interventions. Sustaining the evidence-based or empirically supported interventions and practices with integrity has surfaced as a major challenge for administrators once start up funding or grant funds end. The problem with most of the presently available evidence-based interventions or practices designed to meet the needs of the most vulnerable children and families is that it is not always clear from the research reports what elements of the intervention model or practice are critical in terms of securing hoped for outcomes. Adaptations or changes to these interventions or practice models to reflect real world situations may not produce the same outcomes as were found under the clinical or randomized trial situations. In addition, many of the interventions used in child serving settings have not been tested or replicated by multiple evaluators or researchers independent of the programme initiators.

In the UK, as in other European countries with public welfare systems combining universal and targeted services, there is less emphasis on specific defined programmes with a clear start and end date at which evaluation takes place. Legislation requires the provision of a range of practical and emotional support and therapy to be provided, concurrently or sequentially according to assessed need, often by several agencies and professions. There is also a requirement to consult parents and children about the characteristics of the service to be provided. The multi-faceted and more open-ended or episodic nature of the services therefore makes them less amenable to an RCT research methodology and, to date, there have been very few 'pure model' experimental design studies (Utting et al., 2007). However, within this broad approach, there is growing interest across Europe, both at the prevention and 'heavier end' stages of the work, in incorporating into the service some of the evidence-based approaches developed in the USA.

Researchers use quasi-experimental research designs (sometimes with 'comparison' groups providing for 'natural experiments') or longitudinal studies with 'change over time' as the outcome measure. They often use mixed methods designs with data on a background cohort drawn from records or administrative data complemented by interview data on process and outcome for a small intensive sample. Some of these have used statistical techniques to look for associations between variables about the families and process variables. These have been mainly small scale and service outputs rather than client well-being outcomes have been measured (e.g. Did the family complete the therapy programme? Did the placement disrupt? Did they exit the care system via adoption or return to the biological family?).

For these reasons, most social work interventions are 'best practices' or 'emerging practices', since they are not able to provide evidence of a causal relationship between the specified intervention and the outcomes achieved.

Several meta-analyses, systematic review, and reviews of the literature have been conducted on different interventions specific to particular settings and for particular populations. These reviews suggest that most of the intervention studies reviewed are not replicated or do not transfer easily to settings different from the original research study. The reviews also indicate that the intervention studies do not always address the different diversity dimensions that children, young people and families bring to intervention work in child serving systems. A range of assessment and outcome measures are used in the studies reviewed and many of the measures do not adequately capture change over time.

In the UK some of the rich descriptive and mixed methods research is scoped in books and websites aiming to reach social work practitioners. As well as the *Messages from Research* overviews and the SCIE knowledge reviews referred to above, there are several publications which scope the knowledge in particular areas of practice. These include chapters in Wilson and James' (2007) *Child Protection Handbook* and Sellick et al.'s (2004) *What Works in Adoption and Fostering?* As well as considering the question of disproportionality, Thoburn et al. (2005) scope the literature on services and outcomes for children of minority heritage in receipt of social work services.

Evidence of effectiveness is more robust at the lower levels of need (e.g. parent education groups when problems first start to emerge) or for very specific groups such as young offenders (Kazdin, 2005). At the preventive stage of family work, a series of evidence-based interventions and promising practices focus on parent management training programs across child serving systems. Several parent management training programmes in the UK and the USA have been manualized and use social learning techniques to change the behaviour of children and young people. Some of the parent management training interventions have been tested in randomized clinical trials, while others have emerged as promising practices based on evaluations that are agency specific or population specific. The more promising parent management interventions focus on working with parents/ carers of children and young people experiencing antisocial behaviour, oppositional, defiant or conduct disorders, delinquent behaviour, attention-deficit/hyperactivity disorders and those who are at risk for substance use (Kazdin, 2005; Patterson, 2005). Webster-Stratton (2001) focused on youth, three to eight years, and used culturally and developmentally appropriate curricula to train parents and teachers. The curricula involve the use of video vignettes to help parents learn new skills, teach children important social skills in order to succeed with friends and in school and train teachers to use effective classroom management skills. The manualization of this intervention has allowed for several replications in many sites in the USA. It is also an increasing part of the preventive or early intervention services provided in the UK, especially in the Sure Start`Children's Centres, Extended Schools, and Youth Justice programmes being rolled out through increased government funding. Exemplar 5 highlights a randomized study of a model of practice used in the USA in the juvenile justice, educational and mental health systems. This exemplar also raises some of the issues that researchers and evaluators face when examining effectiveness and focusing on outcomes.

Exemplar 5

The intervention is Multisystemic Family Therapy (MST) developed by Henggeler et al. (1998). This intervention, which is about to be trialled in the UK, has been promoted as being the 'gold standard' for work with high risk youth and their families. The ecologically based, short-term, intensive home and community delivered intervention programme targets work with youth with severe psychosocial and behavioural problems and their families. The intervention provides an alternative to out-of-home placement for these high risk youth. The MST intervention programme is manualized, includes measures to ensure fidelity, requires supervisors and workers to be certified to deliver MST services, and identifies key organizational supports that need to be in place for the MST model to be implemented effectively. MST has a relatively robust evidence base with several RCTs. The MST researchers have reported improvement in youth mental health, school engagement, pro-social behaviour, positive peer relationships and family communication. It has been replicated in many sites in the USA and Canada. While several peer-reviewed

articles document the effectiveness of MST, a systematic review of the effects of MST conducted by Littell et al. (2005) for the Cochrane Collaborative Review showed that there may be no significant differences between MST and usual services. In both conditions, youth improved but MST outcomes were no different then outcomes from usual services. This systematic review raised questions about the MST studies focusing on the inconsistent reports on who is in the sample and how missing cases were identified, the unyoked designs, the unclear randomization procedures, the different observation periods and what was meant by treatment completion. Through this review, Littell (2005) raised several important issues for evaluators, researchers, policy makers, practitioners and administrators who search for effective interventions to use to improve outcomes for children and young people. The issues centre on ensuring that independent evaluations are used to replicate findings before the interventions are promoted as effective in real world settings and that limitations to the intervention and its effects are clearly articulated and transparent. If the outcomes of MST are no different from usual services, then policy makers and administrators need to assess whether to invest scarce resources in the high cost of training and supervision of workers to be certified in the MST intervention, especially when it may not produce better outcomes for their youth and families.

Another approach to bringing evidence-based methods to front line social work has focused on adapting interventions that have been piloted and positively evaluated in clinical settings to the contexts and characteristics of clients referred to mainstream social work teams. Such adaptations have then to be documented and evaluated to see if similar outcomes can be achieved, a step which is all too frequently not taken. Tensions can occur, however, between those who develop the interventions and argue the need for programme fidelity if the reported outcomes are to be achieved, and practitioners and people who use services who argue for adaptations.

There is a rich literature from the UK and other countries in Europe describing populations of children and families referred for a social work or child protection service and the services provided (see for example Quinton's (2004) overview of government funded research on family support services). The prospective longitudinal studies reported by Hunt and Macleod (1999) and by Brandon and Thoburn (2008) of cohorts of children referred for child protection services are examples of the several government-funded longitudinal studies that provide data on child welfare outcomes and look for associations between the characteristics of the children suffering significant harm, the services provided and more or less successful outcomes. However, even when numbers are quite large, the large number of variables, and especially the complexity of services provided, in some cases over several years, precludes the drawing of conclusions about causation.

Moving on to the population of children in out-of-home care, overviews of outcomes for young people leaving care in several countries are provided by the authors in Stein and Munro's (2008) edited book on transitions to adulthood and Bullock et al. (2006) summarize the outcome research from several countries. Exemplar 6 is an example of a mixed methods longitudinal study of children entering care who were subsequently reunified with birth relatives. Other researchers in this field focus on decision making aspects of intervention, and/or on the detailed care and therapeutic interventions provided in group care or by adopters of children with special needs or foster carers.

Exemplar 6

Bullock et al. (1998) combined data from three separate cohort studies of children entering a range of placements in care. A mixed methods approach was followed. Data from case records from total cohorts (n = 875) was combined with detailed information on children, their families, the services provided and the child well-being outcomes obtained from records and in-depth interviews on a sub-sample (n = 31). The characteristics of the extensive and intensive samples were compared to allow for a consideration of the generalizability of the findings. The study concludes with guidance for social workers on assessing the likelihood that children with different characteristics will return safely home. This research and others on the same subject highlight that, for UK children, whether outcome is measured in terms of re-abuse, re-entry into care or general well-being, return to parents is the most 'risky' option once children have been in care for more than a few weeks. Since, as their research shows, a large majority of care entrants sooner or later return to their families of origin, these studies demonstrate the importance of practitioners and researchers working together to improve support and services made available to this most vulnerable group of children and parents.

One programme that has been building a solid evidence base is the Oregon Multidimensional Treatment Foster Care (MTFC) intervention. This intervention programme facilitates opportunities for youth with anti-social problems involved in the juvenile justice, mental health, or child welfare system to live successfully in the community (Chamberlain and Smith, 2003). The MTFC programme involves parent(s), program supervisors, family therapists, individual therapists and behavioural support specialists in working together to deliver the intervention. Youth in this intervention are placed in foster care where the foster parents are trained to be the primary treatment agents and the youth's biological parents and families help to shape the treatment plan. The most recent study of the MTFC intervention was a randomized evaluation focusing on the effects on school attendance and homework completion in girls involved in the juvenile justice system. MTFC was more effective for these girls than group treatment in increasing school attendance and homework completion while in treatment and 12 months post baseline (Leve and Chamberlain, 2007). A trial of MTFC is nearing completion in the UK, but results are not yet available.

Several studies conducted in the UK, other European countries and Australia of children in care or adopted from care (summarized in overviews by Parker, 1999; Sinclair, 2005; and the edited book on transitions to adulthood of Stein and Munro, 2008) have used a longitudinal prospective or cross-sectional cohort design, with placement stability, educational attainment, changes in well-being and/or measures of satisfaction as outcome measures. For example, Sinclair et al. (2004) used case records and postal surveys to provide data on a cross-sectional sample of over 1500 foster carers and 596 foster children, mostly in long-term care.

In the USA, there have been similar studies on re-unification and other foster care outcomes using longitudinal and quasi-experimental designs (Wulczyn., 2004; Pecora et al., 2005; Courtney et al., 2007).

Summary

In summary, despite the large volume of sound descriptive research and the growing number of experimental, quasi-experimental or longitudinal studies, researchers still have significant work to do in the area of describing and evaluating interventions for children, young people and families. More replications of promising and emerging practices need to be conducted with increased focus on process as well as outcomes. These must be independent of the initiators of programmes, and designed around the different populations and levels of need of those referred for a child and family social work service. As the number of experimental studies of programmes developed in controlled, clinical settings expands, it is especially important that adaptations to fit day-to-day practice conditions are developed and evaluated. It is also essential that researchers do not turn their backs on 'practice-based evidence'. As innovative interventions emerge in the course of practice they must be systematically evaluated using research methods most appropriate to the characteristics of the service and client group. This fits with the need for a greater focus on understanding how the context and different moderators influence the intervention.

NEXT STEPS FOR SOCIAL WORK RESEARCH AND EVALUATION IN THE AREA OF CHILDREN, YOUNG PEOPLE AND FAMILIES

In this chapter, we have discussed the key research and evaluation methods being used to inform practice with children, young people and families, and highlighted a few of the key studies that serve as exemplars to illustrate the types of evaluation and research underway. The state of our knowledge of what works and for which children, young people and families, and under what conditions varies across child serving systems.

The limitations to current research and evaluation identified by Pecora et al. (2006) are causes for concern as we move forward in developing new research and evaluation studies. The movement to more integrated services that cross child serving systems and the emphasis on universal and preventive services call for more studies that address what are the most effective models of integrated services, and how are children, young people and families with the highest level of need best served in these new structures. In order to know what works in preventive interventions more longitudinal studies also need to be conducted. In the USA, the fragmented child serving system challenges evaluators and researchers to cross service systems to better understand how to help the 'whole' child or young person, and their families. In addition, the limited number of evidence-based interventions and our understanding of what works for diverse groups of children, young people and families needs to be addressed in future studies. The next steps for social work researchers and evaluators are to continue to build the knowledge base to inform practice and, in partnership with their practitioner colleagues and the children and families they serve, to develop interventions that demonstrate positive outcomes for diverse groups with diverse needs.

We must also close the gap between new interventions and research knowledge and their being rolled out to reach more of the children, young people and families who can benefit from them. To improve the quality of services and to increase the likelihood of positive outcomes, evaluators and researchers need to continue to address: 1) access to services issues; 2) ways to improve organizational structures and coordinating systems across child serving systems; 3) development studies that help social work practitioners and families to change behaviours and make more informed choices, 4) evaluations of the uses made by social work practitioners of risk assessment and other decision support tools at critical points throughout the service system and across child serving systems; and 5) exploration of how best to incorporate into research the variable of the quality of the relationships between social work practitioners and diverse groups of children, young people and families. These studies need to occur in real world settings and address not only outcomes but also the contexts that influence hoped for outcomes.

It is clear that researchers and evaluators are using a range of quantitative and qualitative methods to better understand the context and outcomes for children, young people and families; however, the studies provide limited practical knowledge to help practitioners and managers to know what to do at a particular point in time with a particular child, young person or family. Organizational or clinical interventions that work in one setting are not easily transported or replicated in other settings.

Evaluators and researchers need to consider using more mixed methods research in order to capture the complexity of the service system and clinical interventions. Mixed methods research involves collecting and analysing both quantitative and qualitative data. For example, quantitative data collected from standardized instruments and qualitative data collected during focus group sessions or in-depth research interviews may show similar results or may have different results since different perspectives are being captured. As well as providing data on outcomes, mixed methods research promotes better understanding of context, process and what parents and children find helpful.

Findings and results from research and evaluation studies need to be made more available through a range of dissemination methods to policy-makers, service managers and practitioners, and also to family members and their advocates, in a more timely and responsive way. Evaluators and researchers need to advocate for policy-makers, administrators and first line managers to provide the necessary funds to conduct more studies in real world settings. Practitioners will only use evidence-based or empirically supported interventions if these interventions help them to better serve diverse groups of children, young people and families.

Health and Well-being

Paul Bywaters and Michael Ungar

INTRODUCTION AND DEFINITIONS

This chapter, on social work research on health and well-being, necessarily borders on and overlaps with other contributions to this *Handbook*. Separate discussions of research on disability, on ageing and on mental health provide some boundaries for this chapter which focuses primarily on social work research in relation to physical health and illness and the broader concept of well-being. However, at the outset it has to be recognized that this is not conceptually satisfactory. Separating physical health and well-being from associated 'cognitive, mental, behavioural and emotional dimensions' (Bradshaw, 2002: xiii) is particularly problematic. The International Federation of Social Workers' policy statement on health[1] endorses the World Health Organization's definition of health as 'complete physical, mental, and social well-being and not merely the absence of disease or infirmity'. Separating the physical, the bodily, from the social and emotional is not a position that social workers would normally wish to assert.

Most social work research on health takes this definition for granted although the longstanding emphasis in social work on giving voice to what service users,[2] patients or lay people have to say about their own health (e.g. Broad, 2005) should have led to closer examination of what health means to different actors in different contexts. Research into 'lay' definitions of health from outside social work, for example, by Blaxter (1990) or Flick (2000), makes it clear that 'health' is a contested term. 'Health' can have multiple meanings or dimensions to a person, at different times or in response to different circumstances. It also has different meanings to different people, making talking with service users about their health fraught with problems (Bywaters, 2000). Conceptualizations of health are influenced by the culture and mind-set of those defining the construct (Chan, 2001; 2006; Julia and Kondat, 2005; Murguia et al., 2003; Ungar, 2004).

It is not the purpose of this chapter, however, to discuss the definition and meanings of health and well-being at length. Instead, we must specify two parameters to the discussion that follows. First, we will focus *primarily* on physical health, illness and well-being and not on mental health, although we recognize, of course, that physical health necessarily has mental and emotional, as well as social, dimensions and accompaniments. Second, this chapter also does not provide a focus on research into disability, while recognizing that the impairments which lead to disabling responses are often the result of illness, that illness is commonly stigmatizing, and that it brings discriminatory and disadvantaging socially created consequences.

If those two conditions are set to narrow the focus of the discussion, in two other respects we choose to draw our boundaries broadly. Social work research on health and well-being includes work on the social determinants of health, on prevention and health promotion as well as on the social and practice consequences of illness. We are interested in what influences people's 'health chances' (see below) as well as how they fare when ill, their 'health experience'. In considering the social determinants, we examine what makes for resilience as well as vulnerability (Ungar, 2005b).

Both because of the focus on the determinants of health and because much health work is undertaken by lay people – ill people themselves and informal carers, for example (Stacey, 1988) – in domestic settings, we will not only discuss research about health *care* or social work activity in health *settings* (such as primary care teams or hospitals) but also care provided in communities by informal providers. These informal carers, like social workers in all contexts, deal either with the consequences of ill health or with social and economic circumstances and conditions which may threaten future health (McLeod and Bywaters, 2000).

CONTEXT AND INFRASTRUCTURE

Despite these boundary restrictions the terrain covered by social work research on health and well being internationally remains vast and disparate. For example, we can examine health through different lenses; focusing on individuals and families, communities and populations or institutions and social structures. What follows is necessarily a snapshot, no doubt reflecting the interests of the two authors, both male academics, one from Canada and the other from the UK.

Structural supports

The infrastructure supports for social work research in health are primarily of three kinds: social work journals; social work conferences; and social work networks and associations. Key peer reviewed international social work or social work related journals explicitly focusing on health related practice, policy and research include *Health and Social Work* (HSW), *Social Work in Health Care* (SWiHC) and the *Journal of Psychosocial Oncology*, based in the USA and *Health and Social Care in the Community* (HSCC) based in the UK. This is in addition to the publication of health related articles in the generic social work journals, and social work articles in health journals. The explicitly health focused social work journals are dominated by editorial board members drawn from the USA, with additional input from the United Kingdom and Australia and this is reflected in the content of articles included. There is almost a complete absence of board members or authors from the Indian Sub-continent, South and Central America, Africa, the Middle East (other than Israel), China and Eastern Europe. This must influence the range of work published and any claim the journals have to documenting phenomena with pan-human validity. Genuinely globalizing these supposedly international journals should be a focus of editorial effort.

By comparison to other specialisms *within social work* (although not other disciplines), the availability of conferences at which research can be presented and discussed, and networks built, is relatively strong. The series of triennial social work conferences on health and mental health has been successful in attracting large numbers of participants to venues in Israel, Australia, Finland, Canada and Hong Kong. The annual conferences of the Association of Oncology Social Workers are US based and focused on issues relevant to their health care system, although parallel Oncology Associations in other countries, such as Australia, are beginning to extend the boundaries. The attendance at such conferences reflects both the venues chosen and the ability of participants to meet or find the costs. Once again this skews participation towards wealthy developed countries and towards academics from those countries rather than practitioners or service users.

A third pillar of support is provided by health related social work associations and networks supporting research. Some examples of national and international associations include The Association of Oncology Social Workers and the Society for Social Work Leadership in Health Care which are both based in the USA. The Association of Palliative Care Social Workers is UK based. Sweden has a network of health related social work researchers. Although not formalized as an organization, the pioneering international educational work of the Division of Social Work and Behavioural Science at the Mount Sinai Hospital, New York, has been influential in creating links between practitioners and researchers in the USA, Israel, Australia, Hong Kong and other countries (Rehr et al., 1993). The Social Work and Health Inequalities Network[3] is also international, with members in at least 12 countries, but this does not constitute extensive coverage. Once again these structural mechanisms which support research activity are limited in their reach across the world.

RESEARCH FUNDING

Linked to these limitations in structural supports for health related social work research is the central issue of research funding. A major weakness for social work generally – and health related social work is no

exception – is the limited funding and infrastructure available for research by comparison with other disciplines and particularly in relation to colleagues in other 'health' sciences. This has been documented for the UK by Marsh and Fisher (2005) who estimated that the level of research funding per head of the workforce for social care practitioners was well over 100 times less than that available for health care workers. In the UK, major investments of research funding have been made available through the central government funded research councils for other applied disciplines including nursing, teaching and management but not, as yet, for social work. This lack of underpinning investment is reflected in the relative weakness of research infrastructure in social work, for example, in terms of the training routes and training resources available to aspiring social work researchers, the availability of experienced mentors and role models or opportunities to participate as junior members of research teams on large scale projects. Social workers in health settings or working with health care colleagues usually operate in highly research conscious environments in which evidence of effectiveness carries significant weight and is vital for credibility. Furthermore, evidence is often judged against a perceived hierarchy of research methods with randomized controlled trials (RCTs) second only to systematic reviews (Morago, 2006) and by systems of measurement (for example, the counting of citations as a measure of the 'impact' of journals) which necessarily tip the scales against disciplines with small numbers, poor funding and relatively few research outlets. Add to this the fact that social work researchers often investigate social phenomena using qualitative methods which are often more synchronic with the nature of the field's interventions, and the problem becomes even more exacerbated when it comes to securing research funding (Ungar, 2003b). The problem of legitimacy, which has long existed for social workers working alongside other health professions, is compounded when the discipline is not recognized for its potential contribution.

METHODOLOGICAL ISSUES

One consequence of the limited volume of health related social work research overall (see Auslander, 2001), and the even smaller amount of substantial research employing rigorous methods, is that there are few examples of the systematic reviews or meta-analyses. This approach to consolidating knowledge is a demanding task in disciplines in which RCTs are standard (see below) while methods for the systematic review of non-trial and qualitative research are less well developed (SCIE, 2006). Parker et al. (2006) is one example of a systematic review by a social work research group which examined studies of paediatric home care for evidence of cost-effectiveness. These were not necessarily studies by social workers nor was their focus on social work practice. Kadushin (2004) carried out a systematic review of studies of 'Home Health Care Utilization' to identify which characteristics of service users were associated with home care use. Once again the studies included many which were neither focused on social work services nor on research by social workers. Like numerous others, this study focused on access to services not on outcomes.

The problem is particular relevant to investigations of practice domains typically populated by social workers. Thus, even when investigating the effects of multiple service use on service users in child welfare, corrections, community health and educational counselling settings, social work researchers have had to share the spotlight with researchers from disciplines such as psychology, education and nursing. The irony of the situation is that it is most often social workers who act in the capacity of case managers, helping people cross over between systems, navigating their way to health supporting resources (Cameron, 2003). There is a strong

case to be made for research that can document the processes of concern to social workers: the systemic concerns and processes of service utilization rather than the study of the aetiology of disorder.

There is a range of reasons why it is difficult to establish effective RCTs of social work interventions. In addition to the conceptual, ethical and financial obstacles discussed elsewhere in this *Handbook*, social workers are commonly working with marginalized populations often excluded from medical research trials. These are research participants who are hard to reach and hard to retain in trials. For example, Lewis et al. (2000) wished to conduct a study to establish whether an educational programme could reduce risky behaviours in a population of homeless people with HIV and a history of substance abuse. Almost by definition the clientele of this programme were hard to reach, irregular in attendance at the project and liable to drop out. This precluded a pre-test – post-test model for the study and the validity of resultant comparison between new service users and those still in the programme at six months was inevitably undermined. Conducting rigorous RCTs with this kind of population is practically impossible, leaving aside ethical considerations.

Given that the focus of social work activity is often on groups of people who are marginalized in terms of mainstream services, including very elderly people, members of minority ethnic groups and gay, lesbian, bi- and trans-sexual people, it is not surprising that awareness of the importance of inclusion has become a feature of health related social work research. For example, Cwikel and Behar (1999) discuss this issue at length in their review of social work services with adult cancer patients. While social work research may have been weak in terms of large scale quantitative studies of effectiveness, in part this is because of social work's focus on access and inclusion. A strength of social work research is its willingness to engage with sensitive issues. For example,

Beresford et al. (2007a) in the UK have pioneered qualitative studies of service users' perspectives on palliative care social work.

A second key methodological contribution from health related social work research has been the promotion of practitioner based research (Joubert, 2006). Epstein and Blumenfield's (2002) promotion of the techniques of data mining have opened up the potential for practitioners to conduct small scale studies using existing, routinely collected data and this has assisted in creating a culture of evaluation within some hospital social work teams (Auslander, 2001). Other, more often used, qualitative methods, such as Appreciative Inquiry (Hammond and Royal, 2001), intervention research and case studies, are far better suited to research *in situ* where randomization and controls are impractical and unethical.

DEFINING THE TERRAIN

There have been a number of previous attempts to define the terrain of health related social work research. For example, the Karolinska Institute in Sweden presents its research activity in terms of three key domains:

- The psychological and social background factors that influence onset of disease, the experience of being ill, and adaptation to the disease;
- Psychosocial and social consequences of disease, injury and treatment;
- Methods for developing and evaluating psychosocial work in the health care system and for collaboration among different caregivers and care providers (see http://www.karolinska.se).

This description has a clear rationale: focusing on the human and environmental causes and consequences of ill-health in the first place and then on the effectiveness of service provision and co-ordination. It finds echoes in Ell's (1996) distinction between basic psychosocial research, on the one hand,

and psychosocial treatment and intervention research, and health services research, on the other. However, it can be criticized on two main grounds. First, it is illness rather than health focused and appears to exclude work on well-being, on health promotion or strengths based analysis. Second, it appears not to recognize the relevance for health of social work practice outside the health care system: that social work in all settings is engaged with the health of clients, whether explicitly or implicitly.

With these caveats, the structure for the remainder of this chapter is informed by a similar conceptual distinction between research which focuses on the causes and impact of health and ill-health in people's lives and that which focuses on developing and evaluating service provision; between service user focused research and service provision focused research.

RESEARCH THAT FOCUSES ON SERVICE USERS' HEALTH AND WELL-BEING

This section focuses on research that describes, analyses or tests evidence about the health and well-being of actual or potential social work service users. This falls into two main areas: health chances and health experience (McLeod and Bywaters, 2000).

Research on health chances

Research on health chances examines factors which affect the prospects of good health or the likelihood of poor health and reduced life expectancy in individuals, families, communities or populations. Predominantly, this work focuses on the social, economic, environmental and political determinants of health as they affect people in contact with or at risk of being in contact with social workers. This includes service user perspectives on the potential for and barriers to achieving good health for themselves or others.

There is an extensive international literature on the social determinants of health (Marmot and Wilkinson, 2005; Raphael, 2004) and this is the focus of a major current World Health Organization initiative to reduce health inequalities (http://www.who.int/social_determinants/en/). Given the prevalence of health damaging social and environmental conditions amongst social work service users, it might be anticipated that social work researchers would have made a significant contribution to this arena, but this cannot be claimed. As Auslander (2001) suggests, the majority of research articles focus on 'describing social work interventions or documenting the psychosocial sequelae of acute and chronic illness' (2001: 214). She argues that there is an insufficient focus on outcomes and we would add that there is also an insufficient focus on the social causes of illness. This is, perhaps, in part, because, with notable exceptions (for example, Hudson, 2005), few social work researchers have engaged in epidemiological studies.

There are, of course, some interesting counter examples of basic research on the links between social conditions and health which may not be widely known. For example, Soskolne et al.'s (1996) study of the impact of the Persian Gulf War on physical health, health behaviours and psychological distress in high and low risk areas in Israel is a rare example of explicit linkage being made between international conflict and health outcomes by social work researchers. Soskolne and colleagues have also undertaken a number of studies linking structural socio-economic factors with migration and health outcomes (for example, Soskolne and Shtarkshall, 2002). Two studies from the *Indian Journal of Social Work* (Mor, 2003; Gandhi et al., 2003) examine respectively the impact of working in the brick kiln industry and of the traditional role of fetching water on women's health. But all too often, poor social conditions are the unexplored, taken for granted backdrop to research findings rather than their focus.

Some exceptions exist in more politicized research on well-being that is conscious of the difference between people who face multiple risks and overcoming the odds, and the structural changes that instead help 'change the odds' (Seccombe, 2002) stacked against vulnerable populations. This person-in-environment focus is one of the contributions that social work researchers have made to the burgeoning field of resilience research where initially psychologists focused on individual mental health characteristics and the adaptive nature (plasticity) of individual's interactions in risky environments (Lerner et al., 2003). Though context is a part of these discussions, it has in the main never been given equal consideration. Studies by Garmezy (1985) on children with mothers who have been diagnosed with schizophrenia judged the children resilient if they overcame their disadvantage and secured positive relationships and opportunities to change their life trajectories. The environment is facilitative, but the focus is always on what the child does to compensate, not how service providers and communities can increase resilience by creating resilient contexts in which to grow. This perspective is much more in evidence in the community health promotion literature, such as the International Federation of Red Cross and Red Crescent Societies (2004) world disaster survey which views people's capacity to survive cataclysmic community stressors to be directly related to the social, physical and ecological capital in place in a community before disaster strikes. Healthy high-context communities with networks of support weather severe threats to people's physical well-being better than communities that lack social cohesion.

At the level of individuals at risk, a good example of this need for a more contextualized perspective of health antecedents is an important series of UK research projects exploring the experience of care leavers. Details are presented in Exemplar 1. These studies have been unusual not only in focusing explicitly on the health of the young people concerned but in trying to examine causes of poor and threatened health (Broad, 1994; 1998; 1999; 2005; Broad and Saunders, 1998; Monaghan and Broad, 2003; Smith et al., 2002).

Exemplar 1: The health of care leavers

In the 1990s, Broad and colleagues undertook two national surveys of young people leaving the UK care system and followed up by two further studies: a national survey of the impact of the Children (Leaving Care) Act 2000 and a qualitative study of the views and experiences of young people who had recently left care, reported together in Broad (2005). A third national survey reported by Broad (2005) took the form of a 40 item questionnaire sent to over 300 voluntary and statutory sector teams in England and Wales working with care leavers between 12 and 18 months after the CLCA was enacted. A 20% response rate from teams working with almost 6000 young people made this the largest survey of leaving care services ever reported in the UK. Within a range of pre-coded and open questions, health and well-being was one focus.

The findings make it clear that, while improving, health was still a relatively marginalized issue for the teams. For example, only 2% of staff in the teams were health specialists and no teams had negotiated specialist services from local health providers. There was an almost total absence of effective mental health and substance abuse services and the teams themselves rated health as their least effective area of service. Crucially for the argument here, Broad also identified the failure of the services to recognize that the almost universal poverty and frequently very poor housing conditions of this vulnerable group of young people were damaging to their health. These were not perceived as health issues by the teams, which saw health in terms of the provision of health services.

This perspective is in stark contrast to the understandings of the fifty-seven young people attending three leaving care projects who were interviewed for the second (qualitative) study. The research team engaged about twenty of the young people in carrying out the study which involved collecting data through a variety of methods: semi-structured interview schedules, questionnaires, health diaries, focus groups and an analysis of written documentation about the policies and plans of key local health and social care agencies. Care leavers were involved as researchers in the development and direction of the project, as peer interviewers, and in the identification of recommendations and examples of good practice.

More than one in five of the care leavers identified themselves as having a specific problem with illness or disability. But the young people as a whole identified a much wider range of issues as relevant to their health and well-being. These included key social determinants such as lack of money, poor accommodation and crime as well as problems with relationships, including violence, bullying and abuse, stress and smoking. Their frame of reference included physical, mental, sexual, emotional and psychological aspects of health. They also identified having more money, better accommodation and better support as the three key factors for improving their health.

Research on 'health experience'

'Health experience' research examines the experience of people who have poor physical health, resulting from either acute or longer term conditions. It also investigates the experience of being a carer of someone with poor health. This work explores such topics as the subjective lived experience and meaning of illness; negotiating health and social care services; self-care and self-management; and the interaction of different dimensions of identity (for example, gender, ethnicity, disability, GLBT sexual orientation, age) with this experience.

Developing an understanding of the lived experience of health and illness has been a focus of sociological analysis for over 50 years. Parsons (1951) opened up the terrain by suggesting that sickness involved choice and subjectivity and almost fifty years later Turner (1995) stated that 'A theoretically informed medical sociology would be concerned to criticize the idea of illness as mere behaviour by drawing attention to role of choice, meaning and agency in the experience of illness' (1995: 3–4). Of course, this is not to imply that people choose to be ill, but only that subjective experiences of conditions of disorder and poor functioning cannot be measured without attention to the perceptual frame of the individuals involved. Given social work's occupational focus on understanding the world through the eyes of service users and carers it is not surprising that a considerable volume of social work research has sought to explore the subjective experience of health and illness. A number of strands can be perceived in this work.

The most striking theme is the extent to which this work is about women's experience and conducted by women researchers. For example, recent research has been published on failed pregnancy (Bergart, 2000, O'Dea, 1990), breast cancer (Lethborg et al., 2003; Hirschman and Bourjolly, 2005), the menopause (Jones, 1994) and osteoporosis (Munch and Shapiro, 2006). There is no equivalent writing by social workers about, for example, male infertility, prostate cancer or early male retirement due to ill health. Nor, to our knowledge, is there a male equivalent of the personal exploration of the impact of illness found in Donner and Batliwalla's (2005) account of their joint experience of the onset of blindness in one of the authors. Some work examines the

influence of ethnicity and racism on the experience of health and illness (for example, Bernard and Este, 2005; Richardson et al., 2001) but this and other dimensions of structural inequality are much less prominent than the focus on women's lives. Such structural analysis, however, is still relatively rare. Indeed, much of the work on women's experience does not treat gender as a key analytical variable.

By focusing on gender and race, investigations of health experience broaden their perspective beyond the medical to address the social. For Jones (1994) this is an explicit objective, to reclaim from medicalized conceptions women's understandings of their bodies. Although some studies focus on a specific disease entity, others assert that a common experience of illness can arise across diagnoses. For example, Docherty and McColl (2003) explore commonalities in the response to diagnosis, impact of stress, view of death and search for meaning across respondents with different diagnoses. Similarly Grenier (2006) is interested in the subjective experiences of a descriptor which cuts across diagnostic categories: being and feeling frail (in older women). However, Golub et al. (2006) and Richardson et al. (2001), focusing on HIV, and Jones and Egan (2000) on liver transplants, operate within a diagnostic field. In Golub et al.'s case this is a product of the focus of their studies: Golub et al. are interested in adherence to the particular medication regime involved in HIV. Richardson et al. aimed to discover information about the co-relationship between an HIV diagnosis and symptoms of depression, and the influence of social factors such as ethnic identity, substance use and experiencing violence in relationships on co-morbidity. Jones and Egan use liver transplants as an example on which to base wider conclusions about developments in social work roles in health care.

Another dimension of a social perspective is recognition that illness is not just an individual experience: illness also impacts on those close to the person with the diagnosis, while social support is important for the experience of the ill person. This is drawn attention to in many of the studies to which we have already referred and is a central focus in others, for example Choi and Wodarski (1996) and Grinyer (2006). Choi and Wodarski explore the relationship between the size of a person's social support network and the extent of support available as ill-health worsens, while Grinyer examines the impact on mothers' health of caring for a child with cancer.

Most of the work referred to uses a variety of qualitative approaches including grounded theory and narrative analysis (Docherty and McColl, 2003), intersubjective, autobiographical methods (Donner and Batliwalla, 2005), ethnography, and content analysis (Golub et al., 2006). The use of quantitative approaches by Richardson et al. and Choi and Wodarski is not rare, but less common, with mixed methods favoured where quantitative research is conducted (Ungar, 2006). A linking theme of this work, although it is only sometimes an explicit dimension, is exposing service user – or potential service user – perspectives on health and illness. However, it can be argued that there is a lack of conceptual thinking underpinning many of these studies, an absence drawn attention to by Tangenberg and Kemp (2002) who argue for an emphasis on the physical and sociocultural dimensions of the body: the experiencing body, the body of power, and the client body.

RESEARCH THAT FOCUSES ON SERVICE PROVISION

Research discussed in the previous section provides social work practice with background knowledge of the causes (individual and social) and experience of health and illness. This section focuses on research that directly describes, analyses or tests evidence about the role of social work practice in promoting good health and well-being and in preventing or managing poor health. Again this can be divided into two main parts: social work interventions and the work context of practice.

Research on social work interventions

Research on social work interventions has involved a wide range of descriptive and evaluative studies analysing social work practice which either directly targets service users' health or which aims to promote health, prevent ill-health or mitigate the consequences of illness by the provision of social care, community development or other forms of intervention. In reality, most of this work focuses on social work in health care settings and not on community based practice. Most is concerned with social work with individuals and families rather than populations. Nag (2002) and Nadkarni (2002), both working in India, are interesting exceptions.

Much of the published research has as a sub-text the persistent and continuing problem of legitimacy or, at least, security of social work in health care settings (Sulman et al., 2001). Although, as Auslander (2001) argues, in some countries the place of social work in health settings is required by legislation or, at the very least, certain roles have statutory backing, the situation is far from secure. Where there is legislative support for tasks such as assessment or education, it is often not specified that a social worker has to carry out the role and this weakness has led to challenges from managers and from other professions and occupational groups on grounds of expertise and cost. Moreover, such legislative support is far from universal. In the UK, for example, even the raw numbers of social workers based in health settings is no longer known as national statistics ceased to be collected in the 1980s. The continuing presence of social workers in the majority of National Health Service hospitals has been accompanied by focusing the role on organizational priorities such as length of stay and transfer to community provision with little recognition of the profession's potential to make a wider contribution to holistic patient care.

Thus much of the research can be seen as linked to attempts to provide the evidence base to justify social work's presence despite the cost to – in most countries[4] – hospital or health care provider budgets. Many studies have focused on identifying the need for social work intervention, social work's capacity to reach marginalized patient groups, improved adherence to medical treatments resulting from social worker activities, enhanced patient satisfaction or greater effectiveness in treatment, including cost-effectiveness. In Exemplar 2 we focus particularly on the body of work which explores social work's role in discharge planning.

Exemplar 2: Discharge planning and the role of social work

In the 1970s and 1980s, a series of studies (see Bywaters, 1991) published predominantly in the USA, were built around a recognition that a key lever in achieving legitimacy for the profession would be to demonstrate that hospital social workers could contribute to reducing the length of time that patients stayed in hospital. This offered a 'winning combination' as Boone et al. (1981) described it, promising that if social work could deliver reduced lengths of stay, improved quality of discharge and, hence reduced unplanned readmission rates, it would meet both the desire of hospital managers for reduced costs and of patients for shorter hospital stays and better help to return home. As shorter stays were more likely if social workers had access to patients early in their hospitals stays – or even before admission – this would legitimize social work as a core role in the treatment team, rather than a 'disposal' activity, tagged on when the

medical treatment was finished. Furthermore, if social workers saw patients early in their stays to start discharge planning, this opened up the possibility of offering services which met other aspects of patients' concerns and experiences (Blumenfield and Rosenberg, 1988).

Over a twenty year period from Berkman and Rehr's (1970) first unexpected discovery of the link between screening and length of stay the health social work research community extended and developed its evidence base. There were a number of strands to this work. Some studies focused on validating early access to patients through screening tools, demonstrating that screening could enable social workers to access a more diverse and appropriate range of patients. This developed into studies of pre-admission screening for elective surgery patients (see, for example, Berkman and Rehr, 1973; Berkman et al., 1988; Reardon et al., 1988). These overlapped with other work focusing on demonstrating the impact of social work discharge planning on lengths of stay (for example, Boone et al., 1981; Krell, 1977). A third element examined whether social work's involvement with discharge planning resulted in better quality discharge experiences for patients, including enhanced community services (for example, Oktay, 1992). This led in turn to studies of the impact of new services designed to ease the transfer from hospital (for example, Schwartz et al., 1990). The final element of the care pathway was completed by research which examined the impact of these forms of practice on unplanned re-admission rates (for example, Berkman et al., 1992; Proctor et al., 2000). Subsequently, refinements have included examining how particular populations fared in the discharge process, especially disadvantaged patient groups (Cox, 1996) and extending the focus of attention from patients to care givers (Kane et al., 1999).

This body of work, along with many other studies not mentioned here, constitutes a substantial and comprehensive research series not often found in social work research. Key researchers, especially Barbara Berkman, were central to this endeavour, which met an organizational and practice need in the profession and have been widely influential. A variety of research methods were employed, with quantitative, qualitative and mixed method studies being found. However, in terms of the impact of the work outside social work, two key weaknesses are apparent, reflecting both the complexity of researching the impact of social work interventions and methodological skills gaps in the profession. While many studies comment on the cost conscious environment in which hospital social work services operate and are designed to show the potential efficiency gains for hospitals from social work involvement in discharge planning, very few studies attempt to establish the cost benefits of practice. Secondly, despite awareness of the hostile environment, relatively few studies (Claiborne (2006) is an exception) attempt a 'gold standard' experimental design, such as an RCT. The consequences of these limitations cannot be known for certain, but the absence of this evidence could not have helped when social workers' roles in counselling and discharge planning came under threat in the last decade or so either because they were perceived as superfluous or because other professions were claiming the territory.

Research on the work context of practice

The second sub-section focuses on research into the organizational context of health related social work. This explores issues such as inter-professional and inter-agency collaboration; the structure, administration and organization of service provision; the management, monitoring and evaluation of services.

Once again the background is often a perceived threat to the role and territory of social work in health settings. Such threats are a repeated theme in the 1990s and 2000s as social workers in hospitals responded to the restructuring of health care delivery. For example, Sulman et al. (2001) argued that changes in the organization of health care (shorter lengths of stay, managed care, reduced costs per case) and professional competition for key roles (counselling, discharge planning, community liaison) are 'a real threat to the viability of the acute hospital as a setting for social work' (2001: 315). The paper by Davies et al. (2003) exemplified the results of many studies, finding that clearly articulating the value of social work to the organization, staying current and being flexible were key survival strategies for hospital social work teams in Canada.

Making the case for social work in health care budgets often begins with establishing need and demand. A common concern is how to ensure that social work services reach those for whom they are intended; particularly in health settings where potential service users may be focusing on medical services or where referrals may be filtered through other professions. For example, Cwikel and Behar's (1999) review of empirical evidence about the organization of services for adult cancer patients focused on three questions:

- What proportion of cancer patients are likely to need social workers?
- What types of services social workers provide to meet those needs? and
- Who is likely to be a recipient of those services? (1999: 55)

For social work research, concerns with reach or utilization are not only a matter of responding to organizational imperatives but are often linked to professional values through the issue of social inequality.

Frequently, research has found that the disadvantaged social circumstances which might make interventions by social workers particularly valuable, act as obstacles to referral. For example, Bywaters and McLeod (1996) report on barriers created by poor physical and cognitive health and language differences amongst older hospital patients; Auslander et al. (2005) report the information barriers faced by migrants with high levels of need through a comparison with Israeli veterans.

FUTURE DEVELOPMENTS

There are a number of areas where it might be argued that social work is breaking new conceptual and methodological ground in health research. Among these are service user involvement, resilience (positive growth under stress), and the indigenization of health knowledge.

Service user involvement in research has become vitally important to demonstrating construct validity in quantitative studies and authenticity (the validity of the representation of participant voices) in qualitative research. As Charlton (1998) noted, service users are now insisting 'Nothing about us without us'. Beresford et al.'s (2007b) work exemplifies key developments in health related social work research in this regard. Rather than perceiving service users as subjects of investigation there is an increasing engagement with services users as full participants in research processes. The involvement of service users is increasingly sought as experts in the research process, as contributors to the focus of research, issues of methodology, ethics, methods, analysis and dissemination (Altpeter et al., 1999). Perhaps it is social work's more contextualized understanding of person-in-environment which has made this transition to more inclusive research practices easier than for some allied professions.

A second trend is a shift in the research from illness to health. Throughout this chapter we have highlighted this shift, but it is noteworthy that a good deal of the writing focusing on strengths, coping and resilience under stress is being developed by social workers (for example, Fraser, 1997; Ungar, 2005b). Again, this seems a natural fit with a profession that emerged as a response to the individualizing and pathologizing discourse of psychoanalysis and promoted a more social diagnosis of both problems and capacities. Researching health and related constructs, like resilience, strengths and positive development, are more difficult than researching illness. Randomized controlled studies are seldom possible when conducting health promotion efforts across populations. Nor, in the main, are social workers trained as epidemiologists and statisticians, preferring instead to understand health as it is experienced and lived. Far from marginalizing social work research, these efforts are becoming popular in work with disenfranchised populations who resist the pathologizing discourses of the dominant (illness-oriented) establishment. People with disabilities, for example, argue for a definition as 'differently abled' and want accommodations to ensure their full participation in work and educational settings (Leslie et al., 2003). Natural healers have the respect of their communities (Dawes and Donald, 2000). Children's voices are valued when trying to understand their experiences of trauma (Munford and Sanders, 2005).

A third, related, trend is the indigenization of health knowledge now in evidence in the social work literature. Studies of health, like that with Maori people in New Zealand, inspired Linda Smith (1999) to write *Decolonizing Methodologies: Research and Indigenous Peoples*. Smith argues that health related research should fit with the needs and ways of knowing found among people who live beyond the traditional western discourse of empiricism and objectivity. Emic perspectives, those coming from within a group, rather than etic perspectives, those imposed from beyond, should be central to research. When researching something as complex as health with sensitivity to context (such as decolonization) requires the respectful embrace of difference. More and more the social work health researcher is looking to communities to define their own meaning and methods. This is evident in Lena Robinson's (2007) work on cross-cultural child development. A social worker, Robinson understands that children from minority groups, in particular black children, have very different experiences of development than their white counterparts. Where the tendency has been to normalize the experience of the whites and pathologize the diversity of the blacks, such trends are now being challenged by those who felt marginalized by the arbitrariness of the dichotomy. Those challenges are possible because of the first two of the new directions in research noted above. Members of minority populations are gaining a louder voice in the research process, and there is a greater focus on how people are coping rather than focusing exclusively on breakdown and disorder.

Finally, the analysis presented above suggests three further key areas for development in health related social work research. As we have implied throughout, health related social work research has been excessively, though not exclusively, focused on social work in health settings, especially hospitals. But health care providers are shifting their focus from acute, hospital provision to chronic illness and community based care and a social perspective on health and illness. Their efforts remind us that the vast majority of human experience of health and illness occurs outside health care settings. The emphasis of future health related social work research has to reflect this sea change in the locus and focus of health care, as well as the shift from illness to health outlined above.

Furthermore, as life expectancy rises in most developing countries this experience of chronic illness becomes increasingly widespread, not just the province of the rich 'west'. In the context of a growing infrastructure of social provision in mid-range developing countries, new possibilities for social work are created. Social work researchers will wish to create an infrastructure which does not simply export or import models of research and practice from developed countries. An extended effort should be made by the profession to strengthen the research skills of social workers across the world and to encourage the emergence of training, mentoring, conferences, journals and other publications and funding and other resources to support a truly international social work research community.

Social work research can also make one other important shift. While some work is already international in focus, and we have argued for more, very little social work research has yet come to grips with processes of globalization (Bywaters et al., 2009). Two key dimensions of this are as follows. First, there is the globalization of factors affecting the social determinants of health, such as the impact of neo-liberal economic policies on relative poverty, global warfare and conflict, and environmental degradation and climate change. Second, research should focus on the globalization of health care systems, with particular concern about those who are unable to access basic health care because of poverty, or who have to choose poverty in order to secure treatment. This arena includes the commodification of health. For example, the creation of markets in reproductive technologies and organ transplantation and the role of international corporations in controlling access to health care facilities, health insurance, medication and other forms of treatment should be of concern to social work researchers. The continuing medicalization of people's experience of their bodies, with widespread damaging consequences for health and well-being are a related set of concerns. Tackling such an agenda requires us to develop new global partnerships, both a demanding and an enticing prospect.

NOTES

1. http://www.ifsw.org/en/p38000081.html. Under revision at the time of writing.

2. In the absence of an agreed international language, we are choosing to use the term 'service users' to describe people on the receiving end of social work services, recognizing that 'clients', or 'consumers' and other terms are also widely used.

3. See www.warwick.ac.uk/go/swhin.

4. The UK is an exception here. Almost all hospital based social workers are funded by local government and outposted into hospitals.

Disability

Sally French and John Swain

INTRODUCTION

Research is of fundamental importance to practising social workers and social work students for numerous reasons – from the requirement of students to conduct small scale projects to the general pursuit of evidence-based practice. In this chapter we focus on a shift of thinking in research that is centrally concerned with the relations between those who conduct research and those who are research subjects. The crucial shift is from doing research *on* people to doing research *with* people. This is not to suggest that participatory research (research *with* people) is the only approach that is of value within social work. It is rather a shift within social science research generally that challenges thinking within social work research and offers possible alternatives to more traditional approaches. In this chapter we will concentrate specifically on research in the field of disability while recognizing that the general principles have a wider application.

The chapter begins with an overview of the context, recognizing that changes in disability research are a reflection of and a constituent part of changes within the broader social context of disability. The driving force for change comes from disabled people themselves, with the international growth of the disabled people's movement and the generation of a social model of disability challenging the dominant individual model. The establishment of human and civil rights, inclusion, full participatory citizenship, equality and justice increasingly underpins international policy, practice and provision relating to disabled people, substantiated in part through the mainstreaming of disability issues.

We then turn to disability research and discuss why disabled people are dissatisfied with research done on them. A shift in power relations in disability research needs to be understood and analysed in the context of disabled people's experiences as the subjects of research, their lack of control over the process and production of research and over the role that research can play in reinforcing their oppression rather than enhancing their emancipation.

This takes us to the development of participatory research and an examination of why researchers have moved towards this approach. This is essentially a shift from doing research *on* people to doing research *with* people. Participatory research is an ideal that researchers work towards through different strategies for involving disabled participants in the decision making processes in designing, conducting and evaluating research.

We then look at what has come to be known as emancipatory research and contrast this with participatory research to pinpoint key issues for researchers and disabled people. Whereas participatory approaches are essentially geared towards sharing the control of research processes, emancipatory research is more overtly political and involves the control of research production by disabled people. As the term implies, emancipatory research aims to break down the barriers (structural, environmental and attitudinal) to full participatory citizenship faced by people with impairments in a disabling society.

To develop our discussions further, we highlight a range of examples of research with disabled people that realize, or aim to realize, the shift of power that is the central focus of this chapter. The examples, like the changing research context, are international and provide a basis for critical reflection. Finally, to conclude the chapter, we will consider the specific implications for social workers of the changing thinking and practice in disability research.

THE CONTEXT OF CHANGING DISABILITY RESEARCH

Changing power relations within disability research can only be understood and analysed within the broader context of changing social relations. An in-depth coverage of this is well beyond the scope of this chapter as it includes: globalization; the growing inequalities in health and income; the establishment of human rights policies and anti-discrimination legislation; and the growth of new social movements. The last of these has a particular relevance to changing disability research with the establishment and growth of an international disabled people's movement, particularly through Disabled People's International (DPI). It represents approximately 160 national assemblies, many of which, in turn, represent thousands of disabled individuals with all types of impairments, including people with learning difficulties. In 1992, DPI agreed that it was a human rights organization and that its membership was individually and collectively committed to global justice for disabled people. DPI is also committed to ensuring the voice of disabled people in all policies and programmes, including research programmes that directly affect them. 'Nothing About Us Without Us', is one of the DPI slogans. As a result DPI has had considerable influence in formulating the UN World Programme of Action Concerning Disabled Persons (1983) and the UN Standard Rules on Equalisation of Opportunities for Persons with Disabilities (1993).

In 1992, DPI came together with some of the other international disability organizations to set up an international information network on disability and human rights with the objective of supporting disabled people's actions at the grass-roots to implement those rights. This network, Disability Awareness in Action (DAA), has produced monthly newsletters – the *Disability Tribune* – and numerous resource kits on issues of particular concern, such as organization building, consultation and influence, campaigning and working with the media (Hurst, 2005). Such collective self-empowerment by disabled people has been the catalyst for the social model of disability, challenging the individual model underpinning the traditional approaches to disability research.

Within every society there are competing models of disability, with some being more dominant than others at different times. The most dominant model of disability at the present time is the individual model which is based upon the assumption that the difficulties disabled people experience are a direct result of their individual physical, sensory or intellectual impairments (Oliver and

Sapey, 2006). Thus, the blind person who falls down a hole in the pavement does so because he or she cannot see it, and the person with a motor impairment fails to get into the building because of his or her inability to walk. Problems are thus viewed as residing *within* the individual. The individual model of disability is deeply ingrained and 'taken as given' in the medical, psychological and sociological literature. Even in the literature on the sociology of health and illness disability, as disabled people define it, is basically ignored (Barnes and Mercer, 1996).

The medical model can be regarded as a sub-category of the overarching individual model of disability where disability is conceived as part of the disease process, abnormality and individual tragedy – something that happens to unfortunate individuals on a more or less random basis. Treatment, in turn, is based upon the idea that the problem resides within the individual and must be overcome by the individual's own efforts (French, 2004). Disabled people have, for example, been critical of the countless hours they have spent attempting to learn to walk or talk at the expense of their education and leisure (Oliver, 1996).

None of these arguments imply that considering the medical or individual needs of disabled individuals is wrong; the argument is that the individual model of disability has tended to view disability *only* in those terms, focusing almost exclusively on attempts to modify people's impairments and return them or approximate them to 'normal'. The effect of the physical, attitudinal and social environment on disabled people has been ignored or regarded as relatively fixed, which has maintained the status quo and kept disabled people in their disadvantaged state within society (Oliver and Sapey, 2006).

The social model of disability is often referred to as the 'barriers approach' where disability is viewed not in terms of the individual's impairment, but in terms of environmental, structural and attitudinal barriers which impinge upon the lives of disabled

people, and which have the potential to impede their inclusion and progress in many areas of life, including employment, education and leisure, unless they are minimized or removed (Oliver, 1996). These barriers include inaccessible education or lack of education, inaccessible information and communication systems, inaccessible working environments, inadequate or lack of disability benefits, discriminatory health and social care services and inaccessible transport, housing, public buildings and amenities (Swain et al., 2004). It includes too the tragedy model in all its manifestations, such as the devaluation of disabled people through negative images in the media including films, television and newspapers (Darke, 2004).

The social model of disability locates disability not within the individual disabled person, but within society. Thus the person who uses a wheelchair is not disabled by paralysis but by building design, lack of lifts, rigid work practices, and the attitudes and behaviour of others. Similarly the visually impaired person is not disabled by lack of sight, but by lack of Braille, cluttered pavements and stereotypical ideas about blindness. The social model takes a holistic approach in that specific problems experienced by disabled people are explained in terms of the totality of disabling environments and cultures (Oliver, 2004), and clearly provides the conceptual context for changing disability research.

The social model of disability is an expression of commonality and resistance to the dominant individual/medical/tragedy models. To look globally, however, raises a possibly more complex and controversial picture. To be impaired and disabled in China, in Afghanistan, in Zambia and in the USA encompasses widely differing experiences and encompasses different meanings. The high-income, 'developed' or minority world provides a very different context than the low-income, 'developing' or majority world. Perhaps not surprisingly, however, the picture is complex including both cultural diversity and commonalities (Flood, 2005;

Sheldon, 2005). Provision for disabled people also varies greatly. Most countries in the majority world, for instance, do not have a welfare state.

Though attitudes towards disability are generally universally negative there are cultural differences (Ingstad and Whyte, 1995). First are the ways in which the body and physical characteristics are given value and meaning. Western bio-medical definitions of impairment are not universal and perceptions of the body and mind vary across cultures and also change over time (Hughes, 2002). Religion and the messages various religious doctrines convey about disability is also significant (Ingstad and Reynolds, 1995) as is language and the notion that key concepts may not easily translate into other languages and cultures (Stone, 1999a).

Notwithstanding the importance of cultural differences, subtle and not so subtle, it can be argued that commonality is the overriding picture. Commonality is engendered particularly by experiences of multi-deprivation, predominantly through common experiences of poverty. Disabled people are the poorest of the poor in all countries (Stone, 1999b), and the evidence shows that chronic poverty can lead to higher risk of illness, accidents and impairment, while impairment can lead to poverty and exclusion (Yeo and Moore, 2003).

Turning to social policy, the international shift driven by the social model is evident in the establishment of rights-based policy, both civil and human. Forms of anti-discriminatory legislation have been enacted within at least 40 out of the 189 United Nations Members States (Degener, 2005). There are, however, significant differences in these legislative frameworks and general critiques focus on the lack of clear and effective enforcement mechanisms, with terms such as 'reasonable adjustment' providing broad grounds for non-compliance, i.e. anti-discriminatory legislation that allows for and legalises discrimination against disabled people. Based on international research, Dube et al. (2006) conclude that disabled

people's organizations have been marginalized in the formulization, monitoring and evaluation of disability legislation and policy, both at national and international levels. Furthermore, the social model should not be simplistically equated with what has come to be referred to as the rights-based model. The social model encompasses and informs broader mandates for social change in realizing social justice for disabled people.

In relation to social work and disability research, the specific context is social work policy, provision and practice in relation to disabled people. This is in itself, of course, a substantial and complex topic (Oliver and Sapey, 2006). Recent relevant developments in policy and practice are characterized by the concept of user-involvement (or consumer participation) and related terms such as partnership and empowerment (Kemshall and Littlechild, 2000; French and Swain, 2008) along with a lessening of deference towards 'experts' and an unquestioning belief in their knowledge and skills (McKnight, 1995; Chafetz, 1996). Robson et al. define user involvement as '... the participation of users of services in decisions that affect their lives' (2003: 2) and Croft and Beresford believe that '... speaking and acting for yourself and being part of mainstream society, lies at the heart of social care service user involvement' (2002: 389). The concept of 'user involvement' is now well established within managerial practice and enshrined within legislation. It is no longer the case that managers can or should make decisions on behalf of those they serve. Though the concept of user involvement is well established, it remains fraught with controversy and problematic issues. Few initiatives, however, have been thoroughly evaluated and many have proved ineffective (Beresford et al., 1997; Carr, 2004). Robson et al. (2003) and Carr (2004) note the lack of research, monitoring and evaluation with regard to the impact and outcome of user participation. Agencies tend to focus on the benefits of participation itself rather than on the outcomes achieved, sometimes even viewing participation as a form of 'therapy' to improve the skills, competence and self-esteem of disabled people (Braye, 2000; Carr, 2004). Carr states:

> There is a general lack of research and evaluation on the impact and outcomes of service user participation. Little seems to be formally recorded at local, regional or national levels and the influence of user participation on transforming services has not been the subject of any major UK research studies. (2004: vi)

CHALLENGING DISABILITY RESEARCH

There is what Keith refers to a 'a very large body of work' (2006: 1402) that can be subsumed under the umbrella of 'disability research' and may be pertinent to social work. He offers a rough scheme to categorize types of research, which determine both the goals of research and the methods adopted. He identifies five categories:

- population studies, providing estimates of numbers of disabled people;
- community studies, focusing on a sample of people living in an identified area;
- clinical and educational interventions;
- clinical research; and
- educational research.

Of these the first, studies of prevalence, is dominant in terms of the numbers of participants involved. This whole arena is, however, fraught with controversial arguments. On the positive side, such research can inform decision making about the allocation of resources, the provision of services and determining the effects of the services. It can be argued, too, for instance in relation to people with learning disabilities, that studies of prevalence provides evidence of the numbers of people missing out on needed services (Williams, 2006). However, questions arise in relation to the vagaries of classifying people. There are simplified dichotomies of disabled–nondisabled and labelling of people. Crucially population or prevalence research is not neutral objective research but a political activity

that reverberates through the lives of disabled people. Concluding their review of prevalence studies, Fujiura and Rutkowski-Kimitta state:

> Perhaps the better perspective on counting disability is to interpret measurement operations as imperfect proxies that capture only a fraction of the complex reality that is disablement. (2001: 92)

Analysing the whole field of disability research, Oliver laid down the gauntlet to researchers in the field of disability studies. He stated:

> As disabled people have increasingly analysed their segregation, inequality and poverty in terms of discrimination and oppression, research has been seen as part of the problem rather than part of the solution ... Disabled people have come to see research as a violation of their experiences, as irrelevant to their needs and as failing to improve their material circumstances and quality of life. (1992: 106)

Disability has generally been defined in an individualistic, medicalized way as an internal condition of the individual, and most research on disability, including the British government's large Office of Population Censuses and Surveys (OPCS) reflect this orientation. Writing of the international situation, Yeo states:

> Traditional research often involves wealthy non-disabled outsiders questioning people about their lives. This is not a reliable way of getting information where there are big power differences and where questioners are not trusted friends. To get consent is not sufficient, as few people in situations of poverty and exclusion will refuse to be questioned by those with more power and authority. It is therefore essential that disabled people are fully involved in future research, including setting the agenda. (2001: 35)

Many disabled people view disability in terms of social, physical and attitudinal barriers, which could be removed if only the political will to do so was present (Swain et al., 2004).

If an individualistic stance is taken by researchers, then the questions posed will be based on impairment and not on discriminatory practices and lack of access. Oliver has reworded some of the questions used in a British OPCS survey to illustrate this point. For example, in place of the question 'What complaint causes your difficulty in holding, gripping and turning things?' he substitutes the question, 'What defects in the design of everyday equipment, like jars, bottles and tins, causes your difficulty in holding, gripping and turning them?' and in place of the question, 'Did you move here because of your health problems/disability?' he writes 'What inadequacies in your housing caused you to move here?' (1990: 7). Abberley believes that, 'It is a political decision, conscious or otherwise, to employ questions of the first type rather than the second' (1992: 158). Academic perceptions and interests have dominated disability research to the extent that the work of the researchers has barely been questioned. Whalley Hammell states, 'Rehabilitation researchers' good intentions appear to have been so taken for granted that little attention has been given to the nature of their work' (2006: 171). The way in which disability is understood is a serious issue as these ideas can be translated into practice which impact on every aspect of disabled people's lives.

A further criticism of disability research is that most of the benefits go to the researchers rather than to disabled people themselves (Walmsley and Johnson, 2003; Barnes, 2004). Indeed Barnes et al. (1999) accuse researchers of being 'academic tourists' who use disability as a way of enhancing their career prospects, life style and status. Disabled people have complained that researchers use them to gather information and then disappear without trace (French and Swain, 2007). Similar complaints have been raised by women (researchers have typically been men) and poor people in developing countries who have been investigated by Western researchers (Chambers, 1997). This situation is compounded by the reluctance of funders to sponsor participatory research and to provide the extra resources that involving disabled people entails (Walmsley and Johnson, 2003; Barnes and Mercer, 2006).

Since the early 1990s the way in which disability has been researched has become a major issue for disabled people and their organizations. This is reflected in the importance it is given within the disability studies literature. In 1992 the Joseph Rowntree Foundation in Britain sponsored a series of seminars to discuss the issues of researching disability which culminated in a conference and a special edition of the journal *Disability, Handicap and Society* (now *Disability and Society*). There are now many chapters, articles and books on the topic of researching disability (see, for example, Rioux and Bach, 1994; Barnes and Mercer, 1997; 2004; Moore et al., 1998; Walmsley and Johnson, 2003).

RESEARCH WITH PEOPLE

Brechin states that research, '... tends to be owned and controlled by researchers, or by those who, in turn, own and control the researchers' (1993: 73), for instance those who provide the funding. Researchers who adopt a participatory approach are attempting to change these power relations and to ensure that research is owned and controlled by research participants as well as researchers. In characterizing participatory research, Cornwell and Jewkes argue that, '... the key difference between participatory and conventional methodologies lies in the location of power in the research process' (1995: 1667). You will note that within participatory research the language has changed from 'subjects' to 'participants' to reflect this orientation. Such changes in terminology do not, however, necessarily reflect a change in power relations and all claims to being 'participatory' need to be critically evaluated.

Participatory methodologies have arisen from qualitative research approaches which aim to reflect, explore and disseminate the views, concerns, feelings and experiences of research participants from their own perspective. The aim of participatory research goes beyond this, however, to engage participants in the design, conduct and evaluation of research within non-hierarchical research relations (Zarb, 1992). Feminist research has been particularly influential in this development where the objection has been that male researchers have spoken on behalf of women (Walmsley and Johnson, 2003). Participatory research can also be viewed as an aspect of wider changes within health and social care and society generally.

A crucial tenet of participatory research is that it is research *with* rather than *on* people (Reason and Heron, 1986). The research process is viewed as a potential source of change and empowerment for the research participants as well as a process for influencing professional policy and practice by reflecting the views and opinions of service users. Reason and Heron (1986) believe that participatory research invites people to concur in the co-creation of knowledge about themselves which is achieved by their active involvement at every stage of the research process – from choice of topic to evaluation and dissemination of the findings. Chambers (1997), talking of participatory research within developing countries, identified the following key features:

- It breaks down the mystique surrounding research.
- It ensures that the problems researched are perceived as problems by the community to which the research is directed.
- It helps to develop self-confidence, self-reliance and skills within the research participants.
- It encourages democratic interaction and transfer of power to the research participants.

Participatory research is thus essentially about establishing equality in research relationships.

Involving research participants in wider aspects of the research process is a relatively recent development. The barriers to the fuller involvement of disabled people are numerous. They include practical barriers, such as time and funding, and attitudinal barriers such as disbelief that disabled people are sufficiently 'expert' to be valid researchers or to have a sound and authoritative perspective. Indeed the perspective that disabled people have may feel threatening and be rejected by professionals such as social workers. Failure to ask disabled people for their views and to take them seriously has meant that policies and services have been built and delivered in inappropriate and abusive ways. Talking of people with learning disabilities, Walmsley and Johnson state:

> History shows that medicine and positivist research has objectified them, pursued goals which set them apart from the rest of humanity and has often led to oppressive policies directed towards them. Work around IQ testing in the early twentieth century falls into this category as do many current studies of 'challenging behaviour'... We believe that as researchers we have a responsibility to people with learning disabilities not to add to this history. (2003: 126)

Sometimes disabled people have been considered too vulnerable to take part in research, and in that way have been silenced, or funding for research which explores disabled people's lives or opinions may be difficult to obtain (French et al., 2001).

Research is not justifiable simply on the traditional grounds of furthering knowledge with the presumption that knowledge is intrinsically good. All research is political and research production and processes can further the oppression of those who are the subjects of research. Research into the treatment of a particular disease, for instance, may serve to maintain the status quo by failing to address the social, economic and political factors involved in its aetiology. Likewise the predominance of a medical orientation in research (genetic research for instance) has the potential to lead to abuse and oppression. Qualitative research is not immune from abusive tendencies either and researchers need to justify very clearly why they wish to investigate the lives of marginalized people especially if the area of investigation is sensitive, for instance sexual behaviour.

RESEARCH APPROACHES AND QUESTIONS OF POWER

So far in this chapter we have discussed the meaning of participatory research. Participatory approaches have arisen from qualitative methodologies which have been developed, to a large extent, by non-disabled researchers who wish to break down the traditional hierarchical researcher–researched relationship. Questions of power can be seen as an expression of the interaction or relationship between social workers and disabled people as service users. Sapey states:

> The task for the social worker will involve overcoming the structural, institutional, cultural, professional and personal barriers that contribute to the problem. However, none of them can be achieved if social workers themselves hold on to identity that devalues difference and impairment. Social work is an interpersonal activity and it cannot take place effectively if one person in the working relationship believes himself to be superior to the other. (2002: 188–9)

It is important to understand that the roots of participatory research lie in the development of research methodology itself, rather than the development of a different understanding of disability. Qualitative research is primarily concerned with meaning, interpretation and giving research participants 'a right of voice'. There is a commitment to seeing 'through the eyes' of research participants and a belief that social behaviour cannot be grasped until the researcher has understood the symbolic world of the research participants. Furthermore researchers in the qualitative tradition accept that the research in which they are engaged cannot be independent of their own values and perspectives. Participatory research reflects the concerns and views of disabled people but is not inherently associated with a social model of disability where disability is viewed as a social, political and cultural issue. As Oliver states, '… participatory and action research is about improving the existing social and material relations of research production; not

challenging and ultimately eradicating them' (1997: 26).

Emancipatory research, in the area of disability at least, has its roots in the growth of the disabled people's movement and is underpinned by the social model of disability. It can be argued that emancipatory research, unlike participatory research, is not a research methodology as such, but rather part of the struggle of disabled people to control the decision making processes that shape their lives and to achieve full citizenship. As Barton states, 'The task of changing the social relations and conditions of research production is to be viewed as part of the wider struggle to remove all forms of oppression and discrimination in the pursuit of an inclusive society' (1998: 38).

Emancipatory research goes further than participatory research by aiming to change the social relations of research production, with disabled people taking complete control of the research process. The production of research within an emancipatory paradigm is viewed as part of the liberation of disabled people; that is, part of the process of empowering them and changing society. Barnes explains:

> Emancipatory research is about the systematic demystification of the structures and processes which create disability and the establishment of a workable 'dialogue' between the research community and disabled people in order to facilitate the latter's empowerment. To do this, researchers must learn how to put their knowledge and skills at the disposal of disabled people. (1992: 122)

He later says:

> … the emancipatory research agenda is about nothing less than the transformation of the material and social relations of research production. This means that in contrast to traditional approaches, disabled people and their organisations, rather than professional academics and researchers, should have control of the research process including project finance and the research agenda. (2004: 48)

Barnes (2001) argues that accountability to the disabled community is a key component of emancipatory research and that the outcomes of the research must be meaningful to disabled people. All methods and strategies for gathering data are suitable provided they are placed firmly within an environmental and cultural context which highlights the consequences of a disabling society. As Oliver states, '… what should be researched is … the disablement ingrained in the individualistic consciousness and institutionalised practices of what is, ultimately, a disablist society' (1996: 143). Barnes (2004) believes that doing emancipatory research cannot be conceived in terms of a single project or even a collection of projects, but is a continuous process towards the empowerment of disabled people. Zarb sums up the fundamental difference between participatory and emancipatory research as follows:

> Participatory research which involves disabled people in a meaningful way is perhaps a prerequisite to emancipatory research in the sense that researchers can learn from disabled people and vice versa, and that it paves the way for researchers to make themselves 'available' to disabled people – but it is no more than that. Simply increasing participation and involvement will never by itself constitute emancipatory research unless and until it is disabled people themselves who are controlling the research and deciding who should be involved in and how. (1992: 128)

Although certain features of participatory and emancipatory research may overlap, one common confusion is the equating of emancipatory research with the qualitative paradigm. As noted above, there is no reason inherent within the nature of emancipatory research why it should adopt a qualitative methodology, provided the research agenda is generated by disabled people themselves. Indeed, it could be argued that a quantitative approach is more likely. For instance, emancipatory research into accessible housing for disabled people is likely to take the form of a quantitative survey to produce statistics to influence housing policy. Research undertaken at the Policy Studies Institute in London – Measuring Barriers within Society – for instance, aimed to make a systematic analysis of physical, social, economic and political barriers using both qualitative and quantitative measures (Zarb,

1995). Similarly research into direct payments within the social services departments of Britain by Zarb and Nadash (1994) drew heavily on quantitative data.

The outcomes of emancipatory research are far from certain and the effectiveness of such research can only be evaluated by disabled people themselves and their organizations (French and Swain, 2000). Barnes (2004), however, believes that the emancipatory research paradigm has had a demonstrable and significant impact on organizations and researchers doing disability research. Numerous projects on direct payments and personal assistance, for instance, made a significant contribution to the passing of the Community Care (Direct Payment) Act (1996) in Britain. Barnes is mindful, however, that research is enmeshed within a political and cultural context which may determine how, if at all, it is used. He states:

> Research outcomes in themselves cannot bring about meaningful political and social transformation, but they can reinforce and stimulate the demand for change. Thus the main targets for emancipatory research are disabled people and their allies. (2004: 52)

To complicate the matter even further, Walmsley and Johnson (2003) use the term 'inclusive research' when talking about research with people with learning disabilities. They argue that inclusive research originates from qualitative research and encompasses some aspects of participatory and emancipatory research. Below are listed the major tenets of inclusive research:

- It must address issues that matter to people with learning disabilities. The research problem should be owned (but not necessarily initiated) by people with learning disabilities.
- It should represent the views and experiences of people with learning disabilities.
- It should further the interests of people with learning disabilities.
- Researchers should 'be on the side' of people with learning disabilities.
- It should be collaborative with people with learning disabilities who should be involved in the research.

- People with learning disabilities should have some control over the process and the outcome of the research.
- People with learning disabilities should be treated with respect by the research community.
- All aspects of the research and the research outcomes should be made accessible to people with learning disabilities.

Walmsley and Johnson admit that inclusive research is 'top-down' rather than 'bottom-up' – that is, it is frequently initiated by the researchers rather than people with learning disabilities themselves. They do not, however, believe that this is necessarily a problem and site research questions within the social sciences which have emerged from 'silences', such as that concerned with domestic violence and child abuse. They believe that although people with learning disabilities have an enormous amount of expertise and that those who are less disabled can work as researchers in many ways, it is unrealistic to expect them to fully control the research process which the emancipatory paradigm demands. They go as far as to refer to this expectation as 'unrealistic' and 'oppressive' and state:

> … to argue that they have the expertise to carry out or control all aspects of research is to go beyond the realms of the rational into a world where the reality of intellectual impairment is wished away and difference is denied. (2003: 187)

Walmsley and Johnson argue further that researchers who work within an inclusive ideology are helping people with learning disabilities to understand their situation, rather than oppressing them, and that without this assistance they may not get beyond telling their stories however important and empowering that may be. They state that without allies, research in the area of learning disability may remain '… the untheorised, experienced-based poor relation of its intellectually wealthier cousin in disability studies' (2003: 186).

They also defend the position of researchers who work in this way because, although it is likely that they benefit more from the research than people with learning disabilities, their work does not attract funding or status within academic circles and they are frequently marginalized. The power imbalance between the researcher and the researched cannot, they believe, be resolved until society is a more just place for people with learning difficulties.

INVOLVING DISABLED PEOPLE IN RESEARCH

In this section we shall look at some projects with disabled people that involve them and give their perspectives. These projects have been selected to reflect a range of topics and participant groups relevant to social workers.

The first example comes from research with people with learning difficulties. Atkinson, along with others, have been developing an auto/biographical approach that:

> … has the capacity to combine the political document with the historical – to reflect the lives which have been lived, but to see beyond the individuals to a wider view of learning disability. Auto/biography contains many voices and tells stories at different levels. (Atkinson, 1997: 22)

Individual life stories were recounted and shared in a group context. Nine participants with an age range of 57–77 years met on 30 occasions. One of the themes was 'tales of hospital life' and the following is a short extract in which Margaret tells her story of running away from a mental handicap hospital:

> The sister would keep on at me, saying my work wasn't done properly. She was being horrible. I'd scrubbed the ward and she said I had to do it over again. I said, 'Well I ain't going to do it over again!' I told the doctor. He come round and he wanted to know what I was doing on the stairs again. I said, 'I've been told I've got to do it again, it wasn't done properly.'
>
> I planned it with the other girl, we planned it together. She was fed up. She was doing the dayroom and dining room, cleaning and polishing. Then I was put on it, as well as scrubbing. We planned to get into Bedford, walk across the fields. (Atkinson, 1997: 91)

Next we shall discuss a more fully developed example of participatory research in that the participants were involved in the decision-making process throughout the research. The project was controlled, conducted and reported, with support, by the Bristol Self-Advocacy Research Group, a group of four people with learning difficulties, and was funded by the National Lottery Fund (Palmer et al., 1999). The research involved interviewing other people with learning difficulties about their experiences. The response of the researchers was positive:

> We've all really enjoyed the research visits, meeting new people and making new friends.

> I was looking at my photographs yesterday when I was at home, and all the different places I've been. And I've got the photographs in my photograph album at home. I'm quite proud of what I did. And you feel very important. People say: 'You do do a lot.' They're quite impressed with what I do. I've achieved a lot – too much. (1999: 34)

The themes covered in this research were: What is disability? Cutting out all the labels; Jobs and work; The staff who support us; Transport; and Self-advocacy – what does it mean? Under the theme of support, for example, the research participants speak about being forced to be independent:

> Staff people always think that we all want to be more and more independent. This can be wrong, because they expect us to do too many things ourselves. It should be our choice, not theirs. (1999: 42)

> If you're married, you've got to give and take. One person does one thing, and people help each other out. It's the same in any house – I don't want staff to keep on forcing me to be independent. How would they feel? (1999: 42)

A large-scale international project funded by the Department for International Development (UK) (DFID) was launched in September 2000, entitled Disability Knowledge and Research Programme (Disability KaR). This has become an innovative and wide-ranging programme of research on disability and development and the edited volume (Albert, 2006) contains reports from a number of the projects within this programme which espouse both participatory and emancipatory ideals. The conclusions or messages from the programme are summarized by Albert and Harrison (2006: 11) including:

- Disability is not about health status, it is about discrimination and systematic exclusion. It must be seen and addressed as a question of fundamental human rights.
- meaningful research to support sustainable development demands that disabled people and disabled people's organisations (DPOs) take a leading role and not simply be 'included' or 'consulted';
- development agencies themselves must set an example of good practice by drawing on the experience and expertise of DPOs in both the North and the South;
- DPOs need support which builds and sustains their capacity;
- and governments and development agencies need urgently to tackle the problem of policy evaporation which has meant that good policies on mainstreaming disability in development remain almost entirely trapped on paper.

We hope that these examples give an indication of how the principles of participatory and emancipatory research, to a greater or lesser extent, can be applied to research in order to gain a better understanding of issues from the viewpoint of disabled people. Although the examples we have chosen focus largely on disabled people's attitudes and opinions within the sphere of social science research, there is no reason to believe that disabled people cannot be involved in any type of research although their involvement may bring to the fore different perspectives between disabled people and social workers – not least about what is worth researching.

There are indications that social work research is changing and being shaped by the challenges from disabled people. In his critical commentary, Trevillion states:

> Although the social model was formulated elsewhere, social work has become closely identified with it and, for many social workers, a commitment to it has become an integral part of their

overall commitment to human rights, anti-discriminatory practice and empowerment ... (2007: 978–9)

He goes on to suggest there is a body of social work research that has sought to be explicitly 'emancipatory' in dealing with disability issues and the relationship between professional researchers and disabled people. Trevillion does, however, recognize that some are sceptical of the capacity of social work to truly contribute to the liberation of oppressed groups. Strier (2007) comes to similar conclusions in his analysis of anti-oppressive research in social work. He advocates a 'more participative, action-oriented and emancipatory approach' (2007: 866) to social work research, though also recognizing the challenges this involves.

CONCLUSION

Research of any kind may seem somewhat removed from the everyday pressures of practising social workers, although most will have had considerable exposure to research ideas and practice during their undergraduate education. Sensitive, empowering research can give invaluable insights into clients' complex experiences of disability, which may, in turn, have the potential to improve social work practice as well as client satisfaction. Many clients live with disability and impairment on a daily basis and the knowledge and experience they have gained should not be underestimated, however young they may be.

Disabled people have spoken out about the way their perceptions of disability frequently clash with those of professional workers, and non-disabled people in general, and how the neglect of their perspective has created

inappropriate and abusive policy and practice. Brothers et al. (2002) believe that professionals need to consult with disabled customers, disabled staff and disability organizations in order to prevent discrimination. Beresford and Croft (2004) emphasize the powerful force for change in social work coming from the collective voice of disabled people. They write:

> ... now there is, at least, a force to make 'community control' possible, in the form of service users' movements and organisations. In our view the lesson of recent decades is that without the control of service users, workers and other local people, social work will be an essentially controlling rather than liberating activity. But there are now new chances for change. (2007: 65–6)

With the implementation and strengthening of disability discrimination legislation and the growing philosophy of working with patients and clients in partnership and collaboration, a move towards participatory and emancipatory research in social work is becoming urgent. Such a move would reflect key values associated with social work such as choice, empowerment and partnership and collaboration. It would also be commensurate with public policy such as *Our Health, Our Care, Our Say* (Department of Health, 2006).

We will end this chapter with a question from Mike Oliver who was the first Professor of Disability Studies in Britain and a disabled person himself:

> ... do researchers wish to join with disabled people and use their expertise and skills in their struggles against oppression or do they wish to continue to use these skills and expertise in ways in which disabled people find oppressive? (1992: 102)

Disabled people are being empowered by the disabled people's movement. The question is: Can research by social workers be part of that empowerment?

26

Mental Health

Peter Huxley, Michael Sheppard
and Martin Webber

INTRODUCTION

The history of research in mental health social work (MHSW) is a developmental one, beginning with a very close association with clinical psychiatry, moving through a productive period of partnership with social psychiatry to the present day, entering into a phase of increasing independence and maturity. From an international perspective, this increasing independence is evident in many different places, from Australia to the USA. To attempt to encompass all of this development in a single chapter is barely possible and so we have chosen to focus our attention on some very specific aspects of MHSW research.

Before we outline the chapter content we need to acknowledge that the social research enterprise in mental health is very much a multi-disciplinary one, and that many social scientists as well as social work academics and practitioners have made very valuable and influential contributions (see Huxley, 2001). Again, it is not possible to mention them all by name, but among the disciplines represented in these efforts, notable ones are health economics (such individuals as Richard Frank in the USA and Martin Knapp

in the UK), social policy researchers, psychologists and sociologists (such as Leona Bachrach and Bill Eaton in the USA and Anne Rogers and David Pilgrim in the UK). These individuals and their social work collaborators draw from similar discourses, and are part of an empirical research tradition. Modern multidisciplinary research in mental health now includes service users – as advocated more than a decade ago by Rapp and colleagues (Rapp et al., 1993) – and leans towards an interest in recovery models and the use of participatory and emancipatory research methods (as represented by the contributions of people like Marian Farkas in the USA and Peter Beresford in the UK). MHSW research plays a part in the development of new methods and measures and employs a very wide range of methods appropriate to the question being addressed. The works cited in this chapter reflect this considerable diversity of applications, which we consider to be a sign of academic rigour.

The chapter is in six parts. First, we present a very broad description of the major MHSW research contributions over the past 30–40 years, a period which coincides with the era of deinstitutionalization and the growth of community care

(Goodwin, 1997). This period also saw the development of research into family burden, and familial causation of disorders such as schizophrenia. These commanded quite a great deal of attention at the time, but have since been either remodelled or discredited. Social work researchers have maintained an active contribution to research in relation to the plight of families and carers and research in relation to carer's needs remains a key priority area (see Gould et al., 2007), but relatively speaking is very poorly funded and fails to command a great deal of research attention from other disciplines. For instance, a review of government sponsored research in the UK found only two funded studies over a 20-year period (Thornicroft et al., 2002).

In the second part of the chapter we look at the interface between MHSW research and other social work research domains. We do this because MHSW research continues to be conducted alongside other forms of social work research, and alongside other disciplines. We provide two examples: one on the interface with social work research on maternal depression, and the other on the interface with substance abuse problems. There are many other such interfaces, with the criminal justice system, for instance, but space precludes consideration of all of them.

In the third part of the chapter we look briefly at clinical and practice research where social workers have been at the forefront of developments around the world.

In the fourth part we examine the contribution that MHSW researchers have made to transferable service development and organization, especially those that have travelled across the world. These include research into such matters as case management, disability, stigma and strengths.

In the fifth part of the chapter we examine a selection of the important contemporary diversity and equity-related issues in MHSW, research, in particular social capital, quality of life and social inclusion. Here, MHSW has made important contributions, bringing more holistic than narrow clinical perspectives,

and adding social dimensions to measurement and theory.

Finally, we briefly consider the prospects for MHSW research in the future.

THE CHANGING CONTEXT OF MHSW RESEARCH

The history of the relationship between social work and psychiatry is a long and sometimes troubled one, but always included an element of research and development, possibly because most of the early associations were between academic psychiatrists and social workers (or social scientists) in clinical teaching settings. In the UK one thinks of Hoenig and Hamilton (1969), Wing and Brown (1970), Goldberg and Huxley (1980, 1992), and in the USA of Stein and Test (1980), Hogarty and Anderson (1986) and Segal and Aviram (1978) among others.

These early research collaborations reflect the changing nature of both society and psychiatry during these years. In both the UK and the USA early research was into the harmful effects of institutions, and about ways to improve treatment and foster humane regimes, including the importance of work and similar activity within the confines of the institution (Wing and Brown, 1970). The deinstitutionalization research in both countries turned attention towards the development of community treatment models and in some cases to large area epidemiological studies of considerable duration (e.g. the Environmental Catchment Area (ECA) study in the USA; Bruce et al., 1991). Interest in research into specific therapeutic or treatment models based on social interventions also moved from individual and dynamically oriented models of intervention (e.g. psychosocial casework) through family and group-related interventions to a greater interest in the social systems within which patients now had to survive. This growing interest in what might be broadly termed policy related and whole service systems research (e.g. Robert

Wood Johnson programme; the UK700 trial; PriSM) took centre stage as the more individual treatment research declined in relative importance. So, case management research, still individually focused, gave way to research into more system level issues such as the pathway into psychiatric care (Goldberg and Huxley, 1980), stigma (Pinfold et al., 2005), survival and recovery (Carpenter, 2002). Social scientists had of course been preoccupied with the stigma associated with mental illness since the seminal works of Goffman on the asylum (Goffman, 1961) and stigma (Goffman, 1963), but the newer models had individual elements built into whole systems approaches. The Strengths Model advocated by Charles Rapp and colleagues (Rapp, 1992; Saleebey, 1996, 2005) being an outstanding example of the change of emphasis from an approach based on the assessment of need and deficits to one that takes a much more positive view of people's skills, abilities, aptitudes and preferences, and the contexts in which these can be maximized. The development of this model by mental health social workers underpinned the shift of emphasis from deficit models, which remains a feature of many other professionals' approaches to concepts and measurements in the field of mental health.

More recently, however, two significant societal changes, at least in the USA and the UK and to a lesser extent Australia, have changed the recent focus of research. First, there are concerns about those people in the community who may be a risk to others and themselves, and prompted research into community treatment orders (Segal and Burgess, 2006; Churchill et al., 2007). While this concern is almost universal, it is particularly strong in the USA and the UK, where MHSW plays a unique role in making applications for hospital admission based on medical recommendations; in most other countries the decisions are medical or judicial ones. In the UK, this role has now been extended to other mental health professionals, but at the time of writing it is not clear how many staff from other health disciplines will want to take on this responsibility, and research will

be needed to assess its operation, impact and ethical implications.

Second, welfare to work style programmes have prompted a number of studies of the benefits of different employment programmes, a concern that has not really gone away since this was studied as part of early asylum research (Wing and Brown, 1970).

Ironically, in the UK at least, these recent developments have been accompanied by policy initiatives aimed at enhancing the integration of health and social care services, but the research evidence that closer working produces better outcomes is very weak, with some negative impacts observed (Snooks et al., 2006). These policy initiatives seem to be a peculiarly UK phenomenon, as they appear to be deemed unnecessary in many other parts of the world.

INTERFACES WITH OTHER SOCIAL WORK RESEARCH

Mental health issues feature in all areas of practice, and it is counterproductive to insulate areas on the basis of a commitment to specialization or specialism (Darlington et al., 2005; Gorin, 2006).

Internationally there are many key interfaces. We have chosen two particular ones to consider as prime examples in which social work researchers have made a substantial contribution. The first is the interface between MHSW research and research into child care practice. The second is the interface with substance abuse, formerly known as 'dual diagnosis'.

Exemplar 1: MHSW and child care research (a progression of studies)

Social work intervention in child care in the presence of maternal depression provides a particularly rich area for study. It interfaces two major areas of social work, child care and mental health; it has considerable relevance for inter-professional collaboration; and the widespread nature of maternal depression, particularly amongst deprived groups, makes it a major vulnerability factor in child care. It also demonstrates the extensive relevance of mental health beyond areas defined as MHSW. This exemplar provides a sustained and well developed case of a progression of studies.

Evidence is clearly available – not just in general, but specifically in relation to social work research – on the inter-relationship between child care, maternal depression and social work practice. The research demonstrates not just the close-ness of this relationship, but the critical importance of addressing maternal depres-sion in the conduct of child care practice. In this exemplar we use this key interface as an illustration of the benefits of explor-ing the relationship between different discourses in social work research.

A series of studies, using similar method-ologies (enhancing comparability) has shown that, as we ascend each level of prevention in child care, rates of maternal depression increase. Thus, health visitor clients have rates of 12–13% (Sheppard, 1996, 1997a), there are rates of 18–20% in children's centres (Sheppard, 2008), of 28–30% among children's social care applicants who are nevertheless not allo-cated to caseloads (Sheppard, 2005) and of 40–45% in children's social care services caseload cases (Sheppard, 2001a). We can take this further. Where child pro-tection is an issue, rates are higher still: in health visitor cases where the health visi-tor expresses concerns about child abuse, the rate rises to 31% (Sheppard, 1998a). Although covering different geographical areas, which may well have some impact on rates, these data probably reflect real differences with prevention levels.

Maternal depression, then, is an impor-tant issue in child care social work, dem-onstrating a major overlap with mental health, and also significance far greater than apparent in areas where, arguably, more mental health effort is forthcoming,

such as postnatal depression. Its impor-tance lies in its impact. We have extensive evidence that depression affects maternal social functioning and child care (Cleaver et al., 1999; Smith, 2004b). Maternal depression can present a pernicious factor undermining the mother's capacity to overcome familial problems, and corre-spondingly undermining practitioner efforts.

Identification of maternal depression by child care social workers can be patchy (Sheppard, 1997c), which is unfortunate since mental health professionals often do not consider supporting children to be their role (Webber and Slack, 2008). However, more significant is their 'model of parenting'. Depression, of itself, is not a feature of their definition of parenting, but is an aspect of a 'moral predictive' framework which links key aspects of depression in the mother to risk to the child (Sheppard, 2001a). This yields frame-works ('stoics', the 'genuinely depressed' and 'troubled and troublesome') enabling social workers to act in the light of the 'dangerousness' of the depression for child protection.

Nevertheless, their actions are pro-foundly affected by the presence of mater-nal depression. There is a clear relationship, both between social work parenting assessment frameworks and case status. Thus, for example, 'troubled and trouble-some' parents are far more likely to find their child on the child protection register. Rates of depression in British samples, fur-thermore, escalate with case severity. Some studies show in child protection social work cases three-fifths of mothers were depressed (Sheppard, 1997b, 2001a) compared with around two-fifths overall for caseload cases. These are associated with higher social, material, child care and parenting problems. Other research, though, shows no association between depression and abuse/neglect in a Canadian voluntary agency (Leschied et al., 2005).

Maternal childhood experiences can even affect interventions. Adult maternal depression is often associated with inadequate parenting, even abuse, of the parent when they were children (Bifulco and Moran, 1998; Sheppard, 2001a). These are often parents with deep seated and high needs of their own, irrespective of their status as parents. These needs of the mother herself affect practice strategies. Case status appears to be influenced by mothers' past experience of abuse although the mechanisms by which this occurs are complex (Sheppard, 2003). Yet child care interventions are so child focused that the mother's needs as a person in her own right (as opposed to as a parent) are often ignored (Sheppard, 2001a). Here, policy and its interpretation gives depressed mothers a secondary status, as social workers emphasize that the welfare of the child is paramount (ignoring the importance of the mother's own needs to this).

Despite social support's key position as an intervention framework in social work theory (Dolan et al., 2006) one study indicates that social workers targeting of support was haphazard (when considered in the light of specific support needs) allied to an indiscriminateness in support provision – most women received help in some (but not always the right) area of support need (Sheppard, 2004). One area – relief care for children – seems to have been of most significant help to depressed mothers in reducing their support needs.

The key lesson from these studies at the interface between mental health and child care practice is that child care practitioners neglect maternal depression at their (and the families') peril. It is at the heart of their practice. Skills in the assessment and recognition of depression and the use of effective interventions are in the interests of both parents and families. Obvious approaches include cognitive behavioural work (Cuipers et al., 2008), low intensity/ high volume self help approaches (Anderson et al., 2005) while even some traditional social work approaches may be efficacious (Woodcock, 1995).

The interface between substance abuse and mental health social work research

Social workers are active in the field where mental health problems and substance use disorders (SUD) overlap (sometimes referred to in the past as 'dual diagnosis cases') and have argued against traditional approaches to treatment and care and in support of the alternative harm-reduction model (Brocato and Wagner, 2003; Macmaster, 2004). Most authors, however, identify the need for further research in the field. Bachman et al. (2004) identified topics for a research agenda on the needs of individuals with disabilities who also experience co-occurring substance abuse disorders. Social work research in this area tends to be multidisciplinary, reflecting the nature of the subject area. Metsch and Pollack (2005) pointed out that research in the USA has demonstrated that substance abuse disorders are less widespread among welfare recipients than was originally thought and are less common than other serious barriers to self-sufficiency. The School of Social Work in Michigan conducted early research into the characteristics of people with substance use disorders (Mowbray et al., 1997b) that raised issues about diversity in this population. This study is presented as the next exemplar. The research interest in substance abuse is continued in the school of social work through the work of Delva and colleagues into community and ethnic influences on the epidemiology of substance abuse disorders (Delva et al., 2001, 2002) and preventive interventions (Howard et al., 2005).

Exemplar 2: The interface with substance abuse disorders (using standardized measures)

The study in this exemplar (Mowbray et al., 1997b) provides descriptive data on a large, diverse sample of patients from an urban psychiatric inpatient setting who suffer from substance abuse disorders as well as mental health problems. Such patients are often referred to as 'dually diagnosed'. The focus was on African-Americans in particular. A wide range of standardized clinical, social and community functioning measures were applied over 12 months to all admissions with a DSM-III-R psychiatric diagnosis and substance abuse problems ($n = 486$). The majority were found to have serious economic and employment problems, undesirable living arrangements, limited or conflictive family or social relationships, and some record of arrest. Psychiatric, alcohol and drug abuse problems were paramount, but there were also employment, family/social and legal problems. The most commonly abused substances were alcohol, cocaine and cannabis, and there was a high rate of multiple drug abuse. Some subgroup differences based on gender, age, and race were found which have implications for community treatment planning. The study results reveal the extreme heterogeneity of this population and the existence of multiple treatment needs. The authors conclude that for better treatment planning, future research on dual diagnosis should attempt to establish meaningful subgroups relevant to service needs and should utilize diverse clinical and functioning measures.

CLINICAL AND PRACTICE RESEARCH

Looking beyond these interfaces, it is the case that social workers have been at the forefront of other relevant clinical and practice developments around the world. In the UK, Ramon (2008) cites the following examples:

- self-directed groupwork, which put together community development with empowerment principles (Mullender and Ward, 1991);
- networking and community care (Trevillion, 1992);

- paying attention to institutional abuse, child and elder abuse, and the strong connection between abuse and mental ill health (Stanley et al., 1999);
- anti-discrimination in its implications for ethnic minorities, disabled people, women and poor people has been a much more pronounced feature of training in social work than in any other helping profession;
- empowerment and participation (Beresford and Croft, 1993; Bray and Preston-Shoot, 1995); and
- user involvement in policy making and in research (Barnes and Bowl, 2001; Ramon, 2000).

Few of these initiatives were research led, and MHSW like most other aspects of social work has, as we indicated earlier, a research capacity problem.

A mental health social worker who made an outstanding contribution to the conception of socially based interventions in a clinical research context was the late Gerry Hogarty. During his career he developed four psychosocial interventions specific to schizophrenia, and tested all of them in rigorous randomized trials. This enabled each successive development to be built on the earlier findings, a major feat both in terms of providing a growing knowledge base, but also in terms of the successful continuity of grant funding. In addition he was involved in providing early evidence of the effects of antipsychotic medications and also of the role of the use of antidepressants and anti-anxiety agents in conjunction with these treatments.

Major role therapy (MRT) was the first treatment he developed (Hogarty et al., 1974). It involved social workers and rehabilitation counselors encouraging and supporting service users in their work and family roles. The results were not especially impressive, but there were indications that the newer antipsychotic treatments could be used as a basis for appropriately timed psychosocial interventions. The second development was a family psycho-education approach in combination with social skills training in a series of long-term trials that explored these treatments individually and jointly (Hogarty et al., 1986).

The combination intervention resulted in significant relapse delays but left patients with substantial residual symptoms. The third development was personal therapy (Hogarty et al., 1995, 1997). This added to social skills training by helping service users to better understand their personal interactions with others so that they were better able to develop their interpersonal and instrumental skills. Finally, cognitive enhancement therapy (CET) (Hogarty et al., 2004) linked new understanding in cognitive neuroscience to an intervention that engages service users in exercises that use both interpersonal and computer interactions to gain mastery of personal and social skills.

The paradigm of evidence-based practice has offered a promising heuristic to the further development of MHSW research. As mental health social workers increasingly practice in multi-disciplinary teams with health colleagues, whose decision-making is informed by empirical research to a greater degree, it is perhaps surprising that they show no more aptitude for evidence-based practice than in other fields of social work (Trinder and Reynolds, 2000). The lack of clamour for rigorous evidence to inform practice reflects the meagre contribution to the mental health evidence base that MHSW makes in contrast to health professions (Huxley, 2001; McCrae et al., 2003). However, evidence-based mental health policy increasingly impacts on social work practice (Webber, 2008). For example, the introduction of crisis resolution and home treatment teams in the UK following the implementation of the National Service Framework for Mental Health (Department of Health, 1999), seems to have increased the workload of Approved Social Workers and affected their independence (Furminger and Webber, 2009).

The value, potential and dangers of evidence-based practice continues to be debated around the world (Otto and Ziegler, 2008), and research continues into factors affecting its take-up by practitioners (Mullen et al., 2008), its use by community organizations (Franklin and Hopson, 2007), its place in social work education (Drake et al., 2007; Rubin and Parrish, 2007; Smith et al., 2007) and its relation to social work codes of practice (Gambrill, 2007). The evidence-based practice paradigm provides a rationale for MHSW research, but, in the UK at least, unless there is an adequate and appropriate research infrastructure there is a risk that its development will be slow compared to other parts of the world (Huxley, 2001; McCrae et al., 2003; Tenorio and Hernandez, 2005).

A history of scepticism towards the scientific method has contributed towards a lack of development in the evidence base for MHSW in contrast to medicine and psychology. Additionally, social work interventions are rarely amenable to randomized controlled trials (RCTs), the 'gold standard' in an evidence-based hierarchy of evidence. Clinical guidelines have become skewed towards psychological therapies and drug treatments for this very reason. UK guidelines for the treatment of depression (National Collaborating Centre for Mental Health, 2004), for example, include only one social intervention – befriending – as being potentially effective as there has been a recent RCT which reported its beneficial effect (Harris et al., 1999).

A fundamental critique of the hierarchical approach to evidence is the denigration of social science research methods such as ethnography or discourse analysis, which are demoted to the bottom of the evidential hierarchy. These methods are valuable for exploring processes and interventions which are not amenable to the RCT methodology. The most obvious example of this is the statutory work of a mental health social worker. For example, Alan Quirk and his colleagues (2000) conducted a major ethnographic study of mental health act assessments in the UK and drew some important conclusions about the valuable social role the Approved Social Worker played. Additionally, there are also some inherent difficulties with RCTs such as recruitment difficulties which have led to unrepresentative samples and results with limited clinical applicability (Slade and Priebe, 2001).

RESEARCH INTO MODELS OF CARE

Social workers and the social work research community have contributed to major developments in models of care relevant to mental health. A number of significant research led initiatives have been devised or conducted by MHSWs, usually in collaboration. The work of Stein and Test (1980) stands out as having had a major influence on the development of first hospital and then community services, leading to the creation of assertive outreach treatment teams in the USA and in the UK. It is an interesting reflection on the way in which these teams began and were then adapted (and researched) in the UK that the original fidelity scales in the USA insisted on at least one nurse member, while the UK teams were predominantly nurses. Beinecke and Huxley (2009) explore the reasons for these workforce differences in the two countries, and Huxley is researching the reasoning behind the staffing decisions in UK mental health teams.

Another development from the USA that began in a social work context was case management (Rapp, 1992) and this was adopted in the UK as 'care management', with similar separation of the assessment and care planning aspects from the direct delivery of care. This resulted in the removal of many social workers from the front line of care delivery and into an assessment and brokerage role, which had already been the subject of research in the USA by Charles Rapp and Leona Bachrach and found to be unpopular with service users, and which has continued to prove unpopular with social workers in the UK up to the present day. This recent quote illustrates the point that has been made many times before over the past decades:

It is difficult to believe that so many more senior managers were once, hopefully, enthusiastic and person-centred social workers – too many have now become budget-obsessed/target-driven 'clones' of the State ... We have largely forgotten the origins of social work and it is now seen as bureaucratic and an 'arm' of the State. Where is the 'soul' of our profession? Who really cares any more? Much as he became out of favour are social workers aware of, for instance, 'The Casework Relationship' by Biestek? – he saw social work as having the most positive effect through our caring relationships with those we sought to help. That religious/pseudo-religious approach lost favour but was it not a case of 'throwing the baby out with the bathwater'? We now seem to be far more Case Managers and increasingly distant from our 'Service Users.' (Measures, 2008)

Sir David Goldberg, influenced by his work in primary care in Charleston, USA, wrote, with Peter Huxley, the influential book on the pathway to psychiatric care, using a six-level and five-filter model, showing that psychiatry only became involved at the final stages of care by making a decision about whether to admit the patient to hospital (Goldberg and Huxley, 1980). This model was highly influential in the UK, where universal primary and secondary care systems operated, and perhaps less so elsewhere where they did not. This and the subsequent book on common mental disorder (Goldberg and Huxley, 1992) played a considerable part in removing the focus away from hospital to primary and community care services. Both books were regularly cited by planners developing new community based services.

EXAMPLES OF CURRENT AND EMERGING AREAS OF MHSW RESEARCH

As MHSW research moves further away from mainstream psychiatric research, or looking at it another way, as mainstream psychiatric research moves further into the neuro and genetic sciences, the opportunity to make links with other research constituencies, most of them social science related, increases. As a consequence of these developments current and future MHSW research looks rather different from its historical heritage.

In this growing MHSW research agenda a number of significant linkages are being made by MHSW with key participants, and we outline a number of these examples in this section of the chapter. This research is multidisciplinary, involves social work researchers and other social scientists, and other service constituencies other than the traditional psychiatric or health related. In parallel with developments in service delivery one could think of these emerging areas of research as involving a mainstreaming movement, away from specialist care services and towards those associated with ordinary living and the general population. This movement can be illustrated in two ways. First, by the development of generic quality of life measures relevant to the general population, rather than specific mental illness populations, but which can be used in both to facilitate comparison and quantify exclusion; this work began in the USA in the work of the psychiatrist Tony Lehman and was adapted and adopted by social workers (Joe Oliver, Peter Huxley) and other social scientists (Nijuenhausen Ch. Van., Sherrill Evans) for use in general population contexts. Second, the service user-led research places a great emphasis on the self management of symptoms and on emancipatory and participatory methods aimed at improving ordinary lives in communities in the general population (Tew et al., 2006).

Quality of life research

Oliver (Oliver et al., 1996) originally intended that the Lancashire Quality of Life Profile (LQOLP) should be used by social workers as part of their routine social assessment work, when assessing long-stay hospital patients. It quickly became clear however, that it had potential use as an outcome

indicator, as many clinical and social services were adopting 'improved quality of life' as a service objective. The original profile was used in several sites as a practice tool for assessment and outcome, and individual case studies showing change over time were published. It was also used in major research studies (UK700) (Huxley et al., 2001) and translated into several languages, and a Dutch version was developed (Nieuwenhuizen et al., 2001). The LQOLP was rather lengthy for the measurement of outcomes and a briefer tool was developed (again by a multidisciplinary team in which social workers and social scientists were predominant). The Manchester Short Assessment of Quality of Life (QoL) has also been used as a research and clinical tool (Priebe et al., 1999). The same team went on to develop the QuiLL for older people, which is also being used in service and research settings (Evans et al., 2005). They also made a significant contribution to the debate about the use of QoL measures in mental health by showing that change over time can be measured using these instruments (Evans et al., 2007). They compared people with severe and common mental health problems with the general population, and found that common mental disorders can have an equally devastating effect on quality of life as more severe disorders, and they also showed that the quality of life of people with severe disorders can be improved over time. They also investigated the phenomenon of 'response shift' (Evans and Huxley, 2005) in people with severe disorders. This is said to occur in health-related QoL studies when the patient 'shifts' their subjective rating thresholds to take account of their altered circumstances. Evans and Huxley (2005) showed that contrary to popular opinion at the time, response shift is not common in people with severe mental health problems, and when it does occur it is not mainly in the direction of 'resignation' (adapting to worsened circumstances by raising current subjective ratings) but mainly in the direction of 'aspiration' (aspiring to better circumstances by lowering current subjective ratings).

Service user research

The growing influence of the mental health service user movement has stimulated an increased synergy between MHSW research and user-led research. To some degree this is because both have an interest in the wider quality of life domains, such as work, education, support, safety, etc., rather than addressing the health domain only. The synergy is typified by participative methodologies (Tew et al., 2006) and early partnerships have achieved some local success. For example, Castillo and Ramon influenced the development of user-led services for people with a diagnosis of personality disorder in one locality in the UK following a participative study (Castillo, 2003; Ramon et al., 2001). The growth of academic mental health service user/consumer research units in the UK, Australia and the USA in recent years – encouraged by government policy for consumer involvement in research and stimulated by the growing influence of the service user movement – will undoubtedly influence the future of MHSW research (Doughty and Tse, 2005; Simpson and House, 2002). MHSW and user-led research will continue to share the broad focus on demonstrating real improvements in people's lives (outcomes) in terms of quality of life, social inclusion and social capital. We briefly examine research in these outcome-related areas in the following sections.

Social inclusion research

A report by the European Council on Employment and Social Policy (European Commission, 2001: 1) refers to social exclusion as people being 'prevented from participating fully in the economic, social or political life of the nation'. There appears to be general agreement in the literature about the dimensions of social exclusion, which Atkinson (Atkinson et al., 2002: 4) summarizes as: 'poverty, income inequality, low educational qualifications, labour market disadvantage, joblessness, poor health, poor housing or homelessness, illiteracy and innumeracy'. It is not hard to see how social work in general and MHSW in particular have common interests in these matters, but there is also considerable interest in relation to mechanisms that might prevent children from becoming excluded in later life. Relevant research into the factors that might prevent exclusion in children has been conducted in Australia (Daly et al., 2007) and in the UK (Barnes and Morris, 2008). No coincidence then that Sheppard (2006) in his book on the essence of social work practice entitled *Social Exclusion and Social Work: The Idea of Practice* develops the thesis that social exclusion provides the pivotal point providing the 'social location' for social work.

For some people the concepts of social exclusion and inclusion are still too narrow as a basis for the development of effective local and national social policies (Berman and Phillips, 2000). Beck et al. (1997) have proposed an alternative overarching conceptual framework of *social quality*, defined as:

> The extent to which citizens are able to participate in the social and economic life of their communities, under conditions which enhance their well-being and individual potential. (Beck et al., 1997: 3)

This concept of *social quality* is similar to the conception of quality of life assessment used by MHSW researchers (see above and Oliver et al., 1996) in that it encompasses both objective and subjective interpretations. Social quality has at least four overlapping elements that bear a close resemblance to the life domains of quality of life assessments. They are: social-economic security (protection against unemployment, poverty, ill-health and other material deprivations); social inclusion/exclusion (equal access to supportive infrastructures, labour conditions and collective goods); social cohesion/anomie (the availability of social networks, equal access to services); empowerment/disempowerment (enabling people to develop their full potential in social economic, political and cultural processes). Vogel's (1994) taxonomy of social quality is virtually the same as the life domains covered by quality of life measures, i.e., health, education, work, income, housing, safety, social attachment, leisure (Vogel, 1994: 260).

Arts and social inclusion

Although participation in arts activity is believed to have important mental health and social benefits for people with mental health needs, the evidence base is currently weak. Hacking et al. (2006) report upon the first phase of a study intended to support the development of stronger evidence. The main purpose was to map current participatory arts activity, to identify appropriate indicators and to develop measures for use in the second phase of the research. A survey of participatory arts projects for people with mental health needs aged 16 to 65 in England, identified via the Internet and relevant organizations, was carried out to map the scale and scope of activity and to establish the nature of current approaches to evaluation. The results indicate that the scope of activity, in terms of projects' settings, referral sources, art forms and participation is impressively wide. In terms of scale, however, projects reported low funding and staffing levels that may have implications for the feasibility of routine evaluation in this field. Current approaches to evaluation were limited, but entailed considerable effort and ingenuity, suggesting that projects are keen to demonstrate their benefits. Spandler et al. (2007) explored how arts and mental health projects facilitate some of the key elements of the 'recovery approach' in mental health. The authors argue that the fostering of hope, creating a sense of meaning and purpose, developing new coping mechanisms and rebuilding identities are all outcomes of this activity.

Employment-related service research

Work represents an important goal for many people with severe mental illnesses. Gainful employment addresses practical needs, improving economic independence, as well as therapeutic needs, enhancing self-esteem and overall functioning. Although vocational rehabilitation has been offered in various forms to people with severe mental illnesses for over a century, its role has weakened because of discouraging results from earlier vocational rehabilitation efforts, financial disincentives to work and a general pessimism about outcomes. The traditional model uses a 'train and place' approach, offering training in sheltered workshops and then placing individuals in real life work settings. The Individual Placement and Support (IPS) programme is the reverse, i.e. 'place and train', so that clients are placed in real jobs and then offered variable amounts of direct personal support to be able to retain their work positions.

Service user and carer advocacy groups have set work and occupation as one of their highest priorities, to enhance both functional status and quality of life. Governments in different countries have adopted a variety of welfare to work programmes, and in many cases people with severe mental health problems have benefited from these schemes. This is partly in response to some evidence that there are substantial economic impacts of employment difficulties (unemployment, absenteeism, low productivity) among people with, for example, schizophrenia and depression. Rates of unemployment among people with schizophrenia, for example, often exceed 90%.

Exemplar 3: Research into work (using systematic review methods as developed and advocated by the Cochrane Collaboration)

A UK Health Technology Assessment Review conducted by one of the authors

(P.H.) with clinical colleagues assessed the effectiveness of traditional pre-vocational training (PVT) compared to Supported Employment schemes (SE, a form of Individual Placement and Support (IPS) and to standard care (in hospital or the community) for people with severe mental disorders (Crowther et al., 2001). In addition, the review examined the effectiveness of: particular types of PVT (e.g. 'clubhouse' model) and SE (Individual Placement and Support model); and modifications for enhancing PVT (e.g. payment or psychological interventions).

Eligible studies were RCTs examining the effectiveness of vocational rehabilitation approaches (PVT and SE or modifications) for people of working age and suffering from a severe mental disorder. Eighteen RCTs of reasonable quality were identified: PVT versus hospital controls, three RCTs, $n = 172$; PVT versus community controls, five RCTs, $n = 1204$; modified PVT, four RCTs, $n = 423$; SE versus community controls, one RCT, $n = 256$; and SE versus PVT, five RCTs, $n = 491$. The main finding was that, on the primary outcome (number in competitive employment), SE was significantly more effective than PVT at all time points (e.g. at 12 months, SE 34% employed, PVT 12% employed; the relative risk of not being in competitive employment = 0.76, 95% confidence interval 0.69 to 0.84, number needed to treat = 4.5). Clients in SE also earned more and worked more hours per month than those in PVT.

The main finding was therefore that SE was more effective than PVT for patients suffering from a severe mental disorder who wanted to work. There was no evidence that PVT was more effective than standard community care or hospital care. The implication of these findings is that people suffering from mental disorders who want to work should be offered the option of SE. The systematic review concluded that the cost-effectiveness of SE should be examined in RCTs outside the USA.

Social capital research

As part of their long tradition of engaging with social theory, MHSW researchers are courting the sociological zeitgeist of social capital and are investigating its explanatory potential within social models of mental illness. It is too early to tell whether this romance will blossom, though there are some indications that it may make a meaningful possible contribution to MHSW research (Webber, 2005). Social capital refers to the social context of people's lives. It is a multi-dimensional concept that variously encompasses other concepts such as trust (Coleman, 1988); civic engagement, social norms and reciprocity (Putnam, 1993); features of social structures and networks (Lin, 2001); and the resources embedded within them (Bourdieu, 1986). Social scientists, policy makers and clinicians have seized upon it as a panacea for the post-modern disintegration of grand social theory. It has consequently been applied to fields as diverse as sustainable development (van Bastelaer, 1999), democracy and governance (Putnam, 1993) and public health (Kawachi et al., 1997).

Although the concept has attracted multiple definitions, MHSW researchers have made the case for two distinct social capitals rather than one unified concept (Webber and Huxley, 2004), an idea which is now receiving wider currency (Kawachi, 2006; Kawachi et al., 2007). The communitarian conceptual approach to social capital, derived from the work of political scientist Robert Putnam (1993) has been highly influential in psychiatric epidemiology. This sees social capital as a 'public good' arising from participation in civic activities, mutually beneficial norms of reciprocity and the trust people place in other members of the community. It is often measured at the ecological level to explore associations with prevalence rates of mental disorders (e.g. Boydell et al., 2002; Rosenheck et al., 2001). However, the neo-capital approach derived from sociologists such as Pierre Bourdieu (1986) and Nan Lin (2001) arguably offers more promise to MHSW research.

Predominantly derived from social network analysis, the neo-capital conception maintains a focus on social structure whilst mostly using the individual as the unit of analysis. Lin's definition of social capital as 'investment in social relations by individuals through which they gain access to embedded resources to enhance expected returns of instrumental or expressive actions' (Lin, 1999: 39) emphasizes the dynamic qualities of the concept and its potential utility for mental health.

Social workers have worked with social scientists to derive and validate appropriate measurement strategies. Applied in general population and clinical samples these have demonstrated inequalities in access to social capital for people with a common mental disorders (van der Gaag and Webber, 2007; Webber and Huxley, 2007). They are also being used in intervention research as outcome measures.

The concept of social capital has renewed the focus on the social context of people's lives in mental health research. Its connections with traditional social work concerns of social support and social networks may see the concept as becoming influential in future MHSW practice and research.

Exemplar 4: Social capital and modern data reduction techniques

The development of the Resource Generator-UK (Webber and Huxley, 2007), an instrument to measure an individual's access to social capital, illustrates the contribution of mental health social workers to the measurement of social phenomena and the use of multiple methods. The instrument asks whether a respondent knows someone who could provide them with a specific resource. Each resource represents a concrete sub-domain of social capital and is grouped empirically with others to capture the full diversity of the concept.

Starting from a version of the instrument developed in The Netherlands (van der Gaag and Snijders, 2005), they used focus groups of people recruited from the UK general population to assess the content validity of an item pool identified for the UK. An expert panel using the nominal group technique (van de Ven and Delbecq, 1972) reviewed these group discussions and rated each item on how relevant they believed it to be for members of the UK general population. The remaining items formed the first draft of the instrument which were subjected to cognitive appraisal and a series of field tests.

They used an exploratory non-parametric item response theory model, the 'Mokken scaling method' (Mokken, 1997; Sijtsma and Molenaar, 2002) for item reduction and scaling. Mokken scaling aims to find robust and one-dimensional scales within sets of items. It begins by taking pairs of items with the strongest associations and continues by gradually including other well-fitting items until a scale has been formed that does not improve any further when other items are added (Mokken, 1997). The reliability of the resulting 27-item instrument was tested using the test–retest method. Its validity was assessed using a convergent/divergent validity test and a 'known group' validity test.

The instrument has since been used in two longitudinal studies, although publication of their results is forthcoming. One explored the role of access to social capital in the course of episodes of depression and the other used it as an outcome measure in an evaluation of a volunteering programme for adults with severe mental health problems. Both published (van der Gaag and Webber, 2007; Webber and Huxley, 2007) and unpublished data suggest that social interventions with social capital creation as a goal may have positive effects on mental health.

THE FUTURE MHSW RESEARCH AGENDA

In order to develop a strategic approach to developing capacity in social research, it is necessary to identify the priorities for future research funding. Without programmes of social research to study and improve processes such as social assessment, social interventions and the measurement of the impact of social care, integrated services may tend to rotate users of services through an increasingly medicalized experience of hospital care and community treatment. Likewise, current difficulties in relation to social exclusion, re-admissions, relapses, gender and race issues, people falling through the network of care, serious incidents, housing, vocational services and so on will improve slowly if at all, unless the role of social care provision is taken more seriously and concrete steps are taken to create a better social work and social care evidence base (Huxley, 2001: 120).

A review of all available published and unpublished material on social research priorities in mental health was undertaken as part of a larger programme of work on the development of research groups (Gould et al., 2007). The review was undertaken in 2005 and, in compliance with the national mandate of NIMHE, was based in England. The exercise built upon previous consultation meetings with various mental health stakeholder groups, including service users (e.g. Thornicroft et al., 2002) which sensitized the development of the research approach and instrument.

There were more responses from mental health practitioners than academics and there was a substantial level of response from people who identified themselves as past or current users of mental health services. The two main research priority areas that emerged were research into: social inclusion; social capital; social networks; and into social factors that enable resilience and recovery. MHSW is closely aligned to the user movement in its understanding of the concept of recovery, with a shared emphasis on self-efficacy, hope and empowerment (Carpenter, 2002). Research in this field is dominated by narrative accounts of recovery experiences by service users or survivors (e.g. Faulkner, 2000; Wallcraft, 2002). However, contributions from MHSW research include evaluations of the empowerment capability of psychosocial rehabilitation (Mowbray et al., 1997a) and arts projects (Hacking et al., 2006), for example.

There remains scope to adopt a systems-level approach and investigate barriers to recovery present in wider society. One element of this is anti-stigma work, currently a pre-occupation of social psychiatrists. A further dimension which MHSW researchers are well placed to explore are the social barriers to paid employment, a decent income and good relationships, which survivors say are crucial to recovery. This research agenda neatly maps onto social inclusion policies (e.g. Social Exclusion Unit, 2004), in the UK and Australia, which MHSW researchers are well placed to evaluate. The continued neglect of research into the needs of carers, and interventions to help them in their caring role, should be reversed and this is an area in which MHSW could make a further contribution.

A potentially highly significant but under-researched (at least in the UK) area is the provision of services and supports in rural communities. There is a long tradition of this kind of research in Canada, the USA and Australia among others (Jackson et al., 2007). It is presumably of less priority in England especially due to the nature of the distribution of the population (or some might say because of the dominance of models developed in large urban areas), but it is of considerable interest in the rest of the UK, in Scotland and Wales in particular (Parr et al., 2004).

The increase in globalization means that global issues such as urban–rural differences will receive considerably more attention in future years and we can expect a growth in relevant research from parts of the world which are developing their capacity and stature in social work research. Useful cross-cultural perspectives can be brought to bear on key matters such as child development (Robinson, 2007).

One may expect to see a growth in the development of intercultural research by social workers in the mental health field. Some of this work is already being conducted particularly in relation to culturally sensitive practices (al-Krenawi and Graham, 1997; 2000) and good interethnic communications skills (Robinson, 1998). These are increasingly relevant lessons for multiculturally diverse western nations, where global migrations both forced and voluntary not only diversify client populations but also the workforce. These changes will also bring with them renewed interest in and use of native healing methods (al-Krenawi and Graham, 1999) and perhaps interest in the integration of modern and traditional healing systems (al-Krenawi et al., 1996; al-Krenawi, 1999).

Almost two decades ago, the late Gerry Hogarty, in response to the medicalization of the mental health field that we referred to earlier in this chapter, suggested that a re-examination of contemporary social work research and the profession's practice mandate showed that there remained many 'important and legitimate areas of social work inquiry into mental disorders' (Hogarty, 1991: 5). The subsequent history and development of MHSW research has indeed confirmed that this was the case. We believe that his optimism was well-founded, and we share that optimism for MHSW research in the coming decades.

27

Social Work Research and Aging

Philip McCallion

INTRODUCTION

Aging is a growing focus area for social workers but in general social work researchers have been somewhat absent from much of aging related research. Social work researchers have been focused mostly on specific issues such as Alzheimer's disease, and on populations such as caregivers, and have contributed mostly to the advancement of micro (person) level interventions such as support groups (Toseland et al., 2001b) and less so to mezzo (group and community) and macro (policy) level considerations. Recent decades have seen increased awareness of aging issues, attention to macro and mezzo as well as micro level concerns and a broadening of the interventions in development and being evaluated. This chapter will review current research, consider the related research to practice issues and suggest areas for further research. Guided by the extant research, the chapter will begin with an overview of population growth and the principal theoretical perspectives underlying social work contributions; the areas then covered will comprise: (1) pensions, economic supports and financial literacy; (2) long term care;

(3) aging prepared communities; (4) managing disability and chronic illness; (5) civic engagement and reinventing retirement; (6) caregiver support; (7) intergenerational caregiving and reciprocity; (8) end of life care; and (9) persons with life-long disabilities. The chapter will conclude with some recommendations on research methodology, on the development of research capacity and discuss under- and un-researched areas particularly fruitful for social work consideration.

POPULATION GROWTH

Longevity is a phenomenon in the developed and developing world with numbers aged 65 and over expected to triple by 2050 (from 1999 figures), with the greatest growth in developing countries and with those over 80 and particularly those over 100 representing the population strata with the greatest growth in numbers (U.S. Bureau of the Census, 1999; 2001; Kinsella and Velkoff, 2001). To the extent that social work has been more focused upon younger population groups there is a challenge for social work to position itself to better respond to this demographic. Indeed the aging of the population also has implications for more traditional social work targeted groups, particularly children and families with growing numbers of grandparent caregivers (Janicki et al., 2000) and for oppressed and vulnerable populations with increased longevity, such as immigrants, cultural minorities and persons living in poverty (NYSOFA, 2000).

There is also a growing body of information accumulating in the US through large national longitudinal studies; examples of such studies include the Health and Retirement Study (*hrsonline.isr.umich.edu*). Data on physical and mental health and health care utilization, and on living situations, and financial and social support resources are usually available. Other studies target more specific health concerns, e.g. the Framingham Heart Study (http://www.framinghamheartstudy.org) focused primarily on cardiovascular disease, and the Nun Study on Alzheimer's disease (http://www.mc.uky.edu/nunnet); and on particular populations, e.g. the Nurses' Health Study looking at the health over time of women (http://www.channing.harvard.edu/nhs/history/index.shtml). Several of these studies have included the collection of biomarker material and have informed the development of subsequent national longitudinal studies. In particular, there has been a more prominent featuring of anthropometric measurement (see for example http://www.ifs.org.uk/elsa), collection of genetic materials (see for example www.tilda.ie) and the inclusion of unique populations such as in the Intellectual Disability Supplement to The Irish Longitudinal Study of Aging (McCarron and McCallion, 2008). However, there has been less attention to the extension of measures of well-being, social embeddedness and policy and environmental supports, areas of particular interest for social work and a role for social work researchers lies in expanding such understanding. The challenge for social workers as researchers lies both in finding ways to utilize available datasets to identify needs, support recommended interventions and policy changes and to be active in shaping the questions collected in subsequent waves of studies if relevant questions are not already being considered.

THEORETICAL PERSPECTIVES

A criticism of the research of all applied disciplines is that it is too rarely guided by a theoretical perspective, thereby limiting the ability to cumulatively improve knowledge (Polit and Hungler, 1996). A theoretical perspective is even more important when issues in a research question and their inter-relationships are complex. There are particularly prevalent theoretical perspectives in social work research in aging that focus upon family caregiving, service utilization, quality of life (QoL) and successful aging. Perspectives on dementia and dementia related caregiving are also of particular influence.

Research on family caregiving has been strongly influenced by stress and coping models which recognize that there are subjective as well as objective aspects of stress, that a variety of coping mechanisms may be effective and that appraisals and resources may mediate. The Pearlin Model (Pearlin et al., 1990) has emerged to frame suggestions for avenues to assist caregiving families to cope more effectively. This model includes four major domains: a) background and contextual factors, b) primary and secondary strains, c) mediating factors, and d) outcomes or manifestations of stress. The model has supported the development of interventions to deal with behavioral problems, environmental modifications to address increased dependency and safety needs, and outside supports and education to reduce physical demands of care tasks (Schneider et al., 1999), work (Beeson, 2001), loneliness and depression among spouse caregivers, and distress and burden among informal caregivers after nursing home placement (Garity, 2006).

The Behavioral Model of Health Service Use developed by Anderson and colleagues is also frequently used in social work research, in this case to organize the factors that affect service use into predisposing, enabling, and need categories (Andersen, 1995; Andersen and Davidson, 1996). Developed originally to explain and predict health service use (Andersen, 1968; Anderson and Newman, 1973), the model has been widely used by social work researchers to predict the use of many types of aging focused services (see, for example, Fosu, 1994; McCallion et al., 2004; Smith and Kirking, 1999).

In their use of modified versions of the Andersen model social work researchers have drawn upon caregiving literature that suggests that predisposing factors such as caregiver/care recipient relationship, living arrangement, gender, age and ethnicity, and enabling factors such as rural/urban location, availability of transportation and medical insurance may be as important, if not more important, predictors of service utilization than need variables (Cox, 1993; Coward and Lee, 1985; Hinrichsen and Ramirez, 1992; Kosloski and Montgomery, 1994; Macera et al., 1991; Miller and Cafasso, 1992). However, others have accessed health service utilization literature that suggests that need variables explain more variance in service need than predisposing or enabling variables (see, e.g. Branch et al., 1981; Gill et al., 1998; Wolinsky, 1990). Service utilization studies by social work researchers, particularly work with persons with Alzheimer's disease and their caregivers, have supported the importance of need variables, but have also argued that the contribution of need, predisposing and enabling factors deserves further clarification (Bass et al., 1992; Gill et al., 1998; Kosloski and Montgomery, 1994). Also, the contribution of need, predisposing and enabling factors has been found to differ based upon the type of service use (health versus social services) under consideration (Bass et al., 1992).

Work with persons with dementia has also influenced perspectives on QoL for aging persons. Lawton (1991) suggested that there are four key concepts in a QoL perspective: (1) behavioral competence – continued ability to manage or to be supported to manage critical decisions and day-to-day life, (2) mastery of the environment – continued ability to independently or with support to negotiate living and work areas (assumes ability to remain in familiar places), (3) psychological well-being – freedom from depression and other untreated concerns, and (4) perceived QoL – reflecting the views and desires of the person with dementia. Longston and colleagues (Logsdon et al., 2002) went further, pointing out that behaviors and non-cognitive (and treatable) concerns such as depression and pain do have a negative impact on QoL. Good health and health care have therefore been emphasized as able to impact positively on QoL and this literature suggests that what is important to QoL may change as disease progresses and as living arrangements change. These QoL concerns are perhaps best captured and generalized to all aging persons in concepts of successful aging. Kahn (2002) argues that successful aging occurs when there is a relatively low risk of disease and disease-related disability, high mental and physical functioning, and active engagement with others and in productive activities. He also includes being able to accept age associated decrements in functioning, doing the best with the level of functioning one has, and the need for society to apply external resources to increase opportunities and facilitate behaviors that make for success in older age. These perspectives individually and cumulatively influence much of the research and research needs in aging. The challenge for social work researchers will be both to apply these ideas more broadly to aging issues and to ensure that understandings of the components of QoL in turn influence the development of interventions and are captured in the measures chosen or developed for tests of the effectiveness of interventions.

Guided by these theoretical approaches social work research must address and in some cases does address the following key issues.

Pensions, economic supports and financial literacy

Increases in personal longevity, greater numbers of aging persons and a growing percentage of the overall population being aged over 65 combined with declines in birth rates and the available labor force have led to calls in many countries to modify pension and Social Security eligibility as well as retirement and older age related health benefits.

Extended retirement years Even the choice of traditional retirement ages such as 65 years will mean that many individuals will spend thirty plus years in retirement and for those who retire earlier there is a likelihood that they will spend more years in retirement than in prior employment. This poses challenges in terms of how retirement support will be provided and sustained, and what one's QoL will be during those years. On the one hand there is evidence that levels of disability and chronic illness have been declining but on the other there are reports that 80% of people over 65 have one chronic condition, 50% have two and approximately 40% have some type of disability (Wan et al., 2005). Such findings suggest that the maintenance of health and/or the provision of services to respond to health and independence changes are critical to QoL in retirement (Kahn, 2002); availability of sufficient resources to sustain a chosen life style and meaningful opportunities and activities are also important.

Income and resources Much has been achieved in ensuring sufficient resources for retirement. Pension plans, social security and health insurance from employers and government have been identified as critical components of such retirement 'wealth' but both the value and the security of those resources appears less certain than in the past (Wan et al., 2005). As a result, improving financial literacy is emerging as a new intervention

area for social work (McCallion et al., 2007), but one where the research base is lacking.

Baby boomer issues A largely Western concept to reflect a particularly robust post second world war population cohort, the first wave of this group has turned 60 years of age coinciding with the swelling numbers of older people. Summarizing the findings of a survey of 55 to 70 year olds from across the United States, a MetLife (2006b) study concluded that the definition of retirement for baby boomers (in this survey those aged 50–59) was still essentially freedom from work demands but unlike older cohorts, Boomers saw this as not occurring on some fixed date but as a process likely to stretch into one's seventies and eighties before 'freedom' is actually achieved. Boomers overall did appear to have more resources than older generations but there were concerns that their affluence was being expressed more in spending than in saving and that their retirement income, based upon greater risk and self-directed investment, may not be sufficient for longer years of retirement and is likely to be weighed down by growing health care costs (Gist, 2006). Social workers must also be concerned about those who have not saved and who are only eligible for the most basic of pensions both from a macro advocacy perspective to encourage better pension provision and from a mezzo and micro perspective where particular groups and individuals are disadvantaged by pension availability with actual or potential detrimental effects on QoL.

Early retirement/later retirement Growing affluence, employer incentives and the availability of some pension benefits at earlier ages have all contributed to the growth of a group of individuals who choose to retire early. The data available is not conclusive, but changes in dates for eligibility for full benefits, a decline in the availability of company sponsored pensions and health insurance benefits and reductions in benefits for earlier ages are believed to be discouraging continued growth in this early retirement group and is placing many at risk (Korczyk, 2004).

More importantly for social work research interests, in a series of reports in the US, drawn from census data and surveys, AARP and Medlife have captured many differences for a range of important groups.

Women Although in the US they will live on average at least three years longer after age 65 than men, retired women will more likely live in poverty, be alone and be more dependent upon social security without any additional pension. They are also less likely to continue to be employed after age 65 and therefore will not have opportunities to accrue additional income (AARP, 2005).

African Americans African Americans too are more likely to live in poverty and to depend on Social Security and the proportion of African-American women with an employer pension is much lower than any other group (AARP, 2004a).

Latinos Poverty rates for older Latino men and women are twice those for all persons aged 65 and over and there is also a lower availability of income from pensions (AARP, 2004b).

Gays and lesbians Gay and lesbian older persons, particularly Baby Boomers, appear to be more concerned about their retirement years than other retirees, although many of their concerns are the same: outliving one's income, getting sick or disabled or becoming dependent on others. Nevertheless in MetLife's (2006a) survey of 1000 self identified LGBT people aged 40–61, 40% believed that being gay, lesbian, bisexual or transgender better prepared them for aging.

This snapshot of financial risk for aging subgroups in the US is repeated in other developed nations; a particular concern in many countries is the growing population of financially at risk aging first and second generation immigrant worker groups (Razin and Sadka, 1999). Meanwhile, in developing countries with an absence of developed pension and health insurance programs, the consequences of greater longevity alone will similarly strain the ability of countries to adequately support older persons (Dullemen, 2007).

Social work has been somewhat a consumer of research on economic and family concerns in retirement, for example, in work with elderly victims of abuse and rarely the source of this kind of data and as a result is too silent on the potential for the impoverishment of the elderly. One area where work is emerging is in the understanding of risk of financial exploitation for the elderly and the development of supportive responses. As the resources available to older persons increase and yet their concerns are not allayed about how they will pay for long term care and ensure they have resources for their last years, many seek to improve their retirement resource picture but inadvertently increase their potential for fraud and exploitation. Equally as the number of years of retirement that need to be supported also increase, the consequences of fraud and exploitation are more catastrophic, for example leaving destitute a retiree previously well provided for financially. There are efforts to develop and test educational and other interventions to prevent exploitation and to delay financial spend-down (McCallion et al., 2007), as well as beginning strategies to address the consequences when they do occur. Consistent with social work values and given the negative consequences for the QoL for exploited older people and for those with poor money management skills, this is an important area for social work research and practice. However, in broader terms, if social workers are to be advocates for public policies likely to better support a growing aging population, they must also participate in research that documents the financing of older age and the consequences of public policy for the overall financial security or insecurity of those who are aging.

Long term care

The definition of long term care across time, across nations and across settings continues to be difficult. When a figure of three million people in the US being in nursing homes (CMS, 2003) is quoted there is a need to be careful to define this in terms of type of care (in this case skilled nursing) sources of payment (eligible for Medicaid or Medicare or both) and population of interest (short term rehabilitation, life time disability and long term older person care). The presence of other long term residential alternatives such as assisted living, adult homes and planned retirement communities complicates the picture as do newer programs such as nursing homes without walls (a level of at home nursing care similar to what would be offered in a nursing home) and the reality that in some regions and countries, in the absence of other alternatives, long term stays in acute hospitals are effectively a form of long term care. This very variety in options also speaks to the range of costs involved and perceptions that the long term care system is inefficient, overly expensive and perhaps not fully responsive to both society's and the individual's needs (Kane, 2006). Several issues have emerged as critical research challenges: QoL of nursing home residents (Kane et al., 2003); 'culture change' within existing settings to move away from medical models to better reflect the QoL and self-determination concerns of residents and families and to support personal autonomy even when chronic illness or cognitive impairment are present (Thomas, 2003); rationalization of the growing array of residential options; and support for the diversion of older persons from residential settings to be supported instead in valued community living (Zendell, 2007). Specific nursing home research has focused on reducing incidents and falls, avoiding physical and medical restraints, using routinely collected data to create indicators of quality, increasing the use of psychosocial and recreational support, development of specialized units addressing training and turnover issues among staff and managing costs (Kane, 2006). Social work research is interested in all of these issues but there is a particular challenge for social work to pursue work that will promote independence, self-determination and QoLand support the avoidance of institutional placement while at the same time ensuring quality of delivery

and care when persons are placed outside their own home. This would suggest that social work research should be driven by QoL, culture change and person-centered perspectives.

Aging prepared communities

A new interest for a number of researchers begins with a belief that a key to successful aging is the opportunity to live in a community that offers a conducive social environment and has the capacity to provide the supportive services necessary to promote physical health and emotional well-being. Such communities may occur 'naturally' and it also seems possible for communities to purposefully adapt to better meet these needs and expectations. The consideration of these issues is influenced by prior understandings of predisposing, enabling and need factors in the use of services often gathered in studies using the Andersen Model (McCallion et al., 2004), and efforts have addressed both mezzo and macro level approaches.

Naturally occurring retirement community (NORC) At the mezzo level a NORC is a community with a large concentration of older adults within a geographically defined area (Marshall and Hunt, 1999). Something about this neighborhood caused some people to decide to grow old here and may have also encouraged some other older persons of their own accord to move there. These communities are not planned housing developments; they may comprise apartments, condominiums, or single-family homes (Masotti et al., 2006) and a variety of criteria are used to define them, but generally a geographic area is defined as a NORC if more than 50% of the residents are at least 60 years old; although some groups are satisfied with a concentration as low as 25% and others use a minimum age of 50 (Ormond et al., 2004). What is already known is that there is some preliminary evidence that NORCs may be an effective way to help seniors age in place and avoid moving to a more restrictive residential settings and there is a high life satisfaction among residents of NORCs (Carpenter et al., 2007). As a result and because of the advocacy of existing identified NORCs there is increasing attention to identifying the characteristics and programmatic supports that promote involvement in the community, health and well-being, and a supportive physical and social environment (McLaren et al., 2007). Social workers often play critical roles in the offering and management of such supports. There is also interest in understanding if there are service additions to NORCs (sometimes called supportive services programs) often offered by social workers that will support the beneficial impact of these communities without changing their naturally occurring character (Cohen et al., 2007). Work is also underway to understand what those services should be and how best to deliver them so that the character and ethos of a NORC is preserved and supported (McLaren et al., 2007).

Aging prepared communities At a more macro level there is interest in whether whole neighborhoods, towns, cities and regions may be similarly supportive of aging in place. Various terms are used, aging prepared and elderly friendly among them (Bronstein et al., 2006). Through focus group and community survey data collection a number of necessary community characteristics have been identified:

- accessible and affordable transportation;
- in-home services;
- a range of housing options and services;
- easily accessed health care;
- low crime rates;
- caregiver support services;
- accessible businesses and public buildings;
- support of pedestrians and adequate traffic control;
- age appropriate exercise facilities; and
- a community that sees elders as vital members and central to the community's agenda (adapted from Alley et al., 2007).

In aging prepared community work there are active efforts to both support existing characteristics and to create ways to achieve those not yet realized (Bronstein et al., 2006).

There are also examples of strategies for the engagement of stakeholders such as public and private agency staff, older community members, planning officials, the media, housing providers and developers, philanthropies, medical practices and hospitals and transportation networks (Bronstein, et al., 2006; City of Calgary, 2001).

Participatory action research techniques and qualitative approaches reliant upon focus groups, observation and interviews with key stakeholders are most often used to be responsive to formative and process research questions currently guiding aging prepared work; these approaches are also prevalent in NORC research. Ultimately to justify large scale expenditures in support of these alternatives, demonstration will be needed of delays in nursing home placement, the extension of family caregiver coping, reduction in health care utilization and health morbidity and increase in life satisfaction and community engagement. Measurement of such outcome issues remains to be addressed and will require longitudinal designs and access to health and health care utilizations datasets. Use of existing datasets will also permit the selection of control subjects for comparison purposes. A critical issue that remains to be addressed is the support of older persons living in resource poor communities and with significant health disparities who nevertheless wish to age in place outside of nursing home and other institutional settings. This is a challenge that research must address and will likely involve interdisciplinary perspectives including public health and economics. However, leadership will be needed and a value placed on the continued community living of such persons. Social work is more likely to offer this leadership and is doing so already (Kane et al., 1998).

Managing disability and chronic illness

The rates of disability among older persons have actually been declining. Nevertheless, 36% of people between 55 and 63 years have a disability and this increases to 45% age 65 to 74, to 58% age 75 to 79 and to 74% for those over age 80 (U.S. Census, 2001). Regarding chronic illness:

- Older persons have the highest rates of cancer and the lowest rates of screening (Maramaldi and Lee, 2006).
- Cardiovascular disease is already the leading cause of death in the US and Europe, with one in three persons over age 65 having experienced some type of heart incident, and is expected to be the leading cause in developing countries by 2010 (American Heart Association, 2003).
- Diabetes disproportionately affects the elderly and the highest growth rates are anticipated to be among those over 75 (Boyle et al., 2001).
- Osteoporosis affects approximately 18% of older women and between 3% and 6% of older men, high rates of arthritis among older people appear to be associated with lower educational and socioeconomic levels and age is a prominent risk factor for falls (Samelson, 2002).

In all cases, health disparity populations (ethnic minorities and persons with low socioeconomic status) experience greater morbidity. Obesity is a concomitant concern; Olshansky and colleagues (2004) have warned that diabetes and other chronic diseases are increasing and life expectancy could be cut by five years in the coming decades if obesity continues to increase.

There are two areas for social work practice and social work research: prevention and treatment. In the area of prevention, determining strategies to increase education and screening have been a particular challenge, given controversy at times about the value of screening in older age (Takahashi et al., 2004); social workers in their care management functions have roles in both encouraging screenings and in ensuring that there is appropriate follow-up. In the treatment arena support group interventions, approaches to encourage compliance with treatment protocols and programs to help persons with chronic illness or disability to better navigate health systems have been supplemented with

the promotion of self management strategies particularly as availability of evidence based programs such as the chronic disease self management program (Lorig et al., 1999) has increased. Social work researchers have played roles in advancing the science of translating evidence based interventions offering insights on the preservation of treatment fidelity (see for example Frank et al., 2008). Work in this area has also involved social work researchers in the use of the RE-AIM framework.

There are five elements, or dimensions, of the RE-AIM framework: *reach* – the number, proportion, and representativeness of individuals who participate in a given program; *efficacy/effectiveness* – the impact of an intervention on important outcomes, this includes potential negative effects, QoL, and costs; *adoption* – the number, proportion, and representativeness of settings and staff who are willing to offer a program; *implementation* – at the setting level, implementation refers to how closely staff members follow the program that the developers provide, this includes consistency of delivery as intended (fidelity) and the time and cost of the program; *maintenance* – the extent to which a program or policy becomes part of the routine organizational practices and policies (Glasgow et al., 2006). The emphasis in this framework on effective translation and on the implications for communities and agencies as well as older persons who are the targets of a program fits well with social work micro, mezzo and macro concerns.

By way of example work with grandparent caregivers has resulted in the development of psychoeducational support groups that in randomized trials have resulted in statistically significant reductions in depressive systems and increased ability to manage caregiving responsibilities and family concerns (see e.g. McCallion et al., 2004). This addresses efficacy but one such project also considered the most effective ways to reach the grandparents of interests, and to deliver the program, ensure that the program was delivered as intended and that it would be easily adopted and maintained in the communities targeted (see Janicki et al., 2000; McCallion et al., 2000). In this manner an intervention was developed that holds promise to deliver the same results in communities in need by local agencies and social workers.

Civic engagement and reinventing retirement

There is increasing interest in the value of volunteering for older adults. A recent review of related research summarized findings that those who volunteer have lower mortality rates, greater functional ability, and lower rates of depression later in life than those who do not volunteer. Older volunteers compared to other age cohorts were found to be most likely to receive benefits from volunteering, and volunteers who devote 100 hours per year or more to volunteer activities were most likely to exhibit positive health outcomes (CNCS, 2007). These findings for the benefits of volunteering combine with concerns about the financial security of older adults, growing evidence of a reality if not a desire for older adults to continue working at least part-time and a desire by not for profit service agencies to recruit greater numbers of older volunteers (Burnett, 2006). New terms have emerged such as civic engagement which is seen as including both volunteer and paid employment opportunities that benefit both the community and the older person, and reinventing retirement which reflects that the traditional views of retirement are changing and the absence of work may no longer be the distinguishing characteristic of life in older age (Center for Public Health, 2004; McCallion and Ferretti, 2008).

Although there have always been volunteer and other service opportunities for older persons, the civic engagement perspective begins with a belief that they have often been of the photocopying, receptionist and support staff type; yet there are many older persons who wish to contribute to social causes and to their communities in more meaningful ways. There is increasing concern that the incoming group of older persons, the Baby Boomers with their higher levels of education, health and income, will be particularly hard to engage unless more meaningful roles are created (Gerteis, 2005). There are also concerns about the preparedness of society and potential employers to welcome these volunteers (Center for Public Health, 2004).

Much of the related research to date has drawn upon large survey samples supplemented by smaller anecdotal and qualitative reports. More purposeful, coordinated development of new initiatives such as Respect-Ability (http://www.respectability.org) has relied upon participatory action research approaches, pursued formative and process evaluation and is beginning to explore rate of return methodologies to determine the cost effectiveness of new initiatives in preparation for potential wider application (Lisa A. Ferretti, LMSW, personal communication, 10/1/08).

For social work there is interest in the health and other benefit older persons may accrue through meaningful volunteer and paid participation in public and private agencies. Engagement in literacy and other support efforts for at risk children is particularly recommended as an area for growth for such opportunities (Center for Public Health, 2004), an approach that many social workers would wish to encourage. Finally social workers in their various roles are likely to come in contact with more engaged volunteers working in the same agencies that employ social workers. Given the potential for interaction and to support volunteers who are assisting the same goals social workers are pursuing it seems incumbent on social work research to play roles in developing opportunities and in evaluating their outcomes.

Caregiver support

The average primary caregiver of frail older persons is an adult daughter or daughter-in-law aged 46 with high school or some college education, married with children under 18 and usually still employed. However, 23% of caregivers over 65 are spouses; and stereotypes of men not undertaking personal care are falling; in spousal relationships men are nearly as likely to assume this role when care is needed (Fromme et al., 2005; Greenberg et al., 2006), and spouses are more likely to be caring for someone with significant caregiving needs. Approximately 20% of caregivers are estimated to provide over 40 hours of care per week (NAC & AARP, 2004). Further, this work has been valued in the United States at $306 billion, annually (Arno, 2006).

There are concerns that research to date through its focus on the primary caregivers underestimates the extent and impact of caregiving and views the elderly only as the recipients of care when in many cases care and support is exchanged (Toseland et al., 2001b). There has been a further growing trend for research to document that caregiving is changing – aged family members are more likely to be in poorer health, have more chronic illness issues, to be discharged from hospitals sooner and to function less independently, increasing the need for support (Hooyman and Kiyak, 1996), and as predicted by Cantor (1993), with increases in aged years, caregiving may span multiple generations of families, for example, a grandchild may themselves be a caregiver of children and have responsibilities for an aging parent and for an aged grandparent.

Finally for women in particular, caregiving in their middle years when it disrupts continuous employment will mean they themselves will have less resources in terms of savings and pensions when they too are elderly (SSA, 2002). Greater longevity among women may also mean that the caregiver will have no one to provide care when she, in turn, needs such supports.

Caregiver support has been an important area for social work research (and has also been advanced by the contributions of nurse and psychologist researchers). That caregiver research has addressed the societal context and the role of health delivery systems and employers and has supported calls for public policy responses (Ho et al., 2005). Other areas of research have included the experience of caregivers including caring in different disease conditions, consideration of coping and resilience, benefits and negative consequences of caring for caregivers and the effectiveness of interventions including the value of support versus psychoeducational approaches and leadership by peers versus professionals (for a review see Toseland et al., 2001b). The impact of prolonged care on the physical and psychological health of caregivers has been a particular concern (see for example Lee et al., 2003). There are now sufficient studies that reports of meta-analyses are possible (see for example, Pinquart and Sorensen, 2003). Caregiving has also been an area where there has been considerable work in the development of assessment scales, particularly for the measurement of burden (for a review see Vitaliano et al., 1991). There has also been considerable work undertaken to understand similarities and differences in the caregiving experience across gender (Marks et al., 2002) and across ethnic groups (see e.g. Yong and McCallion, 2003) and in the meaning of care (Farran et al., 1999; Toseland et al., 2004).

Social work research and caregiving stands at something of a crossroads. A famous challenge was laid down in 1989 in the US as to whether we need additional caregiving studies (Zarit, 1989). Do researchers continue to explore the depths of caregiving using qualitative approaches, quantitatively mine large and longitudinal datasets to explain the prevalence, experience, impact and changing nature of caregiving, develop and test new interventions or has enough been done and we should concentrate in the translation and application of existing knowledge?

Intergenerational caregiving and reciprocity

An increasing if new aspect to caregiving in older years is care for grandchildren. The number of children in grandparent headed households has increased dramatically and in the US has been estimated at 4.5 to 6 million children (U.S. Census Bureau, 2001). The number of grandchildren living solely with their grandparents increased 57% between 1992 and 2000 and those numbers are believed to be continuing to grow (Bryson, 2001). Data from several large datasets indicates that all socioeconomic and ethnic groups are presented but there is a higher prevalence in the US among African-Americans and urban areas are over-represented (Bryson, 2001). Also the age of grandparent caregivers appears to range from the mid-30s to the oldest old placing many of these individuals outside the purview of traditional aging focused services (McCallion et al., 2000). There are similar reports in other countries, for example, grandparent caregiving has been identified as one of the fastest growing forms of out-of-home care of children in Australia (Spence, 2004) and in the United Kingdom (Hunt, 2003). Broad (2004) highlights grandparent care as the increasingly preferred placement option for statutory authorities in the UK. Horner et al. (2007) in Australia note that much grandparent caregiving is informal. These issues of formal and informal kinship care are also found in the US as is the realization that society is increasingly dependent upon on grandparents to offer alternatives to institutional care for children and to replace the declining numbers of foster care parents (McCallion et al., 2002). Research findings that there may be both positive and negative consequences for the older person's own health and there are reductions in free time, limitations on housing options, increased demands on resources and even situations where the retiree returns to work to support this new family situation add to the research agenda. Also, unusual for aging services perspectives,

the reasons for grandparent caregiving often involve significant child abuse, addiction and prison/incarceration concerns (Kropf and Yoon, 2006). Therefore research in this area often incorporates policy perspectives, is concerned with the needs of both the grandparent and grandchild (Kolomer et al., 2008) and has informed the development and systematic testing of interventions (McCallion et al., 2004).

Work with census and longitudinal datasets has helped build a picture of these caregiving families and the mining of such datasets is likely to continue to be a significant feature of research in this area. Also, there are opportunities for researchers and advocacy groups to encourage the addition of relevant questions in future waves of such large scale data collection. There has also been investigation of the experiences of unique populations, for example, caring for grandchildren with developmental disabilities (Janicki et al., 2000; McCallion et al., 2000) and multigenerational families where there is a tradition of grandparents caring for grandchildren and in turn the parent generation caring for the grandparents when they are no longer able to care for themselves (see, e.g. Burton, 1996). From all of this research there has also emerged an interest in reciprocity. It remains to be investigated the extent to which grandchildren who have been cared for by their grandparents in turn switch roles in adulthood and provide care to an infirm grandparent.

End of life care

End of life care is one area where there is a disconnect between social work interest and social work presence in related research. With a growing interest and emphasis on advance directives and living wills guiding decision-making at end of life, within hospitals and nursing homes social workers are frequently charged with addressing these issues with individuals and their families (Lacey, 2005). The social work role goes further, offering advice and concrete supports around artificial nutrition and hydration, bereavement, linkage to financial, psychosocial and spiritual resources, social supports and preparing for a good death (Gutheil and Souza, 2006; Lacey, 2005). There is a beginning body of survey and qualitative interview research on surrogate decision-making and end-of-life care, the ethical issues faced by social workers in end-of-life care settings, communication issues in end-of-life and palliative care, the initiation of palliative care earlier in the disease process and social work roles in multidisciplinary team approaches to palliative care (Engelhardt et al., 2006; Guetheil and Sousa, 2006; Lacey, 2005). Most of this research has been conducted with populations in hospitals, hospices, and nursing homes; research on the experiences of families caring for the dying at home is less developed. Social work researchers must decide if their work will continue to support a narrow role for social work in decision-making or if they feel the ethical, family, grief and self-determination issues inherent in treatment decisions and in follow-up after death are also the purview of social work. This is an area where social work has potentially much to offer but where there may be resistance from other professional groups who have traditionally played a larger role. Perhaps a role for research is to offer evidence in support for advocacy.

Persons with life-long disabilities

A challenge was posed by Campbell (1996) to researchers on the absence of data on the aging of persons with life-long disabilities. She defined two groups, those with various forms of intellectual and developmental disabilities (ID) and those with young adult onset of spinal cord, traumatic brain injury and arthritis. There is as yet little on the second group and an emerging literature on the former.

Similar to the general population, over the last decades there have been marked changes in the life expectancy of persons with ID particularly among those aged 55 years and over (Barron and Kelly, 2006). However, the life expectancy of persons with ID remains less than that of the general population, with the average age of death in an Irish population with ID reported at 46 years (Lavin et al., 2006), 66 years for New York State (Janicki et al., 1999), and 58 to 74 years depending on level of disability in the UK (Bittles, 2002). In many countries a majority of adults with ID continue to live with their families and growing longevity and numbers of older persons with ID has major implications for service planning, potentially increasing demand for full-time residential services, support services for ageing caregivers, and services designed specifically to meet the needs of older people with ID. These concerns include:

- As the carers of adults with ID themselves age beyond their caring capacity, additional formal supervised living arrangements will be needed.
- Increased pressure for the creation and support of residential placements is already being experienced by residential services.
- Improved life expectancy among adults with a more severe intellectual disability is placing an increased demand on health services.
- Increased longevity means that fewer residential places are becoming free over time, a higher degree of support within day and residential services is required, and specific support services for older people with ID are needed.

Planning for the future care of these individuals and avoiding crisis situations when family caregivers are no longer available has been and continues to be of paramount importance. Much social work research for this group has been focused upon permanency planning and the promotion of self determination (for a review see McCallion and Kolomer, 2003).

The health and care of people with ID is also of concern. There does seem to be consensus across studies that as a group, individuals with ID have a greater variety of health care needs compared to those of the same age and gender in the general population (US Department of Health and Human Services, 2002); also, health problem experiences may vary by level of disability (Moss et al., 1993). Van Schrojenstein Lantaman-De Valk et al. (2000) compared 318 people with ID within a general practice with others and found that people with learning ID had 2.5 times the health problems of those without ID and that some conditions seem more related to external circumstances, such as lack of information, lack of exercise, poor mobility, poor eating habits, and medication use/misuse. Among the population of older adults with ID, there is also a reported high incidence of mental health problems (Cooper, 1997, 1999). Much recent aging focused research has targeted the higher prevalence of dementia among people with Down syndrome and the challenges this poses for assessment, service delivery, family support and end of life care (McCallion and McCarron, 2004).

There has been controversial evidence that the experience of poor health and early mortality among people with ID may be related to the location and types of health care services people with ID have received over a life time as well as in their older years (see e.g. Strauss et al., 1998). At the very least, for older persons with ID a greater understanding is needed of their access to and utilization of mainstream health services (including health promotion and social support services).

Social work research has played less of a role in addressing health and health access concerns for people with ID, yet many of the same issues of concern for the general population are present here too and social work has much to contribute. Similar efforts are needed to understand the aging of persons with young adult onset disabilities as well as those aging with mental illness, and AIDS/HIV.

CONCLUDING COMMENTS

This review of key issues in social work research in aging has highlighted work in a number of critical areas but does not claim to be exhaustive. This review has focused more upon aspects of the lives of older persons and has chosen areas where there has been considerable work such as caregiving and others where there is a need for more substantial contributions, for example, end of life care. Areas were also chosen to illustrate the range of social work research approaches, qualitative and quantitative; concern with formative, process and outcome issues and inclusion of the subjects of research through participatory action research approaches. The areas chosen also illustrate the growing potential for secondary data analysis, the value of longitudinal studies and the need for different frameworks and research approaches to support translational research work. Many of the areas chosen also benefit from the efforts of multidisciplinary research teams. And it is within this broad swath that the challenge lies for social work research.

Research in any area is often a developmental process, beginning with descriptions of a phenomenon, then seeking to understand underlying issues and concepts and to develop theory and from there develop research questions for more in-depth exploration (Fortune and Reid, 2005). There will often be disputes about whether each stage has been sufficiently exhausted and indeed whether the products are of value, including concerns about the research approaches and methods used. For social work research in aging there are several challenges which hopefully have been illustrated in this review. All research properly carried out is to be valued and narrative and other contributions are equally critical to ensuring a holistic picture. However, we are at a time where there is a large amount of research findings available; these are drawn from a variety of research methods, and often too there are contributions from multiple disciplines. Such a state of the research raises questions about how such findings may be effectively integrated and effectively utilized and as Zarit (1989) raised for caregiving a need to question whether sufficient additional contributions will emerge from replications and further exploration of the same issues. The presence of a large number of existing datasets and improved approaches to combining such datasets should encourage greater exploration of such data rather than encourage new data collection. However, the revising of questionnaires for subsequent waves of longitudinal studies offers some opportunity for new questions and new qualitative and quantitative pursuit of questions is always justified when the data available in incomplete, unsatisfactory or has not addressed the research question of interest.

As stated much of the research reviewed here is of US origin but there are UK, New Zealand, Australian, South Korean, Japanese and Netherlands examples utilized, which helps establish the cross-national saliency of the issues. Also UN reports cited support the value of this research for developing countries too. Clearly, there is additional work, for example, in addressing specific mental health issues as well as newly emerging work in substance abuse and gambling. Social work must continue to pursue a range of research topics in aging, build skills in an array of research approaches, foster the multidisciplinary collaborations that will benefit pursuit of questions that will offer insights to genuinely improve the lives of older persons and ensure that research is translated into action.

Social Work in Criminal Justice

Fergus McNeill, Denis Bracken and Alan Clarke

INTRODUCTION

This chapter comprises four main sections. The first section very briefly outlines the various organizational and professional relationships between social work and criminal justice systems, the many roles that social workers play in criminal justice and the different forms of criminal justice social work (hereafter 'CJSW') research. We go on to present three further and more substantive sections, which consider the historical development and future prospects of inter-related but distinct types of CJSW research: *critical and comparative research* concerned with the character, development, forms and functions of CJSW; *explanatory research* which seeks to explain the issues, problems and processes that CJSW exists to address; and *effectiveness research* which aims to evaluate 'what works?' and what counts as 'evidence-based practice'.

Though we have settled on the term 'CJSW', it is not a term that is widely used. In English-speaking jurisdictions, CJSW is practiced by people who work for 'correctional services', 'offender management services' or 'probation departments'. Some of these people have social work qualifications, others do not. Moreover, the use of the term 'CJSW' immediately raises questions of whether and to what extent the practices concerned are

recognizable as *social work* practices. However, to examine that question at this stage would lead us into wider debates about what social work is and into an invidious position as arbiters of what does and does not count as CJSW. For these reasons, we deliberately use the term loosely.

Before proceeding, we offer two further caveats. Firstly, it is inevitable that our coverage of the questions outlined above will be partial at best and idiosyncratic at worst; we can provide neither a global overview nor a comprehensive analysis. Secondly, we have resisted the temptation to include specific sections on issues concerning relationships between CJSW and poverty, social exclusion, diversity, race, gender and indigenization; this is because we prefer to treat these as recurring issues throughout the chapter.

SOCIAL WORK, CRIMINAL JUSTICE AND RESEARCH

Criminal justice processes and social work

CJSW involves practice in formal criminal justice systems, as well as in alternative and diversionary systems. Of course other areas of social work, such as child protection and mental health, also have connections with the criminal justice system on a regular basis. For the sake of clarity, criminal justice includes systems or processes of criminal law, law enforcement, prosecution and defence, court adjudication and sentencing and the administration of sentences both in the community and in institutions. Separate youth justice systems are common and social work has a long history of involvement with young offenders. Although court missionaries – who may be seen in some senses as the precursors of professional CJSW – ministered to *all* of those in need at court (see Nellis, 2007), services to victims and witnesses are a more recent innovation in the criminal justice system. Since social work with offenders – as opposed to victims – has dominated the history of CJSW and so will dominate this chapter, it makes some sense to dwell briefly here on social work with victims of crime.

The evolution of work with victims owes much to social work's wider interests and loyalties. For example, family violence issues and sexual offending – with their obvious links to both feminist social work and social work's concern with child protection – have become major areas of CJSW involvement. However, for obvious reasons, social work with victims is not always the exclusive preserve of CJSW. Rather, who the victim is, in terms of age and gender, along with the context of her/his victimization may go some way towards pointing to the nature and type of social work contact. For example, child victims of neglect and child sexual abuse are most likely to be involved with child protection social workers, whose primary and proper concern is with the welfare of the child and not with doing justice (in whatever sense) to the offender. People abused by intimate partners (typically women abused by men) may be assisted by specialist teams of social workers, often working in close connection with police and prosecutors. Victims of crime who do not find themselves in categories such as these are more likely to come into contact with more generic victim services in the public or voluntary sectors; sometimes these

services are staffed by social workers. Research in this area has developed rapidly on both sides of the Atlantic (for example, Williams, B., 1999, 2002; Roberts and Springer, 2008).

Where social workers in the criminal justice system are employed, and by whom, has an impact on the character and structure of CJSW practice. Education is also a key factor. Where a social work qualification *is* necessary for practice with offenders in the formal system, there tends to be more direct involvement by the justice-related parts of government in social work education and research as well as greater recognition within social work of CJSW as a distinct area of practice. Smith (2005) for example considers the break with social work training by the Home Office in England and Wales in 1995 as resulting in a decline over the ensuing 10 years in research articles on probation being submitted to and published in the *British Journal of Social Work*. In Scotland and Northern Ireland, a (generic) social work qualification is still required for CJSW practice and this remains the norm in the Republic of Ireland and some other European countries. Elsewhere in the English-speaking world, social work qualifications are not a requirement for practising CJSW. For example, a study of social work employment in Canada (Stephenson, 2000), using data from 1996, found that 18% of probation officers in Canada had a social work qualification. A more recent study of probation (Bracken, 2005) found that no province in Canada required a social work qualification to be a probation officer. The *Canadian Social Work Review*, the only social work academic journal in the country, has published only two articles on CJSW in the past 20 years.[1]

In both the USA and Australia, although social work qualifications are not usually a requirement for work in correctional services, the social work profession has recognized CJSW practice under the name of 'forensic social work' (FSW), defined by Roberts and Brownwell (1999) as 'policies, practices and social work roles with juvenile and adult offenders and victims of crime'

(1999: 360). The American National Association of Social Work sees FSW as a distinct area of practice, and an affiliate of the NASW, the National Association of Forensic Social Workers, is soon to launch its own journal.[2] Despite these developments, Reamer (2004) argues that despite employment of social workers throughout the US criminal justice system, 'the social work profession has largely abandoned the criminal justice field ... And, relatively little serious scholarship on criminal justice issues is authored by social workers' (2004: 213). Green et al. (2005) conducted research among Australian social workers as to how they would describe FSW, which the authors see as 'a (re)emerging area of specialization' (2005: 152). Their research provided support for the idea of FSW as a particular area of practice requiring specialized knowledge and skills.

Criminal justice social work interactions

Although social workers often work in prisons and courts, most CJSW is based in the community and it is probably true to say that the most common tasks involve providing advice to judges (typically through pre-sentence reports), supervising and assisting offenders undertaking community-based sentences, and assisting ex-prisoners in their resettlement or re-entry to the community.

Social work's quest for recognition of a body of knowledge and set of skills necessary for practice typically centres on the idea of generic skills and the transferability of those skills across different areas of practice. Clearly, the practice process in CJSW – engaging, assessing, intervening (and/or case managing) and evaluating – is not dissimilar to that in other forms of social work (McNeill et al., 2005). Whilst the relevance of generic knowledge, values and skills to CJSW has been widely recognized, debates about the degree of more specialist education and training that CJSW requires have been contentious in some jurisdictions. In the UK, Nellis has written extensively on the need for more criminologically focussed training for working with offenders, within a social work context or without. He argued that, in the UK, the Diploma in Social Work which emerged in the early 1990s contained too little of use for probation training and suffered from 'institutionalized genericism' (Nellis, 1993: 30).

Although some element of compulsion or involuntariness is not unique to the practice of social work in criminal justice, some recognition of the 'control' aspects of working with offenders in the community has been the subject of debate and research in CJSW for some time. Parsloe (1976) delineated what she termed three ideologies of welfare, justice and community that underpinned social work involvement with offenders. Her research suggested that all three were at work amongst probation officers in England in the 1970s. Day (1981) reported from a survey of probation officers on the potential for conflict between their 'professional ideology' as social workers and the demands of their work as officers of the court. More recently, in helping practitioners to work through these tensions, Rooney (1992) has explored the involuntary and/or mandated nature of some clients and their interaction with social workers – not just in criminal justice contexts – and he uses social work research which speaks to this aspect of working with offenders. Trotter's (2000, 2006) influential work on engaging with involuntary clients is based on research which he conducted with probation officers in Australia. He found that qualified social workers were more likely to involve themselves in training and to use effective practices; he also found that their clients had lower breach rates.

Criminal justice social work research

If CJSW itself is multifaceted and varied, then the same is true of social work research which can be viewed as both 'complex and multidimensional ... an arena for contested and competing perspectives and practices' (Gibbs, 2001a: 688). Social work itself has undergone many changes in recent decades, mainly in response to wider social, economic and political changes. In particular, the trend towards globalization, the emergence of a neo-liberal political agenda, the introduction of a market-based, mixed economy model of welfare provision, the rise of 'new manageri-alism' and the introduction of privatization have all had a major impact on the nature, organization and delivery of social work (Lesnik, 1997) and on social work research. Recent years have witnessed a shift from casework to case management, the emergence of specialist practice and an increasing emphasis on multi-agency provision and inter-professional working involving both statutory and voluntary sector organizations. There has also been a noticeable shift from the use of psychodynamic therapies in one-to-one work with clients, towards group work based on cognitive-behavioural inter-ventions and task-centred practice initiatives. As a result of these developments, especially in English-speaking countries, the research agendas of social work agencies (in all fields, not just criminal justice) have become increasingly focused on defining and meas-uring effectiveness.

In some respects CJSW has been, for better or worse, an exemplar of these devel-opments; it is probably fair to say that in this area debates about 'what works?' developed earlier and have been running longer. However, though we recount these debates and their relationships to evaluation research later in this chapter, and though this is unde-niably the form of CJSW research that has been most influential in policy and practice, there is much more to CJSW research than 'what works?'. For although the evidence-based practice agenda drives us in the direc-tion of effectiveness research, broader debates about effectiveness require an engagement with research about the nature, character and proper purposes of CJSW as a social practice, and with research which seeks to explain and understand the problems it exists to address

and the processes it exists to support. And so it is to these issues that we turn below.

CRITICAL AND COMPARATIVE RESEARCH *ON* CRIMINAL JUSTICE SOCIAL WORK

In the 1970s, in criminal justice as in the rest of social work, the profession's associations with the 'psy' disciplines came under close scrutiny as a series of scholars, influenced initially by Marxist and later by Foucauldian scholarship, revised traditional accounts of social work's history. They alleged that the emergence of social work as a (semi-) pro-fession was best accounted for by the need for new forms of social control precipitated by social changes associated with industriali-zation and urbanization (for example, Donzelot, 1979).[3] More recently, analytical histories of penal systems have focused on how the 'penal-welfare complex' (Garland, 1985) that developed in the late-nineteenth and early-twentieth centuries has been trans-formed in the more recent past. Accounts of this penal reconfiguration centre on the USA (and sometimes England and Wales) and recount a discursive shift from a preoccupa-tion with the rehabilitation of offenders towards a 'new penology' preoccupied with the management of crime risks or with a new 'culture of control' (see, e.g. Feeley and Simon, 1992, 1994; Garland, 2001; Simon, 2007). Much academic attention has been rightly focused on the emergence of 'mass imprisonment' in the USA[4] as a consequence of this socio-cultural shift – and specifically on the highly racialized character of this phe-nomenon (Wacquant, 2001). But more rele-vant here are related analyses of how societies, cultures and individuals construct (and are constructed by) other penal practices that are less routinely examined than the high drama of imprisonment – in particular CJSW prac-tices.

For Garland (2001), the origins of the emergence of new strategies of crime control lie in a 'crisis of sovereignty' created by two major social 'facts' of the latter part of the twentieth century; '*the normality of high crime rates* and *the acknowledged limitations of the criminal justice state*' (Garland, 2001: 106, emphasis in original). This predicament provokes a 'schizoid' reaction in the state involving the development of two strategies. On the one hand the '*sovereign state strategy*', characterized by 'hysterical denial', deploys a criminology of the alien other to create a suitable enemy for the state to expressively and punitively attack (see also Pratt, 2000). This stands in stark contrast to the 'criminology of the self' which underlies more pragmatic, '*adaptive strategies*' typified in recent approaches to crime prevention and reduction that construct the criminal less as a 'deviant' and more as an 'illicit, opportunistic consumer' (2001: 451–2) whose cost–benefit calculations must be managed. Traditional rehabilitation fits comfortably with neither of these criminologies nor with their related penal strategies; as Garland (1996) notes:

> … the excluded middle ground here is precisely the once-dominant welfarist criminology which depicted the offender as disadvantaged or poorly socialized and made it a *state responsibility* … to take positive steps of a remedial kind. (1996: 461–2, emphasis added)

According to Garland, these developments related to a profound loss of faith in the legitimacy of the traditional rehabilitative aims and purposes of probation partly provoked by adverse research findings (see below). This loss of (political) faith resonated particularly powerfully in terms of changing *public* mentalities and sensibilities about crime and punishment.[5] Indeed, Garland (2001) argues that penal welfarism was eclipsed in large part because of the decline of support for its measures amongst the middle classes, now increasingly insecure as they navigate the risks and uncertainties of late modernity and, partly in consequence, increasingly distrustful of the claims of penal professionals as experts in their field (see also Bauman, 1997). As a result, probation's

traditional justification – as a means of reclaiming or helping disadvantaged people through rehabilitation, in our *collective* interests – lost its cultural purchase and rehabilitation survives only in a hollowed out managerialized form in which the offender need not (perhaps cannot) be respected as an end in himself or herself; he or she has become the means to another end (McCulloch and McNeill, 2007). Rehabilitation is more carefully targeted, rationed and subjected to evaluative scrutiny; it is offence-centred rather than offender-centred; it targets criminogenic need rather than social need.

The discursive reformation of rehabilitation as just another method of risk management undertaken in the public interest has more recently been reflected in significant organizational changes in some jurisdictions. The establishment of the National Offender Management Service for England and Wales in 2004 made Garland seem impressively prescient. The name and the objectives of the new service clearly capture some of the characteristics of the new penology; as a centralized endeavour targeted at, but not for, *offenders* (the 'others'), it exists to *manage* them and in so doing to provide a *service* to the law-abiding public (the 'us'). Its objectives are to punish offenders and to reduce re-offending, affirming respectively the expressive and the instrumental aspects of the new penology.

Nonetheless, Garland's (2001) broader thesis in the 'Culture of Control' has been carefully examined and critiqued on various grounds (see, for example, Braithwaite, 2003; Feeley, 2002; Matthews, 2005; O'Malley, 2004; Zedner, 2002). In the absence of histories of CJSW drawing on practitioner and probationer accounts, it is impossible to judge the nature of the contingent relationships between official *discourses* and frontline *practices*. Fine grained qualitative studies of contemporary penal policies and practices in various jurisdictions (often using ethnographic methods) have in some respects both confirmed and challenged Garland's arguments about the reconfiguration of penality (see e.g. Hannah-Moffat, 2005; Lacombe, 2008; Lynch, 1998, 2000; Robinson, 2002, 2003). Though these studies clearly confirm the emergence of risk and protection as dominant practice discourses – at least in the English-speaking world – they also reveal considerable complexity about how these 'new' discourses interact with existing preoccupations with need and welfare (in Canada and the UK) and with law enforcement (in the USA).[6]

Looking beyond North America and the UK, evidence of similar changes in CJSW in other jurisdictions is even more equivocal. Historically the nature and use of community sanctions in Europe has varied significantly and has not always been tied to rehabilitation (Cid, 2005). In reviewing European probation, Walters (2003) identifies a shift in most jurisdictions from welfare to 'corrections' not dissimilar to that reported in the UK and the USA (see also McNeill, 2004). Canton (2007) notes that:

> A definitive survey of European probation practice (van Kalmthout and Derks, 2000) found a tendency in 'almost all countries' away from social work concepts and values and towards an alignment with the goals of other criminal justice agencies – notably, risk management, public protection and punishment. (2007: 230)

Despite these shifts in discourse, they nonetheless described providing guidance, care and assistance as the most important job of probation services and many services, as we have seen, continue to see probation work as social work. That said, as the shift to 'corrections' suggests, promoting the social inclusion of offenders is increasingly difficult in jurisdictions where the emergence of a focus on public protection has placed considerable strain on the maintenance of a social work ethos in respect of 'offenders'. Rather than recognizing victims and offenders as overlapping social groups, public protection discourses tend to dichotomize them and to cast their interests in a zero-sum game where to be pro-offender is to be anti-victim and vice-versa (McCulloch and McNeill, 2007). There are, however, important differences

between the emphasis on *potential* victims implied by discourses of public protection and, as we have already seen, the emergence of a belated, legitimate and necessary concern with 'real' victims. Canton (2007) notes that while many probation systems in Europe have recognized the political and ethical necessity of responding to the needs of victims as well as offenders, not all have been equally successful in integrating 'victim-centred work in an essentially offender-centred organization' (2007: 230). Amongst those who have progressed this agenda, Canton (2007) cites Austria, Belgium, Norway and parts of Germany as developing victim–offender mediation, as well as noting that some of the newer European services (for example, in the Czech Republic, Latvia and Turkey) have enshrined principles of reparation and mediation in their founding statements.

Looking beyond Europe, different kinds of tensions exist in defining the purposes and character of CJSW. In the Republic of South Africa for example, in the contexts of social, economic and political transition in the post-Apartheid era, probation services have developed rapidly. However, in its changing social context, the character of South African probation is disputed; correctional services see probation strictly as a form of penal supervision, while social development practitioners envision a much broader social work role at every stage in the criminal justice process (Ehlers, 2007). Elsewhere in Africa, in contrast to a focus on public protection, community sentencing tends to focus on community service which Ehlers (2007) suggests 'fits well with cultural traditions of making amends as a response to wrongdoing' (2007: 229).

A further layer of complexity is created by variations *within* different countries of which the USA and Canada provide the clearest examples. Bracken (2007) explains that probation is highly fragmented in the USA partly because of the multiple levels of government (and parts of government) involved, including municipalities, counties and states as well as the federal government itself. In Canada, while the ten provinces and three territories are responsible for delivering probation, it is the federal government and the national parliament that provides the legislative foundation.

Even in less federal nation-states, developments in relation to political devolution – notably in the UK and Spain – are creating new issues and tensions for CJSW. Thus while Scotland remains part of the UK, both social work and criminal justice became devolved matters when the Scottish Parliament was established in 1999; even before devolution, Scotland had taken a different path from England and Wales. Though CJSW continues to be located in social work and remains a service of local authorities, the new Scottish Government is increasingly setting the agenda for CJSW (see McNeill and Whyte, 2007). In this context, McNeill's research (discussed in Robinson and McNeill, 2004) confirmed the emergence of public protection as CJSW practitioners' 'meta-narrative' but noted that they interpreted and operationalized this purpose in particular ways; insisting that it was best achieved through helping offenders via social work methods centred on relationship-building and recognizing the significance of offenders' *social* contexts and problems. Thus there is at least some evidence (as Hannah-Moffat, [2005] and O'Malley [2004] suggest in other jurisdictions) that while CJSW practitioners are increasingly willing to deploy the *discourses* of risk and protection, they do this in particular ways and for particular purposes, often in defence of the traditional *practices* of penal welfarism.

Whether we look to continents, countries or regions, it seems that CJSW is a field of practice in transition. However, those empirical studies referred to above suggest that this is an ongoing process and that it is a process that is mediated by the different histories, cultures and practices of CJSW in different jurisdictions. It follows that a clear priority for the future of critical research on CJSW is to develop more robust frameworks for comparative analysis. In this respect, recent developments in comparative criminological and penological research may provide very useful resources (see Cavadino and Dignan, 2006) – not least in examining to what extent approaches and practices can and should travel across jurisdictions (Jones and Newburn, 2007).

EXPLANATORY RESEARCH

The connections between how we understand social problems and how we tackle them are, at the same time, obvious and complex. Though for CJSW these connections imply the need for considered dialogue between social work and criminology, and though there is some shared or common history between the disciplines, in many jurisdictions – partly because corrections or probation are no longer defined or understood as social work – the links between the two academic disciplines have become tenuous. There have, of course, been honourable and insightful attempts to bridge the gap (see Smith, 1995) and we would argue that CJSW's current transitional position lends salience to such efforts. At such times, developments in research and scholarship which reshape the ways that social problems are understood and addressed are of particular significance and so it is to these forms of criminological research that we now turn.

The problem of reoffending

Sentenced offenders in most jurisdictions are predominantly young, male and unemployed and tend to experience a range of significant personal and social problems. As with prisoners, in respect of whose backgrounds there is a wealth of research evidence (in some jurisdictions at least), offenders under supervision very often face serious and chronic disadvantage and social exclusion. The UK Government's Social Exclusion Unit's (2002) report 'Reducing re-offending by ex-prisoners' revealed that, compared to the general population, prisoners were 13 times more likely to have been in care as a child; 10 times more likely to have been a regular truant from school; 13 times more likely to be unemployed; 2.5 times more likely to have a family member who has been convicted of a criminal offence; 6 times more likely to have been a young father; and 15 times more likely to be HIV positive. In respect of their basic skills, 80% had the writing skills of an 11-year-old; 65% had the numeracy skills of an 11-year-old; 50% had the reading skills of an 11-year-old; 70% had used drugs before coming to prison; 70% suffered from at least two mental disorders; 20% of male prisoners had previously attempted suicide; and 37% of women prisoners had attempted suicide. For younger prisoners aged 18–20 these problems were even more intense; their basic skills, rates of unemployment and previous levels of school exclusion were a third worse even than those of older prisoners (Social Exclusion Unit, 2002: 6).

The associations between some of these kinds of social factors and reconviction rates were explored in an important English study by May (1999). Drawing on 1993 data concerning over 7000 offenders from six probation areas, May (1999) demonstrated that problems with drug use, employment and accommodation were related to reconviction in all six areas and that offenders with multiple problems were more likely to be reconvicted. Of course, whilst it is important to acknowledge the common features within the offender population as a whole, it is equally important to acknowledge the variations in the needs, deeds and characteristics of different individual offenders, of those who have different patterns of offending and of those subject to different court disposals. To give just one example, the literature on women who offend shows that while male and female offenders share common needs, there are key differences in terms of behavioural issues, domestic expectations and risk factors

(Carlen, 2002; McIvor, 2004; Zaplin, 1998). To the extent that we can generalize, what we can say with confidence is that offenders subject to supervision have very high levels of need and that, so long as these needs remain unmet, they are likely to increase the likelihood of them being reconvicted.

In seeking to *predict* reoffending, Andrews and Bonta (1998: 42–3) have argued that the 'Big Four' risk predictors are antisocial attitudes (including values, beliefs, rationalizations, cognitive states), antisocial associates (including parents, siblings, peers and others), a history of antisocial behaviour (early involvement, habits, perceptions of criminal ability), and antisocial personality. They suggest that broader social problems are relevant in the genesis of these risk factors but that these are less proximate causes of reoffending. But moving beyond the identification of risk factors, seeking to *explain* what causes prolonged criminal careers poses considerable challenges for criminologists. Recently, the trend has been towards multi-factorial models. Thus, for example, Farrington (2002) suggests that offending is the result of a four-stage process involving *energizing* (in which motivations develop which may lead to offending); *directing* (in which 'criminal' methods for satisfying those motivations may come to be habitually chosen); *inhibiting* (in which beliefs, values and socialization may take effect to inhibit offending); and *decision-making* (in which situational opportunities, calculations about costs and benefits, the subjective probabilities of different outcomes of offending, and social factors inform decisions about offending). The consequences of offending may then reinforce anti-social tendencies, and the stigmatisation and labelling that often accompanies criminalization may also encourage further offending. Moffitt's (1993, 1997) 'theory of offender types' is also highly pertinent; her distinction between the criminal career types of 'adolescence-limited' and 'life-course persistent' offenders has been well-evidenced in research studies, but the evidence for her related claim that the *causes* of offending in the two groups are different is more contestable (see Smith, 2002).

Though the work of developmental criminologists and those who advocate a life-course perspective has provided very significant insights into criminal careers with some important implications for CJSW, critical criminologists would tend to suggest that the search for 'risk factors' and 'offender types' is fundamentally misconceived in focusing on the individual offender as the main unit of analysis. Thus, although developmental perspectives have underscored the significance of various socio-structural factors, they misdirect our attention towards the individual-level impact of these factors, rather than emphasising that crime, criminality and criminalization are social constructs governed by wider economic, structural, cultural and political forces. It is interesting to note therefore that Laub and Sampson (2003) have recently argued very convincingly that the 'risk factor paradigm' itself needs to be reconsidered. By analysing life-history interviews and other data concerning a cohort of men aged seventy on whom data has been collected since they were aged seven, Laub and Sampson (2003) illustrate the 'inherent difficulties in predicting crime prospectively over the life course' (2003: 290). Essentially, their analysis shows that boys with very similar risk profiles turned out to have very divergent lives.

The promise of desistance

Though criminology's historical quest to understand the causes of crime and criminalization has much to offer CJSW (see Smith, 1995), in many respects studies of how and why offenders desist may have even more to offer; for CJSW it is critically important to understand the change processes involved in desistance. Since desistance can happen independently of interventions but can also be supported (or frustrated) by them, it has been argued recently that CJSW must ground its practices in understandings of

desistance (McNeill, F., 2006). The argument is that CJSW services need to think of themselves less as providers of correctional treatment and more as supporters of desistance processes. It follows that choices about intervention should be based on understandings of individual change processes and of how practitioners can best support these processes, rather than offenders fitting in with pre-designed interventions prescribed for 'types' of offenders.

Maruna (2001) identifies three broad theoretical perspectives on desistance that address how desistance relates to age and maturity, to social ties and social bonds, and to changing personal narratives. Farrall (2002) suggests the integration of all three, stressing the significance of the relationships between 'objective' changes in the offender's life and his or her 'subjective' assessment of the value or significance of these changes:

> ... the desistance literature has pointed to a range of factors associated with the ending of active involvement in offending. Most of these factors are related to acquiring 'something' (most commonly employment, a life partner or a family) which the desister values in some way and which initiates a re-evaluation of his or her own life ... (Farrall, 2002: 11)

Desistance is best understood as emerging from the interfaces between developing personal maturity, changing social bonds associated with certain life transitions, and the individual subjective narrative constructions which offenders build around these key events and changes. It is not just the events and changes that matter; it is what these events and changes *mean* to the people involved. Maruna and Farrall (2004) also suggest that it is helpful to distinguish *primary desistance* (the achievement of an offence-free period) from *secondary desistance* (an underlying change in self-identity wherein the ex-offender labels him or herself as such).

This understanding implies both that desistance is a *process* not an event and that (because of the subjectivities involved) the process is inescapably *individualized*. It is not surprising therefore to discover that there is evidence of age- and gender-related differences in experiences of desistance (see, e.g. Jamieson et al., 1999); variations in the criminal careers of young women and men, perhaps unsurprisingly, reflect differences in age-related and gendered constructions of identity in adolescence and early adulthood. This suggests the significance of developmental processes linked to identity changes in desistance (see also McNeill and Maruna, 2007); a growing body of research which explores offenders' attitudes to, motivations for and narratives of desistance makes the case even more clearly.

Burnett's (1992) important English study of efforts to desist amongst 130 adult property offenders released from custody (see also Burnett and Maruna, 2004) revealed that those who were most confident and optimistic about desisting had greatest success in doing so. For others, the provisional nature of intentions reflected social and personal problems they faced. More recently Burnett and Maruna (2004) have written persuasively about the role of hope in the process of desistance and equally importantly about how social exclusion can suffocate hope (see also Farrall and Calverley, 2006). Burnett also notes that for most of the men involved in her study processes of desistance were characterized by ambivalence and vacillation. However, the over-turning of value systems and all preoccupying new interests that characterized the most successful desisters seem to imply the kind of identity changes invoked in the notion of secondary desistance.

Maruna's (2001) study offers a particularly important contribution to understanding secondary desistance. His research in Liverpool (UK) compared the narrative 'scripts' of 20 persisters and 30 desisters who shared similar criminogenic traits and backgrounds and who lived in similarly criminogenic environments. The persisters' 'condemnation script' evidenced a fatalistic (if realistic) account of their structurally limited prospects for leading different lives. By contrast, the accounts of the desisters revealed a different narrative – a narrative that was arguably less realistic but powerful nonetheless. Their accounts stressed their essential goodness, their 'fall' into and ensnarement in deviance against the backdrop of bleak circumstances, their unlikely escape, typically with the help of someone who believed in them, their accomplishment of what they were 'always meant to do', and their determination to 'give something back' and make good (Maruna, 2001).[7]

In the exemplar below, we focus briefly on a small number of important studies that have explored the implications for practice of this developing evidence base.

Exemplar: Applying desistance research

Rex (1999) explored the experiences of 60 English probationers. She found that those who attributed changes in their behaviour to probation supervision described it as active and participatory. Probationers' commitments to desist appeared to be generated by the personal and professional commitment shown by their probation officers, whose reasonableness, fairness and encouragement seemed to engender a sense of personal loyalty and accountability. Probationers interpreted advice about their behaviours and underlying problems as evidence of concern for them as people, and 'were motivated by what they saw as a display of interest in their well-being' (Rex, 1999: 375). Such evidence resonates with other arguments about the pivotal role that relationships play in effective CJSW interventions (reviewed in McNeill et al., 2005).

Looking beyond the significance of working relationships, studies of young people in trouble suggest that their own resources and social networks are often better at resolving their difficulties than professional staff (Hill, 1999). 'Resilience perspectives' in social work which, in contrast with approaches that dwell on risks and/or needs, consider the 'protective factors and processes' involved in positive adaptation in spite of adversity also seem relevant here. In terms of practice with young people, such perspectives entail an emphasis on the recognition, exploitation and development of their competences, resources, skills and assets (Schoon and Bynner, 2003). In relation to re-entry of ex-prisoners to society, Maruna and LeBel (2003) have made a similar and convincing case for the development of strengths-based (rather than needs-based or risk-based) narratives and approaches.

In looking towards these personal and social contexts of desistance, Farrall (2002) explored the progress achieved by a group of 199 English probationers. Though over half of the sample evidenced progress towards desistance, Farrall found that desistance could be attributed to specific interventions in only a few cases. Although help with finding work and mending damaged family relationships did appear significant, desistance seemed to relate more clearly to the probationers' motivations and to the social and personal contexts in which various obstacles to desistance were addressed.

Farrall (2002) argues that interventions must pay greater heed to the community, social and personal contexts in which they are situated. After all, 'social circumstances and relationships with others are *both* the object of the intervention *and* the medium through which ... change can be achieved' (Farrall, 2002: 212). Necessarily, this requires that interventions be focussed not solely on the individual person and his or her perceived 'deficits'. As Farrall (2002) notes, the problem with such interventions is that while they can build human capital, for example, in terms of enhanced cognitive skills or improved employability, they cannot generate the social capital which resides in the relationships through which we achieve participation and inclusion in society. Vitally, developing social capital is necessary to encourage desistance. It is not enough to build *capacities* for change where change depends on *opportunities* to exercise capacities.

In a recent paper, the material presented in this section has been used to propose a desistance paradigm for CJSW (McNeill, F., 2006). This paradigm deliberately forefronts processes of change rather than modes of intervention; it begins not with what the system or the practitioner does with the offender, but with what the offender is experiencing. Practice under the desistance paradigm would certainly accommodate intervention to meet needs, reduce risks and (especially) to develop and exploit strengths. However, a necessary precursor of such activity would be working out, on an individual basis, how the desistance process might best be prompted and supported. This would require the worker to act as an advocate providing a conduit to social capital as well as a counsellor and educator – building both motivation and human capital. The forms of engagement required by the paradigm would reinstate and place a high premium on collaboration and involvement in the process of co-designing interventions. Critically, such interventions would not be concerned solely with the prevention of further offending; they would be equally concerned with constructively addressing the harms caused by crime by encouraging offenders to make good through restorative processes and community service (in the broadest sense). But, as a morally and practically necessary corollary, they would be no less preoccupied with making good to offenders by enabling them to achieve inclusion and participation in society – and with it the progressive and positive reframing of their identities required to sustain desistance.

EVALUATION RESEARCH AND EVIDENCE-BASED PRACTICE

Though the desistance paradigm is research-based in the sense that it is built upon evidence about desistance processes, it is deliberately advanced as a 'paradigm' rather than a practice 'model' or method. As such it is not directly 'testable' in the way that a specific intervention programme might be. In looking to the history of evaluation research and 'evidence-based practice' in CJSW it is clear that, to date, precisely this type of evaluation research – concerned with questions around 'what works?' in reducing reoffending – has dominated the CJSW field. However, it is important to bear in mind that 'what works?' was preceded by 'nothing works'. The origin of this latter notion is attributed to a US-based narrative review of over 200 offender treatment programmes, which concluded that 'with few and isolated exceptions, the rehabilitative efforts that have been reported so far have no appreciable effect on recidivism' (Martinson, 1974: 25). The phrase 'nothing works' was not used in the original article but, given the changing political climate in the USA and UK, with the rise of neo-liberalism, a growing anti-welfare mentality and a desire to reduce public spending, it represented a convenient new orthodoxy. The threat that this posed for the rehabilitative ideal in general and its implications for probation practice in particular have been much discussed (Newman and Nutley, 2003; Raynor and Robinson, 2005).

With the benefit of hindsight it seems important to distinguish between 'what works?' as a series of research and practice-led developments characterized by a culture of curiosity and 'What Works' as a dogma promulgated through central managerialized initiatives, specifically in England and Wales from the late 1990s onwards. The complicated story of the 'effective practice initiative', which was designed to secure evidence-based offender supervision (Home Office, 1998) and constituted probably the

largest and costliest probation experiment in history is highly pertinent to this discussion but has already been much discussed in the UK literature (Mair, 2004; Raynor, 2004). Commentators have noted that while knowledge about 'what works?' can usefully inform practice and strengthen professional status (Newman and Nutley, 2003), a centrally driven approach to evidence-based practice has the potential to undermine professional autonomy (Hollin, 1995), shift professional boundaries (Newman and Nutley, 2003), threaten the professional status of practitioners (Robinson, 2001) and unduly prioritize only certain forms of evidence and research (see Hollin, 2008; Raynor, 2008). Furthermore, systematic reviews of evidence-based interventions provide mixed findings and commentators on both sides of the Atlantic agree that it is too early to make broad categorical statements about what works and what does not work (Merrington and Stanley, 2004; Aos et al., 2006).

Rather than dwelling further on the detail of these extremely important but nonetheless local developments, it seems more productive in the context of this chapter to examine their salience for wider debates about the relationships between evaluation research, notions of evidence-based practice and CJSW. Perhaps most fundamentally, it now seems very clear that too narrow a view of 'research-into-practice' should be avoided. First, there is a key question as to whether professional practice should be *based* on research evidence or *informed* by such evidence. Whatever the professional domain, as we have implied throughout, practice entails assessing *all* the available evidence (not just that produced as a result of evaluation research) and then making an informed judgement. Research cannot provide all the information practitioners require and what information research does provide needs interpreting and evaluating (Hammersley, 2005). Second, a narrowly focused 'what works?' research agenda may encourage practitioners to 'deliver and replicate' rather than 'develop and refine' (Mantle and Moore,

2004: 303). While replicating a successful initiative is clearly important, it is essential to acquire new knowledge in order for practice to evolve. Third, there is the question of whose job it is to interrogate and use research evidence: Is it a task for the critical and reflective practitioner responding flexibly to individual needs, risks and strengths, or is it a task for managers and consultants who then design 'evidence-based' systems and processes that practitioners must implement more or less slavishly (McNeill, 2001)?

While evaluative studies clearly have the potential to contribute to our understanding of 'what works?', the research literature is littered with disappointing and equivocal findings regarding the extent to which rehabilitative initiatives reduce recidivism. In the case of a specific correctional intervention, a negative evaluation result may be the outcome of one, or a combination of, the following: theory failure; programme or implementation failure; research failure. Theory failure implies that the problem lies with the theory believed to underpin the desired programme outcomes. Programme failure suggests that there was something amiss with the content of the programme or the way it was implemented and administered. Research failure attributes negative findings to methodological shortcomings in the research process.

In a simplistic sense, many programme evaluations would appear to be based on the logic of the medical model. The programme is seen as having the potential to provide a 'cure' and in order to ensure optimum impact the 'treatment' is best delivered in the form of standardized, measured 'doses' to a largely passive group of subjects. In order to produce evidence of sufficient scientific quality, 'evidence hierarchies' have been constructed, which portray a rank ordering of methods of evaluating treatment efficacy. In criminology, one of the first of these was the Scientific Methods Scale (Sherman et al., 1997), which was followed by other similar formulations (U.S. Department of Justice, 2004). Across the various US-based schemes there is a broad consensus that randomized control trials (RCT) constitute a 'gold standard' against which all other methods can be judged, but outwith the USA, the RCT has not been assumed to constitute an unequivocal gold standard in quite the same way (Friendship et al., 2005; Hollin, 2008) and such methods have not been employed very often (Farrington, 2003).

The application of a hierarchy of research standards for judging the quality of evaluations of offender programmes can be challenged on a number of grounds. For example, there are clear qualitative differences between clinical treatments and the kind of interventions promoted in criminal justice. RCT is often viewed as being too rigid a tool when it comes to evaluating social work interventions. Social work does not constitute a 'tidily delimited activity' (Cheetham et al., 1992: 13) and the provision of support involves encounters that 'are not straightforward or linear relationships, but multiple, multilayered, relational and complex' (Trinder, 2000a: 149). From a methodological perspective, the desire to maintain the scientific integrity of the experiment, in an attempt to maximize internal validity, can require exercising strict control over the nature and implementation of an intervention. Ultimately, this can create a situation so far removed from normal circumstances, that any attempt to relate the evaluation findings to the real world becomes meaningless. Thus, as Hollin notes, 'achieving high internal validity may be at the expense of external validity' (2008: 92). Clearly, experimentalism in the context of CJSW has its shortcomings. As Pawson and Tilley assert, in their realist approach to evaluation, 'it is not actual programmes which "work" but the reasoning and opportunities of the people experiencing the programmes which make them work' (1993: 2). We need to ascertain not only *if* an intervention is effective but must also be able explain *how* it works. Kazi (2003) applies the concept of the 'realist evaluation cycle' (Pawson and Tilley, 1997: 85) to social work research and illustrates how this helps to 'penetrate into the realities of practice deeper than the traditionalist view of evidence-based practice' (Kazi, 2003: 816). Realist evaluation is not methods-driven but theory-driven. Such an approach favours a multi-method research strategy incorporating a variety of quantitative and qualitative methods of data collection and analysis. From this perspective, no single method is considered a gold standard; 'the only methodological gold standard is pluralism' (Pawson and Tilley, 2001: 323).

A programme-led approach to 'what works?' represents a marked deviation from the traditional one-to-one supervisory relationship between social worker/practitioner and client (see Burnett and McNeill, 2005). There is a sense in which this can promote a 'one size fits all' approach to programme interventions, which can stifle the creativity of practitioners and lead to intervention strategies and practices becoming less responsive to local conditions and the needs of certain marginalized client groups. As Raynor observes, with reference to England and Wales, 'a target-driven over-concentration on programme development led both to neglect of supportive and motivational offender management of the kind probation officers had traditionally provided' (2008: 78). Indeed, there is evidence of a growing awareness, across a variety of therapeutic contexts, that the variance in treatment outcome is partly attributable to the influence of 'process variables' and the successful creation of a positive therapeutic alliance between practitioner and client (Marshall and Serran, 2004). Writing from within the 'what works?' tradition, Dowden and Andrews (2004) have acknowledged the importance of a 'relationship-based approach' in case management in CJSW.

In their design and delivery, group-based programmes often fail to address individual theories of change and overlook the heterogeneity of offenders.[8] This clearly has implications for programme effectiveness, as it should not be assumed that interventions are universally applicable across all groups of offenders. For example, programmes that prove successful with young white males cannot be guaranteed to produce similar results when targeted at women, other ethnic groups or indigenous offenders (Hannah-Moffat and Shaw, 2000; Shaw and Hannah-Moffat, 2004; Cameron and Tefler, 2004; Worrall, 2000). The apparent failure of some offender programmes to acknowledge the differential impact of individual, cultural and societal factors is somewhat surprising given the emphasis on 'responsivity' (that is, matching the mode of intervention to the learning style of the service user) and the importance attached to cultural diversity training by human service organizations in recent years.

Whereas a programme-led approach to evidence-based practice research has tended to overly focus on *what* works, future studies would do well to address a broader range of questions around issues such as *how* and *why* individuals cease to engage in offending behaviour. As described above, there is already evidence of such a shift with the development of a 'desistance paradigm' for offender management (McNeill, F., 2006). In research terms, the focus on subjectivities in the desistance paradigm necessitates the use of naturalistic, qualitative research methods and methodologies, as opposed to the more positivistic and quantitatively oriented approaches favoured by evaluators using traditional experimental designs to measure programme effectiveness. Practitioners need to understand how to promote and encourage cognitive, behavioural, identity and social changes in their clients and how they can help offenders to sustain such changes. This requires an appreciation of diversity amongst participants, the ability to utilize interpersonal skills in practice (Raynor, 2004) and a detailed knowledge about the wider social contexts in which participants make decisions (McCulloch, 2005). In the largely programme-driven approach to 'what works?', too much emphasis has been placed on offenders' attitudes and behaviour and too little attention devoted to their social and personal circumstances. Thus, there is a danger of separating crime from its social context

(Drakeford and Vanstone, 1996) and ignoring offenders' views as to what works for them (Smith, 1998). Worryingly, with a few notable exceptions (Barry, 2000), there have been limited recent efforts to engage seriously with offenders' perceptions of both CJSW and the various 'what works?' initiatives.

CONCLUSION

As we warned at the outset, this has been a partial and limited overview of the development of and future prospects for CJSW research. Whilst we hope that we have done enough to convince readers that there is and should be much more to CJSW research than 'what works?' evaluations, there are many more questions and issues that we might have addressed. What might moral, political and legal philosophy have to say, for example, about the proper purposes and normative foundations of CJSW? We have also neglected the particular ethical issues that arise for criminal justice researchers partly as a result of the controlling and sometimes coercive nature of criminal justice interventions.[9] We have not addressed what socio-legal studies might have to say, for example, about the uses of discretion and meanings of accountability in CJSW; or about what other contributions social theory and critical and comparative penology might make to making sense of CJSW globally; or about what kinds of histories of CJSW are necessary to make better sense of its past(s) and present(s); or about what other contributions criminology can make to the understanding of offending and the development of new CJSW practices to address it. Perhaps most fundamentally in a collection of this sort, we have had little to say about what CJSW has to learn from *social work* research and vice versa. It is perhaps telling that, although all three authors willing locate themselves within the social work discipline, the reality is that CJSW as a site of study and practice is an intersection between fields and disciplines – an intersection where the character of both

study and practice is disputed and where, in many jurisdictions, the modernist romance between criminal justice and social work has ended in a quintessentially late-modern and very messy divorce. For both normative and empirical reasons, we remain committed to the union, but we do not doubt that if the relationship between social work and criminal justice is to survive, it needs renewed mutual respect, shared commitment of one to the other, and a lot of hard work. Maybe it's time for a second honeymoon.

NOTES

1   One was by an American and used American data. The second was an article by an English academic on the break with social work training by the Home Office.

2   See: http://www.nofsw.org/html/journal.html.

3   For revisionist accounts of probation history in England and Wales, see Young (1976) and Vanstone (2004).

4   For a serious of key papers on this topic, see the journal *Punishment and Society*, Vol. 3, No. 1 (2001).

5   A great deal of important empirical work on public attitudes to punishment has been undertaken in recent years – and some of this research has directly addressed public attitudes to community penalties. Useful recent overviews of this literature can be found in Maruna and King (2004) and Allen and Hough (2007).

6   In some respects, some accounts of penal transformation – and specifically the demise of welfarism – seem at odds with the emergence from the interfaces between criminal justice and mental health in North America of ideas around therapeutic jurisprudence and therapeutic justice (http://www.therapeuticjustice.com/). Related policy and practice initiatives like problem-solving and community courts seem designed to take crime seriously and respond to community concerns, but to do so in a manner which is constructively focused on practical problem-solving rather than risk or punitiveness per se. An analysis of the extent to which these developments represent an exception or counterargument to the culture of control, or whether they represent an expression of it is beyond the scope of this chapter (but for connected arguments see O'Malley, 2004).

7   The potential links to constructive social work and narrative approaches, both of which draw on post-modern perspectives, are obvious but have not

been fully elaborated (see Parton and O'Byrne, 2000; Gorman et al., 2006).

8 Interestingly, 'rolling' programmes – in which individual offenders pursue common treatment processes with peer support but work through the different stages at their own pace – are now emerging as a form of individualized group programme. In some respects these groups resemble AA meetings more than classroom-style didactic learning processes.

9 A special issue of the *British Journal of Criminology* (Vol. 41, No. 3), published in 2001, addressed some of these issues.

Challenges and Directions in Social Work Research and Social Work Practice

Joan Orme, Roy Ruckdeschel and
Katharine Briar-Lawson

INTRODUCTION

This chapter as the last one of the *Handbook* is not intended to arrive at hard and fast conclusions or to provide a 'state of the art' or science overview of social work and social research based on what has gone before. It will, however, attempt to identify themes that have shaped social work practice and their impact on research. It will also provide a mirror to the editorial essay at the commencement of the *Handbook*, acknowledging the purposes of the project as a whole to 'map' the territory. There are many purposes to which maps can be put. However they are most often used when the destination is known and the purpose is to assist in plotting routes but not authoritatively direct – in the way satellite navigation systems tell you where to go (usually sending you in the wrong routes).

The material drawn on to provide the particular mapping exercise in the *Handbook* has revealed some dynamic changes which have contributed to the directions in which social work practice and research have taken. These include:

1. The response of social work to changing demographic, economic, political and social contexts at both national and global levels. This has had implications for the location of social work: its organization, its focus and its practices.
2. The response of social work research to these changes in practice. This has involved changes in the amount of social work research undertaken, its methodological approaches and its utility. It has also led to debates about the distinctiveness of social work research in the wider context of research, inquiry and knowledge creation and transfer.
3. One of the claims for distinctiveness is the iteration between social work practice and social work research. This has been one of the major dynamics during the last decade, and has particular implications for who undertakes social work research, where it is located and who owns it. The relationship between research and practice, the ability of the former to influence the latter and vice versa is a perpetual tension.
4. This tension reflects other influences on both practice and research. These include concepts

of professionalism that eschew a research base for practice and scientific approaches to research that deny the value base of practice. For both therefore the need to look 'outside' of the profession and the discipline, to work with others, draw on their knowledge and methods of knowledge production produces a constantly changing context.

5. The final set of changes includes developments in methods to address the challenges of practice, different understandings and constructions of knowledge. Attention to different voices in both research and practice has led to wider definitions of both and broader understandings of who can contribute to the processes.

These points are not exhaustive, but are indicative of the areas covered in the *Handbook* and are crucial in that they are informed by, and frame, future directions for social work practice and research. In doing so, they also reveal the many challenges that exist for both.

This chapter draws particularly, but not exclusively, on the chapters in this final section, *Domains*. It begins with a consideration of the direction in which social work practice and research has travelled and is still travelling. In doing this it moves to a consideration of challenges. Identifying these provides the opportunity to reflect on where social work research wants/needs to go and what has to be done to get there.

DIRECTIONS

In reflecting on the contributions to the *Handbook* and their implications for directions in social work practice and research a major question to be asked is that posed by Parton and Kirk at the outset to Chapter I: is social work a coherent and single activity moving in a co-ordinated way in the same direction? Or is has it fragmented into a multiplicity of different, vaguely related activities?

The final section of the *Handbook* with chapters on the different domains might suggest that the fragmentation model has prevailed and that each domain or area of social work activity requires separate and distinct research approaches. In the UK this would seem to be borne out by policy developments that over the last decade have removed criminal justice from the ambit of social work and made organizational distinctions between services for adults and children.

Parton and Kirk's reflections lead them to conclude that developments have not challenged an underlying belief that social work has a rich variety and consists of many strands, but remains coherent because of a shared mission and sense of values. An overview of the chapters in this section indicates that although the focus of each is different the influences, the issues addressed and the related developments are not disparate and disconnected but have resonance with one another.

Personal and/or political

An underpinning theme is that social work maintains a focus on individuals while not losing sight of structural issues. Because it operates in the space between the individual and the state, this focus has to be maintained within competing priorities between the personal and policy, the political. This has provided fertile ground for social work research which has had to address the macro agendas of the purpose of social work interventions, and even the purpose of the profession itself. All of the chapters in the *Domains* section have indicated how political and structural changes have influenced research agendas, and how the tension has been to hold to a position that reflects the philosophy that social work is about the 'person in their situation'. However they also recognize the impact of the situation. Perhaps as the sociologist Blumer has suggested the focus ought to be on interaction with the unit of analysis the acting individual (Blumer, 2007). For example the chapter on criminal justice illustrates how emphasis on crime and penal reform deflected attention away from the individual and the circumstances which precipitated them into crime. Recent developments in research, such as that on desistance, have refocused both research and practice.

The chapter on aging highlights different tensions. Demographics and health economics lead to demands for social work research to focus more on the bigger pictures of populations and policies. However, challenges from user movements and policy requirements such as personalization have led to research topics and methods that acknowledge the needs of individuals within the globalizing changes.

Both of these examples remind us that the space between the individual and the state inhabited by social work is becoming increasingly filled by other professionals. The area of children's services requires closer work with educationalists, counsellors and psychologists. In adult services (aging, mental health and disability) the links are more often forged with health professionals. Interprofessional projects and interventions such as single shared assessments illustrate the increasing demand for collaboration. Also, as McCallion's chapter on *aging* illustrates, some practice developments require a renewal of interest in notions of community. Researchers plotting such developments are mindful that policy initiatives can draw on research by other disciplines (see the chapters on aging, mental health and health and well-being) and can threaten the distinctiveness of the social work contribution.

By contrast to these broad issues, focusing on the individual in their situation has led to other significant developments in social work research. Increasingly research is required to answer questions about more personal and private aspects of peoples' lives. While society in general tolerates reality TV and the willingness of so-called celebrities to reveal all, the social work research community tussles with the ethics of inquiring into the intimate aspects of peoples' behaviour and relationships. Research into aspects of familial violence (including violence towards women, adults receiving and requiring care as well as abuse of children) is one example of the need for sensitive approaches, not least because such research has to address and inquire into areas of behaviour that raise political agendas. These include the 'minefield' of researching mothers who abuse (Crinall, 1999) and the personal and methodological challenges of researching male violence (Gilgun, 2008).

Similarly health research requires exploration of intimate experiences, not only of symptoms, but of behaviour that might lead to or exacerbate ill health. It has been suggested (Williams et al., 1999) that attention to inequalities in all aspects of research requires inquiry into aspects of peoples' identity, and the way they construct their identity. How people define and experience their identity is an aspect of the 'personal' in research. The increasing emphasis on risk in social work practice not only involves aspects of individuals' identity it has also required research to investigate, analyse and codify aspects of people's lives and behaviour which indicate aspects of their identity that lead to their vulnerability.

Such developments, alongside growth in the amount of research undertaken, have led to emphasis on research ethics (see for example Peled and Leichtentritt, 2002) and, more recently, governance. The tension between needing to be 'invasive' to understand (for example: What constitutes 'caring'? What leads to violence and abuse?) has to be balanced with people's right to privacy and to be treated with dignity. While the substantive discussion on *Ethics* takes place in Hugman's chapter in Section Three, Briskman's chapter on *Nations* returns to ethics with a different perspective. It illustrates that it is sometimes difficult to hold the balance. Recognition of the humiliating private experiences of migrants who become victims of policy agendas, or the need to understand the individual costs of national practices towards aboriginal peoples requires research that gives voice to hard to reach people. An illustrative exemplar of Indigenous voice by the aboriginal community in Canada is discussed in Chapter 12. Such research has to challenge some of the 'norms' of codes of ethics based on western philosophical tenets.

This chapter, and the chapter on communities, also serves as an important reminder that while much social work practice is individualized there is still an important role for social work practice and research to recognize and investigate social work's role in understanding and working with communities. An individualized approach to both practice and research can often lead to a 'deficit' model in both, exploring what does not work. The development of theories of desistance in criminal justice work, the contribution of theoretical analysis from feminism and the lobbying by social movements, such as those in the field of disability, have all contributed to changing the focus from negatively labelling and stereotyping individuals and communities in need of social work services to seeing them as sources of strength and positive action. The knowledge that comes from oppressed communities and social movements is what Hartman refers to as subjugated knowledge. The task of social work is to listen to and respect this source of knowledge (Hartman, 1992, 1994). These developments have also contributed to important methodological changes.

Routinization and regulation

While the changes listed suggest dynamic and positive movements in social work research celebration should remain muted. The growth in social work research, the increasingly personalized focus and the democratization of methodological approaches are often counteracted by the political agendas that require certain kinds of research evidence and in some cases certain research findings. The insertion of the political into the research agenda is not inherently wrong and is more or less inevitable. Whether the political is a positive or negative force depends on the context (Orme, 2006). As has been

indicated throughout the *Handbook*, and in many of the chapters in this final section, the need to discover 'what works?' provides a permanent backdrop to social work research.

The relationship of social work to the state therefore carries a number of implications for social work research. At a very practical level the focus of research, the involvement of vulnerable communities in research and the growth in the amount of research undertaken by academics, professional researchers, practitioners, students and others has led to an increasing need for ethical committees to gatekeep, monitor and oversee research processes. An industry of local, professional and national ethics committees has developed in organizations and universities (where, in the United States, they take the form of Institutional Review Boards) alongside the more regulatory governance of who should commission research, how it is commissioned and the 'rules' governing research processes.

Social work's position vis-à-vis the state as represented in research governance frameworks has also led to significant developments in the application and utilization of research findings. For example, developments in child care in the UK have been informed by research on assessment frameworks (Ward, 2000) which have implications for both practice initiatives and the development of services. The former is evidenced by the development of an assessment framework that is to be universally applied by practitioners (DoH, 2000), thus routinizing practice and constraining professional judgements in practice (Garrett, 2003c).

A further consequence of the relationship between social work research and the state is the implications for the use of research findings in policy initiatives that have impacted on the organization of services. Such developments raise fundamental questions about the role and purpose of social work intervention. In the UK for example research into child care practices has led to policy initiatives for integrated children's services that involve multi-professional working. These might ultimately reframe and/or marginalize social work with children and families and undermine the professional expertise of social work. This has implications for practice but has spawned major research programmes into the effectiveness of such developments (see e.g. Brandon et al., 2006). In the US, states also require the use of evidence based practice in child welfare and juvenile justice. In some cases this leads to services and programs being promoted which might not be well tailored or applicable to some of the youth and families in care, given that minority youth are disproportionately represented. Such mandates may place very vulnerable populations at more risk. Also, some of the programs legislated for on the basis of received evidence may later be shown to have insufficient evidence (for example multi-systemic therapy as discussed in Chapter 20 and Littell, 2005).

Similar developments have occurred in adult services in the UK with the development of care management and related policy initiatives such as integrated assessments (Clarkson et al., 2006). Finally, the development of 'evidence' in criminal justice social work has led to the development of matrices and indices developed in the US and imported into the UK such as the Offender Assessment System (OASys) or the risk classification tool the Level of Service Inventory – Revised (LSI-R) for predicting offending behaviour and required interventions. It was also the basis for more routinized, programmatic practice interventions as discussed by McNeil et al. in Chapter 28.

All of these developments have been, depending upon the stance taken, enhanced or exacerbated by the use of technology. The need to keep up-to-date with the ever changing landscape of technology represents a significant challenge to social work researchers and is addressed by Ruckdeschel and Chambon in Chapter 12. In considering the impact of domains of practice outcomes from research can be distilled into software

packages for assessment, monitoring and 'evaluating' outcomes. This has meant that they have enabled routinization of practice that has been associated with particular (usually negative) managerialist approaches. The question is how to avoid this. Positive developments in the use of ICT include processes to systematize research findings by codifying, evaluating and cataloguing research by a number of different dimensions, thus making it more accessible. McNeil et al. in discussing criminal justice social work suggest a productive approach which is to consider whose task it is to be research informed. Walter et al.'s (2004) three models of research usage suggest that it is everyone's responsibility: their preferred model is a whole systems approach where different responsibilities pertain throughout the organization.

Achieving this is one of the challenges facing social work practice and research and has implications for the research capacity and capability of the social work workforce. The production of accessible databases makes information widely available, but reflective practice requires both encouraging practitioners to access such databases and, when they do, ensuring they are discerning in their use of the information available.

Voices in knowledge production

However practitioners should not be seen only as the recipients of knowledge. Increasingly trends to have knowledge that emanates *from* practice have led to the involvement of practitioners in undertaking research. Clear arguments for this can be found in the *Nations* chapter, where it is argued that the nature of the issues to be dealt with require the skills and sensitivities demonstrated by practitioners. Also in their practice they have access to and awareness of the complexities of problems experienced by marginalized groups such as aboriginal people and asylum seekers.

Practitioner research is an area that has developed over time (Stock Whitaker and

Archer, 1989; Shaw, 2005; Pain, 2008). The need to involve practitioners in knowledge production is acknowledged by many, but the implications for both the nature of the research undertaken (Hammersley, 2003) and the preparation, education and training of practitioners (McCartt-Hess and Mullen, 1995; Orme and Powell, 2008) is the source of continuing debate.

The democratization of social work services is reflected in policy initiatives such as the use of direct payments in the UK, which enables service users to purchase services to meet their care needs. The increasing involvement of service users in all aspects of social work policy, practice and social work education is evidenced by the wide ranging review of social work conducted by the Scottish Executive, 2006; the special edition on service user involvement in the journal *Social Work Education*, vol. 25 (4), 2006; and the Social Care Institute for Excellence practice guides for the involvement of service users, SCIE, 2007. There are similar developments in involving service users in research. This is not constrained to user groups who are articulate and accessible. For example Tew (2008) discusses developments in social work research into difficult and sensitive areas by reflecting on the involvement of service users in researching compulsory admission to mental hospitals. Gray (2007), writing in the field of mental health, acknowledges that meeting the feminist imperative of 'voice' is sometimes problematic with groups who are unable or unwilling to articulate, for a number of complex reasons.

The contribution of different voices and the involvement of different stakeholders in practice and in research is linked (in the UK) to the recognition of service users as 'experts by experience' and to emancipatory approaches to research. In the United States it has led to the consumer movement in, for example, the delivery of mental health services. It is assumed that such approaches necessarily require qualitative approaches to social work research, but the involvement of service users and carers in research carries with it no

assumptions about methodological approaches (Orme, 2000a). Particular groups may require information about particular circumstances pertaining to their situation. The collection of quantitative data to describe excluded populations, for example, might be just as, or even more, important as qualitative in depth methodologies in terms of understanding the extent and nature of particular problems or describing the world from a particular standpoint.

Such developments are complemented by theoretical developments in the nature and construction of knowledge and methodological approaches that attempt to recognize other 'knowledges' (see Hartman, 1994 for discussion of 'many ways of knowing'). They have been influential in the development of methods for researching sensitive topics and giving voice to those within the situations. These include the use of ethnography to understand communication between professionals (White and Featherstone, 2005), the focus on the interrelationships between practitioners and between practitioners and service users in discourse analysis (Taylor, 2008) and narrative research in organizational practice (Hall, 1999) and research (Riessman and Quinney, 2005). The significance of developments in this area is reflected in the special edition of *Qualitative Social Work: Research and Practice* (vol. 4, no. 4, 2005).

Knowledge production

The growth in the amount of social work research undertaken, the production of searchable research databases and the methodological developments that have led to the recognition of the multiplicity of voices, discourses and 'knowledges' in social work practice and research are all testimony to, and part of the construction of, knowledge for social work.

Analysis over time suggests that we have moved from a period when there was not enough research on and in social work

(Gambrill, 1994) to a period when multiple sources of knowledge are being identified. These include not only evidence from empirical research studies but also epistemological developments that recognize practitioner and service user and carer knowledge. Such distinctions echo the differences between general information and knowledge that can be utilized in and applied to social work practice. In the light of this it is noticeable that there has been limited guidance on how the different knowledge sources can or should be prioritized, how practitioners can judge the quality of the information available. The establishment of the Social Care Institute for Excellence in England has led to the development of systems and processes to evaluate knowledge claims (Pawson et al., 2003), guidance for systematically reviewing relevant research evidence, from social work research and other sources (Coren and Fisher, 2006) and work to identify the kinds and quality of social work research undertaken in universities (Shaw and Norton, 2007).

At the outset of the *Handbook* Parton and Kirk analyse the relationship between science and practice identifying that either social work can be seen as scientific practice in its own right or science (including other social sciences) can be deemed to be the source of knowledge, providing practice guidance and direction. These distinctions could be deemed to be the difference between research *on* and *for* practice. But a further distinction is research *from* practice which acknowledges social work as scientific practice, as the site of the intervention, and therefore the source of knowledge about practice, and the people involved. Drawing on theories of knowledge production research from practice recognizes that those in the situation have specific understandings. This is not in the sense of having a particular standpoint, but of having access to information, feelings and dynamics that can inform understandings of the situation. Therefore they not only provide understanding of the significance of particular words, deeds and processes but also identify compounding factors that

provide a focus for research. As many of the chapters in this section of the *Handbook* illustrate social work practice, and those involved in it, can generate research questions, inform research processes and be the 'test-bed' for new approaches developed as a result of research.

Similarly the involvement of stakeholders in the research process has implications for commitment to the research endeavour and ownership of research processes. This manifests itself in structures for research dissemination but also in analysis of needs across the professional life course (Orme and Powell, 2008) and the requirement to attend to the relationship between practice and research.

Future directions include calls for more (and better) research for practice. In addition to research on populations served, the challenge for the future also includes research on workforce development, the serving practitioner population. As a profession, relatively little research has been fostered to advance knowledge about how to best develop the social work workforce (see Glastonbury and Orme, 1993; Orme, 1995 for examples of limited amount of UK work in this area). In the US workforce research and development using an R&D approach remains a major issue for the twenty-first century as the pipeline into social work has lacked incentives and recruitment tools. Child welfare and aging have most prominently received funding for workforce development. The former may be the most well studied area due to the availability of funds from social security and from the John A. Hartford Foundation. The NASW has recently established a Center for Workforce Studies to further research and analysis. A bill in Congress, led by NASW, called the Reinvestment Act would provide funds for workforce research, workforce innovations and R&D projects. Similar initiatives in the UK involve the government funded Social Care Workforce Research Unit (SCWRU).

Trends identified above, and others highlighted in this section of the *Handbook*, suggest that the impetus is not about *what to research* but about *how* to research. More significantly challenges for social work research involve ensuring research undertaken is both rigorous and significant, although both are contentious issues. Developments in these areas might help fulfil expectations that findings will be disseminated to, and utilized by, policy makers and practitioners. This leads to the challenges for social work research.

CHALLENGES

Challenges to and for social work and social work research are ever present. Chapters in the *Handbook* have identified challenges for social work in responding to economic, social and political changes and to social work research in informing and influencing social policy and social work practice. These challenges have led to methodological developments, but also to explicating issues to be researched. Challenges can be domain specific, as outlined in the chapters in this section, profession-wide, or cross-cutting professions and disciplines pertaining to the nature, purpose and organization of social work, social work education and social work research.

A potential emergent theme, reflected in the scope of the chapters in this section, is that social work research has to be relevant to practice which takes place in diverse locations. Organizationally this includes arrangements for state, public, private and not for profit provision of services. It also includes multi- and inter-disciplinary interventions which can be offered, alongside other professionals, in hospitals, prisons and communities, as well as practice in traditional office-based multi-disciplinary teams. Increasingly services for children, for example, require educationalists, health professionals, counsellors and social workers to work in concert for the benefit of all children not only those who are in need of care and/or protection. Such arrangements have implications for the research to be utilized, and the practice to be evaluated. In elder care, Bernard (2006)

argues for interdisciplinary and intergenerational research: research between policy and practice, between disciplines and between generations. This requires an interconnectedness that has implications for methods. Intergenerational research requires, as highlighted in the chapter on *Aging*, multiple methods, draws on a wide range of data sources and resources, is both cross-cultural and cross-national and requires people involvement (Bernard, 2006: 17).

However, the international scope of the *Handbook* highlights that research should not confine itself to local and/or national boundaries. Increasingly social work has to address social issues that are cross-national such as child trafficking and people movements such as refugees. As the chapter on *Nations* highlights, even when practices are country specific the challenge to the value base of social work is fundamental and requires continual re-appraisal of global ethical standards for social work practice and research. There are global agendas presented by health issues related to HIV/Aids; poverty; social exclusion; diversity; race; gender; faith and indigenization. Alternatively there are themes that cross some borders, relating to similar experiences in specific contexts, such as the experiences of political conflict (Ramon et al., 2006). There are also multi-site global projects testing, or gaining more detailed knowledge about, social work practice such as the international resilience project (Ungar, 2008). All have implications for research and present methodological and other challenges. In our view, the challenges can be grouped into three main categories:

- organizational: purpose and place;
- methodological: process and purpose; and
- credibility: capability and capacity.

Organizational: purpose and place

The various historical accounts of the development of social work research in the *Handbook* chronicle its changing role and purpose.

Early research was closely associated with practice and finding the 'magic bullet' to 'cure' social ills. Later developments that have responded to the challenges of evidence-based practice involve a much closer relationship between research and policy. Practice is still a focus of research but the perspective of social work research has become more top down, emanating from challenges presented by policy initiatives. A further development, identified in 'Directions' above is the burgeoning of information and knowledge from social work research.

Purpose One challenge presented for research related to emerging policies and practices is the tension between being policy driven and wanting to transform policy. The relationship between research, policy and practice discussed in Chapter 3 has emerged in many of the chapters in the *Domains* section. It is therefore not necessary to rehearse the arguments here, but suffice it to say ideally social work research should respond to and critically evaluate policy, while at the same time be independent and innovative in explorations of new practices that might inform policy makers and emergent policy. The challenge is in trying to achieve a balance.

Critiques of the evidence-based policy 'movement' have focused on the paradigm wars associated with the nature of the evidence that is valued (Webb, 2001). There are also suggestions referred to in the beginning of this chapter that the production of research as part of policy agendas is, or can be, associated with managerialist practices or leads to the demise of the practice and profession of social work. However, this does not have to be the case. At times practice innovations, with individuals, groups and families have taken place in social work but have been unresearched: not subject to evaluation. While it is not suggested that social work interventions can be 'tested' in the way that new drugs or engineering solutions can be tested, this does not mean that approaches to practice and practice innovations should be uncritical. The growing number of resources to check data, information and research findings

provide ample opportunity to undertake efficiency studies and effectiveness studies, as well as undertake systematic reviews of existing studies of related practice innovations. All of these processes recognize the transformative power of knowledge but as Chambon (1999) points out transformative knowledge 'rattles certainties', 'shakes complacency' and 'unhinges us from secure meanings' (Chambon, 1999: 53). It is not always comfortable.

The aim should not be to stifle innovation, nor to 'unhinge' social work practitioners, but to learn from the process of research and to disseminate knowledge gleaned. This then becomes part of an iterative process of knowledge creation and knowledge transfer and positive transformation.

Place However such a position may seem to be idealist. If government departments are the major funders of research they will continue to set the research agendas and, as has been argued in the chapter on politics in Section Two, through the provision of funding they will maintain a hold on research agendas. Opportunities for social work research to achieve the necessary levels of funding from non-governmental and independent sources for rigorous, in depth enquiries over time are limited. Drug companies or businesses do not find social work research attractive, and if they did the compromises in accessing such funding are, or would be, problematic.

A further problem of research tied to policy is that the rules for commissioning, carrying out and disseminating research are often such that the independence of the research carried out is limited. The messages gleaned from research may be carefully edited and modified, although the experience of researchers in the US does not bear this out. All funders wish to retain some kind of influence; but social work needs to have properly funded opportunities to achieve the necessary rigour in research, while at the same time retaining autonomy and originality. Developmental research strategies, discussed in Chapter 20, may offset such interference as the outcome goal is set and interventions are tested and retested to approximate the end goal.

Methodological: process and purpose

As has been discussed in the first part of this chapter there is evidence in the chapters in this section, and in other sections in the *Handbook*, of a number of influences on social work research. In summary these include:

- researching the public and the private and the need to address sensitive issues;
- polyvocal research which involves the growing number of stakeholders, both in populations of participants and researchers;
- emancipatory research associated with poly-vocalism has implications for both process and purpose of research; and
- relativism in research agendas derives both from polyvocalism and the emerging purposes of social work research with and on behalf of different stakeholders.

The challenge is to recognize that both the process and purpose of any research project will be perceived differently from different perspectives.

The implications are that research in social work needs to be distinctive: to acknowledge the range of research imperatives (service users, practitioners and policy makers); be clear about its purpose but be able to demonstrate permeability that indicates a maturity and confidence. This permeability is apparent in practice developments that include innovations in multi- and inter-professional working. Shared assessment processes, joint interventions and shared knowledge are features of developments in practice with adults and children. Obvious partnerships are those with health professionals, but increasingly practice partnerships are developed with educationalists, community groups, and independent and for profit providers of services. Research boundaries therefore have to be permeable and

draw on different knowledges. Permeability includes recognizing that lessons can be learnt not only from the results of studies undertaken by different disciplines and with different professions, but also from diverse methodological approaches by these disciplines and professions.

For example in the US the lack of research approaches involving cost–benefit analysis, clinical trials, etc. is hurting the social work profession, mainly because of the willingness of Congress and others to invest because they perceive these to be the gold standards in research and especially in policy and practice relevant research. Therefore research partners, such as economists, are essential to help construct cost–benefit information that can complement and enhance data on effectiveness. This can then be used to inform policy makers as to which practice and programme 'investments' are warranted.

Permeability will lead to challenges of developing multi-disciplinary research teams and grasping the implications of truly mixed methods approaches to research, but it is important to reiterate the point here that claims for the value base of social work wedding its research solely to qualitative methods do a disservice to the profession and to those who require services. Increasingly large scale data sets are available to be mined thus providing important contextual information for both research questions and research findings gleaned from other methodological approaches. On the other hand, hierarchical views of research with quantitative methods built on experimental design viewed explicitly or implicitly as superior to qualitative methods undermine the potential for true and balanced mixed methods research. This issue is more fully discussed in Chapter 19 by Greene, Sommerfeld and Haight.

Credibility: capability and capacity

While it has been argued that social work research is burgeoning it remains a challenge to ensure a continuous, rigorous

CHALLENGES AND DIRECTIONS

and enthusiastic programme of social work research, drawing on a multiplicity of methods while at the same time developing robust systems for reviewing emergent knowledge, in terms of both its rigour and its utility for practitioners (see Chapter 12 for a discussion of the uses of social work research).

Related to this is the question of which approach to knowledge production will prevail, and how developments in social work research relate to and influence both policy and the wider social sciences. How can social work assert its influence? For example Gibbons et al.'s (1994) definition of the differences between what they term mode one and mode two knowledge has been hailed in the social sciences in general and in social work in particular (Gray, 2008). They argue that mode one knowledge is produced to ensure compliance with 'sound scientific practice' while mode two knowledge is trans-disciplinary, transient, socially accountable and reflexive (Gibbons et al., 1994: 3). Emerging out of management studies the description of mode two knowledge fits what has been aspired to in social work research for some time (Orme, 2000a), but social work as a profession or discipline is not acknowledged as a site of such knowledge production. Nor has social work research been able to influence epistemological and methodological agendas in the way other disciplines have. The challenge is to claim what is distinctive about social work research and to celebrate and disseminate this. One such claim would be the democratization of the research process, and the methodological developments associated with this.

However, ironically, such a claim might be seen to be arguing for expertise that has been challenged by the very process of democratization. Knowledge generated from and about practice, whether the research is undertaken by academic, independent or practitioner researchers is questioned by service users and carers who are seen to be 'experts' by virtue of their experience. The slogan of the disability movement 'nothing about us without us' and the arguments in the *Disability*

chapter reflect the standpoint position that only those who are in a situation can truly 'know' that situation. Competing claims for expertise in research and knowledge production have been challenged by some outside social work (Hammersley, 2003), but remain a tension for social work researchers.

The logical consequence of some positions held might be that research agendas become user controlled to the extent that the knowledge and expertise of practitioners and/or researchers is deemed unnecessary and inappropriate. However, there are limitations to such a standpoint approach. It can lead to solutions that are limited to the local (Powell, 2002) or result in uncritical consumerism or the naïve privileging of particular voices: 'to a paralyzing relativism; and possibly to the neglect of theory building' (Butler and Pugh, 2004: 64).

A dialogic approach between researchers and practitioners and between researchers, practitioners and service users and carers is necessary to produce useful and usable knowledge. The challenge is for all knowledge to be recognized, competing accounts to be balanced and meaning created from these creative tensions. This democratic process of knowledge production is not, and will not be, either easy or painless.

A further challenge for social work and social work research is the capacity and capability of the profession and the discipline to both generate and utilize social work research. There are two aspects to this challenge. The first is that social workers do not utilize research findings effectively in their practice. The second is that, in some countries there is either a lack of competence in research or a lack of confidence in the capacity to generate rigorous and significant social work research.

In terms of the first challenge this was specifically the argument behind the move for evidence-based practice (McDonald and Sheldon, 1992; Furniss, 1998; Sheldon and Chilvers, 2001, 2002) and Fischer's earlier argument about the need for scientifically-based practice (Fischer, 1981). The suggestion was that social workers do not use evidence in their practice, and/or that the evidence that is used is not robust enough (McDonald and Sheldon, 1992). However Fisher (1999) suggests that social workers are thought not to synthesize material from different knowledge bases, including research, because they do not report its use. Theories of professional development (Benner, 1984; Eraut, 1994; Fook et al., 2000) and studies on the use of theory in practice (Sheppard et al., 2000) suggest that there are stages in professional development where practitioners do not make specific reference to research, but are drawing on it. Hence Fisher (1999) suggests that the question to be asked is about the kind of knowledge required for practice. He argues that the answer is neither the propositional knowledge of the social sciences nor the rather restricted categories of knowledge suggested by the proponents of evidence based practice.

Chapter 12 explores in more detail the uses of social work research. In referencing the dearth of studies on research utilization (Walter et al., 2004) it suggests that the challenge is to find more effective ways of dissemination. Chapter 20 discusses translational research as a way of bridging this gap. Connected to this is the development of mechanisms and processes for evaluating the evidence, in particular systematic reviews. Some have questioned the compatibility of qualitative methods of enquiry and techniques of systematic review (Staller, 2008). Much of the work undertaken by SCIE is based on an approach to systematic review developed in the UK to adapt and make it suitable to the needs of social work and social care (Coren and Fisher, 2006; Sharland and Taylor, 2006; Braye and Preston-Shoot, 2007).

Such developments are part of the challenge to ensure that research permeates approaches to social work and encourage the use by social work practitioners of research literature. In universities in the US, schools and departments of social work are accredited by the Council on Social Work Education and have to demonstrate how research is embedded in education. How well this is done is of course another matter. Social work education in the US has been an arena in which epistemological debates have played out.

In the UK and in parts of Europe this has been more problematic because research is often not embedded in social work education. Orme and Powell (2008) argue that a circle of resistance develops because educators are required to be expert practitioners. This means they are often less competent or confident as researchers. An audit of research teaching in the UK (Orme et al., forthcoming) found that competent researchers are often researching full time and not educating practitioners. In parts of Europe the problem was an anti-intellectual stance taken by practitioners who were then resistant to what was seen as the 'academicisation' of the profession (Karvinen et al., 1999).

This seeming resistance among practitioners and managers to research has implications for the recruitment of researchers. Commitment to the profession, demands of workloads and limited support, financial and otherwise means that few practitioners are undertaking doctoral studies. Europe, UK and the US have experienced what is called a 'pipeline' problem of practitioners reluctant to undertake doctoral level studies to become researchers (Karvinen et al., 1999; Orme, 2003a; Anastas, 2006).

The picture is not totally negative and measures to foster interest in both the research process and utilizing research results have been evidenced in the UK by initiatives such as *Research in Practice* and *Making Research Count*. The first, established in 1996, is the largest children and families' research implementation project in England and Wales. It is a department of the Dartington Hall Trust run in collaboration with the Association of Directors of Children's Services, The University of Sheffield (http://www.rip.org.uk/aboutus/index.asp). A parallel 'research utilization organization' has been set up for research into adult services. *Making Research Count* is a national collaborative research dissemination initiative, currently run by nine regional centres based in universities. The universities work in partnership with local authorities, National Health Service Trusts and other agencies to promoting knowledge-based, research-informed practice, improve the dissemination of research and strengthen the research-mindedness and critical appraisal skills of social work and social care practitioners. Such initiatives are paralleled in the US by arrangements described by Mullen (2002) who identifies different stages of practitioner involvement in research (see also McCartt-Hess and Mullen, 1995).

However, the close involvement of practitioners in research is not without its challenges. Shaw (2005) draws on empirical evidence to describe some of these, while Meyer in an editorial in *Social Work* (Meyer, 1984) discusses the difficulties of integrating research and practice from the perspective of the practitioner. Hammersley (2003), however, outlines epistemological objections. This latter critique is significant in that it rehearses the arguments identified in Chapter 3 about the implications of applied approaches to research. As discussed there this exacerbates the challenge for social work that research that is truly applied, or knowledge that is generated from and/or by those involved in practice, is in some ways less authentic, less rigorous and therefore less significant.

Some of the uncertainty about the robustness of social work research in the wider social sciences is reflected in responses to Shaw's enquiry into the kinds and quality of social work research in the UK (Shaw and Norton, 2007). These could be seen to be a result of the low morale of social work academics as a result of repeated assessments over the last two decades of research performance in universities (known as the Research Assessment Exercise). The politics of these exercises has repeatedly questioned the research base for social work (Fisher, 1999; Fisher and Marsh, 2001; Orme, 2006). While Australia and New Zealand have adopted forms of this assessment the US and Europe are not subject to such pressure.

However, as has been indicated, the demands of Congress, governments and other funding bodies represent a challenge for social work to demonstrate the quality of the research undertaken. This can only be done by ensuring, as Shaw (2008a) points out, that there is agreement on the quality dimensions of social work research which are at the 'middle range of generality' (Shaw and Norton, 2007: 53) rather than engaging in an irreconcilable tussle between the extremes of constructivists and postmodernists. However these dimensions must include methodological rigour and engaging in epistemological and methodological debates, such as those undertaken in various chapters in this *Handbook*, about the validity of the approaches taken in social work research.

CONCLUSION

This overview of the *Domains* section has presented a series of directions and challenges for social work research in a period of dynamic change that are integrally connected to developments in practice and the profession. The picture is mostly a positive one with evidence of a growing research base for all aspects of practice. The writings in this section illustrate that there are shared themes, or challenges, around methodological developments, what counts as evidence and the influence of the results of research on policy and practice.

In terms of future directions social work is striving, and to some extent succeeding, in becoming a research-based discipline in universities globally. Collaboration with other disciplines and acknowledging shared agendas presents challenges but also opportunities for methodological innovation and development. Such initiatives need to be built on to ensure that policy makers are attentive to the evidence from practice.

However, there needs to be concomitant progress in the workforce in utilizing and supporting the research foundations of the profession. While workload demands remain high and research findings are obscure, meaningless or hard to access there will be limited response among practitioners. This lays open the profession to the potential for practice and programme initiatives to be imposed by policy, rather than developing out of dialogue between service users, practitioners, researchers and policy makers. Chapters in this section have celebrated successes of practice and research informed policy developments, and have also signposted the need for continual vigilance to both challenge such impositions, but more importantly to take the initiative in setting future research agendas.

Bibliography

AARP (2004a) *African-Americans 65 and Older: Sources of Retirement Income*. Washington, DC: AARP Public Policy Institute.

AARP (2004b) *Hispanics 65 and Older: Sources of Retirement Income*. Washington, DC: AARP Public Policy Institute.

AARP (2005) *Women 65 and Older: Sources of Retirement Income*. Washington, DC: AARP Public Policy Institute.

AASW (Australian Association of Social Work) (2002) *AASW Code of Ethics 1999*, 2nd Edn., Kingston ACT: AASW.

Abberley, P. (1992) 'Counting us out: A discussion of the OPCS disability surveys', *Disability, Handicap and Society*, 7: 139–55.

Abbott, E. (1930) 'The university and social welfare', *University Record*, 16: 217–26.

Absolon, K. and Willett, C. (2004) 'Aboriginal research: Berry picking and hunting in the 21st century', *First Peoples Child and Family Review*, 1(1): 5–17.

Achenbach, T. (1991) *Manual for the Child Behavior Checklist/4-18 and 1991 Profile*. Burlington VT: University of Vermont Department of Psychiatry.

Achenbach, T. and Rescorla, L. (2001) *Manual for the ASEBA School-Age Forms and Profiles*. Burlington, VT: ASEBA.

Ackermann, F. and Seek, D. (1999) *Der steinige Weg zur Fachlichkeit. Handlungskompetenz in der Sozialen Arbeit*. Hildesheim, Zürich, New York: Georg Olms Verlag.

Addams, J. (1910) *Twenty Years at Hull House*. New York: Macmillan.

Addams, J. (1999) Twenty Years at Hull-House: *With Autobiographical Notes*. New York: Signet Classic.

Agathonos-Georgopoulou, H. (2003) 'Child maltreatment in sociocultural context: From a syndrome to the Convention on the Rights of the Child', *International Journal of Child and Family Welfare*, 6(1/2): 18–26.

Akinson, G. and Pease, B. (2001) 'The changing role of Indigenous men in community life', in B. Pease and P. Camilleri (eds), *Working with Men in the Human Services*. Sydney: Allen and Unwin.

al-Krenawi, A. (1999) 'Explanations of mental health symptoms by the Bedouin-Arabs of the Negev', *International Journal of Social Psychiatry*, 45(1): 56–64.

al-Krenawi, A. and Graham, J.R. (1997) 'Social work and blood vengeance: The Bedouin-Arab case', *British Journal of Social Work*, 27(4): 515–28.

al-Krenawi, A. and Graham, J.R. (1999) 'Gender and biomedical/traditional mental health utilization among the Bedouin-Arabs of the Negev', *Culture, Medicine, and Psychiatry*, 23(2).

al-Krenawi, A. and Gratham, J.R. (2000) 'Culturally sensitive social work practice with Arab clients in mental health settings', *Health Social Work*, 25(1): 9–22.

al-Krenawi, A., Graham, J.R. and Maoz, B. (1996) 'The healing significance of the Negev's Bedouin dervish', *Social Science and Medicine*, 43(1): 13–21.

Al-Makhamreh, S.S. and Lewando-Hundt, G. (2008) 'Researching "at home" as an insider/outsider: Gender and culture in an ethnographic study of social work practice in an Arab society', *Qualitative Social Work*, 7(1): 9–23.

Alasuutari, P. (2004) *Social Theory and Human Reality*. London: Sage.

Albert, B. (2006) (ed.), *In or Out of the Mainstream? Lessons on Disability and Development Co-operation*, Leeds: The Disability Press.

Albert, B. and Harrison, M. (2006) 'Lessons from the Disability and Research Programme', in Albert, B. (ed.), *In or Out of the Mainstream? Lessons on Disability and Development Co-operation*. Leeds: The Disability Press.

Albert, H. (1967) *Marktsoziologie und Entscheidungslogik*. Neuwied, Berlin, Luchterhand.

Alexander, B.K. (2005) 'Performance ethnography: The reenacting and inciting of culture', in N.K. Denzin and Y.S. Lincoln (eds), *Sage Handbook of Qualitative Research*, 3rd Edn., Thousand Oaks, CA: Sage, pp. 411–41.

Alinsky, S. (1969) *Reveille for Radicals*, 2nd Edn., New York: Vintage Books.

Alinsky, S. (1971) *Rules for Radicals: A Pragmatic Primer for Realistic Radicals*. New York: Random House.

Allan J., Pease, B. and Briskman, L. (eds) (2003) *Critical Social Work: An Introduction to Theories and Practice*. Sydney: Allen and Unwin.

Allen, R. and Hough, M. (2007) 'Community penalties, sentencers, the media and public opinion', in L. Gelsthorpe and R. Morgan (eds), *Handbook of Probation*. Cullompton: Willan, pp. 565–90.

Allen-Meares, P. (1994) 'Are practitioner intuition and empirical evidence equally valid sources of professional knowledge?', in W.W. Hudson and P.S. Nurius (eds), *Controversial Issues in Social Work Research*. Boston: Allyn and Bacon.

Alley, D., Leibig, P., Pynoos, J., Banjaree, T. and Choi, I.H. (2007) 'Creating elder friendly communities: Preparations for an aging society', *Journal of Gerontological Social Work*, 49(1/2): 1–18.

Allnock, D., Akhurst, S. and Tunstill J. (2006) 'Constructing and sustaining a Sure Start Local Programme Partnership: Lessons for future inter-agency collaborations', *Journal of Children's Services*, 1(3).

Altpeter, M., Schopler, J.H., Galinsky, M.J. and Pennell, J. (1999) 'Participatory research as social work practice: When is it viable?', *Journal of Progressive Human Services*, 10(2): 31–53.

Alston, M. and Bowles, W. (2003) *Research for Social Workers: An Introduction to Methods*. Sydney: Allen and Unwin.

Alvarez, A.R. and Gutierrez, L.M. (2001) 'Choosing to do participatory research: An example and issues of fit to consider', *Journal of Community Practice*, 9(1): 1–20.

Alvesson, M. and Geetz, S. (2000) *Doing Critical Management Research*. Thousand Oaks, CA: Sage.

American Heart Association (2003) *Heart Disease and Stroke Statistics 2003 Update*. Dallas, TX: American Heart Association.

Anastas, J.W. (2006) 'Employment opportunities in social work education: A study of jobs for doctoral graduates', *Journal of Social Work Education*, 42(2): 195–209.

Andersen, R. (1968) *A Behavioral Model of Families' Use of Health Services*. Chicago: Center for Health Administration Studies, University of Chicago.

Andersen, R. (1995) 'Revisiting the behavioral model and access to medical care: Does it matter?', *Journal of Health and Social Behavior*, 36: 1–10.

Andersen, R. and Davidson, P. (1996) 'Measuring access and trends', in R. Andersen and P. Davidson (eds), *Changing the U.S. Healthcare System*. San Francisco, CA: Jossey–Bass. (pp. 13–40).

Anderson, L., Lewis, G., Araya, R., Elgie, R., Harrison, G., Proudfoot, J., Schmidt, U., Sharp, D., Weightman, A. and Williams, C. (2005) 'Self help books for depression: How can practitioners and patients make the right choice?', *British Journal of General Practice*, 55: 387–92.

Anderson, L. (2006) 'Analytic autoethnography', *Journal of Contemporary Ethnography*, 35(4): 373–95.

Andersen, R. and Newman, J.F. (1973) 'Societal and individual predictors of medical care utilization in the United States', *The Milbank Quarterly*, 51: 95–124.

Anderson-Nathe, B. and Abrams, L. (2005) 'Getting there is half the fun: Practitioners as researchers and vice versa', *Reflections: Narratives of Professional Helping*, 11(4): 69–77.

Andrews, D.A. and Bonta, J. (1998) *The Psychology of Criminal Conduct*, 2nd Edn., Cincinnati: Anderson.

Angell, M. (2004) *The Truth about the Drug Companies: How They Deceive Us and What to Do About It*. New York: Random House.

Anglin, M.D., Burke, C., Perrochet, B., Stamper, E. and Dawad-Noursi, S. (2000) 'History of methamphetamine problem', *Journal of Psychoactive Drugs*, 32(2): 137–41.

Anis, M. (2005) 'Talking about culture in social work encounters: Immigrant families and child welfare in Finland', *European Journal of Social Work*, 8(1): 3–19.

Ansley, F. and Gaventa, J. (1997) 'Democracy and democratizing research', *Change*, 29(1): 46–54.

Aos, S., Miller, M. and Drake, E. (2006) *Evidence-Based Adult Corrections Programs: What Works and What Does Not*. Olympia: Washington State Institute for Public Policy.

APA (1980) *Diagnostic and Statistical Manual of Mental Disorders (DSM-III)*, 3rd Edn., Washington, DC: American Psychiatric Association.

APA (2000) *Diagnostic and Statistical Manual of Mental Disorders (DSM-IV-TR)*, 4th Edn., text revision edn., Washington, DC: American Psychiatric Association.

Arai, L., Popay, J., Roen, K. and Roberts, H. (2005) 'It might work in Oklahoma but will it work in Oakhampton? What does the effectiveness literature on domestic smoke detectors tell us about context and implementation?', *Injury Prevention*, 11: 148–51.

Arendt, H. (1986) *The Origins of Totalitarianism*. London: Andre Deutsch.

Argyris, C. and Schon, D. (1978) *Organisational learning: A theory of action perspective*. Reading, Mass: Addison Wesley.

Arnd-Caddigan, M. and Pozzuto, R. (2006) 'Truth in Our Time', *Qualitative Social Work: Research and Practice*, 5(4): 423–40.

Arno, P.S. (2006) 'Economic value of informal caregiving: 2004'. Presented at the Care Coordination and the Caregiver Forum, Department of Veterans Affairs, January 25–27, 2006. Available at http://www.va.gov/occ/Conferences/caregiverforum/Docs/Arno-Handout.pdf

Asquith, S., Clark, C. and Waterhouse, L. (2005) *The Role of the Social Worker in the 21st Century*, Edinburgh Scottish Executive.

Atkinson, A.B. (1998) 'Social exclusion, poverty and unemployment', in A.B. Atkinson and J. Hills (eds), *Exclusion, Employment and Opportunity*, CASE Paper 4. Centre for the Analysis of Social Exclusion, London School of Economics. pp 1–20.

Atkinson, A.B., Cantillon, B., Marlier, E. and Nolan, B. (2002) *Social Indicators, the EU and Social Inclusion*. Oxford, New York: OUP.

Atkinson, D. (1997) *An Auto/Biographical Approach to Learning Disability Research*. Ashgate: Aldershot.

Atkinson, D. (2005) 'Research as social work: Participatory research in learning disability', *British Journal of Social Work*, 35: 425–34.

Atkinson, P. (1995) *Medical Talk and Medical Work*. London: Sage Publications.

Atkinson, G. and Pease, B. (2001) 'The changing role of Indigenous men in community and family life', in B. Pease and P. Camilleri (eds), *Working with Men in the Human Services*. Sydney: Allen and Unwin.

Atkinson, P., Coffey, A., Delamont, S., Lofland, J. and Lofland, L. (2001) *Handbook of Ethnography*. London: Sage Publications.

Atkinson, P., Delamont, S. and Hammersley, M. (2008) 'Qualitative research traditions: A British response', *Review of Educational Research*, 58(2): 231–50.

Auslander, A. (2001) 'Social work in health care. What have we achieved?', *Journal of Social Work*, 1(2): 201–22.

Auslander, G.K., Soskolne, V. and Ben-Shahar, I. (2005) 'Utilization of health social work services by older immigrants and veterans in Israel', *Health and Social Work*, 30(3): 241–51.

Austin, C.D. (1983) 'Case management in long-term care: Options and opportunities', *Health and Social Work*, 8(1): 16–30.

Australian Council of Heads of Schools of Social Work (2006) *We've Boundless Plains to Share: The First Report of the People's Inquiry into Detention*. Melbourne: ACHSSW.

Avis, M. (2006) 'Evidence for practice, epistemology and critical reflection', *Nursing Philosophy*, 7: 216–24.

Bachman, S.S., Drainoni, M.L. and Tobias, C. (2004) 'Medicaid managed care, substance abuse treatment, and people with disabilities: Review of the literature', *Health and Social Work*, 29(3): 189–96.

Bäck-Wiklund, M. (1993) Vetenskap och politik i socialt arbete. Rapport 1993: 8 Institutionen för socialt arbete, Göteborgs universitet.

Baehr, P. (2008) 'What are the knowledge conditions of sociology? A response to Gary Wickham and Harry Freemantle', *Current Sociology*, 56(6): 940–8.

Bailey, R. and Brake, M. (1975) *Radical Social Work*. London: Edward Arnold.

Baines, D. (2007a) *Doing Anti-Oppressive Practice: Building Transformative, Politicized Social Work*. Black Point, Nova Scotia: Fernwood.

Baines, D. (2007b) 'Anti-oppressive social work practice: Fighting for space, fighting for change', in D. Baines (ed.), *Doing Anti-Oppressive Practice: Building Transformative Politicized Social Work*. Fernwood: Halifax, pp. 1–30.

Baldwin, M. (1997) 'Day care on the move: Learning from a participative action research project at a day centre for people with learning difficulties', *British Journal of Social Work*, 27: 951–8.

Balen, R. and White, S. (2007) 'Making critical minds: Nurturing "not-knowing" in students of health and social care', *Social Work Education*, 26(2).

Bamba, S. and Haight, W. (2007) 'Helping maltreated children to find their Ibasho: Japanese perspectives on supporting the well-being of children in state care', *Children and Youth Services Review*, 29(4): 405–27.

Bamberger, M. (1999) 'Ethical issues in conducting evaluation in international settings', *New Directions for Evaluation*, 82: 89–98.

Banks, S. (2006) *Ethics and Values in Social Work*, 3rd Edn., Basingstoke: Palgrave-Macmillan.

Barclay, P.M. (1982) *Social Workers: Their Role and Tasks*. London: NISW/Bedford Square Press.

Barnes, C. (1992) *Disabling Imagery and the Media*. The British Council of Organisations of Disabled People. Halifax: Ryburn Publishing.

Barnes, C. (2001) '"Emancipatory" disability research: Project or process?' Public lecture for the Strathclyde Centre for Disability Research, University of Glasgow. Available at: www.leeds.ac.uk/disability-studies/archiveuk/index

Barnes, C. (2004) 'Reflections on doing emancipatory disability research', in J. Swain, S. French, C. Barnes and C. Thomas (eds), *Disabling Barriers – Enabling Environments*, 2nd Edn., London: Sage.

Barnes, C. and Mercer, G. (eds.) (1996) *Exploring the Divide: Illness and Disability*. Leeds: The Disability Press.

Barnes, C. and Mercer, G. (eds) (1997) *Doing Disability Research*. Leeds: The Disability Press.

Barnes, C., Mercer, G. and Shakespeare, T. (1999) *Exploring Disability: A Sociological Introduction*. Cambridge: Polity Press.

Barnes, C. and Mercer, G. (eds) (2004) *Implementing the Social Model of Disability: Theory and Research*. Leeds: The Disability Press.

Barnes, C. and Mercer, G. (2006) *Independent Futures: Creating User-Led Disability Services in a Disabling Society*. Bristol: Policy Press.

Barnes, J. (1979) *Who Should Know What? Social Science, Privacy and Ethics*. Harmondsworth, Penguin.

Barnes, M. and Bowl, R. (2001) *Taking Over the Asylum*. Basingstoke: Palgrave.

Barnes, M. and Morris, K. (2008) 'Strategies for the prevention of social exclusion: An analysis of the Children's Fund', *Journal of Social Policy*, 37(2): 251–70.

Barratt, M. (2003) 'Organizational support for evidence-based practice within child and family social work: A collaborative study', *Child and Family Social Work*, 8: 143–50.

Barron, S. and Kelly, F. (2006) 'National intellectual disability database. Annual report 2006'. Dublin: Health Research Board.

Barry, M. (2000) 'The mentor/monitor debate in criminal justice: What works for offenders', *British Journal of Social Work*, 30 (5): 575–95.

Barth, R.P. and Blackwell, D.L. (1998) 'Death rates among California's foster care and former foster care populations', *Children and Youth Services Review*, 20: 577–604.

Bartley, M. (ed.) (2006) 'Capability and resilience: Beating the odds'. ESRC booklet. Available at: http://www.ucl.ac.uk/capabilityandresilience/beating-theoddsbook.pdf

Barton, L. (1998) 'Developing an emancipatory research agenda: Possibilities and dilemmas', in P. Clough and L. Barton (eds), *Articulating with Difficulty: Research Voices in Inclusive Education*. London: Paul Chapman.

Bass, D., Looman, W. and Ehrlich, P. (1992) 'Predicting the volume of health and social services: Integrating cognitive impairment into the modified Andersen framework', *The Gerontologist*, 32(1): 33–43.

BASW (British Association of Social Workers) (2002) *The Code of Ethics for Social Work*. Birmingham: BASW.

Bateson, Gregory (1972) *Steps to an Ecology of Mind*. Chicago: University of Chicago Press.

Bauman, Z. (1994) *Alone Again: Ethics After Certainty*. London: Demos.

Bauman, Z. (1997) *Postmodernity and its Discontents*. Cambridge: Polity Press.

Bayley, M.J. (1973) *Mental Handicap and Community Care: A Study of Mentally Handicapped People in Sheffield*. London: Routledge and Kegan Paul.

Bazeley, P. (2003) 'Computerized data analysis for mixed methods research', in A. Tashakkori and C. Teddlie (eds), *Handbook of Mixed Methods in Social and Behavioral Research*. Thousand Oaks, CA: Sage, pp. 385–422.

Beange, H., McElduff, A. and Baker, W. (1995) 'Medical disorders of adults with mental retardation: A population study', *American Journal of Mental Retardation*, 99(6): 595–604.

Beauchamp, T.L. and Childress, J.S. (2001) *Principles of Biomedical Ethics*, 5th Edn., New York: Oxford University Press.

Beck, U. (1992) *Risk Society: Towards a New Modernity*. New Delhi: Sage.

Beck, U. and Bonss, W. (eds) (1989) *Weder Sozialtechnologie noch Aufklärung? Analysen zur Verwendung sozialwissenschaftlichen Wissens*. Frankfurt a.M., Suhrkamp.

Beck, W., van der Maesen, L. and Walker, A. (eds) (1997) *The Social Quality of Europe*. The Hague, Netherlands: Kluwer Law International.

Becker, B. (1999) 'Narratives of pain in later life and conventions of storytelling', *Journal of Aging Studies*, 13(1): 73–87.

Becker, H.S. (1967) 'Whose side are we on?', *Social Problems*, 14(winter): 239–47.

Becker, H.S., Geer, B., Hughes, E.C. and Strauss, A.L. (1961) *Boys in White: Student Culture in Medical School*. Chicago: University of Chicago Press.

Becker, S. and Bryman, A. (eds) (2004) *Understanding Research for Social Policy and Practice*. Bristol: Policy Press.

Beeson, R.A. (2001) 'Loneliness and depression in spousal caregivers of persons with Alzheimer's disease', *Dissertation Abstracts International: Section B: The Sciences and Engineering*, 62(1-B): 158.

Beinecke, R. and Huxley, P.J. (2009) 'Mental health social work and nursing in the USA and the UK: Divergent paths coming together?' *International Journal of Social Psychiatry*, 55(May): 214–25.

Bekelman, J.E., Li, Y. and Goss, C.P. (2003) 'Scope and impact of financial conflicts of interest in biomedical research', *Journal of the American Medical Association*, 289(4): 454–65.

Bell, C. and Encel, S. (eds) (1978) *Inside the Whale: Ten Personal Accounts of Social Research*. Rushcutters' Bay NSW: Pergamon.

Belsky, J., Melhuish, T., Barnes, J., Leyland, A.H. and Romaniuk, H. (2006) 'Effects of Sure Start local programmes on children and families: Early findings from a quasi experimental, cross-sectional study', *Child: Care, Health and Development*, 32(6): 753–4.

Benhabib, S. (1992) *Situating the Self: Gender, Community and Postmodernism*. Cambridge: Polity Press.

Benner, P. (1984) *From Novice to Expert: Excellence and Power in Clinical Nursing Practice*. London: Addison Wesley Publishing.

Bennett, M. and Blackstock, C. (2006) 'First Nations child and family services and Indigenous knowledge as a framework for research, policy and practice', in N. Freymond and G. Cameron (eds), *Towards Positive Systems of Child and Family Welfare: International Comparisons of Child Protection, Family Service, and Community Caring Systems*. Toronto: University of Toronto Press.

Beresford, P. (2000) 'Service users knowledges and social work theory: Conflict or collaboration?', *British Journal of Social Work*, 30(4): 489–503.

Beresford, P. (2007a) 'The role of service user research in generating knowledge-based health and social care: From conflict to contribution', *Evidence and Policy*, 3(3): 329–41.

Beresford, P. (2007b) *The Changing Roles and Tasks of Social Work, From Service Users' Perspectives: A Literature Informed Discussion Paper*. London: Shaping Our Lives National User Network/GSCC

Beresford, P. (2007c) 'User involvement, research and health inequalities: Developing new directions', *Health and Social Care in the Community*, 15(4): 306–12.

Beresford, P., Adshead, L. and Croft, S. (2007a) *Palliative care, Social Work and Service Users: Making Life Possible*. London: Jessica Kingsley.

Beresford, P., Adshead, L. and Croft, S. (2007b) '"We don't see her as a social worker": A service user case study of the importance of the social worker's relationship and humanity', *British Journal of Social Work*, Advance Access May. http://bjsw.oxfordjournals.org/cgi/reprint/bcm043v1.pdf

Beresford, P. and Croft, S. (1993) *Citizen Involvement: A Practical Guide for Change*. Basingstoke: Macmillan.

Beresford, P. and Croft, S. (2004) 'Service users and practitioners reunited: The key component for social work reform', *British Journal of Social Work*, 34(1): 53–68.

Beresford, P., Croft, S., Evans, C. and Harding, T. (1997) 'Quality in personal social services: The developing role of user involvement in the UK', in A. Evans, K. Haverinen, K. Leichsering and G. Wistow (eds), *Developing Quality in Personal Social Services*. Aldershot: Ashgate.

Beresford, P. and Evans, C. (1999) 'Research note: Research and empowerment', *British Journal of Social Work*, 29(5): 671–7.

Bergart, A.M. (2000) 'The experience of women in unsuccessful infertility treatment: What do patients need when medical intervention fails?', *Social Work in Health Care*, 30(4): 45–69.

Bergmark, A. and Lundstrom, T. (2002) 'Education, practice and research: Knowledge and attitudes to knowledge of Swedish social workers', *Social Work Education*, 21(3): 359–73.

Berkman, B., Bedell, D., Parker, E., McCarthy, L. and Rosenbaum, C. (1988) 'Pre-admission screening: An efficacy study', *Social Work in Health Care*, 13: 35–50.

Berkman, B., Walker, S., Bonander, E. and Holmes, W. (1992) 'Early unplanned readmissions to social work of elderly patients: Factors predicting who needs follow-up services', *Social Work in Health Care*, 17(4): 103–19.

Berkman, B. and Rehr, H. (1970) 'Unanticipated consequences of the case-finding system in hospital social service', *Social Work*, 15: 63–70.

Berkman, B. and Rehr, H. (1973) 'Early social service case finding for hospitalized patients: An experiment', *The Social Service Review*, 47(2): 256–65.

Berlin, S.B. and Marsh, J.C. (1993) *Informing Practice Decisions*. New York: Macmillan Publishing Company.

Berlin, Sharon B., Mann, K.B. and Grossman, S.F. (1991) 'Task analysis of cognitive therapy for depression', *Social Work Research and Abstracts*, 27(2): 3–11.

Berman, Y. and Phillips, D. (2000) 'Indicators of social quality and social exclusion at national and community level', *Social Indicators Research*, 50: 329–50.

Bernard, M. (2006) 'Research, policy, practice and theory: Interrelated dimensions of a developing field', *Journal of Intergenerational Relationships*, 4(1): 5–21.

Bernard, W. and Este, D. (2005) 'Resiliency and young African Canadian males', in M. Ungar (ed.), *Handbook for Working with Children and Youth: Pathways to Resilience across Cultures and Contexts.* Thousand Oaks, CA: Sage, pp. 433–54.

Berridge, D., Dance, C., Beecham, J. and Field, S. (2008) *Educating Difficult Adolescents: Effective Education for Children in Public Care with Emotional and Behavioural Difficulties.* London: Jessica Kingsley Publishing.

Best, S. and Kellner, D. (1991) *Postmodern Theory: Critical Interrogations.* Basingstoke: Macmillan.

Beverley, J. (2000) 'Testimonio, subalternity, and narrative authority', in N. Denzin and Y. Lincoln (eds), *Handbook of Qualitative Research*, 2nd Edn., Thousand Oaks, CA: Sage, pp. 555–65.

Bhaskar, R. (2000) *The Possibility of Naturalism. A Philosophical Critique of the Contemporary Human Sciences*, 3rd Edn., London and New York: Routledge.

Bickman, L. (1985) 'Improving established statewide programs: A component theory of evaluation', *Evaluation Review*, 9: 189–208.

Biestek, F. (1961) *The Casework Relationship.* London: Allen and Unwin.

Bifulco, A. and Moran, P. (1998) *Wednesday's Child: Research into Women's Experience of Neglect and Abuse in Childhood, and Adult Depression.* London: Routledge.

Billig, M. (2004) 'Methodology and scholarship in understanding ideological explanation' in C. Seale (ed.), *Social Research Methods.* London: Routledge.

Bilson, A. and Barker, R. (1994) 'Siblings of children in care or accommodation: A neglected area of practice', *Practice*, 6(4): 226–35.

Bilson, A. and Barker, R. (1995) 'Parental contact in foster care and residential care after the Children Act', *British Journal of Social Work*, 25(3).

Bilson, A. and Barker, R. (1998) 'Looked after children and contact: Reassessing the social work task', *Research, Policy and Planning*, 16(1): 20–7.

Bingley, A. and Milligan, C. (2007) '"Sandplay, clay and sticks": Multi-sensory research methods to explore the long-term mental health effects of childhood play experience', *Children's Geographies*, 5(3): 283–96.

Bishop, A. (1994) *Becoming an Ally: Breaking the Cycle of Oppression.* Halifax, NS: Fernwood Publishing.

Bishop, R. (2005) 'Freeing ourselves from neocolonial domination in research: A kaupapa Maori approach to creating knowledge', in N.K. Denzin and Y.S. Lincoln (eds), *The Sage Handbook of Qualitative Research*, 3rd Edn., Thousand Oaks: Sage Publications, pp. 109–38.

Bishop, R. (2007) 'Freeing ourselves from neo-colonial domination in research: A Maori approach to creating knowledge', *International Journal of Qualitative Studies in Education*, 11(2): 199–219.

Bittles, A.H. (2002) 'Endogamy, consanguinity and community genetics', *Journal of Genetics*, 81(3): 91–8.

Blackstock, C. (2007) 'An Indigenous envelope for quantitative research'. Unpublished paper. University of Toronto, Faculty of Social Work.

Blackstock, C. (2008) 'Reconciliation means not saying sorry twice: Lessons from Child Welfare in Canada'. Paper prepared for the Aboriginal Healing Foundation.

Blakeslee, A.M., Cole, C. and Conefrey, T. (1996) 'Constructing voices in writing research: Developing participatory approaches to situated inquiry', in G. Kirsch and P. Moretensen (eds), *Ethics and Representation in Qualitative Studies of Literacy.* Urbana, IL: NCTE, pp. 63–75.

Blank, R. (2002) 'Evaluating welfare reform in the United States', *Journal of Economic Literature*, 40(4): 1105–66.

Blaxter, M. (1990) *Health and Lifestyles.* London: Routledge.

Blenkner, M., Bloom, M., Nielson, M. and Weber, R. (1974) *Final Report. Protective Services for Older People: Findings from the Benjamin Rose Institute Study.* Cleveland OH: Benjamin Rose Institute.

Blewett, J. (2007) 'Towards evidence-based care: The challenge of making research count', *Evidence and Policy*, 3(2): 287–300.

Blewett, J., Lewis, J. and Tunstill, J. (2007) *The Changing Roles and Tasks of Social Work: A Literature Informed Discussion Paper.* London: Synergy Research and Consulting/GSCC.

Bloom, M. (1995) 'The great philosophy of science war', *Social Work Research*, 19: 19–23.

Bloom, M. (1999) 'Single-system evaluation', in I. Shaw and J. Lishman (eds), *Evaluation and Social Work Practice.* London: Sage.

Bloom, M. and Fischer, J. (1982) *Evaluating Practice: Guidelines for the Accountable Professional*. London: Prentice–Hall International.

Bloom, M., Fischer, J. and Orme, J.G. (1999) *Evaluating Practice*, 3rd Edn., New York: Free Press.

Blumenfeld, S. and Rosenberg, G. (1988) 'Towards a network of social health services: Redefining discharge planning and expanding the social work domain', *Social Work in Health Care*, 13: 31–48.

Blumenthal, D.S. (2006) 'A community coalition board creates a set of values for community-based research', *Preventing Chronic Disease*, 3. Available at: http://www.cdc.gov/pcd/issues/2006/jan/05_0068.htm

Blumenthal, D.S. and Yancey, E. (2004) 'Community-based research: An introduction', in D.S. Blumenthal and R.J. DiClemente (eds), (2004) *Community-Based Health Research: Issues and Methods*. NY: Springer Publishing Company, pp. 3–24.

Blumer, H. (2007) 'Society in Action', in S. Cahill (ed.), *Inside Social Life, Readings in Sociological Psychology and Microsociology*, 5th Edn., Los Angeles: Roxbury Publishing Co. 312–16.

Blythe, B.J., Tripodi, T. and Briar, S. (1994) *Direct Practice Research in Human Services Agencies*. New York: Columbia University Press.

Boghossian, P. (2006) *Fear of Knowledge*. New York: Oxford University Press.

Böhm, W., Mühlbach, M. and Otto, H.-U. (1989) 'Zur Rationalität der Wissensverwendung im Kontext behördlicher Sozialarbeit', in U. Beck and W. Bonss (eds), *Weder Sozialtechnologie noch Aufklärung*. Frankfurt a.M., Suhrkamp.

Boone, C.R., Coulton, C.J. and Keller S.J. (1981) 'The impact of early and comprehensive social work services on length of stay', *Social Work in Health Care*, 7: 1–9.

Booth, C. (1903) *Life and Labour of the People in London*. London: Macmillan.

Boruch, R. (2007) 'Encouraging the flight of error: Ethical standards, evidence standards, and randomized trials, *New Directions in Evaluation*, 113: 55–73.

Boruch, R., deMoya, D. and Lavenberg, J. (2004) *Reconnaissance on Randomized Trials in OECD Countries*. Unpublished paper. Philadelphia: University of Philadelphia, Graduate School of Education.

Boruch, R., De Moya, D., Snyder, B. (2002) 'The importance of randomized field trials in education and related areas', in F. Mosteller and R. Boruch (eds), *Evidence Matters – Randomized Trials in Education Research*. Washington, DC: Brookings Institute Press, pp. 50–79.

Boser, S. (2007) 'Power, ethics, and the IRB: Dissonance over human participant review of participatory research', *Qualitative Inquiry*, 13(8): 1060–74.

Botvin, G.J., Griffin, K.W. and Nichols, T.R. (2006) 'Preventing youth violence and delinquency through a universal school-based prevention approach', *Prevention Science*, 7: 403–8.

Bourdieu, P. (1986) 'The forms of capital', in J. Richardson (ed.), *Handbook of Theory and Research for the Sociology of Education*. New York: Greenwood Press, pp. 241–58.

Bourdieu, P. (1990) *The Logic of Practice*. Stanford: Stanford University Press.

Boushel, M. (2000) 'What kind of people are we? "Race" anti-racism, and social welfare research', *British Journal of Social Work*, 30: 71–89.

Boydell, J., McKenzie, K., van Os, J. and Murray, R. (2002) 'The social causes of schizophrenia: An investigation into the influence of social cohesion and social hostility. Report of a pilot study', *Schizophrenia Research*, 53: 264.

Boyer, E. (1996) 'The scholarship of engagement', *Journal of Public Outreach*, 1(1): 11–20.

Boyle, J.P., Honeycutt, A.A., K.M., Narayan, V., Hoerger, T.J., Geiss, L.S., Chen, H. and Thompson, T. (2001) 'Projection of Diabetes Burden Through 2050: Impact of changing demography and disease prevalence in the U.S'. *Diabetes Care*, 24: 1936–40.

Bracken, D. (2005) 'Development and trends in Canadian probation', *Vista Perspectives on Probation*, 10(2).

Bracken, D. (2007) 'Probation in the USA and Canada', in R. Canton and D. Hancock (eds), *Dictionary of Probation and Offender Management*. Cullompton: Willan, pp. 231–3.

Brackstone, G. (1999) 'Managing data quality in a statistical agency', *Survey Methodology*, 25: 139–49.

Brackstone, G. (2001) 'How important is accuracy?' Panel discussion presentation to Proceedings of Statistics Canada Symposium, 2001, 'Achieving data quality in a statistical agency: A methodological perspective'.

Bradbury, H. and Reason, P. (2003a) 'Action research: An opportunity for revitalizing research purpose and practices', *Qualitative Social Work*, 2: 155–75.

Bradbury, H. and Reason, P. (2003b) Issues and choice points for improving the quality of action research', in M. Minkler and N. Wallerstein (eds), *Community-Based Participatory Research for Health*. San Francisco, CA: Jossey–Bass, pp. 201–20.

Bradshaw, J. (ed.) (2002) *The Well Being of Children in the UK*. London: Save The Children.

Braithwaite, J. (2003) 'What's wrong with the sociology of punishment?', *Theoretical Criminology*, 7(1): 5–28.

Branch, L.A., Jette, M., Evaschwick, M., Palansky, M. and Diehr, R. (1981) 'Toward understanding elders' health services utilization', *Journal of Community Health*, 7: 80–92.

Brand, V. (1986) 'Social work research in relation to social development in Zimbabwe', *Journal of Social Development in Africa*, 1(1): 67–80.

Brandon, M., Howe, A., Dagley, V., Salter, C. and Warren, C. (2006) 'What appears to be helping or hindering practitioners in implementing the common assessment framework and lead professional working?', *Child Abuse Review*, 15(6): 396–413.

Brandon, M. and Thoburn, J. (2008) 'Safeguarding children in the UK: A longitudinal study of services to children suffering or likely to suffer significant harm', *Child and Family Social Work*. 13: 365–77.

Bray, S. and Preston-Shoot, M. (1995) *Empowerment and Participation in Social Care*. London: Arnold.

Braye, S. (2000) 'Participation and involvement in social care: An overview', in H. Kemshall and R. Littlechild (eds), *User Involvement and Participation in Social Care*. London: Jessica Kingsley.

Braye, S. and Preston-Shoot, M. (2007) 'On systematic reviews in social work: Observations from teaching, learning and assessment of law in social work education', *British Journal of Social Work*, 37: 313–34.

Brechin, A. (1993) 'Sharing', in P. Shakespeare, D. Atkinson and S. French (eds), *Reflections on Research in Practice: Issues in Health and Social Care*. Buckingham: Open University Press.

Brekke, J.S., Ell, K. and Palinkas, L.A. (2007) 'Translational science at the National Institute of Mental Health: Can social work take its rightful place?', *Research on Social Work Practice*, 17(1): 123–33.

Bretherton, I. (1992) 'The origins of attachment theory: John Bowlby and Mary Ainsworth', *Developmental Psychology*, 28: 759–75.

Brettschneider, G. (1989) *Socialutbildningen i Finland och Sverige – tillbakablick och jämförelse* (Social Work Education in Finland and Sweden). Helsingfors: Svenska social- och kommunalhögskolan.

Brewer, J.D. and Hunter, A. (2005) *Foundations of Multimethod Research: Synthesizing Styles*. Thousand Oaks, CA: Sage.

Briar, S. (1979) 'Incorporating research into education for clinical practice in social work: Toward a clinical science in social work', in R. Allen and A. Rosenblatt (eds), *Sourcebook on Research Utilization*. New York: Council on Social Work Education.

Briar, S., Weissman, H. and Rubin, A. (1981) *Research Utilization in Social Work Education*. New York: Council on Social Work Education.

Briar-Lawson, K., Korr, W., White, B., Zabora, J., Vroom, P., Middleton, J., Shank, B. and Schatz, M. (2008) 'Advancing administrative supports for research development', *Social Work Research*, 32(4): 236–241.

Briggs, H.E. and Rzepnicki, T.L. (eds) (2004) *Using Evidence in Social Work Practice: Behavioral Perspectives*. Chicago: Lyceum Books.

Briere, J. (1996) *Professional Manual for the Trauma Symptom Checklist for Children (TSCC)*. Odessa, FL: Psychological Assessment Resources.

Briskman, L. (2003) *The Black Grapevine: Aboriginal Activism and the Stolen Generations*. Sydney: The Federation Press.

Briskman, L. (2007) *Social Work with Indigenous Communities*. Sydney: The Federation Press.

Briskman, L. and Babacan, A. (2008) 'Turning away thy neighbour', in A. Babacan and L. Briskman (eds), *Asylum Seekers: International Perspectives on Interdiction and Deterrence*. Newcastle: Cambridge Scholars Press.

Briskman, L. and Goddard, C. (2007) 'Not in my name: The people's inquiry into immigration detention', in D. Lusher and N. Haslam (eds), *Yearning to Breathe Free*. Sydney: The Federation Press.

Briskman, L., Latham, S. and Goddard, C. (2008) *Human Rights Overboard: Seeking Asylum in Australia*. Melbourne: Scribe.

British Association of Social Workers (2007) 'Ordinary Motion 4', passed at Annual General Meeting, 2 May. Birmingham: BASW.

Britton, M. (2008) '"My regular spot:" Race and territory in urban public space', *Journal of Contemporary Ethnography*, 37(4): 442–68.

Broad, B. (1994) *Leaving Care in the 1990s*. Kent: Rainer.

Broad, B. (1998) *Young People Leaving Care: Life After the Children Act 1989*. London: Jessica Kingsley.

Broad, B. (1999) 'Improving the health and well being of children and young people leaving care', *Adoption and Fostering*, 23(1): 40–8.

Broad, B. (2004) 'Kinship care for children in the UK: Messages from research, lessons for policy and practice'. *European Journal of Social Work*, 7(2): 211–27.

Broad, B. (2005) *Improving the Health and Well Being of Young People Leaving Care*. Lyme Regis: Russell House.

Broad, B. and Saunders, L. (1998) 'Involving young people leaving care as peer researchers in a health research project: A learning experience', *Research Policy and Planning*, 16(1): 1–9.

Broadhurst, K., Wastell, D., White, S., Hall, C., Peckover, S., Thompson, K., Pithouse, A. and Davey, D. (advance access 2009) Performing 'Initial Assessment': Identifying the latent conditions for error at the front-door of local authority children's services, *British Journal of Social Work Advance Access* published 18 January.

Brocato, J. and Wagner, E.F. (2003) 'Harm reduction: A social work practice model and social justice agenda', *Health and Social Work*, 28(2): 117–25.

Brodowski, M., Flanzer, S., Nolan, C., Shafer, J. and Kaye, E. (2007) 'Children's Bureau discretionary grants: Knowledge development through our research and demonstration projects', *Journal of Evidence-Based Practice*, 4(3/4).

Bronstein, L., McCallion, P. and Kramer, E. (2006) 'Developing an aging prepared community: collaboration among counties, consumers, professionals and organizations'. *Journal of Gerontological Social Work*, 48(1/2): 193–202.

Brothers, M., Scullion, P. and Eathorne, V. (2002) 'Rights of access to services for disabled people', *British Journal of Therapy and Rehabilitation*, 9: 232–6.

Brown, J. (2005) 'Challenges faced by aboriginal youth in the inner city', *Canadian Journal of Urban Research*, 14(1): 81–106.

Brown, L. (2006) 'Still subversive after all these years: The relevance of feminist therapy in the age of evidence-based practice', *Psychology of Women Quarterly*, 30: 15–24.

Brown, L. (ed.) (2007) *African Philosophy: New and Traditional Perspectives*. Oxford: Oxford University Press.

Brown, L. and Strega. S. (2005) 'Introduction: Transgressive possibilities', in L. Brown and S. Strega (eds) *Research as Resistance: Critical, Indigenous and Anti-Oppressive Approaches*. London: Canadian Scholars' Press.

Bruce, M.L., Takeuchi, D.T. and Leaf, P.J. (1991) 'Poverty and psychiatric status. Longitudinal evidence from the New Haven Epidemiologic Catchment Area Study', *Archives of General Psychiatry*, 48: 470–4.

Brunnberg, E. (2006) 'Samtliga avhandlingar i socialt arbete' (PhD dissertations in Social Work). Göteborg, Stockholm, Lund, Umeå och Örebro Universitet 1980–2006. Örebro: Örebrö universitet.

Bryant, A. and Charmaz, K. (2007) 'Grounded theory in historical perspective: An epistemological account', in A. Bryant and K. Charmaz (eds), *The Sage Handbook of Grounded Theory*. Thousand Oaks, CA: Sage, pp. 31–93.

Bryman, A. (1988) *Quantity and Quality in Social Research*. London: Unwin Hyman.

Bryson, K.R. (2001) *New Census Bureau Data on Grandparents Raising Grandchildren*. Unpublished manuscript.

Buchanan, A. and Ritchie, C. (2004) *What Works for Troubled Children*, revised edition. London: Barnardo's/Russell House Press.

Buchanan, A., Ritchie, R. and Bream, V. (2002) *Seen and Heard 2, Wiltshire Family Services Study 2001: The Views of Families Who are in Contact with Social Services*. London: Barnardo's.

Budapest Open Access Initiative (2001) Convened in Budapest by the Open Society Institute (OSI). Available at: http://www.soros.org/openaccess/read.shtml

Bullock, R. (2006) 'The dissemination of research findings in children's services: Issues and strategies', *Adoption and Fostering*, 30(1): 18–28.

Bullock, R., Courtney, M., Parker, R., Sinclair, I. and Thoburn, J. (2006) 'Can the corporate state parent?', *Children and Youth Services Review*, 28(11): 1344–58.

Bullock, R., Gooch, D. and Little, M. (1998) *Children Going Home: The Reunification of Families*. Aldershot: Dartmouth.

Bulmer, M. (1982) *The Uses of Social Research*. London: Allen and Unwin.

Bulmer, M. (1984) *The Chicago School of Sociology*. Chicago: Chicago University Press.

Burawoy, M. (1990) 'Marxism as science: Historical challenges and theoretical growth', *American Sociological Review*, 55: 775–93.

Burford, G. and Hudson, J. (eds) (2000) *Family Group Conferencing: New Directions in Community-Centered Child and Family Practice*. New York: Walter de Gruyter.

Burgess, E.W. (1923) 'The interdependence of sociology and social work', *Journal of Social Forces*, 1(4): 366–70.

Burgess, E.W. (1927) 'The contribution of sociology to family social work', *The Family*, October: 191–201.

Burgess, E.W. (1928) 'What social case records should contain to be useful for sociological interpretation', *Social Forces*, 6(4): 524–32.

Burgess, E.W. (1930) 'The value of sociological community studies for the work of social agencies' *Social Forces*, 8(4): 481–91.

Burnett, R. (1992) *The Dynamics of Recidivism*. Oxford: University of Oxford Centre for Criminological Research.

Burnett, R. and Maruna, S. (2004) 'So "prison works" does it? The criminal careers of 130 men released from prison under Home Secretary, Michael Howard', *Howard Journal*, 43(4): 390–404.

Burnett, R. and McNeill, F. (2005) 'The place of the officer–offender relationship in assisting offenders to desist from crime', *Probation Journal*, 52(3): 247–68.

Burnett, P. (2006) *Civic Engagement*. Orno, ME: University of Maine Center on Aging.

Burns, T. (2002) 'The UK700 trial of intensive case management: An overview and discussion', *World Psychiatry*, 1(3): 175–8.

Burrell, G. and Morgan, G. (1979) *Sociological Paradigms and Organisational Analysis*. London: Heinemann.

Burtless, G. (1985) 'Are targeted wage subsidies harmful? Evidence from a wage voucher experiment', *Industrial and Labor Relations Review*, 39: 105–14.

Burton, L.A. (1996) 'Age norms, the timing of family role transitions, and intergenerational caregiving among aging African American women', *The Gerontologist*, 36(2): 199–208.

Busza, J. (2004) 'Participatory research in constrained settings: Sharing challenges from Cambodia', *Action Research*, 2(2): 191–208.

Butler, I. (2002) 'Critical commentary: A code of ethics for social work and social care research', *British Journal of Social Work*, 32(2): 239–48.

Butler, I. and Drakeford, M. (2005) 'Trusting in social work', *British Journal of Social Work*, 35: 639–53.

Butler, I. and Pugh, R. (2004) 'The politics of social work research', in R. Lovelock, K. Lyons and J. Powell (eds), *Reflecting on Social Work – Discipline and Profession*. Aldershot: Ashgate.

Butrym, Z. (1976) *The Nature of Social Work*. London: Macmillan.

Bystydzienski, J. and Schacht, S. (2001) 'Introduction' in J. Bystydzienski and S. Schacht (eds), *Forging Radical Alliances Across Difference*. Lanham: Rowman and Littlefield.

Bywaters, P. (1991) 'Case finding and screening for social work in acute general hospitals', *British Journal of Social Work*, 21(1): 19–39.

Bywaters, P. (2000) 'Talking about inequality: Accounts of ill health', *British Journal of Social Work*, 20(6): 873–8.

Bywaters, P. (2007) 'Tackling inequalities in health: A global challenge for social work' *British Journal of Social Work*. Advance Access doi:10.1093/bjsw/bcm096

Bywaters, P. (2008) 'Learning from experience: Developing a research strategy for social work in the UK', *British Journal of Social Work*, 38(5): 936–52.

Bywaters, P. and McLeod, E. (1996) 'Can social work deliver on health?', in E. McLeod and P. Bywaters (eds), *Working for Equality in Health*. London: Routledge.

Bywaters, P., McLeod, E. and Napier, L. (eds) (2009) *Social work and global health inequalities*. Bristol: Policy Press.

Cabinet Office (1999) *Modernising government* Stationery Office: London. 66pp. Cm 4310. Available via: http://www.archive.official-documents.co.uk/document/cm43/4310/4310.htm

Cahill, C. (2007) 'The personal is political: Developing new subjectivities through participatory action research', *Gender, Place and Culture*, 14(3): 267–92.

Cameron, G. (2003) 'Promoting positive child and family welfare', in K. Kufeldt and B. McKenzie (eds), *Child Welfare: Connecting Research, Policy, and Practice*. Waterloo, ON: Wilfrid Laurier University Press, pp. 79–100.

Cameron, H. and Tefler, J. (2004) 'Cognitive-behavioural group work: Its application to specific offender groups', *Howard Journal*, 43(1): 47–64.

Campbell, D. (1957) 'Factors relevant to the validity of experiments in social setting', *Psychological Bulletin*, 54: 297–312.

Campbell, D. (1969) 'Reforms as experiments', *American Psychologist*, 24: 409–29.

Campbell, D. (1978) 'Qualitative knowing in action research', in M. Brenner, P. Marsh and M. Brenner (eds), *The Social Contexts of Method*. London: Croom Helm, pp. 184–209.

Campbell, D. (1979) 'Degrees of freedom and the case study', in T. Cook and C. Reichardt (eds), *Qualitative and Quantitative Methods in Evaluation Research*. Beverly Hills: Sage.

Campbell, D.T. and Borouch, R.F. (1975) *Evaluation and Experiment – Some Critical Issues in Assessing Social Programs*. New York: Academic Press.

Campbell, D.T. and Stanley, J.C. (1963) *Experimental and Quasi-Experimental Designs for Research*. Chicago: Rand McNally College Publishing Company.

Campbell, D.T. and Stanley, J.C. (1973) *Experimental and Quasi-Experimental Designs for Research*. Chicago: Rand McNally College Publishing Company.

Campbell, M. and Manicom, A. (1995) *Knowledge, Experience and Ruling Relations: Studies in the Social Organization of Knowledge*. Toronto: University of Toronto Press.

Campbell, M.L. (1996) 'A life course perspective: Aging with long-term disability', *Maximizing Human Potential – Quarterly Newsletter of the Aging, Disability and Rehabilitation Network of the American Society on Aging*, 1(3): 1–2.

Campbell, R., Pound, P., Pope, C., Britten, N., Pill, R., Morgan, M. and Donovan, J. (2003) 'Evaluating meta-ethnography: A synthesis of qualitative research on lay experiences of diabetes and diabetes care', *Social Science and Medicine*, 56: 671–84.

Canton, R. (2007) 'Probation in Europe', in R. Canton and D. Hancock (eds), *Dictionary of Probation and Offender Management*. Cullompton: Willan. pp. 230–1.

Cantor, M.H. (1993) 'Families and caregiving in an aging society', in L. Burton (ed.), *Families and Aging*, Amityville, NY: Baywood Publishing Company, pp. 135–44.

Caracelli, V.J. and Greene, J.C. (1993) 'Data analysis strategies for mixed-method evaluation designs', *Educational Evaluation and Policy Analysis*, 15(2): 195–207.

Carey, L. (2004) 'Always, already colonizer/colonized: White Australian wanderings', in K. Mutua and B. Swadena (eds), *Decolonizing Research in Cross-Cultural Contexts*. Albany: State University of New York Press.

Carlen, P. (2002) *Women and Punishment: The Struggle for Justice*. Cullompton: Willan Publishing.

Carnegie Foundation (2008) Available at: http://www.carnegiefoundation.org/classifications/index.asp.?key=785. Last accessed 10 October 2008.

Carniol, B. (2003) 'Generalist skills in social work'. Unpublished chart. Ryerson School of Social Work.

Carniol, B. (2005) 'Analysis of social location and change: Practice implications', in S. Hicks, J. Fook and R. Pozzuto (eds), *Social Work: A Critical Turn*. Toronto: Thompson Educational Publishing.

Carpenter, B.D., Edwards, D.F., Pickard, J.G., Palmer, J.L., Stark, S., Neufeld, P.S., Morrow-Howell, N., Perkinson, M.A. and Morris, J.C. (2007) 'Anticipating relocation: Concerns about moving among NORC residents', *Journal of Gerontological Social Work*, 49(1/2): 165–84.

Carpenter, J. (2002) 'Mental health recovery paradigm: Implications for social work', *Health and Social Work*, 27: 86–94.

Carr, S. (2004) *Has Service User Involvement Made a Difference to Social Care Services?* London: Social Institute for Excellence.

Castillo, H. (2003) *Personality Disorder: Temperament or Trauma? An Account of an Emancipatory Research Study Carried Out by Service Users Diagnosed with Personality Disorder*. London, Jessica Kingsley.

Catalano, R.F., Berglund, L.M. Ryan, A.M.J., Lonczak, S.H. and Hawkins, D.J. (2004) 'Positive youth development in the United States: Research findings on evaluations of positive youth development programs'. *Annals, ASSPSS*, 591(1): 98–124.

Cavadino, M. and Dignan. J. (2006) *Penal Systems: A Comparative Approach*. London: Sage.

Center for Health Communication, Harvard School of Public Health (2004) *Reinventing Aging: Baby Boomers and Civic Engagement*. Boston, MA: Harvard School of Public Health.

Center for Reproductive Rights (2003) *The Bush Global Gag Rule: Endangering Women's Health, Free Speech and Democracy*. Available at: http://www.reproductiverights.org/pub_fac_ggrbush.html. Last accessed 20 February 2008.

Centre for Social Work Research (2005) Available at: http://www.uel.ac.uk./ssmcs/research/cswr/index.htm

Centers for Medicaid and Medicare Services (2003) *Health Care Industry Market Update: Nursing Facilities*. Washington DC: CMS.

Chadwick, E. (1842) *The Sanitary Conditions of the Labouring Population*, Government report.

Chafetz, M.E. (1996) *The Tyranny of Experts*. London: Madison Books.

Chalmers, I. (2005) 'If evidence-informed policy works in practice, does it matter if it doesn't work in theory?' *Evidence and Policy*, 1(1): 227–42.

Chamberlain, P., Leve, L.D. and DeGarmo, D.S. (2007) 'Multidimensional treatment foster care for girls in the juvenile justice system: 2-year follow-up of a randomized clinical trial', *Journal of Consulting and Clinical Psychology*, 75(1): 187–93.

Chamberlain, P. and Smith, D.K. (2003) 'Antisocial behavior in children and adolescents: The Oregon multidimensional treatment foster care model', in A.E. Kazdin and J.R. Weisz (eds), *Evidence-Based Psychotherapies for Children and Adolescents*. New York, NY: Guilford, pp. 282–300.

Chambers, R. (1994) 'The origins and practice of Participatory Rural Appraisal', *World Development*, 22: 953–69.

Chambers, R. (1997) *Whose Reality Counts: Putting the First Last*. London: Intermediate Technology Publications.

Chambon, A. (1999) 'Foucault's approach: Making the familiar visible', in A. Chambon, A. Irving and L. Epstein (eds), *Reading Foucault for Social Work*. New York: Columbia University Press.

Chambon, A. and Fudge-Schormans, A. (2007) *Personhood, Vulnerability, Responsibility: Collaborative Research with Persons Who Have an Intellectual Disability*. Toronto: Joint Centre for Bioethics, University of Toronto.

Chan, C., Ho, P.S.Y. and Chow, E. (2001) 'A body–mind–spirit model in health: An Eastern approach', *Social Work in Health Care*, 34(3–4): 261–82.

Chan, C.L.W. and Chan, T.H.Y. (2006) 'The strength-focused and meaning-oriented approach to resilience and transformation (SMART): A body–mind–spirit approach to trauma management', *Social Work in Health Care*, 43(2–3): 9–36.

Chapin, F.S. (1920) *Field Work and Social Research*. New York: Appleton-Century.

Chapin, F.S. (1947) *Experimental Designs in Sociological Research*. New York: Harper.

Chapin, F.S. and Queen, S.A. (1937) *Research Memorandum on Social Work Research in the Depression*. Social Science Research Council, Bulletin No 39.

Charlton, J. (1998) *Nothing About Us Without Us*. Berkley, CA: University of California Press.

Charlton, J. (2000) *No More About Us Without Us: Disability, Oppression and Empowerment*. California, US: University of California Press.

Cheetham, J., Fuller, R., McIvor, G. and Petch, A. (1992) *Evaluating Social Work Effectiveness*. Buckingham: Open University Press.

Chelimsky, E. (1997) 'Thoughts for a new evaluation society', *Evaluation*, 3(1): 97–118.

Chelimsky, E. (2006) 'The purposes of evaluation in a democratic society', in I. Shaw, J. Greene and M. Mark (eds), *Sage Handbook of Evaluation*. London: Sage Publications, pp. 33–55.

Chen, H.-T. and Rossi, P.H. (1983) 'Evaluating with sense: The theory driven approach', *Evaluation Review*, 7(3): 283–302.

Chief Secretary to the Treasury (2003) *Every Child Matters*. Cm5860. London: Stationery Office.

Childs, V. (2001) 'What does the elephant look like? Problems encountered on a journey to innovation in child protection', in R. Winter and C. Munn-Giddings (eds), *A Handbook for Action Research in Health and Social Care*, pp. 102–15.

Chiu, L.F. (2006) 'Critical reflection: More than nuts and bolts', *Action Research*, 4(2): 183–203.

Choi, N.G. and Wodarski, J.S. (1996) 'The relationship between social support and health status of elderly people: Does social support slow down physical and functional deterioration', *Social Work Research*, 20(1): 52–63.

Chow, J.C.-C. and Crowe, K. (2005) 'Community-based research and methods in community practice', in M. Weil (ed.), *The Handbook of Community Practice*. Thousand Oaks, CA: Sage Publications. pp. 604–19.

Churchill, R., Owen, G., Singh, S. and Hotopf, M. (2007) 'International experiences of using community

treatment orders'. Available at: http://www.dh.gov.uk/en/Publicationsandstatistics/Publications/PublicationsPolicyAndGuidance/DH_072730

Cid, J. (2005) 'Suspended sentences in Spain: Decarceration and recidivism', *Probation Journal*, 52(2): 169–79.

City of Calgary (2001) *A Place To Call Home: Final Report*. Calgary, Alberta: University of Calgary.

Claiborne, N. (2006) 'Effectiveness of a care coordination model for stroke survivors: A randomized study', *Health and Social Work*, 31(2): 87–96.

Clarke, C. (2006) 'Moral character in social work', *British Journal of Social Work*, 36(1): 75–89.

Clarkson, P., Venables, D., Hughes, J., Burns, A. and Challis, D. (2006) 'Integrated specialist assessment of older people and predictors of care-home admission', *Psychological Medicine*, 36: 1011–21.

Cleaver, H., Unell, I. and Aldgate, J. (1999) *Children's Needs – Parenting Capacity: The Impact of Parental Mental Illness, Problem Alcohol and Drug Use, and Domestic Violence on Children's Development*. London: Stationery Office.

Clegg, S. (1999) 'Professional education, reflective practice and feminism', *International Journal of Inclusive Education*, 3(2): 167–79.

Clegg, S. (2005) 'Evidence-based practice in educational research: A critical realist critique of systematic review', *British Journal of Sociology of Education*, 26(3): 415–28.

Clements, J.A. and Rosenwald, M. (2008) 'Foster parents' perspectives on LGB youth in the child welfare system', *Journal of Gay and Lesbian Social Services*, 19(1): 57–69.

Cnaan, R.A. and Dichter, M.E. (2008) 'Thoughts on the use of knowledge in social work practice', *Research on Social Work Practice*. 18(4): 278–84.

CNCS (2007) *The Health Benefits of Volunteering: A Review of Recent Research*. Washington DC: CNCS.

Cochrane, A.L. (1979) '1931–1971: A critical review with particular reference to the medical profession', in *Office of Health Economics Medicines for the Year 2000*. London: Office of Health Economics.

Coghlan, D. and Brannick, T. (2005) *Doing Action Research in Your Own Organization*. London: Sage Publications.

Cohen, S. (2004) 'Breaking the link and pulling the plug', in D. Hayes and B. Humphries (eds), *Social Work, Immigration and Asylum: Debates, Dilemmas and Ethical Issues for Social Work and Social Care Practice*. London: Jessica Kingsley Publishers.

Cohen, C.S., Mulroy, E., Tull, T., Bloom, C.C. and Karnas, F. (2007) 'Integrating services for older adults in housing settings'. *Journal of Gerontological Social Work*, 49(1/2): 145–64.

Coleman, J. (1988) 'Social capital in the creation of human capital', *American Journal of Sociology*, 94: S95–S120.

Collett, J. (2004) 'Immigration is a social work issue', in D. Hayes and B. Humphries (eds), *Social Work, Immigration and Asylum: Debates, Dilemmas and Ethical Issues for Social Work and Social Care Practice*. London: Jessica Kingsley Publishers.

Collins, H. (2000). *Tacit knowledge, trust and the Q of Sapphire*. Cardiff University School of Social Sciences. Working Paper. http://www.cf.ac.uk/socsi/ (subsequently published in *Social Studies of Science*).

Collins, H. and Evans, R. (2002) 'The third wave of science studies: Studies of expertise and experience', *Social Studies of Science*, 32(2): 235–96.

Collins, P.H. (1991) *Black Feminist Thought: Knowledge, Consciousness and the Politics of Empowerment*. London: Routledge.

Connell, R. (2006) 'Northern theory: The political geography of general social theory', *Theory and Society*, 35(2): 237–64.

Connelly, J. (2001) 'Critical realism and health promotion: Effective practice needs an effective theory', *Health Education Research*, 16(2): 115–20.

Connolly, M. and McKenzie, M. (1999) *Effective Participatory Practice: Family Group Conferencing in Child Protection*. New York: Aldine de Gruyter.

Conrad, P. (2007) *The Medicalization of Society: On the Transformation of Human Conditions into Treatable Disorders*. Baltimore: Johns Hopkins University Press.

Cook, T.D. (1987) 'Positivist critical multiplism', in W.R. Shadish and C.S. Relchardt (eds), *Evaluation Studies*. 12 Newbury Park, CA: Sage.

Cooling, T. (2005) 'The search for truth: Postmodernism and religious education', *Journal of Belief and Values*, 26(1): 87–93.

Cooper, A., Hetherington, R., Baistow, K., Pitts, J. and Spriggs, A. (1995) *Positive Child Protection: A View from Abroad*. Lyme Regis: Russell House Publishing.

Cooper, M. (1980) 'Normanton: Interweaving social work and the community', in R. Hadley and M. McGrath (eds), *Going Local: Neighbourhood Social Services*. London: Bedford Square Press/NCVO Occasional Paper 1, pp. 29–40.

Cooper, S.A. (1997) 'A population-based health survey of maladaptive behaviours associated with dementia in elderly people with learning disabilities', *Journal of Intellectual Disability Research*, 41(6): 481–7.

Cooper, S.A. (1999) 'The relationship between psychiatric and physical health in elderly people with intellectual disability' *Journal of Intellectual Disability Research*, 43(1): 54–60.

Cooper, S.P., Heitman, E., Fox, E.E., Quill, B., Knudson, P., Zahm, S.H. et al. (2004) 'Ethical issues in conducting migrant farmworker studies', *Journal of Immigrant Health*, 6(1): 29–40.

Cooper, S.A., Morrison, J., Melville, C., Finlayson, J., Allan, L., Martin, G. and Robinson, N. (2006) 'Improving the health of people with intellectual disabilities: Outcomes of a health screening programme after 1 year', *Journal of Intellectual Disability Research*, 50(9): 667–77.

Copeland, A.L. and Sorensen, J.L. (2001) 'Differences between methamphetamine users and cocaine users in treatment', *Drug and Alcohol Dependence*, 62: 91–5.

Corbin, J. and Strauss, A. (1988) *Unending Work and Care*. San Francisco: Jossey–Bass.

Coren, E. and Fisher, M. (2006) *The Conduct of Systematic Reviews SCIE Knowledge Reviews*. London: Social Care Institute for Excellence.

Cornwell, A. and Jewkes, R. (1995) 'What is participatory research?', *Social Science and Medicine*, 41: 1667–76.

Corporation for National and Community Service (2007) *The Health Benefits of Volunteering: A Review of Recent Research*. Washington, DC: Corporation for National and Community Service.

Corrigan, P. and Leonard, P. (1978) *Social Work Practice under Capitalism: Marxist Approach*. London: Macmillan.

Corsaro, W. (1996) 'Transitions in early childhood: The promise of comparative, longitudinal ethnography', in R. Jessor, A. Colby and R. Shweder (eds), *Ethnography and Human Development: Context and Meaning in Social Inquiry*. Chicago: University of Chicago Press, pp. 419–58.

Coryn, C.L.S. and Scriven, M. (eds) (2008) *Reforming the Evaluation of Research*. New Directions for Evaluation #118. San Francisco: Jossey–Bass.

Costa, R.L. (2006) 'The logic of practices in Pierre Bourdieu', *Current Sociology*, 54(6): 873–95.

Courtney, M.E., Dworsky, A., Cusick, G.R., Havlicek, J., Perez, A. and Keller, T. (2007) *Executive Summary: Midwest Evaluation of the Adult Functioning of Former Foster Youth: Outcomes at Age 21*. Chicago, IL: Chapin Hall Center Center for Children at the University of Chicago.

Coward, R.T. and Lee, G.R. (1985) *The Elderly in Rural Society*. New York: Springer.

Cowger, C.D. and Menon, G. (2001) 'Integrating qualitative and quantitative research methods', in B.A. Thyer (ed.), *The Handbook of Social Work Research Methods*. Thousand Oaks, CA: Sage Publications, pp. 473–84.

Cox, C. (1993) 'Service needs and interests: A comparison of African American and white caregivers seeking Alzheimer assistance', *The American Journal of Alzheimer's Care and Related Disorders and Research*, 8(3): 33–40.

Cox, C. (1996) 'Outcomes of hospitalization: Factors influencing the discharges of African American and white dementia patients', *Social Work in Health Care*, 23(1): 23–38.

Cox, P. and Hardwick, L. (2002) 'Research and critical theory: Their contribution to social work education and practice', *Social Work Education*, 21(1): 35.

Cox, P. and Hardwick, L. (2007) 'Research and critical theory: Their contribution to social work education and practice', *Social Work Education*, 21(1): 35–47.

Coy, M. (2008) 'Young women, local authority care, and selling sex: Findings from research', *British Journal of Social Work*, 38, 1404–28.

Craig, R.W. (2007) 'A day in the life of a hospital social worker: Presenting our role through the personal narrative', *Qualitative Social Work*, 6(4): 431–46.

Crane, K.D. and Ellis, R.A. (2004) 'Benevolent intervention or oppression perpetuated: Minority overrepresentation in children's services', *Journal of Human Behavior in the Social Environment*, 9(1): 19–37.

Crawford, C. and Tilbury, C. (2007) 'Child protection workers' perspectives on the school-to-work transition for young people in care', *Australian Social Work*, 60(3): 308–20.

Cressey, D. (1953) 'The criminal violation of financial trust', *American Sociological Review*, 15(6): 738–43.

Creswell, J. (1994) *Reseach Design. Qualitative and Quantitative Approaches*. Thousand Oaks, London, New Delhi: Sage Publications.

Creswell, J. (2007) *Qualitative Inquiry and Research Design*. Thousand Oaks: Sage Publications.

Creswell, J. and Plano Clark, V.L. (2006) *Designing and Conducting Mixed Methods Research*. Thousand Oaks, CA: Sage.

Creswell, J., Plano Clark, V.L., Gutmann, M.L. and Hanson, W.E. (2003) 'Advanced mixed methods research designs', in A. Tashakkori and C. Teddlie (eds), *Handbook of Mixed Methods in Social and Behavioral Research*. Thousand Oaks, CA: Sage. pp. 209–40.

Cretzmeyer, M., Sarrazin, M.V., Huber, D.L., Block, R.I. and Hall, J.A. (2003) 'Treatment of methamphetamine abuse: Research findings and clinical directions', *Journal of Substance Abuse Treatment*, 24: 267–77.

Crinall, K. (1999) 'Offending mothers: Theorising in a feminist minefield', in B. Pease and J. Fook (eds), *Transforming Social Work Practice. Postmodern Critical Perspectives*. London: Routledge.

Crisp, B. (2000) 'A history of Australian social work practice research', *Research on Social Work Practice*, 10(2): 179–94.

Croft, S. and Beresford, P. (1984) 'Patch and participation: The case for citizen research', *Social Work Today* (17th September), pp. 18–24.

Croft S. and Beresford P. (2002) 'Service users' perspectives', in M. Davies (ed.), *Companion to Social Work*, 2nd Edn., Oxford: Blackwell.

Croft, S., Beresford, P. and Adshead, L. (2005) 'What service users want from specialist palliative care social work – findings from a participatory research project', in J. Parker (ed.), *Aspects of Social Work and Palliative Care*. Trowbridge, Wiltshire: Cromwell Press, pp. 20–37.

Cronbach, L. (1982) *Designing Evaluations of Educational and Social Programs*. San Francisco: Jossey–Bass.

Cronbach, L., Ambron, S., Dornbusch, S., Hess, R., Hornik, R., Phillips, D., Walker, D. and Weiner, S. (1980) *Toward Reform of Program Evaluation*. San Francisco: Jossey–Bass.

Cross, R. (1982) 'The Duhem-Quine Thesis, Lakatos, and the appraisal of theories in macroeconomics', *The Economic Journal*, 92(366): 320–40.

Crowther, R.E., Marshall, M., Bond, G.R. and Huxley, P. (2001) 'Helping people with severe mental illness to return to work: A systematic review', *British Medical Journal*, 322(7280): 204–8.

CSWE (2008) 'Minority fellowship programs'. Available at: http://www.cswe.org/CSWE/scholarships/fellowship/. Last accessed 21 May 2008.

Cuipers, P., Brannmark, J. and Van Straten, A. (2008) 'Psychological treatment of postpartum depression: A meta-analysis', *Journal of Clinical Psychology*, 64(1): 103–18.

Cummings, J.N. and Kiesler, S. (2005) 'Collaborative research across disciplinary and organizational boundaries', *Social Studies of Science*, 35(5): 703–22.

Cwikel, J.G. and Behar, L.C. (1999) 'Organizing social work services with adult cancer patients: Integrating empirical research', *Social Work in Health Care*, 28(3): 55–76.

DHSS (1985) *Social Work Decision in Child Care: Recent Research Findings and their Implications*. London: HMSO.

DoH (1995) *Child Protection: Messages from Research*. London: HMSO.

Dadds, M. and Hart, S. (2001) *Doing Practitioner Research Differently*. London: Routledge.

Dalrymple, J. and Burke, B. (2006) *Anti-Oppressive Practice: Social Care and the Law*. Buckingham: Open University Press.

Daly, A., McNamara, J., Ianton, R., Harding, A. and Yap, M. (2007) *Indicators of Risk of Social Exclusion for Australia's Children: An Analysis by State and Age Group*. Australia: National Centre for Social and Economic Modelling (NATSEM), University of Canberra.

Damasio, A.R. (1994) *Descartes' Error: Emotion, Reason and the Human Brain*. New York: Avon Books.

Darke, P.A. (2004) 'The changing face of representations of disability in the media', in J. Swain, S. French, C. Barnes and C. Thomas (eds), *Disabling Barriers – Enabling Environments*, 2nd Edn., London: Sage.

Darlington, Y., Feeney, J. and Rixon, K. (2005) 'Practice challenges at the intersection of child protection and mental health', *Child and Family Social Work*, 10(3): 239–47.

Datta, L. (2000) 'Seriously seeking fairness: Strategies for crafting non-partisan evaluations in a partisan world', *American Journal of Evaluation*, 21(1): 1–14.

Dausien, B., Hanses, A., Inowlocki, L. and Riemann, G. (2008) 'The analysis of professional practice, the self-reflection of practitioners, and their way of doing things. Resources of biography analysis and other interpretative approaches' [8 paragraphs]. *Forum Qualitative Sozialforschung/ Forum: Qualitative Social Research*, 9 (1), Art. 61. Available at: http://www.qualitative-research. net/fqs-texte/1-08/08-1-61-e.htm. Last accessed 8 March 2008.

Davies, H.T.O., Nutley, S.M. and Smith, P.C. (2000) *What Works? Evidence-Based Policy and Practice in Public Services*. Bristol: Policy Press.

Davies, J.M., Globerman, J., Mullings, D. and White, J.J. (2003) 'Thriving in program management environments: The case of social work in hospitals', *Social Work in Health Care*, 38(1): 1–18.

Davies, M. (1969) *Probationers and their Social Environment*. London: HMSO.

Davies, P., Newcomer, K. and Soydan, H. (2006) 'Government as structural context for evaluation', in I. Shaw, J. Greene and M. Mark (eds), *Sage Handbook of Evaluation*. London: Sage Publications, pp. 163–83.

Dawes, A. and Donald, D. (2000) 'Improving children's chances: Developmental theory and effective interventions in community contexts', in D. Donald, A. Dawes and J. Louw (eds), *Addressing Childhood Adversity*. Cape Town, SA: David Philip, pp. 1–25.

Day, K. and Jancar, J. (1994) 'Mental and physical health and ageing in mental handicap: A review', *Journal of Intellectual Disability Research*, 38(3): 241–56.

Day, P. (1981) *Social Work and Social Control*. London: Tavistock.

D'Cruz, H. and Jones, M. (2004) *Social Work Research: Ethical and Political Contexts*. London: Sage.

de Anda, D. (ed.) (1997) *Controversial Issues in Multiculturalism*. Boston: Allyn and Bacon.

De Montigny, G.A.J. (1995) *Social Working: An Ethnography of Front Line Practice*. Toronto: University of Toronto Press.

Decuir, J.T. and Dixson, A.D. (2004) '"So when it comes out, they aren't that surprised that it is there": Using critical race theory as a tool of analysis of race and racism in education', *Educational Researcher*, 33(5): 26–31.

Deegan, M. (1988) *Jane Addams and the Men of the Chicago School, 1892–1918*. New Brunswick, NJ: Transaction, Inc.

Degener, T. (2005) 'Disability discrimination law: A global comparative approach', in A. Lawson and C. Gooding (eds), *Disability Rights in Europe: From Theory to Practice*. Oxford: Hart Publishing.

Delanty, G. (1997) *Social Science Beyond Constructivism and Relativism*. Buckingham: Open University.

Dellgran, P. and Höjer, S. (2003) 'Topics and epistemological positions in Swedish social work research', *Social Work Education*, 22(6): 565–75.

Delva, J., Allgood, J., Morrell, R. and McNeece, C.A. (2002) 'A state-wide follow-up study of alcohol and illegal drug use treatment', *Research on Social Work Practice*, 12: 642–52.

Delva, J., Mathiesen, S.G. and Kamata, A. (2001) 'Use of illegal drugs among mothers across racial/ethnic backgrounds in the U.S.: A multi-level analysis of individual and community level influences', *Ethnicity and Disease*, 11: 614–25.

Delva, J., Wallace, J.M., Bachman, J., O'Malley, P.M., Johnston, L.D. and Schulenberg, J. (in press) 'The epidemiology of alcohol, cigarettes, and illicit drugs among Mexican American, Puerto Rican, Cuban American, and other Latin American youths in the US: 1991–2002', *American Journal of Public Health*.

Denzin, N. (1989) *Interpretive Interactionism*. Newbury Park, CA: Sage.

Denzin, N. (2000) 'Social work in the 7th moment', *Qualitative Social Work*, 1(1): 25–38.

Denzin, N. (2002) 'Social work in the seventh moment', *Qualitative Social Work*, 1(1): 25–38.

Denzin, N. and Giardina, M. (2008) 'Introduction: The elephant in the living room or advancing the conversation about the politics of evidence', in N. Denzin and M. Giardina (eds) *Qualitative Inquiry and the Politics of Evidence*. Walnut Creek, CA: Left Coast Press.

Denzin, N. and Lincoln, Y. (eds) (2005) *The Sage Handbook of Qualitative Research*, 3rd Edn., Thousand Oaks, CA: Sage.

Department of Health (1999) *National Service Framework for Mental Health*. London: Department of Health.

Department of Health (2006) *Our Health, Our Care, Our Say: A new Direction for Community Services*, Cm 6737. London: TSO.

Department for Education and Skills and Department of Health (2006) *Options for Excellence: Building the Social Care Workforce of the Future*. London: Department of Health.

DePoy, E., Hartman, A. and Haslett, D. (1999) 'Critical action research: A model for social work knowing', *Social Work*, 44(6): 560.

DeRoos, Y.S. (1994) 'Are practitioner intuition and empirical evidence equally valid sources of professional knowledge?', in W.W. Hudson and P.S. Nurius (eds), *Controversial Issues in Social Work Research*. Boston: Allyn and Bacon.

Devore, W. and Schlesinger, E.G. (1996) *Ethnic-Sensitive Social Work Practice*. Boston: Allyn and Bacon.

Dewe, B. (2005) 'Von der Wissenstransferforschung zur Wissenstransformation: Vermittlungsprozesse – Bedeutungsveränderungen', in G. Antos and S. Wichter (eds) *Wissenstransfer durch Sprache als gesellschaftliches Problem*. Peter Lang Europäischer Verlag der Wissenschaften.

Dewe, B., Ferchhoff, W. and Radtke, F.-O. (1992) 'Das "Professionswissen" von Pädagogen. Ein wissenstheoretischer Rekonstruktionsversuch', in B. Dewe, W. Ferchhoff and F.-O. Radtke (eds) *Erziehen als Profession. Zur Logik professionellen Handelns in pädagogischen Feldern*. Opladen: Leske+Budrich.

Dewe, B., Ferchhoff, W., Scherr, A. and Stüwe, G. (1993) *Professionelles soziales Handeln. Soziale Arbeit im Spannungsfeld zwischen Theorie und Praxis*. Weinheim, München: Juventa.

Dewe, B. and Otto, H.-U. (2002) 'Reflexive Sozialpädagogik. Grundstrukturen eines neuen Typs dienstleistungsorientierten Professionshandelns', in W. Thole (ed.), *Grundriss Soziale Arbeit. Ein einführendes Handbuch.* Opladen: Leske+Budrich.

Dewey, J. (1929) *The Sources of a Science of Education*. New York: Liveright.

DfES (2004) *Every Child Matters: Change for Children*. London: The Stationery Office.

DH (Department of Health) (2005) *Research Governance Framework for Health and Social Care*, 2nd Edn., London: Department of Health.

Dick, B. (2007) 'Action research as an enhancement of natural problem solving', *International Journal of Action Research*, 3: 149–67.

Dickersin, K., Scherer, R. and Lefebvre, C. (1994) 'Identifying relevant studies for systematic reviews', *British Medical Journal*, 309: 1286–91.

Diekmann, A. (1995) *Empirische Sozialforschung. Grundlagen, Methoden, Anwendungen*. Hamburg: Reinbek b.

Diner, S.J. (1977) 'Scholarship in the quest for social welfare: A fifty-year history of the *Social Service Review'*, *Social Service Review*, 51(1): 1–66.

Diner, S.J. (1997) 'Department and discipline: The development of sociology at the University of Chicago, 1892–1920', in K. Plummer (ed.), *The Chicago School: Critical Assessments*. London: Routledge.

Dingwall, R. (1997) 'Conclusion: The moral discourse of interactionism', in G. Miller and R. Dingwall (eds), *Context and Method in Qualitative Research*. London: Sage.

Dixon Woods, M., Bonas, S., Booth, A., Jones, D.R., Miller, T., Sutton, A.J., Shaw, R.L., Smith, J.A. and Young, B. (2006) 'How can systematic reviews incorporate qualitative research? A critical perspective', *Qualitative Research*, 6(1): 27–44.

DOAJ (Directory of Open Access Journals) (2008) Lund University Libraries Head Office. Available at: http://www.doaj.org/

Dobash, R.E. and Dobash, R.P. (1979) *Women, Violence and Social Change*. New York: The Free Press.

Dobash, R.E., Dobash, R.P. and Cavanagh, K. (1985) 'The contact between battered women and social change agencies', in J. Pahl (ed.), *Private Violence and Public Policy: The Needs of Battered Women and the Response of the Public Services*. London: Routledge and Kegan Paul.

Docherty, D. and McColl, M.A. (2003) 'Illness stories: Themes emerging through narrative', *Social Work in Health Care*, 37(1): 19–39.

DoH (Department of Health, Department of Employment, Department for Education and Skills and the Home Office) (2000) *Framework for the Assessment of Children in Need and their Families*. London: The Stationery Office.

Dolan, P., Canavan, J. and Pinkerton, J. (2006) *Family Support and Reflective Practice*. London: Jessica Kingsley.

Dominelli, L. (2002) 'Anti-oppressive practice in context', in R. Adams, L. Dominelli and M. Payne (eds) *Social Work: Themes, Issues and Critical Debates*, 2nd Edn., Basingstoke: Palgrave.

Dominelli, L. (2003) *Anti-Oppressive Social Work Theory and Practice*. Basingstoke: Palgrave Macmillan.

Dominelli, L. (2005) 'Social work research: Contested knowledge for practice', in R. Adams, L. Dominelli and M. Payne (eds), *Social Work Futures: Crossing Boundaries, Transforming Practice*. Hampshire: Palgrave Macmillan, pp. 223–36.

Donner, S. and Batliwalla, B. (2005) 'Two social workers' experience with late onset blindness: An intersubjective perspective', *Smith College Studies in Social Work*, 75(1): 49–64.

Donovan, J., Mills, N., Smith, M., Brindle, L., Jacobs, A., Peters, T., Frankel, S., Neal, D., Hamdy, F., for the Protect Study Group (2002) 'Improving the design and conduct of randomized trials by embedding them in qualitative research: ProtecT (prostate testing for cancer and treatment) study', *British Medical Journal*, 325: 766–9.

Donzelot, J. (1979) *The Policing of Families: Welfare versus the State*. London: Hutchinson and Co.

Donzelot, J. (1988) 'The promotion of the social', *Economy and Society*, 17(3): 395–427.

Dorfman, R.A. (1996) *Clinical Social Work: Definition, Practice, and Vision*. Psychology Press.

Doughty, C. and Tse, S. (2005) *The Effectiveness of Service User-Run or Service User-Led Mental Health Services for People with Mental Illness: A Systematic Literature Review*. Wellington, NZ: Mental Health Commission, NZ.

Dowden, C. and Andrews, D. (2004) 'The importance of staff practice in delivering effective correctional treatment: A meta-analytic review of core correctional practice', *International Journal of Offender Therapy and Comparative Criminology*, 48(2): 203–14.

Doyle, R. (1996) 'Breaking the solitudes to improve service for ethnic groups: Action research strategies', in J. Fook (ed.), *The Reflective Researcher*. St. Leonards, Australia: Allen and Unwin, pp. 55–69.

Drake, B., Hovmand, P., Jonson-Reid, M. and Zayas, L.H. (2007) 'Adopting and teaching evidenec-based practice in master's-level social work programs', *Journal of Social Work Education*, 43(4): 431–46.

Drakeford, M. and Vanstone, M. (1996) *Beyond Offending Behaviour*. Aldershot: Arena.

Drury-Hudson, J. (1999) 'Decision making in child protection: The use of theoretical, empirical and procedural knowledge by novices and experts and implications for fieldwork placement', *British Journal of Social Work*, 29: 147–69.

Dube, T., Hurst, R., Light, R. and Malinga, J. (2006) 'Promoting inclusion? Disabled people, legislation and public policy', in B. Albert (ed.), *In or Out of the Mainstream: Lessons from Research on Disability and Development Cooperation*. Leeds: The Disability Press.

Dubois D., Holloway B., Valentine J. and Cooper H. (2002) 'Effectiveness of mentoring programs for youth: A meta-analytic review', *American Journal of Community Psychology*, 30(2): 157–97.

Dullea, K. (2006) 'Women shaping participatory research to their own needs', *Community Development Journal*, 41(1): 65–74.

Dullea, K. and Mullender, A. (1999) 'Evaluation and empowerment', in I. Shaw and J. Lishman (eds), *Evaluation and Social Work Practice*. Thousand Oaks, CA: Sage, pp. 81–100.

Dullemen, C. (2007) V. *Intergenerational Solidarity: Strengthening Economic and Social Ties*. NY: United Nations.

Dunbar, C. Jr. (2008) 'Critical race theory and indigenous methodologies', in Norman K. Denzin and Yvonna S. Lincoln (eds), *Critical Race Theories and Indigenous Methodologies*. Thousand Oaks, CA: Sage, pp. 85–100.

Duncan, S. and Harrop, A. (2006) 'A user perspective on research quality', *International Journal of Research Methodology*, 9(2): 159–74.

Dunn, L.M. and Dunn, L.M. (1997) *Peabody Picture Vocabulary Test*, 3rd Edn., Circle Pines, MN: American Guidance Service.

Eadie, T. and Lymbery, M. (2002) 'Understanding and working in welfare organisations: Helping students survive the workplace', *Social work Education*, 21(5): 515–27.

Eagleton, T. (2003) *After Theory*. London: Allen Lane.

Economist, The (2007, August 25) 'Do not ask or do not answer?', *The Economist*, pp. 69–71.

Edelman, M. (1988) *Constructing the Political Spectacle*. Chicago: University of Chicago Press.

Edleson, J.L. (1999) 'The overlap between child maltreatment and woman battering', *Violence Against Women*, 5(2): 134–54.

Edwards, A. (1987) 'Male violence in feminist theory: An analysis of the changing conceptions of sex/gender violence and male dominance', in J. Hanmer and M. Maynard (eds), *Women, Violence and Social Control*. Basingstoke: Macmillan.

Egger, M., Davey-Smith, G. and Altman, D. (2001) *Systematic Reviews in Health Care: Meta-analysis in Context*, 2nd Edn., London: BMJ Books.

Egger, M., Davey-Smith, G., Schneider, M. and Minder, C. (1997) 'Bias in meta-analysis detected by a simple, graphical test', *British Medical Journal*, 315: 629–34.

Egger, M. and Davey Smith, G. (1998) 'Meta-analysis: Bias in location and selection of studies'. *British Medical Journal*, 316(7124): 61–6.

Ehlers, L. (2007) 'Probation in Africa', in R. Canton and D. Hancock (eds), *Dictionary of Probation and Offender Management*. Cullompton: Willan. pp. 228–9.

Ehrenreich, J. (1985) *The Altruistic Imagination: A History of Social Work and Social Policy in the United States*. Cornell University Press.

Eisler, I. (2002) 'Comment – The scientific practitioner and family therapy: A way forward, a strait-jacket or a distraction?', *Journal of Family Therapy*, 24: 125–33.

Elias, N. (1978) *What is Sociology?* Translated by S. Mennel and G. Morrisey. London: Heinemann.

Ell, K. (1996) 'Social work and health care practice and policy: A psychosocial research agenda', *Social Work*, 41: 583–93.

Ellis, C., Bochner, A., Denzin, N., Lincoln, Y., Morse, J., Pelias, R. and Richardson, L. (2008) 'Talking and thinking about qualitative research', *Qualitative Inquiry*, 14(2): 254–84.

Ellis, K. (2007) 'Direct payments and social work practice: The significance of "street-level bureaucracy" in determining eligibility', *British Journal of Social Work*, 37: 405–22.

Emerson, Robert M., Fretz, Rachel I. and Shaw, Linda L. (1995) *Writing Ethnographic Fieldnotes*. Chicago and London: The University of Chicago Press.

Engel, C. (1992) 'Linköping Collaborative Centre Workshop 5–6 December, 1991', *Journal of Interprofessional Care*, 6(2): 171–2.

Engel, R. and Schutt, R. (2005) *The Practice of Research in Social Work*. Thousand Oaks, CA: Sage.

Engelhardt, J., McClive-Reed, K., Toseland, R., Smith, T., Larson, D. and Tobin, D. (2006) 'Effects of a program for coordinated care of advanced illlness on patients, surrogates, and healthcare costs: A randomized trial'. *The American Journal of Managed Care*, *12(*2): 93–100.

England, H. (1986) *Social Work as Art: Making Sense for Good Practice*. London: Allen and Unwin.

Epstein, I. and Blumenfield, S. (eds) (2002) *Clinical Data-Mining in Practice-Based Research: Social Work in Hospital Settings*. New York: Haworth Press.

Erath, T., Littlechild, B. and Vornanen, R. (eds) (2005) *Social Work in Europe – Descriptions, Analysis and Theories*. Stassfurt: BK Verlag.

Eraut, M. (1994) *Developing Professional Knowledge and Competence*. London: The Falmer Press.

Erickson, F. (2005) 'Arts, humanities, and sciences in educational research and social engineering in federal education policy', *Teachers College Record*, 107(1): 4–9.

Erikson, F. (2008) 'What anthropology of education research could say in current policy discourse'. Paper presented at the 2008 Congress of Qualitative Inquiry at the University of Illinois, Urbana, IL.

Ermarth, F. (1965) 'Political science and sociology in the USSR II', *Open Society Archives*. Available at: http://files.osa.ceu.huholdings/330/8/3/text/62-4-127.shtml. Last accessed 19 August 2008.

Escobar, A. (1995) *Encountering Development: The Making and Unmaking of the Third World*. Princeton: Princeton University Press.

ESRC (Economic and Social Research Council) (2005a) *Postgraduate Training Guidelines*. Available at: http://www.esrc.ac.uk/ESRCInfoCentre/opportunities/postgraduate/.

ESRC (Economic and Social Research Council) (2005b) *Research Ethics Framework*. Swindon: ESRC.

Etowa, J., Bernard, W.T., Oyinsan, B. and Clow, B. (2007) 'Participatory Action Research (PAR): An approach for improving Black women's health in rural and remote communities', *Journal of Transcultural Nursing*, 18: 349–59.

European Commission (2001) 'Structural indicators'. Communication from the Commission (2001) 619 final.

Evaluate Diabetes Self-Management Support Interventions, *AJPM*, 30(1): 67–73.

Evans, C. and Fisher, M. (1999) 'User controlled research and empowerment', in W. Shera and L.M. Wells (eds), *Empowerment Practice in Social Work: Developing Richer Conceptual Frameworks*. Toronto: Canadian Scholars' Press Inc, pp. 348–69.

Evans, S., Banerjee, S., Leese, M. and Huxley, P. (2007) 'The impact of mental illness on quality of life: A comparison of severe mental illness, common mental disorder and healthy population samples', *Quality of Life Research*, 16(1): 17–29.

Evans, S., Gately, C., Huxley, P., Smith, A. and Banerjee, S. (2005) 'Assessment of quality of life in later life: Development and validation of the QuiLL', *Quality of Life Research*, 14(5): 1291–300.

Evans, S. and Huxley, P. (2005) 'Adaptation, response shift and quality of life ratings in mentally well and unwell groups', *Quality of Life Research*, 14(7): 1719–32.

Evans, R. and Plows, A. (2007) 'Listening without prejudice? Re-discovering the value of the disinterested citizen', *Social Studies of Science*, 37(6): 827–54.

Evenhuis, H.M., Mul, M., Lemaire, E.K.G. and Wijs, J.P.M. (1997) 'Diagnosis of sensory impairment in people with intellectual disability in general practice', *Journal of Intellectual Disability Research*, 41(5): 422–9.

Evenhuis, H.M., Theunissen, M., Denkers, I., Verschuure, H. and Kemme, H. 'Prevalence of visual and hearing impairment in a Dutch institutionalized population with intellectual disability', *Journal of Intellectual Disability Research*, 45(5): 457–64.

Everitt, A., Hardiker, P., Littlewood, J. and Mullender, A. (1992) *Applied Research for Better Practice*. London: Macmillan.

Evers, A., Schultz, A.D. and Wiesner, C. (2006) 'Local policy networks in the programme *Social City* – a case in point for new forms of governance in the field of local social work and urban planning', *European Journal of Social Work*, 9(2): 183–200.

Every, D. (2006) *The Politics of Representation: A Discursive Analysis of Refugee Advocacy in the Australian Parliament*. Unpublished PhD thesis. Adelaide: University of Adelaide.

Fabricant, M.B. and Fisher, R. (2002) 'Settlement houses under siege: The struggle to sustain community organizations in New York City', NY: Columbia University Press.

Facchini, C., Campananini, A. and Lorenz, W. (2007) 'Research on the current state of the social work profession in Italy', *The Social Work and Society News Magazine* (*SocMag*). Available at: http://socmag.net/?p57, 14/03/2007. Last accessed 3 March 2008.

Fagerhaugh, S. and Strauss, A. (1977) *Politics of Pain Management. Staff–Patient Interaction*. Menlo Park, CA: Addison-Wesley Publishing Company.

Fahl, R. and Markand, M. (1999) 'The project "analysis of psychological practice" or: An attempt at connecting psychology critique and practice research', *Outlines*, 1: 73–98.

Fahmi, K. (2004) 'Social work practice and research as an emancipatory process', in L. Davies and P. Leonard (eds), *Social Work in a Corporate Era: Practices of Power and Resistance*. Burlington, VT: Ashgate Publishing Ltd, pp. 144–59.

Fahs, M.C. and Wade, K. (1996) 'An economic analysis of two models of hospital care for AIDS patients: Implications for hospital discharge planning', *Social Work in Health Care*, 22(4): 21–34.

Fairclough, N. (2001) *Language and Power*, 2nd Edn., Essex, UK: Pearson.

Faller, K. and Ortega, R. (2008) Reprinted from Children's Bureau Express, February 2007, Workforce Retention in Michigan. Available at: http://cbex-press.acf.hhs.gov/index.cfm?event=website.viewArticlesandissueid=80§ionid=1andarticleid=1270. Last accessed 12 January 2008.

Fals-Borda, O. and Mohammed, R.A. (1991) *Action Knowledge: Breaking the Monopoly with Participatory Action Research*. New York: The Apex Press.

Family Health International (2004) 'Research ethics training curriculum for community representatives'. Available at: http://www.fhi.org/en/RH/Training/trainmat/ethicscurr/retccr.htm.

Fanshawe, P. (2002) 'Seen and heard: Using research findings to develop services', *MCC: Building Knowledge for Integrated Care*, 10(3): 23–7.

Fanshel, D. (ed.) (1980) *Future of Social Work Research*. Washington, DC: NASW.

Fargion, S. (2003) 'Images of contract. An empirical study of the use of theory in practice', *British Journal of Social Work*, 33(4): 517–33.

Fargion, S. (2007) 'Theory and practice: A matter of words. Language, knowledge and professional community in social work', *Social Work and Society*, 5 (1). Available at: http://www.socwork.net/2007/1/articles/fargion

Farmer, P. (2003) *Pathologies of Power: Health, Human Rights and the War on the Poor*. Berkeley: University of California Press.

Farrall, S. (2002) *Rethinking What Works with Offenders: Probation, Social Context and Desistance from Crime*. Cullompton: Willan Publishing.

Farrall, S. and Calverley, A. (2006) *Understanding Desistance from Crime: Theoretical Directions in Rehabilitation and Resettlement*. Maidenhead: Open University Press.

Farran, C.J., Miller, B.H., Kaufman, J.E., Donner, E. and Fogg, L. (1999) 'Finding meaning through caregiving: Development of an instrument for family caregivers of persons with Alzheimer's disease', *Journal of Clinical Psychology*, 55(9): 1107–25.

Farrington, D. (2002) 'Developmental criminology and risk-focussed prevention', in M. Maguire, R. Morgan and R. Reiner (eds), *The Oxford Handbook of Criminology*, 3rd Edn., Oxford: Oxford University Press, pp. 657–701.

Farrington, D.P. (2003) 'A short history of randomized experiments in criminology: A meagre feast', *Evaluation Review*, 27(3): 218–27.

Farrington, D.P. (ed) (2005) *Integrated Developmental and Life-Course Theories of Offending. Advances in*

Criminological Theory, Volume 14. Brunswick: Transaction Publishers.

Faulkner, A.L.S. (2000) *Strategies for Living: A Report of User-Led Research into People's Strategies for Living with Mental Distress.* London: Mental Health Foundation.

Fawcett, B. (2000) 'Researching disability: Meanings, interpretations and analysis', in B. Fawcett, B. Featherstone, J. Fook and A. Rossiter (eds), *Practice and Research in Social Work: Post-Modern Feminist Perspectives.* London: Routledge.

Fawcett, B. and Featherstone, B. (1998) 'Quality assurance and evaluation in social work in a postmodern era', in J. Carter (ed.), *Postmodernity and the Fragmentation of Welfare.* London: Routledge.

Feeley, M. (2002) 'Crime, social order and the rise of neo-Conservative politics', *Theoretical Criminology*, 7(1): 111–30.

Feeley, M. and Simon, J. (1992) 'The new penology: Notes on the emerging strategy of corrections and its implications', *Criminology*, 30: 449–74.

Feeley, M. and Simon, J. (1994) 'Actuarial justice: The emerging new criminal law', in D. Nelken (ed.), *The Futures of Criminology.* London: Sage. pp. 173–201.

Feinstein, L. and Sabates, R. (2006) *Predicting Adult Life Outcomes from Earlier Signals: Identifying Those at Risk*, working paper. Available at www.number-10. gov.uk/files/pdf/PMSU-report.pdf. Last accessed 20 September 2006.

Felce, D. and Emerson, E. (2001) 'Living with support in a home in the community: Predictors of behavioral development and household and community activity', *Mental Retardation and Developmental Disabilities Research Reviews*, 7(2): 75–83.

Felce, D., Lowe, K., Perry, J., Baxter, H., Jones, E., Hallam, A. and Beecham, J. (1998) 'Service support to people in Wales with severe intellectual disability and the most severe challenging behaviours: Processes, outcomes and costs', *Journal of Intellectual Disability Research*, 42(5): 390–408.

Feld, W. (1925) 'Die Fürsorge im Hochschulunterricht und als Wissenschaft', *Schweizerische Zeitschrift für Gemeinnützigkeit*, 64: 424–35.

Feltman, C. (2005) 'Evidence-based psychotherapy and counselling in the UK: Critique and alternatives', *Journal of Contemporary Psychotherapy*, 35(1): 131–43.

Ferdinand, J., Pearson, G., Rowe, M. and Worthington, F. (2007) 'A different kind of ethics', *Ethnography*, 8(4): 519–43.

Ferguson, I. and Lavalette, M. (2004) 'Beyond power discourse: Alienation and social work', *British Journal of Social Work*, 34: 297–312.

Ferguson, I. and Lavalette, M. (2007) '"Social worker as agitator": The radical kernel of British social work', in M. Lavalette and I. Ferguson (eds), *International Social Work and the Radical Tradition.* Birmingham: Ventura Press, pp. 11–31.

Fetterman, D., Kaftarian, S. and Wandersman, A. (1996) *Empowerment Evaluation: Knowledge and Tools for Self Assessment and Accountability.* Thousand Oaks, CA: Sage.

Field, F. (1996) *Stakeholder Welfare.* London: IEA Health and Welfare Unit.

Fielding, M. (2001) 'Learning organization, or learning community: A critique of Senge', *Reason in Practice*, 1(2): 17–29.

Finch, J. (1986) *Research and Policy: The Uses of Qualitative Methods in Social and Educational Research.* London: Falmer Press.

Fine, M., Weis, L., Weseen, S. and Wong, L. (2003) 'For whom? Qualitative research, representations and social responsibilities', in N.K. Denzin and Y.S. Lincoln (eds), *The Landscape of Qualitative Research: Theories and Issues.* Thousand Oaks: Sage, pp. 167–207.

Finkel, A. (2006) *Social Policy and Practice in Canada: A History.* Waterloo, ON: Wilfrid Laurier University.

Finn, J.L., Jacobson, M. and Campana, J.D. (2004) 'Participatory research, popular education and popular theatre', in C.D. Garvin, L.M. Gutiérrez and M.J. Galinsky (eds), *Handbook of Social Work with Groups.* New York: Haworth Press, pp. 326–43.

Finnish National University Network for Social Work 'Academic social work education in Finland', SOSNET. Available at: http://www.sosnet. fi/?deptid=22096. Last accessed 11 December 2008.

Firestone, T. (1990) 'Accommodation: Toward a paradigm-praxis dialectic', in E. Guba (ed.), *The Paradigm Dialog.* Newbury Park, CA: Sage.

Fischer, J. (1973) 'Is casework effective? A review', *Social Work*, 18(1): 5–20.

Fischer, J. (1976) *The Effectiveness of Social Casework.* Springfield, IL: Charles C. Thomas.

Fischer, J. (1981) 'The social work revolution', *Social Work*, 26: 199–209.

Fischer, J. (1984) 'Revolution, schmevolution: Is social work changing or not?', *Social Work*, 29(1): 71–4.

Fischer, J. (1990) 'Problems and issues in meta-analyses', in L. Videka-Sherman and W. Reid (eds), *Advances in Clinical Social Work Research.* Silver Spring, MD: National Association of Social Workers, pp. 297–325.

Fischer, J. (1993) 'Empirically based practice: The end of ideology?', in M. Bloom (ed.), *Single System*

Designs in the Social Services: Issues and Options for the 1990s. New York: Haworth, pp. 19–64.

Fisher, M. (1999) 'Social work research, and social work knowledge and the Research Assessment Exercise', in B. Broad (ed.), *The Politics of Social Work Research and Evaluation.* Birmingham Venture Press.

Fisher, M. (2002a) 'The Social Care Institute for Excellence: The role of a national institute in developing knowledge and practice in social care', *Social Work and Social Sciences Review,* 10(2): 6–34.

Fisher, M. (2002b) 'The role of service users in problem formulation and technical aspects of social research', *Social Work Education,* 21(3): 305–12.

Fisher, M. and Marsh, P. (2001) 'Social work research and the 2001 Research Assessment Exercise: An initial overview', *Social Work Education,* 22(1): 71–80.

Fleck, L. (1979) *Genesis and Development of Scientific Fact.* Chicago: University of Chicago Press.

Flexner, A. (1915) *Is social work a profession?* Paper presented at the National Conference of Charities and Correction, Chicago.

Flexner, A. (2001 [1915]) 'Is social work a profession?', *Research on Social Work Practice,* 11(2): 152–65.

Flick, U. (2000) 'Qualitative inquiries into social representations of health', *Journal of Health Psychology,* 5(3): 315–24.

Flick, U. and Röhnsch, G. (2007) 'Idealization and neglect: Health concepts of homeless adolescents', *Journal of Health Psychology,* 12(5): 737–49.

Flicker, S., Travers, R., Guta, A., McDonald, S. and Meagher, A. (2007) 'Ethical dilemmas in community-based participatory research: Recommendations for institutional review boards', *Journal of Urban Health: Bulletin of the New York Academy of Medicine,* 84(4): 478–94.

Floersch, J. (2002) *Meds, Money, and Manners.* New York: Columbia University Press.

Floersch, J. (2003) 'The subjective experience of youth psychotropic treatment', *Social Work in Mental Health,* 1(4): 51–69.

Flood, M. and Pease, B. (2005) 'Undoing men's privilege and advancing gender equality in public sector institutions', *Policy and Society,* 24(4): 119–38.

Flood, T. (2005) '"Food" or "Thought"? The social model and the majority world', in C. Barnes and G. Mercer (eds), *The Social Model of Disability: Europe and the Majority World.* Leeds: The Disability Press.

Folkard, S. (1974) *IMPACT.* London: HMSO.

Fook, J. (1996) *The Reflective Researcher: Social Workers' Theories of Practice Research.* Sydney: Allen and Unwin.

Fook, J. (2000a) *Social Work: Critical Theory and Practice.* London: Sage.

Fook, J. (2000b) 'Deconstructing and reconstructing professional expertise', in B. Fawcett, B. Featherstone, J. Fook and A. Rossiter (eds), *Practice and Research in Social Work: Post-Modern Feminist Perspectives.* London: Routledge.

Fook, J. (2001) 'Identifying expert social work: Qualitative practitioner research', in I. Shaw and N. Gould (eds), *Qualitative Research in Social Work.* London: Sage Publications.

Fook, J. (2002a) *Social Work: Critical Theory and Practice.* London: Sage Publications.

Fook, J. (2002b). 'Theorizing from practice: Towards an inclusive approach for social work research', *Qualitative Social Work,* 1(1): 79–95.

Fook, J. (2003) 'Social work research in Australia', *Journal of Social Work Education,* 22(1): 45–57.

Fook, J. (2004) 'What professionals need from research: Beyond evidence-based practice', in D. Smith (ed.) *Social Work and Evidence-Based Practice.* London: Jessica Kingsley.

Fook, J. and Askeland, G. (2007) 'Challenges of critical reflection: "Nothing ventured, nothing gained"', *Social Work Education,* 26(5): 1–11.

Fook, J. and Gardner, F. (2007) *Practising Critical Reflection. A Resource Handbook.* Maidenhead: Open University Press.

Fook, J., Ryan, M. and Hawkins, L. (2000) *Professional Expertise: Practice, Theory and Education for Working in Uncertainty.* London, Whiting and Birch.

Fordyce, W. (1990) 'Contingency management', in J. Bonica (ed.), *The Management of Pain.* Philadelphia, PA: Lea and Febiger, pp. 1702–9.

Fordyce, W. (1996) 'Chronic pain: The behavioral perspective', in M.J.M. Cohen and J.N. Campbell (eds), *Progress in Pain Research and Management,* Vol. 7. Seattle, WA: IASP Press, pp. 39–46.

Fortune, A. (1994) 'Ethnography in social work', in E. Sherman and W. Reid (eds), *Qualitative Research in Social Work.* New York: Columbia University Press.

Fortune, A. and Reid, W.J. (2005) *Research in Social Work,* New York: Columbia University press.

Fortune, R., McCallion, P., and Briar-Lawson, K. (in press) *Social Work Practice Research for 21st Century.* New York: Columbia University Press.

Fosu, G.B. (1994) 'Childhood morbidity and health services utilization: Cross-national comparisons of user-related factors from DHS data', *Social Science and Medicine,* 38(9): 1209–20.

Foucault, M. (1980) *Power/Knowledge: Selected Interviews and Other Writings 1972–1977.* Pantheon Books: New York.

France, A. and Utting, D. (2005) 'The paradigm of risk and protection-focussed prevention and its impact on services for children and families', *Children and Society*, 19(2): 77–90.

Frank, J.C. (2008) 'Addressing fidelity in evidence-based health promotion programs for older adults', *Journal of Applied Gerontology*, 27(1): 4–33.

Frank, J. et al. (2008) 'Addressing fidelity in evidence-based health promotion programs for older adults'. *Journal of Applied Gerontology*, 27(1): 4–33.

Franklin, B. and Parton, N. (2001) 'Press-ganged! Media reporting of social work and child abuse', in M. May, R. Page and E. Brunsdon (eds) *Understanding Social Problems: Issues in Social Policy*. Oxford: Blackwell.

Franklin, C. and Hopson, L.M. (2007) 'Facilitating the use of evidence-based practice in community organisations', *Journal of Social Work Education*, 43(4): 377–404.

Fraser, M. (ed.) (1997) *Risk and Resilience in Childhood: An Ecological Perspective*. Washington, DC: NASW Press.

Fraser, M. (2003) 'Intervention research is social work: A basis for evidence-based practice and practice guidelines', in A. Rosen and E.K. Proctor (eds), *Developing Practice Guidelines for Social Work Intervention – Issues, Methods, and Research Agenda*. New York: Columbia University Press. pp. 17–36.

Fraser, M. (2004) 'Intervention research in social work: Recent advances and continuing challenges', *Research on Social Work Practice*, 14(3): 210–22.

Fraser, M. (2005) *Conceptualizing, Designing and Testing Interventions in Social Work: Substantive and Methodological Issues*, OBSSR Summer Institute on Social and Behavioral Research Chapel Hill: University of North Carolina. Available at: http://209.85.173.132/search?q=cache: zUIELLHEY0UJ: ssw.unc.edu/jif/makingchoices/Presentations/Conceptualizing,%2520Designing,%2520and%2520Testing%2520Interventions.ppt+mark+fraser+conceptualsing+and+designing+social+interventionsandhl=enandct=clnkandcd=1andgl=us. Last accessed 12 October 2008.

Fraser, M.W. and Jenson, J. (2007) 'Call for papers, special issue on intervention research in social work', *Social Work Research*.

Freeman, M., de Marrais, K., Preissle, J., Roulston, K. and St. Pierre, Elizabeth A. (2007) 'Standards of evidence in qualitative research: An incitement to discourse', *Educational Researcher*, 36(1): 25–32.

Freeman, S.J. (2000) *Ethics: An Introduction to Philosophy and Practice*. Belmont CA: Wadsworth.

Freire, P. (1970) *Pedagogy of the Oppressed*. New York: Continuum International Publishing.

French, S. (2004) 'Enabling relationships in therapy practice', in J. Swain, J. Clark, K. Parry, S. French and F. Reynolds (eds), *Enabling Relationships in Health and Social Care*. Oxford: Butterworth–Heinemann.

French, S. and Swain, J. (2000) 'Good intentions: Reflecting on researching the lives and experiences of visually disabled people', *Annual Review of Critical Psychology*, 2: 35–54.

French, S. and Swain, J. (2007) 'User involvement in services for disabled people', in R. Jones and F. Jenkins (eds), *Management, Leadership and Development in the Allied Health Professions: An Introduction*. Abingdon: Radcliffe.

French, S. and Swain, J. (2008) 'Understanding disability: A guide for health professionals', Oxford: Elsevier.

French, S., Swain, J. and Reynolds, F. (2001) *Practical Research: A Guide for Therapists*, 2nd Edn., Oxford: Butterworth–Heinemann.

Friedman, J. and Weinberg, D. (1985) 'Experimental housing allowance program: History and overview', in L.H. Aitken and B.H. Kehrer (eds), *Evaluation Studies Review Annual*, Vol. 10. Beverly Hills: Sage Publications.

Friedrichs, J. (1990) *Methoden empirischer Sozialforschung*. Opladen: Westdeutscher Verlag.

Friendship, C., Street, R., Cann, J. and Harper, G. (2005) 'Introduction: The policy context and assessing the evidence', in G. Harper and C. Chitty (eds), *The Impact of Corrections on Re-offending: A Review of "What Works"'*, 2nd Edn., Home Office Research Study 291. London: Home Office, pp. 1–16.

Frohmann, L. (2005) 'The framing of safety project: Photographs and narratives by battered women', *Violence Against Women*, 11(11): 1396–419.

Fromme, E.K., Drach, L.L., Tolle, S.W., Ebert, P., Miller, P., Perrin, N. and Tilden, V.P. (2005) 'Men as caregivers at the end of life', *Journal of Palliative Medicine*, 8(6): 1167–75.

Fuchs, W. (1970–1971) 'Empirische Sozialforschung als politische Aktion', *Soziale Welt*, 21–22: 1–17.

Fudge-Schormans, A. (in preparation), *The Right or Responsibility of Inspection? Social Work, Photographic Re-presentation, and Intellectual and/or Developmental Disability*. Ph.D. Thesis in preparation. University of Toronto, Faculty of Social Work. 2009.

Fujiura, G.T. and Rutkowski-Kimitta, V. (2001) 'Counting disability', in G. Albrecht, K. Seelman and M. Bury (eds), *Handbook of Disability Studies*. Thousand Oaks: Sage.

Fulford, B. and Columbo, A. (2004) 'Six models of mental disorder: A study combining linguistic analysis and empirical methods', *Journal of Philosophy, Psychiatry and Psychology*, 11(4): 129–44.

Fuller, R. and Petch, A. (1995) *Practitioner Research: The Reflexive Social Worker*. Buckingham: Open University Press.

Fullilove, M. (1996) 'Psychiatric implications of displacement: Contributions from the psychology of place', *American Journal of Psychiatry*, 153: 1516–23.

Furlong, J. and Oancea, A. (2005) *Assessing Quality in Applied Educational Research*. Swindon: ESRC. Available at http://www.esrc.ac.uk/ESRCInfoCentre

Furminger, E. and Webber, M. (2009) 'The effect of crisis resolution and home treatment on assessments under the Mental Health Act 1983. An increased workload for Approved Social Workers?', *British Journal of Social Work*, 39(5). doi:10.1093/bjsw/bcm171

Furniss, J. (ed.) (1998) *A Guide to Effective Practice: Evidence Based Practice*. London: HM Inspectorate of Probation.

Gabbay, J. and le May, A. (2004) 'Evidence based guidelines or collectively constructed "mindlines?" Ethnographic study of knowledge management in primary care', *British Medical Journal*, 329(7473): 1013–19.

Gadamer, H. (2004) 'Teorian ylistys' ('Appraisal of theory') in H. Gadamer (ed.), *Hermeneutiikka. Ymmärtäminen tieteissä ja filosofiassa (Hermeneutics. Understanding in Science and Philosophy)*. Vastapaino, Tampere, pp. 152–72.

Galper, J. (1980) *Social Work Practice: A Radical Perspective*. Englewood Cliffs, NJ: Prentice Hall.

Gambrill, E. (1994) 'Priorities and obstacles in research on social work practice', *Research on Social Work Practice*, 4(3): 259–387.

Gambrill, E. (1999) 'Evidence-based practice: An alternative to authority-based practice', *Families in Society: The Journal of Contemporary Human Services*, 80: 341–50.

Gambrill E. (2000) 'The role of critical thinking in evidence-based social work', in P. Allen-Meares and C. Garvin (eds), *The Handbook of Social Work Direct Practice*. CA: Sage Publications.

Gambrill, E. (2001a) 'Social work: An authority based profession', *Research on Social Work Practice*, 11: 166–75.

Gambrill, E. (2001b) 'Educational policy and accreditation standards: Do they work for clients?', *Journal of Social Work Education*, 37: 226–39.

Gambrill, E. (2003) 'Evidence-based practice: Sea change or the Emperor's new clothes?', *Journal of Social Work Education*, 39(1): 1–18.

Gambrill, E. (2007) 'Views of evidence-based practice: Social workers' code of ethics and accreditation standards as guides for choice' *Journal of Social Work Education*, 43(3): 447–62.

Gandhi, S., Dilbaghi, M. and Raina, K. (2003) 'Rural women carry the load of fetching water', *Indian Journal of Social Work*, 64(1): 65–75.

Gardner, F. and Nunan, C. (2007) 'How to develop a research culture in a human services organization: Integrating research and practice with service and policy development', *Qualitative Social Work*, 6: 335–51.

Gardner, R. (2005) *Supporting Families: Child Protection in the Community*. Chichester: John Wiley and Sons.

Garity, J. (2006) 'Caring for a family member with Alzheimer's disease: Coping with caregiver burden post-nursing home placement'. *Journal of Gerontological Nursing*, 32(6): 345–56.

Garland, D. (1985) *Punishment and Welfare: A History of Penal Strategies*. Aldershot: Gower.

Garland, D. (1996) 'The limits of the sovereign state: Strategies of crime control in contemporary society', *British Journal of Criminology*, 36(4): 445–71.

Garland, D. (2001) *The Culture of Control: Crime and Social Order in Contemporary Society*. Oxford: Oxford University Press.

Garmezy, N. (1985) 'Stress-resistant children: The search for protective factors', in J.E. Stevenson (ed.), *Recent Research in Developmental Psychopathology*. New York: Pergamon Press, pp. 213–33.

Garner, Bryan R., Knight, Kevin, Flynn, Patrick M., Morey, Janis T. and Simpson, D. Dwayne (2007) 'Measuring offender attributes and engagement in treatment using the client evaluation of self and treatment', *Criminal Justice and Behavior*, 34(9): 1113–30.

Garrett, P. (2003a) *Remaking Social Work with Children and Families: A critical discussion on the 'Modernisation' of Social Care*. London: Routledge.

Garrett, P. (2003b) 'The trouble with Harry: Why the "new agenda of life politics" fails to convince', *The British Journal of Social Work*, 33(3): 381–97.

Garrett, P. (2003c) 'Swimming with dolphins: The assessment framework, New Labour and new tools for social work with children and families', *British Journal of Social Work*, 33: 441–63.

Garrett, P. (2006) 'How to be modern: New Labour's neoliberal modernity and the *Change for Children* programme', *British Journal of Social Work*, advanced electronic access. http://bjsw.oxfordjournals.org/

Garvin, C. (1981) 'Research-related roles for social workers', in R. Grinnell, Jr. (ed.), *Social Work Research and Evaluation*. Itasca, IL: R.E. Peacock, pp. 547–52.

Gaskins, S., Miller, P. and Corsaro, W. (1992) 'Theoretical and methodological perspectives in the interpretive study of children', in W. Corsaro and P. Miller (eds), *Interpretive Approaches to Children's Socialization: New Directions for Child Development*. San Francisco: Jossey–Bass, pp. 5–23.

Gatrell, A.C. (2005) 'Complexity theory and geographies of health: A critical assessment', *Social Science and Medicine*, 60(12): 2661–71.

Gatrell, A.C., Popay, J. and Thomas, C. (2004) 'Mapping the determinants of health inequalities in social space: Can Bourdieu help us?', *Health and Place*, 10(3): 245–57.

Gaventa, J. and Cornwall, A. (2001) 'Power and knowledge', in P. Reason and H. Bradbury (eds), *Handbook of Action Research: Participative Inquiry and Practice*. London: Sage Publications. pp. 70–90.

Geertz, C. (1973) *The Interpretation of Cultures*. New York: Basic Books.

Geertz, C. (1983) *Local Knowledge*. New York: Basic Books.

Geertz, C. (1987) *Works and Lives: The Anthropologist as Author*. Stanford: Stanford University Press.

Gegeo, D.W. and Watson-Gegeo, K.A. (2001) '"How we know": Kwara'ae rural villagers doing indigenous epistemology', *The Contemporary Pacific*, 13(1): 55–88.

Gerteis, M. (2004) *Re-inventing Aging: Baby Boomer and Civic Engagement*. Cambridge, MA: Harvard School of Public Health.

Gibbons, M., Limoges, C., Nowonty, H., Schwartzman, S., Scott, P. and Trow, M. (eds) (1994) *The New Production of Knowledge: The Dynamics of Science and Research in Contemporary Societies*. London: Sage.

Gibbs, A. (2001a) 'The changing nature and context of social work research', *British Journal of Social Work*, 31: 687–704.

Gibbs, A. (2001b) 'Social work and empowerment-based research: Possibilities, process and questions', *Australian Social Work*, 54(1): 29–39.

Gibbs, L. (2003) *Evidence-Based Practice for the Helping Professions: A Practical Guide*. Pacific Grove, CA: Brooks/Cole.

Gibbs, L. (2007) 'Applying research to making life-affecting judgments and decisions', *Research on Social Work Practice*, 17(1): 143–50.

Gibbs, L.E. and Gambrill, E. (2002) 'Evidence-base practice: Counterarguments to objections', *Research on Social Work Practice*, 12: 452–76.

Giddens, A. (1979) *Central Problems in Social Theory: Action, Structure and Contradiction in Social Analysis*. Basingstoke: Macmillan.

Giddings, L.S. (2006) 'Mixed-methods research: Positivism dressed in drag?', *Journal of Research in Nursing*, 11(3): 195–203.

Giebeler, C., Fischer, W., Goblirsch, M., Miethe, I. and Riemann, G. (eds) (2007) *Fallverstehen und Fallstudien. Interdisziplinäre Beiträge zur rekonstruktiven Sozialarbeitsforschung*. Opladen and Farmington Hills: Verlag Barbara Budrich.

Gilbert, S. (2001) 'Social work with Indigenous Australians', in M. Alston and J. McKinnon (eds), *Social Work Fields of Practice*. Melbourne: Oxford University Press.

Gildemeister, R. (1989) *Institutionalisierung psychosozialer Versorgung. Eine Feldforschung im Grenzbereich von Gesundheit und Krankheit*. Wiesbaden: Deutscher Universitäts-Verlag.

Gilgun, J. (1988) 'Decision-making in interdisciplinary treatment teams', *Child Abuse and Neglect*, 12: 231–9.

Gilgun, J. (1995) 'We shared something special: The moral discourse of incest perpetrators', *Journal of Marriage and the Family*, 57: 265–81.

Gilgun, J. (2002) 'Conjectures and refutations: Governmental funding and qualitative research', *Qualitative Social Work*, 1(3): 359–75.

Gilgun, J. (2004a) 'Fictionalizing life stories: Yukee the wine thief', *Qualitative Inquiry*, 10(5): 691–705.

Gilgun, J. (2004b) 'The 4-D: Strengths-based assessments for youth who've experienced adversities', *Journal of Human Behavior in the Social Environment*, 10(4): 51–73.

Gilgun, J. (2005a) 'Evidence-based practice, descriptive research, and the resilience-schema-gender-brain (RSGB) assessment', *British Journal of Social Work*, 35(6): 843–62.

Gilgun, J. (2005b) 'Qualitative research and family psychology', *Journal of Family Psychology*, 19(1): 40–50.

Gilgun, J. (2005c) 'The four cornerstones of evidence-based practice in social work', *Research on Social Work Practice*, 15(1): 52–61.

Gilgun, J. (2007) 'The legacy of the Chicago School of Sociology for family theory-building'. Pre-conference workshop on theory construction and research methodology. Pittsburgh, PA: National Council on Family Relation.

Gilgun, J. (2008) 'Lived experience, reflexivity, and research on perpetrators of interpersonal violence', *Qualitative Social Work*, 7(2): 181–98.

Gill, C., Hinrichsen, G. and DiGiuseppe, R. (1998) 'Factors associated with formal service use by family members of patients with dementia', *The Journal of Applied Gerontology*, 17(1): 38–52.

Gira, E.C., Kessler, M.L. and Poertner, J. (2004) 'Influencing social workers to use research evidence in practice: Lessons from medicine and the allied health professions', *Research on Social Work Practice*, 14, 68–79.

Giroux, H. (1990) *Curriculum Discourse as Postmodernist Practice*. Geelong: Deakin University Press.

Giroux, H.A. (2000) *Impure Acts: The Practical Politics of Cultural Studies*. New York/London: Routledge.

Gist, J. (2006) *Boomer Wealth – Beware of the Median*. Washington, DC: AARP Public Policy Institute.

Gitlin, T. (1989) 'Postmodernism: Roots and politics', *Dissent*, 36 (Winter): 100–8.

Glad, J. (2006) 'Co-operation in a child welfare case: A comparative cross-national vignette study', *European Journal of Social Work*, 9(2): 223–40.

Glaser, B. (1978) *Theoretical Sensitivity*. Mill Valley, CA: Sociology Press.

Glaser, B. (2007) Doing formal theory', in Antony B. and Kathy C. (eds), *The Sage Handbook of Grounded Theory*. Thousand Oaks, CA: Sage. pp. 97–113.

Glaser, B. and Strauss, A. (1967) *The Discovery of Grounded Theory: Strategies for Qualitative Research*. Chicago: Aldine.

Glasgow, R.E., Nelson, C.C., Strycker, L.A. and King, D.K. (2006) 'Using RE-AIM Metrics to evaluate diabetes self-management support interventions.

Glasgow, R. (2006) 'RE-AIMing Research for application: Ways to Improve Evidence for Family Practice'. *Journal of the American Board of Family Practice*, 19(1): 11–19.

Glass, G.V. (1997) 'Interrupted time series quasi experiments', in R.M. Yeager (ed.), *Complementary Methods for Research in Education*, 2nd Edn., Washington DC: American Educational Research Association.

Glastonbury, B. and Orme, J. (1993) *Care Management: Tasks and Workloads*. Basingstoke: BASW/ Macmillan.

Glisson, C. (2007) 'Assessing and changing organizational culture and climate for effective services', *Research on Social Work Practice*, 17(6): 736–47.

Glisson, C., Dukes, D. and Green, P. (2006) 'The effects of the ARC organizational intervention on caseworker turnover, climate, and culture in children's service systems', *Child Abuse and Neglect*, 30(8): 855–80.

Global Partnership for Transformative Social Work. Available at: http://www.gptsw.net/.

Goddard, C. (2004) 'Baby Ghazal's got a new name', *The Age*, 13 April. Available at: http://www.theage. com.au/articles/2004/04/12/1081621892083.html. Last accessed 1 November 2006.

Goffman, E. (1961) *Asylums: Essays on the Social Situation of Mental Patients and Other Inmates*. New York: Anchor Books.

Goffman, E. (1963) *Stigma: Notes on the Management of Spoiled Identity*. New York: Prentice–Hall.

Goffman, E. (1968) *Asylums: Essays on the Social Situations of Mental Patients and Other Inmates*. Harmondsworth: Pelican.

Gold, M. (ed.) (1993) *The Complete Social Scientist: A Kurt Lewin Reader*. Washington, DC: American Psychological Association.

Goldberg, D. and Huxley, P. (1980) *Mental Illness in the Community: The Pathway to Psychiatric Care*. London: Tavistock.

Goldberg, D. and Huxley, P. (1992) *Common Mental Disorder: A Bio-social Model*. London: Routledge.

Goldman, H.H., Morrissey, J.P. and Ridgely, M.S. (1994) 'Evaluating the Robert Wood Johnson Foundation Program on Chronic Mental Illness', *The Milbank Quarterly*, 72(1): 37–47.

Goldstein, H. (1991) 'Qualitative research and social work practice', *Journal of Sociology and Social Welfare*, 18(4): 109–19.

Goldstein, H. (1994) 'Ethnography, critical inquiry and social work practice', in E. Sherman and W. Reid (eds), *Qualitative Research in Social Work*. New York: Columbia University Press.

Golub, S.A., Indyk, D. and Wainberg, M.L. (2006) 'Reframing HIV adherence as part of the experience of illness', *Social Work in Health Care*, 42(3–4): 167–88.

Gomory, T. (2001a) 'A fallibilistic response to Thyer's theory of theory-free empirical research in social work practice', *Journal of Social Work Education*, 37(1): 26–50.

Gomory, T. (2001b) 'Critical rationalism (Gomory's blurry theory) or positivism (Thyer's theoretical myopia): Which is the prescription for social work research?', *Journal of Social Work Education*, 37(1): 67–78.

Gonzales, J., Ringeisen, H. and Chambers, D. (2002) 'The tangled and thorny path of science to practice: Tensions in interpreting and applying "Evidence"', *Clinical Psychology Science and Practice*, 9(2): 204–9.

Goodwin, D. (2007) 'Upsetting the order of teamwork: is "The same way every time" a good aspiration?', *Sociology*, 41(2): 259–75.

Goodwin, S. (1997) *Comparative Mental Health Policy. From Institutional to Community Care*. London: Sage Publications.

Gopalkrishna, C. (2002) 'What's colour got to do with it? Reflections on messy methodology issues from a multiracial feminist', *Qualitative Research Journal*, 2(3): 62–78.

Gordon, T. (2000) 'Tears and laughter in the margins', *NORA Nordic Journal of Women's Studies*, 8: 149–59.

Gorin, S. (2006) 'Parental mental health problems: Messages from research, policy and practice', *Children and Society*, 20(1): 78–9.

Gorman, K., Gregory, M., Hayles, M. and Parton, N. (eds) (2006) *Constructive Work with Offenders*. London: Jessica Kingsley.

Gosden, D. (2007) 'From humanitarianism to human rights and justice: A way to go', *Australian Journal of Human Rights*, 13(1), 149–76.

Gould, N. (2004) 'The Learning Organisation and reflective practice the emergence of a concept', in N. Gould and M. Baldwin (eds) *Social Work, Critical Reflection and the Learning Organisation*, Aldershot: Ashgate, pp. 1–10.

Gould, N. and Baldwin, M. (2004) *Social Work, Critical Reflection and the Learning Organization*. Abingdon: Ashgate.

Gould, N., Huxley, P. and Tew, J. (2007) 'Finding a direction for social research in mental health: Establishing priorities and developing capacity', *Journal of Social Work*, 7(2): 179–96.

Grant, J. (1993) *Fundamental Feminism: Contesting the Core Concepts of Feminist Theory*. New York: Routledge.

Grasso, A.J. and Epstein, I. (1992) *Research Utilization in the Social Sciences: Innovations for Practice and Administration*. New York: Haworth.

Gray, J. (2007) '(Re)considering voice', *Qualitative Social Work*, 6(4): 411–30.

Gray, M. (2005) 'Dilemmas of international social work: Paradoxical processes in indigenisation, universalism and imperialism', *International Journal of Social Welfare*, 14: 231–8.

Gray, M. (2008) 'Knowledge production in social work: The "gold standard" of Mode 2?'. 34th Biennial Congress of the International Association of Schools of Social Work (IASSW) Transcending Global–Local Divides, Durban, South Africa. Unpublished.

Gray, M., Coates, J. and Yellow Bird, M. (eds) (2008) *Indigenous Social Work Around the World: Towards Culturally Relevant Education and Practice*. Aldershot: Ashgate.

Gray, M. and McDonald, C. (2006) 'Pursuing good practice: The limits of evidence-based practice', *Journal of Social Work*, 6(1): 7–20.

Gredig, D. (2005) 'The co-evolution of knowledge production and transfer. Evidence-based intervention development as an approach to improve the impact of evidence on social work practice', in P. Sommerfeld (ed.) *Evidence-Based Social Work - Towards a New Professionalism?* Bern.

Gredig, D. and Sommerfeld, P. (2008) 'New proposals for generating and exploiting solution-oriented knowledge', *Journal Research on Social Work Practice*, 18: 292–300.

Green G., Thorpe, J. and Traupmann, M. (2005) 'The sprawling thicket: Knowledge and specialisation in forensic social work', *Australian Social Work*, 58(4): 142–53.

Green, J.W. (1995) *Cultural Awareness in the Human Services. A Multiethnic Approach*. Boston: Allyn and Bacon.

Greenberg, D. and Shroder, M. (1997) *The Digest of Social Experiments*. Washington, DC: Urban Institute Press.

Greenberg, J., Seltzer, M.M. and Brewer, E. (2006) 'Caregivers to older adults', in B. Berkman (ed.), *Handbook of Social Work in Health and Aging*. New York, NY: Oxford University Press. pp. 339–54.

Greene, J. (1990) 'Three views on the nature and role of knowledge in social science', in E. Guba (ed.), *The Paradigm Dialog*. Newbury Park: Sage.

Greene, J.A. (2007) *Prescribing By Numbers: Drugs and the Definition of Disease*. Baltimore: Johns Hopkins University Press.

Greene, J.C. (2006) 'Quieting educational reform … with educational reform', *The American Journal of Evaluation*, 27(3): 352.

Greene, J.C. (2007) *Mixed Methods in Social Inquiry*. San Francisco: Jossey–Bass.

Greene, J.C., Benjamin, L. and Goodyear, L.K. (2001) 'The merits of mixing methods in evaluation', *Evaluation*, 7(1): 25–44.

Greene, J.C. and Caracelli, V.J. (eds) (1997) *Advances in Mixed-Method Evaluation: The Challenges and Benefits of Integrating Diverse Paradigms. New Directions for Evaluation no. 74*. San Francisco: Jossey–Bass.

Greene, J.C., Caracelli, V.J. and Graham, W.F. (1989) 'Toward a conceptual framework for mixed-method evaluation designs', *Educational Evaluation and Policy Analysis*, 11(3): 255–74.

Greenhalgh, S. (2001) *Under the Medical Gaze: Facts and Fictions of Chronic Pain*. Berkeley, CA: University of California Press.

Greenwood, D.J. (2002) 'Action research: Unfulfilled promises and unmet challenges', *Concepts and Transformation*, 7: 117–39.

Greenwood, D.J. (2007) 'Pragmatic action research', *International Journal of Action Research*, 3: 131–48.

Greenwood, D.J. and Levin, M. (1998) *Introduction to Action Research: Social Research for Social Change.* Thousand Oaks: Sage.

Greenwood, D.J. and Levin, M. (2004) 'Local knowledge, cogenerative research, and narrativity', in W. Carrroll (ed.), *Critical Strategies for Social Research.* Toronto, Ontario: Canadian Scholar's Press, pp. 281–91.

Gregory, R.L. (ed.) (1987) *The Oxford Companion to the Mind.* Oxford: Oxford University Press.

Grenier, A. (2006) 'The distinction between being and feeling frail: exploring emotional experiences in health and social care', *Journal of Social Work Practice* 20(3): 299–313.

Grinnell, R. and Unrau, Y. (2005) *Social Work Research and Evaluation: Quantitative and Qualitative Approaches.* New York: Oxford University Press.

Griffin, K.W., Botvin, G.J. and Nichols, T.R. (2006) 'Effects of a school-based drug abuse prevention program for adolescents on HIV risk behaviors in young adulthood', *Prevention Science*, 7: 103–12.

Grinyer, A. (2006) 'Caring for a young adult with cancer: The impact on mothers' health', *Health and Social Care in the Community*, 14(4): 311–18.

GSCC (General Social Care Council) (2005) *Post-Qualifying Framework for Social Work Education and Training.* London: GSCC.

GSCC (General Social Care Council) (2008) *Social Work at Its Best: The Roles and Tasks of Social Workers.* London: GSCC.

Guba, E. (ed.) (1990) *The Paradigm Dialog.* Newbury Park, CA: Sage Publications.

Guijt, I. and Shaw, M. (1998) *The Myth of Community: Gender Issues in Participatory Development.* London: IT Publications.

Gunaratnam, Y. (2003) *Researching 'Race' and Ethnicity.* London: Sage Publications.

Gutheil, I. and Souza, M. (2006) 'Psychosocial services at end of life', in B. Berkman (ed.), *Handbook of Social Work in Health and Aging.* New York: Oxford University Press, pp. 325–34.

Guyatt, G. and Rennie, D. (2002) *Users' Guides to the Medical Literature: Essentials of Evidence-Based Clinical Practice.* Chicago: American Medical Association.

Habermas, J. (1981) *Theorie des kommunikativen Handelns.* Frankfurt a.M., Suhrkamp.

Habermas, J. (1984) *The Theory of Communicative Action. Vol. I: Reason and the Rationalization of Society.* Boston, MA: Beacon Press.

Habermas, J. (1987) *The Theory of Communicative Action, Vol. 11: Lifeworld and System – A Critique of Functionalist Reason.* Trans. T. McCarthy. Cambridge: Polity.

Hacking, I. (1999) *The Social Construction of What?* Cambridge: Harvard University Press.

Hacking, S., Secker, J., Kent, L., Shenton, J. and Spandler, H. (2006) 'Mental health and arts participation: The state of the art in England', *Journal of the Royal Society of Health*, 126: 121–7.

Hadley, R. and McGrath, M. (eds) (1980) *Going Local: Neighbourhood Social Services.* London: Bedford Square Press/NCVO Occasional Paper.

Hadley, R. and McGrath, M. (1984) *When Services Are Local – the Normanton Experience.* London: George Allen and Unwin.

Haidt, J. (2001) 'The emotional dog and its rational tail: A social intuitionist approach to moral judgement', *Psychological Review*, 108(4): 814–34.

Hakala, P. (2000) *Learning By Caring. A Follow-Up Study of Participants in a Specialized Training Program in Pastoral Care and Counseling.* Faculty of Theology of the University of Helsinki.

Hall, C.J. (1999) *Social Work as Narrative: Storytelling and Persuasion in Professional Texts.* Aldershot: Ashgate.

Hall, D. and Hall, I. (1996) *Practical Social Research: Project Work in the Community.* London: MacMillan.

Hall, J.R. (2001) 'History of qualitative methods', in N.J. Smelser and P.B. Baltes (eds), *International Encyclopaedia of the Social and Behavioral Sciences*, pp. 12,613–17.

Hall, S. (ed.) (1997) *Representation: Cultural Representations and Signifying Practices.* London: Sage.

Hämäläinen, J. (2003) 'The concept of social pedagogy in the field of social work', *Journal of Social Work*, 3(1): 69–80.

Haight, W., Carter-Black, J. and Sheridan, K. (in press) 'Mothers' experiences of methamphetamine addiction: A case-based analysis of rural, midwestern women', *Children and Youth Services Review.*

Haight, W.L., Jacobsen, T., Black, J., Kingery, L., Sheridan, K. and Mulder, C. (2005) '"In these bleak days": Parent methamphetamine abuse and child welfare in the rural Midwest', *Children and Youth Services Review*, 27: 949–71.

Haight, W., Ostler, T., Black, J., Sheridan, K. and Kingery, L. (2006) 'A child's eye view of parent methamphetamine abuse: Implications for helping foster families to succeed', *Children and Youth Services Review*, 29(1): 1–15.

Haight, W.L. and Taylor, E.H. (2007) *Human Behavior for Social Work Practice: A Developmental–Ecological Framework*. Chicago: Lyceum Books.

Haken, H. (1990) *Synergetik. Eine Einführung*. Berlin, Springer.

Hall, B. (2001) 'I wish this were a poem of practices of participatory research', in P. Reason and H. Bradbury (eds), *Handbook of Action Research: Participative Inquiry and Practice*. London: Sage. pp. 171–8.

Hall, D. and Hall, I. (1996) *Practical Social Research: Project Work in the Community*. London: MacMillan.

Hamburger, F., Hirschler, S., Sander, G. and Wöbcke, M. (eds) (2004–2007) *Ausbildung für Soziale Berufe in Europa* (Vols 1–4). Frankfurt: ISS Verlag.

Hamington, M. (2008) 'Jane Addams', in Edward N. Zalta (ed.), *The Stanford Encyclopedia of Philosophy*, Winter 2008 Edn, Available at: http://plato.stanford.edu/archives/fall2008/entries/addams-jane/

Hammersley, M. (1992) *What's Wrong With Ethnography?* London: Routledge.

Hammersley, M. (1994) 'Ethnography, policy making and practice in education', in D. Halpin, and B. Troyna, (eds), *Researching Education Policy: Ethical and Methodological Issues*. London: Falmer Press.

Hammersley, M. (1995) *The Politics of Social Research*. London: Sage Publications.

Hammersley, M. (1997) 'A reply to Humphries', *Sociological Research Online*, 2(4). Available at: http://www.socresonline.org.uk/socresonline/2/4/6.html

Hammersley, M. (2003) 'Social research today: Some dilemma and distinctions', *Qualitative Social Work*, 2(1): 25–44.

Hammersley, M. (2005) 'Is the evidence-based practice movement doing more good than harm? Reflections on Iain Chalmers' case for research-based policy making and practice', *Evidence and Policy*, 1(1): 85–100.

Hammond, S.A. and Royal, C. (2001) *Lessons from the Field: Applying Appreciative Inquiry*, revised edition. Boulder, CO: Thin Book Publishing.

Haney, L. (2002) 'Negotiating power and expertise in the field', in T. May (ed.), *Qualitative Research in Action*. London: Sage, pp. 286–99.

Hanley, B. (2005) *Research as Empowerment? Report of a Series of Seminars Organised by the Toronto Group*. York: Joseph Rowntree Foundation.

Hannah-Moffat, K. (2005) 'Criminogenic needs and the transformative risk subject: Hybridizations of risk/need penality', *Punishment and Society*, 7(1): 29–51.

Hannah-Moffat, K. and Shaw, M. (2000) 'Thinking about cognitive skills? Think again!', *Criminal Justice Matters*, 39: 8–9.

Hanson, K.L., Morrow, C.E. and Bandstra, E.S. (2006) 'Early intervention with young children and their parents in the U.S.', in C. McAuley, Wendy Rose and P. J. Pecora (eds), *Enhancing the Well-being of Children and Families through Effective Interventions*. London and Philadelphia: Jessica Kingsley Publishers, pp. 58–81.

Hardiker, P., Exton, K. and Barker, M. (1991) *Policies and Practices in Preventative Childcare*. Aldershot: Avebury.

Harding, S. (1986) *The Science Question in Feminism*. Milton Keynes: Open University.

Hardwick, L. and Hardwick, C. (2007) 'Social work research: "Every moment is a new and shocking valuation of all we have been"', *Qualitative Social Work*, 6(3): 301–14.

Harrell-Bond, B. and Voutira, E. (2007) 'In search of "invisible" actors: Barriers to access in refugee research', *Journal of Refugee Studies*, 20(2): 281–98.

Harris, T., Brown, G.W. and Robinson, R. (1999) 'Befriending as an intervention for chronic depression among women in an inner city. 1: Randomised controlled trial', *British Journal of Psychiatry*, 174: 219–24.

Hartman, A. (1992) 'In search of subjugated knowledge', *Social Work*, 37(6): 483–4.

Hartman, A. (1994) 'Setting the theme: Many ways of knowing', in E. Sherman and W. Reid (eds), *Qualitative Research in Social Work*. New York: Columbia University Press, pp. 459–63.

Hasenfeld, Y. (1983) *Human Service Organizations*. Englewood Cliffs, NJ: Prentice–Hall.

Hawkins, J.D., Kostermaan, R., Catalano, R.F., Hill, K.G. and Abbott, R.D. (2005) 'Promoting positive adult functioning through social development intervention in childhood', *Archives of Pediatric and Adolescent Medicine*, 159(1): 25–31.

Haynes, R.B., Sackett, D.L., Gran, J.M., Cook, D.J. and Guyatt, G.J. (1996) 'Transferring evidence from research to practice: 1. The role of clinical care research evidence in clinical decisions', *ACP Journal Club*, 125: A14–A16.

Haynes, R.B., Sackett, D.L., Guyatt, G.L. and Tugwell, P. (2005) *Clinical Epidemiology: How to do Clinical Practice Research?*, 3rd Edn., Philadelphia, PA: Lippincott Williams and Wilkins.

HHS (Department of Health and Human Services) (2004) *Title 45 Public Welfare, Part 46 Protection of Human Research Subjects*. Washington DC: US Department of Health and Human Services.

Available at: http://www.berlinermethodentreffen. de/material/2005/riemann.pdf. Last accessed 8 March 2008.

Health Research Council of New Zealand (2003) *Guidelines on Pacific Health Research.* Auckland: Health Research Council of New Zealand.

Healy, D., Harris, M., Michael, P., Cattell, D., Savage, M., Chalasani, P. and Hirst. D. (2005) 'Service utilization in 1896 and 1996: Morbidity and mortality data from North Wales', *History of Psychiatry,* 16(1): 27–41.

Healy, K. (2000) *Social Work Practices: Contemporary Perspectives on Change.* London: Sage.

Healy, K. (2001) 'Participatory action research and social work: A critical appraisal', *International Social Work,* 44(1): 93–105.

Healy, K. (2005) *Social Work Theories in Context: Creating Frameworks for Practice.* Palgrave Macmillan.

Heatherington, L., Friedlander, M.L. and Greenberg, L. (2005) 'Change process research in couple and family therapy: Methodological challenges and opportunities', *Journal of Family Psychology,* 19(1): 18–27.

Hedrick, T. (1988) 'The interaction of politics and evaluation', *Evaluation Practice,* 9(1): 5–14.

Heller, T., Factor, A.R., Hsieh, K., Hahn, J.E. (1998a) 'Impact of age and transitions out of nursing homes for adults with developmental disabilities', *American Journal of Mental Retardation,* 103(3): 236–48.

Heller, T., Miller, A.B. and Factor, A. (1998b) 'Environmental characteristics of nursing homes and community-based settings, and the well-being of adults with intellectual disability', *Journal of Intellectual Disability Research,* 42(5): 418–28.

Hendrick, H. (2003) *Child Welfare: Historical Dimensions, Contemporary Debate.* Bristol: Policy Press.

Henggeler, S.W. and Borduin, C.M. (1990) *Family Therapy and Beyond: A Multisystemic Approach to Treating the Behavior Problems of Children and Adolescents.* Pacific Grove, CA: Brooks/Cole.

Henggeler, S.W., Schoenwald, S.K., Borduin, C.M., Rowland, M.D. and Cunningham, P.B. (1998) *Multisystemic Treatment of Antisocial Behavior in Children and Adolescents.* NY: Guilford.

Henggeler, S.W., Schoenwald, S.K., Borduin, C.M. and Swenson, C.C. (2006) 'Methodological critique and meta-analysis as Trojan horse', *Children and Youth Services Review,* 28(4): 447–57.

Herising, F. (2005) 'Interrupting positions: Critical thresholds and queer pro/positions', in L. Brown and S. Strega (eds), *Research as Resistance: Critical, Indigenous and Anti-Oppressive Approaches.* London: Canadian Scholars' Press.

Heron, J.C. (1996) *Cooperative Inquiry: Research into the Human Condition.* London: Sage Publications.

Heron, J. and Reason, R. (1997) 'A participatory inquiry paradigm', *Qualitative Inquiry,* 3: 274–94.

Hess, P. and Mullen, E. J. (1995) *Practitioner–Researcher Partnerships: Building Knowledge from, in and for Practice.* Washington, DC: National Association of Social Workers.

Heurtin-Roberts, S. (2002) 'Thoughts on qualitative research methods at the NIH', *Qualitative Social Work,* 1(3): 376–79.

Hick, S. (1997) 'Participatory research: An approach for structural social workers', *Journal of Progressive Human Services,* 8 (2): 63–78.

Higgins, J.P.T. and Green S. (eds) (2008) *Cochrane Handbook for Systematic Reviews of Interventions.* Chichester: John Wiley.

Hill, M. (1999) 'What's the problem? Who can help? The perspectives of children and young people on their well-being and on helping professionals', *Journal of Social Work Practice,* 13(2): 135–45.

Hill, R.B. (2005) 'The role of race in foster care placements', in D.M. Derezotes, J. Poertner and M.F. Testa (eds), *Race Matters in Child Welfare.* Washington, DC: Child Welfare League of America Press, pp. 187–200.

Hinkson, M. (2007) 'Introduction: In the name of the child', in J. Altman and M. Hinkson (eds), *Coercive Reconciliation: Stabilise, Normalise, Exit Aboriginal Australia.* North Carlton: Arena.

Hinrichsen, G. and Ramirez, M. (1992) 'Black and white dementia caregivers: A comparison of their adaptation, adjustment, and service utilization', *The Gerontologist,* 32(3): 375–81.

Hirschman, K.B. and Bourjolly, J.N. (2005) 'How do tangible supports impact the breast cancer experience?', *Social Work in Health Care,* 41(1): 17–32.

Hirst, P. (1981) 'The genesis of the social', *Politics and Power,* 3, 67–82.

Ho, A., Collins, S., Davis, K. and Doty, M. (2005) *A Look at Working-Age Caregivers Roles, Health Concerns, and Need for Support* (Issue Brief). New York, NY: The Commonwealth Fund.

Hodgetts, D., Radley, A., Chamberlain, K. and Hodgetts, A. (2007) 'Health inequalities and homelessness: Considering material, spatial and relational dimensions', *Journal of Health Psychology,* 12(5): 709–25.

Hoenig, J. and Hamilton, M. (1969) *The Desegregation of the Mentally Ill*. London: Routledge.

Hogarth, R. (1985) *Judgment and Choice*. New York: Wiley and Sons.

Hogarty, G.E. (1991) 'Social work practice research on severe mental illness: Charting a future', *Research on Social Work Practice*, 1(1): 5–31.

Hogarty, G.E. and Anderson, C.M. (1986) 'Medication, family psychoeducation, and social skills training: First year relapse results of a controlled study', *Psychopharmacology Bulletin*, 22(3): 860–2.

Hogarty, G.E., Anderson, C.M., Reiss, D.J., Kornblith, S.J., Greenwald, D.P., Javna, C.D. and Madonia, M.J. (1986) 'Environmental–personal indicators in the course of schizophrenia research group: Family psychoeducation, social skills training, and maintenance chemotherapy in the aftercare treatment of schizophrenia. I. One-year effects of a controlled study on relapse and expressed emotion', *Archives of General Psychiatry*, 43(7): 633–42.

Hogarty, G.E., Flesher, S., Ulrich. R. et al. (2004) 'Cognitive enhancement therapy for schizophrenia: Effects of a 2-year randomized trial on cognition and behavior', *Archives of General Psychiatry*, 61: 866–76.

Hogarty, G.E., Goldberg, S., Schooler, N.R. and Ulrich, R.E. (1974) 'Drug and sociotherapy in the aftercare of schizophrenic patients: Two year relapse rates', *Archives of General Psychiatry*, 31: 603–8.

Hogarty, G.E., Kornblith, S.J., Greenwald, D., DiBarry, A.L., Cooley, S., Flesher, S., Reiss, D., Carter, M. and Ulrich, R. (1995) 'Personal therapy: A disorder-relevant psychotherapy for schizophrenia', *Schizophrenia Bulletin*, 21(3): 379–93.

Hogarty, G.E., Kornblith, S.J., Greenwald, D., DiBarry, A.L., Cooley, S., Ulrich, R.F., Carter, M. and Flesher, S. (1997) 'Three-year trials of personal therapy among schizophrenic patients living with or independent of family, I: Description of study and effects on relapse rates', *American Journal of Psychiatry*, 154(11): 1504–13.

Holden G., Thyer, B., Baer, J.C., Delva, J., Dulmus, C. and Shanks, T.R.W. (2008) 'Suggestions to improve social work journal editorial and peer review processes: The San Antonio Response to the Miami Statement', *Research on Social Work Practice*, 18: 66–71.

Hollin, C.R. (1995) 'The meaning and implications of "programme integrity"', in J. McGuire (ed.), *What Works: Reducing Offending*. Chichester: Wiley. pp. 195–208.

Hollin, C.R. (2008) 'Evaluating offending behaviour programmes: Does only randomization glister?', *Criminology and Criminal Justice*, 8(1): 89–106.

Hollinsworth, D. (1997) 'The work of anti-racism', in G. Gray and C. Winter (eds), *The Resurgence of Racism: Howard, Hanson and the Grace Debate*. Clayton: Monash Publications in History, No. 24.

Hollstein, W. (1973) 'Hilfe und Kapital. Zur Funktionsbestimmung von Sozialarbeit', in W. Hollstein and M. Meinhold (eds), *Sozialarbeit unter kapitalistischen Produktionsbedingungen*. Frankfurt a.M., Fischer.

Hollway, W. (2001) 'The psycho-social subject in "evidence-based practice"', *Journal of Social Work Practice*, 15(1): 9–22.

Holman, B. (1987) 'Research from the underside', *British Journal of Social Work*, 17(6): 669–83.

Home Office (1998) *Effective Practice Initiative: A National Implementation Plan for the Effective Supervision of Offenders*. Probation Circular 35/1998, London: Home Office.

Hooks, B. (1990) *Yearning: Race, Gender, and Cultural Politics*. Boston: South End Press.

Hooyman, N. and Kiyak, H. (1996) *Social Gerontology: A Multidisciplinary Perspective*, 4th Edn., Boston: Allyn & Bacon.

Horner, B., Downie, J., Hay, D. and Wichmann, H. (2007) 'Grandparents who parent their grandchildren in Western Australia: An evaluation of an agency-based psychosocial support program'. *Journal of Family Issues*, 28: 77–84.

Horwitz, A.V. (2002) *Creating Mental Illness*. Chicago: University of Chicago.

Hough, G. and Briskman, L. (2003) 'Responding to the changing socio-political context of practice', in J. Allan, B. Pease and L. Briskman (eds), *Critical Social Work: An Introduction to Theories and Practices*. Sydney: Allen and Unwin.

House, E. (1991) 'Evaluation and social justice: where are we now?' in M. McLaughlin and D. Phillips, (eds), *Evaluation and Education: At Quarter Century*. Chicago: Chicago University Press.

House, E. (1993) *Professional Evaluation*. Newbury Park: Sage.

House, E. and Howe, K. (1999) *Evaluation and Values*. Thousand Oaks: Sage Publications.

Houston, S. (1995) 'Transcending the fissure in risk theory: Critical realism and child welfare', *Child and Family Social Work*, 6: 219–28.

Houston, S. (2001) 'Beyond social constructionism: Critical realism and social work', *British Journal of Social Work*, 31(6): 845–62.

Houston, S. (2004) 'Garrett contra Ferguson: A Meta-Theoretical Appraisal of the "Rumble in the Jungle"'. *British Journal of Social Work.* 34(2): 261–7.

Howard, J. (2006) *Address to the National Press Club*, 26 January. Available at: www.theage.com.au/news/national/pms-speech/2006/01/25/1138066849045.html. Last accessed 30 May 2007.

Howard, M.O., Delva, J., Jenson, J.M., Edmond, T. and Vaughn, M.G. (2005) 'Prevention interventions for adult emotional and mental problems: Substance abuse', in C.N. Dulmus and L. Rapp-Paglicci (eds), *Handbook of Preventive Interventions for Adults.* New York: John Wiley and Sons.

Howard, M.O. and Jenson, J.M. (1999) 'Special section: Practice guidelines and clinical social work', *Research on Social Work Practice*, 9(3): 283–364.

Howe, D. (1992) 'Child abuse and the bureaucratization of social work', *Sociological Review*, 40(3): 491–508.

Howe, D. (1993) *On Being a Client: Understanding the Process of Counselling and Psychotherapy.* London: Sage.

Howe, D. (1996) 'Surface and depth in social work practice', in N. Parton (ed.), *Social Theory, Social Change and Social Work.* London: Routledge.

Howe, K.R. (1988) 'Against the quantitative–qualitative incompatibility thesis (or dogmas die hard)', *Educational Researcher*, 17(8): 10–16.

Howe, K.R. (2003) *Closing Methodological Divides.* Boston: Kluwer Academic Publishing.

Huberman, M. (1985) 'What knowledge is of most worth to teachers? A knowledge-use perspective', *Teaching and Teacher Education*, 1: 251–62.

Hudson, B. (2004) 'Analyzing network partnerships', *Public Management Review*, 6(1): 75–94.

Hudson, B. (2007) 'Modernising adult care', *Community Care*, October, 4(1693): 34–5.

Hudson, C. (2005) 'Socioeconomic status and mental illness: Tests of the social causation and selection hypotheses', *American Journal of Orthopsychiatry*, 75(1): 3–18.

Hudson, W. (1978) 'First axioms of treatment', *Social Work*, 23(1): 3–4.

Hughes, B. (2002) 'Disability and the body', in C. Barnes, M. Oliver and L. Barton (eds), *Disability Studies Today.* Cambridge: Polity Press.

Hughes, E.C. (1984a) 'The cultural aspect of urban research', in *The Sociological Eye: Selected Papers.* New Brunswick, NJ: Transaction Books. pp. 106–17.

Hughes, E.C. (1984b) 'The dual mandate of social science: Remarks on the academic division of labor', in *The Sociological Eye: Selected Papers.* New Brunswick, NJ: Transaction Books, pp. 443–54.

Hugman, R. (1992) 'Rehabilitation and community support: A case study of social care', *Applied Community Studies*, 1(2) [Monograph], 93 pp.

Hugman, R. (2005) *New Approaches in Ethics for the Caring Professions.* Basingstoke: Palgrave–Macmillan.

Human Rights and Equal Opportunity Commission (1997) *Bringing Them Home: Report of the National Inquiry into the Separation of Aboriginal and Islander Children from their Families.* Sydney: HREOC.

Humphries, C., Berridge, D., Butler, I. and Ruddick, R. (2003) 'Making research count: The development of knowledge based practice', *Research Policy and Planning*, 21(1): 41–9.

Humphries, B. (1997) 'From critical thought to emancipatory action: Contradictory research goals?', *Sociological Research Online*, 2(1): 1–10.

Humphries, B. (1998) 'The baby and the bath water: Hammersley, Cealey Harrison and Hood-Williams and the emancipatory research debate', *Sociological Research Online*, 3 (1). Available at: http://www.socresonline.org.uk/socresonline/3/1/9.html

Humphries, B. (1999) 'Feminist evaluation', in I. Shaw and J. Lishman (eds), *Evaluation and Social Work Practice.* London: Sage, pp. 118–32.

Humphries, B. (2003) 'What *else* counts as evidence in evidence-based social work?' *Social Work Education*, 22(1): 81–91.

Humphries, B. (2004a) 'The construction and reconstruction of social work', in D. Hayes and B. Humphries (eds), *Social Work, Immigration and Asylum: Debates, Dilemmas and Ethical Issues for Social Work and Social Care Practice.* London: Jessica Kingsley.

Humphries, B. (2004b) 'Taking sides: Social work research as a moral and political activity', in R. Lovelock, K. Lyons and J. Powell (eds), *Reflecting on Social Work – Discipline and Profession.* Aldershot: Ashgate.

Humphries, B. (2005) 'From margin to centre: Shifting the emphasis of social work research', in R. Adams, L. Dominelli and M. Payne (eds), *Social Work Futures: Crossing Boundaries, Transforming Practice.* Hampshire: Palgrave Macmillan, pp. 279–92.

Humphries, B. (2008) *Social Work Research for Social Justice.* Basingstoke, Hampshire: Palgrave Macmillan.

Hunt, J. (2003) *Family and Friends Carers: Scoping paper prepared for the Department of Health – November 2001* (31177). London: Department of Health. Retrieved July 30, 2005, from http://www.dfes.gov.uk/childrenandfamilies/04016168%5B1%5D.pdf

Hunt, J. and Macleod, A. (1999) *The Best-Laid Plans: Outcomes of Judicial Decisions in Child Protection Proceedings*. London: The Stationery Office.

Hurley, M. (2007) 'Who's on whose margins?', in M. Pitts and A. Smith (eds), *Researching the Margins: Strategies for Ethical and Rigorous Research with Marginalised Communities*. Houndmill: Palgrave Macmillan.

Hurst, R. (2005) 'Disabled People's International: Europe and the social model of disability', in C. Barnes and G. Mercer (eds), *The Social Model of Disability: Europe and the Majority World*. Leeds: The Disability Press.

Husband, C. (1995) 'The morally active practitioner and the ethics of anti-racist social work', in R. Hugman and D. Smith (eds), *Ethical Issues in Social Work*. London: Routledge.

Huxley, P. (2001) 'The contribution of social science to mental health services research and development: A SWOT analysis', *Journal of Mental Health*, 10(2): 117–20.

Huxley P., Evans S., Burns T., Fahy T. and Green J. (2001) 'Quality of life outcome in a randomized controlled trial of case management', *Social Psychiatry and Psychiatric Epidemiology*, 36(5): 249–55.

Huxley, P. and Thornicroft, G. (2002) 'Social inclusion, social quality and mental illness', *British Journal of Psychiatry* (editorial), 182: 289–90.

IASWR (Institute for the Advancement of Social Work Research) (2007) 'Partnerships to integrate evidence-based mental health practices into social work education and research'. Available at: http://charityadvantage.com/iaswr/EvidenceBasedPractice-Final.pdf. Last accessed 25 November 2008.

IASWR (Institute for the Advancement of Social Work Research) (2008) *'Directory of social work research grants awarded by the National Institutes of Health, 1993–2008'. Available at: http://charityadvantage.com/iaswr/NIHSWRDatabaseNovember2008.pdf. Last accessed 25 November 2008.*

Ife, J. (1997) *Rethinking Social Work: Towards Critical Practice*. Melbourne: Longman.

Ife, J. (2001) *Human Rights and Social Work: Towards Critical Practice*. Cambridge: Cambridge University Press.

Ife, J. and Tesoriero, F. (2006) *Community Development: Community-Based Alternatives in an Age of Globalisation*, 3rd Edn., French Forest, NSW: Pearson Longman.

IFSW (International Federation of Social Workers) (2004) *IFSW General Meeting 2004, Proposal for a New Ethical Document Agenda Item 11.1*. Available at: http://ifs.org/GM-2004/GM-Ethics.html.

IFSW (International Federation of Social Workers) (2008) *Definition of Social Work*. Available at: http://www.ifsw.org/en/f38000138.html. Last accessed 1 December 2008.

IFSW/IASSW (International Federation of Social Workers/International Association of Schools of Social Work) (2001) *The Definition of Social Work*. Available at: http://www.ifsw.org/en/p38000208.html. Last accessed 31 October 2007.

IFSW/IASSW (International Federation of Social Workers/International Association of Schools of Social Work) (2007) *International Definition of the Social Work Profession*. Supplement of *International Social Work*. London: Sage Publications.

IMS (2008) *Working Paper*. 2008-02-19. Stockholm: Socialstyrelsen.

Ingstad, B. and Reynolds Whyte, S. (1995) *Disability and Culture*. Los Angeles: University of California Press.

Ingamells, A. (1996) 'Constructing frameworks from practice: Towards a participatory approach', in J. Fook (ed.), *The Reflective Researcher*. St. Leonards, Australia: Allen and Unwin, pp. 151–66.

Institute of Medicine (IOM) (2001). *Crossing the Quality Chasm*. Washington, DC: National Academy Press.

International Federation of Red Cross and Red Crescent Societies (2004) *World Disasters Report 2004*. Geneva.

International Federation of Social Workers (2000) 'Definition of social work'. Available at: http://www.ifsw.org/en/p38000208.html. Last accessed 13 August 2007.

Ioannidis, J.P.A. (2005) 'Why most published research findings are false', *Plos Medicine*, 2(8): e124.

Irving, A. (1986) 'Leonard Marsh and the McGill Social Science Research Project', *Journal of Canadian Studies*, 21(2): 6–25.

Irving, A. (1992) 'The scientific imperative in Canadian social work: Social work and social welfare research in Canada, 1897–1945', *Canadian Social Work Review*, 9(1): 9–27.

Israel, B., Schulz, A.J., Parker, E.A. and Becker, A.B. (1998) 'Review of community-based research: Assessing partnership approaches to improve public health', *Annual Review of Public Health*, 19: 173–202.

Israel, B., Schulz, A.J., Parker, E.A., Becker, A.B., Allen III, A.J. and Guzman, J.R. (2003) 'Critical issues in developing and following community based participatory research principles', in M. Minkler and N. Wallerstein (eds), *Community-Based Participatory Research for Health*. San Francisco, CA: Jossey–Bass, pp. 53–76.

Jackson, H., Judd, F., Komiti, A., Fraser, C., Murray, G., Robins, G. (2007) 'Mental health problems in rural contexts: What are the barriers to seeking help from professional providers?', *Australian Psychologist*, 42: 147–60.

Jacob, M.C. (1992) 'Science and politics in the late twentieth century', *Social Research*, 59(3): 487–503.

Jakob, G. and Von Wensierski, H.-J. (eds) (1997) *Rekonstruktive Sozialpädagogik. Konzepte und Methoden sozialpädagogischen Verstehens in Forschung und Praxis*. Weinheim and Munich: Juventa.

Jamieson, J., McIvor, G. and Murray, C. (1999) *Understanding Offending Among Young People*. Edinburgh: Scottish Executive.

Janicki, M.P., Dalton, A.J., Henderson, C.M. and Davidson, P.W. (1999) 'Mortality and morbidity among older adults with intellectual disability: Health services considerations', *Disability & Rehabilitation*, 21(5–6): 284–94.

Janicki, M.P., McCallion, P., Grant-Griffin, L. and Kolomer, S.R. (2000) 'Grandparent caregivers I: Characteristics of the grandparents and the children with disabilities they care for', *Journal of Gerontological Social Work*, 33(3): 41–62.

Janowitz, M. (1972) *Sociological Models and Social Policy*. Morristown, NJ: General Learning Systems.

Jasso, G. (1988) 'Principles of theoretical analysis', *Sociological Theory*, 6(1): 1–20.

Jayartne, S. and Levy, R.L. (1979) *Empirical Clinical Practice*. New York: Columbia University Press.

Jenson, J.M. (2005) 'Connecting science to intervention: Advances, challenges and the promise of evidence-based practice', *Social Work Research*, 29(3): 131–4.

Jenson, J.M. (2008) 'Editorial: Keeping pace with methodological and analytic advances in social research', *Social Work Research*, 32(2): 67–9.

Johnson, M. and Austin, M.J. (2006) 'Evidence-based practice in the social services: Implications for organizational change', *Administration in Social Work*, 30(3): 75–103.

Johnson, R.B. and Onwuegbuzie, A.J. (2004) 'Mixed methods research: A research paradigm whose time has come', *Educational Researcher*, 33(7): 14–26.

Johnson, R.B., Onwuegbuzie, A.J. and Turner, L.A. (2007) 'Toward a definition of mixed methods research', *Journal of Mixed Methods Research*, 1(2): 112–33.

Johnsson, E. and Svensson, K. (2005) 'Theory in social work – some reflections on understanding and explaining interventions (Teori i socialt arbete – några

reflektioner om att förstå och förklara interventioner)', *European Journal of Social Work*, 8(4): 419–33.

Joint University Council Social Work Education Committee (2006) *A Social Work Research Strategy in Higher Education 2006–2020*. Available at: http://www.kcl.ac.uk/content/1/c6/03/18/32/Strategy-Final2.pdf. Last accessed 12 October 2008.

Jones, C. (1983) *State Social Work and the Working Class*. Basingstoke: Macmillan.

Jones, C. (1996) 'Anti-intellectualism and the peculiarities of British social work education', in N. Parton (ed.), *Social Theory, Social Change and Social Work*. Routledge, pp. 191–210.

Jones, J. (1994) 'Embodied meaning: Menopause and the change of life', *Social Work in Health Care*, 19(3–4): 43–65.

Jones, J.B. and Egan, M. (2000) 'The transplant experience of liver recipients: Ethical issues and practice implications', *Social Work in Health Care*, 31(2): 65–88.

Jones, M. (2004) 'Supervision, learning and transformative practices', in Nick G. and Mark B. (eds), *Social Work, Critical Reflection and the Learning Organization*. Abingdon: Ashgate, pp. 11–22.

Jones, R.G. and Kerr, M.P. (1997) 'A randomized control trial of an opportunistic health screening tool in primary care for people with intellectual disability', *Journal of Intellectual Disability Research*, 41(Pt 5): 409–15.

Jones, S.H. (2005) 'Autoethnography: Making the personal political', in Norman K. Denzin and Yvonna S. Lincoln (eds), *Sage Handbook of Qualitative Research*, 3rd Edn., Thousand Oaks, CA: Sage, pp. 763–91.

Jones, T. and Newburn, T. (2007) *Policy Transfer and Criminal Justice: Exploring US Influence over British Crime Control Policy*. Maidenhead: McGraw–Hill/Open University Press.

Jonson-Reid, M. and Barth, R.P. (2000) 'From placement to prison: The path to adolescent incarceration from child welfare supervised foster or group care', *Children and Youth Services Review*, 22: 493–516.

Jordan, B. (1984) *Invitation to Social Work*. Oxford: Martin Robertson.

Jordan, B. (1997) 'Social Work and Society', in M. Davies (ed.) *The Blackwell Companion to Social Work*. Oxford: Blackwell Publications.

Jordan, B. and Jordan, C. (2000) *Social Work and the Third Way: Tough Love as Social Policy*. London: Sage.

Joubert, L. (2006) 'Academic-practice partnerships in practice research: A cultural shift for health social workers', *Social Work in Health Care*, 43(2–3): 151–61.

Journal of Community Practice (2004) 12 (3/4).

Journal of Social Work Values and Ethics. Marson, Stephen and Finn, Jerry (eds). Available at: http://socialworker.com/jswve/.

JUC SWEC (Joint University Council Social Work Education Committee) (2006) *A Social Work Research Strategy in Higher Education, 2006–20*, Social Care Workforce Unit. London: Kings College London.

Juhila, K. and Pösö, T. (1999) 'Local cultures in social work', in S. Karvinen, T. Poso and M. Satka (eds), *Reconstructing Social Work Research.* University of Jyvaskyla: SoPhi.

Julia, M. and Kondat, M.E. (2005) 'Health care in the social development context: Indigenous, participatory and empowering approaches', *International Social Work*, 48(5): 537–52.

Kadushin, G. (2004) 'Home health care utilization: A review of the research for social work', *Health and Social Work*, 29(3): 219–32.

Kahlberg, S. (2000) 'Max Weber', in G. Ritzer (ed), *The Blackwell Companion to Major Social Theorists.* Malden, Mass: Blackwell Publishers. pp. 144–204.

Kahn, R.L. (2002) 'On successful aging and well-being', *The Gerontologist*, 42(6): 725–6.

Kahneman, D., Slovic, J.C. and Tversky, A. (1982) *Judgment under uncertainty: Heuristics and biases.* Cambridge, UK: Cambridge University Press.

Kahneman, D. and Tversky, A. (1972) 'Subjective probability: A judgement of representativeness', *Cognitive Psychology*, 3: 237–51.

Kane, R.A. (2006) 'A social worker's historical and future perspective on residential care'. In B. Berkman (ed.), *Handbook of Social Work in Health and Aging.* New York: Oxford University Press, pp.7–18.

Kane, R.L., Kane, R.A. and Ladd, R.C. (1998) *The Heart of Long-Term Care.* NY: Oxford University Press.

Kane, R.A., Reinardy, J., Penrod, J.D. and Huck, S. (1999) 'After the hospitalization is over: A different perspective on family care of older people', *Journal of Gerontological Social Work*, 31(1/2): 119–41.

Kane, R.A., King, K.C., Bershadsky, B., Kane, R.L., Giles, K., Degenholtz, H.B. et al., (2003) Quality of life measures for nursing home residents. *Journal of Gerontology: Medical Sciences,* 58A(3): 240–8.

Karpf, M.J. (1931) *The Scientific Basis of Social Work. A Study in Family Case Work.* New York: Columbia University Press.

Karvinen, S., Pösö, T. and Satka, M. (eds) (1999) *Reconstructing Social Work Research.* University of Jyväskylä, SoPhi.

Karvinen-Niinikoski, S. (2005) 'Research orientation and expertise in social work – challenges for social work education', *European Journal of Social Work*, 8(3): 259–71.

Kaseke, E. (2001) 'Social development as a model of social work practice: The experience of Zimbabwe', in L. Dominelli, W. Lorenz and H. Soydan (eds), *Beyond Racial Divides: Ethnicities in Social Work Practice.* Aldershot: Ashgate, pp. 105–16.

Kaskisaari, M. (1991) *Beatrice Webb tiedenaisena: radikaalifeministinen näkökulma elämänkertaan (Beatrice Webb as a Researcher: A Radical Feminist View of Her Biography).* Jyväskylä: University of Jyväskylä.

Kassirer, J. (2008, April 6) 'Tainted medicine', *Los Angeles Times*, M6–7.

Kawachi, I. (2006) 'Commentary: Social capital and health: Making the connections one step at a time', *International Journal of Epidemiology*, 35: 989–93.

Kawachi, I., Kennedy, B.P., Lochner, K. and Prothrow-Stith, D. (1997) 'Social capital, income inequality, and mortality', *American Journal of Public Health*, 87: 1491–8.

Kawachi, I., Subramanian, S.V. and Kim, D. (eds) (2007) *Social Capital and Health.* New York: Springer–Verlag.

Kazdin, A.E. (2005) *Parent Management Training: Treatment for Oppositional, Aggressive and Antisocial Behavior in Children and Adolescents.* New York, NY: Oxford.

Kazi, M. (1998) *Single Case Evaluation by Social Workers.* Surrey: Ashgate.

Kazi, M. (2000) 'Contemporary perspectives in the evaluation of practice', *British Journal of Social Work*, 30: 755–68.

Kazi, M. (2003) 'Realist evaluation practice', *British Journal of Social Work*, 33(6): 803–18.

Keeling, Margaret L. and Piercy, Fred P. (2007) 'A careful balance: Multinational perspectives on culture, gender, and power in marriage and family therapy practice', *Journal of Marital and Family Therapy*, 33(34): 443–63.

Keith, R.A. (2006) 'Research', in G. Albrecht et al. (eds), *Encyclopedia of Disability.* Thousand Oaks: Sage.

Kellogg Commission on the Future of State and Land Grant Universities (1999) *Returning to our Roots: The Engaged Institution.* Washington, DC: National Association of State Universities and Land-Grant Colleges.

Kelly, G.A. (1955) *The Psychology of Personal Constructs.* New York: Norton.

Kemmis, S. and McTaggart, R. (2005) 'Participatory action research: Communicative action and the public sphere', in N.K. Denzin and Y.S. Lincoln (eds), *The Sage Handbook of Qualitative Research*. Thousand Oaks, CA: Sage, pp. 559–604.

Kempe, R.S. and Kempe, C. (1978) *Child Abuse*. Cambridge, Massachusetts: Harvard University Press.

Kemshall, H. and Littlechild, R. (eds) (2000) *User Involvement and Participation in Social Care: Research Informing Practice*. London: Jessica Kingsley.

Kerlinger, F.N. (1973) *Foundations of Behavioral Research*, 2nd Edn., London, New York, Sydney, Toronto: Holt, Rinehart and Wiston.

Kerr, A.M., McCulloch, D., Oliver, K., McLean, B., Coleman, E., Law, T., Beaton, P., Wallace, S., Newell, E., Eccles, T. and Prescott, R.J. (2003) 'Medical needs of people with intellectual disability require regular reassessment, and the provision of client- and carer-held reports', *Journal of Intellectual Disability Research*, 47(Pt 2): 134–45.

Kerr, M., Dunstan, F. and Thapar, A. (1996) 'Attitudes of general practitioners to caring for people with learning disability', *British Journal of General Practice*, 46(403): 92–4.

Kessler, M.L., Gira, E. and Poertner, J. (2005) 'Moving best practice to evidence-based practice in child welfare', *Families in Society*, 86(2): 244–50.

Khinduka, S.K. (2007) 'Toward rigor and relevance in US social work education', *Australian Association of Social Workers*, 60(1): 18–28.

Kiikeri, M. and Ylikoski, P. (2004) *Tiede tutkimuskohteena: filosofinen johdatus tieteentutkimukseen (Science as a Research Topic: A Philosophical Introduction to Science Research)*. Helsinki: Gaudeamus.

Kincheloe, J. and McLaren, P. (2005) 'Rethinking critical theory and qualitative research', in N. Denzin and Y. Lincoln (eds), *The Sage Handbook of Qualitative Research*, 3rd Edn., London: Sage.

Kinsella, K. and Velkoff, V.A. (2001) *Life Expectancy and Changing Mortality*. U.S. Census Bureau, Series P95/01-1. An Aging World. Washington, DC: U.S. Government Printing Office, pp. 23–35.

Kirk, S. (1979) *Understanding Research Utilization in Social Work. Sourcebook on Research Education*. New York: Council on Social Work Education, No. 12.

Kirk, S.A. (1999) 'Good intentions are not enough: Practice guidelines for social work', *Research on Social Work Practice*, 9(3): 302–10.

Kirk, S.A. (2004) 'Are children's *DSM* diagnoses accurate?', *Brief Treatment and Crisis Intervention*, 4(3): 255–70.

Kirk, S.A. and Kutchins, H. (1988) 'Deliberate misdiagnosis in mental health practice', *Social Service Review*, 62(2): 225–37.

Kirk, S.A. and Kutchins, H. (1992) *The Selling of DSM: The Rhetoric of Science in Psychiatry*. Hawthorne, NY: Aldine de Gruyter.

Kirk, S.A. and Reid, W.J. (2002) *Science and Social Work: A Critical Appraisal*. New York, Columbia University Press.

Knowles, G. and Cole, A. (eds) (2007) *Handbook for Arts-Informed Research in the Social Sciences*. CA: Sage.

Kohli, Ravi K.S. (2005) 'The sound of silence: Listening to what unaccompanied asylum-seeking children say and do not say', *British Journal of Social Work*, 36(5): 707–21.

Kohn, N. and Amatucci, K.B. (2007) 'Desire among platform agnostics'. Paper presented at the 2007 Congress of Qualitative Inquiry at the University of Illinois, Urbana, IL.

Kolomer, S., McCallion, P. and Van Vorbis, C. (2008) 'School based support group intervention for children in the care of their grandparent', in B. Hayslip and P. Kaminski (eds), *Parenting the Custodial Child*. NY: Springer, pp. 545–64.

Korczyk, S.M. (2004) *Is Early Retirement Ending?* Washington, DC: AARP Public Policy Institute.

Kosloski, K. and Montgomery, R. (1994) 'Investigating patterns of service use by families providing care for dependent elders', *Journal of Aging and Health*, 6: 17–37.

Kraemer, H.C., Kazdin, A.E., Offord, D.R., Kessler, R.C., Jensen, P.S. and Kupfer, D.J. (1997) 'Coming to terms with the terms of risk', *Archives of General Psychiatry*, 54(April): 337–43.

Krell, G.I. (1977) 'Overstay among hospital patients', *Health and Social Work*, 2: 163–78.

Kreuger, L. and Neuman, W. (2006) *Social Work Research Methods: Qualitative and Quantitative Applications*. Boston: Allyn and Bacon.

Kropf, N. and Yoon (2006) 'Grandparent caregivers: Who are they?', in B. Berkman (ed.), *Handbook of Social Work in Health and Aging*. New York, NY: Oxford University Press, pp. 355–62.

Kuhlmann, C. (2003) 'Gender and theory in the history of German social work – Alice Salomon, Herman Nohl and Christian Klumker', in S. Hering and B. Waaldijk (eds), *History of Social Work in Europe (1900–1960): Female Pioneers and Their Influence on the Development of International Social Organizations*. Leske + Budrich, Opladen. pp. 95–104.

Kuhn, T. (1962) *The Structure of Scientific Revolutions*. Chicago: University of Chicago Press.

Kuhn, T. (1994) *Tieteellisten vallankumousten rakenne* (Orig.: The Structure of Scientific Revolutions). Finnish Translation by Kimmo Pietiläinen. Helsinki: Art House.

Kumsa, M.K. (2007) 'Home and exile', *Qualitative Social Work*, 6(4): 483–7.

Kundnani, A. (2007) *The End of Tolerance: Racism in 21st Century Britain*. London: Pluto Press.

Kvale, S. (2004) *Interviews: An Introduction to Qualitative Interviewing*. London: Sage Publications.

Lacey, D. (2005) 'Predictors of social service staff involvement in selected palliative care tasks in nursing homes: An exploratory model', *American Journal of Hospice and Palliative Medicine*, 22(4): 269–76.

Lacombe, S. (2008) 'Consumed with sex: The treatment of sex offenders in risk society', *British Journal of Criminology*, 48(1): 55–74.

Ladson-Billings, G. and Donnor, J. (2005) 'The moral activist role of critical race theory scholarship', in N. Denzin and Y. Lincoln (eds), *The Sage Handbook of Qualitative Research*, 3rd Edn., Thousand Oaks, CA: Sage.

Larner, G. (2004) 'Family therapy and the politics of evidence', *Journal of Family Therapy*, 26: 17–39.

Larson, M.S. (1977) *The Rise of Professionalism: A Sociological Analysis*. Berkeley, CA: University of California Press.

Lather, P. (1992) 'Critical frames in educational research: Feminist and poststructural perspectives', *Theory into Practice*, 31(2): 87–99.

Laub, J. and Sampson, R. (2003) *Shared Beginnings, Divergent Lives: Delinquent Boys to Age Seventy*. Cambridge, MA: Harvard University Press.

Lavalette, M. and Ferguson, I. (2007) 'Democratic language and neo-liberal practice: The problem with civil society', *International Social Work*, 50(4): 447–59.

Lave, J. and Wenger, E. (1991) *Situated Learning: Legitimate Peripheral Participation*. Cambridge, UK: Cambridge University Press.

Lavin, K.E., McGuire, B.E. and Hogan, M.J. (2006) 'Age at death of people with an intellectual disability in Ireland' *Journal of Intellectual Disability*, 10(2): 155–64.

Lavoie, C. (2005) 'Participatory Action Research in a diverse, low-income neighborhood: Reflections from a white researcher', *Annual Conference of the Canadian Sociological and Anthropological Association (CSAA)*. London, Ontario.

Lavoie, C. (2006) 'Hiring people to work in their own community', in B. Lee and S. Todd (eds), *A Casebook of Community Practice: Problems and Strategies*. Mississauga: Common Act Press. pp. 114–19.

Lawrence, R. (2006) 'Research dissemination: Actively bringing the research and policy worlds together', *Evidence and Policy*, 2(3): 373–84.

Lawson, H. (1999) 'Journey analysis: A framework for integrating consultation and evaluation in complex change initiatives', *Journal of Educational and Psychological Consultation*, 10: 145–72.

Lawton, M.P. (1991) 'A multidimensional view of quality of life in frail elders', in J.E. Birren, J.E. Lubben, J.C. Rowe and G.E. Deutchman (eds.), *The Concept and Measurement of Quality of Life in the Frail Elderly*. New York: Academic Press, pp. 4–27.

Layard, R. (2005) *Happiness: Lessons from a New Science*. London: Allen Lane.

Layder, D. (1997) *Modern Social Theory: Key Debates and New Directions*, London: UCL Press.

Lazega, E. (1997) 'Network analysis and qualitative research: A method of contextualization', in G. Miller and R. Dingwall (eds), *Context and Method in Qualitative Research*. London: Sage Publications.

Leadbeater, B., Banister, E., Benoit, C., Jansson, M., Marshall, A. and Riecken, T. (eds) (2006) *Ethical Issues in Community-Based Research with Children and Youth*. Toronto: University of Toronto Press.

Lederman, Cindy S., Osofsky, Joy D. and Katz, Lynne (2007) 'When the bough breaks the cradle will fall: Promoting the health and well-being of infants and toddlers in juvenile court', *Infant Mental Health Journal*, 28(4): 440–8.

Lee, S.L., Colditz, G.A., Berkman, L.F. and Kawachi, I. (2003) 'Caregiving and risk of coronary heart disease in U.S. women: A prospective study', *American Journal of Preventive Medicine*, 24(2): 113–19.

Lee, Y.-J. and Greene, J.C. (2007) 'The predictive validity of an ESL placement test: A mixed methods approach', *Journal of Mixed Methods Research*, 1(4): 366–89.

Leiby, J. (1978) *A History of Social Welfare and Social Work in the United States*. New York: Columbia University Press.

Lekoko, R.N. (2007) 'Storytelling as a potent research paradigm for indigenous communities', *Alternative: An International Journal of Indigenous Scholarship*, 3(2): 82–95.

Lengermann, P. and Niebrugge, G. (2007) 'Thrice told: narratives of sociology's relation to social work', in C. Calhoun (ed.), *Sociology in America: A History*. Chicago: University of Chicago Press, pp. 63–114.

Lennox, N.G. and Kerr, M.P. (1997) 'Primary health care and people with an intellectual disability: The evidence base', *Journal of Intellectual Disability Research*, 41(Pt 5): 365–72.

Leonard, P. (1997) *Postmodern Welfare: Reconstructing an Emancipatory Project.* London: Sage.

Lerner, R.M., Dowling, E.M. and Anderson, P.M. (2003) 'Positive youth development: Thriving as the basis of personhood and civil society', *Applied Developmental Science*, 7(3): 172–80.

Leschied, W., Chiodo, D., Whitehead, P. and Hurley, D. (2005) 'The relationship between maternal depression and child outcomes in a child welfare sample: Implications for treatment and policy', *Child and Family Social Work*, 10(4): 281–91.

Leslie, D.R., Leslie, K. and Murphy, M. (2003) 'Inclusion by design: The challenge of social work in workplace accommodation for people with disabilities', in W. Shera (ed.), *Emerging Perspectives on Anti-Oppressive Practice.* Toronto: Canadian Scholars' Press, pp. 157–69.

Lesnik, B. (ed.) (1997) *Change in Social Work.* Hampshire: Arena.

Lethborg, C.E., Kissane, D. and Burns, W.I. (2003) '"It's not the easy part": The experience of significant others of women with early stage breast cancer, at treatment completion', *Social Work in Health Care*, 37(1): 63–85.

Leve, L.D. and Chamberlain, P. (2007) 'A randomized evaluation of multidimensional treatment foster care: Effects on school attendance and homework completion in juvenile justice girls', *Research on Social Work Practice*, 17(6): 657–63.

Lewin, K. (1946) 'Action research and minority problems', *Journal of Social Issues*, 2(4): 34–46.

Lewin, K. (1953) *Die Lösung sozialer Konflikte.* Bad Nauheim, Christian.

Lewis, J. (2002) 'Fluctuating fortunes of the social sciences since 1945. A working paper for the commission on the future of the social sciences'. Academy of Learned Societies for the Social Sciences.

Lewis J.R., Boyle, D.P., Lewis L.S. and Evans, M. (2000) 'Reducing AIDS and substance abuse factors among homeless, HIV-infected, drug-using persons', *Research on Social Work Practice*, 10(1): 15–33.

Lieberman, Alicia F. (2007) 'Ghosts and angels: Intergenerational patterns in the transmission and treatment of the traumatic sequelae of domestic violence', *Infant Mental Health Journal*, 28(4): 422–39.

Lightman, E. (1992) *A Community of Interests: The Report of the Commission of Inquiry into Unregulated Residential Accommodation.* Ontario: Queen's Printer for Ontario.

Lin, N. (1999) 'Building a network theory of social capital', *Connections*, 22: 28–51.

Lin, N. (2001) *Social Capital. A Theory of Social Structure and Action.* Cambridge: Cambridge University Press.

Lincoln, Y. and Guba, E. (2000) 'Paradigmatic controversies, contradictions and emerging confluences', in N. Denzin and Y. Lincoln (eds), *Handbook of Qualitative Research*, 2nd Edn., Thousand Oaks, CA: Sage.

Lincoln, Y.S. and Tierney, G.W. (2004) 'Qualitative research and institutional review boards', *Qualitative Inquiry*, 10(2): 219–34.

Lindblom, C. (1959) 'The science of "muddling through"', *Public Administration Review*, 19(2): 79–88.

Ling, H.K. (2004) 'The search from within: Research issues in relation to developing culturally appropriate social work practice', *International Social Work*, 47(3): 336–45.

Ling, H.K. (2007) *Indigenising Social Work: Research and Practice in Sarawak.* Petaling Jaya, Selangor, Malaysia: Strategic Information and Research Development Centre (SIRD). Available at: www.gerakbudaya.com.

Linhorst, D.M. (2006) *Empowering People with Severe Mental Illness: A Practical Guide.* New York, NY: Oxford University Press.

Linton, S. (1998) *Claiming Disability: Knowledge and Identity.* New York, NY: New York University Press.

Lipsey, M.W. (1993) 'Theory as method: Small theories of treatments', *New Directions for Program Evaluation*, 57: 5–38.

Lipsey, M.W. et al. (1985) 'Evaluation. The state of the art and the sorry state of the science', in D.S. Cordray (ed.), *Utilizing Prior Research in Evaluation Planning. New Directions for Program Evaluation.* San Francisco: Jossey–Bass, pp. 7–28.

Lipsey, M.W. and Wilson, D.B. (1993) 'The efficacy of psychological, educational, and behavioral treatment: Confirmation from meta-analysis', *American Psychologist*, 48: 1181–209.

Lipsey, M.W. and Wilson, D.B. (2000) *Practical Meta-Analysis.* New York: Sage.

Lipsky, M. (1980) *Street-Level Bureaucracy. Dilemmas of the Individual in Public Services.* New York: Russel Sage Foundation.

Lister, R. (1997) *Citizenship: Feminist Perspectives.* Sydney: The Federation Press.

Littell, J.H. (2005) 'Lessons from a systematic review of effects of multisystemic therapy', *Children and Youth Services Review*, 27(4): 4.

Littell, J.H. (2006) 'The case for multisystemic therapy: Evidence or orthodoxy?', *Children and Youth Services Review*, 28(4): 458–72.

Littell, J.H., Corcoran, J. and Pillai, V. (2008) *Systematic Reviews and Meta-Analysis (Pocket Guides to Social Work Research Methods)*. New York: Oxford University Press.

Littell, J.H., Popa, M. and Forsythe, B. (2005) 'Multisytemic therapy for social, emotional and behavioral problems in youth aged 10–17', *Cochrane Database of Systemic Reviews*, Issue 4, Art. No: CD004797.pub4.DOI:10.1002/15671838. CD004797.pub4.45–463.

Lloyd, R.M. (1992) 'Negotiating child sexual abuse: The interactional character of investigative practices', *Social Problems*, 39(2): 109–24.

Logsdon, R., Gibbons, L.E., McCurry, S. and Teri, L. (2002) 'Assessing quality of life in older adults with cognitive impairment'. *Psychosomatic Medicine*, 64, 510–19.

Longres, J. (2000) *Human Behavior in the Social Environment*, 3rd Edn., Itasca, Illinois: Peacock Publishers, Inc, pp. 336–7.

Lopez, J. and Potter, G. (2001) *After Postmodernism: An Introduction to Critical Realism*. London: Athlone.

Lorenz, W. (1994) *Social Work in a Changing Europe*. London: Routledge.

Lorenz, W. (2003) 'European experiences in teaching social work research', *Journal of Social Work Education*, 22(1): 7–18.

Lorenz, W. (2004) 'Research as an element in social work's ongoing search for identity', in R. Lovelock, K. Lyons and J. Powell (eds) *Reflecting on Social Work – Discipline and Profession*. Aldershot: Ashgate.

Lorenz, W. (2006) *Perspectives on European Social Work: From the Birth of the Nation to the Impact of Globalization*. Opladen and Farmington Hills: B. Budrich.

Lorenz, W. (2007) 'Practising history: Memory and contemporary professional practice', *International Social Work*, 50(5): 597–612.

Lorenz, W. (2008a) 'Paradigms and politics: Understanding methods paradigms in an historical context: the case of social pedagogy', *British Journal of Social Work*, 38(4): 625–44.

Lorenz, W. (2008b) 'Towards a European model of social work', *Australian Social Work*, 61(1): 7–24.

Lorig, K.R., Sobel, D.S., Stewart, A.L., Brown Jr., B.W., Ritter, P.L., González, V.M., Laurent, D.D. and Holman, H.R. (1999) 'Evidence suggesting that a chronic disease self-management program can improve health status while reducing utilization and costs: A randomized trial', *Medical Care*, 37(1): 5–14.

Lovelock, R., Lyons, K. and Powell, J. (eds) (2004) *Reflecting on Social Work: Discipline and Profession*, Aldershot: Ashgate.

Lovelock, R. and Powell, J. (2004) 'Habermas/Foucault for social work: Practices of critical reflection', in Robin Lovelock, Karen Lyons and Jackie Powell (eds), *Reflecting on Social Work – Discipline and Profession*. Aldershot, UK: Ashgate, pp. 181–223.

Lubove, R. (1965) *The Professional Altruist*. Cambridge: Harvard University Press.

Lüders, C. (1987) 'Der "wissenschaftlich ausgebildete Praktiker" in der Sozialpädagogik. Zur Notwendigkeit der Revision eines Programms', *Zeitschrift für Pädagogik*, 33: 635–52.

Lüders, C. (1991) 'Spurensuche. Ein Literaturbericht zur Verwendungsforschung', *Zeitschrift für Pädagogik*, Sonderheft 27, 415–37.

Lüders, C. (1998) 'Sozialpädagogische Forschung – was ist das? Eine Annäherung aus der Perspektive qualitativer Sozialforschung', in T. Rauschenbach and W. Thole (eds) *Sozialpädagogische Forschung. Gegenstand und Funktionen, Bereiche und Methoden*. Weinheim, München: Juventa.

Lüders, C. and Rauschenbach, T. (2001) 'Sozialpädagogische Forschung', in H.-U. Otto and H. Thiersch (eds), *Handbuch der Sozialarbeit/ Sozialpädagogik*, 2nd Edn., Neuwied, Kriftel: Luchterhand.

Lum, D. (1996) *Social Work Practice and People of Color. A Process Stage Approach*. Monterey, CA: Brooks/Cole.

Lundy, C. (2004) *Social Work and Social Justice: A Structural Approach to Practice*. Peterborough, Ontario: Broadview Press.

Lygo, I. (2004) *News Overboard: The Tabloid Media, Race Politics, and Islam*. Sydney: Southerly Change Media.

Lykes, M.B., Blanche, M.T. and Hamber, B. (2003) 'Narrating survival and change in Guatemala and South Africa: The politics of representation and a liberatory community psychology', *American Journal of Community Psychology*, 31(1/2): 79–90.

Lykes, M.B. and Coquillon, E. (2007) 'Participatory and action research and feminisms: Towards transformative praxis', in S.N. Hesse-Biber (ed.), *Handbook of Feminist Research*. Thousand Oaks, CA: Sage. pp. 296–326.

Lymbery, M. and Butler, S. (2004) *Social Work Ideals and Practice Realities*. Hampshire: Palgrave Macmillan.

Lynch, M. (1998) 'Waste managers? The new penology, crime fighting and parole agent identity', *Law and Society Review*, 32(4): 839–69.

Lynch, M. (2000) 'Rehabilitation as rhetoric: The ideal of reformation in contemporary parole discourses and practices', *Punishment and Society*, 2(1): 40–65.

Lyons, K. (1999) 'The place of research in social work education'. Paper presented at the ESRC Seminar, Theorising Social Work Research, 26 May 1999, Brunel.

Lyons, K. (2007) 'Historical portraits: Dame Eileen Younghusband (Jan. 1902 – May 1981), United Kingdom', *Social Work and Society*, 5 (2). Available at: http://www.socwork.net/2003/1/historicalportraits/404

Lyons, K. (2000) 'The place of research in social work education', *British Journal of Social Work*, 30(4): 433–47.

Lyons, K. and Lawrence, S. (eds) (2006) *Social Work in Europe: Education for Change*. Birmingham, UK: Venture Press.

Lyons, K., Manion, K. and Carlsen, M. (2006) *International Perspectives on Social Work: Global Conditions and Local Practice*. Houndsmill: Palgrave Macmillan.

Lyons, K. and Taylor, I. (2004) 'Gender and knowledge in social work', in R. Lovelock, K. Lyons and J. Powell (eds) *Reflecting on Social Work – Discipline and Profession*. Aldershot: Ashgate, pp. 72–94.

Lyotard, J.F. (1984) 'The Postmodern condition: A report on knowledge'. (La condition postmodern) Translation from the French by Geoff Bennington and Brian Massumi; foreword by Frederic Jameson. Minneapolis: University of Minnesota Press.

Maas, H. (1966) *Five Fields of Social Service: Reviews of Research*. New York: NASW.

Macafee, D.F. (1999) 'Predictors of perceived emotional distress', *Dissertation Abstracts International: Section A: Humanities Social Sciences*, 59(9-A): 3364.

Macaulay, A.C., Delormier, A., McComber, E., Cross, L., Porvin, G., Paradis, R. et al. (1998) 'Participatory research with the native community of Kahnawake creates innovative code of research ethics', *Canadian Journal of Public Health*, (March–April): 105–8.

McCallion, P., Ferretti, L. and Benoit, L. (2007) *Facing the Challenges: Financial Literacy and Exploitation and the PSA Client*. Albany, NY: NYS OCFS. A cd-rom.

McCallion, P. and Ferretti, L.A. (2008) 'Retirement', in T. Mizrahi and L.E. Davis (eds.), *Encyclopedia of Social Work* Washington, DC & NY: NASW Press & OUP, pp. 533–6.

McCallion, P., Janicki, M.P., Grant-Griffin, L. and Kolomer, S.R. (2000) 'Grandparent caregivers II:

Service needs and service provision issues', *Journal of Gerontological Social Work*, 33(3): 63–90.

McCallion, P., Toseland, R.W., Gerber, T. and Banks, S. (2004) 'Increasing the use of formal services by caregivers of persons with dementia', *Social Work*, 49(3): 441–50.

McCallion, P. and Kolomer, S.R. (2003) 'Aging persons with developmental disabilities and their aging caregivers', in B. Berkman and L. Harootyan (eds.), *Social Work and Health Care in an Aging World*. New York: Springer, pp. 201–25.

McCallion, P. and McCarron, M. (2004) 'Aging and Intellectual disabilities: A review of recent literature'. *Current Opinion in Psychiatry*, 17(5): 349–52.

McCarron, M., Gill, M., McCallion, P. and Begley, C. (2005) 'Health co-morbidities in ageing persons with Down syndrome and Alzheimer's dementia', *Journal of Intellectual Disability Research*, 49(Pt 7): 560–6.

McCarron, M. and McCallion, P. (2008) *The Intellectual Disability Supplement to The Irish Longitudinal Study on Ageing*. Dublin: Trinity College Dublin.

McClean, S. and Shaw, A. (2005) 'From schism to continuum?: the problematic relationship between expert and lay knowledge', *Qualitative Health Research*, 15(6): 729–49.

McCartt-Hess, P. and Mullen, E. (1995) 'Bridging the gap: Collaborative considerations in practitioner–researcher knowledge-building partnerships', in P. McCartt-Hess and E. Mullen (eds), *Practitioner–Researcher Partnerships: Building Knowledge from, in and for Practice*. Washington, DC: NASW Press.

McCracken, S.G. and Marsh, J.C. (2008) 'Practitioner expertise in evidence-based practice decision making', *Research an Social Work Practice*, 18: 301–10.

McCrae, N., Murray, J., Huxley, P., Thornicroft, G. and Evans, S. (2003) *The Social Care Contribution to Mental Health Research*. London: Health Services Research Department, Institute of Psychiatry, King's College London.

McCulloch, P. (2005) 'Probation, social context and desistance: Retracing the relationship', *Probation Journal*, 52(1): 8–22.

McCullough, J. (in press) 'Enemies everywhere: (In)security politics, asylum seekers and other enemies within', in A. Babacan and L. Briskma (eds), *Asylum Seekers: International Perspectives on Interdiction and Deterrence*. Newcastle: Cambridge Scholars' Press.

McCulloch, P. and McNeill, F. (2007) 'Consumer society, commodification and offender management', *Criminology and Criminal Justice*, 7(3): 223–42.

McDonald, C. (2006) *Challenging Social Work: The Context of Practice*. Basingstoke, UK: Palgrave Macmillan.

McDonald, C., Harris, J. and Wintersteen, R. (2003) 'Contingent or context? Social work and the state in Australia, Britain and the USA', *British Journal of Social Work*, 33: 191–208.

McGrath, A. (1995) *Contested Ground: Australian Aborigines under the British Crown*. Sydney: Allen and Unwin.

McIntyre, A. (2003) 'Through the eyes of women: Photovoice and participatory research as tools for reimagining place'. *Gender, Place and Culture*, 10(1): 47–66.

McIvor, G. (ed.) (2004) *Women Who Offend*. London: Jessica Kingsley.

McKernan, S.-M. and Ratcliffe, C. (2006) *The Effect of Specific Welfare Policies on Poverty*. Washington, DC: The Urban Institute.

McKnight, J. (1995) *The Careless Society*. New York: Basic Books.

McLaren, C., Landsberg, G. and Schwartz, H. (2007) 'History, accomplishments, issues and prospects of supportive services programs'. *Journal of Gerontological Social Work*, 49(1/2): 127–44.

McLaughlin, H. (2007) *Understanding Social Work Research*. London: Sage.

McLaughlin, H., Young, A. and Hunt, R. (2007) 'Edging the chance: Action research with social workers and deaf and hard of hearing service users to achieve "best practice standards"', *Journal of Social Work*, 7: 288–306.

McLeod, E. and Bywaters, P. (2000) *Social Work, Health and Equality*. London: Routledge.

McNeill, F. (2001) 'Developing effectiveness: Frontline perspectives', *Social Work Education*, 20(6): 671–87.

McNeill, F. (2004) 'Desistance, rehabilitation and correctionalism: Developments and prospects in Scotland', *Howard Journal of Criminal Justice*, 43(4): 420–36.

McNeill, F. (2006) 'A desistance paradigm for offender management', *Criminology and Criminal Justice*, 6: 39–62.

McNeill, F., Batchelor, S., Burnett, R. and Knox J. (2005) *21st Century Social Work*. Scottish Executive: Edinburgh.

McNeill, F. and Maruna, S. (2007) 'Giving up and giving back: Desistance, generativity and social work with offenders', in G. McIvor and P. Raynor (eds), *Developments in Work with Offenders*. London: Routledge, pp. 224–39.

McNeill, F. and Whyte, B. (2007) *Reducing Reoffending: Social Work and Community Justice in Scotland*. Cullompton: Willan.

McNeill, T. (2006) 'Evidence-based practice in an age of relativism: Towards a model for practice', *Social Work*, 51 (2): 147–57.

McTaggart, R. (1997) *Participatory Action Research: International Contexts and Consequences*. Albany, NY: SUNY.

Macdonald, G. (1994) 'Developing empirically-based practice in probation', *British Journal of Social Work*, 24: 405–27.

Macdonald, G. (1997a) 'Social work research: The state we are in', *Journal of Interprofessional Care*, 11(1): 57–66.

Macdonald, G. (1997b) 'Social work: Beyond control?' in A. Maynard and I. Chalmers (eds) *Non-Random Reflections on Health Services Research. On the 25th Anniversary of Archie Cochrane's Effectiveness and Efficiency*. Plymouth: BMJ Publishing Group. pp. 122–46.

Macdonald, G. (1999) Social work and its evaluation: A methodological dilemma?' in F. Williams, J. Popay and A. Oakley (eds), *Welfare Research: A Critical Review*. London: UCL Press.

Macdonald, G. (2000) 'Assessing systematic reviews and clinical guidelines', In V.A. Moyer, E.J. Eilliott, R.L. Davis, R. Gilbert, T. Klassen, S. Logan., C. Mellis and K. Williams (eds), *Evidence-based Pediatrics and Child Health*. London: BMH Publishing.

Macdonald, G. (2001) *Effective Interventions for Child Abuse and Neglect, An Evidence-Based Approach to Assessment, Planning and Evaluation*. Chichester: John Wiley.

Macdonald, G. (2003) *Using Systematic Reviews to Improve Social Care*. London: Social Care Institute for Excellence.

Macdonald, G. (2008) 'Evidence-based practice', in M. Davies (ed.), *The Blackwell Encyclopaedia of Social Work*, 3rd Edn., Oxford: Basil Blackwell.

Macdonald, G. and Macdonald, K. (1995) 'Ethical issues in social work research', in R. Hugman and D. Smith (eds), *Ethical Issues in Social Work*. London: Routledge.

Macdonald, G. and Sheldon, B. (1992) 'Contemporary studies of the effectiveness of social work', *British Journal of Social Work*, 22: 615–43.

Macdonald, G. and Sheldon, B. (1998) 'Changing one's mind: The final frontier? [evidence based social work]' *Issues in Social Work Education*, 18(1): 3–25.

Macdonald, G., Sheldon, B. and Gillespie, J. (1992) 'Contemporary studies of effectiveness in social work', *British Journal of Social Work*, 22(6): 615–43.

MacDonald, J. (2005) 'Untold stories: Women, in the helping professions, as sufferers of chronic pain restorying (dis)Ability – Professional findings', *Proceedings for Care, Work and Family Conference*. Manchester, UK: University of Manchester.

MacDonald, J. (2006) 'Storying both sides of the desk: Women in the helping professions use chronic pain experiences to inform practices', *Narrative Matters Conference*. Wolfville, N.S.: Acadia University.

MacDonald, J. (2008a) 'Untold stories: Women, in the helping professions, as sufferers of chronic pain (re) storying (dis)Ability'. Doctoral dissertation, Memorial University of Newfoundland, 2006. Library and Archives Canada, Ottawa (microform – AMICUS 33872393).

MacDonald, J. (2008b) 'Anti-oppressive practices with chronic pain sufferers', *Social Work in Health Care*, 47(2): 135–56.

Macera, C., Still, C., Brandes, D., Abramson, R. and Davis, D. (1991) 'The South Carolina Alzheimer's disease patient registry: A progress report', *The American Journal of Alzheimer's Care and Related Disorders and Research*, 6(1): 35–8.

Mackenzie, C., McDowell, C. and Pittaway, E. (2007) 'Beyond "do no harm": The challenge of constructing ethical relationships in refugee research', *Journal of Refugee Studies*, 20(2): 299–319.

Macmaster, S.A. (2004) 'Harm reduction: A new perspective on substance abuse services', *Social Work*, 49(3): 356–63.

Maguire, P. (1987) *Doing Participatory Research: A Feminist Approach*. Amherst, MA: University of Massachusetts.

Maguire, P. (2001) 'Uneven ground: Feminisms and action research', in P. Reason and H. Bradbury (eds), *Handbook of Action Research: Participative Inquiry and Practice*. London: Sage. pp. 59–69.

Mair, G. (ed.) (2004) *What Matters in Probation*. Cullompton: Willan.

Majors, R. and Billson, J.M. (1992) *Cool Pose: The Dilemmas of Black Manhood in America*. New York: Simon and Schuster.

Mallinson, S., Popay, J., Elliott, E., Bennett, S., Bostock, L., Gatrell, A., Thomas, C. and Williams, G. (2003) 'Historical data for health inequalities research', *Sociology*, 37(4): 771–780.

Maluccio, A.N., Canali, C. and Vecchiato, T. (eds) (2002) *Assessing Outcomes in Child and Family Services*. New York: Aldine de Gruyter.

Mancini, Michael A. (2007) 'The role of self-efficacy in the recovery from serious psychiatric disability', *Qualitative Social Work*, 6(10): 49–74.

Mandell, N. (1988) 'The least adult role in studying children', *Journal of Contemporary Ethnography*, 16(4): 433–67.

Mantle, G. and Moore, S. (2004) 'On probation: Pickled and nothing to say', *Howard Journal*, 43 (3): 299–316.

Mäntysaari, M. (2005a) 'Hyvinvointivaltiota kehittämässä – Richard Titmuss ja sosiaalihuolto' ('Developing the welfare state – Richard Titmuss and social administration'), in J. Saari (ed.), *Hyvinvointivaltio. Suomen mallia analysoimassa*. Helsinki: Gaudeamus, pp. 388–405.

Mäntysaari, M. (2005b) 'Realism as a foundation for social work knowledge', *Qualitative Social Work*, 4(1): 87–98.

Mäntysaari, M. (2005c) 'Propitious omens? Finnish social work research as a laboratory of change', *European Journal of Social Work*, 8 (3): 247–58.

Mäntysaari, M. and Haaki, R. (2007) 'Suomalainen sosiaalityön väitöskirjatutkimus vuosina 1982–2006', (Finnish PhD research from 1982 to 2006). *Janus*, 15(4): 357–66.

Maramaldi, P. and Lee, J. (2006) Older adults with cancer, in B. Berkman (ed.), *Handbook of Social Work in Health and Aging*. New York: Oxford University Press, pp. 7–18.

Maren, M. (1997) *The Road to Hell: The Ravaging Effects of Foreign Aid and International Charity*. New York: The Free Press.

Mark, M., Greene, J. and Shaw, I. (2006) 'The evaluation of policies, programmes and practices', in I. Shaw, J. Greene and M. Mark (eds) *Sage Handbook of Evaluation*. London: Sage Publications.

Marks, N., Lambert, J.D. and Choi, H. (2002) 'Transitions to caregiving, gender, and psychological well-being: A prospective U.S. national study', Journal of Marriage and Family, 64: 657–67.

Marlow, C. and Boone, C. (2005) *Research Methods for General Social Work*. Toronto: Thompson.

Marmot, M. and Wilkinson, R. (eds) (2005) *Social Determinants of Health*. Oxford: Oxford University Press.

Marsh, J., Cha, T. and Kuo, E. (2004) 'Social work readers describe useful knowledge'. *Social Work*, 49(4): 533–4.

Marsh, L. (1943) 'Report on Social Security for Canada: Prepared for the Advisory Committee on Reconstruction'. Ottawa: Kings Printer for Canada.

Marsh, P. and Fisher, M. (2005). *Developing the Evidence Base for Social Work and Social Care Practice*. London: Social Care Institute for Excellence.

Marsh, P., Fisher, M, Mathers, N. and Fish, S. (2005) *Developing the Evidence Base for Social Work and Social Care Practice*. Using Knowledge in social care report 10. London, UK: Social Care Institute for Excellence. Available at: www.scie.org.uk. Last accessed 1 December 2008.

Marshall, L.J. and Hunt, M.E. (1999) 'Rural naturally occurring retirement communities: A community assessment procedure'. *Journal of Housing for the Elderly*, 13(1/2): 19–34.

Marshall, W.L. and Serran, G.A. (2004) 'The role of the therapist in offender treatment', *Psychology, Crime and Law*, 10(3): 309–20.

Marston, G. and Watts, R. (2003) 'Tampering with the evidence: A critical appraisal of evidence-based policy making', *The Drawing Board: An Australian Review of Public Affairs*, 3(3): 143–63.

Martin, M. (2007) 'Crossing the line: Observations from East Detroit, Michigan USA', *Qualitative Social Work*, 6(4): 465–75.

Martin, J. and Nakayama, T. (1999) 'Thinking dialectically about culture and communication', *Communication Theory*, 9(1): 1–25.

Martin, S. (2004) 'Reconceptualising social exclusion: A critical response to the neoliberal welfare reform agenda and the underclass thesis', *Australian Journal of Social Issues*, 39(1): 79–94.

Martinez-Brawley, E. (2001) 'Searching again and again, inclusion, heterogeneity and social work research', *British Journal of Social Work*, 31(2): 271–85.

Martinez-Brawley, E.E. and Zorita, P.M.B. (1998) 'At the edge of the frame: Beyond science and art in social work', *British Journal of Social Work*, 28(2): 5–27.

Martinson, R. (1974) 'What works? – Questions and answers about prison reform', *The Public Interest*, 10: 22–54.

Maruna, S. (2001) *Making Good*. Washington, DC: American Psychological Association.

Maruna, S. and Farrall, S. (2004) 'Desistance from crime: A theoretical reformulation', *Kvlner Zeitschrift fur Soziologie und Sozialpsychologie*, 43: 171–94.

Maruna, S. and King, A. (2004) 'Public opinion and community penalties', in A.E. Bottoms, S. Rex and G. Robinson (eds), *Alternatives to Prison. Options for an Insecure Society*. Cullompton: Willan. pp. 81–112.

Maruna, S. and LeBel, T. (2003) 'Welcome home? Examining the "re-entry court" concept from a strengths-based perspective', *Western Criminology Review*, 4(2): 91–107.

Marx, K. and Engels, F. (1969) 'Manifesto of the Communist Party (1847–1848)', *Selected Works*, Vol. I. Moscow: Progress Publishers, pp. 108–37.

Mason, J. (1996) *Qualitative Researching*. London: Sage.

Masotti, P.J., Fick, R., Johnson-Masotti, A. and MacLeod, S. (2006) 'Healthy naturally occurring retirement communities: A low-cost approach to facilitating healthy aging. *American Journal of Public Health*, 96: 1164–70.

Massey University (2006) *Code of Ethical Conduct for Research, Teaching and Evaluations Involving Human Participants*. Palmerston North: Massey University.

Masten, A.S., Burt, K. and Coatsworth, J.D. (2006) 'Competence and psychopathology in development', in D. Cicchetti and D. Cohen (eds), *Developmental Psychopathology, Vol. 3: Risk, Disorder and Psychopathology*, 2nd Edn., New York: Wiley. pp. 669–738.

Matthewman, S. and Hoey, D. (2006) 'What happened to postmodernism?', *Sociology*, 40(3): 529–47.

Matthews, R. (2005) 'The myth of punitiveness', *Theoretical Criminology*, 9(2): 175–201.

Maunsell, E., Brisson, J., Deschenes, L. and Frasure-Smith, N. (1996) 'Randomized trial of a psychological distress screening program after breast cancer: Effects on quality of life', *Journal of Clinical Oncology*, 14(10): 2747–55.

Maxwell, J. (2002) 'The role of the researcher in qualitative psychology', in Mechthild Kiegelmann (ed.), *Qualitative Psychology Nexus*, 2, Die Deutsche Bibliothek.

Maxwell, J. (2008) 'The value of a realist understanding of causality for qualitative research', in N. Denzin and M. Giardina (eds), *Qualitative Inquiry and the Politics of Evidence*. Walnut Creek, CA: Left Coast Press.

May, T. (1996) *Situating Social Theory*. Buckingham: Open University Press.

May, T. (1999) *Explaining Reconviction Following a Community Sentence: The Role of Social Factors*. Home Office Research Study 192. London: Home Office.

Mayall, B. (2001) 'Introduction', in L. Alanen and B. Mayall (eds), *Conceptualising Child–adult Relations*. London: Routledge–Falmer, pp. 1–10.

Mayer, J.E. and Timms, N. (1970) *The Client Speaks: Working Class Impressions of Casework*. London: Routledge and Kegan Paul.

Maynard, A. and Chalmers, I. (1997) *Non-Random Reflections on Health Services Research. On the 25th Anniversary of Archie Cochrane's Effectiveness and Efficiency*. Plymouth: BMJ Publishing Group.

Maynard, M. (1985) 'The response of social workers to domestic violence', in J. Pahl (ed.), *Private Violence and Public Policy: The Needs of Battered Women and the Response of the Public Services*. London: Routledge and Kegan Paul.

Meagher, G. (2002) *The Politics of Knowledge in Social Service Evaluation*. Sydney: Uniting Care Burnside.

Measures, P. (2008) Comment on 'Service users and social care practitioners: Making ourselves felt', The Social Care Experts Blog, *Community Care*, March 6. Available at:

Meeuwisse, A., Sunesson, S. and Swärd, H. (2006) *Socialt arbete: en grundbok* (Social Work: An Introduction) 2. utg., 1. tr Edn., Stockholm: Natur och Kultur.

Meltsner, Arnold J. (1972) 'Political feasibility and policy analysis' in *Public Administration Review*, 32(6): 859–67.

Merrick, J., Davidson, P.W., Morad, M., Janicki, M.P., Wexler, O. and Henderson, C.M. (2004) 'Older adults with intellectual disability in residential care centers in Israel: Health status and service utilization. *American Journal of Mental Retardation*, 109(5): 413–20.

Merrington, S. and Stanley, S. (2004) '"What works?": Revisiting the evidence in England and Wales', *Probation Journal*, 51(1): 7–20.

Mertens, D.M. (2003) 'Mixed methods and the politics of human research: The transformative–emancipatory perspective', in A. Tashakkori and C. Teddlie (eds), *Handbook of Mixed Methods in Social and Behavioral Research*. Thousand Oaks, CA: Sage. pp. 135–64.

MetLife (2001) *The MetLife Survey of American Attitudes Towards Retirement*. New York, NY: Metropolitan Life Insurance Company.

MetLife (2006a) *Out and Aging: The MetLife study of Lesbian and Gay Baby Boomers*. New York, NY: Metropolitan Life Insurance Company.

MetLife (2006b) *Living Longer, Working Longer: The Changing Landscape of the Aging Workforce – A MetLife Study*. New York, NY: Metropolitan Life Insurance Company.

Metsch, L.R. and Pollack, H.A. (2005) 'Welfare reform and substance abuse', *The Milbank Quarterly*, 83 (1): 65–99.

Meyer, C. (1984) 'Integrating research and practice', *Social Work*, 28: 323.

Michigan State University (1996) *Points of Distinction: A Guidebook for Planning and Evaluating Quality Outreach*, revised. East Lansing, MI: Michigan State University Board of Trustees.

Middleman, R. and Goldberg, G. (1974) *Social Service Delivery: A Structural Approach to Social Work Practice*. New York: Columbia University Press.

Midgley, J. (1981) *Professional Imperialism: Social Work in the Third World*. London: Heinemann.

Midgley, J. (1983) *Professional Imperialism. Social Work in the Third World*. London: Heinemann.

Midgley, J. (1992) 'The challenge of international social work', in M.C. Hokenstad, S. Khinduka and J. Midgley (eds), *Profiles in International Social Work*. Washington, DC: NASW Press.

Miethe, I. (2007) 'Rekonstruktion und Intervention. Zur Geschichte und Funktion eines schwierigen und innovativen Verhältnisses', in I. Miehte, W. Fischer, C. Giebeler, M. Goblirsch and G. Riemann (eds) *Rekonstruktion und Intervention. Interdisziplinäre Beiträge zur rekonstruktiven Sozialarbeitsforschung*. Opladen: Barbara Budrich.

Miles, M.B. and Huberman, A.M. (1994) *Qualitative Data Analysis: An Expanded Sourcebook*, 2nd Edn., Thousand Oaks, CA: Sage.

Miller, B. and Cafasso, L. (1992) 'Gender differences in caregiving: Fact or artifact?' *The Gerontologist*, 32: 498–507.

Miller, G. and Dingwall, R. (1997) (eds) *Context and Method in Qualitative Research*. London: Sage Publications.

Milligan, C. (2001) *Geographies of Care: Space, Place and the Voluntary Sector*. Aldershot: Ashgate.

Milligan, C. and Fyfe, N. (2004) 'Putting the voluntary sector in its place: Geographical perspectives on voluntary activity and social welfare in Glasgow', *Journal of Social Policy*, 33(1): 73–93.

Milligan, C., Gatrell, A.C. and Bingley, A. (2004) 'Cultivating health: Therapeutic landscapes and older people in Northern England', *Social Science and Medicine*, 58(9): 1781–93.

Mills, C.W. (1943) 'The professional ideology of social pathologists', *American Journal of Sociology*, 49(22): 165–80.

Mills, C.W. (1959) *Sociological Imagination*. Harmondsworth: Penguin.

Mills, C.W. (2004 [1959]) 'On intellectual craftsmanship', in C. Seale (ed.), *Social Research Methods; A Reader*. London: Routledge.

Mills, D., Jepson, A., Coxon, T., Easterby-Smith, M., Hawkins, P. and Spencer, J. (2006) *Demographic Review of the UK Social Sciences*. Swindon: ESRC. Available at: http://www.esrc.ac.uk/ESRCInfoCentre.

Minkler, M. and Wallerstein, N. (eds) (2003a) *Community-Based Participatory Research for Health*. San Francisco, CA: Jossey–Bass.

Minkler, M. and Wallerstein, N. (2003b) 'Introduction to community based participatory research', in M. Minkler and N. Wallerstein (eds), *Community-Based Participatory Research for Health*. San Francisco, CA: Jossey–Bass, pp. 3–26.

Mitchell, F., Lunt, N. and Shaw, I. (2008) *Practitioner Research in Social Services: An Overview*. Report to Institute for Research and Innovation in Social Services, Dundee, Scotland.

Mitchell, G. (1999) 'Evidence-based practice: Critique and alternative view', *Nursing Science Quarterly*, 12(1): 30–5.

Moffitt, T. (1993) '"Life-course-persistent" and "adolescence-limited" anti-social behaviour: A developmental taxonomy', *Psychological Review*, 100: 674–701.

Moffitt, T. (1997) 'Adolescence-limited and life-course persistent offending: A complementary pair of developmental theories', in T.P. Thornberry (ed.), *Advances in Criminological Theory, 7: Developmental Theories of Crime and Delinquency*. New Brunswick and London: Transaction, pp. 11–54.

Mokken, R.J. (1997) 'Nonparametric models for dichotomous responses', in W.J. Van Der Linden and R.K. Hambleton (eds), *Handbook of Modern Item Response Theory*. New York: Springer, pp. 351–68.

Mokuau, N., Braun, K.L., Wong, L.K., Higuchi, P. and Gotay, C.C. (2008) 'Development of a family intervention for native Hawaiian women with cancer: A pilot study', *Social Work*, 53(1): 9–19.

Molloy, J.K. (2007) 'Photovoice as a tool for social justice workers', *Journal of Progressive Human Services*, 18(2): 39–55.

Monaghan, M. and Broad, B. (2003) *Talking Sense: Messages from Young People Facing Social Exclusion about their Health and Well Being*. London: The Children's Society.

Monette, D. (2002) *Applied Social Research: Tools for the Human Services*, 5th Edn., Orlando, FL: Harcourt College.

Moon, Jennifer A. (2006) *Learning Journals. A Handbook for Reflective Practice and Professional Development*. London and New York.

Moore, M., Beazley, S. and Maelzer, J. (1998) *Researching Disability Issues*. Buckingham: Open University Press.

Mor, D.P.S. (2003) 'Living conditions of women workers in brick kilns: Reflecting the agenda for social work intervention', *Indian Journal of Social Work*, 64(3): 388–400.

Morad, M. (2004) 'Talking hypothetically: The Duhem–Quine thesis, multiple hypotheses and the demise of hypothetico-deductivism', *Geoforum*, 35(2004): 661–8.

Morago, P. (2006) 'Evidence-based practice: From medicine to social work', *European Journal of Social Work*, 9(4): 461–77.

Morgan, D. (1992) *Discovering Men*. London: Routledge.

Morris, P.M. (2008) 'Reinterpreting Abraham Flexner's speech, "Is Social Work a Profession?": Its meaning and influence on the field's early professional development', *Social Service Review*, 82(4): 29–60.

Morris, T. (2006) *Social Work Research: Four Alternative Paradigms*. Thousand Oaks, CA: Sage.

Moser, H. (1977a) *Methoden der Aktionsforschung. Eine Einführung*. München: Kösel.

Moser, H. (1977b) *Praxis der Aktionsforschung*. München: Kösel.

Moser, H. (1995) *Grundlagen der Praxisforschung*. Freiburg i.Br., Lambertus.

Moss, S., Patel, P., Prosser, H., Goldberg, D., Simpson, N., Rowe, S. and Lucchino, R. (1993) 'Psychiatric morbidity in older people with moderate and severe learning disability. I: Development and reliability of the patient interview (PAS-ADD)', *British Journal of Psychiatry*, 163: 471–80.

Mowbray, C.T., Moxley, D.P., Jasper, C.A. and Howell, L.L. (Eds.), (1997a) *Consumers as Providers in Psychiatric Rehabilitation*. Columbia, MD: International Association of Psychosocial Rehabilitation Services.

Mowbray, C.T., Ribisl, K.M., Solomon, M., Luke, D.A. and Kewson, T.P. (1997b) 'Characteristics of dual diagnosis patients admitted to an urban public psychiatric hospital: An Examination of individual, social, and community domains', *The American Journal of Drug And Alcohol Abuse*, 23(2): 309–26.

Moyb, S. (2005) *Origins of the other: Emmanuel Levinas between revelation and ethics*, Ithaca, N.Y.: Cornell University Press.

MRC (Medical Research Council) (2000) *A Framework for Development and Evaluation of RCTs For Complex Interventions to Improve Health*. London: MRC.

Mullaly, B. (1993) *Structural Social Work: Ideology, Theory and Practice*. Toronto: McClelland and Stewart.

Mullaly, B. (1997) *Structural Social Work*. Oxford: Oxford University Press.

Mullaly, B. (2002) *Challenging Oppression: A Critical Social Work Approach*. Don Mills, Ontario: Oxford University Press.

Mullaly, B. (2006) *The New Structural Social Work: Ideology, Theory, Practice*. New York: Oxford University Press.

Mullen, E. (2002) 'Problem formulation in practitioner and researcher partnership: A decade of experience at the Centre for the Study of Social Work Practice', *Social Work Education*, 21(3): 323–36.

Mullen, E., Bellamy, J., Bledsoe, S., and Francois, J. (2007) 'Teaching evidence-based practice', *Research on Social Work Practice*, 17: 574–82.

Mullen, E., Bledsoe, S.E. and Bellamy, J.L. (2008) 'Implementing evidence based social work practice', *Research on Social Work Practice*, 18(4): 325–38.

Mullen, E. and Dumpson, J.R. (eds) (1972) *The Evaluation of Social Intervention*. San Francisco, CA: Jossey–Bass.

Mullen, E., Shlonsky, A., Bledsoe, S.E. and Bellamy, L. (2005) 'From concept to implementation: challenges facing evidence-based social work', *Evidence and Policy*, 1(1): 61–84.

Mullen, E. and Streiner, D. (2002) 'The evidence for and against evidence-based practice', in A. Roberts and K. Yeager (eds), *Foundations of Evidence-Based Social Work Practice*, pp. 21–34. Oxford: Oxford University Press.

Mullender, A. (1996) *Rethinking Domestic Violence: the Social Work and Probation Response*. London: Routledge.

Mullender, A. and Ward, D. (1991) *Self-directed Groupwork*. London: Birch and White.

Munch, S. and Shapiro, S. (2006) 'The silent thief: Osteoporosis and women's health care across the life span', *Health and Social Work*, 31(1): 44–53.

Munford, R. and Sanders, J. (2003) *Making a Difference in Families: Research that Creates Change*. Sydney, Australia: Allen and Unwin.

Munford, R. and Sanders, J. (2004) 'Recruiting diverse groups of young people to research: Agency and empowerment in the consent process', *Qualitative Social Work: Research and Practice*, 3(4): 469–82.

Munford, R. and Sanders, J. (2005) 'Borders, margins and bridges: Possibilities for change for marginalized young women', *Community Development Journal*, July, 1–13.

Munford, R., Sanders, J., Mirfin-Veitch, B. and Conder, J. (2008) 'Ethics and research: Searching for ethical practice in research', *Ethics and Social Welfare*, 2(1): 50–66.

Munford, R. and Walsh-Tapiata, W. (2000) *Strategies for Change*. Palmerston North: School of Sociology, Social Policy and Social Work, Massey University.

Munro, E. (1998) *Understanding Social Work: An Empirical Approach*. London: Athlone Press.

Munro, E. (2002a) 'The role of theory in social work research: A further contribution to the debate', *Journal of Social Work Education*, 38(3): 461–70.

Munro, E. (2002b) *Effective Child Protection*. London: Sage Publications.

Munro, E. (2004) 'The impact of audit on social work practice', *British Journal of Social Work*, 34(8): 1075–95.

Munro, E. and Parton, N. (2007) 'How far is England in the process of introducing a mandatory reporting system?', *Child Abuse Review*, 16: 5–16.

Murguia, A., Peterson, R.A. and Zea, M.C. (2003) 'Use and implications of ethnomedical health care approaches among Central American immigrants', *Health and Social Work*, 28(1): 43–51.

Mutua, K. and Swadener, B. (2004) 'Introduction', in K. Mutua and B. Swadena (eds), *Decolonizing Research in Cross-Cultural Contexts*. Albany: State University of New York Press.

NAC and AARP (2004) *Factsheet on Family Caregiving*. Washington, DC: NAC & AARP.

Nadkarni, V. (2002) 'Interventions on garbage pollution using integrated social work practice framework', *Indian Journal of Social Work*, 63(3): 313–39.

Nag, M. (2002) 'Empowering female sex workers for AIDS prevention and far beyond: Sonagachi shows the way', *Indian Journal of Social Work*, 63(4): 473–501.

NAS (National Association of Scholars) (2007) 'NAS study declares social work education to be a national academic scandal'. Email communication, socwork-bounces@dbnmail2.ukzn.ac.zal.

NASW (National Association of Social Workers) (1999) *Code of Ethics*. Washington, DC: NASW.

National Collaborating Centre for Mental Health (2004) 'Depression: Management of depression in primary and secondary care'. National Institute for Health and Clinical Excellence. Available at: www.nice.org.uk. Last accessed: 4 July 2008.

National Institute of Mental Health (1999) *Bridging Science and Service: A Report by the National Advisory Mental Health Council's Clinical Treatment and Services Research Workgroup*. Bethesda, MD: National Institute of Mental Health.

Neil, A. and Wolf, D. (2003) 'Implementing intervention research in doctoral education: Maximizing opportunities in training for outcome evaluation', *Journal of Teaching in Social Work*, 23(1/2): 3.

Nellis, M. (1993) 'CCETSW, criminal justice and the idea of a probation stream', in *Probation Training Issues and CCETSW's Training Curriculum*. London: CCETSW.

Nellis, M. (2007) 'Humanising justice: The English Probation Service up to 1972', in L. Gelsthorpe and R. Morgan (eds), *Handbook of Probation*. Cullompton: Willan, pp. 25–58.

Nesbitt, R. and Ross, L. (1980) *Human Inference: Strategies and Shortcomings of Social Judgment*. Englewood Cliffs, NJ: Prentice Hall.

Neuman, L. (2003) *Social Research Methods: Qualitative and Quantitative Approaches*, Boston: Allyn and Bacon.

Neuman, W. and Kreuger, L. (2005) *Social Work Research Methods: Qualitative and Quantitative Approaches*. Boston: Allyn and Bacon.

New Freedom Commission on Mental Health (2003) *Achieving the Promise: Transforming Mental Health Care in America. Final Report*. Rockville, MD: DHHS Pub. No. SMA-03-3832.

Newman, J. and Nutley, S. (2003) 'Transforming the probation service: "what works", organisational change and professional identity', *Policy and Politics*, 31(4): 547–63.

NHMRC (National Health and Medical Research Council) (2003) *Values and Ethics: Guidelines for Research in Aboriginal and Torres Strait Islander Health Research.* Canberra: NHMRC.

NHMRC/ARC/AVCC (National Health and Medical Research Council/Australian Research Council/ Australian Vice-Chancellors' Committee) (2007) *National Statement on Ethical Conduct in Human Research.* Canberra: NHMRC.

Nichols, S. (2004) *On the Natural Foundations of Moral Judgment.* Oxford: Oxford University Press.

Nieuwenhuizen Ch. van., Schene, A.H., Koeter, M.W.J. and Huxley, P.J. (2001) 'The Lancashire quality of life profile: Modification and psychometric evaluation', *Social Psychiatry and Psychiatric Epidemiology*, 36: 36–44.

NIH (National Institutes of Health) (2003) *NIH Plan for Social Work Research.* Available at: http://obssr. od.nih.gov/Documents/Publications/SWR_Report. pdf. Last accessed 29 February 2008.

NIH (2008a) Dissemination and Implementation Research (Program Announcement (PA) Number: PAR-07-086). Retrieved May 4, 2009 from http://grants.nih.gov/grants/guide/pa-files/PAR-07-086.html

NIH (2008b) Community Participation in Research (Program Announcement Number: PA-08-074). Retrieved May 4, 2009 from http://grants.nih.gov/ grants/guide/pa-files/PA-08-074.html

Noyes, J. and Popay, J. (2007) 'Directly observed therapy and tuberculosis: How can a systematic review of qualitative research contribute to improving services? A qualitative meta-synthesis', *Journal of Advanced Nursing*, 57(3): 227–43.

Noyes, J., Popay, J., Pearson, A., Hannes, K. and Booth, A. (Forthcoming 2009) 'Qualitative Research and Cochrane Reviews', in Higgins, J.P.T. and Green, S. (eds), *Cochrane Handbook for Systematic Reviews of Interventions*, Wiley-Blackwell (also published by The Cochrane Collaboration, 2008. www.cochrane-handbook.org

NSCAW Research Group (2002) National Survey of Child and Adolescent Well-being: Introduction to Wave 1. Ithaca, NY: Cornell University, National Data Archive on Child Abuse and Neglect.

Nunno, M. (2006) 'The effects of the ARC organizational intervention on caseworker turnover, climate, and culture in children's services systems', *Child Abuse and Neglect*, 30(8): 849–54.

Nuremberg Code (1949) *The Trials of War Criminals Before the Nuremberg Military Tribunals Under Control Council Law No. 10.* Nuremberg/Washington DC: US GPO.

Nutley, S.M., Walter, I. and Davies, H.T.O. (2007) *Using Evidence: How Research Can Inform Public Services.* Bristol: Policy Press.

NYSOFA (2000) *Project 2015: The Future of Aging in New York State.* Albany, NY: New York State Office for the Aging.

Oakley, A. (1998) 'Experimentation and social interventions: A forgotten but important history', *British Medical Journal*, 317: 1239–42.

Oakley, A. (2000) *Experiments in Knowing: Gender and Method in the Social Sciences.* Cambridge: Polity Press.

Oakley, A., Strange, V., Bonnell, C., Allen, E. and Stephenson, J. (2006) 'Process evaluation in randomised controlled trials of complex interventions', *British Medical Journal*, 332: 413–16.

Oates, R.K. and Bross, D.C. (1995) 'What have we learned from treating physical abuse?' *Child Abuse and Neglect*, 19(4): 463–73.

O'Brien, M., Bachman, M., Husbands, C., Shreeve, A., Jones, N., Watson, J. and Shemilt, I. (2006) 'Integrating children's services to promote children's welfare: Early findings from the implementation of children's trusts in England', *Child Abuse Review*, 15: 377–95.

OBSSR (Office of Behavioral and Social Sciences Research) (2001) *Qualitative Methods in Health Research.* Washington DC: National Institutes for Health. Available at: http://obssr.od.nih.gov/publications/qualitative.pdf

OBSSR (Office of Behavioral and Social Sciences Research) (2008) 'About OBSSR'. Available at: http://obssr.od.nih.gov/about_obssr/about.aspx. Last accessed 8 December 2008.

O'Dea, C. (1990) 'The experience and effects of loss and bereavement in failed pregnancy', *Journal of Social Work Practice*, 4: 66–89.

Oevermann, U. (1996) 'Theoretische Skizze einer revidierten Theorie professionalisierten Handelns', in A. Combe, and W. Helsper, (eds) *Pädagogische Professionalität.* Frankfurt a.M., Suhrkamp.

Office of National Drug Control Policy (2006) *Pushing Back Against Meth: A Progress Report on the Fight Against Methamphetamine in the United States.* Washington, DC: Government Publishing Office.

Office of National Statistics (2003) 'The mental health of young people looked after by local authorities'. Available at: http://www.statistics.gov.uk/ pdfdir/hel0603.pdf. Last accessed 22 November 2008.

Oktay, J.S. (1992) 'Evaluating social work discharge planning services for elderly people: Access, complexity, and outcome', *Health and Social Work*, 17(4): 290–8.

Olds, D., Henderson, C.R. and Kitzman, H. (1994) 'Does prenatal and infancy nurse home visitation have enduring effects on qualities of parental caregiving and child health and 25 to 50 months of life?', *Pediatrics*, 93: 89–98.

Oliver, J.P.J., Huxley, P.J., Bridges, K. and Mohamad, H. (1996) *Quality of Life and Mental Health Services*. London: Routledge.

Oliver, M. (1990) *The Politics of Disablement*. London: Macmillan.

Oliver, M. (1992) 'Changing the social relations of research production', *Disability, Handicap and Society*, 7: 101–15.

Oliver, M. (1996) *Understanding Disability: From Theory to Practice*. London: Macmillan.

Oliver, M. (1997) 'Emancipatory research: Realistic goal or impossible dream?', in C. Barnes and G. Mercer (eds), *Doing Disability Research*. Leeds: The Disability Press.

Oliver, M. (2004) 'If I had a hammer: The social model in action', in J. Swain, S. French, C. Barnes and C. Thomas (eds), *Disabling Barriers – Enabling Environments*, 2nd Edn., London: Sage.

Oliver, M. and Sapey, B. (2006) *Social Work with Disabled People*, 3rd Edn., Basingstoke: Macmillan.

Olshansky, S.J. et al. (2005) 'A potential decline in life expectancy in the United States in the 21st century', *NEJM*, *352*, 1138–45.

O'Malley, P. (2004) 'The uncertain promise of risk', *Australian and New Zealand Journal of Criminology*, 37(3): 323–43.

ONED (Observatoire National de l'Enfance en Danger) (2008) Available at: http://www.oned.gouv.fr/. Last accessed 10 October 2008.

Onken, S.J., Dumont, J.M., Ridgeway, P., Dorman, D.H. and Ralph, R.O. (2002) *Mental Health Recovery: What Helps and What Hinders*. New York: Columbia University. Available at: http://www.nasmhpd.org/ntac/reports/index.html

Onwuegbuzie, A.J. and Johnson, R.B. (2006) 'The validity issue in mixed research', *Research in the Schools*, 13(1): 48–63.

Osmond, J. and O'Connor, I. (2004) 'Formalizing the unformalized: Practitioners' communication of knowledge in practice', *British Journal of Social Work*, 34(5): 677–92.

Orcutt, B.A. (1990) *Science and Inquiry in Social Work Practice*. New York: Columbia University Press.

Orme, J. (1995) *Workloads: Measurement and Management*. Aldershot: Avebury (in association with CEDR).

Orme, J. (1997) 'Research into practice', in G. McKenzie, J. Powell and R. Usher (eds), *Understanding Social Research: Perspectives on Methodology and Practice*. Hove: Falmer Press.

Orme, J. (2000a) 'Interactive social sciences: patronage or partnership?' *Science and Public Policy*, 27(3): 211–19.

Orme, J. (2000b) 'Social work: "The appliance of social science" – a cautionary tale', *Social Work Education*, 19(4): 323–34.

Orme, J. (2001) *Gender and Community Care*. Basingstoke: Palgrave-Macmillan.

Orme, J. (2003a) 'Why social work need doctors', *Social Work Education*, 22(6): 541–54.

Orme, J. (2003b) '"It's feminist because I say so!" Feminism, social work and critical practice in the UK', *Qualitative Social Work*, 2(2): 131–53.

Orme, J. (2004) 'It's feminist because I say so: Feminism, social work and critical practice in the UK', *Qualitative Social Work*, 2(2): 131–54.

Orme, J. (2006) 'What are we producing knowledge for?' *Janus (Finnish)*, 2: 196–208.

Orme, J. and Glastonbury, B. (1993) *Care Management: Tasks and Workloads*. Basingstoke: BASW/Macmillan, Practical Social Work.

Orme, J. and Powell, J. (2008) 'Building research capacity in social work: Process and issues', *British Journal of Social Work*, 38(5): 988–1008.

Orme, J., Fook, J., MacIntyre, G., Paul, S. Powell, J. and Sharland, E. (forthcoming) 'An audit of research teaching in the Social Work degree' in J.Orme, ed. *An Audit of Baseline Resources for Social Work Research: Finances. Staff, Teaching*. Swindon: ESRC.

Ormond, B.A. et al. (2004) 'Supportive Services Programs in Naturally Occurring Retirement Communities', U.S. Department of Health and Human Services, Office of the Assistant Secretary for Planning and Evaluation, Office of Disability, Aging, and Long-Term Care Policy.

Ortega, D.M. and Richey, C.A. (1998) 'Methodological issues in social work research with depressed women of color', *Journal of Social Service Research*, 23(3–4): 47–70.

Ostler, T., Haight, W., Black, J., Choi, G., Kingery, L. and Sheridan, K. (2007) 'Case series: Mental health needs and perspectives of rural children reared by parents who abuse methamphetamine', *Journal of the American Academy of Child and Adolescent Psychiatry*, 46(4): 500–7.

Otto, H.-U. (1971) 'Zum Verhältnis von systematisiertem Wissen und praktischem Handeln in der Sozialarbeit', in H.-U. Otto and K. Utermann (eds) *Sozialarbeit als Beruf. Auf dem Weg zur Professionalisierung?* München: Juventa.

Otto, H.-U. and Schneider, S. (eds) (1973) *Gesellschaftliche Perspektiven der Sozialarbeit.* Neuwied, Berlin: Luchterhand.

Otto, Hans-Uwe and Ziegler, Holger (2008). 'The notion of causal impact in evidence-based social work: An introduction to the special issue on *What Works?*', *Research on Social Work Practice*, 18(4): 273–7.

Outhwaite, W. (2000) 'Jurgen Habermas', in G. Ritzer (ed.), *The Blackwell Companion to Major Social Theorists.* Malden, Massachusetts: Blackwell Publishers.

Oxfam (2007) *A Price Too High: The Cost of Australia's Approach to Asylum Seekers.* Melbourne: Oxfam.

Oyen, E. (2002) 'Poverty production: A different approach to poverty understanding'. Paper presented at the International Conference on Social Science and Social Policy in the 21st Century, Vienna.

Padgett, D. (1998) *Qualitative Methods in Social Work Research.* Thousand Oaks, CA: Sage.

Pahl, J. (2007) *Ethics Review in Social Care Research: Report From the Planning Group on Ethics Review in Social Care Research to the Department of Health.* London: Department of Health.

Pain, H. (2008) 'Practice research in social work and social care'. Southampton Practice Research Initiative Network Group (SPRING). Unpublished discussion paper.

Palmer, N., Peacock, C., Turner, F., Vasey, B. and Williams, V. (1999) 'Telling people what you think', in J. Swain and S. French (eds), *Therapy and Learning Difficulties: Advocacy, Participation and Partnership.* Oxford: Butterworth–Heinemann.

Palshaugen, O. (2007) 'On the diversity of action research', *International Journal of Action Research*, 3: 9–14.

Park, P. (1993) 'What is participatory research? A theoretical and methodological perspective', in P. Park (ed.), *Voices of Change: Participatory Research in the United States and Canada.* Connecticut: Bergin and Harvey, pp. 1–20.

Park, P. (2001) 'Knowledge and participatory research', in P. Reason and H. Bradbury (eds), *Handbook of Action Research: Participative Inquiry and Practice.* London: Sage Publications, pp. 81–90.

Parker, G., Bhatka, P., Lovett, C., Olsen, R., Paisley, S. and Turner, D. (2006) 'Paediatric home care: A systematic review of randomized trials on cost and effectiveness', *Journal of Health Services Research and Policy*, 11(2): 110–19.

Parker, J. (2001) 'Social movements and science: The question of plural knowledge systems', in J. Lopez and G. Potter (eds), *After Postmodernism: An Introduction to Critical Realism.* New York: Athlone Press.

Parker, R. (1999) *Adoption Now: Messages from Research.* Chichester: Wiley.

Parker, R.A., Ward, H., Jackson, S., Aldgate, J. and Wedge, P. (eds) (1991) *Looking After Children: Assessing Outcomes in Child Care.* London: HMSO.

Parr, H., Philo, C. and Burns, N. (2004) 'Social geographies of rural mental health: Experiencing inclusion and exclusion', *Transactions of the Institute of British Geographers*, 29: 401–19.

Parsloe, P. (1976) 'Social work and the justice model', *British Journal of Social Work*, 6(1): 71–89.

Parsons, T. (1951) *The Social System.* London: Routledge and Kegan Paul.

Parton, N. (1985) *The Politics of Child Abuse.* Basingstoke: Macmillan.

Parton, N. (1996) *Social Theory, Social Change and Social Work.* London: Routledge.

Parton, N. (1999) *Theorising Social Work Research.* Paper presented in seminar 'Social work: What kinds of Knowledge?' 26th May 1999, Brunnel. Available at: http://www.scie.org.uk/publications/misc/tswr/seminar1/parton.asp. Last accessed 14 September 2008.

Parton, N. (2000) 'Some thoughts on the relationship between theory and practice in and for social work', *British Journal of Social Work*, 30(4): 449–64.

Parton, N. (2002) 'Postmodern and constructionist approaches to social work', in R. Adams, L. Dominelli and M. Payne (eds), *Social Work: Themes, Issues and Critical Debates.* Palgrave, pp. 237–46.

Parton, N. (2003) 'Rethinking *professional* practice: the contributions of social constructionism and the feminist "ethics of care"', *British Journal of Social Work*, 33(1): 1–16.

Parton, N. (2005) *Safeguarding Childhood.* Basingstoke: Palgrave.

Parton, N. (2006) *Safeguarding Childhood: Early Intervention and Surveillance in a Late Modern Society.* Basingstoke: Palgrave/Macmillan.

Parton, N. (2008) 'Changes in the form of knowledge in social work: From the "social" to the "informational"?', *British Journal of Social Work*, 38(2): 253–69.

Parton, N. and O'Byrne, P. (2000) *Constructive Social Work: Towards a New Practice.* Basingstoke: Macmillan.

Patterson, G.R. (2005) 'The next generation of PMTO models', *The Behavior Therapist*, 28(2): 27–33.

Patton, M.Q. (2002) *Qualitative Research and Evaluation Methods*. Thousand Oaks, CA: Sage.

Pawson, R. (2002) 'Evidence-based policy: The promise of "realist synthesis"', *Evaluation*, 8(3): 840–58.

Pawson, R. (2006) *Evidence-Based Policy: A Realist Perspective*. Sage: London.

Pawson, R., Boaz, A., Grayson, L., Longon, A. and Barnes, C. (2003) *Types and Quality of Knowledge in Social Care*, Knowledge Review 3. London: Social Care Institute for Excellence.

Pawson, R. and Tilley, N. (1993) 'OXO, Tide, brand X and new improved evaluation', paper presented at the British Sociological Association Annual Conference, University of Essex, England.

Pawson, R. and Tilley, N. (1997) *Realistic Evaluation*. London: Sage.

Pawson, R. and Tilley, N. (2001) 'Realistic evaluation bloodlines', *American Journal of Evaluation*, 22(3): 317–24.

Payne, G., Dingwall, R., Payne, J. and Carter, M. (1981) *Sociology and Social Research*. London: Routledge and Kegan Paul.

Payne, M. (2005) *Modern Social Work Theory*, 3rd Edn., Basingstoke: Palgrave.

Payne, M. (2006) *What is Professional Social Work?* Bristol: Policy Press.

Peake, K. and Epstein, I. (2004) 'Theoretical and practical imperatives for reflective social work organizations in health and mental health: The place of practice-based research', in *Social Work in Mental Health*, Haworth Press, pp. 23–37.

Pearlin, L.I., Mullan J.T., Semple, S.J. and Scaff, M.M. (1990) 'Caregiving and the stress process: An overview of concepts and their measures', *Gerontologist*, 30: 583–94.

Pearson, G. (1973) 'Social work as the privatized solution to public ills', *British Journal of Social Work*, 3(2): 209–28.

Pearson, G. (1975) *The Deviant Imagination: Psychiatry, Social Work and Social Change*. Basingstoke: Macmillan.

Pease, B. (1987) *Towards a Socialist Praxis in Social Work*. Unpublished Masters Thesis, La Trobe University, Melbourne.

Pease, B. (1990) 'Towards collaborative research on socialist theory and practice in social work', in J. Petrucenia and R. Thorpe (eds), *Social Change and Social Welfare* Practice. Sydney: Hale and Iremonger.

Pease, B. (2000) *Recreating Men: Postmodern Masculinity Politics*. London: Sage.

Pease, B. (2002) 'Rethinking empowerment: A postmodern reappraisal for emancipatory practice', *British Journal of Social Work*, 32: 135–47.

Pease, B. (2004) 'Deconstructing white men: Critical reflections on masculinity and white studies', in A. Moreton-Robinson (ed.), *Whitening Race: Essays in Social and Cultural Criticism*. Canberra: Aboriginal Studies Press.

Pease, B. (2006a) 'Encouraging critical reflections on privilege in social work and the human services', *Practice Reflexions*, 1(1): 15–26.

Pease, B. (2006b) 'Masculine migrations', in A. Jones (ed.), *Men of the Global South*. London: Zed Books.

Pease, B. (2007) 'Critical social work theory meets evidence-based practice in Australia: Towards critical knowledge-informed practice in social work', in K. Yokota (ed.), *Emancipatory Social Work*. Kyoto: Sekai Shisou-sya, pp. 103–38.

Pease, B., Allan, J. and Briskman, L. (2003) 'Introducing critical theories in social work', in J. Allan, B. Pease and L. Briskman (eds), *Critical Social Work: An Introduction to Theories and Practice*. Sydney: Allen and Unwin.

Pease, B. and Crossley, P. (2005) 'Migrant masculinities: The experiences of Latin-American migrant men', *Journal of Iberian and Latin-American Studies*, 11(1): 133–40.

Pease, B. and Fook, J. (eds) (1997) *Transforming Social Work Practice: Postmodern Critical Perspectives*. Sydney: Allen and Unwin.

Pease. B. and Fook, J. (eds) (1999a) *Transforming Social Work Practice: Postmodern Critical Perspectives*. Sydney: Allen and Unwin.

Pease, B. and Fook, J. (1999b) 'Postmodern critical theory and emancipatory social work practice', in B. Pease and J. Fook (eds), *Transforming Social Work Practice: Postmodern Critical Perspectives*. Sydney: Allen and Unwin.

Pecora, P., Kessler, R.C., Williams, J., O'Brien, K., Downs, A.C., English, D. et al. (2005) *Improving Family Foster Care: Findings from the Northwest Foster Care Alumni Study*. Seattle: Casey Family Programs.

Pecora, P.J., McAuley, C. and Rose, W. (2006) 'Effectiveness of child welfare interventions: Issues and challenges', in C. McAuley, P.J. Pecora and W. Rose (eds), *Enhancing the Well-being of Children and Families through Effective Interventions*. Philadelphia. PA: Jessica Kingsley Publishers. pp. 14–20.

Pedersen, A., Clarke, S., Dudgeon, P. and Griffiths, B. (2005) 'Attitudes towards Indigenous Australians and asylum seekers: The role of false beliefs and other social-psychological variables', *Australian Psychologist*, 40(3): 170–8.

Peele, S. and Brodsky, A. (1991) *The Truth About Addiction and Recovery*. New York: Simon and Schuster.

Peile, C. and McCouat, M. (1997) 'The rise of relativism: The future of theory and knowledge development in social work', *British Journal of Social Work*, 27: 343–60.

Peled, E. and Leichtentritt, R. (2002) 'The ethics of qualitative social work research', *Qualitative Social Work*, 1(2): 145–69.

Pence, E. (1987) *In our Best Interest: A Process for Personal and Societal Change*. Duluth, MN: Minnesota Program Development Inc.

Pence, E. and Paymar, M. (1986) *Power and Control: Tactics of Men Who Batter. An Educational Curriculum*. Duluth, MN: Minnesota Program Development Inc.

Penheiro, P.S. (2005) 'An end to violence against children'. New York, NY: United Nation's Secretary General's Study on Violence Against Children. Available at: http://www.violencestudy.org/IMG/pdf/I._World_Report_on_Violence_against_Children.pdf. Last accessed 22 November 2008.

Pennrod, J., Preston, D.B., Cain, R.E. and Starks, M.T. (2003) 'A discussion of chain referral as a method of sampling hard-to-reach populations', *Journal of Transcultural Nursing*, 14(2): 100–7.

Perera, S. (2002) 'A line in the sea', *Race and Class*. 44 (2): 23–39.

Petrosino A., Turpin-Petrosino C. and Buehler J. (2002) '"Scared Straight" and other juvenile awareness programs for preventing juvenile delinquency', *Cochrane Database of Systematic Reviews*, 2002, Issue 2. Art. No.: CD002796. DOI: 10.1002/14651858. CD002796.

Phillips, D. (1987) *Philosophy, Science and Social Inquiry*. New York: Pergamum.

Phillips, D. (1990) 'Postpositivistic science: Myths and realities', in E. Guba (ed.), *The Paradigm Dialog*. Newbury Park: Sage.

Phillips, L. and Jorgensen, W. (2002) *Discourse Analysis as Theory and Method*. London: Sage.

Philp, M. (1979) 'Notes on the form of knowledge in social work', *Sociological Review*, 27(1): 83–111.

Pickering, M. (2000) 'Auguste Comte', in G. Ritzer (ed.), *The Blackwell Companion to Major Social Theorists*. Malden, Mass: Blackwell Publishers, pp. 25–52.

Pieper, M. (1988) '"Gebrauchsfertiges" Wissen? Von den Schwierigkeiten, Wissenschaft in der Praxis sozialer Arbeit zu nutzen', in K.-D. Ulke (ed.), *Ist Sozialarbeit lehrbar? Zum wechselseitigen Nutzen von Wissenschaft und Praxis*. Freiburg i.Br., Lambertus.

Pinfold, V., Thornicroft, G., Huxley, P. and Farmer, P. (2005) 'Active ingredients in anti-stigma programmes in mental health', *International Review of Psychiatry*, 17(20): 123–31.

Pinquart, M. and Sorensen, S. (2003) 'Differences between caregivers and noncaregivers in psychological health and physical health: A meta-analysis', *Psychology and Aging*, 18(2): 250–67.

Pithouse, A. (1999) *Social Work: The Social Organisation of an Invisible Trade*. Aldershot: Avebury Gower.

Pittaway, E., Bartolomei, L. and Rees, S. (2007) 'Gendered dimensions of the 2004 tsunami and a potential social work response in post-disaster situations', *International Social Work*, 50(3): 307–19.

Pittman, K., Gaines, E. and Faigley, I. (2007) *State Children's Cabinets and Councils: Getting Results for Children and Youth*. Washington, DC: The Forum for Youth Investment. Available at: http://www.forum-fyi.org/files/Getting%20%Results%20Final.pdf. Last accessed 16 June 2008.

Plath, D. (2006) 'Evidence-based practice: Current issues and future directions', *Australian Social Work*, 59(1): 56–72.

Platt, A. (1969) *The Child Savers: The Invention of Delinquency*. Chicago: University of Chicago Press.

Platt, Jennifer (1996) *A History of Sociological Research Methods in America. 1920–1960.* Cambridge: Cambridge University Press.

Plummer, K. (1997) 'Introducing Chicago sociology' in Plummer, K. (ed.), *The Chicago School: Critical Assessments Vol I, A Chicago Canon?* London: Routledge.

Polit, D. and Hungler, B.P. (1996). *Essentials of Nursing Research: Methods, Appraisal, and Utilization*. Philadelphia, PA: J.B. Lippincott.

Polkinghorne, D. (2000) 'Psychological inquiry and the pragmatic and hermeneutic traditions', *Theory and Psychology*, 10(4): 453–79.

Polanyi, M. (1958) *Personal Knowledge: Towards a Post-Critical Philosophy*. University of Chicago Press.

Polanyi, M. (1967) *The Tacit Dimension*. New York: Doubleday.

Popay, J., Thomas, C., Williams, G., Bennett, S., Gatrell, A. and Bostock, L. (2003) 'A proper place to live: Health inequalities, agency and the normative dimensions of space', *Social Science and Medicine*, 57: 55–69.

Popay, J., Williams, G., Thomas, C. and Gatrell, A.C. (1998) 'Theorising inequalities in health: The place of lay knowledge', in M. Bartley, D. Blane and G. Davey Smith (eds), *The Sociology of Health Inequalities*. Oxford: Blackwell.

Pope, C.E. and Snyder, H.N. (2003) *Race as a Factor in Juvenile Arrests*. Washington, DC: US Department of Justice.

Popkewitz, T. (1990) 'Whose future, whose past? Notes on a critical theory and methodology', in E. Guba (ed.), *The Paradigm Dialog*. Newbury Park, CA: Sage.

Popper, K. (1966) *Die Logik der Forschung*. Tübingen, Mohr Siebeck.

Popper, K. (1980) *The Logic of Scientific Discovery*. London: Inwin Hyman.

Potter, G. and Lopez, J. (2001) 'After postmodernism: The millenium', in J. Lopez and G. Potter (eds), *After Postmodernism: An Introduction to Critical Realism*. New York: Athlone Press.

Potts, K. and Brown, L. (2005) 'Becoming an anti-oppressive researcher', in L. Brown and S. Strega (eds), *Research as Resistance: Critical, Indigenous and Anti-Oppressive Approaches*. London: Canadian Scholars' Press.

Potts, K., and Brown, L. (2005) 'Becoming an anti-oppressive researcher' in L. Brown and S. Strega (eds), *Research as Resistance: Critical, indigenous and Anti-Oppressive Approaches*. Toronto: Canadian Scholars' Press, pp. 255–85.

Potvin, L., Cargo, M., McComber, A.M., Delormier, T. and Macaulay, A.C. (2003) 'Implementing participatory intervention and research in communities: Lessons from the Kahnawake Schools Diabetes Prevention Project in Canada', *Social Science and Medicine*, 56(6): 1295–305.

Powell, F. (2001) *The Politics of Social Work*. London: Sage.

Powell, J. (2002) 'The changing conditions of social work research', *British Journal of Social Work*, 32(1): 17–33.

Powell, J. (2005) '"Value talk" in social work research: Reflection, rhetoric and reality', *European Journal of Social Work*, 8(1): 21–37.

Powell, J. (2007) 'Promoting older people's voices – the contribution of Social Work to interdisciplinary research', *Social Work in Health Care*, 44(1/2): 111–26.

Powell, J. and Goddard, A. (1996) 'Cost and stakeholder views: A combined approach to evaluating services', *British Journal of Social Work*, 26(1): 93–108.

Powers, E. and Witmer, H. (1951) *An Experiment in the Prevention of Delinquency – the Cambridge–Somerville Youth Study*. New York: Columbia University Press.

Praglin, L.J. (2007) 'Ida Cannon, Ethel Cohen and early medical social work in Boston: The foundations of a model of culturally competent social service', *Social Service Review*, 81(1): 27–45.

Pratt, J. (2000) 'The return of the wheelbarrow man; or, the arrival of postmodern penality?', *British Journal of Criminology*, 40(1): 127–45.

Preston, S.M. (2007) 'Whose lives and whose learning? Whose narratives and whose writing? Taking the next research and literature steps with experts by experience', *Evidence and Policy*, 3(3): 343–59.

Priebe, S., Huxley, P.J., Knight, S. and Evans, S. (1999) 'Application and results of the Manchester Short Assessment of Quality of Life (MANSA)', *International Journal of Social Psychiatry*, 45(1): 7–12.

Prins, E.H. (2008) '"Maturing out" and the dynamics of the biographical trajectories of hard drug addicts' [114 paragraphs], *Forum Qualitative Sozialforschung/Forum: Qualitative Social Research*, 9 (1), Art. 30. Available at: http://www.qualitative-research.net/fqs-texte/1-08/08-1-30-e.htm. Last accessed 8 March 2008.

Printz, J.J. (2007) *The Emotional Construction of Morals*. Oxford: Oxford University Press.

Proctor, E. (in press) 'The question of questions: An agenda for social work practice research', in R. Fortune, P. McCallion, and K. Briar-Lawson (eds), *Social Work Practice Research for the 21st Century*. New York: Columbia University Press.

Proctor, E., Morrow-Howell, N., Li, H. and Dore, P. (2000) 'Adequacy of home care and hospital readmission for elderly congestive heart failure patients', *Health and Social Work*, 25(2): 87–96.

Proctor, E. and Rosen, A. (2008) 'From knowledge production to implementation: Research challenges and imperatives', *Research on Social Work Practice*, 18(4): 285–91.

Prosser, J. (1998) *Image-Based Research: A Sourcebook for Qualitative Researchers*. London; Bristol, PA: Falmer Press.

Pugh, R. (n.d.) 'What happened to our ideas and understandings of community? Thinking and theorizing local context and practice'. Paper presented in the UK to the 2006 Joint Social Work Education Conference (JSWEC), Homerton College, Cambridge.

Putnam, R. (1993) *Making Democracy Work: Civic Traditions in Modern Italy*. Princeton, NJ: Princeton University Press.

Quigley, D. (2006) 'A review of improved ethical practices in environmental and public health research: Case examples from native communities', *Health Education and Behaviour*, 33(2): 130–47.

Quine, W. Van Orman (2008 [1951]) 'Two dogmas of empiricism', *The Philosophical Review*, 60 (1951): 20–43. Available at: http://www.ditext.com/quine/quine.html. Last accessed 22 November 2008.

Quinn, M. (2003) 'Immigrants and refugees: Towards anti-racist and culturally affirming practices', in J. Allen, B. Pease and L. Briskman (eds), *Critical Social Work: An Introduction to Theories and Practices.* Sydney: Allen and Unwin.

Quinton, D. (2004) *Supporting Parents: Messages from Research.* London: Jessica Kingsley.

Quirk, A., Lelliott, P., Audini, B. and Buston, K. (2000) *Performing the Act: A Qualitative Study of the Process of Mental Health Act Assessments.* Final report to the Department of Health. London: The Royal College of Psychiatrists' Research Unit.

Qualitative Report, The. ISSN 1052-0147. Chenail, Ronald J. (ed.). Nova Southeastern University, Fort Lauderdale, Florida. Available at: http://www.nova. edu/ssss/QR/index.html.

Qualitative Social Work: Research and Practice (2007) Special issue on 'New Voices in Social Work'. 6(4).

Qureshi, H. (2004) 'Evidence in policy and practice', *Journal of Social Work*, 4(1): 7–23.

Rachman, S.J. and Wilson, G.T. (1980) *The Effects of Psychological Therapy.* Oxford: Pergamon.

Radkau, J. (2005) *Max Weber: Die Leidenschaft des Denkens* (*Max Weber: The Passion of a Thinker*). München: Hanser.

Radley, A., Hodgetts, D. and Cullen, A. (2005) 'Visualizing homelessness: A study in photography and estrangement', *Journal of Community and Applied Social Psychology*, 15(4): 273–95.

Ramon, S. (2000) (ed.) *A Stakeholder's Approach to Innovation in Mental Health Services: A Reader for the 21st Century.* Brighton: Pavilion Publishing.

Ramon, S. (2008) 'Options and dilemmas facing british mental health social work'. Anglia Plytechnic University, Cambridge, UK. Available at: http://www.critpsynet.freeuk.com/Ramon.htm

Ramon, S., Campbell, J. and Lindsay, J. (2006) 'The impact of political conflict on social work: Experiences from Northern Ireland, Israel and Palestine', *British Journal of Social Work*, 36: 435–50.

Ramon, S., Castillo, H. and Morant, N. (2001) 'Experiencing personality disorder: A participative research', *International Journal of Social Psychiatry*, 47: 1–15.

Ramos, B. (2004) 'Culture, ethnicity, and caregiver stress among Puerto Ricans', *Journal of Applied Gerontology*, 23(4): 469–86.

Raphael, D. (2004) *Social Determinants of Health: Canadian Perspectives.* Toronto: Canadian Scholars Press.

Rapp, C.A. (1992) 'The strengths perspective of case management with persons suffering from severe mental illness', in D. Saleeby (ed.), *The Strengths Approach in Social Work.* New York: Longman. pp. 45–58.

Rapp, C.A., Shera, W. and Kishardt, W. (1993) 'Research strategies for consumer empowerment of people with severe mental illness', *Social Work*, 38(6): 727–35.

Ratcliffe, P. (2004) *Race, Ethnicity and Difference: Imagining the Inclusive Society.* New York: Open University Press.

Rawson, R.A., Anglin, M.D. and Ling, W. (2002) 'Will the methamphetamine problem go away?', *Journal of Addictive Diseases*, 21(1): 5–19.

Raynor, P. (2004) 'Rehabilitative and reintegrative approaches', in A. Bottoms, S. Rex and G. Robinson (eds), *Alternatives to Prison: Options for an Insecure Society.* Cullompton: Willan, pp. 195–223.

Raynor, P. (2008) 'Community penalties and Home Office research: On the way to "nothing works"?', *Criminology and Criminal Justice*, 8(1): 73–87.

Raynor, P. and Robinson, G. (2005) *Rehabilitation, Crime and Justice.* Basingstoke: Palgrave Macmillan.

Razin, A. and Sadka, E. (1999) 'Migration and pension with international capital mobility', *Journal of Public Economics*, 74(1): 141–50.

Reamer, F.G. (1998) *Ethical Standards in Social Work. A Review of the NASW Code of Ethics.* Washington, DC: NASW Press.

Reamer, F. (2004) 'Social work and criminal justice: The uneasy alliance', *Journal of Religion and Spirituality in Social Work*, 23: 213–31.

Reardon, G.T., Blumenfield, S., Weissman, A.L. and Rosenberg, G. (1988) 'Findings and implications from pre-admission screening of elderly patients waiting for elective surgery', *Social Work in Health Care*, 13: 51–64.

Reason, P. (1994) 'Three approaches to participative inquiry', in N.K. Denzin and Y.S. Lincoln (eds), *Handbook of Qualitative Research.* Thousand Oaks, CA: Sage Publications, pp. 324–39.

Reason, P. and Heron, J. (1986) 'Research with people: The paradigm of co-operative experiential enquiry', *Person-Centred Review*, 1: 456–76.

Redmond, M. (2005) 'Co-researching with adults with learning disabilities', *Qualitative Social Work*, 4(1): 75–86.

Reducing Re-offending: Key Practice Skills. Edinburgh: Scottish Executive. Available online at: www.socialworkscotland.org.uk/resources/pub/Reducing Reoffending.pdf. Last accessed 21 May 2008.

Redwood, S. and Todres, L. (2006) 'Exploring the ethical imagination: Conversation as practice versus committee as gatekeeper', *Forum Qualitative Sozialforschung/Forum: Qualitative Social Research*, [electronic journal], 7(2), March, Article 26, 25 paragraphs. Available at http://www.qualitative-research. net/fqs-texte/2-06/06-2-34-e.htm. Last accessed 3 October 2007.

Rees, S. and Pease, B. (2006) 'Domestic violence in refugee families in Australia: Rethinking settlement policy and practice', *Journal of Immigrant and Refugee Studies*, 5(2): 1–19.

Rees, S. and Pease, B. (2007) 'Domestic violence in refugee families in Australia: Rethinking settlement policy and practice', *Journal of Immigrant and Refugee Studies*, 5(2): 1–20.

Rehr, H., Rosenberg, G. and Blumenfield, S. (1993) 'Enhancing leadership skills through an international exchange: The Mount Sinai experience', *Social Work in Health Care*, 18(3/4): 13–33.

Reichert, E. (2006) *Understanding Human Rights: An Exercise Book*. Thousand Oaks: Sage Publications.

Reid, P. and Vianna, E. (2001) 'Negotiating partnerships in research on poverty with community-based agencies', *Journal of Social Issues*, 57(2): 337–54.

Reid, W. (1988) 'Service effectiveness and the social agency', in R. Patti, J. Poertner and C. Rapp (eds), *Managing for Effectiveness in Social Welfare Organisations*. New York: Haworth.

Reid, W. (1990) 'Change-process research: A new paradigm?', in L. Videka-Sherman and W.J. Reid (eds), *Advances in Clinical Social Work Research*. Silver Spring, MD: NASW, pp. 130–48.

Reid, W. (1994) 'The empirical practice movement', *Social Service Review*, 68: 165–84.

Reid, W. (1998) *Empirically-Supported Practice: Perennial Myth or Emerging Reality?* Distinguished Professorship Lecture. New York: State University at Albany.

Reid, W. (2002a) 'Knowledge for direct social work practice: An analysis of trends', *Social Service Review*, 76(1): 6–33.

Reid, W. (2002b) 'In the land of paradigms, methods rules', *Qualitative Social Work*, 1(3): 291–5.

Reid, W. and Epstein, L. (1972) *Task-Centered Casework*. New York: Columbia Press.

Reid, W. and Shyne, A. (1969) *Brief and Extended Casework*. New York: Columbia University Press.

Reim, T. and Riemann, G. (1997) 'Die Forschungswerkstatt', in Gisela Jakob and Hans-Jürgen von Wensierski (eds), *Rekonstruktive Sozialpädagogik. Konzepte und Methoden sozialpädagogischen Verstehens in Forschung und Praxis*. Weinheim and Munich: Juventa, pp. 223–38.

Reissman, C. and Quinney, L. (2005) 'Narrative in social work: A critical review', *Qualitative Social Work*, 4(3): 391–412.

Research on Social Work Practice http://intl-rsw. sagepub.com/

Rex, S. (1999) 'Desistance from offending: Experiences of probation', *Howard Journal*, 38(4): 366–83.

Richards, L. (2005) *Handlung Qualitative Data. A Practical Guide*. London, Thousand Oaks, New Delhi: Sage Publications.

Richardson, J., Barkan, S., Cohen, M., Back, S., FitzGerald, G., Feldman, J., Young, M. and Palacio, H. (2001) 'Experience and covariates of depressive symptoms among a cohort of HIV infected women', *Social Work in Health Care*, 32(4): 93–111.

Richmond, M. (1917) *Social Diagnosis*. New York: Russell Sage Foundation.

Richmond, M.E. (1922) *What is Social Case Work?* New York: Russell Sage Foundation.

Riemann, G. (2003) 'A joint project against the backdrop of a research tradition: An introduction to "doing biographical research"' [36 paragraphs]. *Forum Qualitative Sozialforschung/Forum: Qualitative Social Research* [On-line Journal], 4(3). Available at: http://www.qualitative-research.net/ fqs-texte/3-03/3-03hrsg-e.htm. Last accessed 16 March 2008.

Riemann, G. (2005a) 'Ethnographies of practice – practising ethnography. Resources for self-reflective social work', *Journal of Social Work Practice*, 19(1): 87–101.

Riemann, G. (2005b) 'Zur Bedeutung von Forschungswerkstätten in der Tradition von Anselm Strauss. Mittagsvorlesung', *1. Berliner Methodentreffen Qualitative Forschung, 24–25. Juni 2005*.

Riemann, G. (2006) 'Ethnographers of their own affairs', in Sue White, Jan Fook and Fiona Gardner (eds), *Critical Reflection in Health and Social Care*. Maidenhead: Open University Press, pp. 187–200.

Riessman, C.K. and Wuinney, L. (2005) 'Narrative in social work: A critical review', *Qualitative Social Work*, 4(4): 391–412.

Rigney, L. (1999) 'Internationalisation of an Indigenous anti-colonial critique of research methodologies: A guide to Indigenist research methodology and its principles', *Wicazo Sa Review*, 14: 109–21.

Rioux, M.H. and Bach, M. (1994) *Disability Is Not Measles: New Research Paradigms in Disability*. North York, Ontario: Roeber Institute.

Rist, R.C. (2000) 'Influencing the policy process with qualitative research', in N. Denzin and Y. Lincoln (eds), *Handbook of Qualitative Research*, London: Sage.

Ristock, J. and Pennell, J. (1996) *Community Research as Empowerment: Feminist Links and Postmodern Interruptions*. New York: Oxford University Press.

Roberts, A. and Brownwell, P. (1999) 'A century of forensic social work: Bridging the past to the present', *Social Work*, 44(4): 359–69.

Roberts, A. and Springer, D. (eds) (2008) *Social Work in Juvenile and Criminal Justice Settings*. Springfield, Illinois: Charles Thomas.

Roberts, A., Yeager, K. and Regehr, C. (2006) 'Bridging evidence-based health care and social work', in A. Roberts and K. Yeager (eds), *Foundations of Evidence-Based Social Work Practice*. Oxford: Oxford University Press, pp. 3–20.

Roberts, B. (2002) *Biographical Research*. Buckingham: Open University Press.

Roberts, H. and Petticrew, M. (2006) *Systematic Reviews in the Social Sciences; A Practical Guide*. Oxford: Blackwell Publishing.

Roberts, K. and Bea, R. (2001) 'Must accidents happen? Lessons from high reliability organizations', *Academy of Management Executive*, 15(3): 70–8.

Roberts, R.E., Attkisson, C. and Rosenblatt, A. (1998) 'Prevalence of psychopathology among children and adolescents', *American Journal of Psychiatry*, 155: 715–25.

Robinson, G. (2001) 'Power, knowledge and "what works" in probation', *Howard Journal*, 40(3): 235–54.

Robinson, G. (2002) 'Exploring risk management in the probation service: Contemporary developments in England and Wales', *Punishment and Society*, 4(1): 5–25.

Robinson, G. (2003) 'Technicality and indeterminacy in probation practice: A case study' *British Journal of Social Work*, 33(5): 593–610.

Robinson, G. and McNeill, F. (2004) 'Purposes matter: Examining the "ends" of probation', in G. Mair (ed.), *What Matters in Probation*. Cullompton: Willan. pp. 277–304.

Robinson, J. (1970) 'Experimental research in social casework', *British Journal of Social Work*, 1(4).

Robinson, L. (1998) *'Race', Communication and the Caring Professions*. Buckingham: Open University Press.

Robinson, L. (2007) *Cross-Cultural Child Development for Social Workers*. London, UK: Palgrave Macmillan.

Robson, P., Begum, N. and Locke, M. (2003) *Developing User Involvement*. Bristol: Policy Press.

Roen, K., Arai, L., Roberts, H. and Popay, J. (2006) 'Extending systematic reviews to include evidence on implementation: Methodological work on a review of community-based initiatives to prevent injuries', *Social Science and Medicine*, 63: 1060–71.

Rogoff, B. (1990) *Apprenticeship in Thinking: Cognitive Development in Social Context*. New York: Oxford University Press.

Romm, N. (1997) 'Becoming more accountable: A comment on Hammersley and Gomm', *Sociological Research Online*, 2(3). Available at: http://www.socresonline.org.uk/socresonline/2/3/2.html.

Romm, N. (1998) 'Interdisciplinary practice as reflexivity', *Systemic Practice and Action Research*, 11(1): 63–77.

Romm, N. (2000) *Accountability in Social Research: Issues and Debates*. New York: Plenum Publishers.

Rooney, R. (1992) *Strategies for Work with Involuntary Clients*. New York: Columbia University Press.

Rose, A. (1958) *Regent Park: A Study in Slum Clearance*. Toronto: University of Toronto Press.

Rose, A. (1966) *Prospects For Rehabilitation In Housing In Central Toronto*. Report of Research Submitted to City of Toronto Planning Board and Central Mortgage And Housing Corporation, September 1966. Toronto.

Rose, A. (1980) *Canadian Housing Policies, 1935–1980*. Toronto: Butterworths.

Rosen, A. and Proctor, E.K. (2003) *Developing Practice Guidelines for Social Work Intervention – Issues, Methods, and Research Agenda*. New York: Columbia University Press.

Rosen, A., Proctor, E.K., Staudt, M.M. (1999) 'Social work research and the quest for effective practice', *Social Work Research*, 23(1): 4–14.

Rosenheck, R., Morrissey, J., Lam, J., Calloway, M., Stolar, M., Johnsen, M., Randolph, F., Blasinsky, M. and Goldman, H. (2001) 'Service delivery and community: Social capital, service systems integration, and outcomes among homeless persons with severe mental illness', *Health Services Research*, 36: 691–710.

Rossi, P. (1992) 'Strategies for evaluation', *Children and Youth Services Review*, 14: 167–91.

Rossi, P., Lipsey, M. and Freeman, H. (2004) *Evaluation: A Systematic Approach*, 7th Edn., Thousand Oaks, California: Sage Publications.

Rossi, P.H. and Wright, J.D. (1984) 'Evaluation research: An assessment', *Annual Review of Sociology*, 10: 331–52.

Rossiter, A. (2000) 'The postmodern feminine condition: New conditions for social work', in B. Fawcett, B. Featherstone, J. Fook and A. Rossiter (eds), *Practice and Research in Social Work: Postmodern Feminist Perspectives*. London: Routledge.

Rothman, J. and Thomas, E.J. (eds) (1994a) *Intervention Research: Design and Development for Human Service*. New York: Haworth.

Rothman, J. and Thomas, E.J. (1994b) 'An integrative perspective on intervention research', in J. Rothman and E.J. Thomas (eds), *Intervention research: Design and Development for Human Service*. New York: Haworth, pp. 3–23.

Rounsaville, B., Alcarcon, R., Andrews, G., Jackson, J.S., Kendell, R.E. and Kendler, K. (2002) 'Basic nomenclature issues for DSM-V', in D.J. Kupfer, M.B. First and D.A. Regier (eds), *A Research Agenda for DSM-V*. Washington, DC: American Psychiatric Assocation, pp. 1–29.

Rowntree, J. (1901) *Poverty, A Study of Town Life*. London: Macmillan.

Royal Commission on Aboriginal Peoples (1996) *Report of the Royal Commission on Aboriginal Peoples*. Ottawa, ON: Indian and Northern Affairs Canada.

Rubin, A. (2006, 2007) 'Proceedings of the conference on improving the teaching of evidence-based practice in social work'. Paper presented at the Conference on Improving the teaching of evidence-based practice in social work, University of Texas School of Social Work.

Rubin, A. (2007) Improving the teaching of evidence-based practice: Introduction to the special issue. *Research on Social Work Practice*, 17: 541–7.

Rubin, A. and Babbie, E. (2008) *Research Methods for Social Work*. Belmont, CA: Thomson.

Rubin, A. and Parrish, D. (2007) 'Challenges to the future of evidence-based practice in social work education', *Journal of Social Work Education*, 43(3): 405–28.

Ruckdeschel, R.A. (1994) 'Does emphasizing accountability and evidence dilute service delivery and the helping role – yes response', in Hudson, Walter and Nurius, Paula (eds), *Controversial Issues in Social Work Research*. Needham Heights, MA: Allyn and Bacon.

Ruckdeschel, R. and Farris, B. (1981) 'Assessing practice, a critical look at the single case design' *Social Casework*, 62(7): 413–19.

Rutman, D., Hubberstey, C., Barlow, A. and Brown, E. (2005) 'Supporting young people's transitions from care: Reflections on doing participatory action research with youth from care', in L. Brown and S. Strega (eds), *Research as Resistance: Critical, Indigenous and Anti-Oppressive Approaches*. Toronto: Canadian Scholars' Press, pp. 153–79.

Rutter, M. (2006a) 'The promotion of resilience in the face of adversity', in A. Clarke-Stewart and J. Dunn (eds), *Families Count: Effects on Child and Adolescent Development*. New York and Cambridge: Cambridge University Press, pp. 26–52.

Rutter, M. (2006b) *Genes and Behaviour: Nature–Nurture Interplay Explained*. Oxford: Blackwell Publishing.

Rutter, M. (2007a) 'Resilience, competence and coping', *Child Abuse and Neglect*, 31: 205–9.

Rutter, M. (2007b) 'Proceeding from observed correlation to causal inference: The use of natural experiments', *Perspectives on Psychological Science*, 2(4): 377–95.

Rutter, M. and Sroufe, L.A. (2000) 'Developmental psychopathology: Concepts and challenges', *Development and Psychopathology*, 12: 265–96.

Ryan, J.P., Marsh, J.C., Testa, M.F. and Louderman, R. (2006) 'Integrating substance abuse treatment and child welfare services: Findings from the Illinois alcohol and other drug abuse waiver demonstration', *Social Work Research*, 30(2): 95–107.

Sabo, K. (ed.) (2003) *Youth Participatory Evaluation: A Field in the Making*. San Francisco, CA: Jossey–Bass.

Sackett D., Richardson W., Rosenberg W. and Haynes R. (2000) *Evidence-Based Medicine: How to Practice and Teach EBM*, 2nd Edn., London: Churchill–Livingstone.

Sackett, D., Rosenberg, W., Muir Gray, J., Haynes, R. and Richardson, W. (1996) 'Evidence based medicine: What it is and what it isn't', *British Medical Journal*, 312: 71–2.

Sainsbury, E., Nixon, S. and Philips, D. (1982) *Social Work in Focus: Clients' and Social Workers' Perceptions in Long-Term Social Work*. Routledge and Kegan Paul.

Saleebey, D. (1996) 'The strengths perspective in social work practice: Extensions and cautions', *Social Work*, 41(3): 296–305.

Saleebey, D. (2005) *The Strengths Perspective in Social Work Practice*. Boston: Pearson/Allyn and Bacon.

Salkind, N. (2006) *Exploring Research*. New Jersey: Pearson Prentice Hall.

Salomon, A. (2003 [1933]) 'Die wissenschaftlichen Grundlagen der sozialen Arbeit', in A. Feustel (ed.), *Alice Salomon. Frauenemanzipation und soziale Verantwortung. Ausgewählte Schriften Band 3: 1919–1948*. Opladen: Luchterhand.

Samelson, E.J., Zhang, Y., Kiel, D.P., Hannan, M.T. and Felson, D.T. (2002) 'Effect of birth cohort on risk of hip fracture: Age-specific incidence rates in the Framingham Study'. *American Journal of Public Health*, 92: 858–62.

Samuel, M. (2005) 'Social care professionals overwhelmed by paperwork', *Community Care*, 14 December, 8.

Sandelowski, M. (2003) 'Tables or tableaux? The challenges of writing and reading mixed methods studies', in A. Tashakkori and C. Teddlie (eds), *Handbook of Mixed Methods in Social and Behavioral Research*. Thousand Oaks, CA: Sage, pp. 321–50.

Sanders, J. and Munford, R. (2005) 'Activity and reflection: Research and change with diverse groups of young people', *Qualitative Social Work*, 4(2): 197–209.

Sanders, J. and Munford, R. (in press) 'Participatory action research', in M. Ungar and L. Liebenberg (eds), *Researching Youth Across Cultures and Contexts.* Canada: University of Toronto Press.

Sandoval, C. (1997) 'Theorising white consciousness for a post-empire world: Barthes, Fanon and the rhetoric of love', in R. Frankenburg (ed.), *Displacing Whiteness: Essays in Social and Cultural Criticism.* London: Duke University Press.

Sanjek, R. (ed.) (1990) *Fieldnotes. The Makings of Anthropology.* Ithaca, NY and London: Cornell University Press.

Saraceno, C. (ed.) (2002) *Social Assistance Dynamics in Europe. National and Local Poverty Regimes.* Bristol: The Polity Press.

Satka, M. (1995) *Making Social Citizenship. Conceptual practices from the Finnish Poor Law to professional social work.* Jyväskylä: SoPhi.

Satka, M. and Harrikari, T. (2008) 'The present Finnish formation of child welfare and history', *British Journal of Social Work*, 38(4): 645–61.

Schellhammer, E., Aeberli, M., Egli, O., Winiker, J. and Zurschmiede, U. (1978) 'Merkmale und Problemsicht der erzieherisch Tätigen in Jugendheimen der deutschsprachigen Schweiz', *Fachblatt für Schweizerisches Heimwesen*, 49: 255–65.

Scheyett, A. (2006) 'Silence and surveillance: Mental illness, evidence-based practice and a Foucauldian lens', *Journal of Progressive Human Services*, 17(1): 71–92.

Schiepek, G., Eckert, H. and Weihrauch, S. (2002) *Assessment of Dynamic Systems – Data Based Real-Time Monitoring in the Management of Change Processes.* Aachen: Universitätsklinikum.

Schiepek, G., Weihrauch, S., Eckert, H., Trump, T., Droste, S., Picht, A. and Spreckelsen, C. (2003), Datenbasiertes Real-Time Monitoring als Grundlage einer gezielten Erfassung von Gehirnzuständen im psychotherapeutischen Prozess', in G. Schiepek (ed.), *Neurobiologie der Psychotherapie.* Stuttgart: Schattauer, pp. 235–72.

Schilling, R. (1997) 'Developing intervention research programs in social work', *Social Work Research*, 21(3): 173–80.

Schmidt, M. (1993) 'Grout: Alternative kinds of knowledge and why they are ignored', *Public Administration Review*, 53(6): 525–30.

Schneider, J., Murray, J., Banerjee, S. and Mann, A. (1999) 'Eurocare: A cross-national study fo co-resident spouse cares for people with Alzheimer's disease: 1- factors associated with cared burden', *International Journal of Geriatric Psychiatry*, 14: 651–61.

Schnurr, S. (2005) 'Evidenz ohne Reflexivität? – Zur Debatte um Evidenzbasierte Praxis in der Sozialen Arbeit', *Zeitschrift Forschung und Wissenschaft Soziale Arbeit*, 5: 19–31.

Schön, D. (1983) *The Reflective Practitioner: How Practitioners Think in Action.* New York: Basic Books.

Schön, D. (1987) *Educating the Reflective Practitioner: Towards a New Design for Teaching and Learning in the Professions.* San Francisco: Jossey–Bass.

Schön, D. (1992) 'The crisis of professional knowledge and the pursuit of an epistemology of practice', *Journal of Interprofessional Care*, 6(1): 49–63.

Schoon, I.J. and Bynner, H. (2003) 'Risk and resilience in the life course: Implications for interventions and social policies', *Journal of Youth Studies*, 6(1): 21–31.

Schuldberg, J. (2005) *The Challenge of Cross-Cultural Competency in Social Work: Experiences of Southeast Asian Refugees in the United States.* Lewiston, NY: Edwin Mellen Press.

Schultz, K.F., Chalmers, I., Hayes, R.J. and Altman, D.G. (1995) 'Empirical evidence of bias: Dimensions of methodological quality associated with estimates of treatment effects in controlled trials', *Journal of the American Medical Association*, 273: 408–12.

Schultz, R.L. (2005) *Hull-House Maps and Papers by the Residents of Hull-House.* Urbana and Chicago: University of Illinois Press.

Schütze, F. (1994) 'Ethnographie und sozialwissen-schaftliche Methoden der Feldforschung. Eine mögliche methodische Orientierung in der Ausbildung und Praxis der Sozialen Arbeit?' in N. Groddeck and M. Schumann (eds), *Modernisierung Sozialer Arbeit durch Methodenentwicklung und – reflexion.* Freiburg: Lambertus, pp. 189–297.

Schütze, F. (2000) 'Schwierigkeiten bei der Arbeit und Paradoxien professionellen Handelns. Ein grundla-gentheoretischer Aufriss', *Zeitschrift für qualitative Bildungs-, Beratungs- und Sozialforschung*, 1(1): 49–96.

Schütze, F. (2007a) 'Biography analysis on the empirical base of autobiographical narratives: How to analyse autobiographical narrative interviews—part I. Module B.2.1', *INVITE—Biographical counselling in rehabilitative vocational training—further education curriculum.* Available at: http://www. biographicalcounselling.com/download/B2.1.pdf. Last accessed 8 March 2008.

Schütze, F. (2007b) 'Biography analysis on the empirical base of autobiographical narratives: How to analyse autobiographical narrative interviews—part II.

Module B.2.2', *INVITE—Biographical counselling in rehabilitative vocational training—further education curriculum*. Available at: http://www.bio-graphicalcounselling.com/download/B2.2.pdf. Last accessed 8 March 2008.

Schwab, J. (1969) 'The practical: A language for curriculum', *School Review*, November: 1–23.

Schwandt, T. (1997) Evaluation as practical hermeneutics. *Evaluation*, 3(1): 69–83.

Schwandt, T. (ed.) (1998) 'Scandinavian perspectives on the evaluator's role in informing social policy', *New Directions for Evaluation*, No. 77. San Francisco: Jossey–Bass Publishers.

Schwandt, T. (2000) 'Three epistemological stances for qualitative inquiry: Interpretivism, hermeneutics and social constructionism', in N. Denzin and Y. Lincoln (eds), *Handbook of Qualitative Research*. Thousand Oaks: Sage.

Schwandt, T. (2002) *Evaluation Practice Reconsidered*. New York: Peter Lang Publishers.

Schwandt, T. and Dahler-Larsen, P. (2006) 'When evaluation meets the "rough ground" in communities', *Evaluation*, 12(4): 496–505.

Schwartz, P.J., Blumenfield, S. and Simon, E.P. (1990) 'The interim homecare program: An innovative discharge planning alternative', *Health and Social Work*, 15: 152–60.

SCIE (2006) *Using Qualitative Research in Systematic Reviews: Older People's Views of Hospital Discharge*. London: Social Care Institute of Excellence.

SCIE (Social Care Institute for Excellence) (2007) *The Participation of Adult Service Users, Including Older People, in Developing Social Care*. London: Social Care Institute for Excellence.

Scott, M.B. and Lyman, S.M. (1968) 'Accounts', *American Sociological Review*, 33: 46–62.

Scottish Executive (2006) *Changing Lives: Report of the 21st Century Social Work Review*. Edinburgh: Scottish Executive.

Scourfield, J. (2001) 'Interviewing interviewees and knowing about knowledge', in I. Shaw and N. Gould (eds), *Qualitative Research in Social Work*. London: Sage.

Scriven, M. (1986) 'New frontiers of evaluation', *Evaluation Practice*, 7(1): 7–44.

Scriven, M. (1997) 'Truth and objectivity in evaluation', in E. Chelimsky and W. Shadish (eds), *Evaluation for the 21st Century*. Thousand Oaks: Sage.

Seccombe, K. (2002) '"Beating the odds" versus "changing the odds": Poverty, resilience, and family policy', *Journal of Marriage and Family*, 64(2): 384–94.

Segal, S.P. and Aviram, U. (1978) *The Mentally Ill in Community-Based Sheltered Care*. New York: Wiley.

Segal, S.P. and Burgess, P.M. (2006) 'Conditional release, a less restrictive alternative to hospitalization?', *Psychiatric Services*, 57: 1600–6.

Seligman, M.E.P. (1995) 'The effectiveness of psychotherapy: The consumer reports study', *American Psychologist*, 50: 965–74.

Sellars, W. (1963) *Science, Perception and Reality*. London – New York: Routledge and Kegan Paul.

Sellick, C., Thoburn, J. and Philpot, T. (2004) *What Works in Adoption and Fostering?* Barkingside: Barnardos.

Senge, P.M. (1990) *The Fifth Discipline: The Art and Practice of the Learning Organization*. London: Century Business.

Sennett, R. (2003) *Respect in a World of Inequality*, 1st Edn., New York: W.W. Norton.

Sevenhuijsen, S. (1998) *Citizenship and the Ethics of Care: Feminist Considerations on Justice, Morality and Politics*. London: Routledge.

Shadish, W., Cook, T. and Leviton, L. (1990) *Foundations of Program Evaluation: Theories of Practice*. Newbury Park: Sage Publications.

Shapiro, V. (2009) 'Reflections on the work of Professor Selma Fraiberg: A pioneer in the field of social work and infant mental health', *Clinical Social Work Journal*. Available at: http://www.springerlink.com.floyd.lib.umn.edu/content/700862721301xj51/fulltext.pdf.

Sharland, E. and Taylor, I. (2006) 'Social care research: A suitable case for systematic review?' *Evidence and Policy*, 2(w): 503–23.

Shaw, I. (1996) *Evaluating in Practice*. Aldershot: Ashgate.

Shaw, I. (1999) *Qualitative Evaluation*. London: Sage.

Shaw, I. (2003a) 'Qualitative research and outcomes in health, social work and education', *Qualitative Research*, 3(1): 57–77.

Shaw, I. (2003b) 'Critical commentary: Cutting edge issues in social work research', *British Journal of Social Work*, 33: 106–16.

Shaw, I. (2004) 'William J. Reid: An appreciation', *Qualitative Social Work*, 3(2): 109–15.

Shaw, I. (2005) 'Practitioner research: Evidence or critique?', *British Journal of Social Work*, 35(8): 1231–48.

Shaw, I. (2006) 'Evaluation of social work and the human services', in I. Shaw, J. Greene and M. Mark (eds), *Handbook of Evaluation: Policy, Programme and Practice*. London: Sage Publications.

Shaw, I. (2007) 'Is social work distinctive?', *Social Work Education: The International Journal*, 26(7): 659–69.

Shaw, I. (2008a) 'Merely experts? Reflections on the history of social work, science and research', *Research, Policy and Planning*, 26(1): 57–65.

Shaw, I. (2008b) 'Ways of knowing in social work', in M. Gray and S. Webb (eds), *Social Work Theories and Methods*. London: Sage Publications.

Shaw, I. (2009) 'Rereading *The Jack-Roller*: Hidden histories in sociology and social work', *Qualitative Inquiry*, 15(7): 1241–64.

Shaw, I., Arksey, H. and Mullender, A. (2004) *ESRC Research and Social Work and Social Care*. London: Social Care Institute for Excellence.

Shaw, I., Arksey, H. and Mullender, A. (2006) 'Recognizing social work', *British Journal of Social Work*, 36(2): 227–46.

Shaw, I., Bell, M., Sinclair, I., Sloper, P., Mitchell, W., Dyson, P., Clayden, J. and Rafferty, J. (2009) 'An exemplary scheme? An evaluation of the Integrated Children's System', *British Journal of Social Work*.

Shaw, I. and Faulkner, A. (2006) 'Practitioner evaluation at work', *American Journal of Evaluation*, 27(1): 44–63.

Shaw, I. and Gould, N. (2001a) 'Introduction', in I. Shaw and N. Gould (eds), *Qualitative Research and Evaluation*. Sage: London.

Shaw, I. and Gould, N. (2001b) 'The social work context for qualitative research', in I. Shaw and N. Gould (eds), *Qualitative Research and Evaluation*. Sage: London.

Shaw, I. and Gould, N. (2001c) 'Inquiry and action: Qualitative research and professional practice', in I. Shaw and N. Gould (eds), *Qualitative Research and Evaluation*. Sage: London.

Shaw, I. and Gould, N. (eds) (2001d) *Qualitative Research in Social Work*. London: Sage Publications.

Shaw, I. and Norton, M. (2007) *The Kinds and Quality of Social Work Research in UK Universities*. London: Social Care Institute for Excellence.

Shaw, I. and Shaw, A. (1997) 'Game plans, buzzes and sheer luck: Doing well in social work', *Social Work Research*, 21(2): 69–79.

Shaw, M. and Hannah-Moffatt, K. (2004) 'How cognitive skills forgot about gender and diversity', in G. Mair (ed.), *What Matters in Probation*. Cullompton: Willan, pp. 90–121.

Sheldon, A. (2005) 'One world, one people, one struggle? Towards the global implementation of the social model of disability', in C. Barnes and G. Mercer (eds), *The Social Model of Disability: Europe and the Majority World*. Leeds: The Disability Press.

Sheldon, B. (1995) *Cognitive-Behavioural Therapy. Research, Practice and Philosophy*. London: Routledge.

Sheldon, B. and Chilvers, R. (2001) *Evidence-Based Social Care: Problems and Prospects*. Lyme Regis, Russell House.

Sheldon, B. and Chilvers, R. (2002) 'An empirical of the obstacles to evidence-based practice', *Social Work and Social Sciences Review*, 10: 6–26.

Sheppard, M. (1995) 'Social work, social science and practice wisdom', *British Journal of Social Work*, 25(3): 265–93.

Sheppard, M. (1996) 'Depression in the work of British health visitors: Clinical facets', *Social Science and Medicine*, 43(11): 1637–48.

Sheppard, M. (1997a) 'Depression in female health visitor consulters: Social and demographic factors', *Journal of Advanced Nursing*, 26: 921–9.

Sheppard, M. (1997b) 'Double jeopardy: The link between child abuse and maternal depression in child and family social work', *Child and Family Social Work*, 2(2): 91–108.

Sheppard, M. (1997c) 'Social work practice in child and family care: A study of maternal depression', *British Journal of Social Work*, 27(6): 815–47.

Sheppard, M. (1998a) 'Social profile, maternal depression and welfare concerns in clients of health visitors and social workers: A comparative study', *Children and Society*, 12: 125–35.

Sheppard, M. (1998b) 'Practice validity, reflexivity and knowledge for social work', *British Journal of Social Work*, 28: 763–81.

Sheppard, M. (2001a) *Social Work Practice with Depressed Mothers in Child and Family Care*. London: Stationery Office.

Sheppard, M. (2001b) 'Depressed mothers' experience of partnership in child and family care', *British Journal of Social Work*, 32: 93–112.

Sheppard, M. (2003) 'The significance of past abuse to current intervention strategies with depressed mothers in child and family care', *British Journal of Social Work*, 33(6): 769–87.

Sheppard, M. (2004) 'An evaluation of social support interventions with depressed mothers', *British Journal of Social Work*, 34: 939–60.

Sheppard, M. (2005) 'Mothers' coping strategies as child and family care service applicants', *British Journal of Social Work*, 35: 743–59.

Sheppard, M. (2006) *Social Exclusion and Social Work: The Idea of Practice*. Aldershot: Ashgate.

Sheppard, M. (2008) 'Depression in children's centre users', Unpublished paper.

Sheppard, M., Newstead, S., Di Caccavo, A. and Ryan, K. (2000) 'Reflexivity and the development of process knowledge in social work: A classification and empirical study', *British Journal of Social Work*, 30(4): 465–88.

Sherman, L.W., Gottfredson, D.C., MacKenzie, D.L., Eck, J.E., Reuter, P. and Bushway, S.D. (1997) *Preventing Crime: What Works, What Doesn't, What's Promising*. Washington, DC: Department of Justice, National Institute of Justice.

Shewell, H. (2000) *'Enough to Keep Them Alive': Indian Welfare in Canada, 1873–1965*. Toronto: University of Toronto Press.

Shirilla, J.J. and Weatherston, D.J. (eds) (2002) *Case Studies in Infant Mental Health: Risk, Resiliency, and Relationships*. Washington, DC: Zero to Three, pp. 1–13.

Shulman, L. (2006) *'The Skills of Helping Individuals, Families, Groups, and Communities*, 5th Edn., Belmont, CA: Thomson Higher Education.

Shweder, R.A., Goodnow, J.J., Hitano, G., LeVine, R.A., Markus, H.R. and Miller, P.J. (2006) 'The cultural psychology of development: One mind, many mentalities', in W. Damon and Lerner R.M. (eds), *Handbook of Child Psychology, Vol. 1: Theoretical Models of Human Development*, 6th Edn., Hoboken, NJ: Wiley, pp. 716–92.

Side, K. (2005) 'Snapshot on identity: Women's contributions addressing community relations in a rural northern Irish District', *Women's Studies International Forum*, 28(4): 315–27.

Sierminska, E., Brandolini, A. and Smeeding, T.M. (2006) *Comparing Wealth Distribution Across Rich Countries: First Results From The Luxembourg Wealth Study*. Available at: http://www.lisproject.org/publications/lwswps/lws1.pdf. Last accessed 10 September 2008.

Sijtsma, K. and Molenaar, I.W. (2002) 'Introduction to nonparametric item response theory', in R.M. Jaeger (ed.), *Measurement Methods for the Social Sciences 5*. Thousand Oaks: Sage.

Silverman, D. (1997) 'The logics of qualitative research', in G. Miller and R. Dingwall (eds), *Context and Method in Qualitative Research*. London: Sage Publications.

Simon, J. (2007) *Governing Through Crime: How the War on Crime Transformed American Democracy and Created a Culture of Fear*. New York: Oxford University Press.

Simpson, E.L. and House, A.O. (2002) 'Involving users in the delivery and evaluation of mental health services: Systematic review', *British Medical Journal*, 325: 1265.

Sin, R. (2007) 'Community action research: Lessons from the Chinese communities in Montreal', in D. Baines (ed.), *Doing Anti-Oppressive Practice: Building Transformative Politicized Social Work*. Halifax: Fernwood Publishing, pp. 160–75.

Sinclair, I. (2000) *Methods and Measurement in Evaluative Social Work* http://www.scie.org.uk/publications/misc/tswr/seminar6.asp

Sinclair, I. (2005) *Fostering Now: Messages from Research*. London: Jessica Kingsley.

Sinclair, I., Baker, C., Lee, J. and Gibbs, I. (2007) *The Pursuit of Permanence: A Study of the English Child Care System*. London: Jessica Kingsley.

Sinclair, I. and Thomas, D.N. (1983) *Perspectives on Patch*. London: NISW, Paper 14.

Sinclair, I., Wilson, K. and Gibbs, I. (2004) *Foster Placements: Why They Succeed and Why They Fail*. London: Jessica Kingsley.

Singer, P. (2007) 'Giving till it doesn't hurt', *The Age*, 6 January, 17.

Skehill C. (2007) 'Researching the history of social work: Exposition of a history of the present approach', *European Journal of Social Work*, 10(4): 449–63.

Skidmore, W. (1975) *Theoretical thinking in sociology*. New York: Cambridge University Press.

Slade, M. and Priebe, S. (2001) 'Are randomised controlled trials the only gold that glitters?', *British Journal of Psychiatry*, 179: 286–7.

Smith, A. (1996) 'Mad cows and ecstasy: Chance and choice in an evidence-based society', *Journal of the Royal Statistical Society A*, 159(3): 367–83.

Smith, A. and Pitts, M. (2007) 'Researching the margins: An introduction', in M. Pitts and A. Smith (eds), *Researching the Margins: Strategies for Ethical and Rigorous Research with Marginalised Communities*. Houndmills: Palgrave Macmillan.

Smith, C. (2001) 'Trust and confidence: Possibilities for social work in high modernity', *British Journal of Social Work*, 32(2): 287–306.

Smith, C. (2004a) 'Trust and confidence: Making the moral case for social work', *Social Work and Social Sciences Review*, 11(3): 5–15.

Smith, C.A., Cohen-Callow, A. and Hall, D.M.H. (2007) 'Impact of a foundation-level MSW research course on students' critical appraisal skills', *Journal of Social Work Education*, 43(30): 481–95.

Smith, D. (1995) *Criminology for Social Work*. London: Macmillan.

Smith, D. (1998) 'Social work with offenders: The practice of exclusion and the potential for inclusion', in M. Barry and C. Hallett (eds), *Social Exclusion and*

Social Work: Issues of Theory, Policy and Practice. Dorset: Russell House, pp. 107–17.

Smith, D. (2005) 'Probation and social work', *British Journal of Social Work*, 35: 621–37.

Smith, D.E. (1987) *The Everyday as Problematic: A Feminist Sociology.* Toronto: University of Toronto Press.

Smith, D.J. (2002) 'Crime and the life course', in M. Maguire, R. Morgan and R. Reiner, (eds), *The Oxford Handbook of Criminology*, 4th Edn., Oxford: Oxford University Press.

Smith, L.T. (1999) *Decolonising Methodologies: Research and Indigenous Peoples.* Dunedin: University of Otago Press.

Smith, M. (2004b) 'Parental mental health: Disruptions to parenting and outcomes for children', *Child and Family Social Work*, 9(1): 3–11.

Smith, M.K. (1999, 2007) 'Social pedagogy' in *The Encyclopaedia of Informal Education.* Available at: http://www.infed.org/biblio/b-socped.htm. Last accessed 1 September 2008.

Smith, M.K. (2001) 'Kurt Lewin, groups, experiential learning and action research', *The Encyclopedia of Informal Education.* Available at: http://www.infed.org/thinkers/et-lewin.htm. Last accessed 12 September 2008.

Smith, M.L. and Glass, G.V. (1977) '*Meta-analysis* of psychotherapy outcome studies'. *American Psychologist*, 32: 752–60.

Smith, R. (2004c) 'A matter of trust: Service users and researchers. *Qualitative Social Work*, 3(3): 335–46.

Smith, R., Monaghan, M. and Broad, B. (2002) 'Involving young people as co-researchers: Facing up to methodological issues', *Qualitative Social Work*, 1(2): 191–207.

Smith, S.R. and Kirking, D.M. (1999) 'Access and use of medications in HIV disease'. *Health Services Research*, 34(1.1): 123–44.

Snooks, H., Peconi, J. and Porter, A. (2006) *An Overview of the Evidence Concerning the Effectiveness of Services Delivered Jointly by Health and Social Care Providers and Related Workforce Issues.* Cardiff: AWARD.

Social Care Institute for Excellence (2004) *Learning Organizations: A Resource Pack.* Available at: http://www.scie.org.uk/publications/learningorgs/index.asp. Last accessed 4 August 2008.

SDRG (Social Development Research Group) (2008) Available at: http://depts.washington.edu.sdrg/. Last accessed 10 October 2008.

Social Exclusion Unit (2002) *Reducing Reoffending by Ex-prisoners.* London: Office of the Deputy Prime Minister.

Social Exclusion Unit (2004) *Social Exclusion and Mental Health.* Social exclusion unit report. London: Office of Deputy Prime Minister.

Social Research Association (2003) *Ethical Guidelines.* Available at: http://www.the-sra.org.uk/ethical.htm. Last accessed 3 November 2008.

Socialstyrelsen (2006) Barn och unga-insater ar 2006. Stockholm: National Board of Health and Welfare. (Children in public care in 2008 – some tables and summaries in English.)

socwork-bounces@dbnmail2.ukzn.ac.zal. 'Social work education a national academic scandal – USA, email distribution list.

Sohng, S.S.L. (1996) 'Participatory research and community organizing', *Journal of Sociology and Social Welfare*, 23(4): 77–95.

Solomon, P. and Draine, J. (2004) 'Outcome measurement scale with families of the serious mentally ill', in A. Roberts and K. Yeager (eds), *Evidence-Based Practice in Health Care and Human Services.* New York: Oxford University Press.

Solomon, P. and Marshall, T. (2002) 'Competencies for collaborating with families of persons with severe mental illness: Improving client outcomes', in A. Roberts and G. Greene (eds), *Social Workers' Desk Reference.* New York: Oxford University Press.

Somers, M.R. (1998) '"We're no angels": Realism, rational choice, and relationality in social science', *The American Journal of Sociology*, 104(3): 722–84.

Sommerfeld, P. (1998) 'Erkenntnistheoretische Grundlagen der Sozialarbeitswissenschaft und Konsequenzen für die Forschung', in E. Steinert, B. Sticher-Gil, P. Sommerfeld and K. Maier (eds), *Sozialarbeitsforschung: was sie ist und leistet.* Freibrug i. Br.: Lambertus.

Sommerfeld, P., Calzaferri, R., Hollenstein, L. and Schiepek, G. (2005) 'Real-time monitoring. New methods for evidence-based social work', in P. Sommerfeld (ed.), *Evidence-Based Social Work – Towards a New Professionalism?* Bern, Frankfurt, New York: Peter Lang Verlag. S. 201–34.

Sommerfeld, P. and Koditek, T. (1994) '"Wissenschaftliche Praxisberatung" in der Sozialen Arbeit', *Neue Praxis*, 24: 230–49.

Soska, T.M. and Butterfield, A.K.J. (eds) (2004) *University Community Partnerships.* Binghamton, NY: Hayworth Press.

Soskolne, V., Baras, M., Palti, H. and Epstein, L. (1996) 'Exposure to missile attacks: The impact of the Persian Gulf War on physical health, health behaviours and psychological distress in high and low risk areas in Israel', *Social Science and Medicine*, 42(7): 1039–47.

Soskolne, V. and Shtarkshall, R.A. (2002) 'Migration and HIV prevention programmes: Linking structural factors, culture, and individual behaviour: An Israeli experience', *Social Science and Medicine*, 55(8): 1297–307.

Soydan, H. (1993) 'Audy of the history of ideas in social work – a theoretical framework', *Scandinavian Journal of Social Welfare*, 2: 204–14.

Soydan, H. (1999) *The History of Ideas in Social Work*. Birmingham: Venture Press/Social Work Research Association Series.

Soydan, H. (2007) 'Improving the teaching of evidence-based practice: Challenges and priorities', *Research on Social Work Practice*, 17(5): 612–18.

Soydan, H. (2008a) 'Towards the gold standard of impact research in social work – avoiding threats to validity', in H.-U. Otto, A. Polutta and H. Ziegler (eds), *Evidence-Based Practice – Modernising the Knowledge Base of Social Work?*, Leverkusen, Opladen: Barbara Budrich Publisher. Forthcoming.

Soydan, H. (2008b) Intervention research. *Encyclopedia of social work* (20th edition). New York: Oxford University Press, Volume 2: pp. 536–39.

Soydan, H. (2008c) 'Applying randomized controlled trials and systematic reviews in social work research', *Research on Social Work Practice*, 18(4): 311–18.

Soydan, H., Jergeby, U., Olsson and Harms-Ringdal, M. (1999) *Socialt arbete med etniska minoriteter. En litteraturöversikt* [Social work with ethnic minorities. A literature review]. Stockholm: Liber.

Spandler, H., Secker, J., Kent, L., Hacking S. and Shenton, J. (2007) 'Catching life: The contribution of arts initiatives to recovery approaches in mental health', *Mental Health Today*, 7(6): 34–6.

Specht, H. and Courtney, M. (1994) *Unfaithful Angels: How Social Work has Abandoned its Mission*. NY: Free Press.

Spence, N. (2004) Kinship care in Australia. *Child Abuse Review*, 13(4): 263–76.

Spencer, L., Ritchie, J., Lewis, J. and Dillon, L. (2003). *Quality in Qualitative Evaluation: A Framework for Assessing Research Evidence*. London: Cabinet Office.

Spencer, P. and Wollman, H. (2007) 'Nationalism and the problem of humanitarian intervention', *Australian Journal of Human Rights*, 31(1): 79–111.

Sperry, L.L. and Sperry, D.E. (1996) '*Early development of narrative skills*', *Cognitive Development*, 11: 443–65.

Spitzer, R., Davies, M. and Barkley, R. (1990) 'The DSM-III-R field trial of disruptive behavior disorders', *Journal of the American Academy of Child and Adolescent Psychiatry*, 29: 690–7.

Spong, S. (2007) 'Scepticism and belief: Unraveling the relationship between theory and practice in counseling and psychotherapy', in S. Smith (ed.), *Applying Theory to Policy and Practice*. Aldershot: Ashgate.

Sprague, J. (2005) *Feminist Methodologies for Critical Researchers: Bridging Differences*. Walnut Creek, CA: Rowman and Littlefield.

Springer, J. and Phillips, J. (1994) 'Policy learning and evaluation design: Lessons from the community partnership demonstration project', *Journal of Community Psychology*, 22 (Special Summer Issue): 117–39.

Sroufe, L. Alan, Egeland, B., Carlson, E. and Collins, A. (2005) *The Development of the Person: The Minnesota Study of Risk and Adaptation from Birth to Adulthood*. New York: Guilford.

SSA (2002) Women and Social Security (Fact Sheet). Washington, DC: Social Security Administration.

St. Pierre, Elizabeth Adams (2006) 'Scientifically based research in education: Epistemology and ethics', *Adult Education Quarterly*, 56(4): 239–66.

Stacey, M. (1988) *The Sociology of Health and Healing*. London: Unwin Hyman.

Stein, M. and Munro, E.R. (2008) *Young People's Transitions from Care to Adulthood*. London: Jessica Kingsley.

Stainton, T. (2004) 'Reason's other: The emergence of the disabled subject in the Northern Renaissance', *Disability and Society*, 19(3): 225–43.

Stake, R. (2004) *Standards-Based and Responsive Evaluation*. Thousand Oaks: Sage Publications.

Stake, R. and Schwandt, T.A. (2006) 'On discerning quality in evaluation', in I. Shaw, J. Greene and M. Mark (eds), *Sage Handbook of Evaluation*. London: Sage Publications. Ch. 18.

Stake, R. and Trumbull, D. (1982) 'Naturalistic generalizations', *Review Journal of Philosophy and Social Science*, 7(1): 1–12.

Staller, K. (2007) 'Metalogue as methodology: Inquiries into conversations among authors, editors and referees', *Qualitative Social Work*, 6(2): 137–52.

Staller, K. (2008) 'Systematic reviews and qualitative enquiry: Oil and water?' *Qualitative Social Work*, 7(3): 380–91.

Stanley, L. (1990) *Feminist Praxis: Research, Theory and Epistemology*. London: Routledge.

Stanley, N., Manthorpe, J. and Penhale, B. (eds) (1999) *Institutional Abuse*. London: Routledge.

Staples, L.H. (1999) 'User controlled research and empowerment', in W. Shera and L.M. Wells (eds),

Empowerment Practice in Social Work: Developing Richer Conceptual Frameworks. Toronto: Canadian Scholars' Press, pp. 119–41.

State of Hawaii, Department of Health (2008) Available at: http://hawaii.gov/health/mental-health/camhd/library/webs/ebs/ebs-index.html. Last accessed 29 June 2008.

State of Oregon, Department of Human Services (2008) Available at: http://www.oregon.gov/DHS/mentalhealth/ebp/main.shtml. Last accessed 3 July 2008.

Statham, D., Brand, D. and Reith, T. (2005) 'The need for social work intervention – a discussion paper for the *Scottish 21st Century' Social Work Review.* http://www.21csocialwork.org.uk/docDetails.php?id=267&sec=reports

Statham, J., Cameron, C. and Mooney, A. (2006) *The Tasks and Roles of Social Workers: A Focused Overview of Research Evidence.* London: Thomas Coram Research Unit, Institute of Education, University of London.

Staub-Bernasconi, S. (2007a) 'Social work: Theories and methods', in G. Ritzer (ed.), *The Blackwell Encyclopedia of Sociology.* Malden, MA: Blackwell, pp. 4541–6.

Staub-Bernasconi, S. (2007b) *Soziale Arbeit als Handlungswissenschaft.* Bern, Stuttgart, Wien: Haupt Verlag.

Stedman Jones, G. (1971) *Outcast London.* Oxford: Clarendon Press.

Stein, L. and Test, M.A. (1980) 'Alternatives to hospital treatment: Conceptual model treatment program and clinical evaluation', *Archives of General Psychiatry,* 37(4): 392–7.

Stein, M. and Munro, E. (eds) (2008) *Young People's Transitions from Care to Adulthood: International Research and Practice. (Child Welfare Outcome Series).* London: Jessica Kingsley.

Steinberg, R.M. and Carter, G.W. (1984) *Case Management and the Elderly.* Lexington, MA: Lexington Books.

Stephenson, M. (2000) *In Critical Demand: Social Work in Canada.* Ottawa: CASSW-ACESS.

Stern J.M. and Simes, R.J. (1997) 'Publication bias: Evidence of delayed publication in a cohort study of clinical research projects', *British Medical Journal,* 315: 640–5.

Stock Whitaker, D. and Archer, J.L. (1989) *Research by Social Workers; Capitalizing on Experience.* London: CCETSW.

Stoecker, R. (2005) *Research Methods for Community Change: A Project-Based Approach.* Thousand Oaks, CA: Sage.

Stone, E. (1999a) 'Modern slogan, ancient script: Impairment and disability in the Chinese language', in M. Corker and S. French (eds), *Disability Discourse.* Buckingham: Open University Press.

Stone, E. (1999b) *Disability and Development: Learning from Action and Research on Disability in the Majority World.* Leeds: The Disability Press.

Stövesand, S. (2007) Neighbourhoods mobilise the troops [1] – Community organising, violence and governmentality. Available at: http://www.socwork.net/2007/1/articles/stoevesand: 1–14.

Strand, K., Marullo, S., Cutforth, N., Stoecker, R. and Donohue, P. (2003) *Community-Based Research and Higher Education.* San Francisco, CA: Jossey–Bass.

Straus, Murray A., Gelles, Richard J. and Steinmetz, Suzanne K. (2006 [1980]) *Behind Closed Doors: Violence in the American Family.* Edison, NJ: Transaction Publishers.

Strauss, A. (1987) *Qualitative Analysis for Social Scientists.* New York and Cambridge: Cambridge University Press.

Strauss, A.L. and Corbin, J. (1990) *Basics of Qualitative Research: Grounded Theory Procedures and Techniques.* Newbury Park: Sage.

Strauss, A., Fagerhaugh, S., Suczek, B. and Wiener, C. (1985) *Social Organization of Medical Work.* Chicago and London: The University of Chicago Press.

Strauss, A. and Glaser, B. (1970) *Anguish. A Case History of a Dying Trajectory.* Mill Valley, CA: The Sociology Press.

Strauss, D., Kastner, T.A. and Chavelle, R. (1998) 'Mortality of adults with developmental disabilities living in California institutions and community care, 1985–1994', *Mental Retardation,* 36(5): 360–71.

Strauss, S. and McAlister, F. (2000) 'Evidence-based medicine: A commentary on common criticism', *Canadian Medical Association Journal,* 163: 837–41.

Strauss, S.E., Richardson,W.S., Glasziou, P. and Haynes, R.B. (2005) *Evidence-Based Medicine: How to Practice and Teach EBM,* 3rd Edn., Edinburgh, UK: Elsevier.

Strega, S. (2005) 'The view from poststructural margins: Epistemology and methodology reconsidered', in L. Brown and S. Strega (eds), *Research as Resistance: Critical, Indigenous and Anti-Oppressive Approaches.* Toronto: Canadian Scholars' Press.

Strier, R. (2007) 'Anti-oppressive research in social work: A preliminary definition', *British Journal of Social Work,* 37(5): 857–71.

Stringer, E. (2007) *Action Research,* 3rd Edn., Thousand Oaks, CA: Sage.

Stringer, E. and Dwyer, R. (2005) *Action Research in Human Services*. New Jersey: Pearson Prentice Hall.

Stuart, C. and Whitmore, E. (2006) 'Using reflexivity in a research methods course: Bridging the gap between research and practice', in S. White, J. Fook and F. Gardner (eds), *Critical Reflection in Health Care and Social Care*. Berkshire, England: Open University Press, pp. 156–71.

Stuart, C. and Whitmore, E. (2008) 'Negotiating partnerships: Community-based research and the classroom', *Manifestations, 1*. Available at: http://www.manifestationjournal.org/.

Studies in Social Justice. Basok, Tanya and Ilcan, Suzan (eds). University of Windsor, Canada, Centre for Studies in Social Justice, Windsor, Canada. Available at: http://ojs.uwindsor.ca/ojs/leddy/index.php/SSJ/index

Substance Abuse and Mental Health Services Administration (SAMHSA), Center for Substance Abuse Treatment (1999) Treatment for Stimulant Use Disorders (Treatment Improvement Protocol Series #33), (DHHS Publication No. 02–3745). Rockville, MD: U.S. Department of Health and Human Services.

Suchman, E.A. (1967) *Evaluative Research: Principles and Practice in Public Service and Social Action Programs*. New York: Russell Sage Foundation.

Sulman, J., Savage, D. and Way, S. (2001) 'Retooling social work practice for high volume, short stay', *Social Work in Health Care*, 34(3/4): 315–32.

Sunesson, S. (2003) 'Socialt arbete – en bakgrund till ett forskningsämne', in *Socialt arbete: en nationell genomlysning av ämnet (Högskoleverkets rapportserie 2003:16 R), s. 75–131*. Högskoleverket 2003. Available at: http://web2.hsv.se/publikationer/rapporter/2003/0316R.pdf. Last accessed 11 September 2008.

Sunesson, S. (2006) 'Socialt arbete som internationellt forskningsområde', in Meeuwisse and Sunessonand Svärd (eds), *Socialt arbete. En grundbok*. Stockholm: Natur och kultur, pp. 334–47.

Sung-Chang, Pauline and Yeung-Tsang, Angelina (2008) 'Our journey nurturing the voices of unemployed women in China through collaborative-action research', *Qualitative Social Work*, 7(1): 61–80.

Sutton, C., Utting, D. and Farrington, D. (2004) *Support from the Start: Working with Young Children and their Families to Reduce the Risks of Crime and Anti-Social Behaviour*. London: Department for Education and Skills (Research Report 524).

Swain, J., French, S., Barnes, C. and Thomas, C. (eds) (2004) *Disabling Barriers – Enabling Environments*, 2nd Edn., London: Sage.

Swain, J., Finkelstein, V., French, S. and Oliver, M. (eds) (1993) *Disabling Barriers – Enabling Environments*, 2nd Edn., London: Sage.

Swedner, H. (1983) *Socialt arbete. En tankeram (Social Work. A Frame to Analysis)*. Lund: LiberFörlag.

Swigonski, M. (1993) 'Feminist standpoint theory and the question of social work research', *Affilia*, 8(2): 171–83.

Szto, P., Furman, R. and Langer, C. (2005) 'Poetry and photography: An exploration into expressive/creative qualitative research', *Qualitative Social Work: Research and Practice*, 4(2): 135–56.

Tagg, J. (1988) *The Burden of Representation: Essays on Photographies and Histories*. Basingstoke: Macmillan.

Takahashi, R. and Asakawa, Y. (2005) Young–old and old–old motivation in cooperative fall-prevention programmes. *Age Ageing*, 34: 90.

Tangenberg, K.M. and Kemp, S. (2002) 'Embodied practice: Claiming the body's experience, agency, and knowledge for social work', *Social Work*, 47(1): 9–18.

Tashakkori, A. and Teddlie, C. (2003) *Handbook of Mixed Methods in Social and Behavioral Research*. Thousand Oaks, CA: Sage.

Task Force on Social Work Research (1991) *Building Social Work Knowledge for Effective Services and Policies: A Plan for Research Development*. Available at: http://www.iaswresearch.org. Last accessed 20 March 2008.

Taylor, B.J., Dempster, M. and Donnelly, M. (2007) 'Grading gems: Appraising the quality of research for social work and social care', *British Journal of Social Work*, 335–54.

Taylor, C. (2006) 'Narrating significant experience: Reflective accounts and the production of (self) knowledge', *British Journal of Social Work*, 36(2): 189–206.

Taylor, C. (2008) 'Trafficking in facts: Writing practices in social work', *Qualitative Social Work*, 7(1): 25–42.

Taylor, C. and White, S. (2000) *Practising Reflexivity in Health and Welfare: Making Knowledge*. Buckingham: Open University Press.

Taylor, C. and White, S. (2006) 'Knowledge and reasoning in social work: Educating for humane judgement', *British Journal of Social Work*, 35: 1–18.

Teddlie, C. and Tashakkori, A. (2003) 'Major issues and controversies in the use of mixed methods in the social and behavioral sciences', in A. Tashakkori and C. Teddlie (eds), *Handbook of Mixed Methods in Social and Behavioral Research*. Thousand Oaks, CA: Sage, pp. 3–50.

Teddlie, C. and Tashakkori, A. (2006) 'A general typology of research designs featuring mixed methods', *Research in the Schools*, 13(1): 12–28.

Tenorio, R. and Hernandez, N. (2005) 'State of social work research within the scope of mental health', *Salud Mental*, 28(4): 18–32.

Tew, J. (2008) 'Researching in partnership: Reflecting on a collaborative study with mental health service users into the impact of compulsion', *Qualitative Social Work*, 7(3): 271–88.

Tew, J., Gould, N., Abankwa, D., Barnes, H., Beresford, P., Carr, S., Copperman, J., Ramon, S., Rose, D., Sweeney, A. and Louise, W. (2006) *Values and Methodologies for Social Research in Mental Health*. Bristol: Policy Press.

Thane, P. (1982) *Foundations of the Welfare State*. London: Longman.

Thoburn, J. (2007) *Globalisation and Child Welfare: Some Lessons from a Cross-National Study of Children in Out-of-Home Care*. Norwich: UEA Social Work Monographs.

Thoburn, J., Chand, A. and Procter, J. (2005) *Child Welfare Services for Minority Ethnic Families*. Philadelphia, PA: Jessica Kingsley Publishers.

Thole, W. and Küster-Schapfl, E.-U. (1997) *Sozialpädagogische Profis*. Opladen, Leske + Budrich.

Thomas, E. (1984) *Designing Interventions for the Helping Professions*. CA: Sage.

Thomas, W.H. (2003) *Life Worth Living*. Action, MA: Van derWejk & Burnham Publishers.

Thomas, P. and Bracken, P. (2004) 'Critical psychiatry in practice', *Advances in Psychiatric Treatment*, 10(5): 361–70.

Thomlison, B. and Corcoran, K. (2008) *The Evidence-Based Internship – A Field Manual*. New York: Oxford University Press.

Thompson, N. (1997) *Anti-Discriminatory Practice*. Basingstoke: Macmillan.

Thompson, N. (2000) *Understanding Social Work: Preparing for Practice*. Basingstoke: Macmillan.

Thompson, N. (2003) *Promoting Equality: Challenging Discrimination and Oppresssion*, 2nd Edn., Basingstoke: Palgrave/Macmillan.

Thompson-Robinson, M., Hopson, R. and SenGupta, S. (eds) (2004) 'In search of cultural competence in evaluation', in *New directions for Evaluation*, No. 102. San Francisco: Jossey–Bass Publishers.

Thornicroft, G., Bindman, J., Goldberg, D., Gournay, K. and Huxley, P. (2002) 'Researchable questions to support evidence based mental health policy concerning adult mental illness', *Psychiatric Bulletin*, 26: 403–6.

Thornicroft, G., Rose, D., Huxley, P., Dale, G. and Wykes, T. (2001) 'What are the research priorities of mental health service users?', *Journal of Mental Health*, 11(1): 1–5.

Thornicroft, G., Strathdee, G., Phelan, M., Holloway, F., Wykes, T., Dunn, G., McCrone, P., Leese, M., Johnson, S. and Szmukler, G. (1998) 'Rationale and design. PRiSM Psychosis Study I', *British Journal of Psychiatry*, 173: 363–70.

Thyer, B. (1989) 'First principles of practice research', *British Journal of Social Work*, 19(4): 309–23.

Thyer, B. (2001a) 'What is the role of theory in research on social work practice?', *Journal of Social Work Education*, 37(1): 9–25.

Thyer, B. (2001b) *The Handbook of Social Work Research Methods*. Thousand Oaks, CA: Sage.

Thyer, B. (2002) 'Developing discipline specific knowledge for social work: Is it possible?', *Journal of Social Work Education*, 38(1): 101–13.

Thyer, B. (2003) 'Principles of evidence-based practice and treatment development', in G. Greene and A. Roberts (eds), *Social Worker's Desk Reference*. New York: Oxford University Press.

Thyer, B. (2004) 'Science and evidence-based social work practice', in H.E. Briggs and T. Rzepnicki (eds), *Using Evidence in Social Work Practice: Behavioral Perspectives*. Chicago: Lyceum, pp. 75–89.

Thyer, B. (2007) 'Evidence-based social work: An overview', in B. Thyer and J.S. Wodarski (eds), *Social Work in Mental Health: An Evidence-Based Approach*. New York: Wiley, pp. 1–28.

Thyer, B. (2008) 'The quest for evidence-based practice?: We are all positivists!', *Research on Social Work Practice*, 18(4): 339–45.

Thyer, B. and Kazi, M. (eds) (2004) *International Perspectives on Evidence-based Practice in Social Work*. Birmingham: British Association of Social Workers.

Tierney, W. (2000) 'Undaunted courage: Life history and the post-modern challenge', in N. Denzin and Y. Lincoln (eds), *Handbook of Qualitative Research*, 2nd Edn., Thousand Oaks, CA: Sage Publications. pp. 537–53.

Tilbury, C. (2004) 'The influence of performance measurement on child welfare policy and practice', *British Journal of Social Work*, 34: 225–41.

Tilbury, C. and Thoburn, J. (2008) 'Children in out of home care in Australia, International Comparisons'. *Children Australia*, 33(3): 5–12.

Tilbury, C. and Thoburn, J. (in Press) 'Disproportionate representation of indigenous children in child welfare systems: international comparisons', in K. Kufeldt and B. McKenzie (eds), *Child Welfare: Connecting Research, Policy and Practice*. Waterloo, Canada: Wilfrid Laurier University Press.

Tilley, C. (1990) 'Towards an archaeology of archeology', in C. Tilley (ed.), *Reading Material Culture: Structuralism, Hermeneutics, Poststructuralism.* Cambridge: Cambridge University Press.

Timms, N. (1968) *The Language of Social Casework.* London: Routledge and Kegan Paul.

Titchkosky, T. (2001) 'From the field – coming out disabled: The politics of understanding', *Disability Studies Quarterly*, 21 (4). Available at: http://www.cds.hawaii.edu/dsq/_articles_html/

Titmuss, R.M. (1973) *Commitment to Welfare*, 4th Edn., London: George Allen and Unwin Ltd.

Titterton, M. (1992) 'Managing threats to welfare: The search for a new paradigm of welfare', *Journal of Social Policy*, 21(1): 1–23.

Titterton, M. and Smart, H. (2008) 'Can participatory research be a route to empowerment? A case study of a disadvantaged Scottish community', *Community Development Journal*, 43(1): 52–64.

Tiumalu-Faleseuga, K. (1993) 'Pacific island development in New Zealand', in A.C. Walsh (ed.), *Development that works! Lessons from Asia-Pacific.* Palmerston North: Amokura Publications, Massey University, pp. D4.1–4.

Tjora, A.H. (2006) 'Writing small discoveries: An exploration of fresh observers' observations', *Qualitative Research*, 6(4): 429–51.

Toikko, T. (2001) *Sosiaalityön amerikkalainen oppi: yhdysvaltalaisen caseworkin kehitys ja sen yhteys suomalaiseen tapauskohtaiseen sosiaalityöhön (The American Doctrine of Social Work: The Development of U.S. Casework and its Connections to Finnish Casework),* Seinäjoen ammattikorkeakoulu. Tampereen yliopisto, sosiaalipolitiikan ja sosiaalityön laitos.

Tonkiss, F. (2005) *Space, the City and Social Theory.* Cambridge, UK: Polity Press.

Toroyan, T., Roberts, I. and Oakley, A. (2000) 'Randomization and resource allocation: A missed opportunity for evaluating health care and social interventions', *The Journal of Medical Ethics*, 26: 319–22.

Torrance, H. (2008) Discussant at plenary session on evidence: Questions of evidence in policy research at the 2008 Congress of Qualitative Inquiry at the University of Illinois, Urbana, IL.

Torres, R.D., Miron, L.F. and Inda, J.X. (eds) (1999) *Race Identity, Citizenship: A Reader.* Mass: Blackwell Publishers.

Toseland, R., McCallion, P., Smith, T., Huck, S., Bourgeois, P. and Garstka, T. (2001a) 'Health education groups for caregivers in an HMO', *Journal of Clinical Psychology*, 57(4): 551–70.

Toseland, R.W., Smith, G. and McCallion, P. (2001b) 'Helping family caregivers', in A. Gitterman (ed.), *Handbook of Social Work Practice with Vulnerable Populations.* New York: Columbia University Press, pp. 548–81.

Toseland, R.W., McCallion, P., Smith T. and Banks, S. (2004) 'Supporting caregivers of frail older adults in an HMO setting'. *American Journal of Orthopsychiatry*, 74(3): 349–64.

Touraine, A. (2000) *Can We Live Together? Equality and Difference.* Cambridge: Polity Press.

Tower, R.B. and Krasner, M. (2006) 'Marital closeness, autonomy, mastery, and depressive symptoms in a U.S. internet survey', *Personal Relationships*, 13: 429–49.

Townsend, P. (1979) *Poverty in the United Kingdom: A Survey of Household Resources and Standards of Living, 1967–1969.* Harmondsworth: Penguin.

Tregaskis, C. and Goodley, D. (2005) 'Disability research by disabled and non-disabled people: Towards a relational methodology of research production', *International Journal of Social Research Methodology*, 8(5): 363–74.

Trevillion, S. (1992) *Caring in the Community: A Networking Approach to Community Partnership.* London: Longman.

Trevillion, S. (1999) *Networking and Community Partnership*, 2nd Edn., Aldershot: Ashgate/Arena.

Trevillion, S. (2000) 'Social work, social networks and network knowledge', *British Journal of Social Work*, 30(4): 505–17.

Trevillion, S. (2007) 'Health, disability and social work: New directions in social work research', *British Journal of Social Work*, 37(5): 937–46.

Trevillion, S. (2008) 'Research, theory and practice: Eternal triangle or uneasy bedfellows?', *Social Work Education*, 27(4): 440–50.

Trinder, L. (1996) 'Social work research: the state of the art (or science)', *Child and Family Social Work*, 1: 233–42.

Trinder, L. (2000a) 'Evidence-based practice in social work and probation', in L. Trinder with S. Reynolds (eds), *Evidence-Based Practice: A Critical Appraisal.* Oxford: Blackwell Science, pp. 138–62.

Trinder, L. (2000b) 'A critical appraisal of evidence-based practice' in L. Trinder and S. Reynolds (eds), *Evidence-Based Practice: A Critical Appraisal.* Oxford: Blackwell Science.

Trinder, L. and Reynolds, S. (2000) *Evidence-Based Practice. A Critical Appraisal.* Oxford: Blackwell Science.

Tripodi, T. (1994) *A Primer on Single-Subject Design for Clinical Social Workers*. Washington DC: NASW.

Trocme, N., Knoke, D. and Blackstock, C. (2004) 'Pathways to the overrepresentation of Aboriginal children in Canada's child welfare system', *Social Service Review*, 78(4): 557–600.

Tronto, J. (1993) *Moral Boundaries: A Political Argument for an Ethic of Care*. New York: Routledge.

Trotter, C. (2000) 'Social work education, pro-social orientation and effective probation practice', *Probation Journal*, 47(4): 256–61.

Trotter, C. (2006) *Working with Involuntary Clients: A guide to practice*, 2nd Edn., London: Sage.

Truman, C. (1999) 'User involvement in large-scale research: Bridging the gap between service users and service providers?', in B. Broad (ed.), *The Politics of Social Work Research and Evaluation*. Birmingham: Venture Press.

Truman, C. and Humpheries, B. (1994) 'Rethinking social research in an unequal world', in B. Humpheries and C. Truman (eds), *Rethinking Social Research: Anti-discriminatory Approaches in Research Methodology*. Aldershot: Avebury.

Tunstill, J. (2003) 'Political and technical issues facing evaluators of family support', in: I. Katz and J. Pinkerton (eds), *Evaluating Family Support: Thinking Internationally, Thinking Critically*. West Suffix: John Wiley and Sons.

Tunstill, J., Meadows, M., Akhurst, S., Allnock, D. and Garbers, C. (2005) *Implementing Sure Start Local Programmes: An Integrated Overview of the First Four Years*. London: DfES.

Turner, B. (1995) *Medical Power and Social Knowledge*. London: Sage.

U.S. Department of Health and Human Services (1999) *Mental Health: A Report of the Surgeon General*. Rockville, MD: U.S. Department of HHS, SAMHSA, CMHS, NIH, NIMH.

U.S. Department of Justice (2004) *Implementing Evidence-Based Practice in Community Corrections: The Principles of Effective Intervention, National Institute of Corrections*, Community Corrections Division, U.S. Department of Justice. Available at: www.nicic.org/pubs/2004/019342.pdf. Last accessed 5 May 2008.

U.S. Bureau of the Census (1999/2001) Grandchildren living in the home of their grandparents: 1970 to present [Historical time series tableCH-7]. Retrieved November 10th 2006 from http://www.census.gov/population/socdemo/hh-fam/tabCH-7.pdf

U.S. Department of Health and Human Services (2002) *Closing the Gap: A National Blueprint for Improving the Health of Individuals with Mental Retardation – Report of the Surgeon General's Conference on Health Disparities and Mental Retardation*. Washington, DC: Author.

U.S. Department of Health and Human Services (HHS). (2008). Office of Research Integrity: Welcome. Retrieved May 4, 2009 from http://ori.hhs.gov/

U.S. Drug Enforcement Agency (2006) *National Drug Threat Assessment 2007*. Washington, DC: Government Publishing Office.

Uehara, E., Sohng, S., Bending, R., Seyfried, S., Richey, C., Morelli, P., Spencer, M., Oretaga, D., Keenan, L. and Kanuha, V. (1996) 'Towards a values-based approach to multicultural social work research', *Social Work*, 41(6): 613–21.

Ungar, M. (2003a) 'Stale'. *Toronto Star* (Canada), July 29, p. D15.

Ungar M. (2003b) 'Qualitative contributions to resilience research', *Qualitative Social Work*, 2(1): 85–102.

Ungar, M. (2004) *Nurturing Hidden Resilience in Troubled Youth*. Toronto: University of Toronto Press.

Ungar, M. (ed.) (2005a) *Handbook for Working with Children and Youth: Pathways to Resilience across Cultures and Contexts*. Thousand Oaks: Sage.

Ungar, M. (2005b) 'Introduction: Resilience across cultures and contexts', in M. Ungar (ed.), *Handbook for Working with Children and Youth: Pathways to Resilience across Cultures and Contexts*. Thousand Oaks, CA: Sage Publications, pp. xv–xxxix.

Ungar, M. (2006) '"Too ambitious": What happens when funders misunderstand the strengths of qualitative research design?', *Qualitative Social Work*, 5(2): 261–77.

Ungar, M. (2008) 'Research note resilience across cultures', *British Journal of Social Work*, 38(2): 218–35.

University of Birmingham and Institute of Education (2006) *Working to Prevent Social Exclusion of Children and Young People: Final Lessons from the National Evaluation of the Children's Fund*. London: Department for Education and Skills. Research report RR734.

Utting, D, Monteiro, H. and Ghate, D. (2007) *Interventions for Children at Risk of Developing Antisocial Personality Disorder*. Cabinet Office/Policy Research Bureau.

Valandra, Gilgun, J.F. and Sharma, A. (2008) 'Critical Race Theory and Critical Discourse Analysis as Tools to Examine Race and Racism in Social Work Practice and Research'. Paper presented at a symposium on Children in Conflict with the Law. *Fourth International Congress on Qualitative Research*, May 17, Urbana, IL.

van Bastelaer, T. (1999) 'Does social capital facilitate the poor's access to credit? A review of the micro-economic literature'. *Social Capital Initiative Working Paper*, 8.

van de Ven, A. and Delbecq, A. (1972) 'The nominal group as a research instrument for exploratory health studies', *American Journal of Public Health*, 62: 337–42.

van der Gaag, M. and Snijders, T.A.B. (2005) 'The resource generator: Social capital quantification with concrete items', *Social Networks*, 27: 1–29.

van der Gaag, M. and Webber, M. (2007) 'Measurement of individual social capital: Questions, instruments, and measures', in I. Kawachi, S.V. Subramanian and D. Kim (eds), *Social Capital and Health*. New York: Springer–Verlag, pp. 29–49.

van Kalmthout, A. and Derks, J. (eds) (2000) *Probation and Probation Services – a European Perspective*. Nijmegen: Wolf Legal Publishers.

van Maanen, John (1988) *Tales of the Field. On Writing Ethnography*. Chicago and London: The University of Chicago Press.

van Schrojenstein Lantman-De Valk, H.M., Metsemakers, J.F., Haveman, M.J. and Crebolder, H.F. (2000) 'Health problems in people with intellectual disability in general practice: A comparative study', *Family Practice*, 17(5): 405–7.

Vanstone, M. (2004) *Supervising Offenders in the Community: A History of Probation Theory and Practice*. Aldershot: Ashgate.

Varela, Francisco J. (1992) *Ethical Know-How: Action, Wisdom and Cognition*. Stanford, CA: Stanford University Press.

Vedung, Evert (1998), 'Policy instruments: Typologies and theories', in Marie-Louise Bemelmans-Videc, Ray C. Rist and Evert Vedung (eds), *Carrots, Sticks and Sermons. Policy instruments and their evaluations*. New Brunswick: Transaction Publishers.

Vitaliano, P., Russo, J., Young, H., Becker, J. and Maiuro, R. (1991) 'The screen for caregiver burden', *The Gerontologist*, 31(1): 76–83.

Vogel, J. (1994) 'Social indicators and social reporting', *Statistical Journal of the United Nations*, 11: 241–60.

Völter, B. (2008) 'Verstehende Soziale Arbeit. Zum Nutzen qualitativer Methoden für professionelle Praxis, Reflexion und Forschung' [58 paragraphs]. *Forum Qualitative Sozialforschung/Forum: Qualitative Social Research*, 9 (1), Art. 56. Available at: http://www.qualitative-research.net/fqstexte/1-08/08-1-56-d.htm. Last accessed 8 March 2008.

Von Wensierski, H.-J. (1997) 'Verstehende Sozialpädagogik. Zur Geschichte und Entwicklung qualitativer Forschung im Kontext der Sozialen Arbeit', in G. Jakob and H.-J. Von Wensierski (eds) *Rekonstruktive Sozialpädagogik*. Weinheim, München, Juventa.

Von Wensierski, H.-J. and Jakob, G. (1997) 'Rekonstruktive Sozialpädagogik. Sozialwissenschaftliche Hermeneutik, Fallverstehen und sozialpädagogisches Handeln – eine Einführung', in G. Jakob and V. Wensierski (eds), *Rekonstruktive Sozialpädagogik. Konzepte und Methoden sozialpädagogischen Verstehens in Forschung und Praxis*. Weinheim, München, Juventa.

von Wright, G.H. (1982) Logiikka, filosofia, kieli. Helsinki: Otava.

Wacquant, L. (2001) 'Deadly symbiosis: When ghetto and prison meet and merge', *Punishment and Society*, 3(1): 95–134.

Wade, K. and Neuman, K. (2007) 'Practice-based research: Changing the professional culture and language of social work', *Social Work in Health Care*, 44(4): 49–64.

Wadsworth, Y. and Hargreaves, K. (1993) *What is Feminist Research?*, Melbourne: Action Research Issues Association.

Wagner, G. (1988) *Residential Care: A Positive Choice*. National Institute for Social Work. London: HMSO.

Wahab, S. (2004) 'Tricks of the trade: What social workers can learn about female sex workers through dialogue', *Qualitative Social Work*, 3: 139–60.

Wakefield, J.C. and Kirk, S.A. (1996) 'Unscientific thinking about scientific practice: Evaluating the scientist–practitioner model', *Social Work Research*, 20(2): 83–95.

Waldegrave, C. (2000) 'Just therapy with family group conferencing', in G. Burfod and J. Hudson (eds), *Family Group Conferencing: New Directions in Community-Centered Child and Family Practice*. New York: Walter de Gruyter.

Waldfogel, J. (1998) *The Future of Child Protection. How to Break the Cycle of Abuse and Neglect*. Cambridge, MA: Harvard University Press.

Walker, J.S., Briggs, H.E., Koroloff, N. and Friesen, B.J. (2007) 'Special section: Promoting and sustaining evidence-based practice', *Journal of Social Work Education*, 43(3): 361–496.

Walker, S., Anaru, E. and Gibbs, A. (2006) 'An exploration of Kaupapa Maori research, its principles, processes and applications', *International Journal of Social Research Methodology*, 9(4) 331–44.

Wallace, W.L. (2004) 'The logic of science in sociology', in C. Seale (ed.), *Social Research Methods: A Reader*. London: Routledge.

Wallcraft, J. (2002) '"Turning towards recovery?" A study of personal narratives of mental health crisis and breakdown'. Unpublished PhD thesis. London: London South Bank University.

Wallerstein, I. (1997) 'Eurocentrism and its avatars: The dilemmas of social sciences', *New Left Review*, 1/226: 93–107. http://www.newleftreview.org/?page=article&view=1934. Printed on May 5, 2009

Wallerstein, I. (2001) *Unthinking Social Science: The Limits of Nineteenth-Century Paradigms*, 2nd Edn., Philadelphia: Temple University Press.

Wallerstein, N. and Duran, B. (2003) 'The conceptual, historical, and practice roots of community based participatory research and related participatory traditions', in M. Minkler and N. Wallerstein (eds), *Community-Based Participatory Research for Health*. San Francisco, CA: Jossey–Bass, pp. 27–52.

Walmsley, J. and Johnson, K. (2003) *Inclusive Research with People with Learning Disabilities: Past, Present and Futures*. London: Jessica Kingsley.

Walter, I., Nutley, S., Percy-Smith, J., McNeish, D. and Frost, S. (2004) 'Improving the use of research in social care practice'. Social Care Institute for Excellence (SCIE). Available at: http://www.scie.org.uk/.

Walters, J. (2003) 'Trends and issues in probation in Europe', paper delivered to the PACCOA conference, Hobart, Tasmania, 1 September. Available at: http://www.paccoa.com.au/PDF%20files/John%20Walters.pdf. Last accessed 21 May 2008.

Walton, R.G. (1975) *Women and Social Work*. London: Routledge.

Wamsley, Gary L. and Zald, Mayer N. (1973) 'The political economy of public organizations', *Public Administration Review*, 33(1): 62–73.

Wan, H., Sengupta, M., Velkopf, V.A. and DeBarros, K.A. (2005) *Current Population Reports: P23–209, 65+ in the United States*. Washington, DC: U.S. Government Publishing Office.

Wang, C.C. (2003) 'Using photovoice as a participatory assessment and issue selection tool: A case study with the homeless in Ann Arbor', in M. Minkler and N. Wallerstein (eds), *Community-Based Participatory Research for Health*. San Francisco, CA: Jossey–Bass, pp. 179–96.

Ward, H. (2000) *The Development Needs of Children: Implications for Assessment*. London: Department of Health.

Washington State Institute for Public Policy (2008) 'Intensive family preservation services: Program fidelity influences effectiveness', revised. Available at: http://www.wsipp.wa.gov/pub.asp?docid+06-02-3901. Last accessed 10 October 2008.

Webb, S. (2001) 'Some considerations on the validity of evidence based practice in social work', *The British Journal of Social Work*, 31(1): 57–79.

Webb, S. (2006) *Social Work in a Risk Society: Social and Political Perspectives*. Basingstoke, UK: Palgrave Macmillan.

Webber, M. (2005) 'Social capital and mental health', in J. Tew (ed.), *Social Perspectives in Mental Health. Developing Social Models to Understand and Work with Mental Distress*. London: Jessica Kingsley Publishers, pp. 90–111.

Webber, M. (2008) *Evidence-Based Policy and Practice in Mental Health Social Work*. Exeter: Learning Matters.

Webber, M. and Huxley, P. (2004) 'Mental health and social capitals (letter)'. *British Journal of Psychiatry*, 184: 185–6.

Webber, M. and Huxley, P. (2007) 'Measuring access to social capital: The validity and reliability of the Resource Generator-UK and its association with common mental disorder', *Social Science and Medicine*, 65: 481–92.

Webber, M. and Slack, K. (2008) 'Do we care? Adult mental health professionals' attitudes towards supporting service users' children', *Child and Family Social Work*, 13(1): 72–9.

Weber, L. (2006) 'Future directions of feminist research', in S. Hesse-Biber (ed.), *Handbook of Feminist Research: Theory and Praxis*. Thousand Oaks, CA: Sage.

Weber, M. (1948) 'Science as a vocation', in H.H. Gerth and C.W. Mills (eds), *From Max Weber: Essays in Sociology*. London: Routledge and Kegan Paul.

Weber, M. (1949) *The Methodology of the Social Sciences*. New York: The Free Press.

Weber, M. (2004). *The Vocation Lectures*. Indianapolis: Hackett Publishing Company.

Webster-Stratton, C. (2001) 'The incredible years: Parents, teachers, and children training series', in S.I. Pfeiffer and L.A. Reddy (eds), *Innovative Mental Health Interventions for Children: Programs That Work*. New York, NY: Haworth, pp. 31–48.

Weeks, Linton (2007) 'The eye generation prefers not to read all about it', *Washingtonpost.com*, July 6, 2007.

Weick, Ann (2000) 'Hidden voices', *Social Work*, 5(5): 395–402.

Weidner, J., Kilb, R. and Jehn, O. (eds) (2003) *Gewald im Griff. Band 3. Weiterentwicklung des Coolness- und Anti-Aggressivitäts-Trainings*. Weinheim, Basel, Berlin: Beltz.

Weidner, J. and Malzahn, U. (2004) 'Zum Persönlichkeitsprofil aggressiver Jungen und Männer', in J. Weidner, R. Kilb and D. Kreft (eds), *Gewalt im Griff 1: Neue Formen des Anti-Aggressivitäts-Trainings*, 4th Edn., Weinheim, München: Juventa.

Weiss, C.H. (1995) 'Nothing as practical as good theory: Exploring theory-based evaluation for comprehensive community-based initiatives for children and families', in J.P. Connell, A.C. Kubisch, L.B. Schorr and C.H. Weiss (eds), *New Approaches to Evaluating Community Initiatives: Concepts, Methods and Contexts*. Washington, DC: Aspen Institute.

Welshman, J. (2004) 'The unknown Titmuss', *Journal of Social Policy*, 33(2): 225–47.

Wendell, S. (1996) *The Rejected Body: Feminist Philosophical Reflections on Disability*. New York: Routledge.

Wenocur, S. and Reisch, M. (2001) *From Charity to Enterprise: The Development of American Social Work in a Market Economy*. IL: University of Illinois Press.

Wenstrop, F. and Myrmel, A. (2006) 'Structuring organizational value statements', *Management Research News*, 29(11): 673–83.

Western, D. and Bradley, R. (2005) 'Empirically supported complexity: Rethinking evidence-based practice in psychotherapy', *Current Directions in Psychological Science*, 14(5): 266.

Werthington, E. et al. (2007) 'The CITRA pilot studies program: Mentoring translational research', *The Gerontologist*, 47(6): 845–50.

Whalley H.K. (2006) *Perspectives on Disability and Rehabilitation: Contesting Assumptions, Challenging Practice*. Oxford: Elsevier.

Whisman, M.A. and Gary Hl. McClelland (2005) 'Designing, testing, and interpreting interactions and moderator effects in family research', *Journal of Family Psychology*, 19(1): 111–20.

White, S. (1997) 'Beyond retroduction? Hermeneutics, reflexivity and social work practice', *British Journal of Social Work*, 27: 739–53.

White, S. (2001) 'Auto-ethnography as reflexive inquiry: The research act as self-surveillance', in I. Shaw and N. Gould (eds), *Qualitative Research in Social Work*. London: Sage, pp. 100–15.

White, S. (2009) 'Fabled Uncertainty in Social Work: A Coda to Spafford et al.', *Journal of Social Work*, 9(2): 222–35.

White, S. and Featherstone, B. (2005) 'Communicating misunderstandings: Multi-agency work as social practice', *Child and Family Social Work*, 10: 207–16.

White, S., Fook, J. and Gardner, F. (eds) (2006) *Critical Reflection in Health and Social Care*. Maidenhead: Open University Press.

White, S. and Wastell, D. (2008) 'Unsettling evidence and lively language: Reflexive practitioner as trickster', in H.-U. Otto, A. Polutta and H. Ziegler (eds), *Evidence-based Practice – Modernising the Knowledge Base of Social Work?* Opladen: Barbara Budrich (in press).

Whitmore, E. (1994) 'To tell the truth: Working with oppressed groups in participatory approaches to inquiry', in P. Reason (ed.), *Participation in Human Inquiry*. Thousand Oaks, CA: Sage, pp. 82–98.

Whitmore, E. (2001) '"People listened to what we had to say": Reflections on an emancipatory qualitative evaluation', in I. Shaw and N. Gould (eds), *Qualitative Research in Social Work*. London: Sage Publications, pp. 83–99.

Whitmore, E. and Mckee, C. (2001) 'Six street youth who could ...' in P. Reason and H. Bradbury (eds), *Handbook of Action Research: Participative Inquiry and Practice*. Thousand Oaks, CA: Sage. pp. 396–402.

Whittaker, J.K. (1994) Foreword to *A Primer on Single-Subject Design for Clinical Social Workers*, by T. Tripodi. Washington, DC: NASW Press, pp. xi–xii.

Whittaker, J.K. (1999) 'Foreword' to M. Connolly and M. McKenzie (eds), *Effective Participatory Practice: Family Group Conferencing in Child Protection*. New York: Aldine de Gruyter.

Wickham, G. (2008) 'Competing uses of history in researching the social: A reply to Peter Baehr', *Current Sociology*, 56(6): 949–54.

Wickham, G. and Freemantle, H. (2008) 'Some additional knowledge conditions for sociology', *Sociology*, 56(6): 922–39.

Williams, A. (ed.) (2007) *Therapeutic Landscapes*. Aldershot: Ashgate.

Williams, B. (1999) *Working with Victims of Crime*. London: Jessica Kingsley Publishers.

Williams, B. (ed.) (2002) *Reparation and Victim-Focused Social Work*. London: Jessica Kingsley Publishers.

Williams, B. and Harris, B. (2001) 'Learning logs: Structured journals that work for busy people', in S. Shankaran, B. Dick, R. Passfield and P. Swepson (eds), *Effective Change Management Using Action Learning and Action Research*. Lismore, NSW: Southern Cross University Press, pp. 97–112.

Williams, C., Soydan, H. and Johnson, M.R.D. (eds) (1998) *Social Work and Minorities. European Perspectives*. London: Routledge.

Williams, F. (1999) 'Exploring the links between old and new paradigms: A critical review', in F. Williams, J. Popay and A. Oakley (eds), *Welfare Research: A Critical Review*. London: UCL Press.

Williams, F., Popay, J. and Oakley, A. (eds) (1999) *Welfare Research: A Critical Review*. London: UCL.

Williams, G. (2000) 'Knowledgeable narratives', *Anthropology and Medicine*, 7: 135–40.

Williams, J., Netten, A. and Ware, P. (2007a) 'Managing the care home closure process: Care managers' experiences and views', *British Journal of Social Work*, 37(5): 909–24.

Williams, P. (2006) *Social Work with People with Learning Difficulties*. Exeter: Learning Matters Ltd.

Williams, R. (1958) *Culture and Society 1780–1950*. London: Chatto and Windus.

Williams, R. (1983) *Keywords: A Vocabulary of Culture and Society*. London: Fontana.

Williams, S., Calnan, M. and Dolan, A. (2007b) 'Explaining inequalities in health: Theoretical, conceptual and methodological agendas', in E. Dowler and N. Spencer (eds), *Challenging Health Inequalities: from Acheson to 'Choosing Health'*. Bristol: Policy Press.

Willis, J. and Saunders, M. (2007) 'Research in a post-colonial world: The example of Australian Aborigines', in M. Pitts and A. Smith (eds), *Researching the Margins: Strategies for Ethical and Rigorous Research with Marginalised Communities*. Houndsmill: Palgrave Macmillan.

Willson, K. (2006) 'Looking out: Prairie women use photovoice methods to fight poverty', *Canadian Woman Studies*, 25(3/4): 160–6.

Wilson, E. (1977) *Women and the Welfare State*. London: Tavistock.

Wilson, E. (1980) 'Feminism and social work', in R. Bailey and M. Brake (eds), *Radical Social Work and Practice*. London: Edward Arnold.

Wilson, K. and James, A. (eds) (2007) *The Child Protection Handbook*, 3rd Edn., Philadelphia: Elsevier.

Wilson, M. (1993) 'DSM-III and the transformation of American psychiatry: A history', *American Journal of Psychiatry*, 150: 399–410.

Wilson, V. (2006) 'Critical realism as emancipatory action: The case for realistic evalaluation in practice development', *Nursing Philosophy*, 7: 45–57.

Wilson, S. J., Lipsey, M. W. and Soydan, H. (2003) 'Are mainstream programs for juvenile delinquents less effective with minority youth than majority youth? A meta-analysis of outcome research'. *Research on Social Work Practice*, 13(1): 3–26.

Wing, J.K. and Brown, G. (1970) *Institutionalism and Schizophrenia*. Cambridge: Cambridge University Press.

Witkin, S. (1996) 'If empirical practice is the answer, then what is the question?', *Social Work Research*, 20(2): 69–75.

Witkin, S. (2000) 'Writing social work', *Social Work*, 45(5): 389–94.

Witkin, S. (2001) 'Reading social work', *Social Work*, 46(1): 5–8.

Witkin, S.L. and Chambon, A. (2007) 'New voices in social work: Writing forms and knowledge production', *Qualitative Social Work: Research and Practice*, 6(4): 387–97.

WMA (World Medical Association) (1964) *Declaration of Helsinki*. (As amended 2004.) Ferney-Voltaire, WMA.

Wodak, R. (2001) 'What CDA is about', in R. Wodak and M. Myers (eds), *Methods of Critical Discourse Analysis*. London: Sage, pp. 1–13.

Wolfensberger, W. (2003) 'Social role valorization: A new insight and a new term for normalization', in D.G. Race (ed.), *Leadership and Change in Human Services: Selected Readings from Wolf Wolfensberger*. London: Routledge.

Wolfinger, Nicholas H. (2002) 'On writing fieldnotes: collection strategies and background expectancies', *Qualitative Research*, 2(1): 85–95.

Wolinsky, F.D. (1990) *Health and Health Behavior among Elderly Americans*. New York: Springer.

Wolpert, L. and Richards, A. (1997) *Passionate Minds: The Inner World of Scientists*. Oxford: Oxford University Press.

Wood, G. and Tully, C. (2006) *The Structural Approach to Direct Practice in Social Work: A Social Constuctionist Perspective*. New York: Columbia University Press.

Woodcock, J. (1995) 'Group work using task-centred methods as a potential way of helping with maternal depression', *Journal of Social Work Practice*, 9(1): 73–84.

Woodroofe, K. (1962) *From Charity to Social Work in England and the United States*. London: Routledge and Kegan Paul.

Worrall, A. (2000) 'What works at one arm point? A study in the transportation of a penal concept', *Probation Journal*, 47(4): 243–9.

Wright, A. (2004) *Religion, Education and Postmodernity*. London: Routlege Falmer.

Wulczyn, F. (2004) 'Family Reunification', *The Future of Children*, 14(1): 95–113.

Wulczyn, F., Kogan, J. and Harden, B.J. (2003) 'Placement stability and movement trajectories', *Social Services Review*, pp. 212–23.

Yang, K.S. (2000) 'Monocultural and cross-cultural Indigenous approaches: The royal road to a balanced global psychology', *Asian Journal of Social Psychology*, 3(3): 241–63.

Yegedis, Y. and Weinbach, R. (2002) *Research Methods for Social Workers*. Boston: Allyn and Bacon.

Yelloly, M. and Henkel, M. (eds) (1995) *Learning and Teaching in Social Work: Towards Reflective Practice*. London: Jessica Kingsley Publishers.

Yeo, R. (2001) *Chronic Poverty and Disability*, Manchester: Chronic Poverty Research Centre.

Yeo, R. (2004) 'Chronic poverty and disability, ADD and chronic poverty research centre'. Available at: http://www.chronicpoverty.org/pdfs/04Yeo.pdf.

Yeo, R. and Moore, K. (2003) 'Chronic poverty and disability: 'Nothing about us, without us', *World Development*, 31(3).

Yong, F. and McCallion, P. (2003) Hwabyung as caregiving stress among Korean-American caregivers of a relative with dementia', *Journal of Gerontological Social Work*, 42(2): 3–19.

Young, I.M. (2000) 'Five faces of oppression', in M. Adams (ed.), *Readings for Diversity and Social Justice*. New York: Routledge.

Young, P. (1976) 'A sociological analysis of the early history of probation', *British Journal of Law and Society*, 3: 44–58.

Zald, M.N. (1970) 'Political economy: A framework for comparative analysis', in Zald, Mayer N. (ed.), *Power in Organizations*. Nashville: Vanderbilt University Press.

Zald, M.N. (1981) 'Political economy: A framework for comparative analysis', in Zey-Ferrel and Aiken (eds), *Complex Organizations: Critical Perspectives*. Glenview, IL: Scott Foresman.

Zaplin, R. (ed.) (1998) *Female Offenders: Critical Perspectives and Effective Interventions*. Gaithersburg: Aspen.

Zarb, G. (1992) 'On the road to Damascus: First steps towards changing the relations of research production', *Disability, Handicap and Society*, 7: 125–38.

Zarb, G. (1995) 'Modelling the social model of disability', *Critical Public Health*, 6: 21–9.

Zarb, G. and Nadash, P. (1994) *Cashing in on Independence: Comparing the Costs and Benefits of Cash and Services*. York: Joseph Rowntree Foundation.

Zarit, S.H. (1989) 'Do we need another stress and caregiving study?', *The Gerontologist*, 29(2): 147–8.

Zedner, L. (2002) 'Dangers of dystopias in penal theory', *Oxford Journal of Legal Studies*, 22(2): 341–66.

Zeira, A., Canali, C., Jergeby, U., Neve, E., Thoburn, J. and Vecchiato, T. (2008) 'Evidence-based social work practice with children and families?', *European Journal of Social Work*, 11(1): 57–72.

Zendell, A. (2007) 'Impact of the Olmstead decision five years later', *Journal of Gerontological Social Work*, 49(1/2): 97–114.

Zentralarchiv für Empirische Sozialforchung (2004) *ISSP 2002: Family and changing gender roles III. Codebook ZA study 3880*. Köln: Zentralarchiv.

Zima, P.V. (2004) *Was ist Theorie?: Theoriebegriff und Dialogische Theorie in den Kultur- und Sozialwissenschaften (What is a Theory? The Concept of Theory and Dialogical Theory in Cultural and Social Sciences)*. Tübingen u.a: Francke.

Ziman, J. (2000) *Real Science. What It Is and What It Means*. Cambridge: Cambridge University Press.

Zimbalist, S. (1977) *Historic Themes and Landmarks in Social Welfare Research*. New York: Harper and Row.

Name Index

Subject Index

Supporting researchers for more than forty years

Research methods have always been at the core of SAGE's publishing. Sara Miller McCune founded SAGE in 1965 and soon after, she published SAGE's first methods book, *Public Policy Evaluation*. A few years later, she launched the Quantitative Applications in the Social Sciences series – affectionately known as the 'little green books'.

Always at the forefront of developing and supporting new approaches in methods, SAGE published early groundbreaking texts and journals in the fields of qualitative methods and evaluation.

Today, more than forty years and two million little green books later, SAGE continues to push the boundaries with a growing list of more than 1,200 research methods books, journals, and reference works across the social, behavioural, and health sciences.

From qualitative, quantitative and mixed methods to evaluation, SAGE is the essential resource for academics and practitioners looking for the latest in methods by leading scholars.

www.sagepublications.com

Research Methods Books
from SAGE

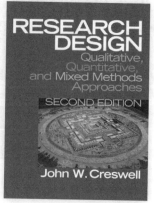

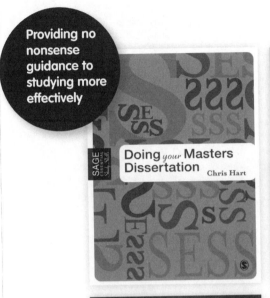

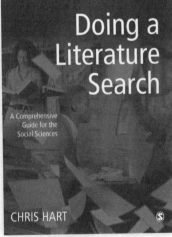